The Art of
Colour Photography

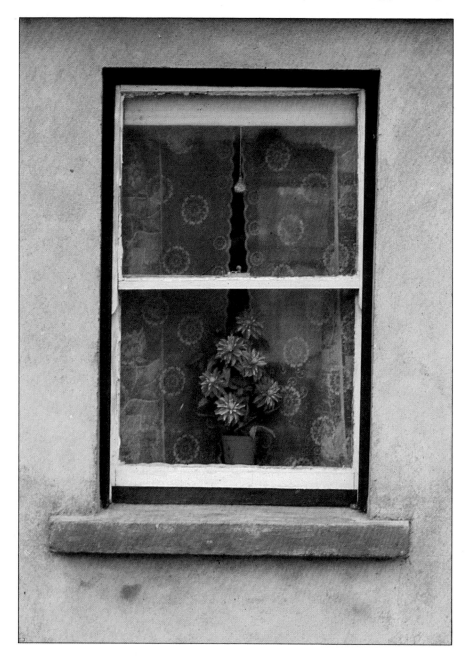

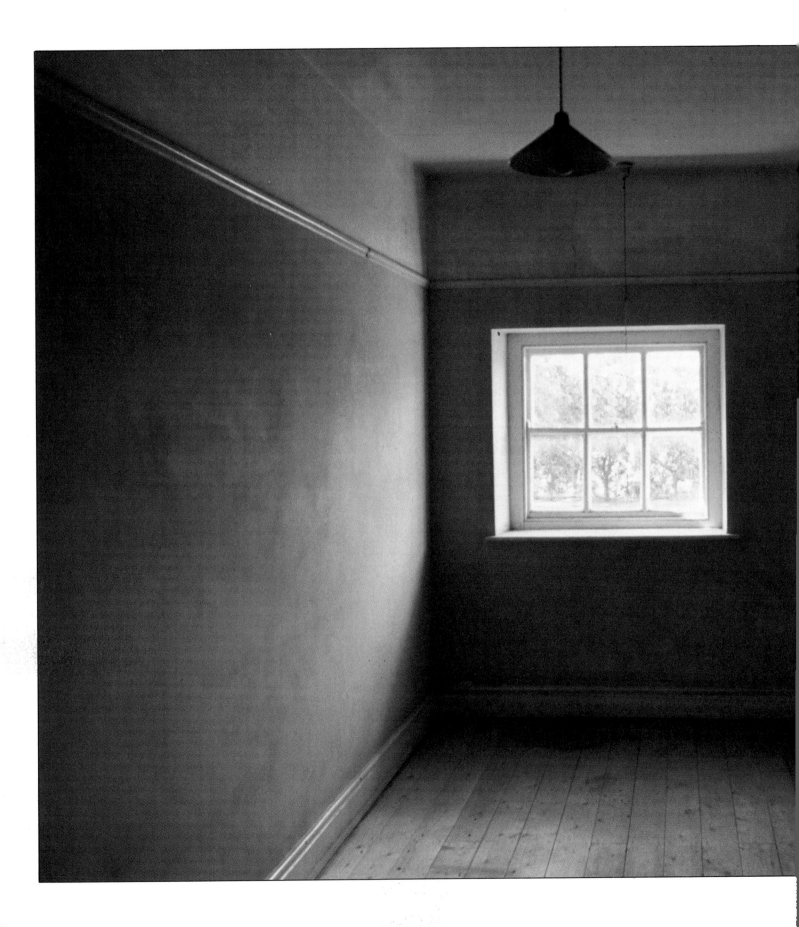

The Art
of Colour
Photography

John Hedgecoe

Mitchell Beazley

Editor
Jack Tresidder

Art Editors
Ted McCausland and Mel Petersen

Technical Editor
Arnold Desser

Assistant Editors
Sam Elder, Jonathan Hilton

Designer
Anne-Marie Hughes

Editorial Assistant
Charlotte Kennedy

Production
Barry Baker

Scientific and Technical Consultants

Christopher Cooper
Fred Dustin,
London College of Printing
Neville Maude
Dr C. McManus,
Psychological Laboratory, Cambridge
Dr J. D. Mollon,
Psychological Laboratory, Cambridge

Artists

Dave Ashby
John Davis
Richard Lewis
Jim Robins
Leslie D. Smith

The Art of Colour Photography
was edited and designed by
Mitchell Beazley Publishers Limited,
Mill House, 87–89 Shaftesbury Avenue,
London W1V 7AD

Photographs by John Hedgecoe

Text by John Hedgecoe and Jack Tresidder

The Art of Colour Photography
© Mitchell Beazley Publishers 1978
Photographs by John Hedgecoe
© John Hedgecoe, 1978
Text © jointly by John Hedgecoe
and Mitchell Beazley Publishers 1978
All rights reserved

Reprinted 1981

Typeset by Servis Filmsetting Limited

Reproduction by Gilchrist Bros. Ltd, Leeds

Printed in the Netherlands by Smeets BV Weert

ISBN 0 85533 139 9

Contents

Introduction

Photography is the most accessible of all art forms. It is a medium open to anyone and requires no exceptional faculty of hand or mind. Yet there is a profound difference between a good photographer and someone who simply aims a camera at the world and presses the shutter. The difference is a matter partly of technical knowledge and partly of intuition, imagination and trained perception. The aim of this book is not to display photographs and make artistic claims for them; it is to encourage you to develop your own skill and insight and to make you more aware of the creative choices that are involved every time you take a picture. As you make these choices you may find that what began as a pastime has become an art.

Until recent years the photographs most usually regarded as "art" were black and white abstractions of reality. This attitude was a result both of an historical accident and of a fundamental misunderstanding of what is unique about the photographic image. The reason why the pioneers of photography made black and white pictures was that they lacked the technical means to make coloured ones. Colour was potentially always a vital ingredient, as it has been in graphic art since the first cave paintings. Just as the belated introduction of sound in the movies at first created the impression that cinema was essentially a silent art, so the comparatively recent development of reliable colour film persuaded some that photography was essentially a black and white medium of art. Photographers who used colour film when it gradually became available for mass use after 1935 had to overcome the idea that their pictures were somehow too explicit to be art—too literal a representation of reality. Painting, by comparison, seemed to offer a greater range of colour and a greater capacity to transcend its source material.

The error in all this was a failure to recognize that photography and painting are two distinct and separate art forms. In a painting, the hand of the artist is always evident and nobody thinks the picture he paints is the literal truth. The photographer is far less obtrusive. Although his picture is not objective but subjective, affected by all the choices he has made about it, in looking at many photographs we are hardly aware of his presence at all. A photographic image seems to place us in direct contact with reality—or a faithful copy of it. It is this apparent closeness to reality that makes some photographs so poignant. A portrait, for instance, can seem to bring us nearer to a living person than any other image can. And yet we are also aware that the subject of the photograph is infinitely far removed from us. He does not breathe and cannot move. He is transfixed in time on a two-dimensional surface, his fleeting expression frozen for us to dwell on. The unique quality of photography is its capacity to convey the sense of life with such directness that nothing seems to stand between us and the image. When colour film is used to create mood and atmosphere, depth and form, it can add enormously to the evocative quality of a picture. It is for this reason that a detailed analysis of colour forms the introductory sections of this book and that the photographs explore the moods of different light sources primarily in terms of their effects on colour.

Although intuitively we respond more immediately to colours than to shapes, our perception of colour and our sensitivity to its nuances is usually undeveloped. We tend to think in stereotyped ways of foliage being green in summer and brown in autumn, for instance. Yet the first step in understanding colour is the realization that everything in the world changes its hue according to the light by which we view it. Colours may appear unnatural, but no colour can really be called true or untrue. Our capacity to accept unfamiliar colours is being extended rapidly with advances in dye- and pigment-making, in television and in printing. At the same time, manufactured pigments are becoming generally bolder and stronger. The readiness of people to respond to vivid colour combinations gives photographers who want to experiment with colour considerable creative scope. But it is worth remembering that colour levels, like sound levels, can become deafening. Although any colours can live together if they are properly balanced, strong competing colours tend to overwhelm forms and flatten a picture. In nature, strong hues are usually balanced by strong sunlight, and landscapes are often dominated by subdued and harmonious colours. Likewise, many of the photographs in this book make discreet use of quite a limited and subtle palette.

By no means all the pictures are intended to be "art". They reveal, in their many hundreds, a strong and cohesive personal style. But many were taken as a deliberate exercise to show the elements that go to make up a total picture. There is more than a little pretentiousness about the artistic labels that are sometimes attached to photographs—often borrowed from painting styles. Photographs that consciously set out to be art are usually self-indulgent and sterile. A good picture will last and live—and may then be called art. It is good if its imagery extends beyond the frame, provoking thought, capturing atmosphere or providing a surprise that upsets our visual preconceptions. Such pictures are the result less of mechanical skill than of intuition and forethought. The ease or difficulty of taking them is no measure of their value. Photography, like any other art, rests on a foundation of knowledge and skill, and can be spontaneous only when its fundamentals are understood. But a preoccupation with technique and with the merits of different cameras, lenses or filters is unlikely to produce pictures with the flavour of life. Photographs of the utmost clarity and definition can be static and unimaginative, while a blurred picture may be full of human insight.

The elements that go to make up an effective colour photograph are explained in detail in this book. In addition to hue, form, tone, pattern, line, texture and shape—the basic compositional ingredients of most graphic arts—they include the special and often subtle relationships between different colours. The ways in which colours are affected by different backgrounds, and the overriding importance of the angle of view in relation to the changing light, are also fundamental aspects of colour photography. But when these lessons have been absorbed it is your individual response to a scene that will determine whether or not you take a good picture. For a successful photograph depends on a series of personal choices the photographer has made about it—about the elements he wants to include, the range of tones, the mood and, above all, the decisive moment at which to press the shutter.

The pictures on the next few pages show a variety of subjects, ordinary in themselves, that have been transformed by individual decisions about viewpoint or shutter speed, selection or abstraction, lighting or colour accent. They range from the simplicity of a formal dance to the whirling light enveloping a ski racer; from a ruffled sea in an aerial photograph to a dream-like image of swans floating in a skein of grey silk. Our emotions and senses, dreams and fears have their own mysterious colours and in realizing them colour photography moves far beyond mere representation. It is in using the interpretive potential of a unique medium that you will find yourself beginning to capture not merely the scene as it appears in your camera viewfinder but its very essence.

The
world of colour

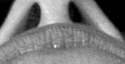

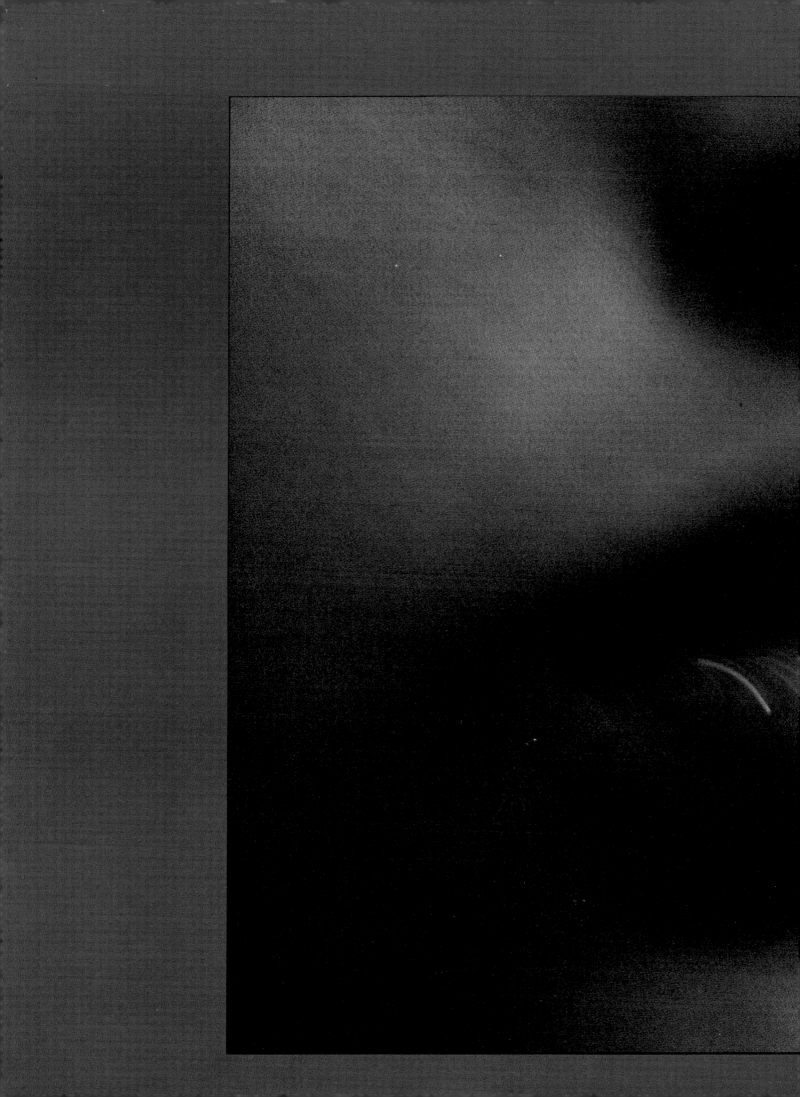

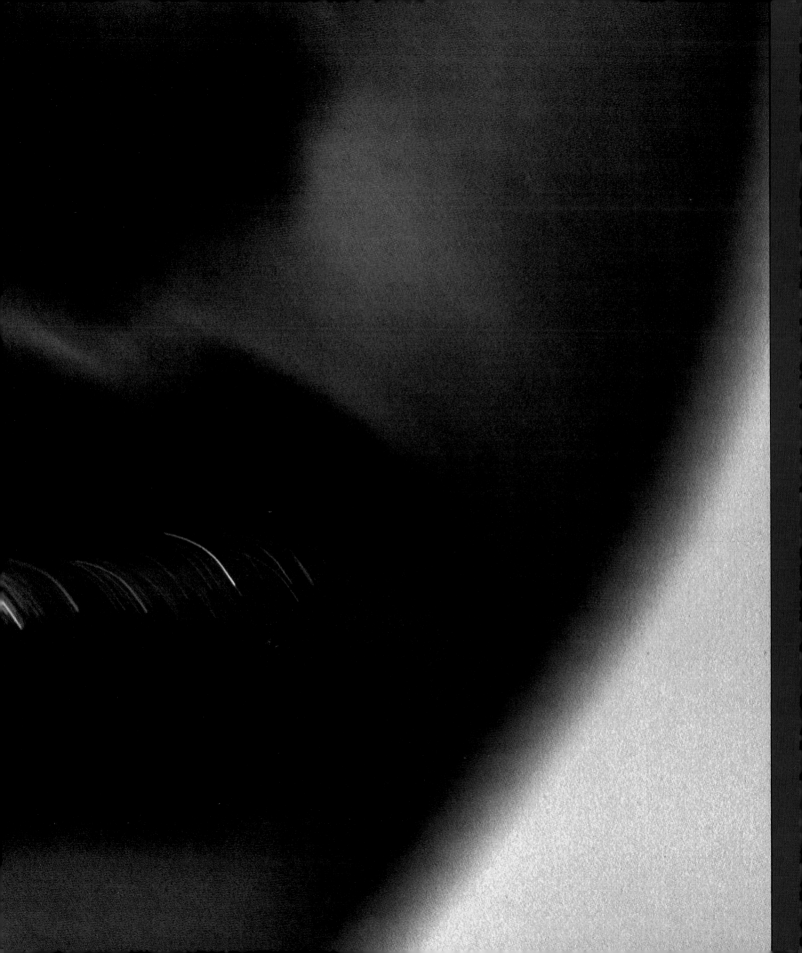

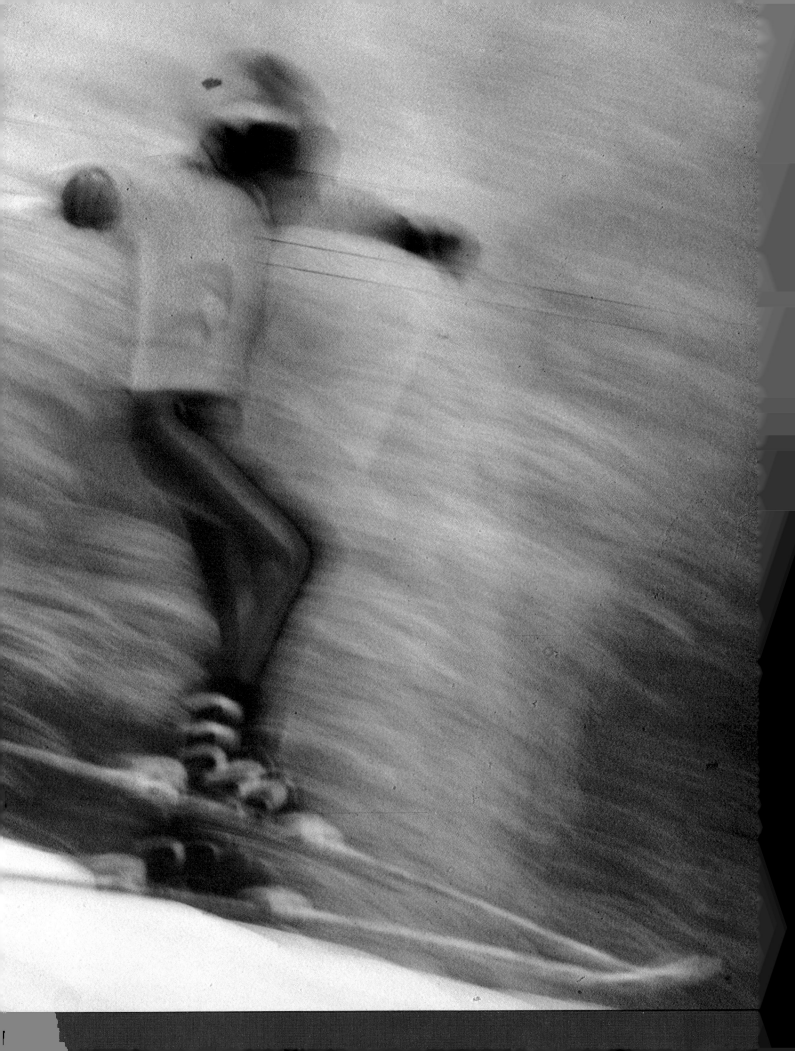

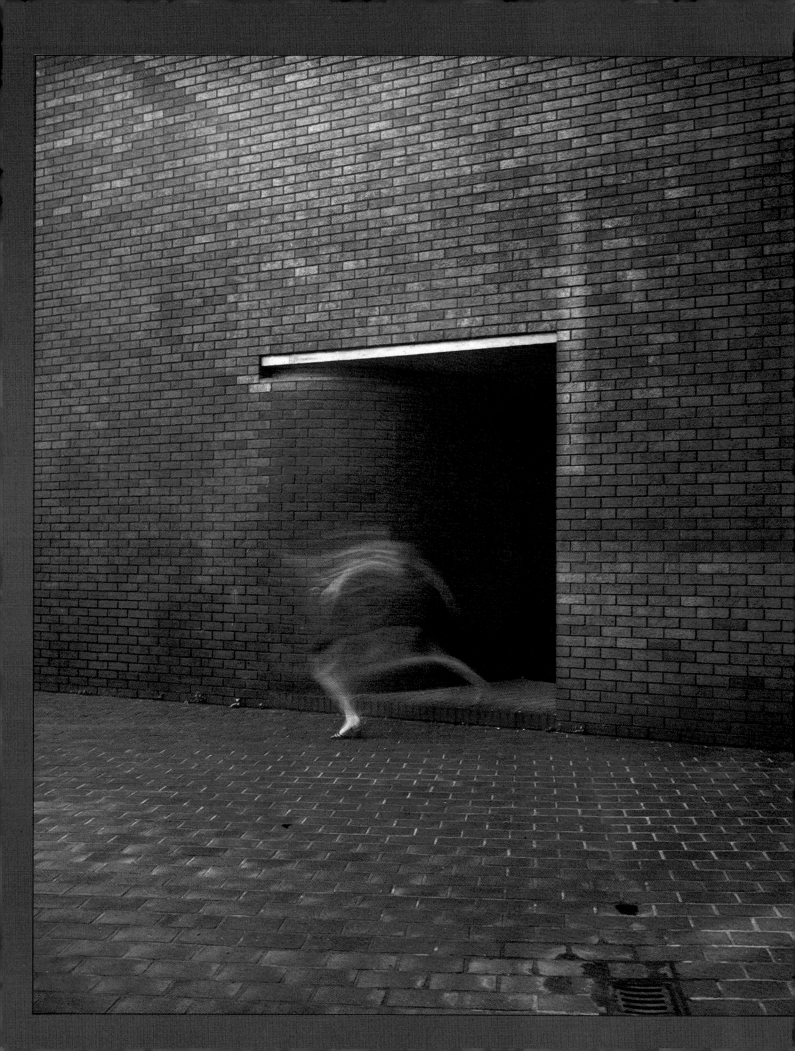

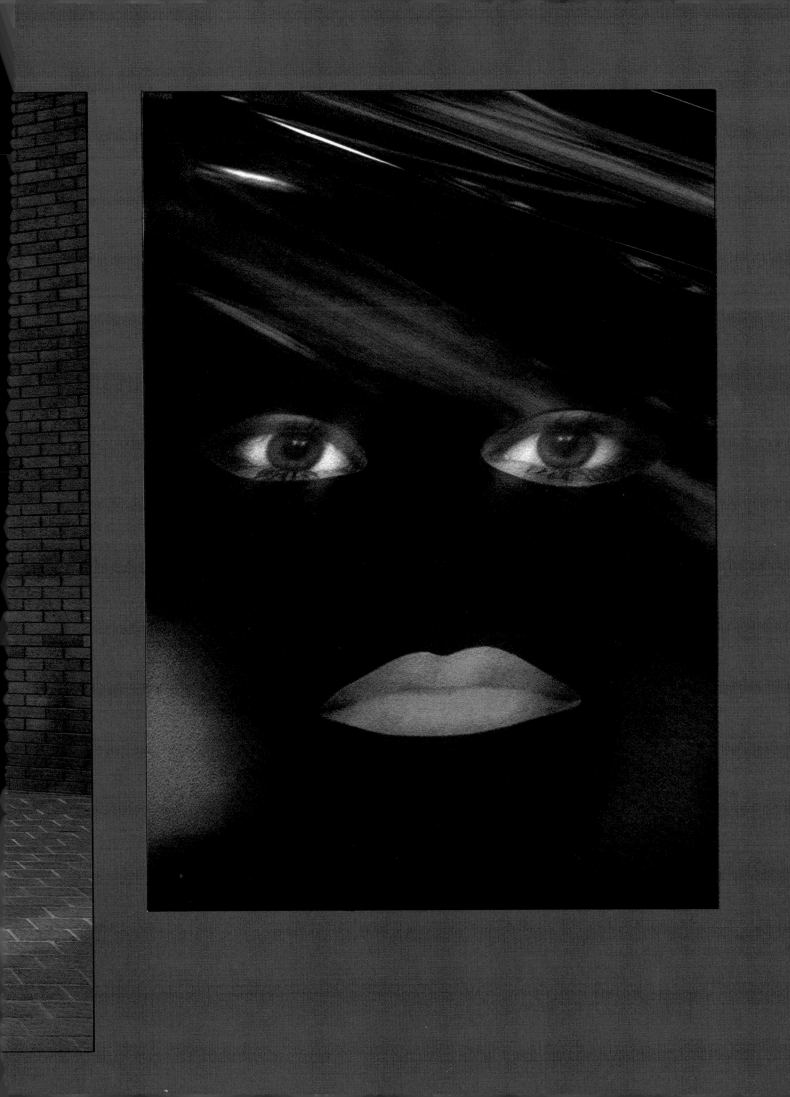

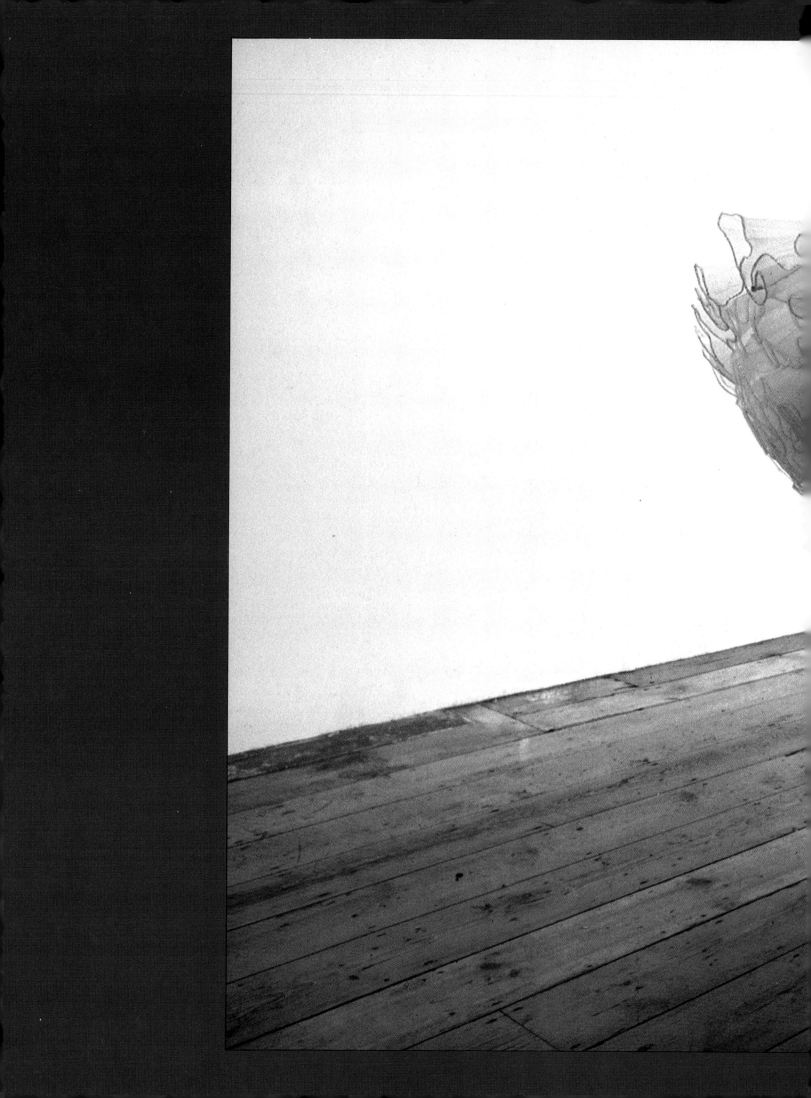

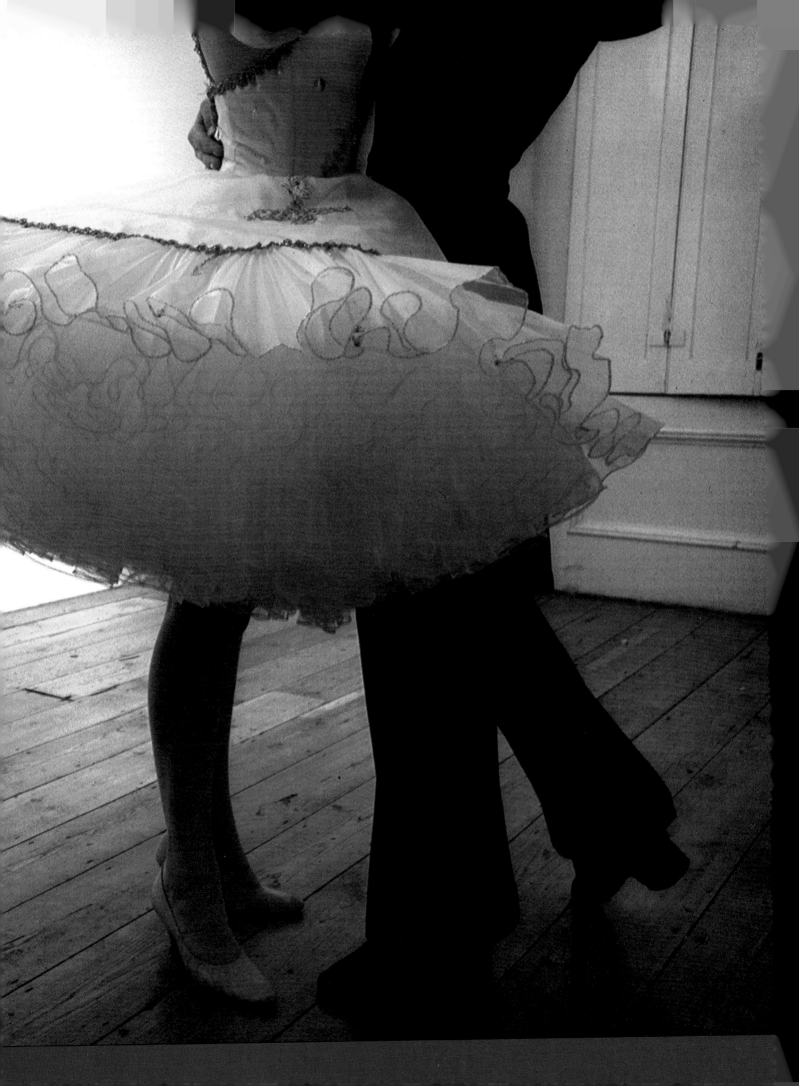

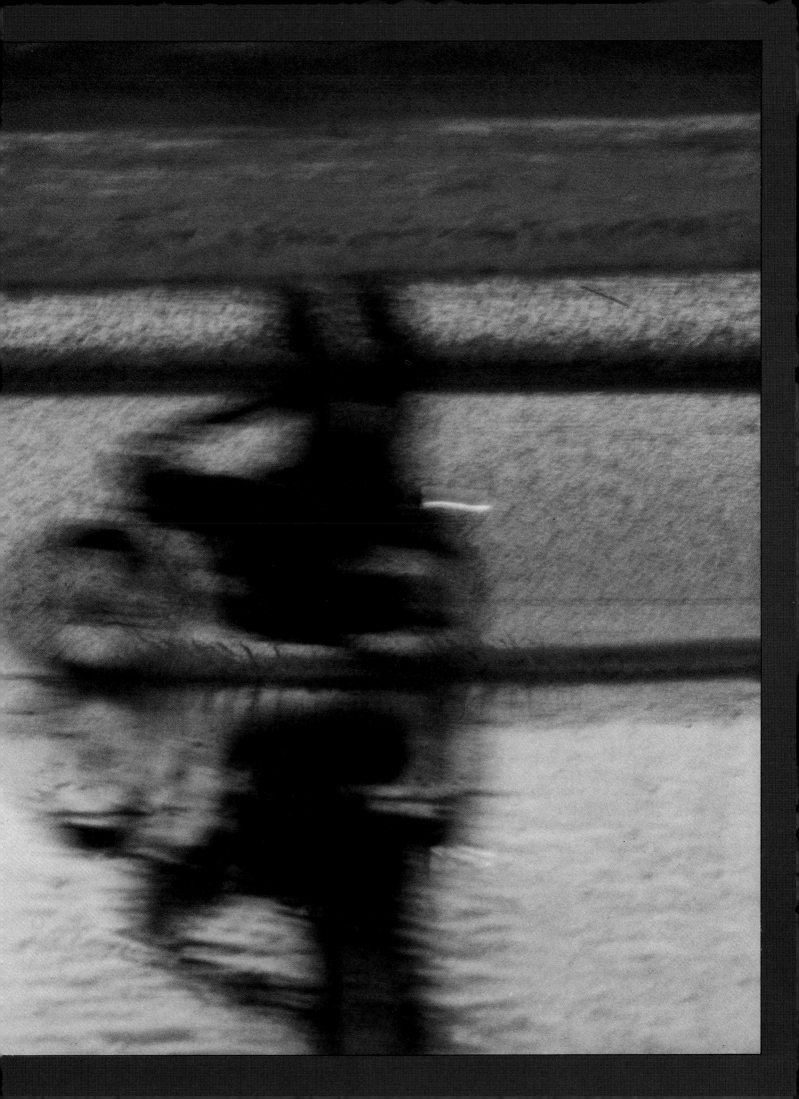

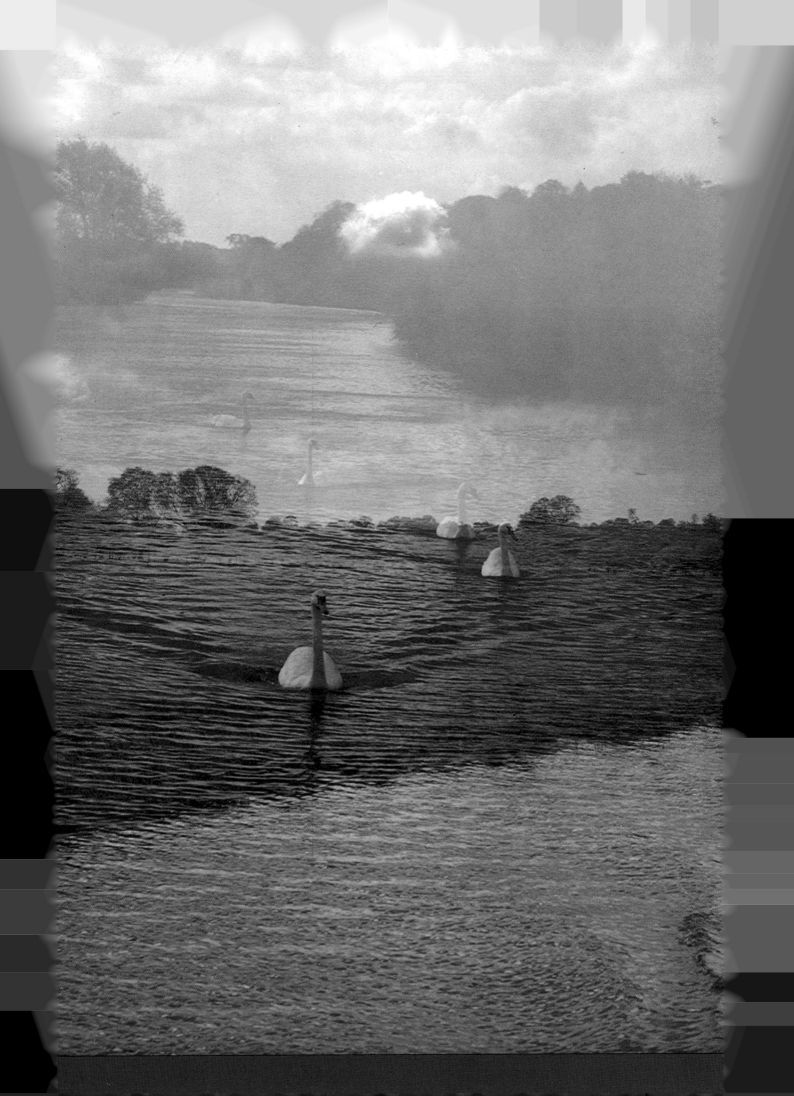

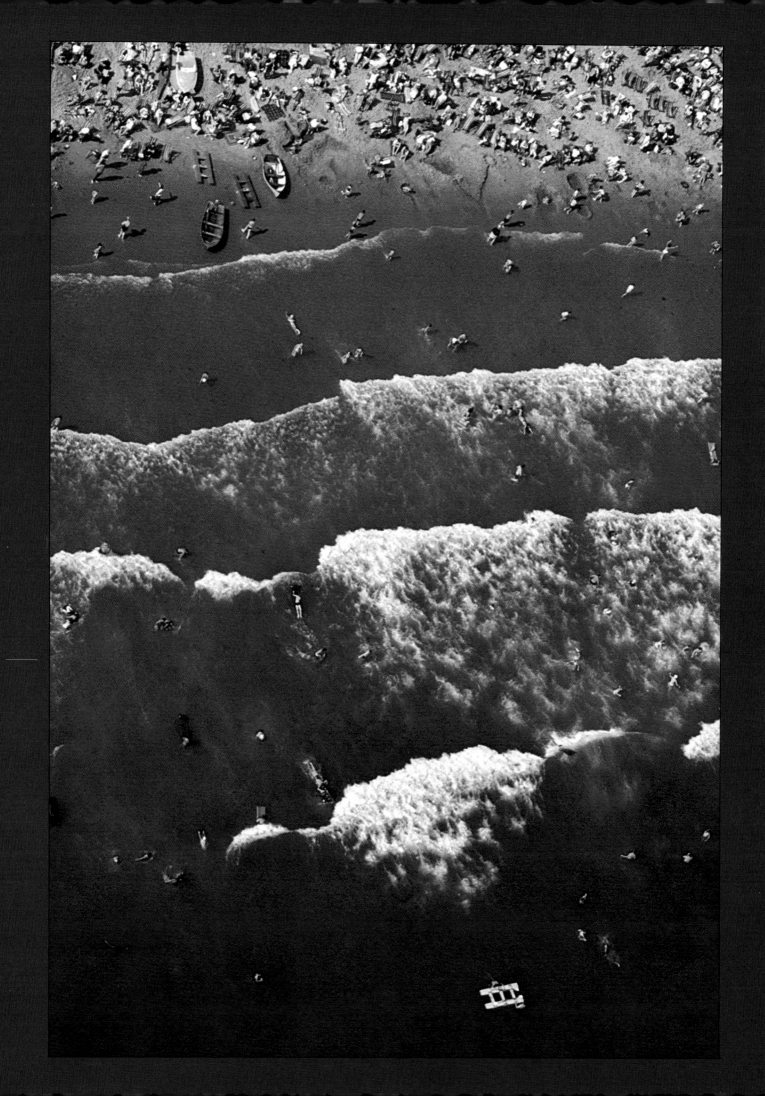

Pentax, 100 mm macro lens,
Ektachrome 200, 1/250, f8,
oblique sunlight.

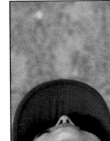

Leicaflex, 90 mm, Ektachrome
160, 1 sec., f16, frontal
spotlight, subject movement
during exposure.

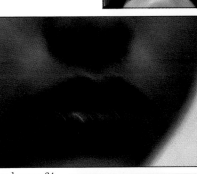

Pentax, 55 mm, Ektachrome 64,
1/30, f16, panned during slow
exposure in overcast light.

Hasselblad, 80 mm, Ektachrome 64,
1/4, f16, subject movement during
exposure, overcast light.

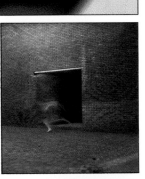

Leicaflex, 135 mm, Ektachrome 64,
cut-outs from two photographs
superimposed on black plastic and
reflected on to flexible plastic.

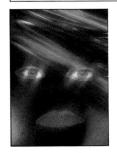

Pentax, 28 mm, Ektachrome 160,
1/30, f8, hand-held, four
500-watt photofloods, angled.

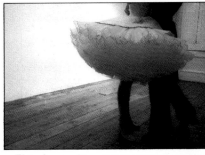

Pentax, 50 mm, Ektachrome 64,
1/30, f5.6, slow subject movement
during exposure at sunset.

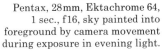

Pentax, 28 mm, Ektachrome 64,
1 sec., f16, sky painted into
foreground by camera movement
during exposure in evening light.

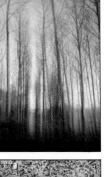

Leicaflex, 90 mm and 35 mm, Ektachrome 64, 1/250, f8, double
exposure with change of lenses
and horizon levels, overcast light.

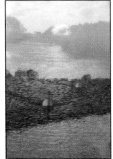

Pentax, 35 mm, Ektachrome 200,
1/500, f8, from light aircraft
at 500 ft (152 m), bright sunlight.

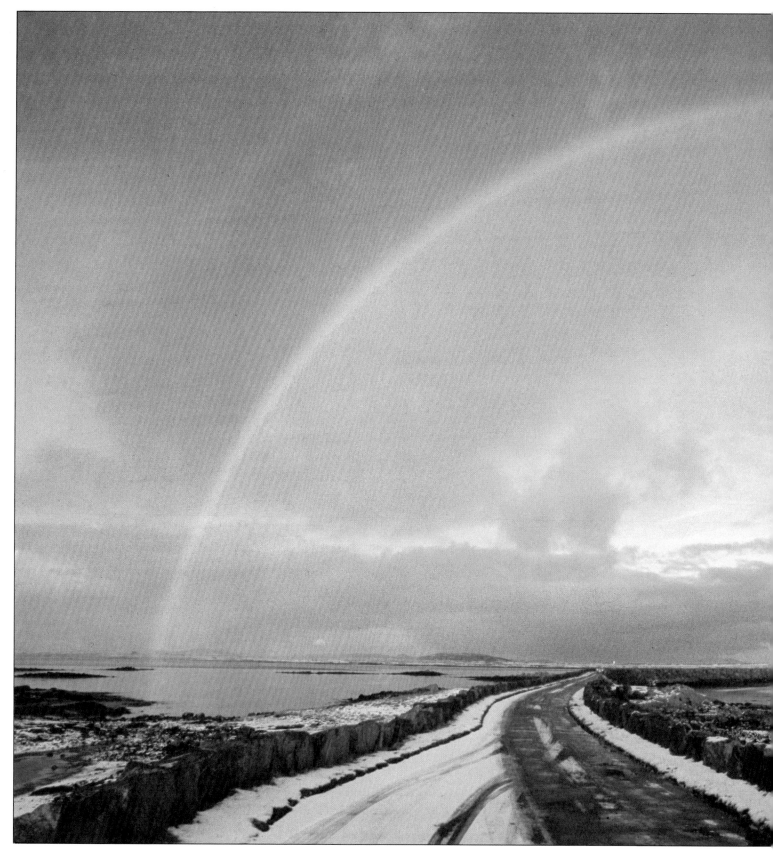

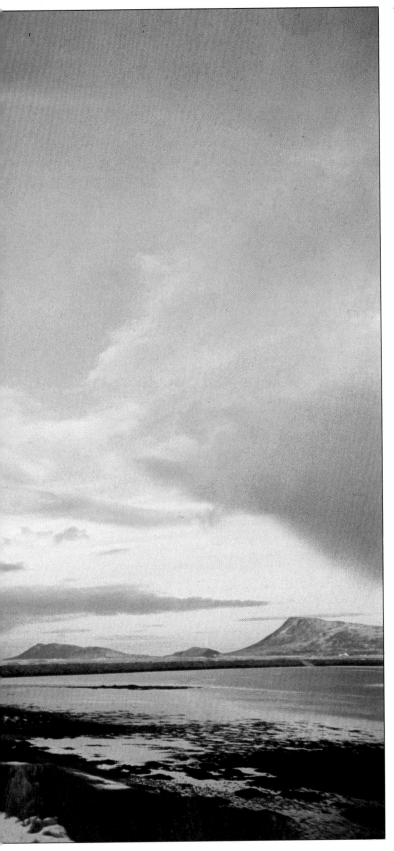

What is colour?

The photographer, like the artist and the scientist, seeks to control colour. Often this means recording as accurately as possible the hues in a given scene. At other times it means achieving the colour that best evokes the mood he seeks in an image—by manipulating light sources or angles and by controlling the processing and printing of the film. Far from being simple to control, colour is as transient as light itself. To master it the photographer must learn to observe it sensitively and to manipulate its trace on the film with understanding as well as experience. The key to the understanding of colour is the realization that it is a property not only of objects but also of the light that strikes them.

The photographer who attends to the play of colour in the world around him soon becomes aware of its infinite subtlety. The vocabulary we normally use in describing colours rarely rises much above the level of "the sky is blue, the grass is green". The colour labels of a child's paint-box are likely to defeat us. How many people can confidently match such closely related terms as umber and ochre, or chrome and saffron, or cobalt and indigo, with the colours they name? Yet even the most elaborate colour charts name only a few of the thousands of hues that human beings can distinguish. Anyone who works closely with colour is soon made aware of the extent to which his own eye and brain affect what he sees. He finds that it is hard to tell whether two colours are the same or different when nearby colours influence his judgement of hue.

There are important differences in the response to colour of the eye and of film and these need to be understood. It is helpful also to know something of how colours are added to and subtracted from each other in the varied technologies of colour reproduction—in television, in colour film and in printing. Accordingly the pages that follow deal with these and with the processes of perception, as well as with the more subtle responses of the mind to colour.

To answer the basic question "What is colour?", however, we must begin with the nature of light itself, because we see colours in nature only by means of light, whether created by the sun, a flashbulb or a tungsten filament. Spectacular evidence of the existence of colours in sunlight is provided by the rainbow, which separates out the colours that, mixed together, we normally perceive as white light. Red apples or yellow daffodils owe their colours to the fact that they absorb some colours of light and reflect others. From the subtraction, addition and mixing of rainbow hues in thousands of permutations arises our whole world of colours.

The colours of light

White light is synthesized *when coloured light in a spectrum is recombined by a converging lens (above). But if part of the spectrum is blocked out, the mixture takes on the "complementary" colour. When green is blocked out (right) the recombined light is coloured magenta, which is the complementary of green.*

In 1666 Isaac Newton, then 23 years old, became fascinated by the behaviour of rays of sunlight passing through a prism—a glass block of triangular cross-section. His studies led to the realization that colour arises from the interaction of light with matter. Each ray of light was. *refracted* by the prism; that is, it emerged travelling in a different direction from that in which it entered. But not only was the sunlight bent by the prism—it emerged as a spreading beam of multicoloured light, displaying the hues seen in a rainbow, and in the same order. Although there were seven main hues in the spectrum he saw—red, orange, yellow, green, blue, indigo and violet—these merged into one another.

Newton concluded that white sunlight was a mixture of different kinds of light, each kind being of one pure colour, and that a prism bent these colours by different amounts— red the least, violet the most, and the other colours by an intermediate amount. He found that when he mixed the colours of a spectrum—for example, by bringing its light to a focus with a lens—he obtained white light. By blocking out some colours before recombining the others, he obtained a coloured mixture of light. Furthermore, this colour was quite different from any found in the spectrum.

What Newton had discovered was that the colour of anything in nature depends on the kind of light it sends to the eye. This depends on both the nature of the light falling on an object and the individual colours in that light that its surface reflects, absorbs or transmits. If the light falling on a surface lacks some colours, the light reflected from the surface will also lack those colours. But the "true" colour of a reflective surface—the colour it looks in a standard white light—can be completely specified by stating in the form of a table of numbers, or displaying as a graph, the proportion of light of each spectral colour that it reflects.

If the proportion of reflected colours is similar to the balance found in sunlight (with blue-green predominating and the proportion of other colours tailing off towards the ends of the spectrum) the surface will appear white. But if, for example, there is a greater proportion of the colours towards the red end of the spectrum than in sunlight, then the surface will have a reddish cast; if bluish colours tend to dominate in the reflected light the surface will have a blue cast. The balance of spectral colours that produces particular hues is complex. But it is generally true to say that if a surface looks strongly coloured when viewed in white light,

The gamut of colours appears in a soap bubble. Light reflected from the bubble's inner surface interferes with that reflected from the outer surface. Some colours are reinforced, others weakened according to the surface thickness and the angle of view. The altered colour balance of the reflected light results in a great diversity of colours. Similar effects appear when two glass surfaces are not quite in contact, producing coloured rings.

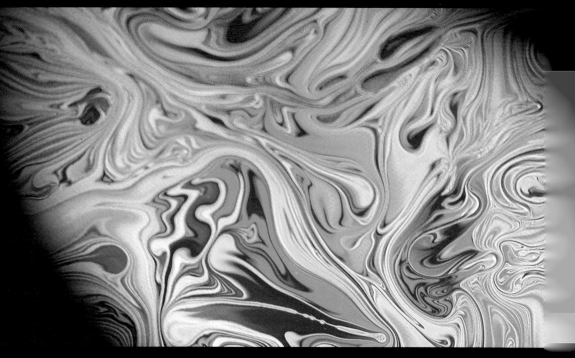

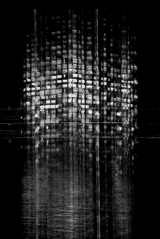

Light is fragmented by a filter specially engraved with parallel lines in this picture of a riverside building at night. A vertical string of images is formed from each point of light in the subject. Each of these, apart from the central main image, is spread into its components by a process called diffraction. A street light seen through the fabric of an umbrella is similarly fragmented by the partly opaque material.

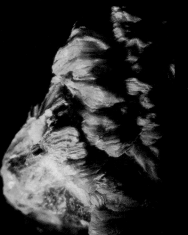

Autunite in ordinary light.

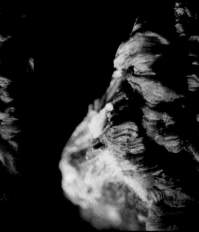

Fluorescence in ultra-violet light.

Invisible light is made visible by this sample of the uranium ore mineral autunite. The mineral ranges in colour from yellow to green in ordinary light (far left) with brownish shades contributed by other minerals coating the sample. When it is lit with ultraviolet light (near left) autunite fluoresces, glowing a brilliant yellowish-green. The other minerals glow in other colours, including a striking purple. The energy of UV light is being converted into visible form. Minerologists use UV lamps to assist them in identifying various mineral samples.

it is reflecting certain colours from the light falling on it and strongly absorbing others. If it looks black, it is absorbing all the spectral colours.

Certain substances not only absorb some of the light energy falling on them but also re-emit it as light of a different colour and these substances are called *luminescent*. The gemstones ruby and spinel, for example, will absorb blue hues in light and emit red. Ultraviolet light, which is an invisible component of light beyond the violet end of the spectrum, stimulates many substances to emit visible light. If re-emission ceases immediately when the stimulating light ceases, the effect is called *fluorescence*. If the glow lingers, it is called *phosphorescence*. The extra brightness brought about by some washing powders is achieved by a fluorescent component that is retained in clothes and is stimulated by the ultraviolet part of sunlight. The extra light that is emitted is sufficient to make the clothes noticeably brighter. Fluorescent poster paints are also stimulated by the ultraviolet component of sunlight.

Light that is absorbed by a material is converted into heat energy. In 1800 the English astronomer William Herschel discovered an invisible component of sunlight by its warming effect on the bulb of a thermometer. It lay beyond the red end of the spectrum, so he named it *"infra-red"* (below the red) light. Specialized film will respond to this light.

Finally, there are the colours we see transmitted by transparent substances. It might be thought surprising that, say, a portion of a colour transparency looks the same colour by reflected light as by the light it transmits. Why does it not reflect and absorb some combination of colours and transmit the remainder? The answer is that the light by which we view a transparency, from whichever direction, has been both reflected and transmitted. Light passing through film dye is reflected from countless pigment particles suspended in a clear medium. The light may emerge in any direction from the film, and so the film looks the same colour from any angle.

The case is different for certain very thin films, such as the anti-reflection coatings used on lenses. The coating can minimize reflection only for a narrow range of spectral colour, determined by the coating's thickness. The colour wavelength chosen is in the central regions of the spectrum. Hence the light reflected from the coating is poor in yellow or green, and the colour of the "bloom" is that obtained when yellow or green is subtracted from white, namely purple.

The balance of colour

Visible light is generated in the outermost regions of atoms that have been heated. Every atom consists of a cloud of electrons orbiting a central nucleus and the number of electrons in each orbit is limited. When a material is heated, its atoms vibrate faster and jostle each other more violently so that some electrons jump to higher-energy orbits, absorbing heat energy as they do so. Later they fall back into the vacancies created in lower levels, losing energy. The lost energy appears as electromagnetic radiation, travelling away from the atom.

As the amount of energy lost by an electron in a particular jump varies, so does the colour of the radiation sent out. If a comparatively large amount of energy is released, it will appear as a burst of, say, blue or ultraviolet light. A lower-energy transition gives rise to a burst of red or infra-red light. But all the colours of visible light together with infra-red and ultraviolet light represent only a small part of a band of radiation extending from high-energy X-rays to low-energy radio waves. The lower the energy, the longer the wavelength.

More important to the photographer is that the balance of the different colours in visible light varies between one source of light and another. In photography the mixture in a particular kind of light is often described in terms of *colour temperature*. Colour temperature is expressed in kelvins (K), the international scientific unit of temperature measurement. To convert a temperature from kelvins to Celsius, simply subtract 273.

Imagine a piece of iron being heated from room temperature. When the iron is at 1,000 K it sends out radiation of a wide range of wavelengths, but the bulk of it is infra-red radiation, which can be felt as heat. When the iron is heated to 3,000 K it continues to send out radiation of all kinds, but now enough of it is in the form of visible light to make the iron glow visibly. Most of the emission is still infra-red radiation, however, and proportionately more red light is sent out than is present in sunlight, so the glow appears red.

When the iron is heated to 6,000 K, roughly the temperature of the sun's surface, most of its radiation is within the visible spectrum and blue-green predominates. To the eye, the iron is glowing white-hot. Any light source with a similar spectrum is described as having a colour temperature of 6,000 K and in this light colours look natural.

If the iron is heated until it vaporizes and the vapour is then further heated to 20,000 K, the temperature of some of the hottest stars, its peak emission will be in the ultraviolet. To the naked eye the glowing vapour will appear to be a dazzling blue colour. Because blue sky light in some conditions has a similar spectrum it is said to have a colour temperature of 20,000 K. This figure has no relation to the actual temperature of the air at any altitude, because sky light is not being *emitted* by air gases, but *scattered* by them. Colour temperature is a useful way of summarizing the different colour mixtures within various kinds of daylight and artificial light, but it must not be confused with a measurement of heat.

At noon on a clear day, the colour of sky light (not direct sunlight) is affected by scattering by individual molecules (groups of linked atoms) in the air. A small proportion of sunlight is absorbed and immediately reradiated by a molecule in all directions. Blue light is scattered far more strongly than red, and ultraviolet light even more strongly.

When the air is full of water vapour, dust or smog particles, it is again the shorter wavelengths that are most affected. But because these particles *absorb* some blue, the light from a hazy sky is less blue than that from a clear sky

and has a colour temperature of about 9,000 K. The light transmitted by cloud has still less preponderance of blue. Daylight colour film is balanced to a mixture of direct sunlight and light from a clear sky with a few white clouds. But in the morning and evening, when the sun is low in the sky, sunlight has to traverse a great thickness of atmosphere. The greater absorption of blue light, even when the air is relatively clear, causes the familiar red appearance of the dawn and evening sun and of photographs taken in this light.

Colour reversal film must be adapted to the reddish cast of light from a relatively low-temperature artificial source, such as a tungsten-filament lamp. The differing balance of colours in other kinds of artificial light is sometimes adjusted by means of filters—illumination from fluorescent lamps, for instance, which peaks in certain colours (and therefore cannot be assigned a colour temperature).

The colour of daylight *can be seen changing through the day in the photographs at the right. At sunrise, it is reddened by atmospheric absorption of blue. At midday, the snow illuminated by direct sunlight is white, but in shadow areas, light reflected from the sky, with a high proportion of scattered short wavelengths, produces a strong blue cast. Fog in the right-hand picture gives a weaker overall blue cast.*

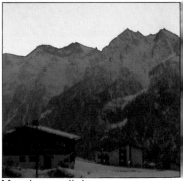

Morning sunlight

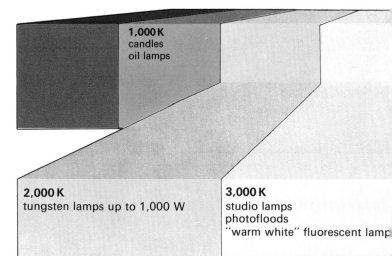

1,000 K
candles
oil lamps

2,000 K
tungsten lamps up to 1,000 W

3,000 K
studio lamps
photofloods
"warm white" fluorescent lamp

With daylight film, *most forms of artificial light give a reddish cast, as in the first two pictures here. Light from the oil lamp shown in the left-hand picture is redder than that of tungsten lighting, which has produced the pale orange cast seen in the central picture. The shot on the right was taken with a diffused electronic flash, balanced to a colour temperature similar to that of daylight, which has recorded the scene in colours that by comparison look "natural".*

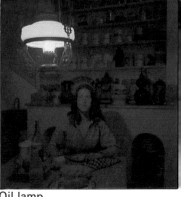

Oil lamp

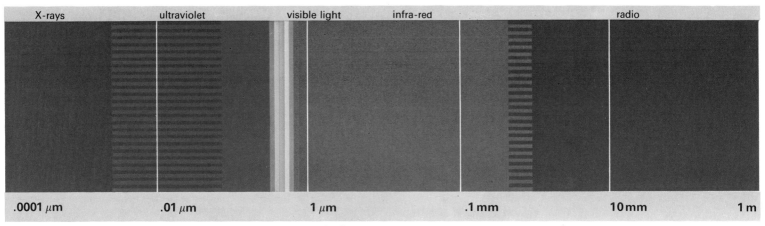

.0001 μm   .01 μm   1 μm   .1 mm   10 mm   1 m

Longest wavelength of visible light is just below 1 μm = one-millionth of a metre

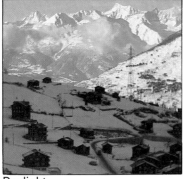

Daylight

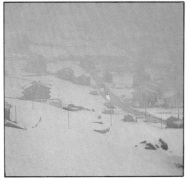

Fog

Invisible radiation *flanks a narrow spectrum of visible light. The human eye is sensitive only to wavelengths between 0.4 and 0.7 of a micrometre—the range of light that can be perceived as the colours between violet and red. There is some ultraviolet light in daylight, especially in sky light. Ultra-violet wavelengths overlap with those of longer X-rays. Daylight has no X-rays, which are absorbed from sunlight by the atmosphere. But artificially generated X-rays are invaluable in industry and medicine for their penetrating power and ability to show on film things the eye cannot see.*

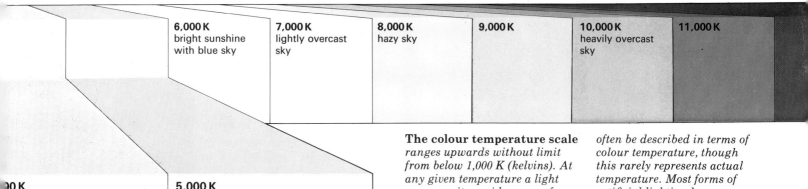

6,000 K
bright sunshine
with blue sky

7,000 K
lightly overcast
sky

8,000 K
hazy sky

9,000 K

10,000 K
heavily overcast
sky

11,000 K

...0 K
...r flashbulbs
...e photofloods
...ol white" fluorescent lamps

5,000 K
blue flashbulbs
electronic flash
average daylight

The colour temperature scale *ranges upwards without limit from below 1,000 K (kelvins). At any given temperature a light source emits a wide range of wavelengths, but some are predominant and result in an overall colour. Hence the colour of radiant light can often be described in terms of colour temperature, though this rarely represents actual temperature. Most forms of artificial lighting have a colour temperature in the range from 2,000 K to 6,000 K. Beyond this, daylight becomes bluer as short wavelengths predominate.*

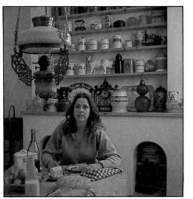

Tungsten lighting

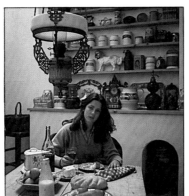

Daylight flash

Infra-red light *reflected from the foliage of a tree shows up as a brilliant magenta in this "false-colour" picture. Infra-red film not only reveals the presence of infra-red radiation in the light reflected from everyday objects but also gives unpredictable colours from other wavelengths. Hot objects emit a great deal of infra-red radiation, and foliage reflects it strongly. Specialized films respond to the shortest infra-red wavelengths, those up to about one micrometre.*

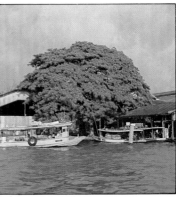

Infra-red light

Forming images

In general the photographer can regard light as travelling in straight lines. But to understand its behaviour in some circumstances a knowledge of the wave nature of light is helpful. This is basic, for example, to understanding what happens to light when it is polarized.

The colour and texture of a surface are revealed when the surface absorbs some wavelengths of the light that falls on it and sends other wavelengths to the eye or to a camera lens. But this diffuse reflection can be masked by specular, or mirror-like, reflection. Glossy paper, glass, metal or still water appear glaring when virtually all the light falling on the surface is reflected. To cut out this glare and show the qualities of the surface the photographer has to overcome the polarization of this specularly reflected light.

Light consists of rapidly varying electric and magnetic fields. These vibrations are transverse—that is side to side, rather like the waves in a shaken rope. The light from the sun or from nearly all artificial sources of light is unpolarized—the vibrations occur at all angles around the line of movement of the ray. Diffusely reflected light is also unpolarized. But after being specularly reflected, light is polarized, so that its vibrations are largely in one plane. A polarizing filter can be aligned to block the light in this specific plane while passing diffusely reflected light.

Light waves spread outwards from light sources. Because they are spread ever more thinly, the brightness of the light shed by a lamp, for instance, falls off with distance—a fact of importance in studio lighting. For each cone of light rays diverging from the object a converging lens will form a cone of rays bending back to a small disc and then diverging as it travels on from there. The image of an object cast on a screen or film is most sharply focused when the latter is placed where its intersection with each cone of refracted rays forms the smallest possible disc.

The farther an object is from a converging lens the closer behind the lens a sharp image is formed. A photographic image is brought into focus by changing the distance of the lens from the film. The focal length of a particular lens is the lens–image distance when the object is "at infinity"—very far from the lens—and the lens is therefore fully retracted.

Polarization

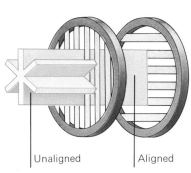

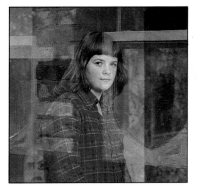

Unaligned   Aligned

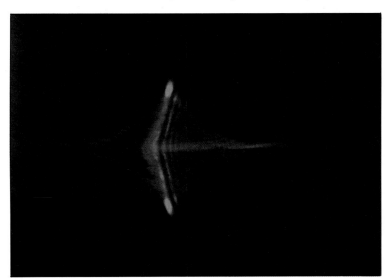

Lens aperture *affects image sharpness (below right). An object is in focus when rays from each point on it are brought to a point focus (middle film plane). When the lens is nearer or farther from the film the converging rays from the object form a "circle of confusion" on the film. If the lens aperture is reduced (far right) the cone of rays from the object is narrowed as it leaves the back of the lens. The position of best focus is unchanged, but at other*

The distorted image *of an off-axis pinpoint of light (above) was formed by a low-quality lens. It has been photographed through a microscope to show the colours caused by chromatic aberration, and a lozenge shape, caused by coma, both faults in focusing.*

A polarizing filter *(above) blocks some light and causes the light that it does pass on to vibrate at only one angle. If light reaching the filter is already largely polarized, as it is when reflected from glass, the filter can be rotated to block this light. Normal light, vibrating at all angles around the line of motion, will partly pass through the filter to give a slightly dimmed view of the scene previously masked by the reflections.*

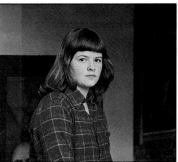

Reflections *(top) are subdued by a polarizing filter in a shot taken through the same window.*

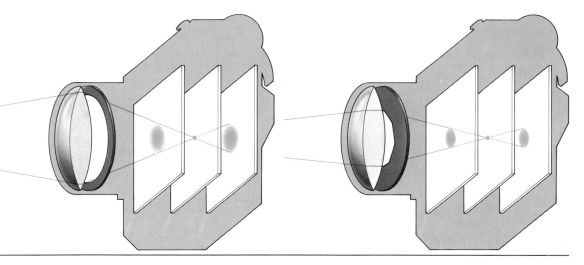

lens–film distance settings the circles of confusion are reduced. So an unfocused image, though blurred, will be sharper than it would be with the lens set at full aperture.

Nearly all lenses have spherical surfaces. Because of this and because of the differing wavelengths and refractive characteristics of any package of light rays, simple lenses are subject to a variety of aberrations, some of which are illustrated here. To eliminate these defects and to reduce internal reflections, a typical modern compound lens for ordinary photographic use will consist of six or more elements—individual simple lenses of differing kinds of glass (and hence refractive powers) and degrees of curvature.

Though lenses differ greatly in their construction, focal lengths and physical dimensions, they are readily compared in terms of the f number, which determines the brightness of the image that the lens will form under particular conditions. The brightness of the image is essentially the intensity of the light falling on to the film, which is equal to the rate at which light energy falls on a unit area. The larger the aperture of the lens iris, the greater the brightness of the image. On the other hand, the larger the image and hence the greater the area over which the light is spread, the fainter the image will be. The size of the image increases with its distance from the lens, which for all but close subjects can be taken to be equal to the focal length of the lens. So the ratio between the focal length and the aperture is a good measure of the brightness of the image that the lens will produce of a scene of standard brightness. When a lens's aperture setting is described as being f4, the diameter of the iris opening is $\frac{1}{4}$ of the lens's focal length. The familiar series of f stops (f2.8, f4, f5.6, f8 . . .) corresponds to successive halvings of the image brightness, calling for doublings of the exposure time.

The intensity of the light entering the human eye is controlled by an iris in just the same way as that entering a camera. The human eye lens, however, focuses by changing its curvature. In photographic terms it is by no means a perfect lens, being subject to nearly all conceivable aberrations. But since only the central part of the visual field is "read" in detail, poor peripheral image quality is tolerable. And the extraordinarily complex "wiring" of the human retina, discussed next, gives the eye a delicacy and flexibility in colour discrimination that no man-made instrument can match.

Spherical aberration *is the inability of a lens to focus light from the whole area of the lens. When rays passing through the centre of the lens are recorded sharply (inset left) rays passing through the edge come into focus closer to the lens and form a halo around each point (inset right). Soft-focus lens attachments use a controlled amount of spherical aberration to diffuse the image.*

Chromatic aberration *can cause colour fringes around highlights in a photograph. As light enters a lens it is refracted, or bent. In a simple lens (near right) the coloured constituents of light are refracted by different amounts and are brought into focus at different points: here only red is correctly focused in the recorded image (rear film plane). Green would focus nearer the lens and blue nearer still. A combination of lenses, such as the achromatic doublet (far right) made of two materials with different refractive indices, focuses colours at the same point.*

Coma *affects off-axis images. Light rays passing through all parts of a lens should be focused to a single point (inset left). But when coma is present a teardrop-shaped patch is formed (inset right). Coma is hard to cure, especially in a wide-angle lens, and even in a corrected lens it can distort parts of a picture as a result of unsymmetrical light patches recorded on the image.*

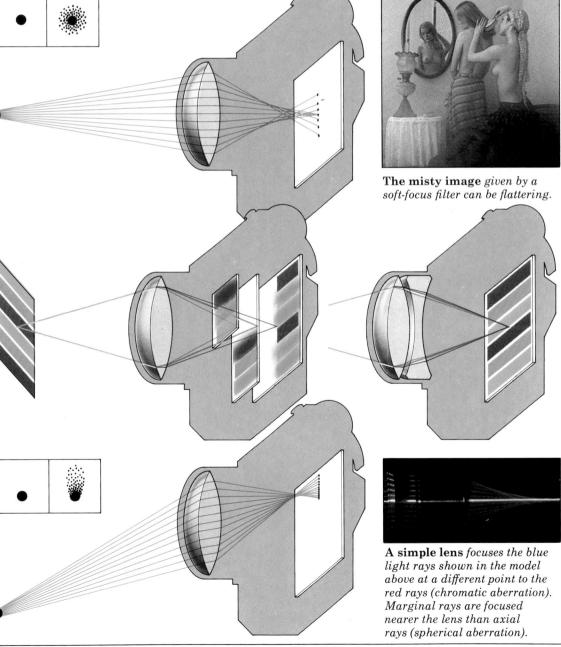

The misty image *given by a soft-focus filter can be flattering.*

A simple lens *focuses the blue light rays shown in the model above at a different point to the red rays (chromatic aberration). Marginal rays are focused nearer the lens than axial rays (spherical aberration).*

Colour vision

All human beings are colour-blind. For, as we have seen on the preceding pages, a given colour can be formed by many different mixtures of coloured light, among which the eye cannot discriminate. This is because information about hue is represented in the eye by the relative strengths of just three signals, from cells sensitive to the red, green and blue parts of the spectrum. As a result, three so-called "primary" colours are sufficient to match any hue, a feature that is known as trichromacy.

The cornea, the transparent horny layer fronting the eyeball, together with the eye lens, form images of external scenes on the retina, the inner surface of the eye. In some respects, therefore, an analogy can be drawn between the eye and the camera, which also has a lens, a "screen" on which the image is formed and a means of varying focus. Whereas the camera lens is responsible for all the convergence of the incoming light, most of the eye's focusing power is due to its curved form and only a little extra power is contributed by the lens. The fact that the eye lens can rapidly change its curvature in order to form sharp images of objects at different distances does, however, give the eye a flexibility in changing focus that cannot be matched by a camera, in which the lens has to be moved back and forth. It is difficult to produce a film image that shows extremely close and distant objects simultaneously in focus.

When it comes to the effect of light on the retina, any analogy with a camera ceases. Within the retina are specialized cells, called rods and cones, which absorb light and transform it into electrical signals, these in turn causing changes in a long chain of cells leading to the cortex, or outer layer, of the brain. The retina contains several types of nerve cells, which partly analyse the information from the rods and cones before transmitting it to the brain.

Human vision in dim light depends on the rods, but normal daylight vision and discrimination of colour depend on the cones. In the normal eye there are three different kinds of cones, each containing a different kind of pigment. Each pigment absorbs light of a certain colour more strongly than any other. Thus one absorbs blue light most strongly, another green and a third red. But each kind of cone absorbs all colours of light to some extent, and gives an electrical response. As shown in the diagram below, the overlap is particularly marked in absorption curves for red and green

light. The response of, say, a "red-sensitive" cone to a faint red light could be the same as its response to a bright light from the green wavelength region of the spectrum.

Thus if the brain is to sense colour there must be mechanisms that compare the outputs of the three different classes of cones. To reach the brain, signals must pass via intermediate stages to ganglion cells, which provide the final output from the retina. The cones are connected in complex ways to the ganglion cells. A certain type of ganglion cell, called an "opponent" cell, may receive "excitatory" signals from a cone of one type—signals that, occurring alone, would stimulate the cell to send a signal to the brain. But it may "switch off" if it receives simultaneous "inhibitory" signals from cones of another type. Diagrams on the opposite page show how the outputs of opponent ganglion cells represent comparisons of the inputs from the cones.

Other ganglion cells are "non-opponent"; they receive, say, excitatory signals from both red-sensitive and green-sensitive cones. These cells thus signal the brightness of the light, rather than its colour.

Rods are of only one type, most sensitive to blue-green light. That is why in twilight, when only the rods are functioning, we cannot discriminate colours; and objects that in daylight would look blue appear much brighter than objects that in daylight would be red.

The blue-sensitive cones give little information about brightness, though they are important in perceiving hue. Their signals appear to be transmitted only to the opponent type of ganglion cell. In an experiment, the red- and green-sensitive cones can be fatigued by being exposed to yellow light, which excites both of them. The observer then becomes wholly dependent on the blue cones, and has difficulty resolving fine detail or detecting flicker in the stimulus light.

For very small details or very faint light, normal vision is like that of a colour-blind man who lacks blue cones altogether. This is why it is unwise in colour drawings to use thin blue lines: they will be difficult to distinguish from black lines.

Much of this is to be explained by the fact that there are almost no blue-sensitive cones in the centre of the fovea, the otherwise most sensitive region of our retina, corresponding to the line of sight. We are particularly insensitive to small or faint blue details when we look directly at them.

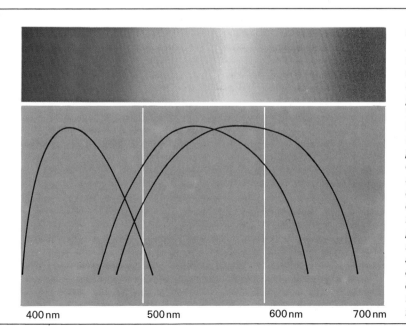

The responses of three types of cones *enable us to judge the colour of light. There are more than six million cones in the retina, each only two-thousandths of a millimetre thick. The absorption curves of pigments in each type of cone are broad and overlapping (right). Blue light of short wavelength triggers a strong response—an electrical signal to other cells—from B cones, but little or none from the other two types. Green (medium-wavelength) or red (long-wavelength) light triggers considerable response from G and R cones, but maximum response to green comes from the G cones and to red from the R cones.*

400 nm   500 nm   600 nm   700 nm

Ganglion cells *(labelled A, B and C in the diagrams at the right) receive signals from the cones (marked as red-, green- or blue-sensitive) and pass on further signals to the brain. The signals are represented as balls falling down chutes. Some cells (B and C) compare signals from two classes of cones and either fire or switch off— symbolized by the closing of a valve. For simplicity, each cone is shown as either responding or not when light falls on it; in fact each cone may produce strong or weak signals. Many other patterns of cell connection between cones and ganglion cells influence the final information received by the brain.*

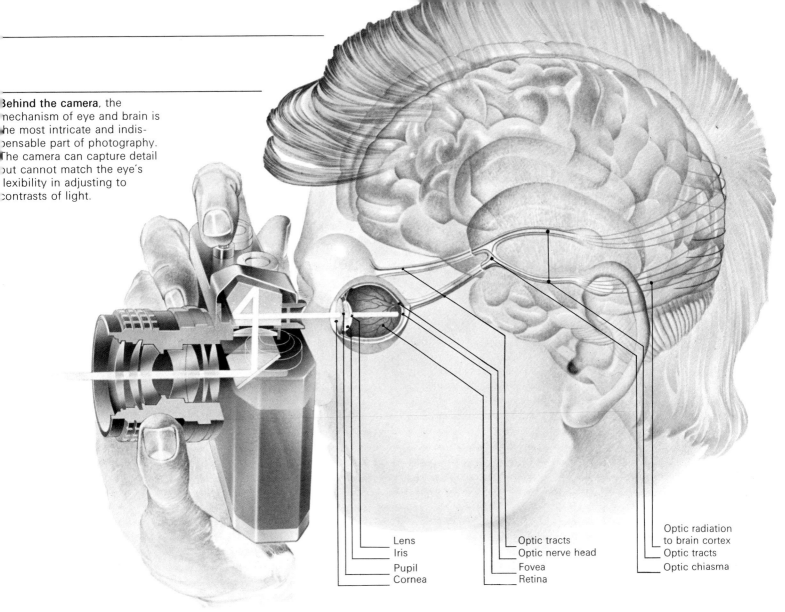

Lens
Iris
Pupil
Cornea

Optic tracts
Optic nerve head
Fovea
Retina

Optic radiation
to brain cortex
Optic tracts
Optic chiasma

The photographer controls the
exposure of his film by varying
shutter speed and the iris
diaphragm. The eye also
regulates light entering it, partly
by varying the aperture of the
iris. A more important variable,
however, is the sensitivity of

the cones and rods. Light
must penetrate the whole
thickness of the retina before
reaching these sensitive receptors
forming the image-receiving
"screen" at the back of the eye.
The rods come into play when
the light intensity falling on

the eye is low. Although highly
sensitive they cannot provide
colour discrimination and
this task is left to the cones.
Information about the intensity
and wavelengths of light received
by the rods and cones is sorted
in the retina and signals are

sent through the optic nerves
along pathways leading to higher
nerve cells at the back of the
brain for final analysis. A
partial cross-over of nerve
fibres (the optic chiasma)
relays some signals from each
eye to both sides of the brain.

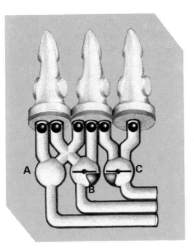

When no light reaches the
cones, no signals are dropped
into the bulge representing
the ganglion cells.

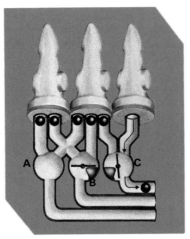

When blue light bathes the
cones, the blue-sensitive cone
releases a message and this is
sent on by the ganglion cell.

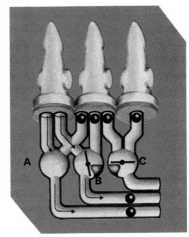

In red light, signals go to
both cell A and cell B, which
receives no opposing signal.
Both pass the signal on.

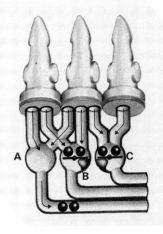

White light activates all three
cones, but only cell A fires,
relaying information triggered
by both red and green cones.

Colour vision

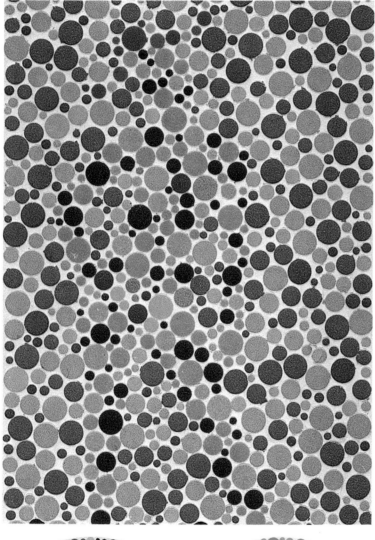

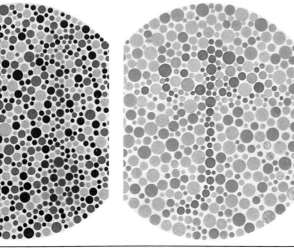

The brightest light that the eye can handle is 10,000 million times as bright as the faintest. The eye must adjust its sensitivity to the prevailing intensity of light, as does an automatic camera. The eye has a variable aperture, the pupil, which contracts in brighter light. But the amount of light admitted to the eye can be reduced only by one-sixteenth by contraction of the pupil. Most of the variation in the eye's sensitivity is due to automatic adjustment of the sensitivity of cells in the retina.

Each kind of cone has its own independent sensitivity control. It is this independence that gives the eye the ability to adjust to the colour of the surrounding illumination. A piece of paper that looks white in daylight will still look white when we have adjusted to the tungsten light of a domestic room—even though the proportion of blue light in the illumination is now very much lower. But how does the eye make the adjustment?

In normal daylight, which contains all wavelengths in roughly equal proportions, the three types of cones will be about equally sensitive. The piece of white paper will appear white because it reflects a balance of all wavelengths. When we have been in tungsten illumination for a little time, the blue-sensitive cones will become more sensitive than the red- and green-sensitive cones, to compensate for the lack of blue in the light. Although the white paper now reflects less blue light than red or green light, the blue-sensitive cones will give the same signal as before.

Such adjustments as these have the useful result that we see a given object as constant in brightness and hue despite large changes in the intensity and quality of the illumination. However, the adjustments of the eye are not instantaneous and so may occasionally cause errors or create illusions. One such illusion is the complementary after-image. If we stare for a little time at a piece of red paper and then look at a white surface, we will see a blue-green (cyan) patch that moves around with the direction of our gaze. The sensitivity of the red-sensitive cones has decreased through fatigue in the small part of the retina that was stimulated by the image of the paper. When we now look at the white surface those cones give less response than they would normally give in white light, while the signals from the blue- and green-sensitive cones are little changed. So the overall pattern of signals reaching the brain resembles the pattern of signals normally resulting from an actual cyan patch.

Colour information from the retina is passed through several intermediate stages to the occipital cortex, the outer layer of the back of the brain. One of the most interesting questions now being investigated by visual scientists is this:

The McCollough effect *indicates a link between form and colour at some stage in the brain's processing of signals from the eye. Stare at the pattern on the near right, letting your eyes wander freely over the pattern for at least one minute in a strong light. Resist the temptation to tilt your head. Then look at the black and white pattern. The left tilted bars in the second pattern seem tinged with a pale blue-green complementary to the hue of the left-tilted bars in the first pattern. And the right-tilting bars seem*

to take on a pink hue, complementary to the green of the bars in the first pattern. The colours are "tied" to the bars and do not move with the direction of gaze. Even more remarkably, when the black and white pattern is turned through 90 degrees the bars in a given area will change in their apparent colour as their tilt changes. This indicates that it is the alignment of the bars rather than their position which is important. The effect can persist for days if the black-and-white pattern is not viewed too frequently.

do we have separate neural mechanisms for analysing colour, brightness, form, movement, distance and so on? Experiments on monkeys suggest that there is a region in the brain that deals solely with the analysis of colour. Possibly there is a corresponding area in the human brain, and damage to it accounts for some cases of total colour blindness.

The remarkable McCollough effect (shown below), however, suggests that colour and form are analysed together at some stage in the visual system. When one has looked at the left-hand coloured pattern for several minutes, illusory colours are seen on the black and white pattern—pale greens where the bars are tilted to the left and pinks where they are tilted to the right.

The McCollough effect is very different from an ordinary after-image, for each point on the retina has been stimulated equally by red and green light during adaptation to the coloured pattern. It suggests that in the human brain there are nerve cells that respond only to a bar of a particular colour *and* of a particular orientation. Such cells have indeed been found in the brains of monkeys. The apparent colour of a tilted bar may depend on the relative activity of cells tuned to that orientation, but differing in the colour that causes them to respond. While the coloured pattern is being viewed, cells specific to, say, green bars tilted 45 degrees to the right (and others specific to red bars tilted 45 degrees to the left) grow fatigued. Then a black and white pattern tilted 45 degrees to the right will look pink, since the fatigued cells are not contributing their normal response. But there are other proposed explanations of the curious McCollough effect.

Complete colour blindness, a total inability to discriminate colours, is very rare indeed, but some deficiency of colour vision is rather common. About eight per cent of all men have some hereditary defect in their colour vision, although less than one in two hundred women are so affected. Some people ("dichromats") appear to lack either the red- or green-sensitive cones. The result is that they may confuse, say, red with green or yellow with green and will match any other colour they are given by an appropriate mixture of only two primary colours (instead of three as in normal people). Others ("anomalous trichromats") appear to have three types of cones, but one class of these cones has its peak sensitivity somewhere between the peak sensitivities of normal red- and green-sensitive cones. Like the rest of us, such people need three wavelengths to match all the colours. The matches that they make are not the usual ones, but there is no sense in which they can be said to be less correct than those made by the majority of people.

Complementary after-images
form after a few seconds of viewing any bright scene. Look at the picture below under bright light for a minute or so and then look at the blank space. The film packaging will appear in the colours familiar to photographers. The illusory colours are the result of an under-response to white by temporarily fatigued cones.

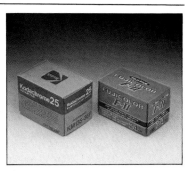

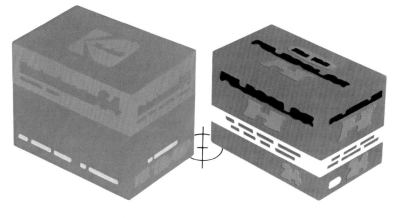

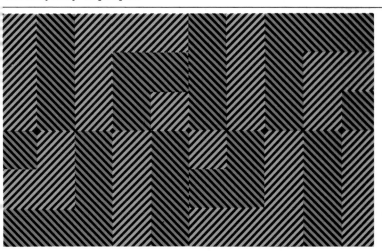

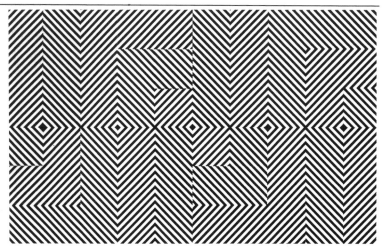

Colour psychology

The emotional or psychological effects of colour are not so easy to measure as the physiological aspects of colour perception, yet most of us have colour preferences and feel that these affect our moods. Many people find it difficult to live or work in rooms with colour schemes that strike them as inappropriate. Colours are thought of as strong or weak, restful or arousing—even heavy or light.

Although many such reactions are highly individual, research seems to show that others are widely shared. But our beliefs about colour are easily overridden by other sensory experience and the distinctions we make in assigning a certain quality to one colour or another are subtle and elusive, tending to produce conflicting evidence when scientific tests are made.

For example, laboratory experiments made as long ago as 1907 showed that people agreed about the apparent weight of colours. Red seemed heaviest, followed by orange, blue and green (all similar in weight), then yellow and finally white. Pairs of colour patches of identical shapes looked unstable when the "heaviest" colour was on top. Yet this visual impression is not strong enough to influence people's estimation of the weights of different coloured objects held in the hand.

Colour modifies the apparent size of objects, the colours that look heavy also looking small. Among equal-sized squares, red ones look smallest, blue larger and white largest of all. The French tricolour is normally designed with vertical blue, white and red bands of equal breadth. But the version used at sea has bands in the proportions 33:30:37 so that, viewed from a distance, the bands will look equal.

The familiar classification of colours into "warm" and "cool" (see pages 40–1) does not seem to be strongly related to our actual judgement of temperature. In one experiment a blue or green bar at a temperature of 42°C (108°F) seemed warmer to people who held it than a red or orange bar at the same temperature. A test of whether or not the colour of the lighting in a room affected judgements of its warmth or comfort suggested that illuminating a room with "warm" light is no substitute for heating it.

Industrial psychologists are interested in the effects of colour on the efficiency of workers. It has been claimed that workmen spend less time in lavatories painted red than in those painted blue. Monkeys have certainly been shown to spend less time in red lighting than in lighting of other colours if they are given a choice. It has been suggested that this is due less to a preference for other colours than to a speeding up of their "biological clocks" in red lighting—the monkeys feel they have spent longer in the red environment. But if human beings' "clocks" are similarly affected, this does not seem to affect the direct estimates they make of how long they have spent in environments of various colours.

If people are asked in experiments to draw a semicircle slowly, they can carry out the task better under green lighting than under red, which increases hand tremor—shown also by increased difficulty in holding a needle in a small hole without touching the edge. It seems that red light does have an arousing effect, as is popularly believed, for it increases the electrical conductance of the skin, which is a measure of the rate of sweating. Yet red light has no appreciable effect on pulse or respiration rates. Here, as in most areas of colour psychology, the evidence is conflicting. There is a wide range of manual tasks, as well as most mental tasks, that seems to be unaffected by the colour of the lighting in use.

Aesthetic reactions to colours, both singly and in

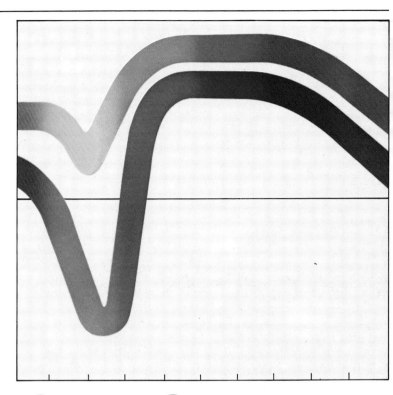

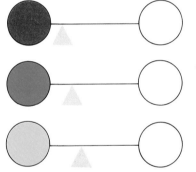

The order of preference in which most people place colours is shown in these graphs, with brighter tints (top band) being preferred to darker shades.

Relative weights of colours seemed something like this to volunteers who were asked to position the pointers so that coloured luminous discs would appear to balance the white ones. Red seemed heaviest.

combination, have fascinated artists and writers for centuries. Only a few well-controlled scientific studies have been made, but they seem to show a surprising degree of agreement in colour preference among different people. Shown specimens of single colours on a neutral grey background, people generally prefer bluish hues, ranging from blue-green to purple-blue. A greenish yellow is liked least. All colours are liked more when they are lighter.

Researchers have also asked people to judge the pleasantness of pairs of colours and found that large differences in hues are generally preferred to small ones, with an even more marked preference for colour pairs that show large differences in saturation or brightness.

The impact of abstract colour designs can be predicted to some extent from these preferences for single and paired colours. Some psychologists believe that such simple preferences are biologically based and influence even the complex aesthetic judgements we make of paintings or photographs, viewed as colour designs.

We are more likely to be struck by the variety of responses to colour in different cultures than by the similarities. White, traditionally a bridal colour in many countries, is the colour of mourning in some others. A Westerner is not surprised that in the costuming and make-up of Vietnamese opera, red should symbolize anger, but could hardly guess that white symbolizes treachery and black symbolizes boldness.

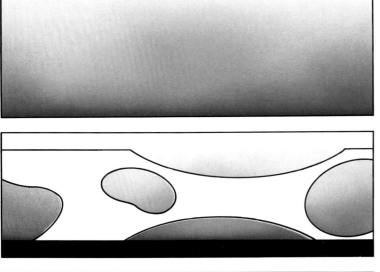

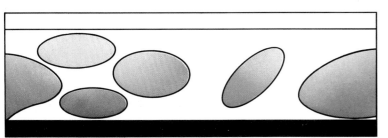

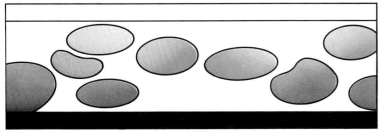

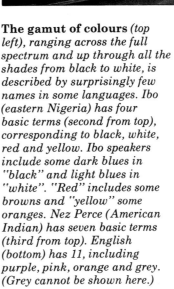

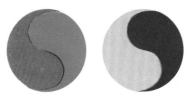

The gamut of colours (top left), ranging across the full spectrum and up through all the shades from black to white, is described by surprisingly few names in some languages. Ibo (eastern Nigeria) has four basic terms (second from top), corresponding to black, white, red and yellow. Ibo speakers include some dark blues in "black" and light blues in "white". "Red" includes some browns and "yellow" some oranges. Nez Perce (American Indian) has seven basic terms (third from top). English (bottom) has 11, including purple, pink, orange and grey. (Grey cannot be shown here.)

The saffron robes worn by Buddhist monks may affect the unusually high evaluation of yellow in Thailand.

Hues in the yin-yang symbols below show combinations of the kind people prefer in colour pairs. Contrasting hues such as green and magenta are liked, or large differences in lightness if the hues are the same.

Careful research has shown that there is much common ground, nevertheless, in human reactions to colour around the world. Red, yellow, green and blue seem to be "focal" colours for mankind. Before they have learned to talk, children tend to prefer these colours and to avoid the "boundary" colours lying between them. The names of the focal colours are the first to be learned.

Furthermore, when languages are arranged in order of the complexity of their colour terminology, it is found that colour names appear in a definite order. Some languages, including several in New Guinea, have only two "basic" colour terms, corresponding to black and white, or dark and light. Other colour terms are non-basic because, for example, they are restricted to specific objects. The anthropologists Brent Berlin and Paul Kay claim that even in the most complex languages there are no more than 11 basic colour terms. And they propose that, as societies discriminated colours ever more finely, these basic terms appeared in this historical sequence: black and white; red; yellow and green, in either order; blue; brown; and purple, pink, orange and grey (the last four appearing in any order). Clearly there are many more colour names in a language such as English; but crimson, for example, is not regarded as basic because it covers part of the range of red, and words such as "blond" are discounted because they apply only to certain kinds of objects or materials in much the same way as

object-related colour terms in more primitive societies.

Corresponding colour terms in different languages may not cover the same range of colours. But the "foci" of the terms—the most typical examples of the colours denoted—always agree closely.

Many people make strong associations between colours and other sensory experiences. Thus the poet Rimbaud thought of each vowel as having its own colour: A, black; E, white; I, red; O, blue; and U, green. And Rimsky-Korsakov felt the different musical keys had their own colour associations: C major, white; D major, yellow; E major, blue; and F major, green.

Leaving aside such personal reactions, some qualities do seem to be generally assigned to colours. To an extent, these are influenced by differences of culture or environment. On a "good-bad" evaluation, white is regarded more highly in Asia than in the West. Yellow is evaluated more highly in Thailand than anywhere else—possibly for religious reasons. In terms of potency, green is regarded as a strong colour in arid countries. The overall impression, however, is of the uniformity rather than the diversity of colour "meaning" across cultures. Grey, yellow and white are usually regarded as weak, while red is almost always seen as potent and active. Blue is evaluated nearly everywhere as a "good" colour. In their perception of colour and response to it, human beings seem to be much alike.

Colour description

The infinite variety of colour can be reduced to order with the help of analytic terms based on those first used by artists and now taken over and refined by scientists. Three "dimensions" of colour are usually recognized—three characteristics that can vary independently of each other and which, when specified, serve to define any possible colour. One of many ways of defining these dimensions is in terms of hue, saturation and lightness or darkness.

Hue is the essential quality that distinguishes one colour from another—red from blue, purple from yellow, and so on. Each hue can vary over a continuous range of saturation, or purity. Thus while crimson is a highly saturated colour, crimson light can be desaturated by mixing it with white light, degrading it to a pink. Physically this effect can be achieved by mixing a pure paint with a white one to make what painters call a tint of the original hue.

Saturation determines the apparent vividness, or chroma, of a colour. The spectrum displays perfectly saturated hues, but most of the colours we see every day are highly unsaturated. Various natural processes can further desaturate the colours of a scene by introducing white light. Thus the light scattered from mist droplets desaturates the colours of a scene and makes them "weaker". The varying amounts of white light reflected from a rich, red velvet according to the angle of illumination will give rise to various tints of the vivid hue seen with frontal lighting. And the white light reflected in a window desaturates the colours of objects viewed through the window. Pigments show saturated colours when they are ground to a consistency that allows full absorption of certain wavelengths of light and full reflection of other wavelengths without light escaping out of the back of the pigment layer.

The third important quality of a colour is its lightness or darkness. This essentially depends on the proportion of light reflected by a surface of that colour—equivalent to its brightness relative to other colours under a given illumination. A colour's absolute brightness (in the physicist's sense of the amount of light energy coming from it in each second) depends on this lightness and also on the intensity of the illuminating light. But the eye's powers of adaptation are such that normally we are unaware of the absolute brightness of a surface. Thus we do not realize that, say, the black sleeve of a jacket in daylight can be brighter than a hand seen in moonlight. We are normally aware only of relative brightnesses in given conditions.

Desaturated colours may be lighter than the saturated colours and then, as we have seen, they are called tints of that hue. (They can never be as light as a pure white—the colour of a surface that reflects all the visible light falling on it.) But a hue can also be desaturated by being darkened. The painter makes these "shades" of a hue by mixing black with the pure colour. Mustard and olive are shades of yellow and green, respectively. The darkest possible colour is a pure black, which would absorb all the visible light falling on it; no real material is quite as dark as this theoretical ideal. Fully saturated colours, however, vary absolutely in their degree of lightness or darkness.

Still more subtle discriminations in the world of colour can be made. For example, volume colour (the translucent colour of a liquid) may be distinguished from area colour (of, say, a wall under ordinary illumination). But hue, saturation and brightness are the terms most essential to an understanding of the reproduction of colours and their interactions with each other, in nature, in photography and in the human mind.

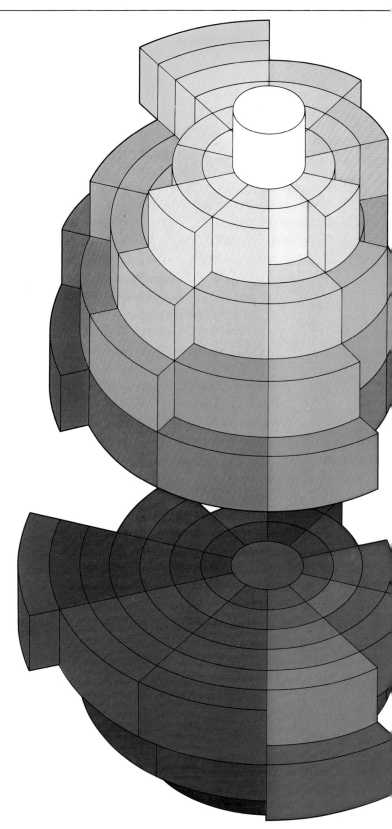

A colour solid *is an orderly arrangement of colours in three dimensions, corresponding to hue, lightness and saturation. The diagrams above are based on a system published by Albert Munsell in 1915. Hues are arranged cyclically around a central spine, which consists of the achromatic colours from black through the greys to white. Colours become lighter in ascending order on this spine according to the extent to which they reflect light. They become more vivid moving out from the spine as they are mixed less and less with grey.*

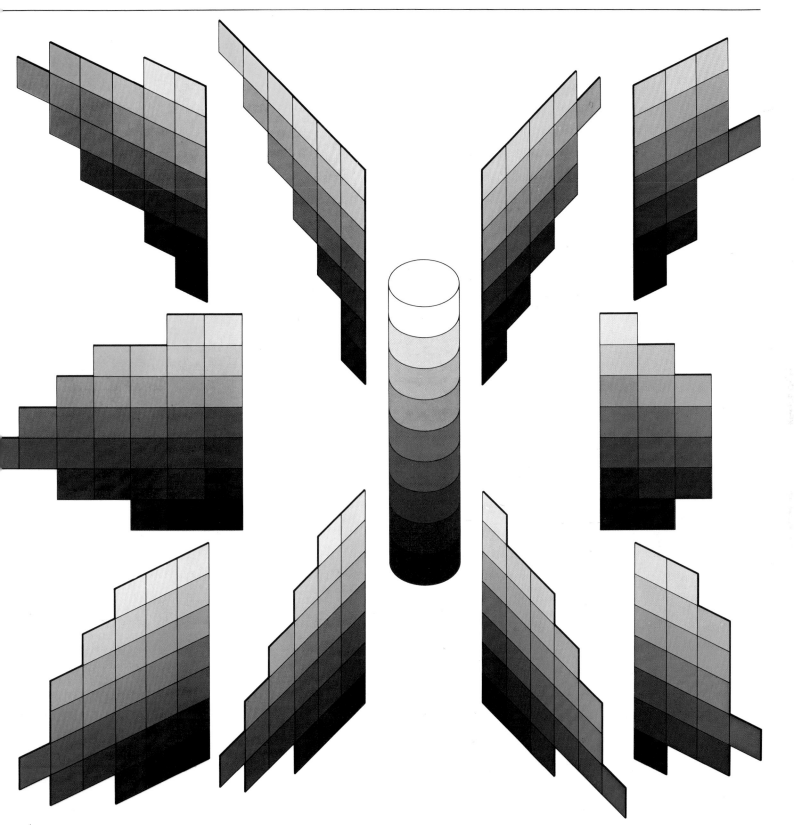

This vividness of appearance, closely related to saturation, is called chroma in the Munsell classification system. In the diagram on the left, the solid has been sliced just below the level of medium lightness. The increases in chroma between successive chips are intended to appear equal. It can be seen that some hues reach higher chromas than others. This is due partly to the limitations of the pigments available in printing. But even, say, an "ideal", perfectly saturated blue (not attainable in practice) would have less chroma than a fully saturated red. Of the very light colours, the yellows have the highest chroma, while the purples are the most colourful of the very dark shades. In the exploded diagram on the right, the wings represent the five main and five intermediate hues; the interior of the colour solid can now be seen. The hues range from dark shades to tints, with the most saturated samples at the extremity of each wing. Yellow is the lightest saturated hue. The colours shown do not exactly reproduce the standard hues in the Munsell Book of Color.

Colour mixing

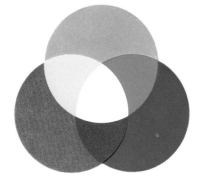

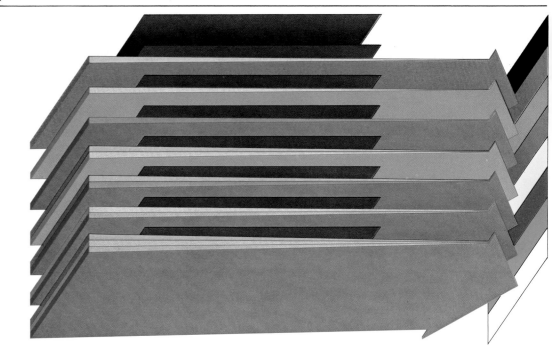

Addition *of primary-coloured lights gives new colours where they overlap (above). Colours formed by mixing any two of the primaries, red, green and blue, are called secondaries and include the magenta, cyan and yellow seen here. When all three of the primaries are mixed in equal amounts, white is obtained. The right-hand diagram shows the results of various mixtures of the three primaries in light beams projected on to a screen.*

Below the dark band at the top of the screen where no light is projected at all are bands of red, green and blue where these colours are projected alone. Next, red and green lights are combined to give a yellow band, red and blue lights to give magenta, and blue and green lights to give cyan. Red, green and blue together form the white band at the bottom.

Since the eye has only three different kinds of cones, the colour receptors in the retina, it cannot respond differently to all the mixtures of wavelengths that reach it. For example, in relatively pure light the eye will see a yellow if it receives a narrow range of wavelength from the yellow part of the spectrum. But it will respond in exactly the same way to certain mixtures of red and green light. White sunlight is a mixture of all the spectral colours; but a mixture of only two wavelengths, one in the red and the other in the blue-green, can give a good white.

Not only can a certain perceived colour correspond to a wide range of wavelength compositions; a limited selection of coloured lights of fixed wavelengths can be mixed in varying proportions to match almost any colour. This fact is of prime importance to printers and photographers, for it makes possible virtually all the modern forms of colour reproduction on film and paper.

If a deep red, a deep blue and a deep green light are projected on to a white screen in the right proportions they will produce a white mixture where they overlap. Varying their relative brightnesses can lead to the production of almost any desired colour. For example, a brown could be made from a mixture of a dim green light with a slightly brighter red one, with little or no blue. Increasing the brightness of all three lamps would cause the brown to lighten and become a yellowish-red.

For this *additive* mixing of colours a saturated red, blue and green are described as "primaries". By mixing àny two primaries a "secondary" is obtained. For example, mixing the red with progressively more green will produce highly saturated yellow-reds, yellows, yellow-greens and greens. When green is mixed with progressively more blue, various deep blue-greens are obtained. And when blue is mixed with varying amounts of red, a series of deep purples is obtained.

When a third primary is mixed in with such a secondary the mixture begins to move towards a white (that is, towards the central spine of the Munsell colour tree shown on the

previous pages). These are the unsaturated hues known as "tertiary" colours.

The additive mixing of colours was used in photography by the physicist James Clerk Maxwell in the 1860s. He recorded the brightnesses of the red, green and blue light in a scene on separate black and white negatives, each of which received light of only one colour. He made these into positive transparencies and projected each on to a screen with light of the appropriate colour, making sure that the images were accurately in register. The observers' eyes responded to the mixture of light reflected from the screen roughly as they would have done to the original scene.

This kind of additive colour reproduction is not used today because of the inconvenience of making separate images and projecting them in exact coincidence. But *partitive* colour reproduction, which depends in part on a form of additive mixing, was the basis of the first commercially successful colour photography and is used today in colour television and in Polavision instant movie film. When an image made of multicoloured dots is viewed from a distance the eye cannot resolve the individual spots and their colours seem to be combined. The colour perceived in a small area of the picture depends on the relative numbers, sizes and brightnesses of the dots of each colour in that area. Thus a mixture of red and green dots of equal sizes in equal numbers would give a yellow result when viewed from a distance. The Autochrome process, which the Lumière brothers marketed as early as 1907, used the partitive principle. Their pictures consisted of a black and white photographic transparency coated with transparent starch grains dyed red, green and blue in roughly equal numbers. They made up a mosaic of spots the brightness of which depended on the density of the photo-graphic image (see page 254). Polavision movie film consists of a black and white image fronted by a grid of red, blue and green stripes. And a modern colour TV image is similarly composed of glowing red, blue and green spots or stripes.

Colour printing employs arrays of tiny dots arranged at

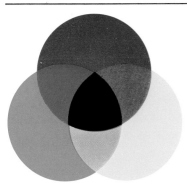

Subtraction *of colours from white light by filters or dyes can also form any colour. Above are three filters against a white background. The cyan filter absorbs red light, the yellow absorbs blue and the magenta absorbs green. Where two overlap, either red, blue or green is passed, as the diagram on the right illustrates more fully. The secondaries, magenta, cyan and yellow, are thus the "primaries" for subtractive colour reproduction.*

A variety of different colours is produced from white light (which can be regarded broadly as a mixture of red, green and blue) as it passes in turn through various combinations of cyan, yellow and magenta filters. Magenta and cyan filters pass blue only; cyan and yellow pass green only; and yellow and magenta pass red only. No light at all can pass all the filters.

slightly different alignments so that some of them overlap while others lie side by side. These dots are printed in three colours and in black. However, the colours used are yellow (reflecting red and green light), magenta (red and blue) and cyan (blue and green). To understand the reason for this choice of colours one must understand the principle of *subtractive* colour reproduction.

As explained on page 24, the colours of all objects are due to the subtraction of other colours from the illuminating light. Thus a red paint sends predominantly red light to the eye because most of the blue and green components in the light falling on it are absorbed, leaving mainly red light to be reflected. When this paint is mixed with another one, each continues to subtract its share of the light and so the mixture reflects still less light. Thus when red and green paints are mixed the red paint pigment will absorb a great deal of green and blue light, while the green pigment will subtract yet more blue and most of the red light. The result will be a dark colour, but it is unlikely to be a grey. For the colours reflected by the unmixed red and green are far from pure. They consist of bands of colour, which are likely to overlap to some extent. The red will probably reflect considerable amounts of yellow light and the green paint is likely to reflect appreciable amounts both of yellow and of blue. So both components reflect some yellow and the colour of the mixture is a dark yellow—that is, a brown. This is called subtractive colour mixing.

When red paint is mixed with yellow the result will probably be an orange since that is the only wavelength that is relatively strongly reflected by both components. Yellow and blue paints in general give a dull green when mixed, and so will combined yellow and blue filters, although theoretically these two colours subtract all the primary colours of light.

Colours are always darkened by subtractive mixing, for the mixture necessarily contains less light than any of its components. This was one of the reasons why the

Impressionists painted colours in dots and dashes of vivid spectral hues, rather than by using mixed paints.

The overlapping dyes that form colours in film must contain the red, blue and green primaries, but must not be too dark. Transparent cyan, magenta and yellow dyes are therefore used in photographic film and papers. Cyan absorbs red light and transmits blue and green; magenta absorbs green and transmits red and blue; and yellow absorbs blue and transmits red and green. Where cyan and magenta overlap the mixture formed will be blue, and so on. Yellow, cyan and magenta are the main secondary colours because each of them contains equal components of two primary colours of light and each can on its own subtract the remaining primary colour.

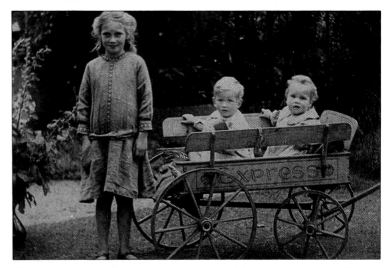

Partitive colour synthesis *was used in this Paget photograph of 1914. Ordinary film was exposed through a grid of red, green and blue squares, printed as a trans-* *parent black and white positive on glass, and viewed through a similar grid. This process was essentially similar to that used in the Autochrome screen.*

Colour relationships

We think of colours as having "natural" brightnesses—yellow as brightest and purple, or perhaps blue, as darkest. And it is true that the extent to which any colour can be lightened while retaining its purity is limited. Thus, a rich red paint is of medium darkness. It can be lightened by diluting it with white to make pink, and it can be darkened by mixing it with black to make reddish brown. But in each case its purity, or redness, is reduced. Yellow, on the other hand, can be very light and colourful at the same time. A darkened yellow is a tan, inevitably sombre and greyish by contrast with the vividness of a deep blue, even though the blue is low in brightness. Such relationships can be seen in the Munsell colour tree on pages 36–7.

Striking effects can be achieved when juxtaposed colours violate our expectations about their relative brightness. We are surprised by an area of olive next to a pink—a green-yellow that is darker than normal adjacent to a red lighter than normal.

The perceived lightness of a colour depends on its colour context. A particular pale colour will seem darker in a picture dominated by light colours. Other properties are also influenced by relationships between neighbouring colours. Our judgement of hue may be altered when certain colours are juxtaposed. In general a vivid colour will make the colour next to it appear more like its complementary. Thus red will "induce" a green-blue tinge in neighbouring colours.

It is extremely difficult to generalize about the merits of a particular colour balance in a picture or colour scheme. But there are objective characteristics of colour contrast and harmony. Colours harmonize if they are close to each other in hue, saturation and lightness. Closeness in only one of these aspects may also contribute to colour harmony. Thus pale tints, even of very different hues, can often harmonize successfully and so can very sombre shades, because they agree in lightness and darkness respectively.

Varying tints of a narrow range of hues—that is, drawn from a single sector of the colour wheel shown here—harmonize with each other. But this is subject to the qualification that small areas of weaker, greyer colours sit uneasily with large areas of more vivid ones; small pale green areas among large emerald-green ones, for example.

The effect of juxtaposing contrasting colours is to create a vibrancy different from the more placid mood created by harmonic colours. Where colours have clearly been chosen to contrast, the evidence of a clear principle of selection can be as pleasing as a clear selection of closely related colours.

Reddish hues are often described as warm, bluish ones as cold. Red may owe its suggestion of warmth to its association with the warmth and snugness of domestic scenes lit by candles, oil lamps or fires. Blue is the dominant cast of overcast days and alpine or arctic snow scenes.

Red colours also seem to "advance" towards the viewer, while blues seem to recede. This impression may have to do with the greater "potency" that nearly all cultures associate with red (see pages 34–5). But it may also be due to the simple physiological fact that red light is focused less easily than blue light; that is, the eye has to accommodate more—become more strongly curved—to bring it to a focus. The eye has to do the same to transfer its focus from more distant objects to nearer ones, and this may be why red objects seem closer than blue ones that are actually at the same distance. On the other hand, our sense of the "recession" of blue may be influenced by our observation that the horizon and distant hills often look blue through hazy air, an effect created by the scattering of blue light by molecules in the atmosphere.

Hues vary continuously around the colour wheel. In addition, each of the hues ranges through paler tints to merge with white light at the centre of the wheel. Another wheel could show the same hues in a range of shades darkening towards black.

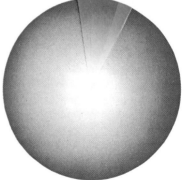

Hues that are similar—drawn from a small sector of the colour wheel—harmonize, and

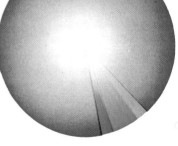

the closeness of this harmony increases as the related hues are tinted towards white.

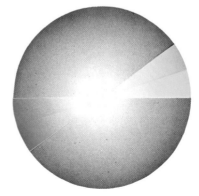

Hues opposite each other on the colour wheel are complementary; if added, they make white.

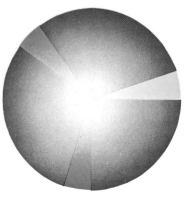

Widely separated hues contrast, but they can be used together in many striking compositions.

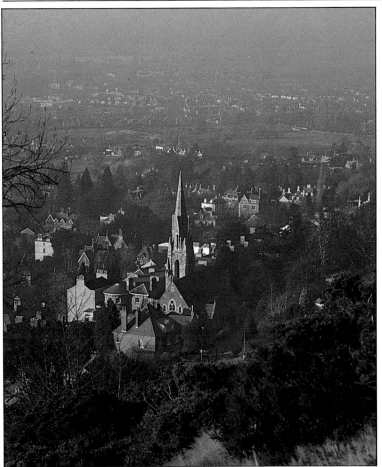

The central area seems to retreat and advance in Josef Albers's **Homage to the Square: Departing in Yellow** (above).

In the context of these carefully calculated areas, hues and shades, even the vivid yellow seems tranquil.

The distance is blue in this English landscape at evening. The common feeling that in a picture bluish hues recede may derive from their association with the blue cast of distant scenes. The colour is caused by scattering of sunlight, especially the blue part, by airborne dust and moisture. As it is caused by the atmosphere, the resulting impression of distance is called ''aerial perspective''

Neighbouring colours can modify not only the effect of a colour in a composition but also our very judgement of what it is. Until the surrounding circles are masked, it is hard to believe that exactly the same colour appears in the discs in the upper and lower halves of these diagrams. The discs seem lighter when surrounded by a darker colour, and vice versa. Apparent change of hue is more elusive; it is often said that a colour takes on a tinge that is complementary to its neighbour, but there is usually more disagreement over whether this effect occurs.

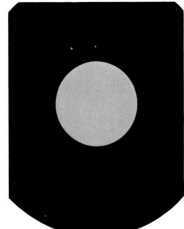

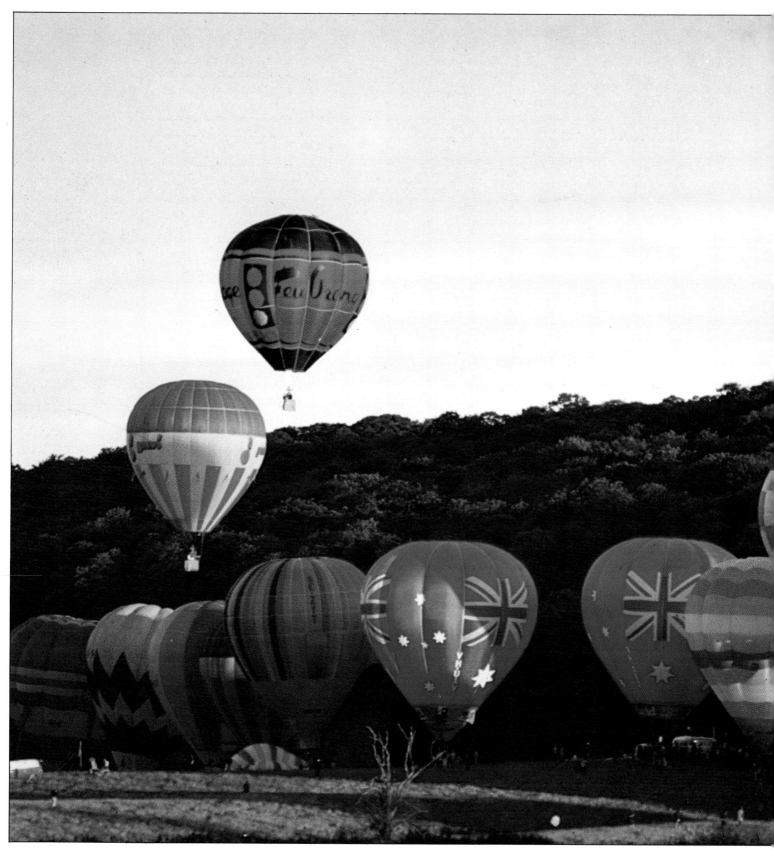

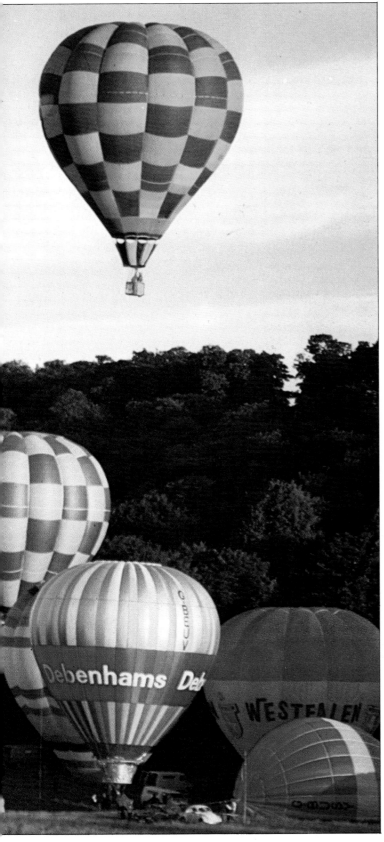

Handlling colour

Hot air balloons *rising into a pale morning sky reveal subtleties of colour, form and pattern in an apparently simple image. Modelled by the play of light and shade or flattened against the shadowed hillside, the balloons vary in colour from deeply saturated hues to silvery highlights where their fabric reflects the autumn sunlight. The field, patterned in russet and grey, itself shows the extent to which colour depends on light. Knowing how to handle colour depends on a complex relationship between subject, camera and the light that reaches both.* Leicaflex, 90mm, Ektachrome 200, 1/500, f8.

Using the changing light

Colour is constant only under constant light. Outdoors, it changes continually as the sky lightens and darkens, as the earth warms or cools towards evening, and as clouds mass or mist gathers. The first essential in handling colour is to be aware of this variety in tone and hue. Expect change and be ready to respond to it and exploit the ever-shifting scene presented to the camera.

As we have already seen, many colour changes are not registered by the untrained eye at all, because the brain has its own built-in filtering system and tends to see colours as it expects them to look. Photographically, however, the inherent colour of any object can vary greatly depending on camera angle and on each area's exposure to light. In direct light one of the simplest ways in which you can influence the colours of your picture is simply to shift your angle of view. By shooting into the sun instead of with it, you can turn white into black. Alternatively, you can wait until the subject itself moves, presenting a reflective surface to the light and the camera instead of one that absorbs most of the available light. Only in the diffused light of an overcast day can you expect inherent colour not to change from minute to minute.

Film emulsions are balanced to the colour temperature of either daylight or artificial light. But daylight itself has a wide range of different colour temperatures. White daylight (about 6,000 kelvins) is a combination of direct sunlight and scattered light from a blue sky. Between sunrise and sunset, however, daylight may change from pink through orange, white and pale blue back to pink.

As different qualities of light play on subjects, shaping and colouring them, the photographer must anticipate the most effective moment to shoot. Even without changing your camera angle, the possibilities are endless. The direction and quality of light can blend together discordant colours, emphasize a single hue or balance one with another. If the day is cloudy, you can wait until sunlight picks out a single facet of a scene, highlighting a spot of vivid colour, or shadows create a pattern of tones with flat areas of subdued colour. In a real sense, therefore, your choice of viewpoint in relation to the direction of light is the first step in handling colour. Only after you have assessed the direction of light in relation to camera angle can you begin to compose your picture.

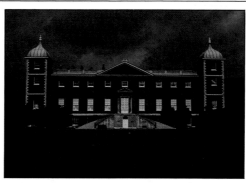

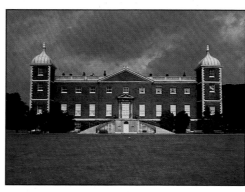

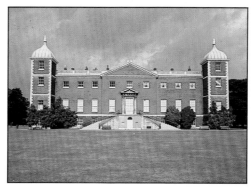

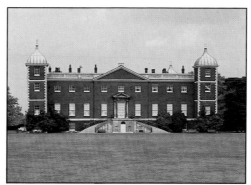

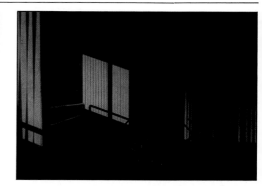

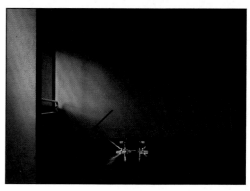

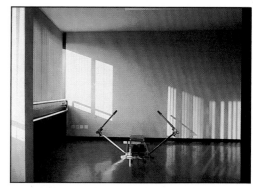

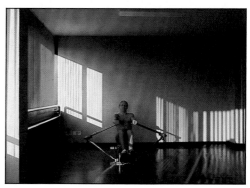

Colour changes *produced by storm light are shown in a sequence of four shots taken within half an hour. Leaden skies matching darkened brickwork (top) began to clear in the next picture, showing redder bricks but still subdued vegetation. A shaft of sun lightening the building and grass brought out colour in the trees, but made the third shot less dramatic. Finally, under a paler but completely overcast sky, the bricks appeared brown and detail was shown with sober clarity.*

Pentax, 55mm, Ektachrome 64, 1/125, f8, except for the third picture, shot at 1/250.

The mood of a hotel exercise room *altered startlingly when exposure changes were combined with fluctuating light. The pattern of shadows (top) made me expose for contrast. More diffused light in the second shot created an eerie mood, the machine seeming to generate light. As the sun reappeared I exposed for shadow detail, which gave less mystery. Lastly, I balanced exposure for both shadows and highlights, but felt human interest was needed for this more prosaic treatment.*

Pentax, 28mm, Agfachrome 50s, 1/250 (top and bottom), 1/125 (middle two), all at f8.

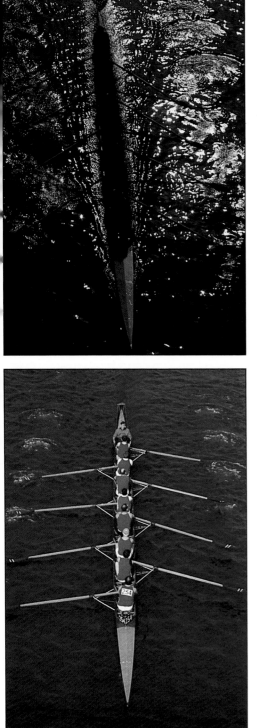

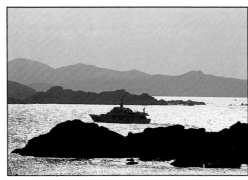

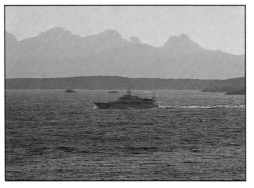

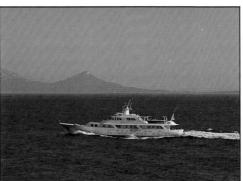

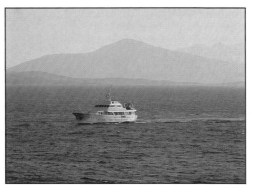

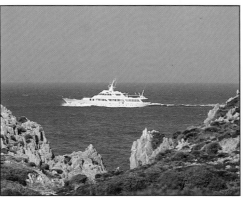

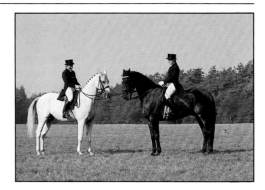

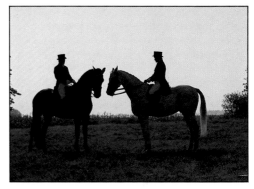

The two rowing pictures *were taken from a bridge over the Thames. In the first, low morning sun was reflecting into the camera from the water so all colour was lost. The shot concentrated on the glittering surface ripples, silhouetting the boat. With the sun striking the backs of a crew rowing in the opposite direction, I turned to shoot with the light behind the camera. Contrast was reduced, showing colour and pattern clearly but lessening the drama.*

Pentax, 50mm, Ektachrome 200, 1/1000, f8 (top), 1/250, f6.3 (above).

Camera angle *affects both form and colour in the pictures of the two horses. Shooting with the sun at a 45° angle (top), representative colour and modelling were shown in a rather prosaic way. For the second shot I moved to the other side and photographed into the sun. Exposing for the shadows, I burnt out the sky and created the impression of two riders against the early morning light. Shape now is more important than form or colour.*

Pentax, 35mm, Ektachrome 64, 1/250, f16 (top), 1/125, f11 (above).

Changing angles of light *produced the wide range of colours in the shots of the motor yacht. Without altering my position, I took the whole sequence in 15 minutes using a Pentax and exposing for highlights. In the first picture (top) the camera was aimed straight into a high sun. My 200mm lens pulls the mountains up, but they are in almost total shadow, as is the boat. As the yacht moves away slightly from the sun's path in the next picture, light creeps round the stern. More aerial perspective is evident in the mountains. In the next shot, the sun strikes the boat from the rear, illuminating it like a searchlight and modelling its detail. Flag colours can be seen, and a brown tender. At this angle, the reflected wake gives a strong sense of momentum, and the background is much sharper. As the yacht moves into two-thirds sunlight in the fourth picture, its superstructure reflects blue from the sea, which has turned much lighter. Finally, the yacht has rounded the headland and moved into full sun. Direct light has made the sea a brilliant blue, but the boat looks flat. The tender can now be seen to be red, not brown.*

Exploring light and angle

Changes of camera position can greatly alter the angle at which light strikes a subject and its effect on the colours and forms that it reveals. The exploration of colour, therefore, can begin quite simply. You should first experiment with the permutations of hue that are possible using a single subject photographed from different angles. Try to find a setting that is not full of distracting background detail, then move around your subject, seeing the ways in which the colours change.

In the early morning or evening, when the intensity of light is shifting quite rapidly, you will need to make quick adjustments to timing and aperture. But these are among the most interesting times of day, especially when large areas of sky and water add reflected light to the picture. The sequence of shots shown here were all taken within about 15 minutes on a beach in Bali. Most of the colour differences were produced by changing the angle between camera and subject in evening light.

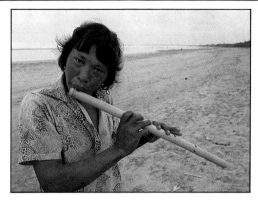

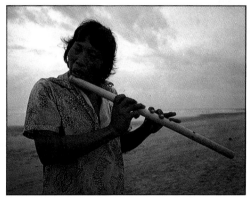

The sequence of the flute player *begins with a conventional shot in full light, composed to give most of the emphasis to the instrument and to bring out the strong diagonal line of the playing position. The exposure reading was taken from the man's skin and shirt, and the predominant browns create a harmonic but rather neutralizing effect.* Pentax, 35mm, Ektachrome 64, 1/125, f8.

Taken from a lower angle *and exposed for the highlight of the sky, this picture gives even greater emphasis to the angle and colour of the flute, but the change to a smaller aperture has darkened the skin tones and the colour of the sand, with some loss of detail as a result.* 1/125, f11.

Mood and atmosphere increase *dramatically with the player crouching. The damp sand now casts reflections from the pale blue sky on to both man and instrument. The muted blue-pink tones and water reflections extending into the calm ocean unify the whole picture, giving it impressive depth and providing a soft and sympathetic backdrop to the solitary figure.* 1/125, f11.

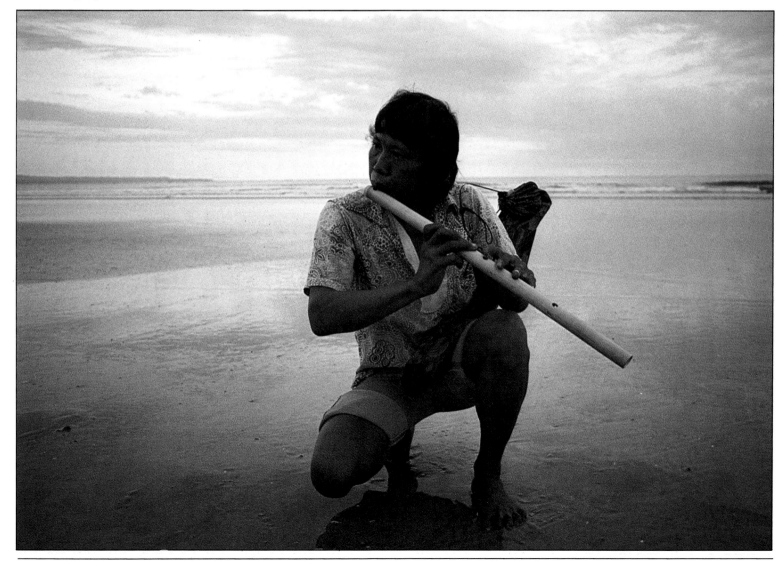

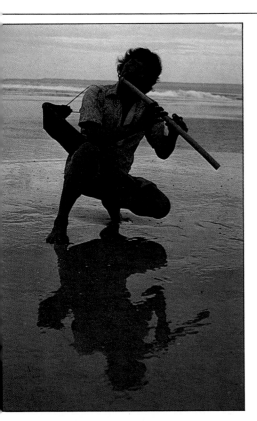

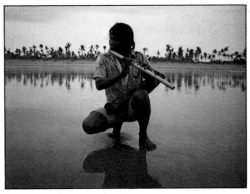

In the vertical shot, *I took up a lower camera position and exposed for the sky only, losing detail in favour of shape, shadow and subtle pinks in the sky. The reflection of man and sky in the wet sand provides most of the interest.* 1/250, f11.

By moving round the player *and shooting back towards the trees on the skyline I have positioned him so that the weak light shines directly upon him. There is now more colour in his shirt.* 1/60, f8.

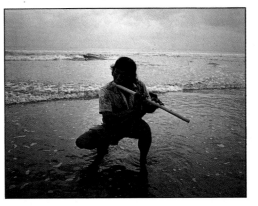

The colours of the sea *are picked up when the man moves round again and out into the shallows, where the breaking waves provide background activity. For this picture I exposed for the light on the water and also on the man's shirt.* 1/60, f11.

For the final shot *I wanted to catch the light striking the flute directly, so I stood over the crouching man. Exposure was for the shadows and the shutter speed has not stopped the movement of the water. The angle makes this an emphatic picture.* 1/30, f4.

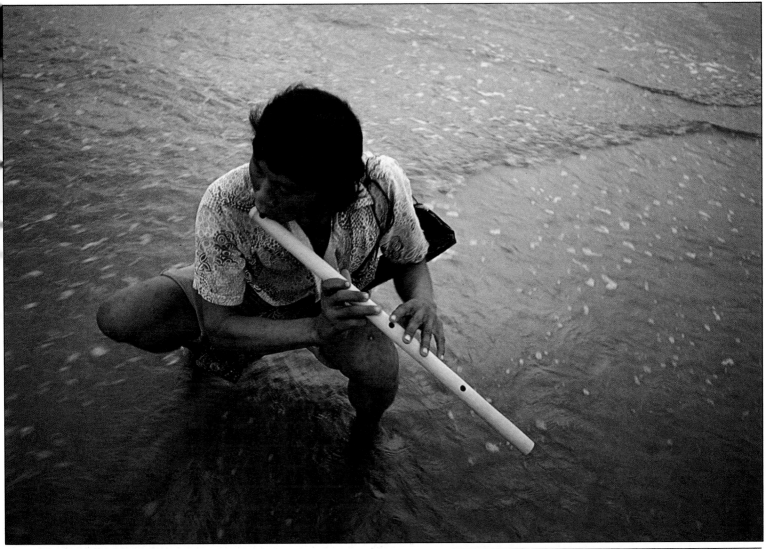

Angle of view

In its technical meaning, the term angle of view refers to the area of a subject that can be taken in by a camera lens. But in a compositional sense, the view that appears on your film—and the impact of the whole picture—depends largely on the camera position you select and the angle from which you view a subject.

In colour photography, selection of viewpoint is affected by special considerations in addition to general ones such as scale, balance or perspective. Apart from the angle at which light is striking surfaces, you need to note colours in the background and foreground, which may harmonize or contrast with the main subject.

Such obvious measures as gaining height to reduce background or shooting upwards to eliminate foreground can produce striking changes in shape and patterns as well as in the colours of objects. Professional photographers take up some extraordinary camera positions to explore a given subject and you should experiment to find how subjects that seem ordinary can be transformed.

High or low angles of view *can enable you to study patterns and compositions that would not become apparent from a normal viewpoint. Nearly all the photographs on these two pages are the result of adopting a camera angle different from the normal eye-level position. The shot of a girl's painted toe-nails under a trestle table shows how an unusual angle of view can not only reveal an interesting symmetry, formed by her legs and the trestles, but also say something in an oblique way about mood and personality, leaving the rest to our imagination.*
Pentax, 50mm, Ektachrome 64, 1/125, f5.6.

A high-level shot *looking down on the Piazzetta, Venice, isolates people promenading in the evening and allows them to be studied without conflicting shadows.*
Pentax, 50mm, Ektachrome 64, 1/125, f8.

My object in the next picture *was to capture the dynamic lines of a skyscraper in Vancouver. Shot from below with a wide-angle lens, the shadowed base of the building has a solidity that contrasts well with the towering glass walls and their reflections of the blue sky.*
Leicaflex, 35mm, Ektachrome 200, 1/500, f16.

A downward angle *(from the roof of my car) was needed to outline an Indonesian farmer against his paddy-field. In the fading light his face would otherwise have merged into background vegetation and his farming tools would have formed less interesting angles than they do here.*
Pentax, 50mm, Agfachrome 50s, 1/125, f3.5.

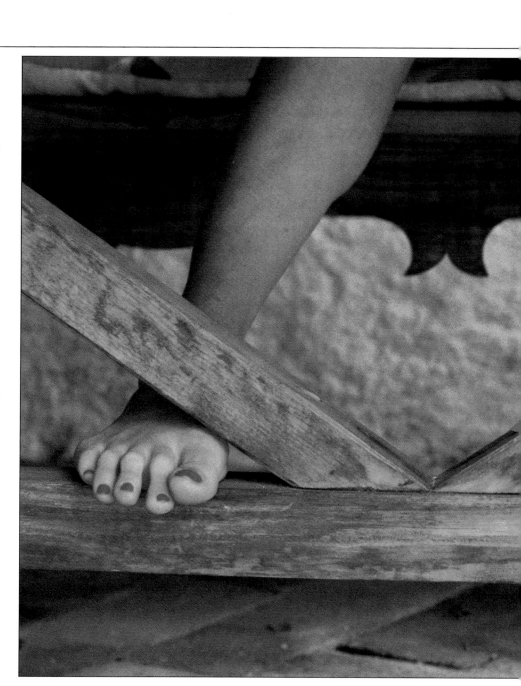

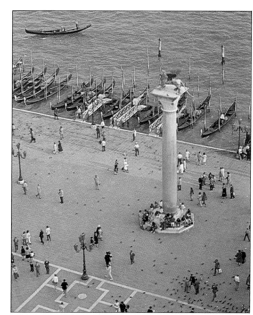

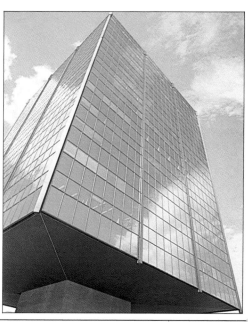

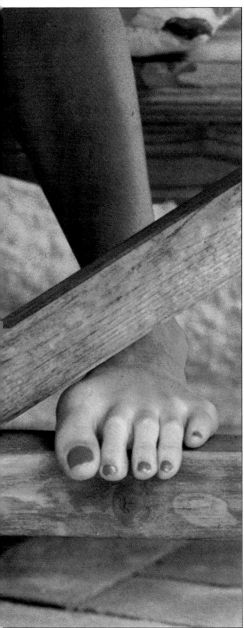

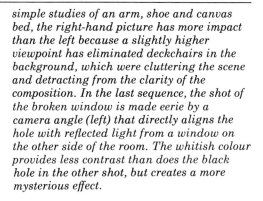

Background and foreground colour *must be considered carefully in selecting camera angles. The house below is a rectory near Sligo, Ireland, where the poet W. B. Yeats once lived. To make it less forbidding, I first shot through a clump of daffodils so that the pale greens and yellows conveyed a more lyrical mood. The other shot exploits the shape of the trees, which I noticed had a similar line to the roof. I moved farther back, used a 250mm lens with tripod on my Hasselblad and shot at 1/60, f8. The longer lens enabled me to compress both wood and house into an effective image. In the two*

simple studies of an arm, shoe and canvas bed, the right-hand picture has more impact than the left because a slightly higher viewpoint has eliminated deckchairs in the background, which were cluttering the scene and detracting from the clarity of the composition. In the last sequence, the shot of the broken window is made eerie by a camera angle (left) that directly aligns the hole with reflected light from a window on the other side of the room. The whitish colour provides less contrast than does the black hole in the other shot, but creates a more mysterious effect.

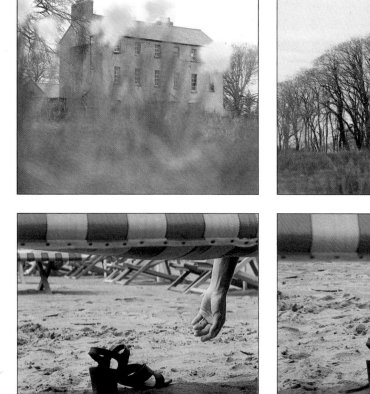

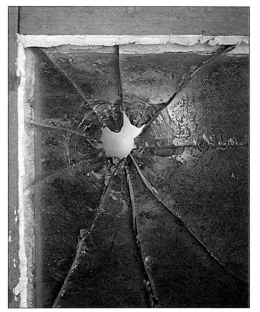

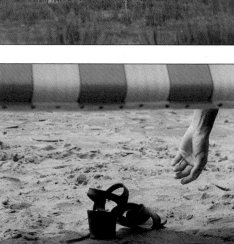

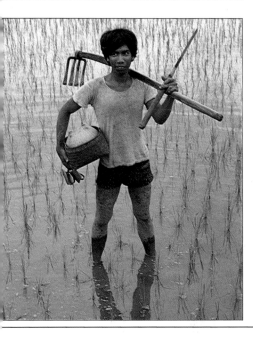

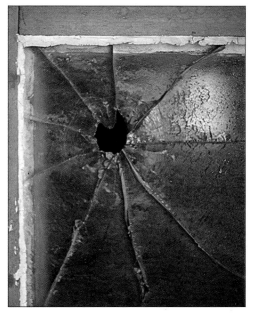

Light and shade

Except in flat lighting, the camera always records the world as a combination of light and shade, and it is tonal variations that give the illusion of three-dimensional form in a two-dimensional photograph. Shadows can be used as graphic shapes in contrast to areas of light and colour. In the picture of a modern glass and concrete building (far right), for example, shade has both suppressed the distracting background and created an intriguing design in the foreground. Shadows can be simply informative, indicating the direction of light, the time of day and even the weather. Aesthetically, they can also create powerful atmospheric effects of drama or mystery.

It is worth remembering that, in colour photography, a range of subtle hues not found in bright light can appear in areas of pale shadow. As shadows are illuminated only by reflected light, your film will often pick up a blue cast from the sky in these areas, or a cast from another colour reflected from a nearby surface. Conversely, deep shadows surrounding lighted colours can, by contrast, give them a marvellous radiance.

In the picture on the left, taken with a 90 mm lens, the soft, rounded form and misty texture of the cloud are suggested entirely by the play of light and shade. To increase contrast, I took a general light reading from the sky and closed down one stop to f16 at 1/250.

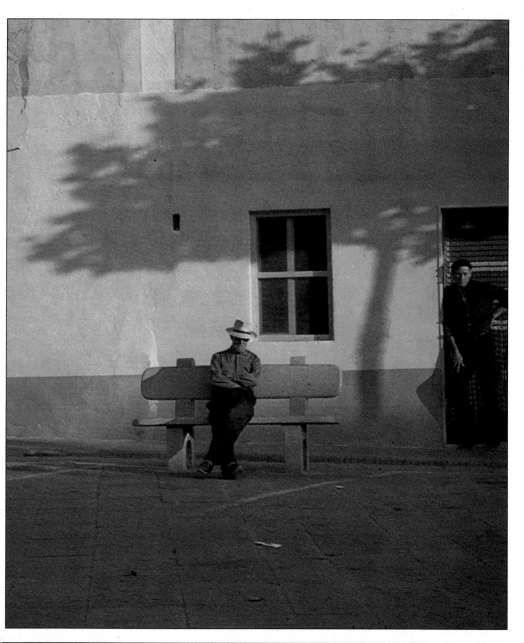

The mild temperature *of a Spanish evening is precisely evoked by the pale shadow of a tree providing illusory shade for an old man on a bench. Directional light is being reflected into the shadow areas so that they balance and blend with the washed-out colours of the buildings.* Contax, 50 mm, Ektachrome 64, 1/50, f11.

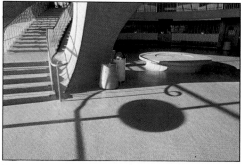

Because unwanted detail is in shadow *a sense of order has been brought to a picture that otherwise would have looked cluttered. The foreground shadows make an intriguing abstract design, which is in keeping with the geometric architecture of this spacious concrete and glass building. The picture thus becomes interpretative, rather than merely informative.* Pentax, 50 mm, Ektachrome 200, 1/125, f11.

With bright light next to deep shadow, *the contrast range may make it impossible to choose an average exposure to suit both areas. In this picture the meter reading was taken for the outside light conditions. If a larger aperture had been used to retain some interior detail, the richness of the stained glass and the delicate colours of horse and rider would have been overexposed. As it is they glow against the shadow area.* Pentax, 35 mm, Agfachrome 50s, 1/125, f8.

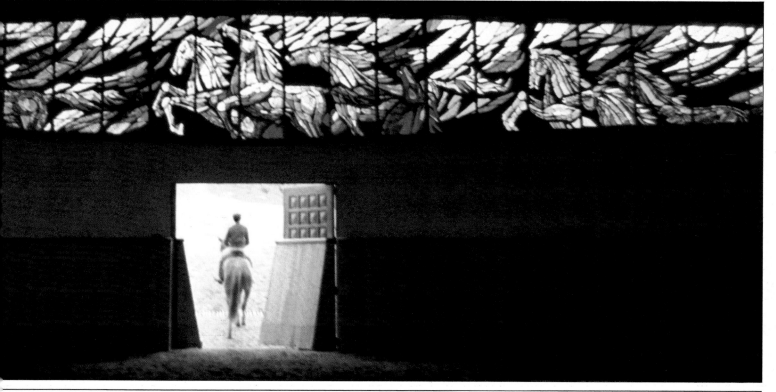

Monochromatic colour

The term monochromatic colour seems to embody a contradiction. Photographs are often described either as coloured or as monochromatic—incorrectly supposed to mean black and white. Strictly, a monochromatic photograph means one that uses a single colour from any part of the spectrum. The term can even be extended to mean a photograph that gives the effect of a single colour, although actually it has several different hues. In composing this kind of photograph, judgements very similar to those of black and white photography come into play.

The idea that bright is beautiful is hard to resist. But as the pictures on these pages show, colour does not have to be vivid to be effective. The evocative scene (right) might almost have been painted by a watercolour artist, using colour as a delicate wash to create the feeling of first light and calm typical of early morning. A colour that did not blend in would have marred the picture.

The literal quality of colour—its tendency to identify in prosaic detail each individual element in a picture—is often criticized by those who believe black and white photography conveys mood more effectively. Monochromatic pictures in fact show how powerfully colour can itself create mood. Other than colour, there is little difference between the imagery of the two pictures shown here. But in one we feel the approach of a warm, saturating rain; in the other, a silvery blue haze suffusing the water and shoreline suggests the chill of an early morning mist that will give way to a cold, fine day. Mist, fog and late or early light often give opportunities for monochromatic photographs without the need for filters, especially where areas of water pick up reflected colour from the sky.

Colour and detail are so muted (below) *that they are almost abstract areas of dense and less dense tone. The trees were green and the boat red, but to capture the atmosphere of a cold, still morning in North Wales I exposed for the highlights, shooting against the emerging light, which gives an overall blue cast.*
Olympus, 100mm, Kodachrome 25, 1/125, f11.

The beautiful scene (right) *was also photographed early in the morning, but in warmer conditions. The water-laden air dissolved into heavy rain a few minutes after the shot was taken. Low cloud encloses the whole scene, acting as a blanket to hold in the little available light and colouring every element a soft, luminous sepia.*
Leica, 90mm, Kodachrome 25, 1/125, f11.

Monochromatic colour

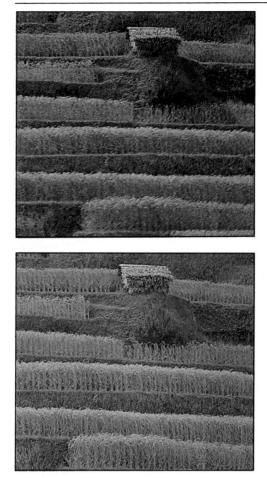

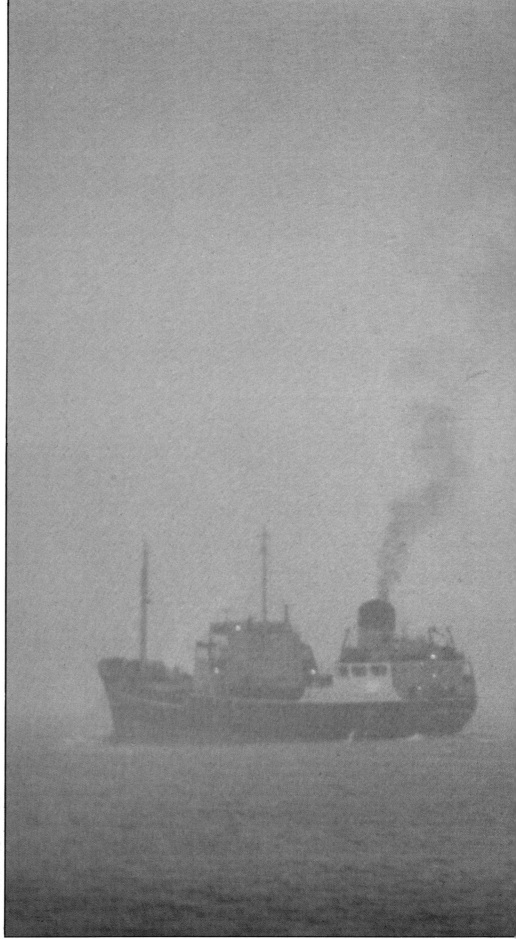

These pictures of an Indonesian paddy-field *were taken within minutes of each other. In the top picture, bright directional sunlight produced well-defined modelling and tonal separation. As a cloud moved across the sun, diffused light made the picture more soft and monochromatic.* Pentax, 150mm, Kodachrome 25, 1/125, f11 (top), f16 (above).

Photographed through a steamed-up window *partially cleared by my hand, the rising sun has given an overall yellow cast to the window and to a curtain, which was actually white with a blue pattern.* Pentax, 50mm, Ektachrome 64, 1/500, f16.

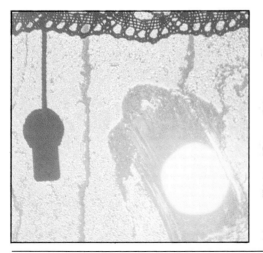

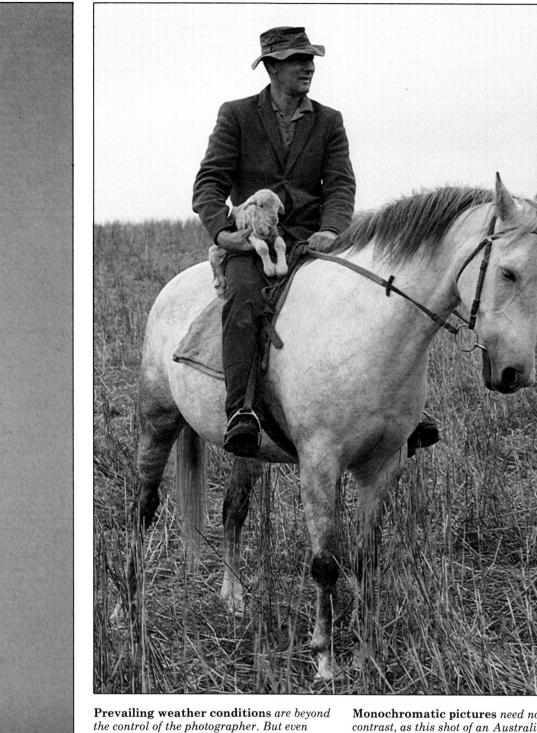

Prevailing weather conditions *are beyond the control of the photographer. But even most daunting situations can be turned to advantage. Here, a range of strongly contrasting colours has been desaturated in the misty, diffused light to produce a picture full of the atmosphere of the sea. Although the hull of the steamer at the water line is bright red, as is the funnel, the superstructure is orange and white and the sails of the yacht deep blue, an overall monochromatic impression of greyish pink is created. To achieve this kind of truthful effect and convey the atmosphere of the mist you need to expose very accurately. Over- or underexposure will destroy the fragile image and colour.*
Leica, 50mm, Kodachrome 25, 1/125, f11.

Monochromatic pictures *need not lack contrast, as this shot of an Australian drover with a new-born lamb shows. The Australian outback is characteristically subtle in colouring, with faded browns, reds and greens blending into each other. Here, the beige colour of the dried-up stubble mediates between the dark grey of the rider's clothes and the light grey of his horse. Echoing this, the similar beige of the horse's mane prevents the outline of the animal merging into a bleached-out sky. Although there is quite a range of hues in the picture, the differences between them are slight enough to leave a monochromatic impression, very much in sympathy with the subject matter and with the landscape itself.*
Leicaflex, 50mm, Kodachrome 25, 1/125, f11.

Dominant colour

In composing an effective colour picture, something more is involved than the considerations of shape, line, tone, texture or balance that apply to black and white photography. For colour can itself set a mood, express an emotion or appeal to our senses in a purely abstract way. Colours can be manipulated to create or destroy the illusion of depth and, according to their selection or placement, can establish balance or set up a jarring tension. Many modern painters are now exploring the optical sensations induced by the interplay of colours. In photography, effective colour composition is a matter of sensitivity, intuition and experience, but some basic guidelines can be laid down so those new to the art of photography can avoid the more obvious pitfalls.

"Actually, one works with few colours," said Picasso, "but when each is in its right place it seems a lot." If you try to cram too many colours into a picture, the struggle for dominance will create confusion. The most successful pictures usually have one colour that outweighs the rest. Dominance may be established by a large area of subdued colour or a smaller area of bright colour, and it is worth remembering that lightness is a relative thing. Lemon yellow, for instance, may appear shrill in one part of a picture but call no attention to itself in another.

Whatever the dominant colour is, it must be carefully related to the centre of interest in the picture. If the dominant colour is not itself the point of interest, it should at least support or enhance it. When a single strong colour predominates, pattern tends to become more important, giving interest to what might otherwise become monotonous. Best of all, as Picasso suggested, are a few colours balanced in an overall relationship within the picture.

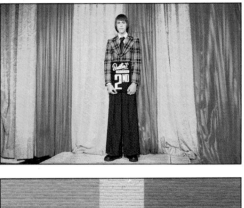

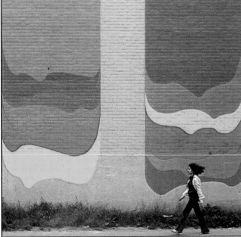

Photographing people *against overwhelming colour holds both dangers and rewards. In the upper shot, sickly red and yellow curtains overpower the hesitant runner-up in a holiday camp contest. But in the lower shot the background is of central importance. The walking girl simply locates the mural and gives it scale.*
Top: Pentax, 50mm, Ektachrome 160, 1/30, f4.
Above: Leica, 50mm, Ektachrome 64, 1/125, f8.

One way of increasing colour dominance *is to use tungsten film in daylight, as in the shot of a girls' dormitory (right). The film has strengthened the blue of the daylight, which is screened by a blind over the upper window. It has also intensified the blue of the coloured perspex that has been pasted over the lower window.*
Hasselblad, 60mm, Ektachrome 160, 1/15, f5.6.

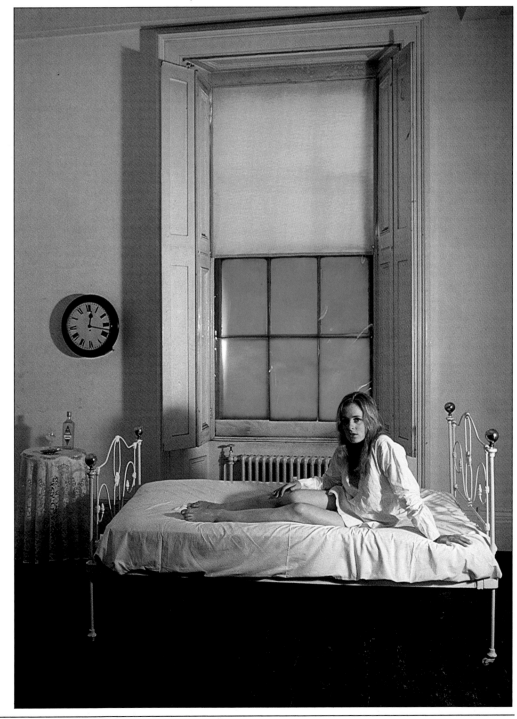

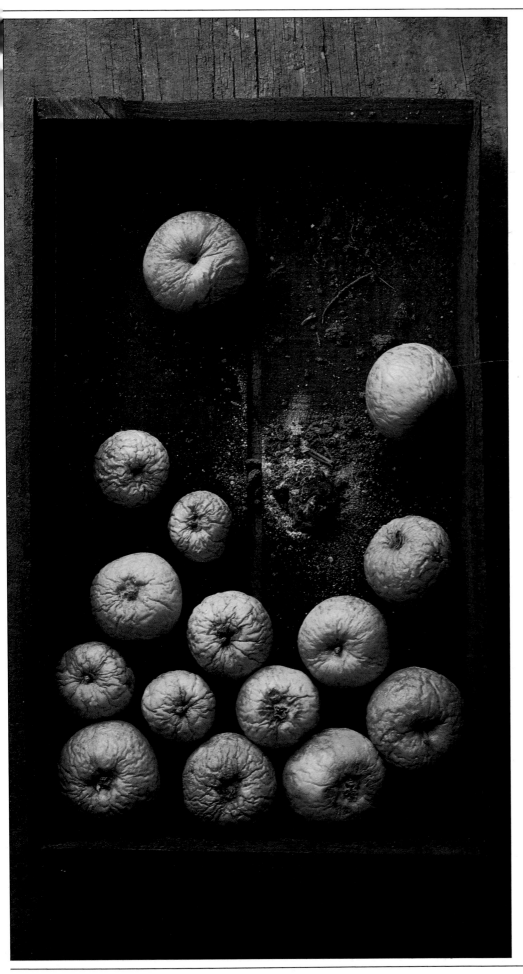

The form and texture of wrinkled apples
*in a box (left) has been brought out by the
dominance of their yellow, red and brown
hues over a subdued background, which
contains muted echoes of the same colours.
A brighter background—of a different
colour—would have fought for interest and
destroyed the impact of the picture.*
MPP 5x4in, 150mm, Ektachrome 64, 1 sec., f22.

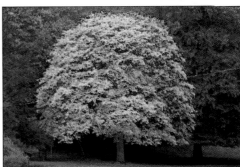

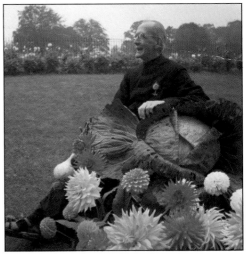

Specimen trees *are often placed where
their dominant colours will look best. The
yellow maple (top) has an ideal backdrop.*
Minolta, 50mm, Ektachrome 64, 1/250, f11.

Father Simplicity, *master gardener
(above), grew these flowers and the almost
miraculous cabbage in an English
monastery. To photograph them together I
placed the vivid flowers in the foreground so
that attention is immediately drawn there.
The eye is then carried back with the natural
recession of darker greens. As the
background was rather untidy, I used a
pyramid shape as a compositional device to
strengthen the picture. Colour dominance
can sometimes be offset by this kind of
emphasis on pattern in the more subdued
areas of a photograph.*
Hasselblad, 60mm, Ektachrome 64, 1/60, f16.

A touch of colour

The vitality of colour depends more on placement than size. Some of the most striking colour pictures exploit a spot of intense colour in a scene otherwise dominated by gently blending hues. Confronted by an overall uniformity, the eye welcomes variety.

Most hues look brightest against a neutral background. This is particularly true of reds and yellows, which advance strongly, often giving a three-dimensional effect and turning a scene that might have looked drab into a sparkling shot. If sunlight picks out a bright colour against a shadowed area, the effect is doubly dramatic.

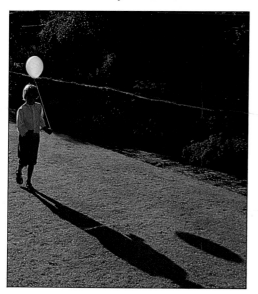

A translucent balloon *held aloft by a small boy implies a party somewhere just out of sight of the camera. This shot says much about the virtue of patience. Moments before, the boy had been running and the balloon was lost against the sunlit grass. As he slowed, the balloon began to rise against the shadowy foliage, its string backlit, like the boy, by the low evening sun. The composition and the angle of the sunlight produce a delicate balance of light and shade.*
Pentax, 50mm, Ektachrome 64, 1/125, f11.

Without the strong red *of the neon signs, the picture of a Toronto skyline at dusk would be dominated by the luminous evening sky. As it is, the eye is drawn into the bottom of the scene and can then rise gradually with the buildings to explore the sweep of clouds. The touch of colour, echoed by the soft pink of the sky, here becomes woven throughout the photograph. To retain detail in the sky-scrapers and the clouds I took one light reading from the sky and another from the buildings, then averaged the two.*
Leicaflex, 90mm, Ektachrome 64, 1/60, f8.

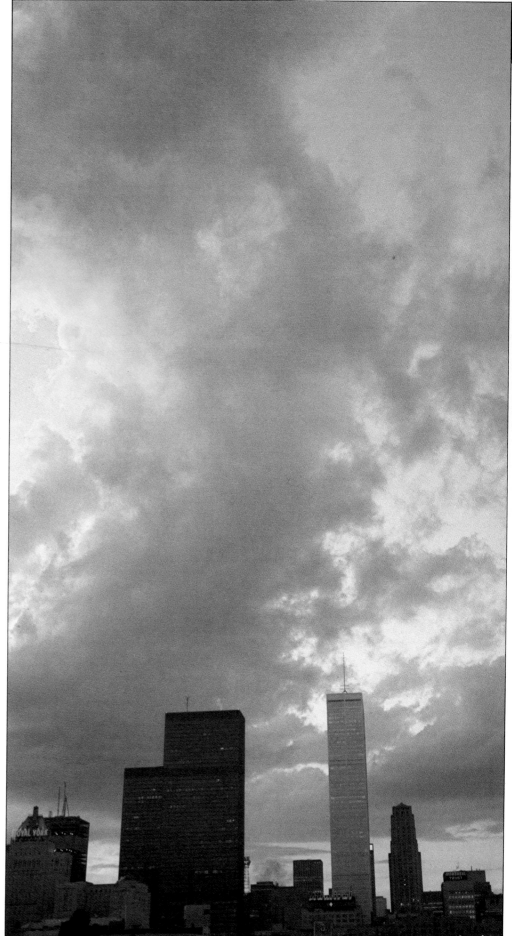

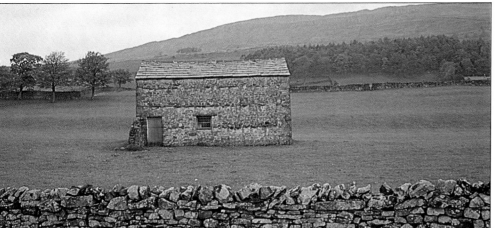

The red barn door *comes as a complete surprise in this picture of a Yorkshire farm. Its colour almost glows out of its grey surroundings, seeming by its gaiety to contradict the austerity of the landscape.* Olympus, 50mm, Ektachrome 64, 1/125, f16.

In the right proportion, *a touch of colour need not monopolize attention. I waited for a shaft of sunlight to highlight the boat and gulls against the shadow area, but their relatively small scale leaves the eye free to explore the detail of an immense, shattered cliff face in Wales.* Hasselblad, 150mm, Ektachrome 64, 1/250, f8.

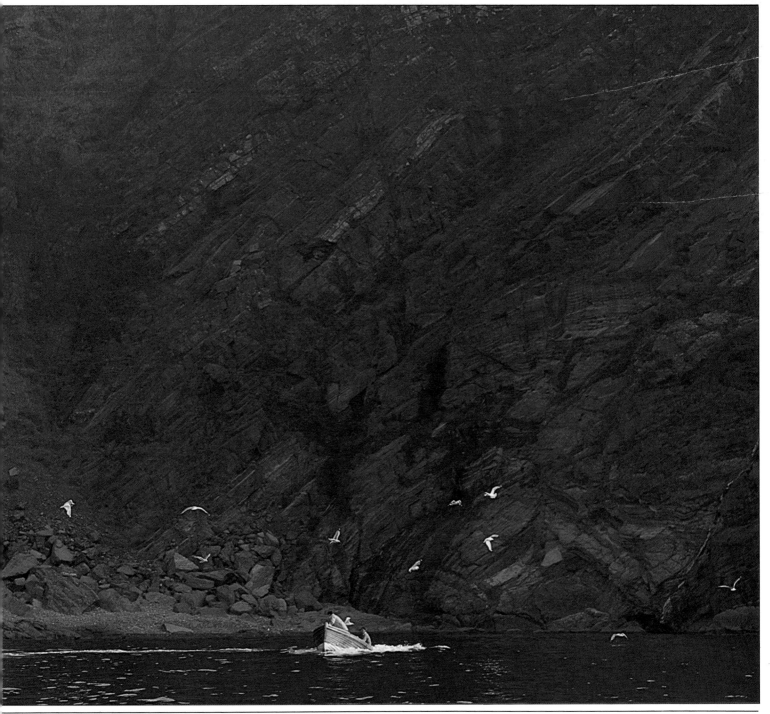

Contrasting colour

Contrast in black and white photography is simply the difference between the lightest and darkest parts of a scene. But in colour photography, while light and shade remain important, the relationships and varying intensities of colour become added elements in composition. Boldly contrasting colours, provided they are used in a balanced way, give pictures drama and impact, even without light and shade.

Colours that contrast most strongly lie opposite each other on the colour wheel (see pages 40–1). Although the primaries, red, green and blue, are themselves clearly demarcated, even sharper contrasts are formed by red against cyan, green against magenta and blue against yellow. The vibrancy of these combinations has a physiological basis, as the wavelengths representing different colours do not fall into exact focus at the same time at the back of the eye. Focal length is longer for reds and yellows than for blues and greens. When we look at these colours together, tiny muscular adjustments constantly take place to cope with the differences in wavelength.

Large areas of contrasting colour jostling each other in a picture therefore create a restless duality of interest and also tend to flatten out space, creating pure pattern. On the other hand, a small colourful accent is emphasized by being placed next to a contrasting colour and you should exploit the vitality of such colour schemes. It is important to remember, however, that when light and shade enter the picture, the highlighted area may produce a contrast range that is too great for your colour film to handle. As a result, the colours may be altered drastically. For accurate rendition, special measures will be needed if light readings from different parts of the subject exceed two diaphragm stops.

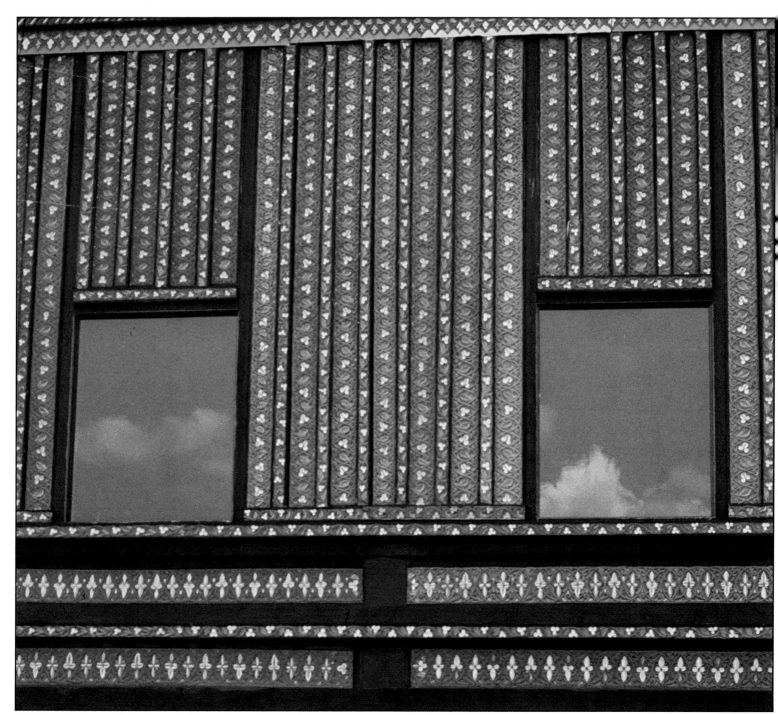

The balloon *is both attractive and easily seen because of its bold design in fully saturated colours. The rich, unblemished sky provides a backdrop of equal density. Maximum contrast between complementary colours is achieved where blue sky meets the sunlit yellow of the translucent bag.* Pentax, 100mm, Agfachrome 50s, 1/250, f11.

Sister and brother *confront the bleak Outer Hebrides in protective clothes of vigorous colours that contrast strongly, particularly the light blue of the boy's anorak against its complementary, red. The fence, which has muted echoes of the same colours, makes a good background.* Pentax, 50mm, Ektachrome 64, 1/125, f8.

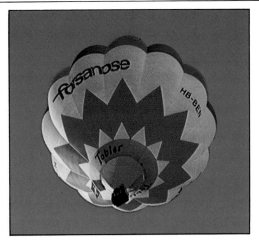

Bright colours in a billowing spinnaker *create an illusion of momentum. This sail is usually hoisted when the boat is moving at speed and its colours are chosen for their good visibility as well as their gaiety. In this picture they provide an excellent example of the striking effect that can be achieved when the three primaries are juxtaposed. The most vivid area of the sail, a line of solid red sandwiched between bands of green, is set against the deep blue of the sea. Muted blue tones on either side of the green highlight well the central band and echo the water's blue. The white of the mainsail, deck and hull add crispness.* Leicaflex, 90mm, Ektachrome 200, 1/500, f8.

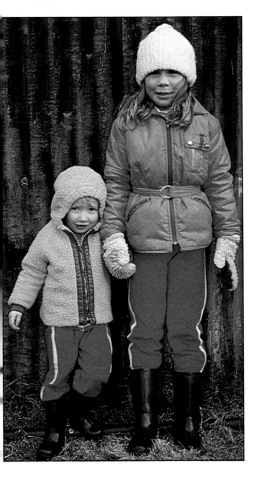

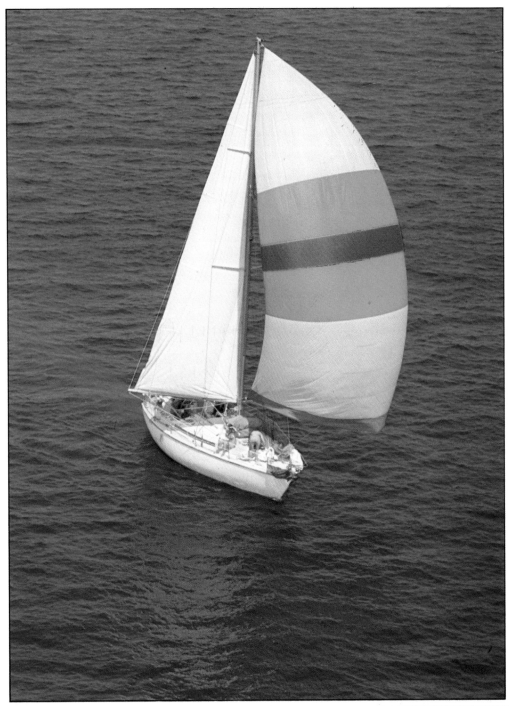

The Javanese building *in this photograph could easily be mistaken for an outdoor mural of elaborate design. The shot shows contrasting colours used effectively but in a subdued way. Patches of sky, reflected in the window panes of the building, provide a link with the darker blue of the building's decoration. The pattern itself is full of accents of light and colour, which combine to soften a rather severe façade painted in a dominant colour that would otherwise be overpowering. By picking out structural lines in blue the architect has given added interest to the design, both through the use of contrasting colour and by pointing up lateral and vertical lines.* Pentax, 50mm, Ektachrome 64, 1/125, f11.

Harmonic and discordant colour

Mood can be established as easily by colour harmony as by colour contrast, but it is a gentler mood with more subtle pleasures. Harmonic colours are grouped closely together on the colour wheel and make up only a restricted palette, consisting usually of two colours in desaturated hues. The absence of aggressive colours, however, makes it easier to appreciate fine distinctions between similar hues.

Although harmony is partly a matter of inherent colour characteristics, it can be achieved also by tone, scale or placement. If a calm, restful atmosphere is needed it is often possible to subdue contrasting colours either by dissipating them in strongly reflective light or by slightly underexposing to produce a low-key picture.

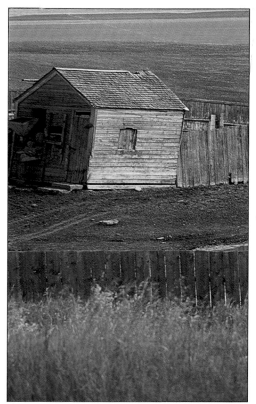

Colour harmony *is found everywhere in nature and even the colours introduced by man seem, in the process of time, to be blended into their surroundings. In a Canadian landscape lit by late sun, the weathered boards of the shed combine in so subtle a way with the earth and fields that the range of hues from greys to greens and browns is hardly noticed. Once a bright turquoise, the faded and rusted water pipe (right) lives amicably with the greenish-brown seaweed in a harmony increased by mutual reflections.*

Above: Leica, 50mm, Ektachrome 64, 1/125, f11.
Right: Pentax, 100mm, Ektachrome 64, 1/30, f8.

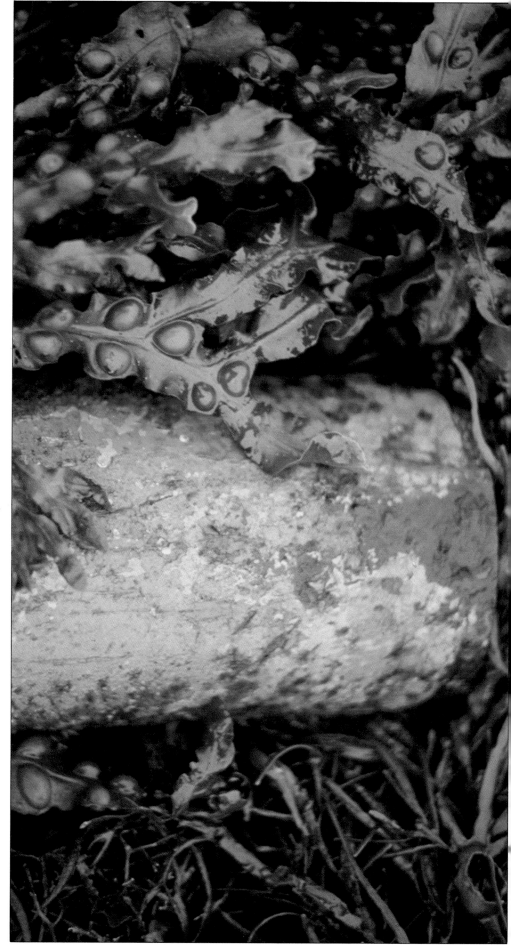

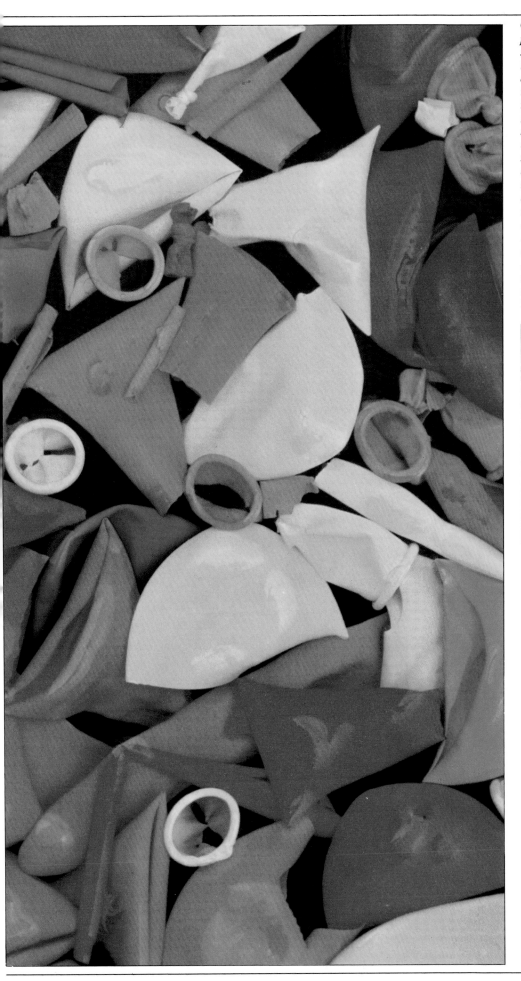

Colour discord can be created by placing contrasting colours together in such a way that they are uncomfortable to look at. Each pure colour has its own level of brightness and when this is changed in manufacturing, some hues—pinks for instance—can look "shocking" alongside hues of the same brightness. To avoid discord, such hues need to be used carefully in composing pictures. But dissonance can sometimes be as useful as harmony. And although some colours were commonly thought to be inherently discordant, art and fashion now prove that they can be used effectively in the right mixtures and proportions. The shot of torn balloons shows the vigour of dissonant colours. In spite of small areas of shadow and high-light, the strength of the colours has turned the picture into a flat design that, at the same time, has great vitality.
Pentax, 100mm, Agfachrome 50s, 1/60, f8.

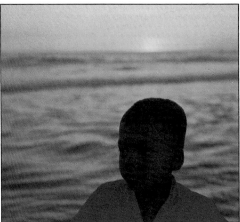

Jarring colours can be muted by the use of light and angle of view. The boy's shirt (above) was an almost fluorescent red, but blends with the background when shot against the diffused yellow light of a sunset in Sri Lanka. The couple in the garden (below) are surrounded by violent colours, but a balanced composition helps to hold the picture together and strong reflected light has dissipated some colour.
Rolleiflex, 80mm, Agfachrome 50s.
Above: 1/125, f8. Below: 1/250, f11.

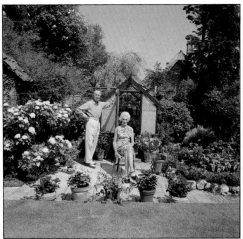

Composition and line

Composition is simply the organization of subject matter in the camera viewfinder so that the final picture conveys your intention. Though usually it implies order it could equally imply disorder. Experienced photographers compose instinctively rather than in a calculated way, but there are principles that help the beginner.

Special aspects of composing in colour have already been discussed. The pages that follow deal with more general aspects of line, shape, tone, texture, proportion and perspective. Angle of view is fundamental, of course, as it determines the relative emphasis given to objects within a view as well as selection of the picture area itself. A close-up of a smart house in an otherwise seedy street could give a deceptive impression of the whole area.

Line is important both in its strict meaning as a linear mark or outline and in the general sense of the direction taken by the eye in looking at a picture. A good composition should lead the eye to a single main subject and then let it explore the rest of the picture. In a picture with depth, the line of movement is often from the foreground through the middle distance to the background. In pictures with more surface interest, the movement may be circular. Photo-reportage often needs pictures that give and show everything instantly. But successful pictures make an initial impact and then offer more.

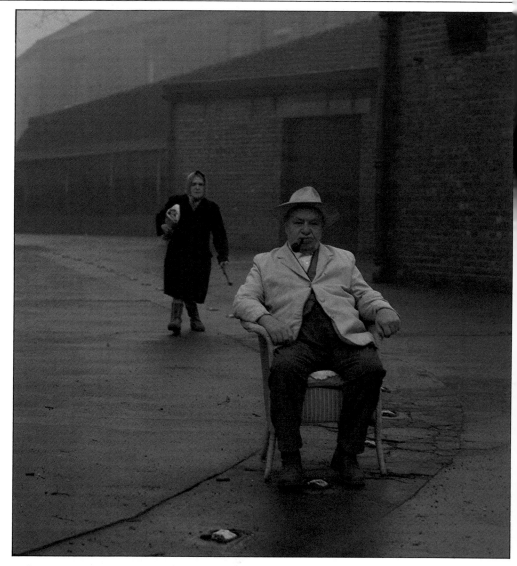

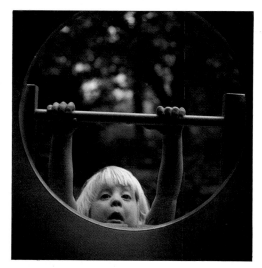

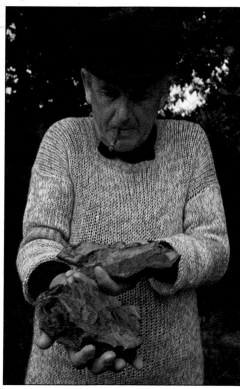

A simple circular frame *acts as a funnel, directing the eye to the anxious concentration with which the boy is struggling to lift himself up to the bar. The subdued colour of the porthole emphasizes the highlight on the child's face and the surface nature of the composition is reinforced by an out-of-focus background. Rolleiflex, 80mm, Ektachrome 64, 1/30, f8.*

Percy Shaw, *inventor of cat's-eyes for safer driving, is photographed here in conditions in which he has a special interest—the industrial smog of Halifax. Line, scale, colour, tone and positioning all make him the immediate centre of attention and then take the eye back in a curve marked by the cat's-eyes. Colours receding in the fog are matched by a recession of tones as his white hat aligns exactly with the package carried by the woman in the middle distance. Her black dress links up with the dark tones of the buildings farther back, their lines giving the picture enormous depth. Hasselblad, 80mm, Ektachrome 64, 1/30, f8.*

Rocks lead from the bottom of the frame *like two stepping stones, carrying attention towards the face of Graham Sutherland, an artist who often paints natural materials of this kind. By crouching down and using a wide-angle lens I have exaggerated the perspective effect. The picture is balanced by the texture and colour of his jersey. Leicaflex, 28mm, Ektachrome 64, 1/125, f8.*

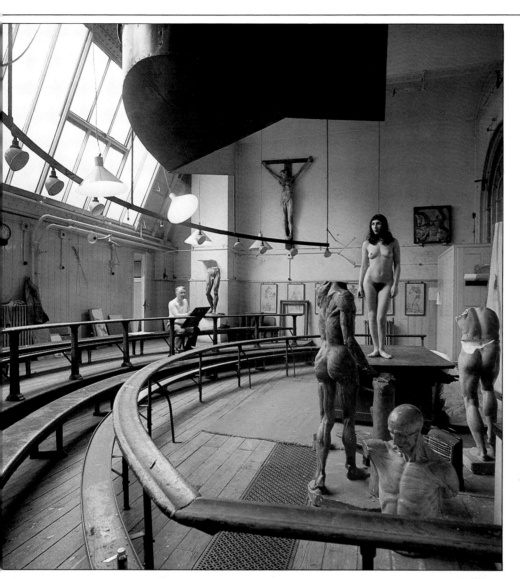

The artist at work in the drawing studio of the Royal Academy, London, is only a small figure in the composition, but is given importance by his position. Curved railings lead to him from the foreground and then carry the eye on into the background. Although this is a highly descriptive picture, taken in a mixture of daylight and artificial light and full of differing elements, it is balanced and given depth by a series of further links—the naked statues leading to the model and then to the crucifix on the wall, and the flesh tones of the artist at his drawing board, the model and the brown mat.
Hasselblad, 60mm, Ektachrome 200, 1/30, f8.

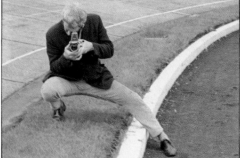

Linear perspective in the sweep of the kerb takes the eye through and out of this picture, but is counterbalanced by the arch formed by the photographer's legs. The colour balance between his coat and the dark grey road reinforces this sense of equipoise. It is completed by the fact that the photographer is shooting back towards me as I photograph him.
Pentax, 50mm, Ektachrome 64, 1/30, f8.

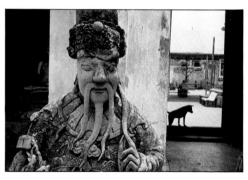

For a composition to work, luck sometimes plays a part. Had I not waited for something to appear in the middle ground, as the dog did, this picture might have looked flatter. With the statue acting as a half-frame, the eye moves into the alley and past the dog into the sunlight. The alley makes up about a third of the picture, an apt proportion in composition.
Pentax, 50mm, Agfachrome 50s, 1/125, f11.

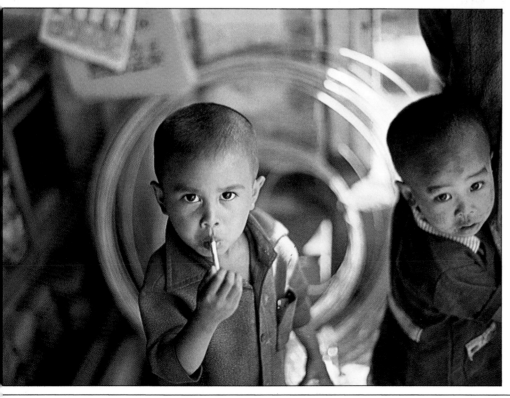

A coiled hose and shallow depth of field give an effective surface composition, in which the centre of interest is the expressions of the two boys.
Pentax, 50mm, Ektachrome 64, 1/30, f8.

Balance, position and scale

Rules of composition in photography are useful guidelines, even though they are made to be broken. A fundamental principle is that colours, lines and shapes should be balanced so that they help to convey the main statement of the picture instead of causing conflict. Balance need not necessarily mean symmetry, however. As we have seen, two equally dominant colours will compete for attention. If colours, shapes or areas of differing sizes or strengths are positioned in the right way they can provide a more effective pictorial balance.

The position of the horizon is a significant factor in landscape shots. If the horizon is in the middle of the frame the effect tends to be static. Altering the proportions within the image—by moving the camera down to emphasize the ground or up to emphasize the sky—will give a more dynamic composition.

On a less obvious level, the classical divisions of space used in painting can be equally effective in photography. If you mentally divide whatever you intend to photograph into thirds, both horizontally and vertically, objects positioned on these divisions, and especially at intersections, are given added emphasis. This can be particularly useful in positioning people for portraits. The "Rule of Thirds" also provides a rough guide for dividing pictures into foreground, middle distance and background.

To establish a sense of the comparative size of objects, some sort of scale has to be introduced. Lenses can influence the apparent size of objects, while camera positions can greatly alter the apparent relationships between their sizes. Equally, a vast sweep of scenery is only as large as the paper it is printed on unless the viewer can gauge its size by comparing it to something of known size—an animal, for instance, or a human figure. In the top picture there is little indication of the scale of the object that produced the wide ripples—in fact quite small.

Cropping is an obvious way to improve the balance of a picture. There is nothing sacrosanct about format or picture size, and it is often useful in composing pictures to allow for masking off some of the area in the viewfinder, especially when the camera format does not suit the proportion you may want of sky to land or subject to setting. Retaining superfluous information will spoil more pictures than it helps.

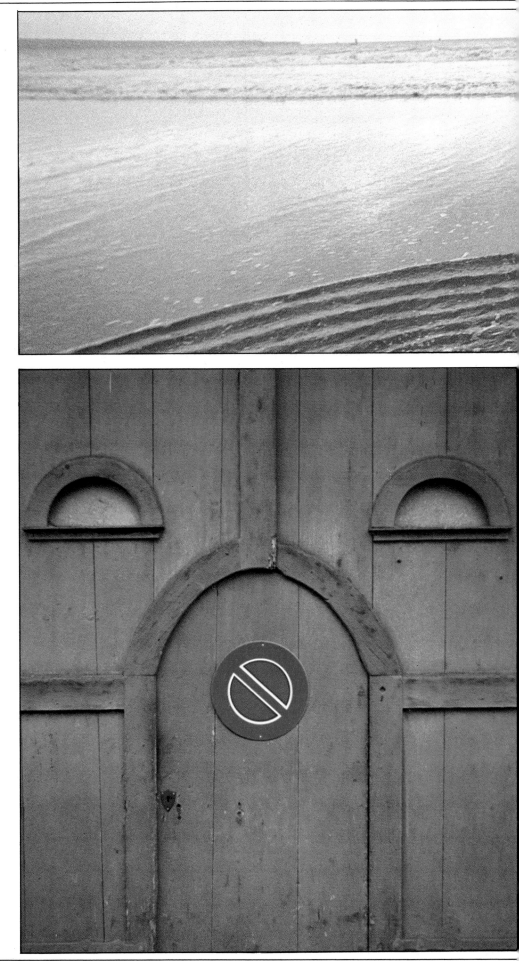

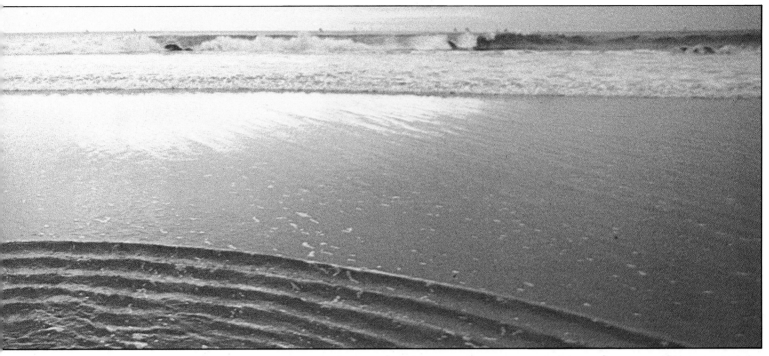

The tidal movement of a wave *gathering and breaking has a natural rhythm and balance, but winds, currents and the changing light create patterns that are never repeated. The evocative picture above balances contrasts between the line of surf and the semicircle of ripples, and between the subtle highlights and the darker tones. The streaks of light across the sand form a link with the thin strip of bright sky above the sea.*
Pentax, 21mm, Agfachrome 50s, 1/250, f5.6.

Even on a small scale, *the right combination of colours in the right position can hold the eye, as the sign on a door in a Parisian goods yard demonstrates. At eye level, in bold contrasting colours of red, white and blue against a greenish-yellow background, it is placed to gain maximum impact, and to warn off motorists blocking the entrance. I cropped the picture out of a much larger image area in order to bring about complete symmetry and the impression of a face with lidded eyes. The drawing power of a small area of contrasting colour must be considered carefully in determining the balance of colour pictures.*
Pentax, 100mm, Ektachrome 64, 1/125, f8.

A small pyramid of white *at the intersection of lines on a tennis court becomes a focal point in a pattern that balances sombre browns and greens. Scale, perspective and colour are all in perfect counterpoise and the recession of perspective lines is so strong that at first one does not notice the tennis net bisecting them. The illusion of white lines of the service courts floating above the fainter brown lines adds further optical interest.*
Pentax, 35mm, Ektachrome 200, 1/60, f11.

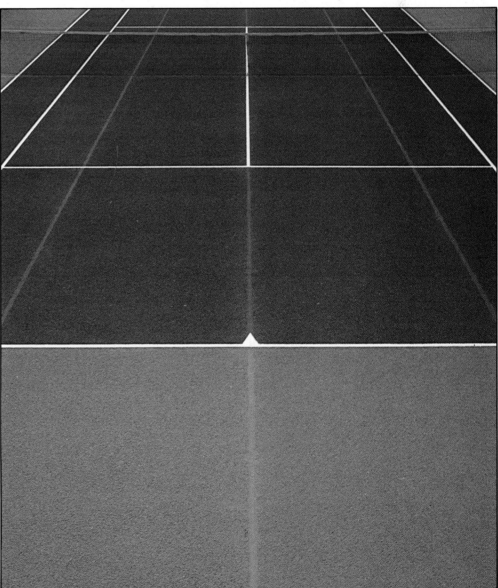

Point of interest

Photographs need not always have a dominant point of interest; there are times when it is the overall effect that counts. What is true, however, is that whether or not a single area is emphasized, the most effective pictures are those that make a single statement. If an artist uses several points of interest they are usually of varying importance and are carefully related.

As a general rule the point of interest should be placed off-centre to give a sense of movement. A colour accent can often provide the point of interest, but a whole range of other devices can be used to focus attention on the main message—angle of view, change of scale, perspective, light, movement, texture or pattern. People, particularly when they are caught in movement, can exert an attraction that is out of all proportion to their scale through the viewer's tendency to relate to them. Human interest then becomes the main point of interest.

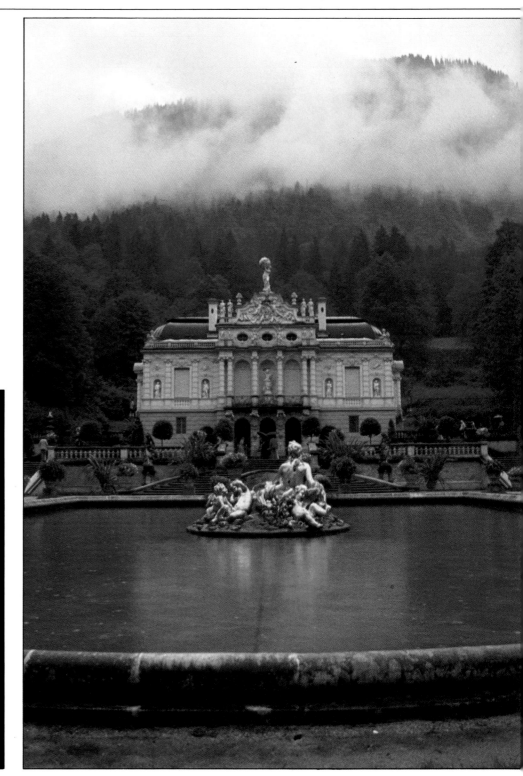

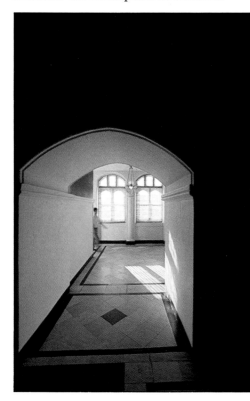

The point of interest, *unequivocal here, is dictated both by perspective and the pattern of light and shade, which together draw the eye towards the windows at the end of the corridor. There, signalled by the line of the wall and the patch of light on the floor, is a moving figure, itself an intriguing image, encroaching upon a serene and empty space in a blur of motion that contrasts well with the distinct lines of the hallway, its floor pattern and area of reflected light.* Pentax, 35mm, Ektachrome 64, 1/30, f5.6.

An overcast day *sealed in the light and saturated the colours to give added brilliance to the golden fountain that seems to glow in the centre of a circular pool in the grounds of Linderhof Palace, Bavaria. The fountain, the immediate point of interest, also directs attention to the palace itself and the sombre, mist-shrouded hill behind. The three-dimensional effect created by the foreground prevents the palace looking like a flat façade.* Nikkormat, 24mm, Agfachrome 50s, 1/30, f3.5.

A chance play of light *has illuminated vividly the painting of a hen and its chicks, so that the Singhalese artist and his family seem almost transfixed by the image. The picture has become an imperative feature in an otherwise overcomplicated domestic scene. In a sense, it does not seem to belong in the room at all, its white contrasting starkly with the dark background. At the same time it illustrates the important place given to pictures in Sri Lanka's sparsely furnished houses.* Rolleiflex, 80mm, Ektachrome 200, 1/30, f8.

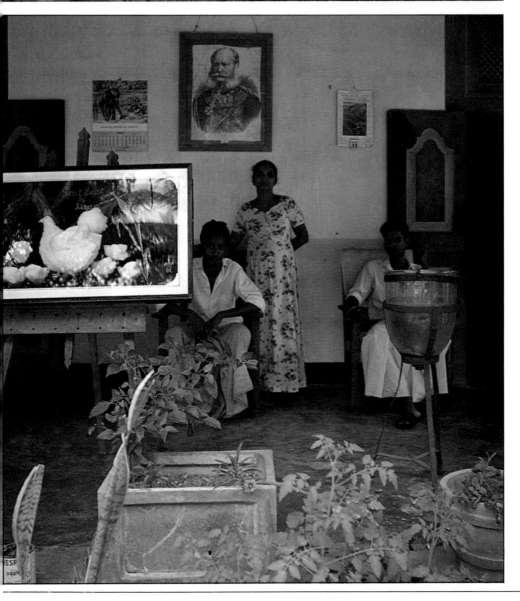

Small in scale *but significant in the humour and interest he brings to the picture, a naked Sumatran boy capers near the edge of a weir. It was the contrast between the placid water near the lip of the falls and the translucent curtain below that first attracted me to the location. This in itself would have given me a picture with a good contrast of colours and textures. But then, suddenly, the boy appeared, well positioned on the bend of the bank and impressively supported by the rushing water about him, completely stealing the scene.* Pentax, 100mm, Agfachrome 50s, 1/125, f8.

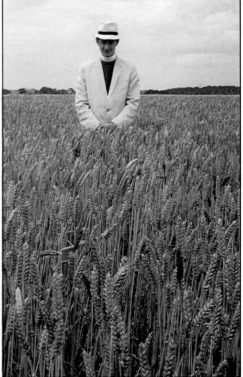

Waist-deep in a wheatfield, *the vicar is given strength and authority by being placed on a neutral-coloured base so that he projects far above the horizon into a subdued sky. Although every element in the composition contributes to the dominance of the figure, the eye can travel beyond him to the distant trees and is also directed back to the foreground by his downward look. I used a small aperture to keep the ears of wheat in sharp focus.* Leicaflex, 35mm, Ektachrome 200, 1/125, f22.

Shape and silhouette

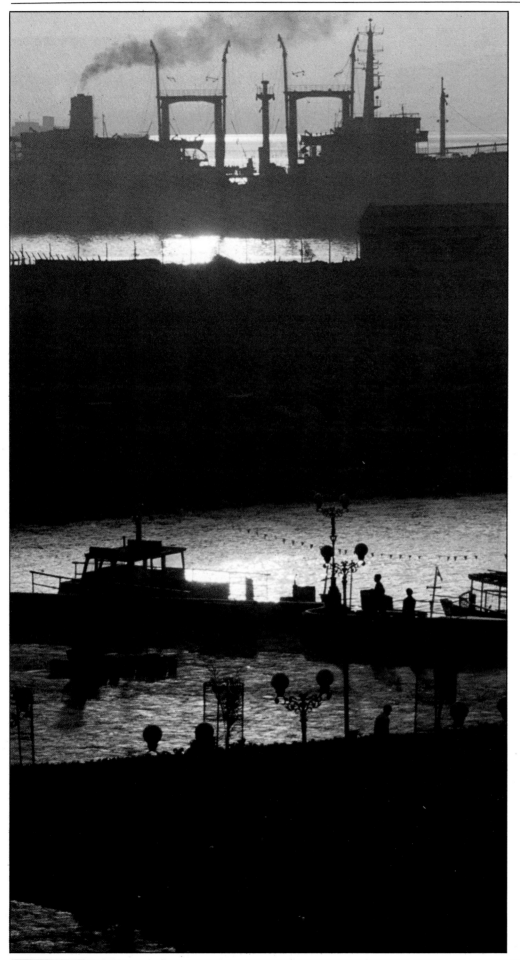

The camera is the most accurate pictorial recording device we have. Almost no complexity of line, colour, tone or texture is beyond its descriptive capacity. But it can be used also to simplify the world, reducing detail and accentuating the most basic element of objects, their shape. The uses of shape as a swift pictorial code range from road signs to advertising; people we know can be recognized by shape alone when they are too far away for colour or detail to be distinguished.

The ability to manipulate shape is important in colour photography, where sharply defined areas of strong colour often flatten form and emphasize outline. But the boldest shapes are created by silhouette. Photographed against the light, objects can look as two-dimensional as cut-out images, making us instantly and powerfully aware of their essential message.

Bulky silhouettes *alternate with golden highlights in an impressionistic picture of Bombay harbour at sunset. My use of a long lens has compressed the silhouettes, creating a perspective confusion that is increased by the smaller shapes in the foreground. I exposed for the highlights and medium tones so that the pattern of black and pale yellow would dominate.*
Pentax, 200mm, Ektachrome 64, 1/250, f16.

Two versions of the same scene *(right) dramatize the effect of turning a mainly descriptive picture into a silhouette. In weak sunlight the crumbling stones of Whitby Abbey, Yorkshire, can be studied in their natural surroundings. Photographed against an evening sky, the abbey takes on more ominous proportions. Gone is the feeling of familiarity as the colours begin to fade towards monochrome and the building's flattened shape is dominant.*
Above right: Hasselblad, 80mm, Ektachrome 200, 1/250, f11.
Right: Leicaflex, 50mm, Ektachrome 200, 1/500, f8.

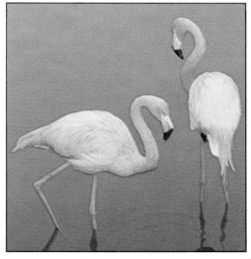

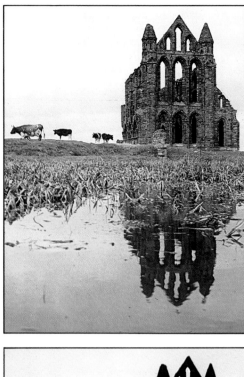

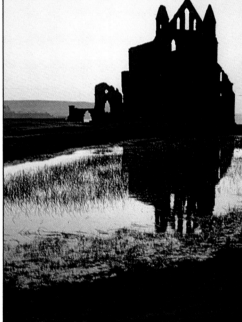

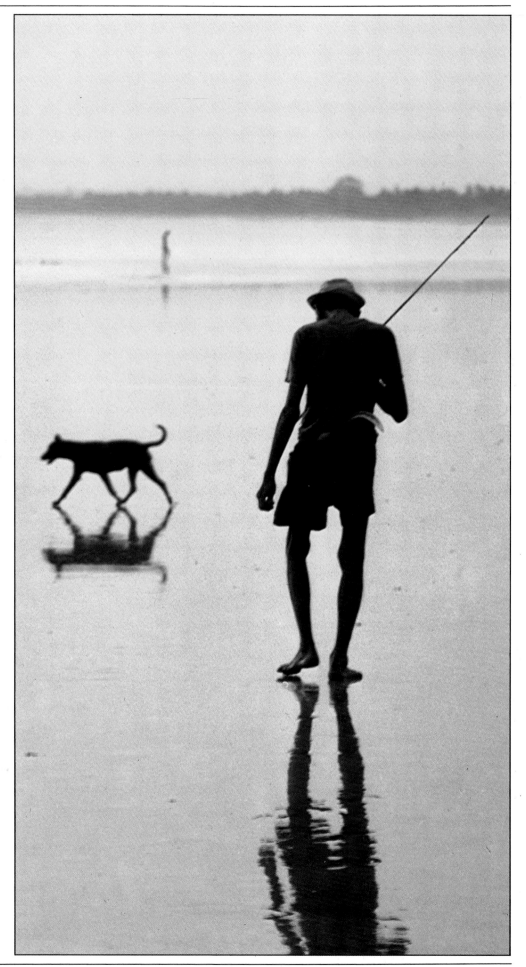

Flat areas of subtle pinks *(left) on a background of pale blue make this picture close to a purely abstract design in the shape of flamingos. Because the photograph is taken against the light, there is no modelling on the bodies and so their form is described entirely by our knowledge that birds are rounded and by the shape their feathers take.*
Contax, 50 mm, Ektachrome 64, 1/125, f8.

A simple picture *conveys through shape alone all that is necessary about this stooped old man searching for shellfish. The dog and the diamond shapes within its reflected legs balance the composition and limited colour provides atmospheric support.*
Pentax, 100 mm, Ektachrome 64, 1/125, f8.

Form and modelling

Creating a convincing illusion of three-dimensional form on the flat surface of film by means of the camera's single, fixed eye is the most exciting aspect of photography. Since bright hues seem to advance from darker ones, colour can itself sometimes indicate form. But in suggesting the volume and weight of an object, lighting is crucial, because our visual memory of form is prompted mainly by the way in which varying surfaces are differently illuminated by light and by resulting tonal gradations.

Sharp contrasts of light and shade produced by strong side-lighting can convey the powerful angles of geometric objects. But more subtle forms tend to be flattened by overlighting or lost in deep shadow. The rounded contours of living things are best conveyed by the gentle modelling of diffused light.

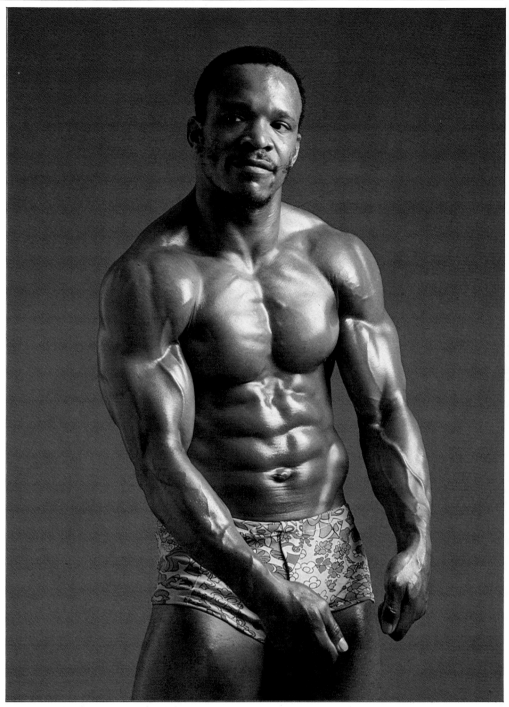

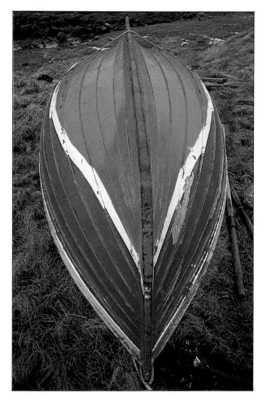

Colour creates form *almost unaided in the picture of the upturned boat. With overcast lighting creating little shadow, the rise of the hull is conveyed mainly by the red advancing above the dark blue. If you cover the red, the turquoise rim advances, suggesting that the surface is concave rather than convex.*
Pentax, 35mm, Ektachrome 64, 1/30, f8.

The smooth red shapes of tomatoes *in a box are given three-dimensional form by the colour and texture of the background and the contrast between shadows and toplit surfaces. The tomatoes have a firm roundness that appears tangible.*
Pentax, 50mm, macro lens, Agfachrome 50s, 1/15, f8.

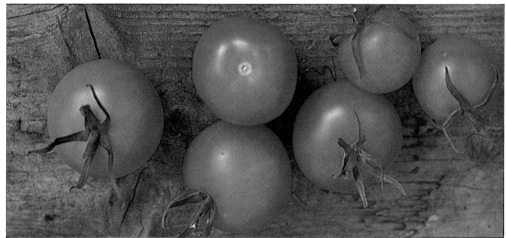

The form of the body builder *is here emphasized by strong diffused side-lighting and a plain background of a sympathetic colour that reveals his muscular strength with greater emphasis. The highlights are accentuated by oil, which helps to bring out the texture and colour of his skin as it varies from dark brown to cream.* Hasselblad, 150mm, Balcar electronic flash, 1200 joules 6ft (2m) obliquely from subject, Ektachrome 64, f11.

Muted colours *and the use of weak diffused directional lighting reveal the subtleties of this classical Greek sculpture, giving it substance and solidity while softening the cold smoothness of the marble. This is the perfect light for the female form and for delicate sculptures. The shadow on the wall gives depth to the picture.* Nikon, 85mm, Ektachrome 200, 1/30, f5.6.

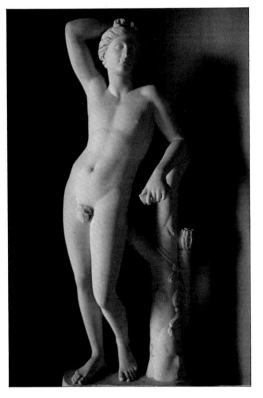

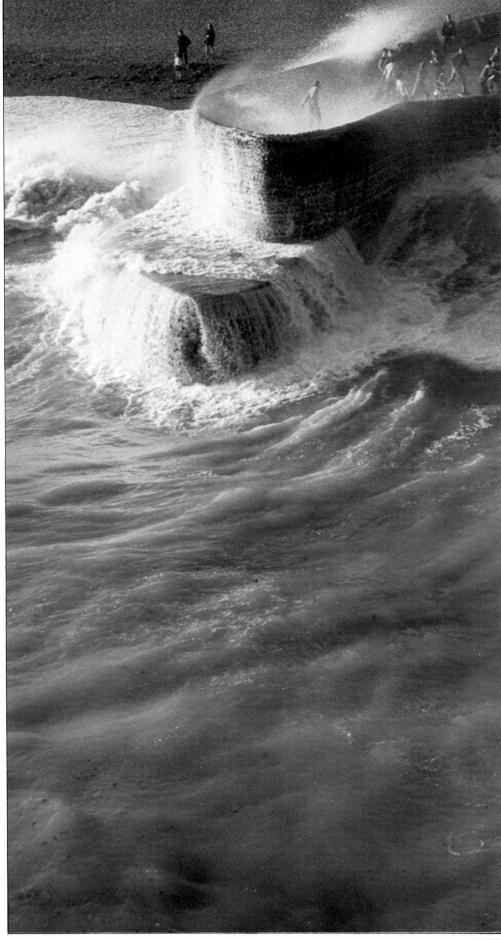

A storm on the sea front *at Brighton, England, is dramatically captured in a picture that contrasts static and mobile forms. Late afternoon sun has provided strong side-lighting, which is reflected from the breaking surf and which gives deep tonal modelling to the turbulence of the waves in the foreground. The form of the pier is described not only by light and shade but also by the shape of the water cascading from the rounded end of the stone wall. The contrasts between the strength and solidity of the pier and the power of the rolling sea, between sun and shadow and between stationary and running children on the breakwater all contribute to the excitement of the shot.* Leica, 50mm, Ektachrome 64, 1/250, f5.6.

Tone and hue

In photography, as in music, the effect of a composition depends largely on the interest of its tonal variations. Tone in photography simply means the range of lightness and darkness within a picture. The range can extend from black to brilliant white depending on the reflection or absorption of light. As we have seen, tonal gradations are crucial in suggesting three-dimensional form. Dramatic tonal contrasts emphasize the solidity of forms, while more gentle tones reveal their subtleties in diffused light.

Many subjects suit a rather restricted tonal range. In portraiture, for instance, a high-key photograph confined to bright tones near the white end of the scale can help to capture delicate features. Low-key pictures using dim light and dark surfaces convey a more sombre mood.

Colour photography extends the tonal range because variations of brightness can be produced by changes of hue as well as of light intensity. Inherently, colours have differing brightness values. Of the four most distinctive colours, red, green, blue and yellow, blue is the darkest and yellow the brightest. Within each of these colours are countless individual hues with subtly different intensities (maroon, scarlet and pink, for instance, all being hues of red). A range of hues can therefore itself provide some tonal variety in a picture taken in strong but flat lighting.

Tone becomes a much more important compositional element than hue in monochromatic pictures and in dim or misty light, which tends to blend colours and disguise their differences. But sensitivity to both tone and hue, and to their interplay, is needed to produce effective pictures.

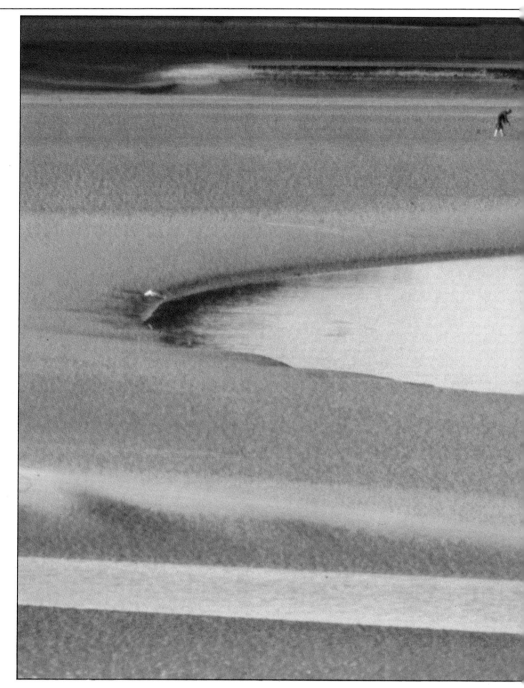

Early morning light *on an estuary in Wales has filtered the colours of the sand, sea and grass to simple tones of grey-blue and beige. The tones in the water and on the sand change in value according to the way in which light from the sky is being reflected or absorbed. Growing light would reveal a much greater range of hues.* Leicaflex, 90mm, Ektachrome 200, 1/30, f11.

A British industrial town, *wrapped in the smog and sea mist of a winter morning, is reduced to a tonal pattern ranging from near-black to near-white highlights. Clear light would have shown strong reds and greens in the scene as well as the predominant grey slate, but scattering of light caused by the misty conditions has produced an overall blue cast.* Praktica, 135mm, Agfachrome 50s, 1/125, f11.

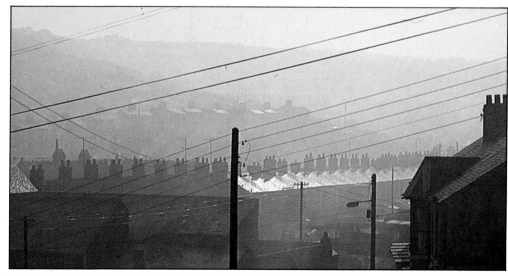

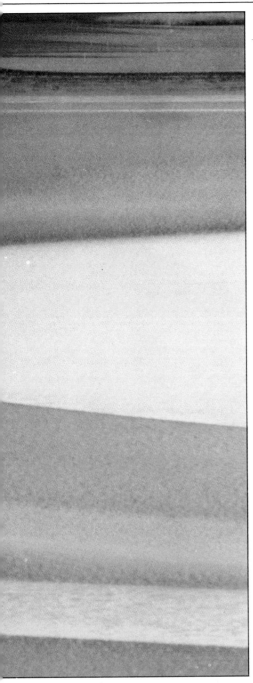

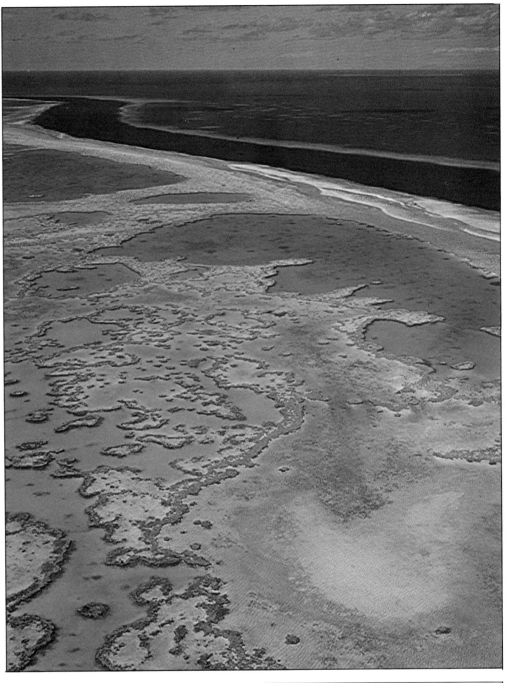

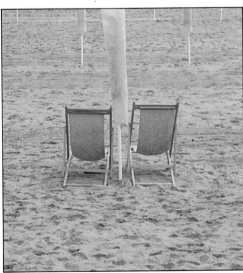

The range of hues *in this shot of the Great Barrier Reef is created by the varying depth of water and nearness of the coral to the surface. Taken from a Cessna at a height of about 200ft (65m), the picture is given interest by a variety of harmonic colours ranging from the dark blue of a channel between the inner and outer reefs to the hues of the shallower water, where an analogous colour—turquoise to green—begins to appear.*
Leicaflex, 21 mm, Ektachrome 64, 1/250, f8.

Yellow hues, *ranging from the orange of the deckchair through the umber sand to the lemon of the umbrella, are the main compositional element in this picture. The diagram shows only a few of the many subtly different hues of yellow.*
Leica, 135 mm, Ektachrome 64, 1/60, f8.

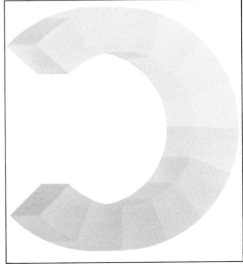

Texture

The truism that raking light best reveals texture needs to be treated with care in colour photography, for the quality of light should always match the subject. Shadows cast by harsh, oblique lighting may suit the character of a weatherbeaten face, but not the creamy skin of a girl. Texture is an important way of indicating depth, but hard shadow may destroy subtle hues.

Texture and colour *play major roles in describing the form of this tree trunk. The inverted V formed by the shadow area is the only discernible shape, and the soft directional light brings out a play of yellow and green against purple shadow areas that would have been lost in stronger light. Such enigmatic images suggest other associations—a landscape seen from the air, or the scaly limbs of a giant.*
Pentax, 100mm macro, Agfachrome 50s, 1/60, f8.

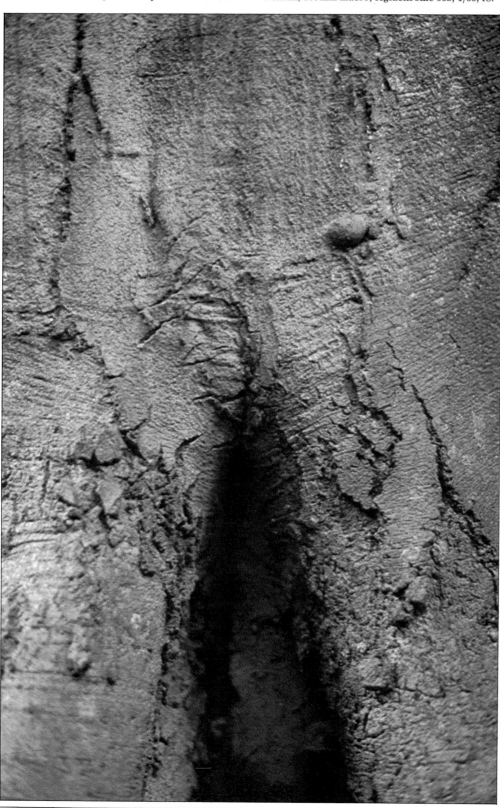

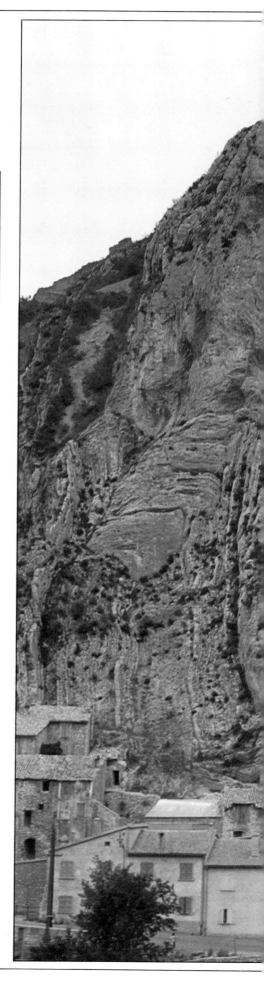

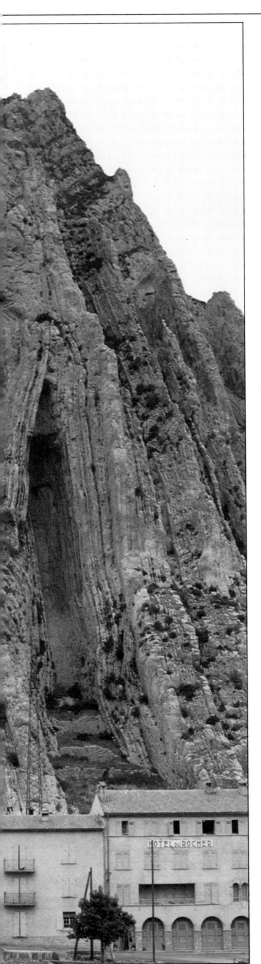

An overcast day *has brought out a warm harmony of colour and texture in the photograph of an eroded rock face behind a small French village. The soft orange in the hollows of the cliff suggests the crumbling texture of the surface and there is further variation of colour and texture in the tiles of the houses, sloping at differing angles to the light and contrasting with a reflective tin roof.* Rolleiflex, 80mm, Ektachrome 64, 1/125, f8.

A bale of wool *has been transformed from a mundane object into a dramatic one by an intriguing combination of textural surfaces. Diffused sunlight striking the shining golden fibre of the bale has accurately revealed fine variations of texture, conveying the tactile sensations of taut wire, harsh fibre, prickly hair and soft wool behind a film of smooth plastic.* Pentax, 50mm macro, tripod, Ektachrome 64, ¼ sec, f11.

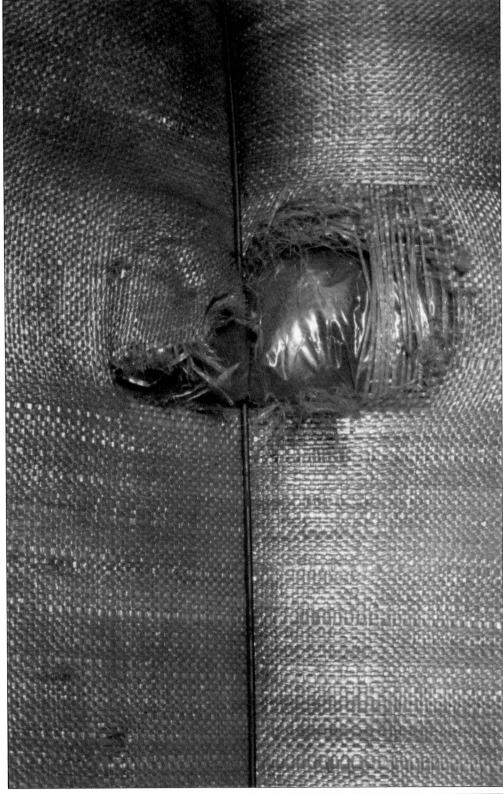

Pattern

Patterns surround us all, reflecting not only our own instinct for order but also the repetitive sequences of nature, dappled, or mottled, striped, spotted or grained. Photographs based simply on pattern do not pretend to be anything more than decorative. But they are often intriguing, especially when the pattern is created by accident or a momentary trick of light and shade. Apart from delighting us by their sheer novelty, such pictures sometimes have a curious power, perhaps because they show a design beneath the apparently random surface of things.

Pattern pictures in black and white tend to be abstract. Their main interest lies in the vitality and texture given to the picture surface by repeated tonal accents. Colour patterns arouse a more emotional response. In a scatter of deckchairs dampened by rain, the eye will seek a balance of colour and be unsettled if it is not shown.

Unsuspected patterns can be found by shooting from a distance or close up, or by choosing an unorthodox angle of view. I took the picture of the ceiling opposite by lying on my back in the foyer of the Bali Beach Hotel and using a 28mm lens on my Pentax with an exposure of 1/30 at f11. The point of focus is offset slightly and the linear pattern created by the bamboo frames is of such force that the chandelier almost seems to have been sheared off.

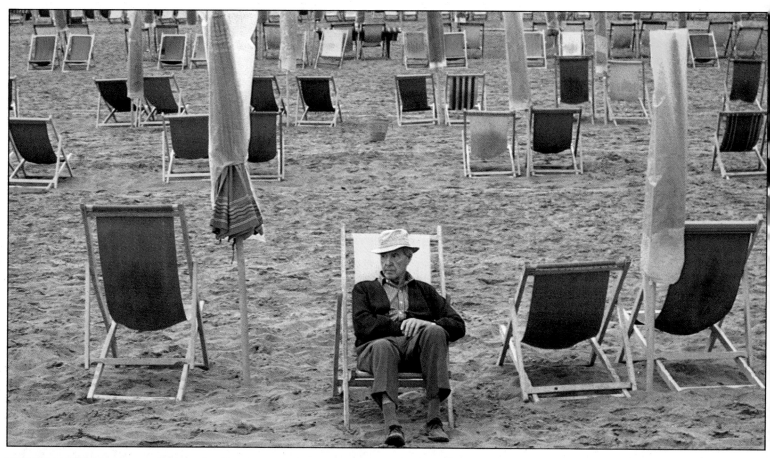

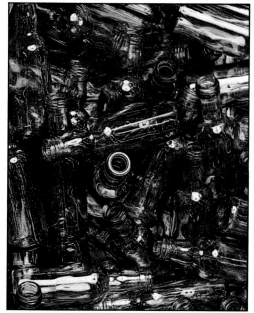

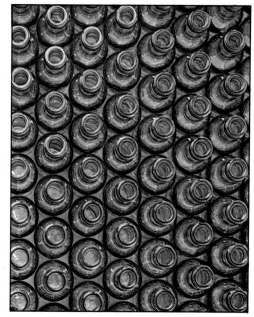

Henry Moore, *a sculptor sensitive both to colour and form, is the focal point of a colour pattern created quite accidentally on an Italian beach deserted after rain. Damp patches give the impression that some deck chairs are still occupied. The balance of colour patches, united by the neutral sand and receding to more subdued hues brings a sense of order to an otherwise rather disorganized background.*
Leicaflex, 35mm, Ektachrome 64, 1/30, f8.

A haphazard collection of bottles *makes a busy picture (far left) in which shape is delineated mainly by reflections. Surfaces that catch the light provide the only hint of a pattern in a basically random picture. When arranged neatly, the same bottles form a symmetrical pattern, which is enlivened by a network of black lines and an overall sloping effect.*
Olympus, 50mm, Ektachrome 64, 1/30, f8.

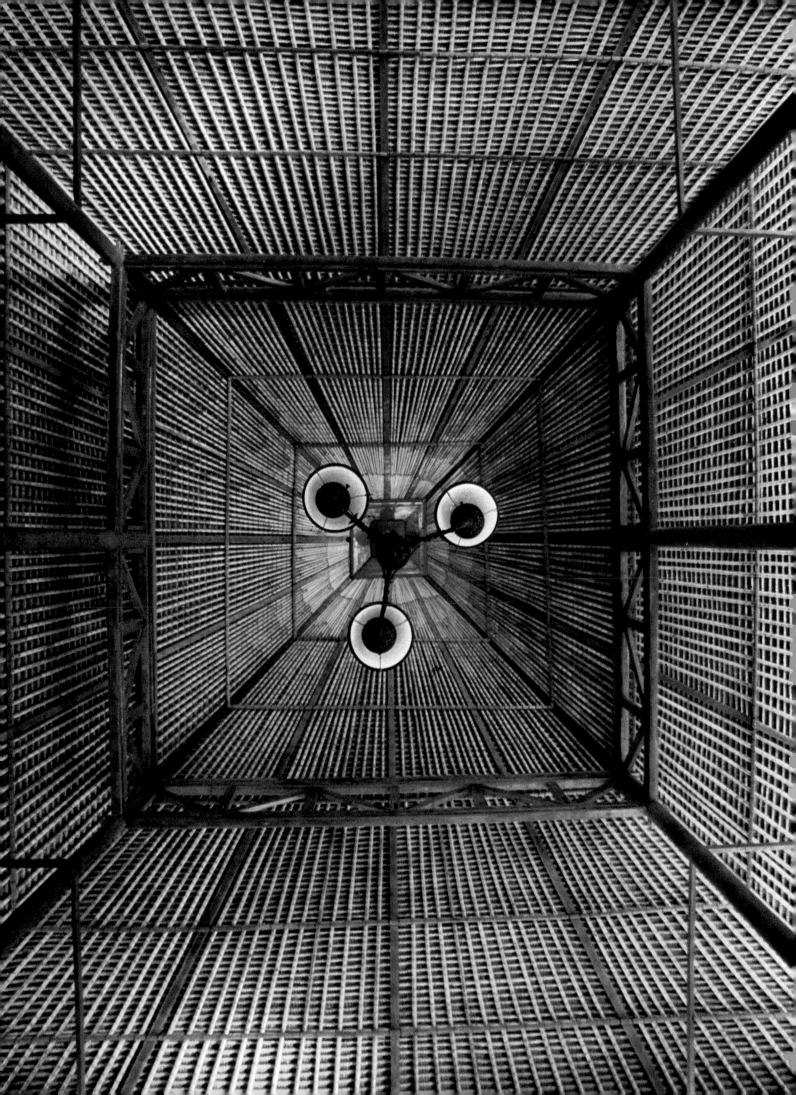

Pattern

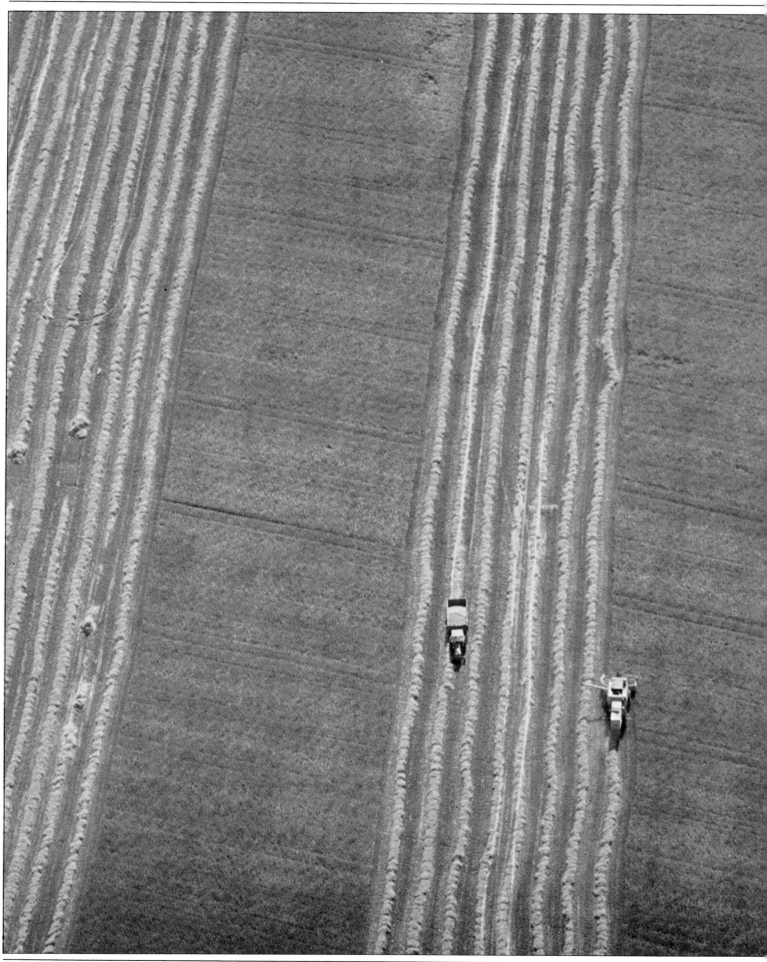

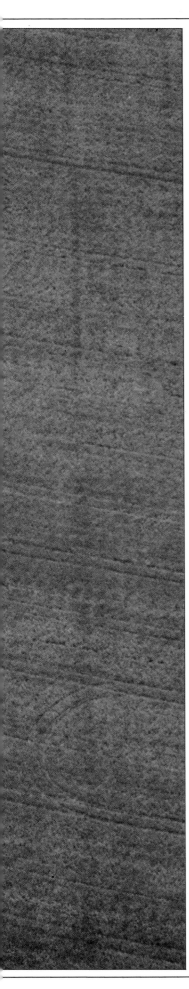

Man creates patterns *wherever he works or settles. Sometimes planned for decorative effect, they are more often the result of chance or convenience, following and emphasizing the natural contours of the land. The patterns produced by these transformations may show up best in diffused light, though shadows can give added interest provided they do not conflict. In the picture (left) of the Canadian prairies, harvesters crossing at right angles to the planting lines create a pattern that is given a texture rather like beige wool by the light and shade striking the standing crop.* Leicaflex, 50mm, Ektachrome 64, 1/250, f8.

Terraced rice-fields *(top right) in Indonesia produce marvellous patterns through the interplay of line and colour, reflection and shadow. The wooden shelters, resembling sentinels, are objects themselves of delicate design. Their brown and beige tones harmonize with the surrounding variety of greens, yet their geometric lines contrast with the snaking form of the terraces.* Pentax, 35mm, Ektachrome 64, 1/125, f8.

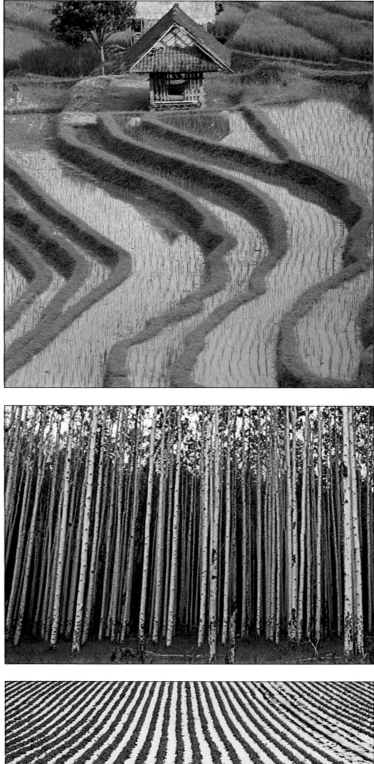

Silver birch trees *(centre) in the Rockies are made interesting by the pattern of white trunks alternating with shadow. The interplay of light and shade leads the eye in and out of the scene, creating the impression of a wall that is impenetrable but that has considerable depth.* Olympus, 28mm, Ektachrome 64, 1/250, f11.

Frost or snow *can accentuate landscape patterns by covering distracting detail or crisply highlighting an existing point of interest. In the shot (bottom right) of a potato-field in Scotland, heavy frost has dramatized a scene that would otherwise have lacked strong colour contrast. A wide-angle lens gives the effect of sagging and converging furrows.* Pentax, 28mm, Ektachrome 64, 1/30, f8.

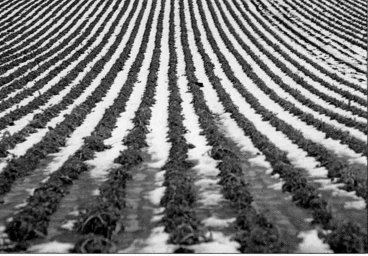

Perspective

Perspective in the two-dimensional art of photography recreates the world's third dimension—its depth. As we have seen, the tonal modelling provided by light and shade can suggest depth and volume in an individual object. But the illusion that one object in a picture is farther back than another is created by four main kinds of perspective.

Of particular interest in colour photography is *aerial perspective*, the tendency for colours and tones to fade with distance due to atmospheric diffusion. *Overlapping forms*, one partly obscuring another, are a second indicator of depth. In *diminishing scale*, objects look smaller the farther away they are. Finally, *linear perspective* is the gradual converging of planes or lines as they recede from us.

Just as a strong pattern will tend to flatten a picture, so all these types of perspective can be used to give pictures depth. A subsidiary, but more ambiguous, indicator of depth is *selective focus*, the eye's knowledge that a sharp and an unfocused object must be on two different planes. In the shot of rose hips below, an aperture of f1.2 lifts the foreground hips away from those out of focus behind them, but destroys background depth.

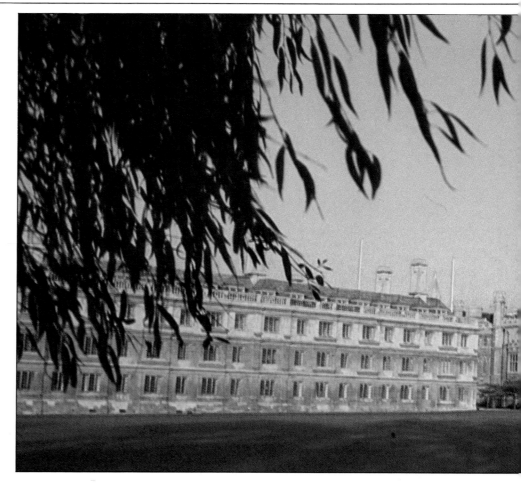

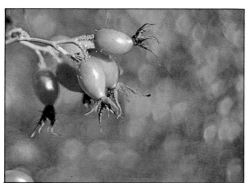

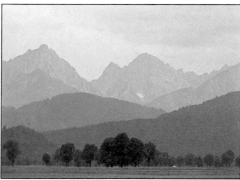

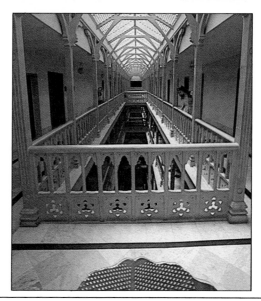

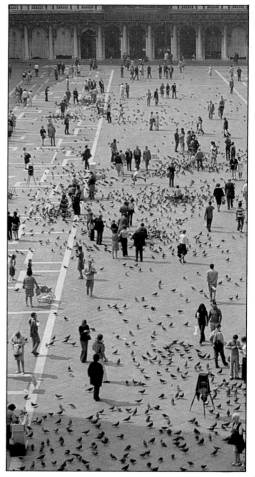

Aerial perspective *in the picture of Bavarian mountains carries the eye back from the brighter colours of closer vegetation to overlapping peaks, their colour dissipated by haze and distance.*
Pentax, 50mm, Agfachrome 50s, 1/125, f11.

The linear perspective *of a balcony in a Bombay hotel is accentuated by my aiming downwards with a wide-angle lens from a glass table on which I was standing.*
Pentax, 18mm, Ektachrome 200, 1/30, f8.

A diminishing scale *of figures and birds in the shot of St Mark's Square is partly concealed by their continuous pattern. Note the difference when you cover the middle area. As the red banner draws the eye, the shot might have looked flat without the strong linear perspective on the ground.*
Leicaflex, 50mm, Agfachrome 50s, 1/125, f11.

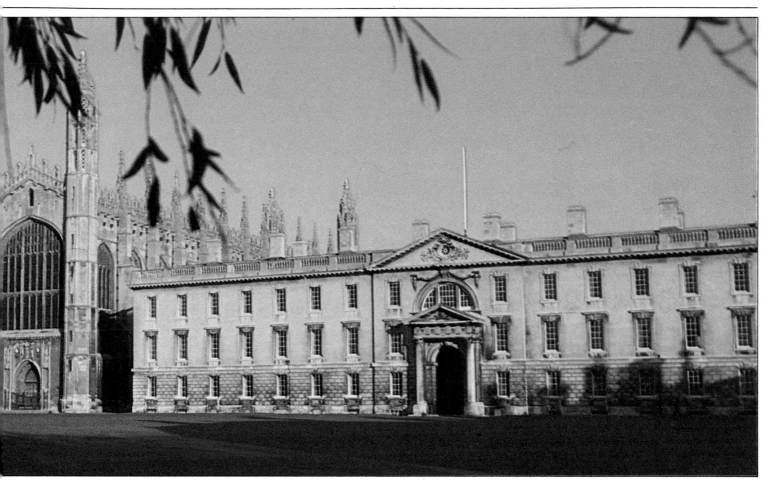

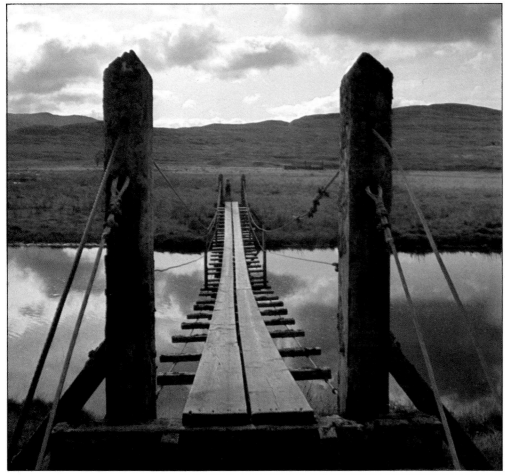

All the main perspective devices *are illustrated in the picture of King's College, Cambridge, giving it considerable depth in spite of strong lateral lines, which might have tended to flatten it. The dark shadows lying at the base of the buildings add definition to the linear perspective of the colleges, which converge slightly towards the chapel. There is subtle aerial perspective, both in the changing golden tones of the buildings and in the blues of the sky. The changing size of the windows also directs the eye towards the chapel, while the overlapping leaves, because we know their actual scale, give an immediate sense of depth to the picture by appearing relatively large. Framing of this kind is a powerful way of suggesting distance.* Pentax, 28mm, Agfachrome 50s, 1/125, f8.

This compelling picture *forces the eye to pass between the uprights and across a footbridge in Scotland. Cables supporting the uprights in the foreground converge, repeating the outer lines of the bridge, although the centre line is quite straight. Diminishing scale is provided not only by the dwindling cross-members but also by the uprights on the far side, which appear tiny. Evening light from an overcast sky is reflected from the planks, carrying the eye from the foreground into a sombre background, which widens outwards.* Leicaflex, 35mm, Ektachrome 64, 1/30, f16.

Framing

Framing as a pictorial device has been used for centuries to display paintings in a surrounding of a colour, size or texture that balances and complements them. Exactly the same considerations apply in photography, but the device has additional possibilities here as the frame can be included in the picture.

The most obvious effect of framing in photography is to concentrate attention on a specific area within the field of view. But the primary intention may be to hide distracting detail or to fill in an uninteresting foreground—a frequent compositional problem for beginners. Half-framing can be equally effective and helps to give a sense of scale or distance in a picture. Low-hanging leaves, doorways, arches, walls and other architectural details all make convenient frames. In the absence of anything else it is quite easy to improvise frames, which can range from a piece of scrap paper or a torn handkerchief held in front of the camera to a smear of butter round the outside of a glass filter.

The colour of the frame is obviously important if you are using colour film. It may introduce a lively contrast or alternatively help to harmonize the range of hues in the picture. The white frame used in the photograph below, for instance, was a distinct advantage, as one of the objectives of this shot was to create a high-key composition in whites and browns, providing a link with the style of the paintings on which the artist was working—one of them can be seen just behind the chair. In the picture of the cathedral on the opposite page, coppery leaves thrown out of focus by their closeness to a long lens, provide a warm colour contrast with the neutral stone of the building.

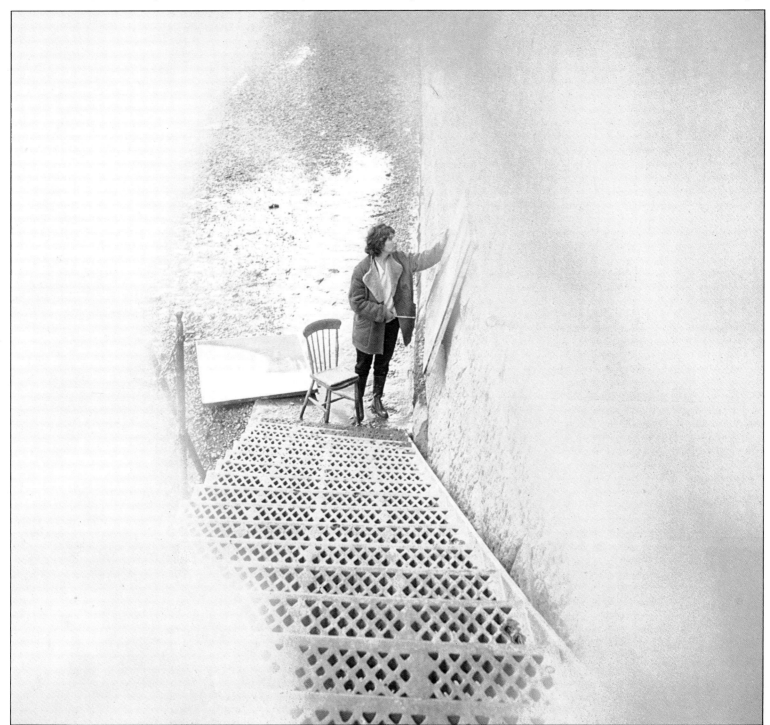

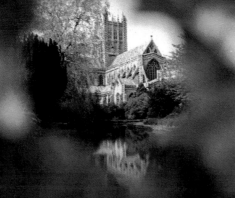

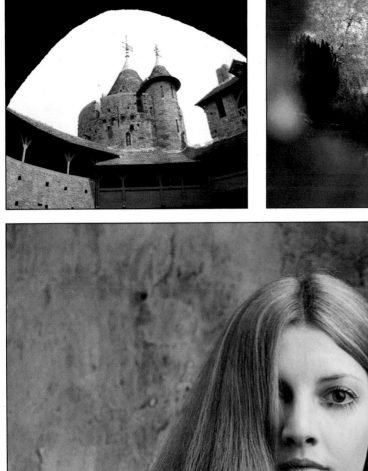

The garden surrounding the cathedral *(left) was so attractive that it diverted attention from the building I wanted to photograph. By moving back and using a long lens and wide aperture I was able to make the cathedral the focal point by masking the foreground with the leaves of a copper beech. In the picture alongside, I used an arch to mask the sun, which was flaring into the camera, and the frame both suits the shapes of this Welsh castle and captures its enclosed feeling, while drawing attention to the architectural detail.*

Far left: Hasselblad, 250mm, Ektachrome 64, 1/250, f5.6.
Left: Hasselblad, 60mm, Ektachrome 200, 1/60, f22.

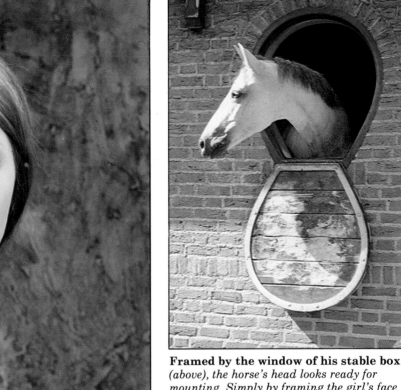

Framed by the window of his stable box *(above), the horse's head looks ready for mounting. Simply by framing the girl's face with her own hair (left), I have emphasized its beautiful colour and texture. At the same time the impression of a disembodied head makes an intriguing image.*

Above: Pentax, 50mm, Ektachrome 64, 1/125, f8.
Left: Hasselblad, 150mm, Ektachrome 64, 1/60, f11.

This dream-like image *was created by holding a torn film carton a few centimetres in front of the lens—a framing technique available to every photographer. The painter, Sandra Blow, was actually standing on the shoreline of the River Thames at low tide, surrounded by black mud and at the foot of a black iron staircase. But by positioning myself so that the maximum light was reflected into the lens, I was able to achieve a picture that makes use of a colour scheme in sympathy with the mood and tone of the artist's work. High-key photographs can often be created simply by reflections.*

Hasselblad, 80mm, Ektachrome 64, 1/30, f8.

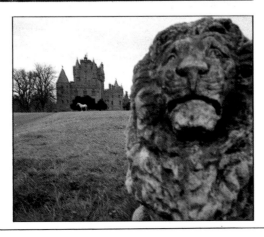

Half-framing, *accomplished with the statue of a lion, is the first of a series of linked devices that carry the eye into this picture of Glamis Castle, the location for the murder of the Scottish King Duncan in Shakespeare's Macbeth. Beyond the stone beast, and greatly reduced in scale, a distant white horse is itself framed by trees, which are in turn framed by the castle. The lion establishes a sense of proportion, being slightly out of focus so that it leads the eye forwards while creating the uncanny impression that the viewer is actually standing beside it.*

Hasselblad, 80mm, Ektachrome 64, 1/125, f8.

Existing backgrounds

While framing can be used to hide a distracting foreground, it is often more difficult in outdoor photography to eliminate an unsuitable background. Selective focusing with a wide aperture or long lens can help to isolate your subject from its setting, and a slow shutter speed will provide a similar effect through blur if there is movement in the background. Lighting is another means of control. But remember that a background need not always be subordinate, as the name implies, and finding an effective one is sometimes only a matter of looking and of bearing in mind its importance in composition.

A main subject *can often be effectively presented as a background, as in the shot of the New York skyline, its shapes echoed by the silhouettes of battered timbers on a Brooklyn wharf. Sympathetic shapes linked in this way will enliven the most prosaic view. The distant outlines are softened by slight haze and early morning sun reflected from the water.* Hasselblad, 150mm, Ektachrome 64, 1/250, f16.

The office worker *on his lunch break, whose vivid red socks caught my attention while I was walking in a Montreal park, seemed unlikely on that day to get closer to nature than the painted forest against which he is posed. Here the background, the key element in the picture, seems to make a wry statement about the quality of life in an urban environment.* Leicaflex, 50mm, Agfachrome 50s, 1/250, f8.

Selective focusing *becomes an advantage in photographing animals, which often have to be picked out from backgrounds that provide them with natural camouflage. This shot, taken with a long lens, has isolated the impala while taking in delicate blades of grass that perfectly match the animal's nervous alertness.* Leicaflex, 400mm, Ektachrome 200, 1/500, f5.6.

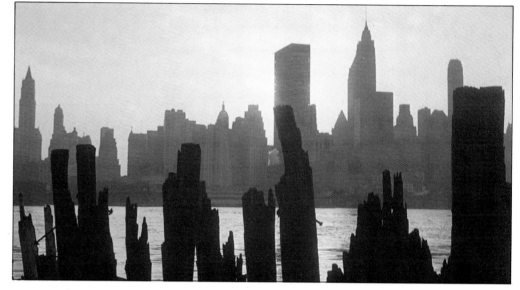

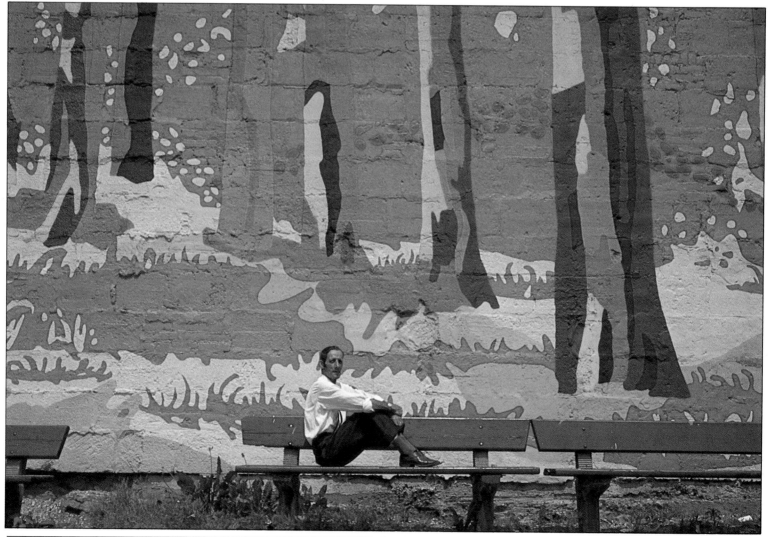

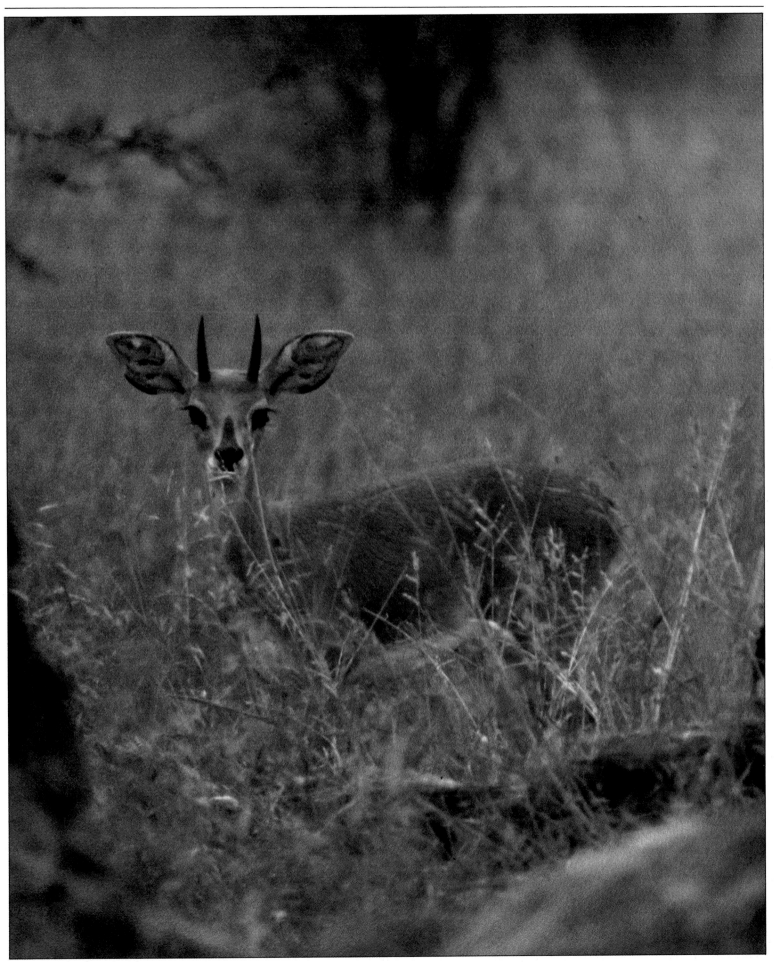

Planned backgrounds

Because its purpose is to support a subject, not overpower it, a planned background involves an important creative decision. The background can be dramatic, softly atmospheric or narrative, placing the subject in context. Its lighting should generally be one stop less than on the subject.

Paper rolls provide convenient plain backdrops. Elaborate subjects look well against them, especially when the colour harmonizes with the subject's or forms a contrast that emphasizes the main point of interest. Black or pure white, although sometimes effective, should be used with caution, as they can make subjects appear to sink into gloom or float on the surface. Things normally need to be posed against a solid base that has tonal variety.

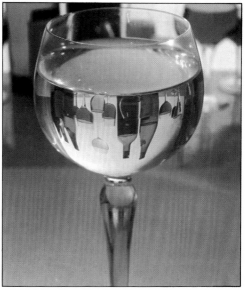

Glass and bottles, *whether clear or coloured, are usually lit in one of two ways. Backlighting gives bold, hard outlines with few highlights and little modelling, emphasizing the shape and colours of both container and liquid. Soft, directional lighting gives a more delicate effect, showing form and transparency. White or grey backgrounds with shadows help to achieve this effect, and side-lighting from a single window, balanced by a reflector, will bring out all the subtleties of glass. The top picture shows how liquid in a glass can be used as a kind of lens, reflecting other images. To convey an impression of the scene at a wine-tasting, I moved in close to one glass with an MPP 5 × 4in camera and exposed at 1/10, f8. The other picture, exposed at 1/125, f8, was backlit with two photofloods bounced off a wall and another placed behind the bottles.*

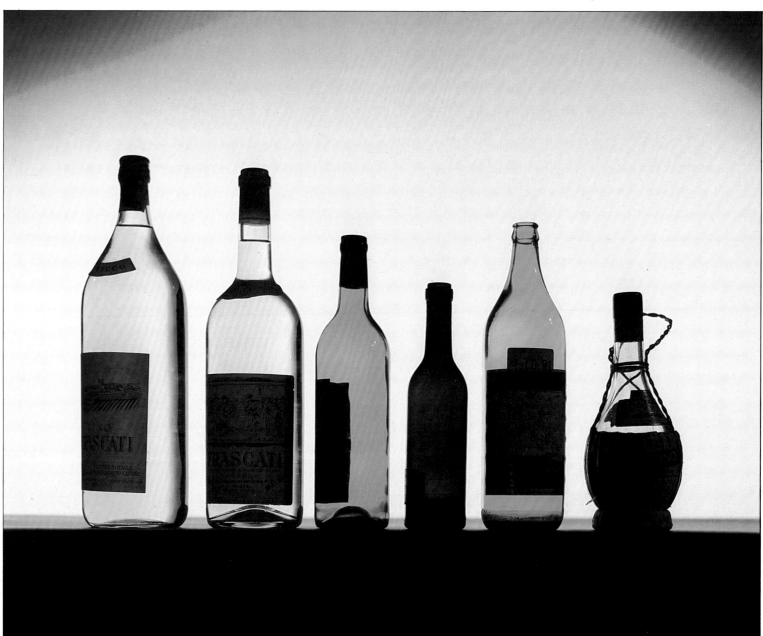

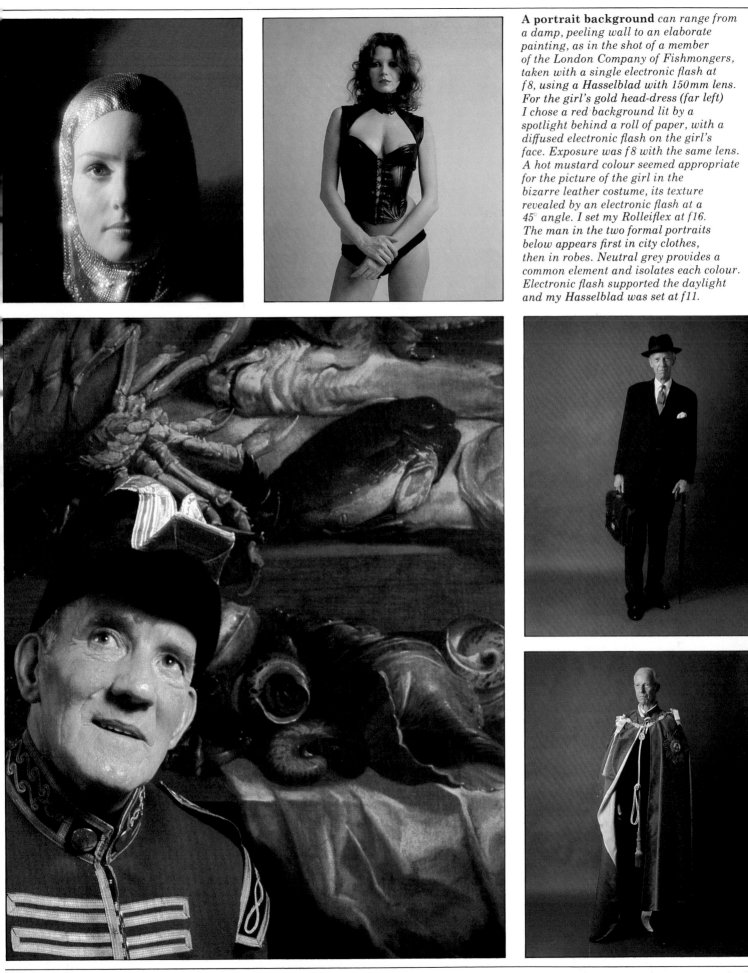

A portrait background *can range from a damp, peeling wall to an elaborate painting, as in the shot of a member of the London Company of Fishmongers, taken with a single electronic flash at f8, using a Hasselblad with 150mm lens. For the girl's gold head-dress (far left) I chose a red background lit by a spotlight behind a roll of paper, with a diffused electronic flash on the girl's face. Exposure was f8 with the same lens. A hot mustard colour seemed appropriate for the picture of the girl in the bizarre leather costume, its texture revealed by an electronic flash at a 45° angle. I set my Rolleiflex at f16. The man in the two formal portraits below appears first in city clothes, then in robes. Neutral grey provides a common element and isolates each colour. Electronic flash supported the daylight and my Hasselblad was set at f11.*

Movement

Photography may seem better equipped in some ways to arrest movement than to convey it. If a photographer's judgement is bad, the result will be the paralysis of a subject that was full of vitality. Yet properly understood, the techniques of capturing movement can be used to produce pictures bursting with life.

The basics are simple. Movement can be shown by a sequence of pictures that add up to a visual story with its own ebb and flow. Secondly, it can be shown by an exposure that will record, as a blur, movement either by the subject or by the camera itself. Thirdly, a sharp picture can be taken at such a vital moment during an action that the mind of the viewer completes the movement. A diving boy, a leaping footballer or a charging bull all have a momentum that is irresistible.

Sometimes, movement can be conveyed by pattern alone, or by the force of perspective. Colour adds its own impact to photographs of moving objects, and hues can also be radically altered by the movement of highlights into shadow during long exposures. This technique allows a moving image to be devoured by light, often diffusing and smearing hues together to create beautiful colour effects.

It is always worth experimenting with the effects of slight blur, especially when the subject is rather pedestrian, although a scene that is already full of vitality is usually better taken straight. Effective contrasts are possible when there are static and moving subjects in the same scene—a girl on a street corner, for instance, with a blur of traffic behind her. Similar effects are achieved by panning to capture a moving object sharp while blurring the background. The nearer you are to a moving subject the faster the shutter speed needed to reveal sharp detail. The angle of movement to the camera is obviously important also, with subjects approaching head-on allowing slower shutter speeds to be used than would be possible with subjects moving across the field of view.

If you want slight blur to emphasize motion, calculate the shutter speed that would freeze the action and then shoot at half that speed. A car crossing your line of vision at 70 mph (112 km/h) could be frozen at 1/1000 or blurred at 1/500. When taking action shots of a particular subject for the first time, work out a method of prefocusing and then experiment with a range of different exposures.

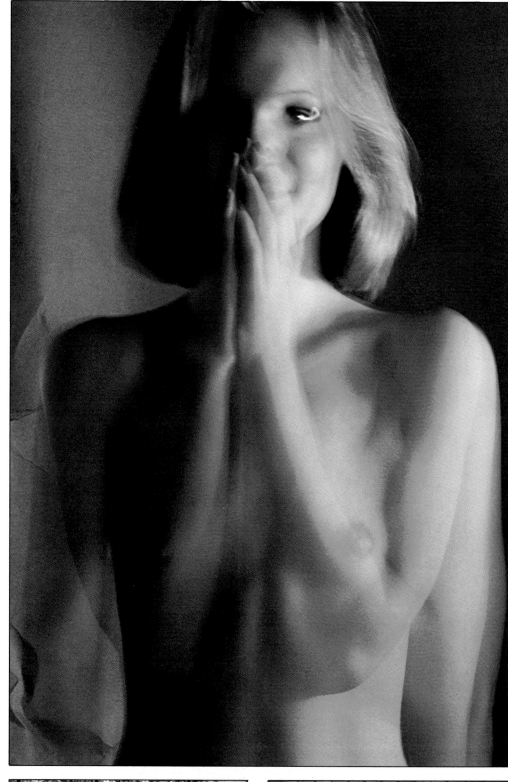

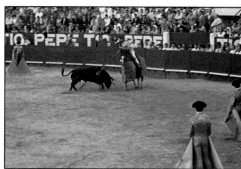

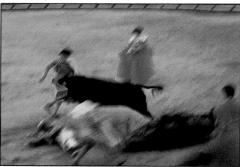

The girl has simply raised her hands from her sides to her face in the course of a 1/2 second exposure in tungsten lighting. There is a fascination about pictures in which, during a long exposure, random elements enter an otherwise calculated scene, giving an unpredictable result. The deliberate combination of chance and intention is one of the attractions of taking photographs.
Pentax, 135mm, Ektachrome 160, 1/2, f8.

Horse and rider assume ghostly form in an indoor picture at the German national riding school at Warendorf. Rays of sunlight were falling on the sawdust of the arena from high windows and the horse was crossing the floor at a slow trot that required an exposure of 1/125 to retain full detail. I panned at a speed of 1/15 to spread shadow into the highlights and give depth to the scene. Instead of being shown as alternate bars

of gold and dark brown, the floor has been transformed to a glowing russet colour. Movement has lightened the dark red jacket of the rider to crimson and highlights have begun to dissolve the horse. Details parallel to the pan, such as the reins, remain sharp, as does the horse's forelock, which has been caught as it emerged from shadow in the instant before the shutter finally closed.
Pentax, 50mm, Ektachrome 160, f11.

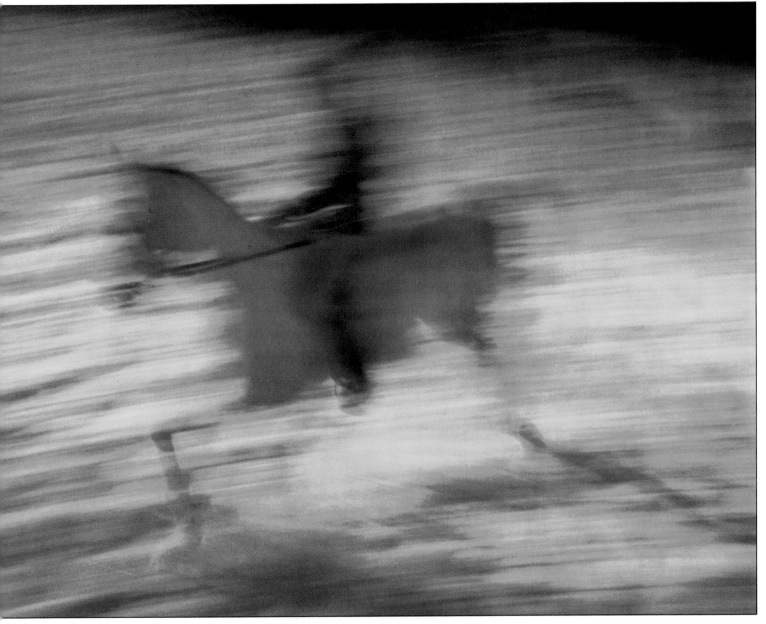

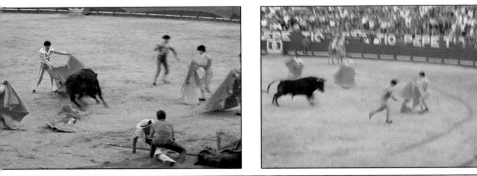

A sequence of pictures can be taken at a rate of almost one a second with a quality 35mm camera, even without a motor drive. I like this bullfight sequence because for the moment the bull has come out on top, disrupting the usual train of events and creating a few dramatic moments of shock and turmoil. The day was overcast and by shooting for slight blur at 1/15 I achieved a better result than a faster speed would have given.

Leicaflex, 90mm, Ektachrome 64, 1/15, f16.

Movement

Panning can powerfully convey lateral speed and at the same time allow a fast-moving subject to be photographed successfully with a comparatively long exposure time. Cameras with direct viewfinders are best for panning, but any can be used. However, with SLR cameras the image will be blacked out during exposure, so that the subject cannot be seen during the whole pan.

For best results, the pan must be smooth and the speed and movement of the subject should be consistent. Variations such as those produced by a bumpy road will cause double images. This may well add drama to the shot, provided the movement is only slight,

as in the picture of a motorcyclist, below. This shot also shows the effectiveness of panning bright colours against a subdued background.

As a moving object will rarely travel in a consistent arc at the same distance from you, a small aperture giving greater depth of field is usually an advantage. Take up a firm stance, keep the subject in the centre of the viewfinder and swing from the waist without moving your feet. Follow through beyond the exposure time to avoid a jerky result. As a rough guide, a speed of 1/15 can be used to pan a vehicle moving at 30mph (48km/h), or 1/30 for 60mph (96km/h).

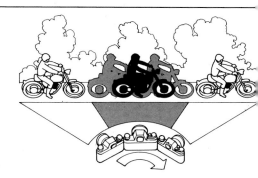

As shown in the diagram, *a pan should begin some distance before the button is pressed and continue after exposure is completed. Prefocusing, as in the shot of the motorcyclist (below left), is essential.* Fujica, 50mm, Ektachrome 64, 1/500, f11.

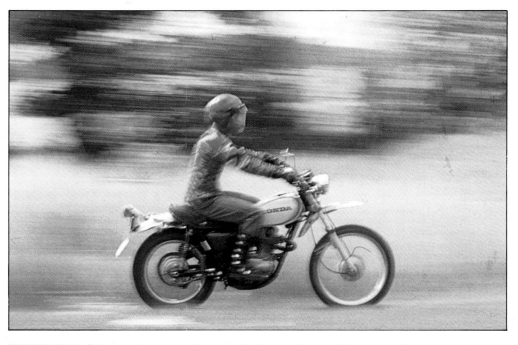

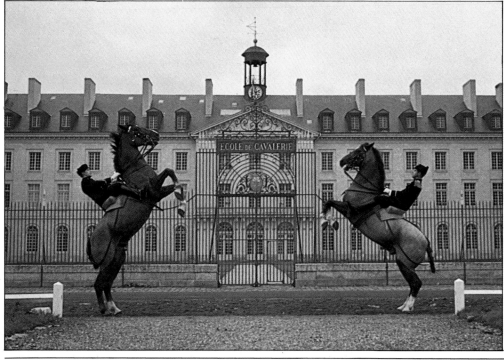

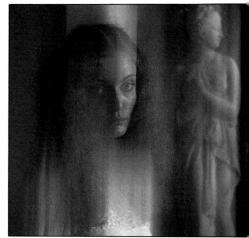

Film movement *can spread colour and create unusual effects. For the shot above I used a motorized camera to wind the film on during the exposure, but a tripod and hand winder would do.* Hasselblad, 150mm, Ektachrome 64, 1/4, f8.

Motion and formal rigidity *combine in a picture at the French national military riding school. Such shots need careful planning in advance. After gauging the height to which the horses would rear without breaking the roofline, I centred the gate and tower to simplify the background and shot at ground level, using a normal lens to balance horses and building.* Leicaflex, 55mm, Ektachrome 64, 1/500, f5.6.

The hurtling motorcyclist *opposite is actually balancing on a stationary machine. The speed lines have been created by a zoom lens focused on the 24 on his shirt and then moved back. Although these lines actually suggest movement away from the camera, the powerful illusion of forward momentum relies on our assumption (heightened by the lighted headlamp) that a motorcyclist in this position must be bearing down on the viewer.* Pentax, 85-210 zoom lens, Agfachrome 50s, 1/30, f11.

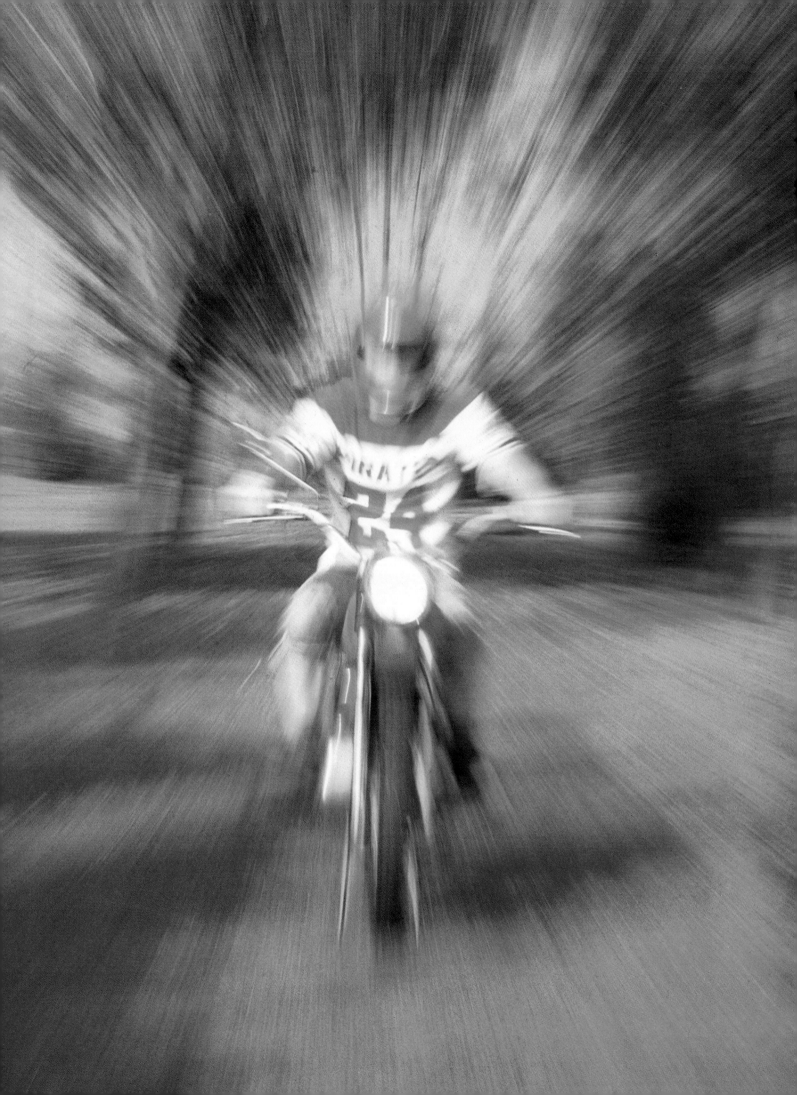

Movement

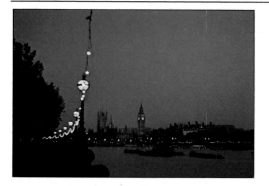

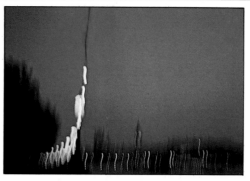

This high-speed motor-boat *was shot from a helicopter travelling at approximately the same speed, 30 knots. I could therefore have used a relatively slow shutter speed to achieve a sharp image, but taking photographs from an aircraft is complicated by the possibility of a suddenly bumpy ride and so I chose to shoot at 1/500 to cut out camera shake. The picture is given a powerful sense of movement by the shape and colour of the wake, tearing the dark, placid water. Composition is helped by the camera angle, which creates a diagonal thrust. For this shot I wanted to concentrate interest on the speed-boat and I therefore used a polarizing filter in order to both eliminate reflection and increase contrast between boat and sea. The water shows a considerable range of tone.*
Pentax, 135mm, Ektachrome 64, 1/500, f11.

A view of London *from across the Thames at night becomes something quite different in the second shot (above right). Simply by jarring the camera during a slightly longer exposure time I have created a picture in which the colours, reds and greens* especially, *are made clearer and lighter by movement. What the first view showed as spots of light have been transformed to resemble oil flares and dancing wraiths hovering above the water.*
Pentax, 135mm, Ektachrome 64, ½ and 1 sec, f16.

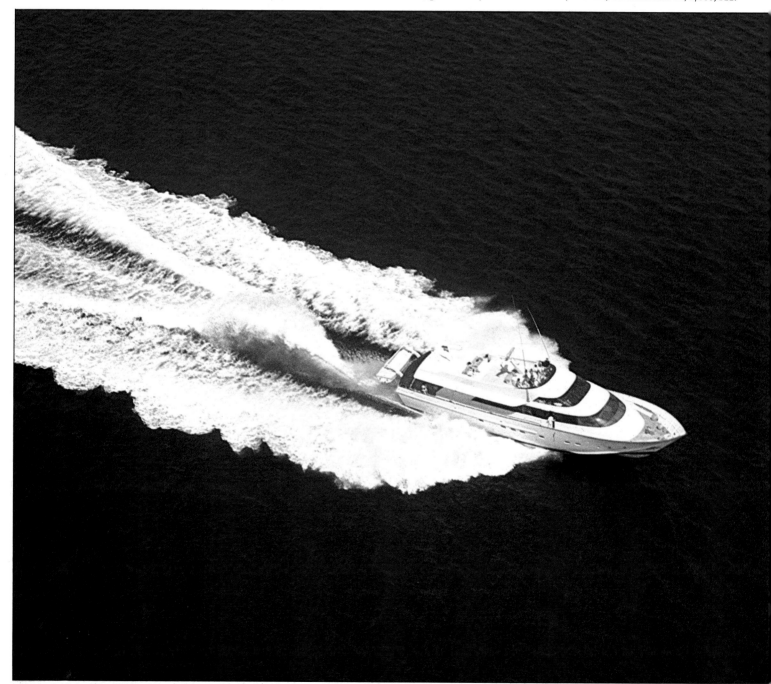

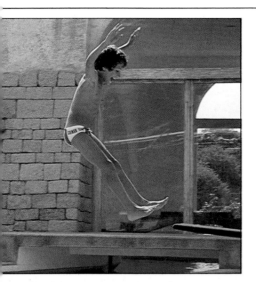

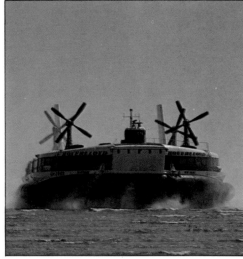

The position and shape of the boy *was central to the feeling of exuberance, so I shot at high speed to arrest his movement and expression. The sun falling from behind lifts him out of a subdued background, while the arch echoes the arc of his body. In the hovercraft shot, freezing the action has stopped the spray but a slower exposure of 1/500 would have been a better choice as I wanted to show the props as a blurred outline, not as apparently static.*

Far left: Pentax, 85mm, Ektachrome 200, 1/500, f3.5.
Left: Leicaflex, 180mm, Ektachrome 200, 1/2000, f8.

Neon lights *can be easily transformed into attractive patterns at night. To achieve the flowing lines of this picture I simply waved the camera during a long exposure.*
Canon, 50mm, Ektachrome 64, 2sec, f16.

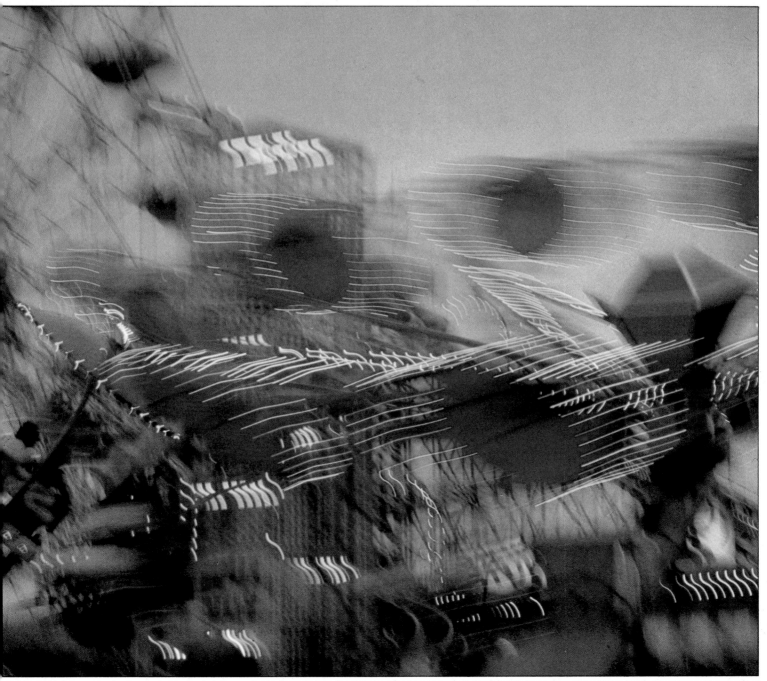

High-speed movement

Photography alone is able to reveal what the human eye cannot see unaided —arrested movement at high speed. Very high-speed photography usually has a scientific purpose rather than an aesthetic one, but the pictures that it produces can be both beautiful and informative. Subjects can range from a dripping tap to a flying bird, and your equipment need not be expensive.

To take the pictures of the bursting water-filled balloon I used a Minolta with a 100mm macro lens at f11, but depending on the subject any lens can be used. The only other equipment was a tripod, a portable flash giving an exposure time of about 1/1000, an air-pistol and a piece of softboard covered with black cloth to provide a background and absorb the pellets.

I filled the balloons with sufficient water to give them a good shape and suspended them from nylon threads, which, by imparting spin on release of their tension, may have helped retain the shape of the water after the balloon had split. I prefocused on the balloon from 6ft (about 2m) with the flashlight at the same distance and at an angle of 45° and placed a large silverized mirror 6ft from the subject, opposite the flash.

The whole difficulty lay in synchronizing the flash with the balloon burst. To test my ability to do this manually I held the gun in my right hand, the cable release in my left and fired both simultaneously from a kneeling position behind the camera. A Polaroid showed the balloon still intact, so I deduced that a slight delay was needed before triggering the camera in order to allow time for the bullet to reach the balloon and cause it to burst. Being right-handed I switched the gun to my left hand and triggered the camera with my right an instant after I had fired the gun.

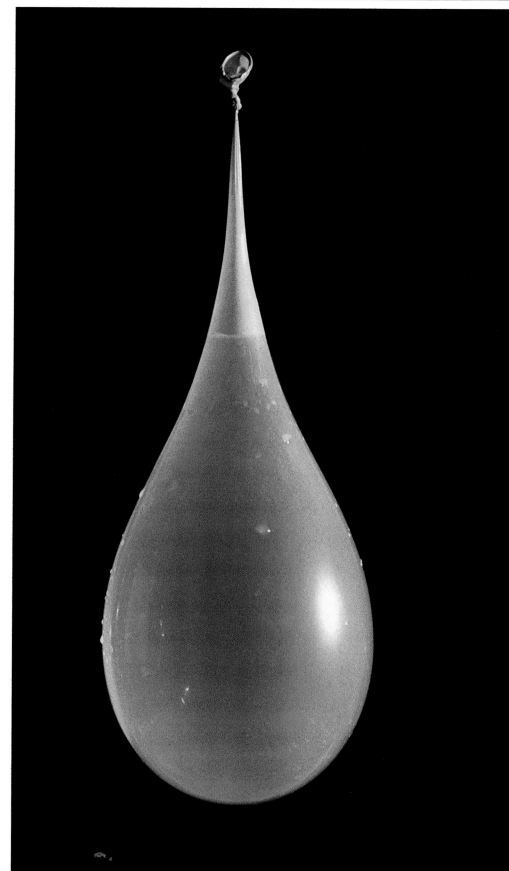

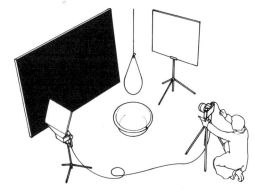

Using the arrangement shown in the diagram *I took these three pictures consecutively, but used a new balloon for the last shot. The first shot simply shows an* *intact balloon. In the second picture the bullet has struck and burst the balloon, although the rubber at the bottom has yet to fall away. Water has begun to flow up and* *out from the point of impact, producing slight feathering and crystalline spearing. The third shot shows the whole weight of water before it exploded. The liquid is moving*

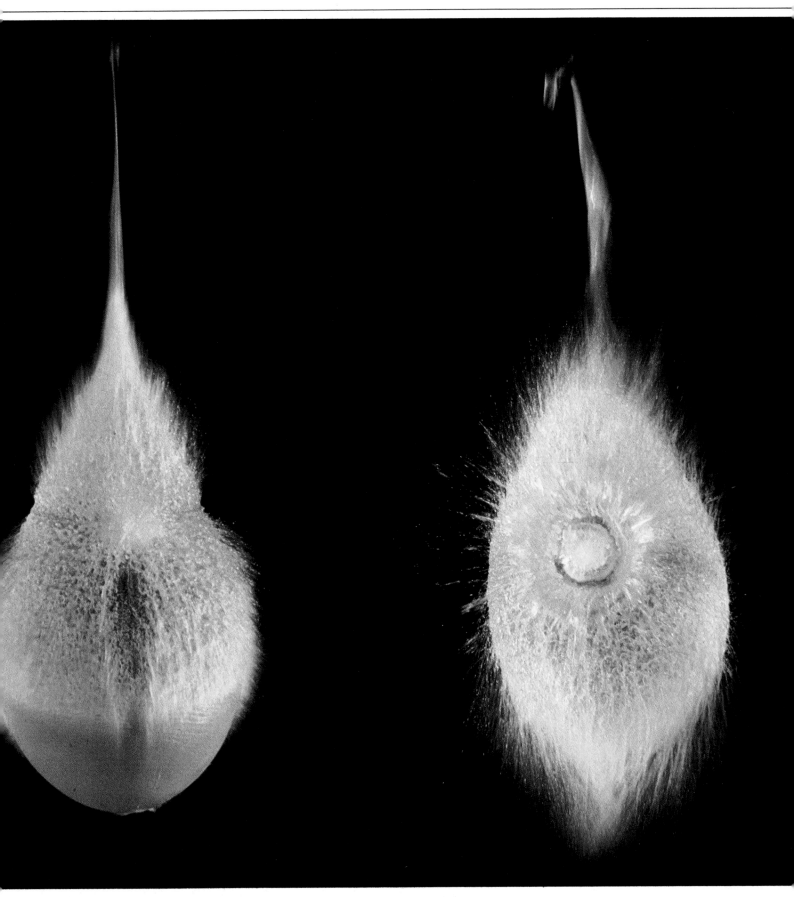

faster than the electronic flash. Specialized
equipment, or a flash speed of 1/5000, would
probably have been needed to freeze the
action completely, although the movement

helps to give the impression of an explosion.
In the course of the experiment I found that
thin, cheap balloons gave the best results and
that after a little practice I could achieve

the effect I wanted nine times out of ten.
If you want to try a similar sequence
at home you should have a large basin to
catch the flying water—and wear oilskins.

Close-ups

Photography at close range can produce startling colour pictures particularly where magnification reveals an unsuspected richness of colour in things so small they would normally pass unnoticed. As several pictures here show, deep colour saturation can also be achieved in close-ups taken with ordinary lenses. A masked-down area of colour usually gains in intensity because it does not have to compete with nearby highlights or light sources. In the shot of autumn leaves, for instance, the colours would have been dissipated had I tried to include the whole tree. The close-up of leaves says much about the beauty of the tree and the approaching season. Small areas revealed are often more telling than the whole panorama.

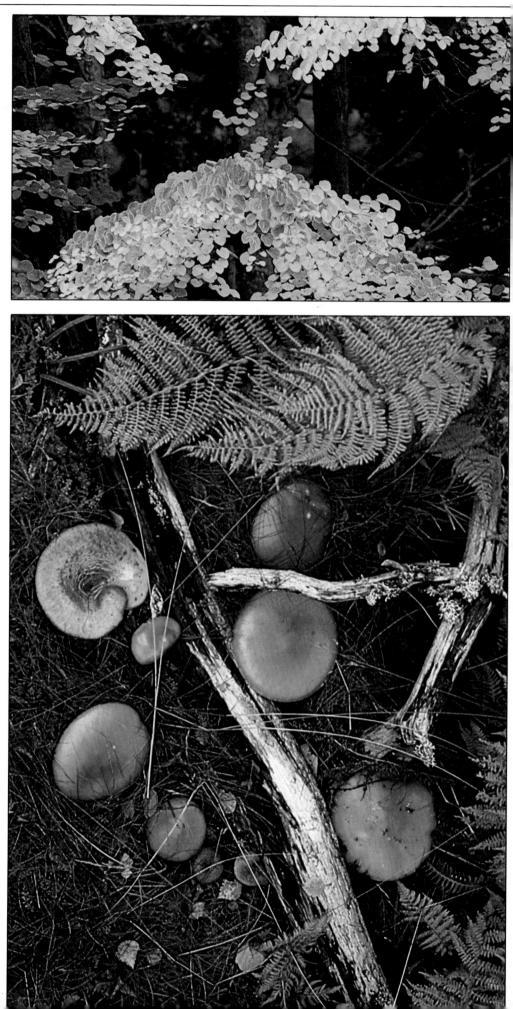

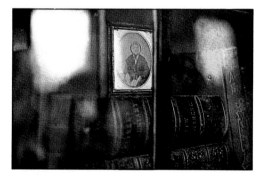

Picture stories *to evoke atmosphere and a sense of time past often depend on small details. This view into a bookcase with an old calotype portrait among bound volumes was photographed through smeary glass, which had picked up white and green reflections. These both balance the portrait's gold frame and suggest the faded colours of Victorian gas lamps.* Pentax, 50mm, Ektachrome 64, 1/500, f16.

Autumnal colours *in the close-up of a Katsura tree (top right) gain brilliance through the contrast of yellows and greens against the darkness of the wood behind. The delicate fan-like patterns heighten the impression of cascading leaves, and there is further interest in the gradation of hues towards the stronger yellows on the right-hand side of the picture.* Leica, 21mm, tripod, Kodachrome 25, 1/60, f8.

Underexposure *by half a stop can help to increase colour saturation in close-ups, as in the reddish fungi found near the foot of the tree in the top picture. In the half-light of the wood, the grass and ferns are quite dark, heightening the reds and the white dead wood. It is better in such shots to take advantage of debris already in place than to try to arrange a composition artificially—especially if you are interested in botanical accuracy.* Leica, 50mm, Kodachrome 25, 1/30, f8.

Painted signs, *such as this eye on a French optician's shop window, are a kind of folk art that, like graffiti, is worth photographing, if only to document a period or style. The camera is marvellously equipped to catalogue impermanent things and there is a wealth of material, needing no special talent to photograph. Include only the immediate area, then do another shot to establish location. When I took this picture the window was covered with a cleaning fluid that made the glass opaque.*
Pentax, 100mm, Ektachrome 64, 1/125, f8.

By cropping the head and arms *of the boy this close-up has given impact to a strong design, echoing the shape of the trade-mark on the tee-shirt. Like the eye, the shirt records a fashion and pins down a period. The colours have been strengthened by the warm evening sun.*
Pentax, 50mm, Agfachrome 50s, 1/125, f11.

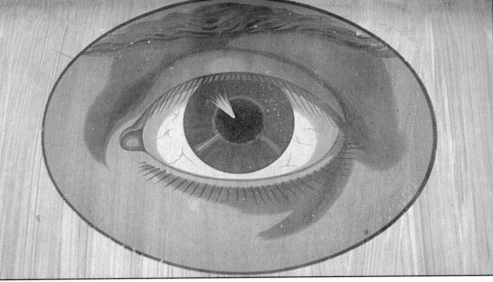

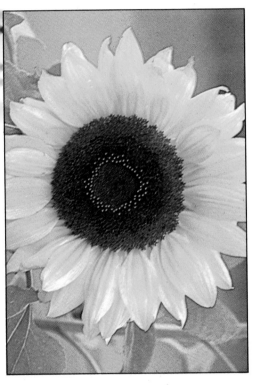

Photographing a single bloom *without the assistance of image magnifying equipment such as bellows or extension tubes, or at least close-up filters, usually means that your subject fills only a small part of the frame and may be lost against a mass of distracting background colour. This problem can be largely overcome by the careful selection of the right type of subject material. The sunflower (above) is a good example. As its size leaves little competing background, the colours of the bloom are intensified and the finer detail of the stamens exposed. However, inexpensive extension tubes or, better, a macro lens are really essential for close-ups. As slow shutter speeds are normally used, a wind shield is sometimes needed to prevent movement of the flower.*
Pentax, 100mm, Agfachrome 50s, 1/125, f8.

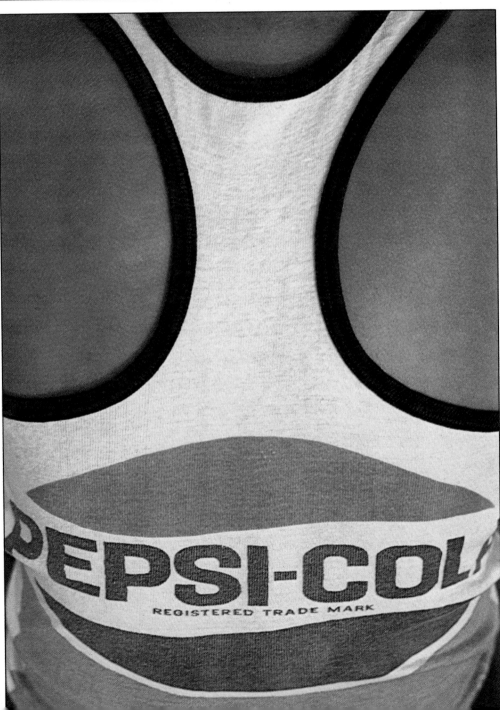

Macrophotography

The capacity of a close-up to reveal colour and detail is extended in macrophotography, which allows subjects to be photographed between life-size and ten times life-size. An array of equipment, including extension rings, bellows, macro lenses, or combinations of these, is available to achieve this. Specialized macro lenses have the added flexibility of being able to double for general photographic work. If you do not need a fast lens, 55mm or 100mm macro lenses can be used instead of the equivalent "normal" focal length lenses. Of the two macro focal lengths, I prefer the 100mm, as this lens allows close-ups to be taken at a reasonable working distance from the subject, making it easy to compose the picture and avoid casting shadows on it.

Normal lenses are built primarily for photography at a normal distance and although their capacity can be stretched by magnifying attachments, they cannot compare with specialized macro lenses designed specifically for close-ups, which can focus at distances of less than 6 in (15 cm). Magnification beyond life size requires attachments for either type of lens, and the closer the focus the more shallow the depth of field. If the light is good, stopping down will help to avoid focusing errors, although this nearly always involves lengthy exposures. A tripod and long cable release are therefore essential to minimize camera shake. Any format camera can be used as long as it has a reflex-type focusing system, which will avoid parallax error.

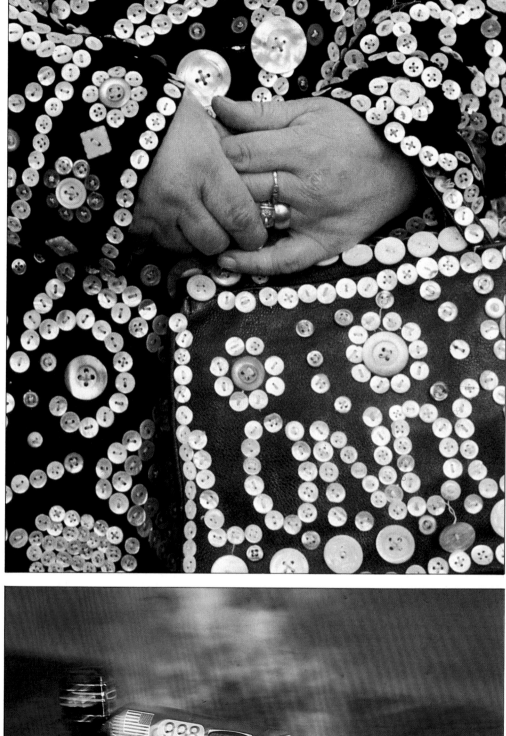

The pearly queen's costume, *in close-up, though not strictly a macrophotograph, shows some of the virtues of a macro lens, allowing colour and fine detail to be revealed while not actually intruding on the subject. The macro lens brings out not only the pattern of buttons on her costume but also the contrast between them and the more restrained decoration of her middle-aged motherly hands.*
Pentax, 100mm macro, Ektachrome 200, 1/125, f8.

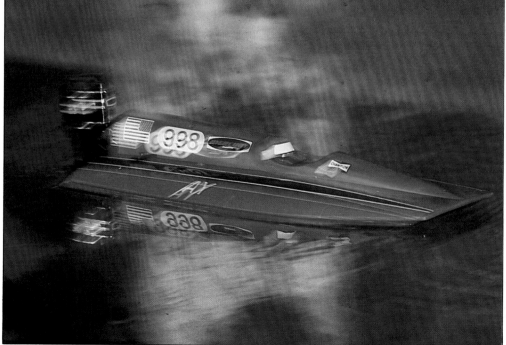

To photograph models *in a realistic way I have found a 100mm macro lens easiest to use, giving a reasonable-sized image while allowing the shot to be taken from a distance. For this picture of a toy boat I put the camera on a tripod at a distance of about 3ft (1m) and panned the shot, jarring the camera slightly at the same time to suggest the throbbing of a motor.*
Pentax, 100mm macro, Ektachrome 64, 1/125, f11.

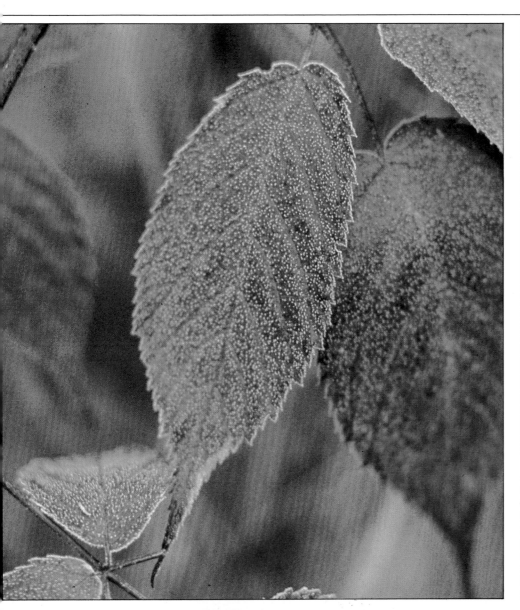

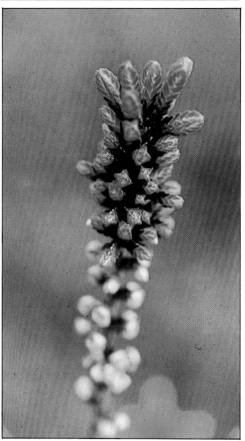

A sprig of heather, *its colour showing up brilliantly against a completely out-of-focus background, shows how lenses not specifically constructed for macro work give an extremely narrow depth of field. This picture was taken with two extension tubes magnifying the subject about five times with a depth of field hardly more than a centimetre.*
Nikon, 50mm, Ektachrome 64, 1/125, f16.

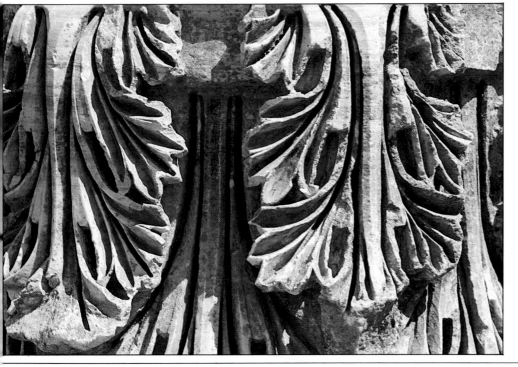

Frost-covered leaves, *taken with a macro lens and at very close range, seem to gleam in the early morning light of a Canadian autumn. The lens has picked the leaves out of the background quite sharply but given a depth of field of only a few centimetres. With hand-held outdoor close-ups it is best to use fairly wide apertures and fast shutter speeds to minimize subject and camera movement, although pegs can be used to stabilize plants if there is a breeze.*
Pentax, 50mm macro, Ektachrome 64, 1/250, f5.6.

Using extension tubes *greatly extends the range of the normal lens and is particularly useful for architectural detail. In the picture of the top of a Corinthian column (left), raking light reveals texture without too much shadow—a 30°–40° angle is best. I stopped down for maximum definition and underexposed by half a stop to improve colour saturation.*
Hasselblad, 150mm with extension tube, Ektachrome 64, 1/30, f22.

Photographing through microscopes

The magnification of photographic images made possible by using microscopes opens up a world of colours and forms hidden from the human eye. Images greater than about ten times life size fall within the definition of photomicrography and are made by positioning the camera above a microscope—preferably an SLR attached by an adaptor. The lens is either detached or, if this is impossible, it is set at infinity and full aperture. Exposure is controlled by shutter speed and focusing by the microscope lens. A cable release is essential to avoid the worst effects of vibration.

For purely creative purposes, our concern, here lighting, need not be sophisticated. An Anglepoise lamp will do. Transparent or semi-transparent subjects are best lit from below, with the microscope mirror angled to reflect an even light. Lighting from above without the mirror reflection suits opaque substances, such as a mineral sample, giving a dark background that will show the colours of the subject.

Polarized light can create beautiful colour effects, which are enhanced by the microscope. The picture opposite shows sugar crystals magnified about 50 times. White light, a mixture of all colours, was shone through a polarizing filter and then through the crystals. The emerging light then passed through a second polarizing filter, which produced a changing kaleidoscope of colours as it was rotated for the effect I chose to convey.

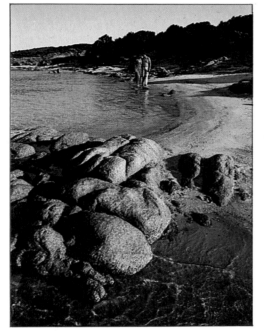

Rephotographing a small area *of a negative can create an impressionistic picture that reveals the grain of the photograph and begins to break up the colour. I magnified the couple walking on the beach tenfold, using a Leicaflex with a microscope. The grainy quality has enhanced the romantic mood. Very small colourful images provide the most suitable material for such experiments.*

The flea *was taken from a mole's nest then dyed and mounted in gum chloral, a medium well suited to photomicrography because of its superior refractive qualities. The amount of detail visible gives the shot the clarity of a finely worked drawing.*

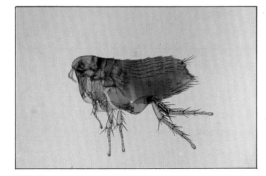

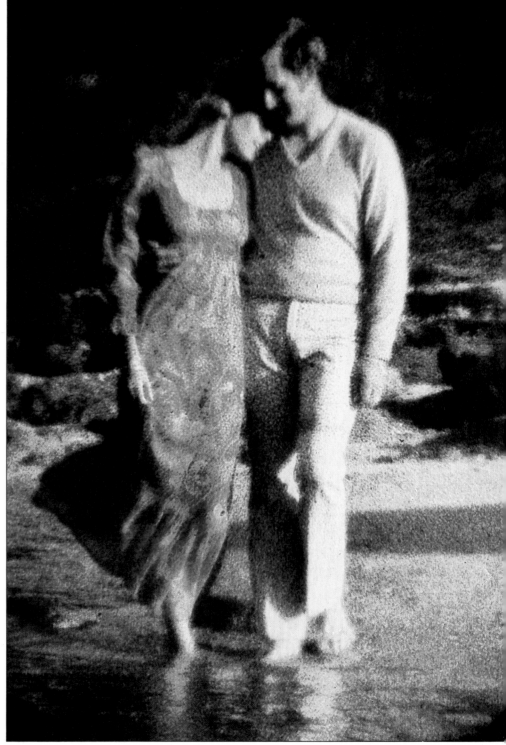

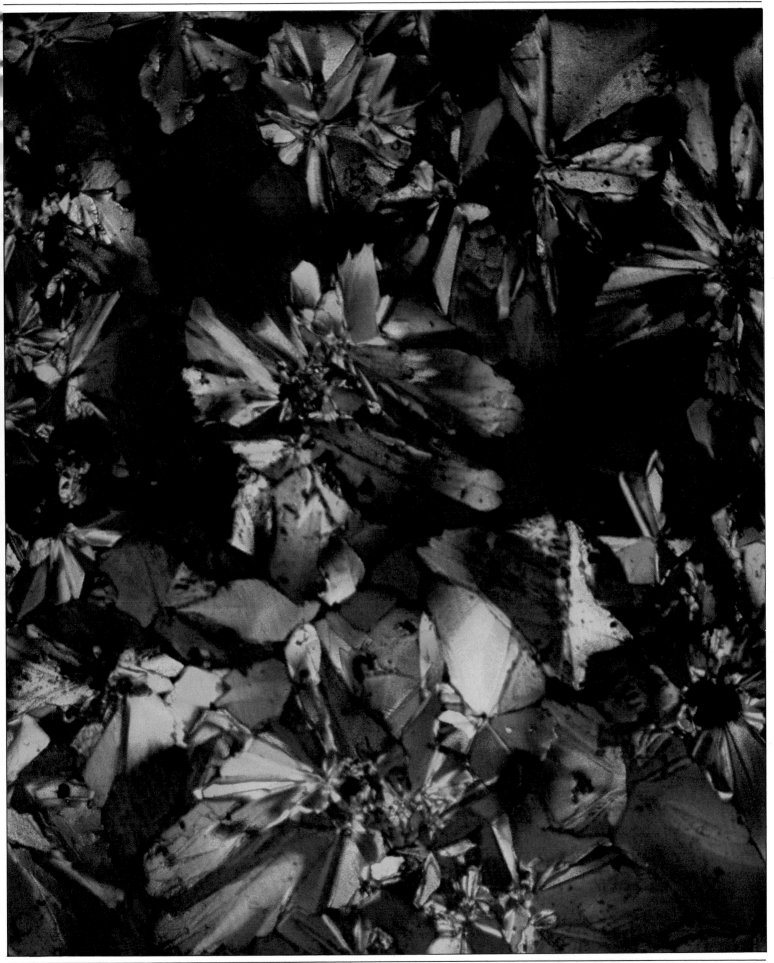

Using reflected images

An important way of extending the dimensions of photography is by the use of mirrors or other reflective surfaces, which can show parts of a scene usually hidden from the single fixed eye of the camera. The form of a subject can thus be shown from two different angles, often with interesting changes of colour. Anything is valid to extend the camera's range, and you should be prepared to exploit the distortions and illusions produced by polished surfaces, all of which can be used to transform the commonplace world. As people are used to accepting lack of definition in reflected images, convincing illusions can be created in mirrors by the use of painted backdrops. Even taken straight, mirror images have a degree of mystery that makes them intriguing, particularly in portraiture.

The hotel sign *below stands out brilliantly against the patterned background of a reflected arcade roof. I crouched to capture reflected light from the lettering at the right angle and to avoid more confusing detail reflected by the glass door at eye level.*
Leicaflex, 50mm, Ektachrome 200, 1/30, f8.

Shot through the glass door *of a small Parisian hotel, the bottom picture combines a sharp mirrored image with the ghostly forms of the counter and winding stairway inside the hall and the reflections from the street outside. Its evocative quality depends largely on the curiosity it arouses.*
Leicaflex, 50mm, Ektachrome 200, 1/30, f4.

A wet pavement *makes an abstract colour pattern that suggests the garish night life of a big city.*
Minolta, 55mm, Ektachrome 64, 2sec., f8.

Reflections *give light and depth to the picture of a Geneva hotel frontage (top right). The clowning girl appeared unexpectedly and posed on the X where her precise positioning seemed to be appropriate to the stylized composition. The window curtaining at each side of the entrance has softened the reflections.*
Pentax, 28mm, Agfachrome 50s, 1/125, f8.

The colour of a van *makes a good frame for the view of Winchester Cathedral reflected in its windscreen. The curve of the windscreen has distorted the cathedral in an interesting way and there is an effective contrast between the building's mellow age and the modernity of the van. The colour of the stonework is remarkably accurate for a windscreen reflection. If cars are parked in front of buildings you want to shoot, make use of them. They will one day provide an historic record.*
Rolleiflex, 80mm, Ektachrome 200, 1/250, f8.

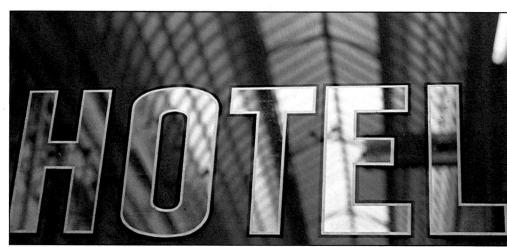

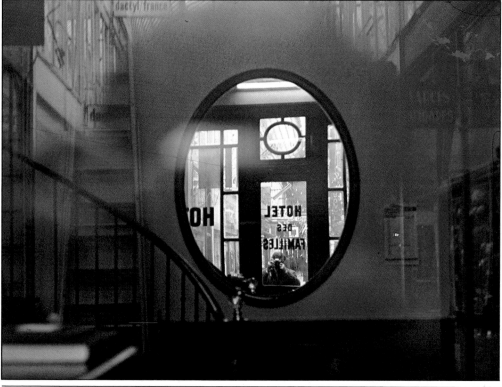

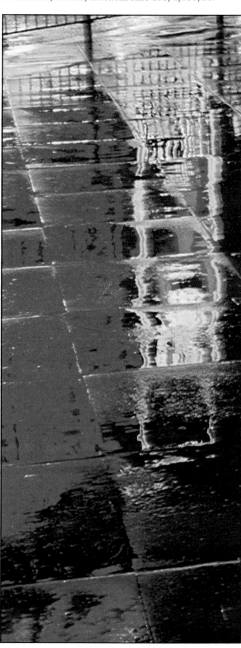

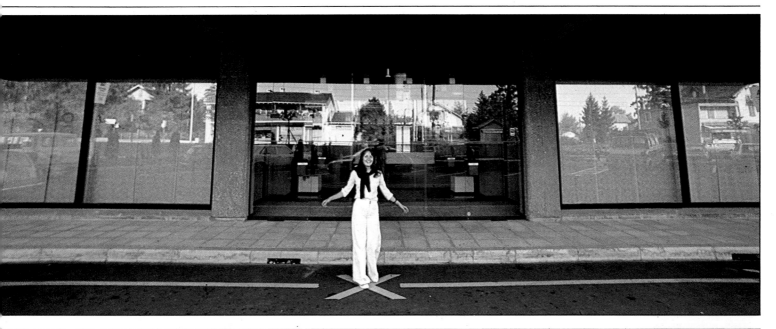

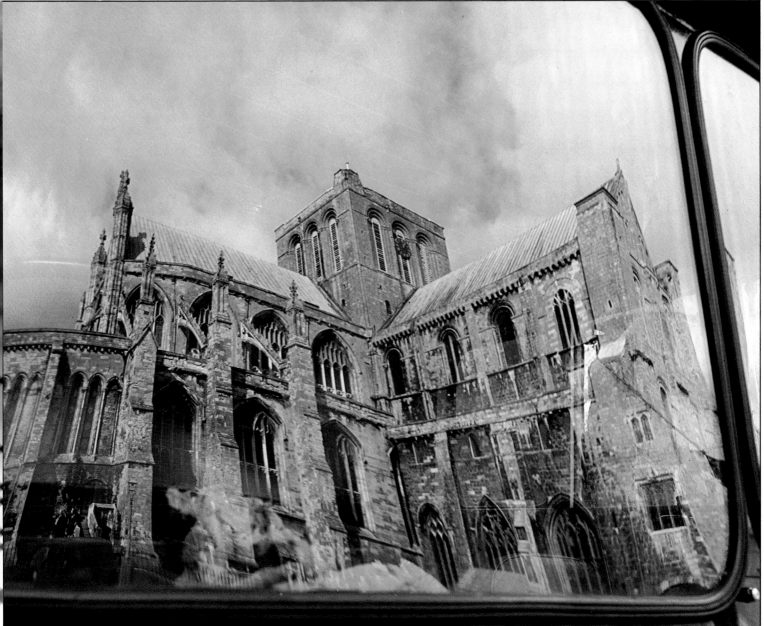

Colour in abstract design

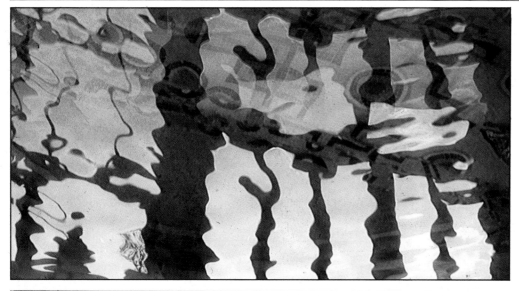

The imaginative possibilities of colour photography are just as great as its workaday role of providing a literal record of reality—and frequently more stimulating. It is always exciting to explore the ways in which common objects and unremarkable scenes can be translated into pictures that puzzle the eye and provoke the imagination. The ability to capture the many transformations constantly wrought by light, nature or circumstances depends mainly on being able to look further than simple representation. The photographer must "see" the world in a new way, attending to its subjective aspects and to the compositional elements of line and tone, shape, colour and texture for their own interest.

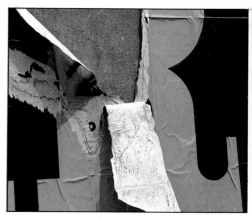

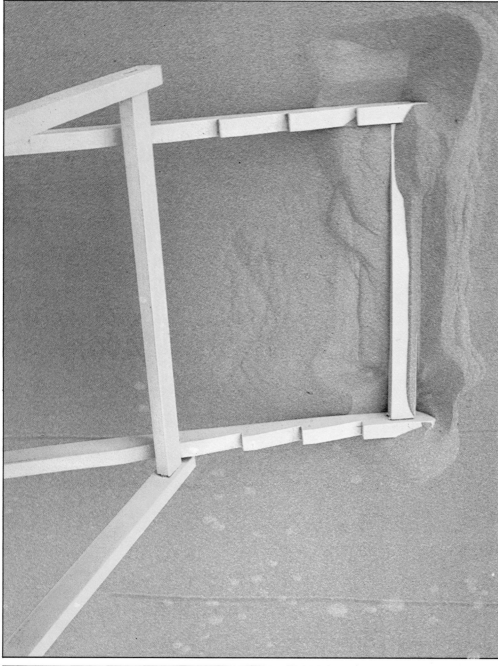

Reflections in gently moving water *can produce fascinating shapes and patterns. Light reflected from a glass window in strong sunlight gives an eerie illusion in blues and greens of human faces and seahorses in the waters of a pool.* Pentax, 35mm, Ektachrome 64, 1/60, f8.

Torn posters *with bold colours and unusual designs are a favourite photographic subject, best shot in a strong light. The debris of urban life provides a multiplicity of similar examples, ranging from peeling paint on doors to squashed cans.* Pentax, 50mm, Agfachrome 50s, 1/250, f8.

A deckchair sinking into soft sand *is a common enough sight, but it is isolated in this picture, which becomes an economical abstract pattern of solid colour against a muted background of contrasting texture.* Praktica, 135mm, Ektachrome 64, 1/60, f8.

The tide carves out a wealth of abstract forms *along shorelines, particularly in soft rock. This area of eroded slate is full of varied colours, forms and textures, with pools of water, trapped sand and limpet population all helping to give the picture depth and tonal interest.* Pentax, 100mm, Ektachrome 64, 1/60, f8.

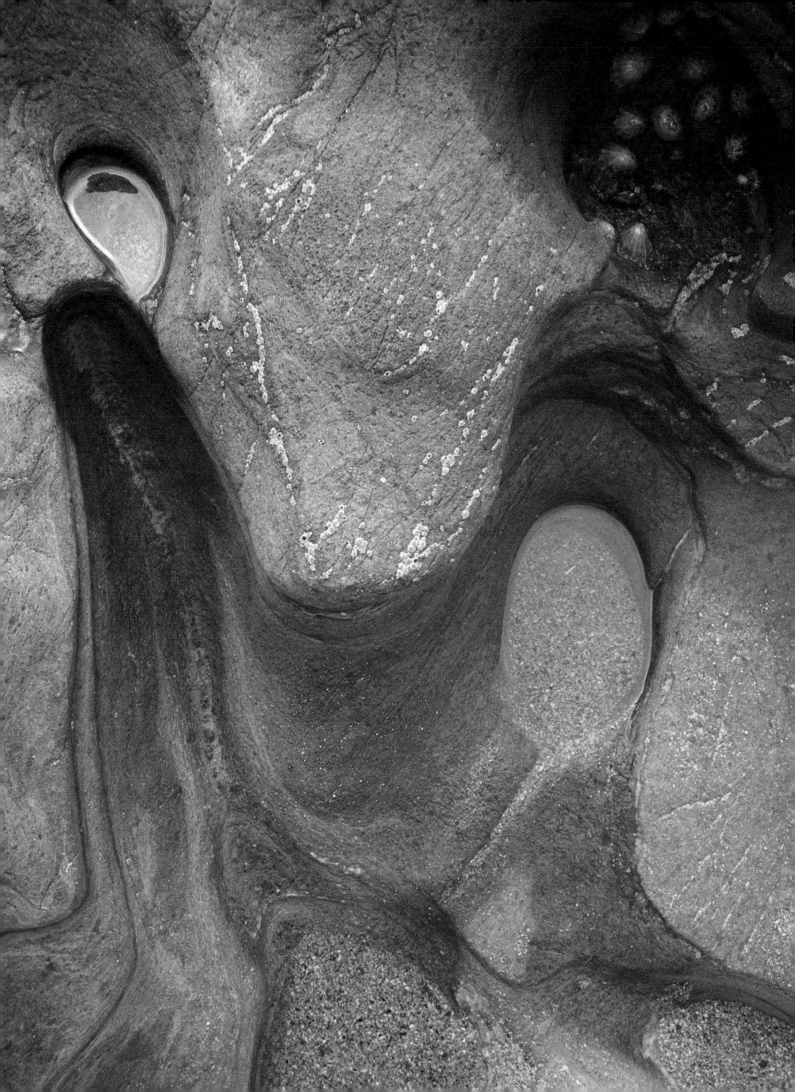

Mixed images and media

The freedom of photography to interpret the world creatively goes far beyond abstract selections of reality. Photographers have always been interested in the visual surprises produced by the deliberate or accidental mixing of images. In addition to the studio and darkroom techniques discussed later, striking images can be made from film collages, combinations of more than one frame, or the interaction of film with other materials and media.

The montage on the opposite page combines six separate images, which were projected in turn on to the same piece of tracing paper. To assess the final result, each image was first positioned and pencilled in on the paper at the appropriate scale. Prints were then made at the selected size, cut out and pasted together to form the composite. After some retouching to disguise the joins (a problem with heavy printing paper), the whole image was rephotographed.

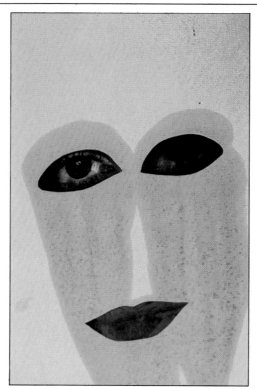

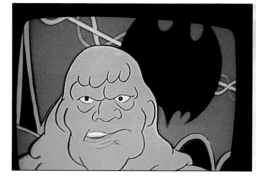

Television *or cinema screens provide a marvellous source of images. A shutter speed no faster than 1/30 should be used for photographing TV, as the picture is re-formed many times a second and several scans are needed during the exposure to record a complete image. I used full colour contrast for the shot above, a mixture of three media.* Pentax, 100mm, Ektachrome 64, 1/15, f8.

The sad mask *(left) is a photograph of eyes and a mouth cut from a magazine and pasted on to paper dabbed with oil.*

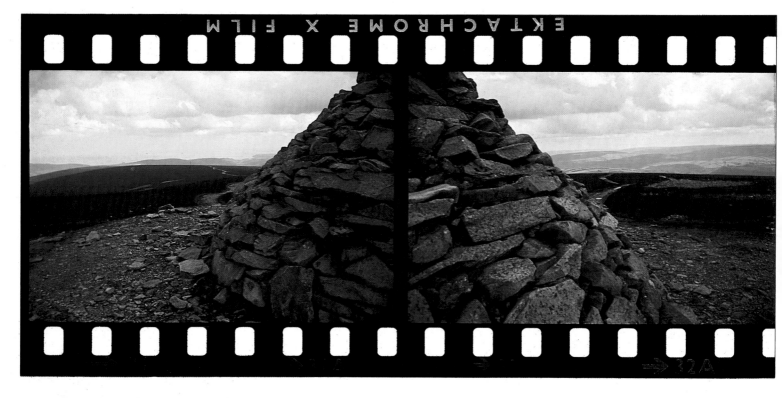

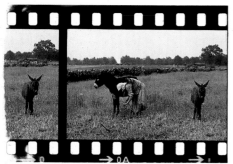

Repetition *of part of an image has the result of completely removing the picture from a literal representation. I took the donkey pictures at the beginning of a roll. Although the images are not exactly the same, the reappearance of the solitary donkey has a curiously static and comical effect. The woman, who seems to form the back legs of the central donkey, is neatly framed by the other two.* Leicaflex, 90mm, Ektachrome 200, 1/250, f8.

To create the obelisk *in a strangely changing landscape, I used different lenses to photograph either side of a pile of granite boulders. I shot first with a 50mm lens and with the centre of the pile at the right-hand edge of the frame. After marking the horizon line on the screen I moved to the right, switched to a 90mm lens, aligned the horizon and took the next shot at the same exposure, 1/250, f8, but with the pile centred on the left of the frame.*

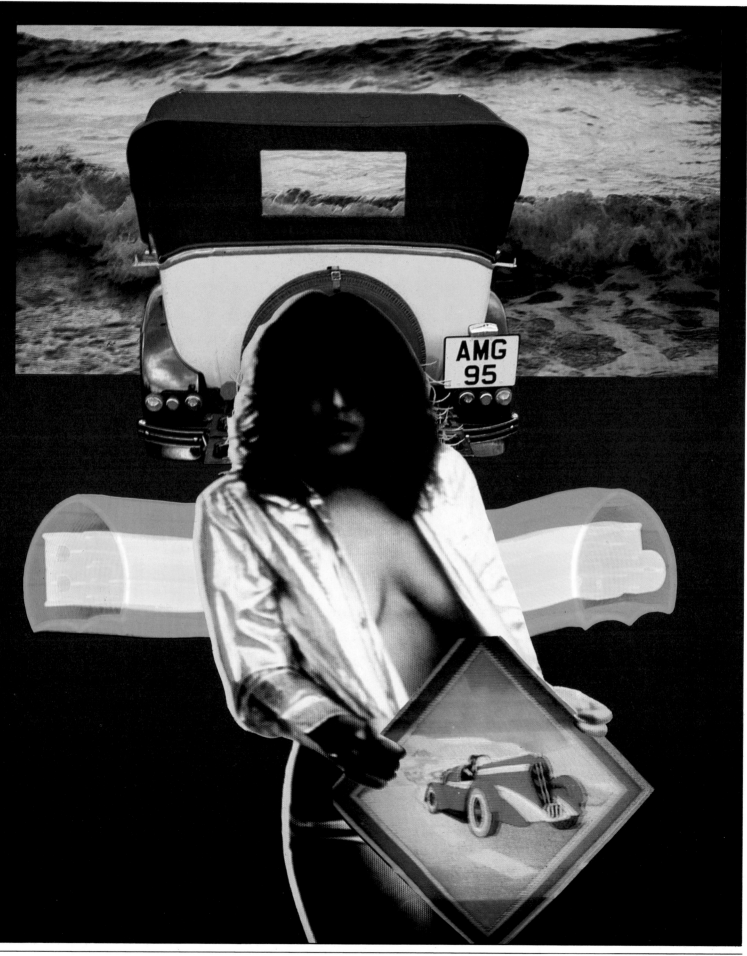

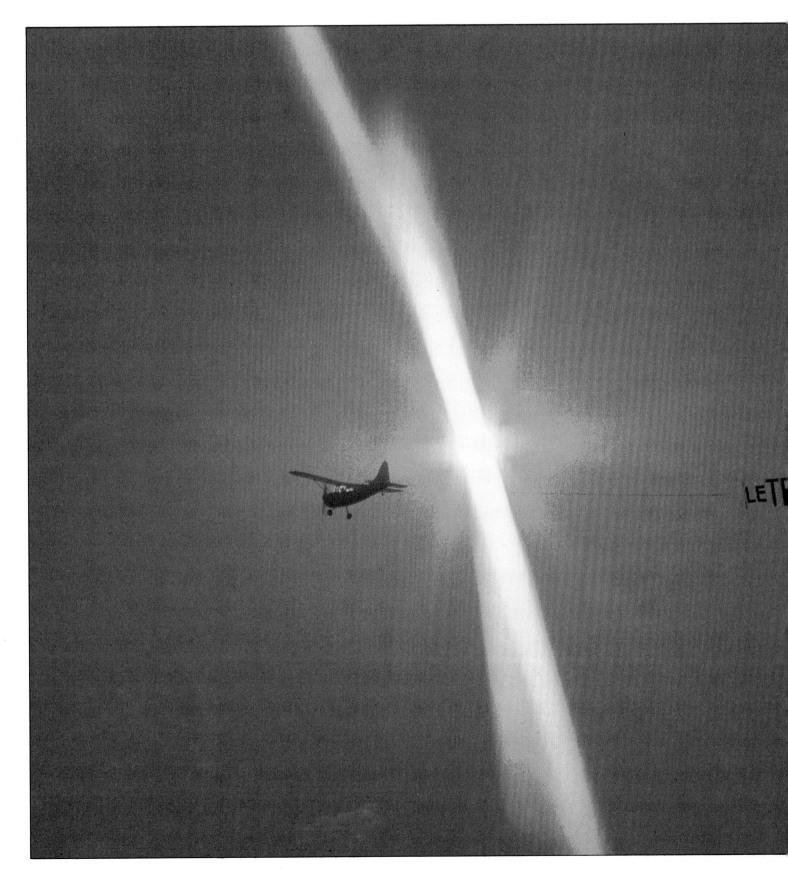

The moods of natural light

MONTECATINI VI ATTENDONO

The power and blinding intensity of natural light, *and the photographer's capacity to control it, are summed up in a picture that was taken straight into the light of a clear summer's day. It records not only the strength of the sun but also the delicate point of light reflected from the cabin of the aircraft. The highlight of the sun was diffused by a rapid zoom combined with panning and aided by some lens flare. This has enabled the aircraft, its message, and even the frail towline to be seen clearly, backlit against the sky.* Pentax, 85–210 mm zoom lens, Ektachrome 200, 1/125, f22.

The sun

The sun, source of natural light and of life itself, is a potent photographic image, stirring feelings and memories that lie below the level of consciousness. Although its sheer energy and intensity make it difficult to handle, its presence never fails to give vitality to landscapes or seascapes, and its hues, varying from white to blood red, may decide the whole balance and mood of a colour photograph.

Taken straight, in the middle of the day, the sun will burn out a picture, causing flare or halation, and may even damage the focal plane shutter. But there are many ways of avoiding this, some of them illustrated here. By photographing the sun when it is rising or setting, obscured by cloud or haze, shining through translucent materials or half-hidden by foreground objects, accurate exposures can be calculated, especially if half-filters, polarizing or neutral-density filters are used. A reading from a weak sun should be taken about 25° off-centre. Remember, however, that the light intensity changes rapidly at dawn or sunset. So recheck constantly and vary exposures by one stop either side. Use of a long lens and the inclusion of a distant object, particularly one with a sympathetic shape, will help to show the sun at a suitable size. Unless you are prepared to leave the body of the picture to reproduce as a complete silhouette, it is usually necessary to allow the sun to burn out a little.

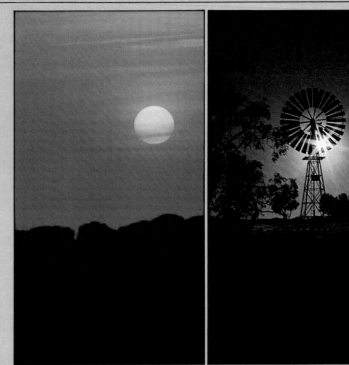

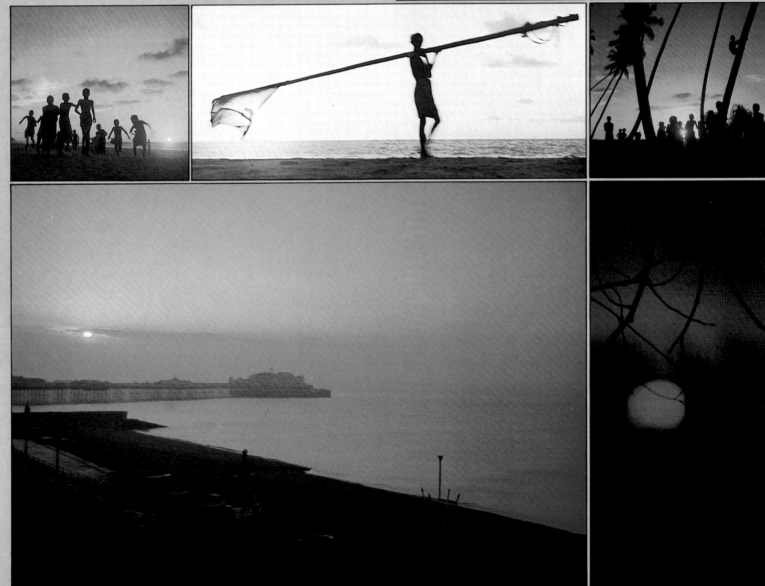

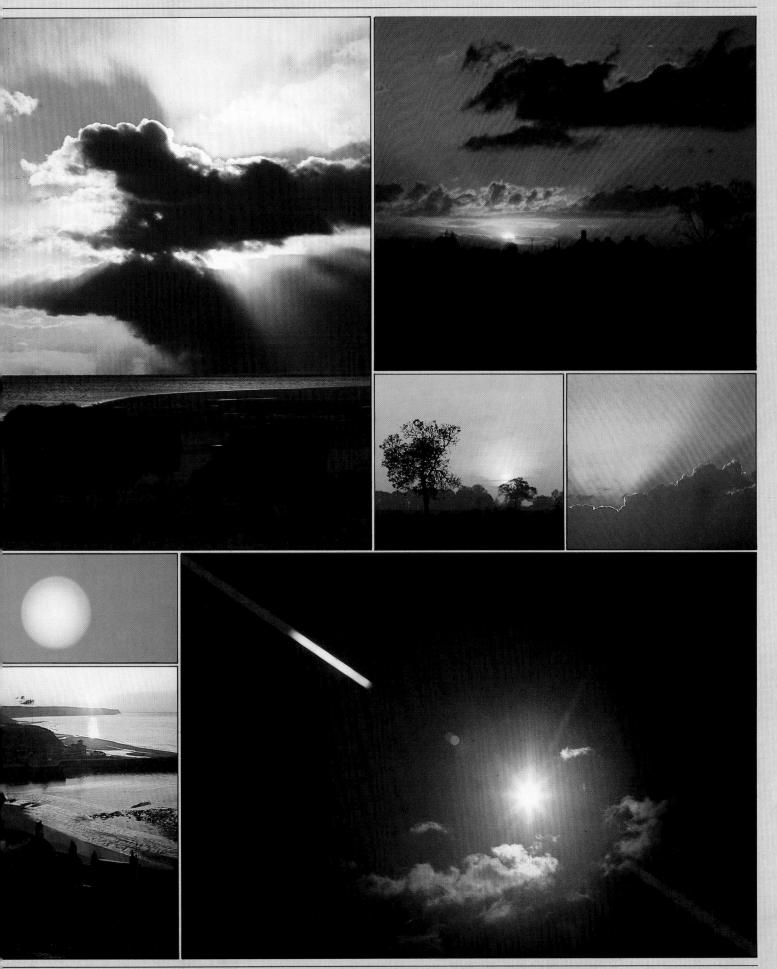

Skies

Although the sun is the ultimate source of natural illumination, the sky, in its infinite variety of atmospheric moods, is the great mediating influence in all outdoor photographs. Purely as a background, its colours, varying from blood red to the palest shades of blue, can determine whether the atmosphere of a picture is calm or turbulent, ominous or happy. Depending on whether it is clear or overcast the sky constantly alters the hues of the world below. And as a subject in its own right, it offers a marvellous range of material as cumulus clouds form and re-form in sculptural shapes, or as cirrus clouds create delicate patterns of light and shade, tone and hue.

The best cloud effects are found at times of change and transition—in autumn and spring, at dawn or at dusk, before or after storms—often when most people are still in bed or huddled round fires. In mountainous country, thermals give added interest as wind currents push clouds up and over the peaks. When travelling you should look out for landscape features or buildings that will record well against the sky, which can bring alive even the least interesting countryside or dullest stretch of water.

In photographing the sky, either as a substantial part of the background or as the main subject, exposure is often a problem, especially if foreground detail is to be included. A bright sky may need up to four stops less exposure than the land it illuminates. If exposure is calculated for the sky alone the foreground will block up into dense shadow with silhouetted features. Exposure for the foreground, on the other hand, will show the sky as a flat, featureless area of white. Averaging the two meter readings does not always solve the problem, although an adjustment of the angle or view will help. A better solution is to watch out for reflective surfaces—a road, wall, or stretch of water—that will act as a link between sky and ground, reducing the contrast. Partial filters can be used to filter the light from only half the scene and a polarizing filter will darken the sky and increase cloud contrast without creating a colour cast.

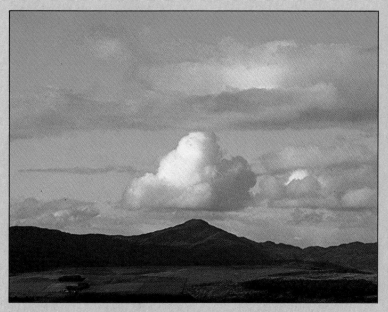

Moulded by thermal currents, *these clouds seem to have taken on the shape of the landscape over which they float. The play of changing colours and shadows on the ground repeats their patterns. Skyscapes like this reverse the ratio of two-thirds land to one-third sky usual in landscapes. The picture is given depth by the colour changes and spreading cloud formation.* Pentax, 35mm, Agfachrome 50s, 1/250, f8.

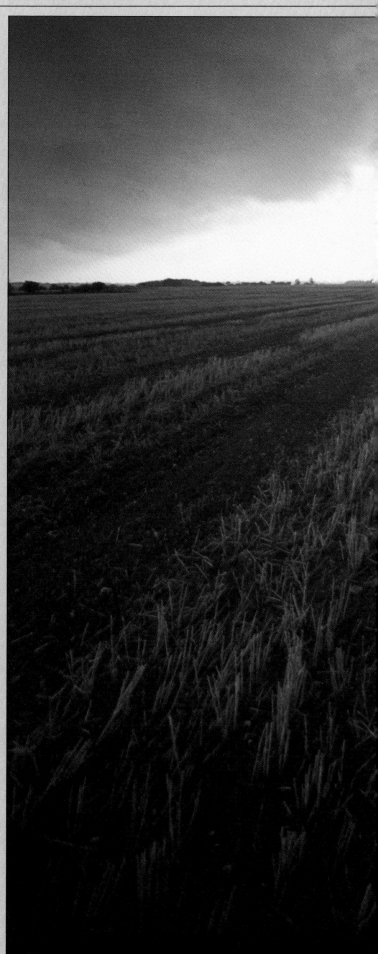

A stormy sky *with an intense light on the horizon from the setting sun gives this picture of an English landscape a great sense of expanse and distance. The failing light has been trapped between a field of stubble and low, misty rain clouds, colouring the whole scene a luminous sepia.*

Minolta, 35mm, Agfachrome 50s, 1/125, f8.

Two aspects of light *are caught in one photograph of crofters' cottages on the west coast of Scotland. I was standing in autumn sunlight looking towards a cloudburst. Minutes later the whole sky had blackened. Speed in capturing the vital moment can be as essential in landscape shots as in photo-journalism.*

Pentax, 28mm, Ektachrome 64, 1/250, f8.

Drama and impact *in this shot of a sky reflected in a Canadian lake have been achieved by exposing only for the sky, throwing the land into shadow and silhouetting the cloud pattern against a sinking sun. I used a wide-angle lens, which helps the feeling of sky extending over the viewer's head.*

Leicaflex, 21mm, Agfachrome 50s, 1/250, f8.

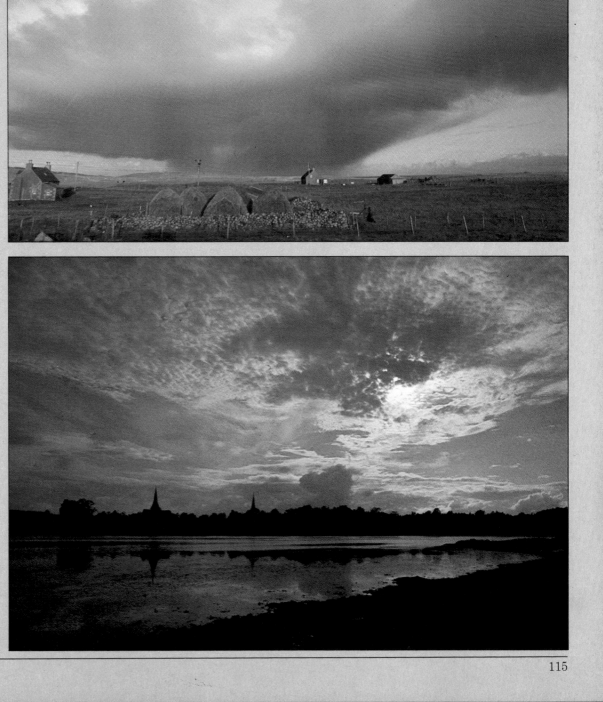

Skies

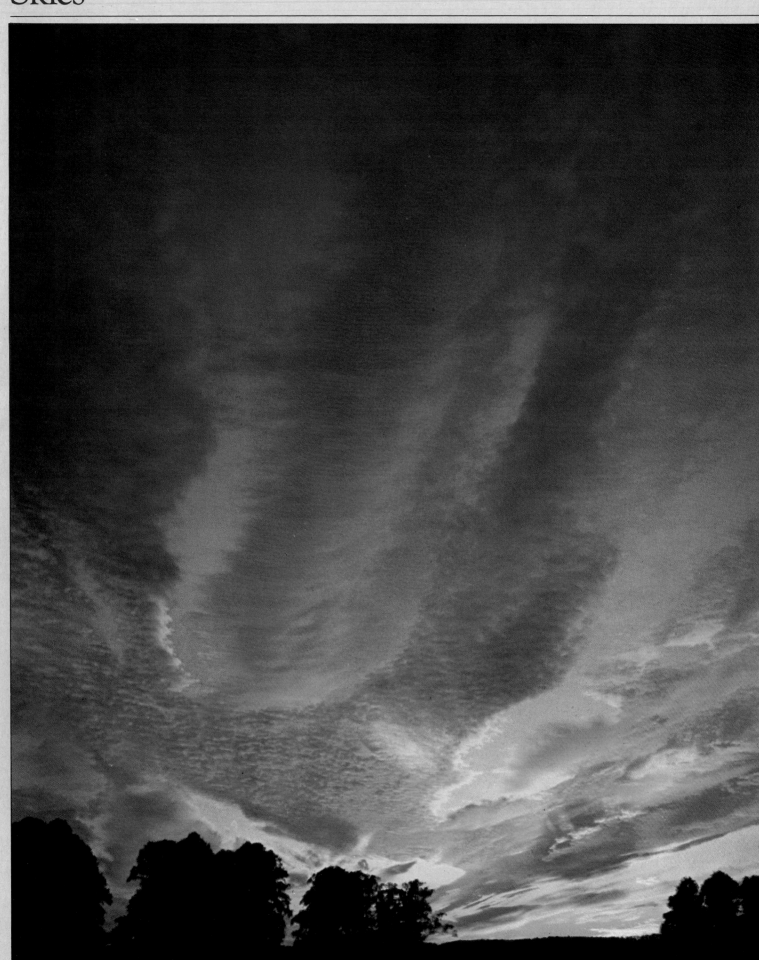

A burning New Hampshire sky *dramatizes the dawn, illuminating oak trees on the horizon in silhouette and giving the effect of flames and smoke bursting from the skyline. Photographing such effects is quite easy; being in the right place at first light takes effort. On this occasion I exposed for the highlights and used a wide-angle lens, which is necessary to capture scenes of this scope.*

Pentax, 28mm, Ektachrome 64, 1/250, f8.

A rainstorm *divided into tones of light grey and darker grey by a barrier of glowing colours gives this rainbow extraordinary definition. The effect was produced by a summer storm in England and lasted only a few minutes—time for me to stop my car and take three shots. Flat countryside is ideal for pictures of the sky. Here, the colours and patterns contrast well with the plain greys of the raincloud.*

Leicaflex, 35mm, Agfachrome 50s, 1/250, f8.

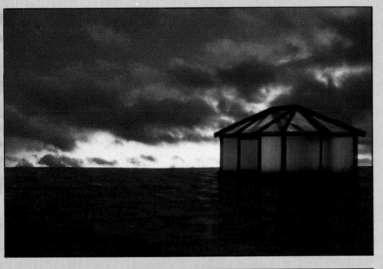

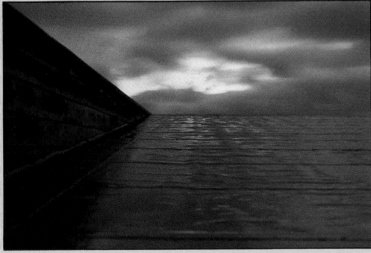

Light glows golden, *trapped in the fanlight of a roof shot from an attic window after an evening rainstorm (top). Colour and tone have transformed something mundane into an exciting, abstract image. The roof looks almost flat and could be mistaken for a broad stretch of water full of reflections. The fanlight is strongly three-dimensional, but there is little real indication of its dimensions.*

Nikon, 35mm, Ektachrome 64, 1/30, f4.

The same roof *half an hour later but photographed from another angle gives a totally different picture. The side of a gable shows the tilt of the roof and provides a hard, angular line against a muted sky, its moving clouds blurred by a long exposure time. The powerful planes still provide the imagination with an ambiguous setting and the bluish-purple hues give the picture a haunting quality.*

Nikon, 35mm, Ektachrome 64, 1sec, f8.

Water

In outdoor photography, water acts as a powerful yet sensitive mirror of the sky, its light and colour changing as the sky darkens or clears and its form and shape responsive to winds or currents. Strong light reflected from calm water, especially seen against dark land masses, can dominate a picture and determine the highlight exposure as well as the mood of the whole scene, which can change according to the angle from which the water is photographed. Sea that from a height resembles a sheet of beaten silver can look turbulent and menacing when photographed from a low angle and against the light. Water often provides an effective main subject. Not only has it a marvellous range of hues, from translucent green to dense blue, but the spray or mist that rises from water can transform other colours, as some of these pictures show. Because water refracts light, however, the colours of submerged objects tend to be dissipated.

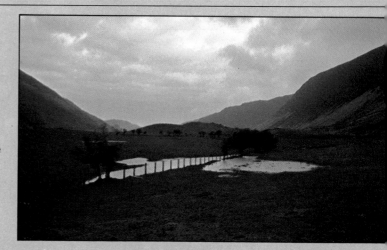

Calm water *in a sheltered Irish estuary reflects the last light of day, its subtle blue-green hue seeming to extend into the sky. The boat, moving so gently that it hardly breaks the surface, has picked up a warm glow of reflected light on its brown planking. Exposure is critical in such shots. I underexposed half a stop for richer colour.* Hasselblad, 150mm, Ektachrome 200, 1/250, f5.6.

The mirror image *below is disturbed only by a slight breeze sweeping across one patch of water like an artist's brush. Apart from providing a middle distance, this has prevented the picture from appearing static because of the centred horizon.* Rolleiflex, 80mm, Ektachrome 64, 1/500, f8.

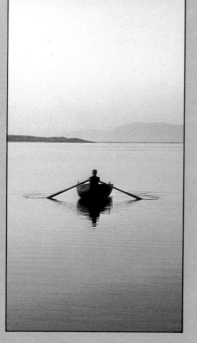

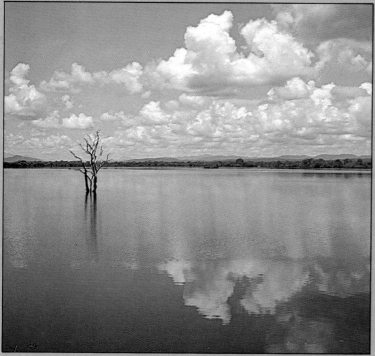

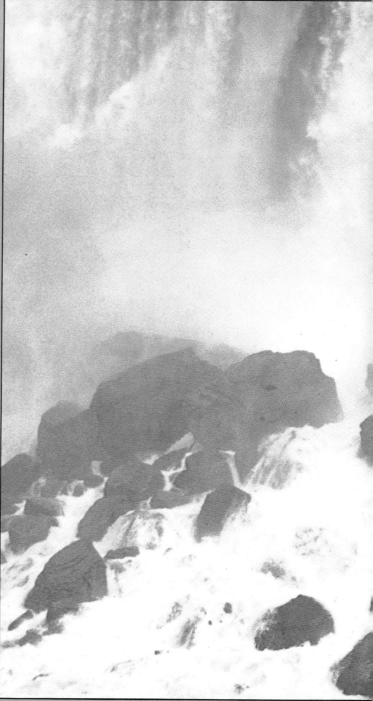

Reflected light *from surface water lying in an open field after a storm created a picture (left) in the fading light of an evening in the Scottish Highlands. The water, balanced by the trees, holds down the valley floor and itself makes an interesting pattern. It also silhouettes the line of the fence, which is completely lost within the dark field. Purple hues are picked up, but against the light the water looks silver.*

Rolleiflex, 80mm, Ektachrome 200, 1/250, f5.6.

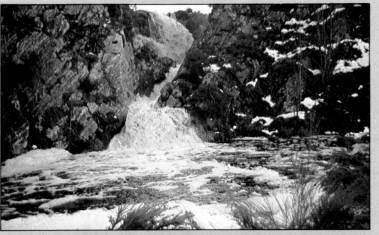

In photographing waterfalls *or any running water, shutter speeds are hard to estimate. To stop movement, a speed of 1/2000 may be needed. Yet 1/250 often gives an image closer to normal vision, and even slower speeds can suggest the velocity of smooth river water flowing around a rock. In the picture (left) I froze the water to heighten the cold look of the rocks and moss, shooting against the light for a chilly blue cast.*

Pentax, 50mm, Ektachrome 200, 1/500, f8.

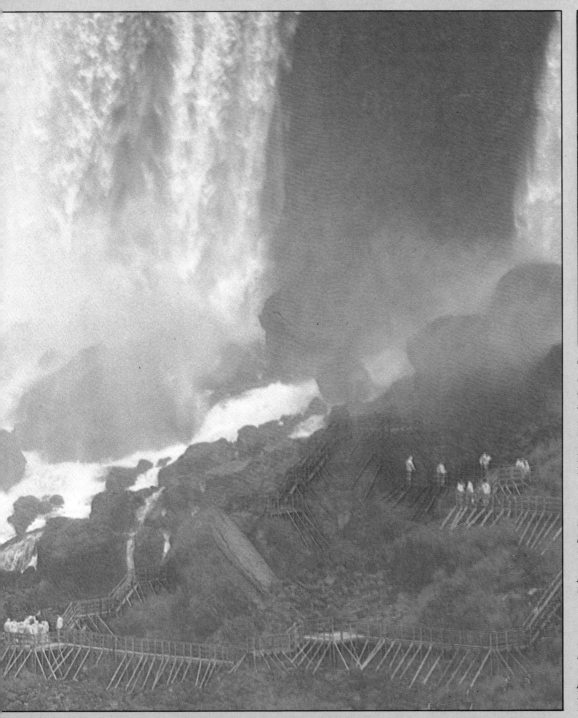

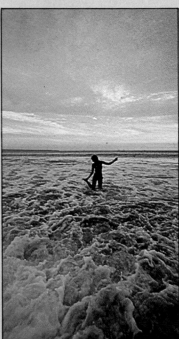

The turbulent surf *is only ankle deep. I photographed into a setting sun to silhouette the swimmer and darken the water. A long lens and slow shutter help to give the foreground water its apparent solidity.*
Leicaflex, 21mm, Agfachrome 50s, 1/60, f16.

Spray *has diffused the light, adding to the sombre majesty of falling water in the shot of the American falls at Niagara. The contrast between elemental power and human insignificance is emphasized by the oilskins the spectators are wearing, which are mere yellow specks. The picture ignores the conventional view of the overall scene to take in the precarious-looking viewing ramp, which provides scale and drama.*
Leicaflex, 250mm, Ektachrome 200, 1/250, f8.

119

Backlighting in direct sunlight

The characteristic feature of photography in strong, direct sunlight is high contrast between areas of deep shade and bright light. Unless light and shade are balanced in an interesting way, the results may be rather prosaic, with harsh sunlight dissipating colour and bouncing off reflective surfaces. An alternative is to place the subject between the camera and the sun. Backlighting (sometimes called contre-jour) requires careful judgement of exposure to avoid turning subjects into complete silhouette. Depending on the angle and strength of the light, an allowance of at least two stops is needed to reveal detail in the shadow. Against very strong sunlight, the camera itself should also be shielded to prevent ambient light flaring into the lens. With these precautions, backlighting or delicate rimlighting enables you to create atmosphere by contrast alone, and to take portraits in soft light, kinder and more sympathetic to the nature of your subject.

The different moods of frontal sun and backlighting are well illustrated in the two pictures of the sailboat. In the first shot, three-quarters frontal light gives good modelling to the boy's body, but the colours of sail and water are weakened by mutual reflections and the boat tends to merge with the background. The second shot, against the light, strengthens tonal contrast, separates the different planes and deepens the colour of the sail, which is now projected on to the water not as a reflection but through transmission of light. In silhouette, the picture is much more dramatic with a greater sense of movement. I used a 200mm lens on my Pentax and took the first photograph at 1/250, f8 and the second at 1/500, f16.

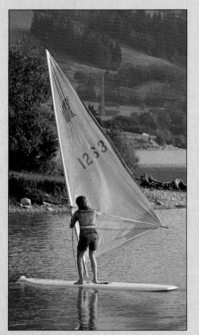

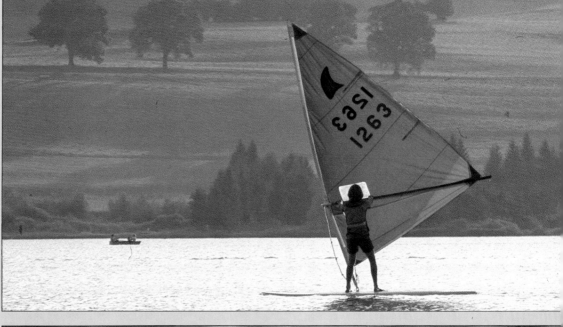

Rimlighting and high backlighting *effectively isolate the Balinese dancer from a darker background and help to emphasize the rhythm of the dance and shape of her limbs. I exposed for the shadow to record her skin tones and the colours of her costume, enriched by being placed in shadow. As a counterbalance, the highlight on her headdress helps to convey the intensity of the sunlight.*
Pentax, 100mm, Ektachrome 200, 1/250, f8.

Shot against a low sun, *the figure of the Buddhist monk has become insubstantial and the tracery of the umbrella and palm trees is brought out. The picture remains full of colour, while avoiding the literal quality of a postcard. The monk's features were unimportant as I was more interested in the composition than in a portrait.*
Rolleiflex, 80mm, Ektachrome 64, 1/250, f8.

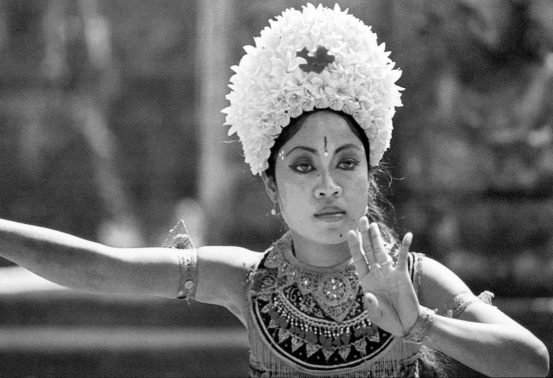

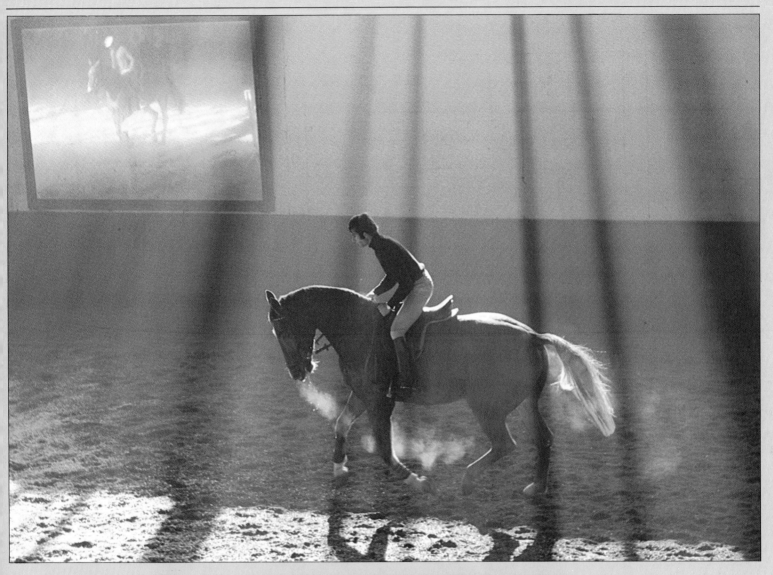

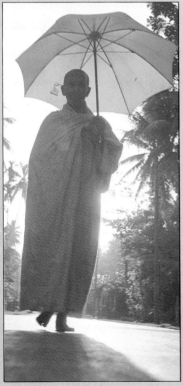

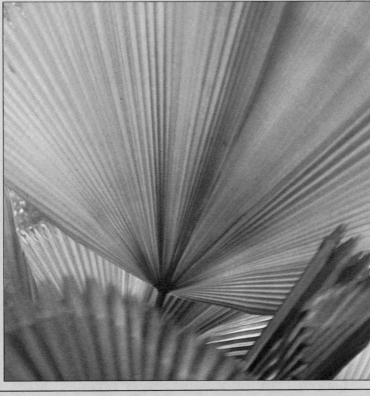

Dramatic shafts *of early morning sun rimlight a horse and backlight the delicate trail of its breath in a circular pattern that emphasizes the rider's control. The interplay of light and shade shows the power of backlighting to simplify shapes and enliven a dull setting. The shot was timed to catch a rider reflected in the mirror as a frontally lit reverse image.* Pentax, 100mm, Ektachrome 200, 1/250, f4.

A contrast *of directly lit and backlit palm leaves reveals the intricate design of nature. The greens would have appeared quite solid and uniform had the shot been taken in ordinary reflected light. But with the light shining through the leaf membrane, all the different densities of hue and layered patterns are shown in well-defined fan-like shapes.* Pentax, 100mm, Ektachrome 64, 1/250, f5.6.

Indirect and reflected light

In addition to backlighting, a way of softening the harshness of direct light is to try to position your subjects where they can be illuminated by the more delicate light reflected from nearby colourless surfaces. Alternatively, indirect light surrounding a shaded area can often provide adequate illumination and bring out glowing, saturated colours, similar to those seen in diffused or overcast light.

In the picture of the little girl peering into the shop window, the bright but diffused light reflecting back from the wall behind the girl has shown the interior of the shop as well as the reflections in the glass. The colours are subdued by the shadowless light, but because of the white surfaces I took a meter reading from my hand to ensure correct recording of skin tones and exposed at 1/125, f8. In direct sun, the film could not have handled the lighting contrasts.

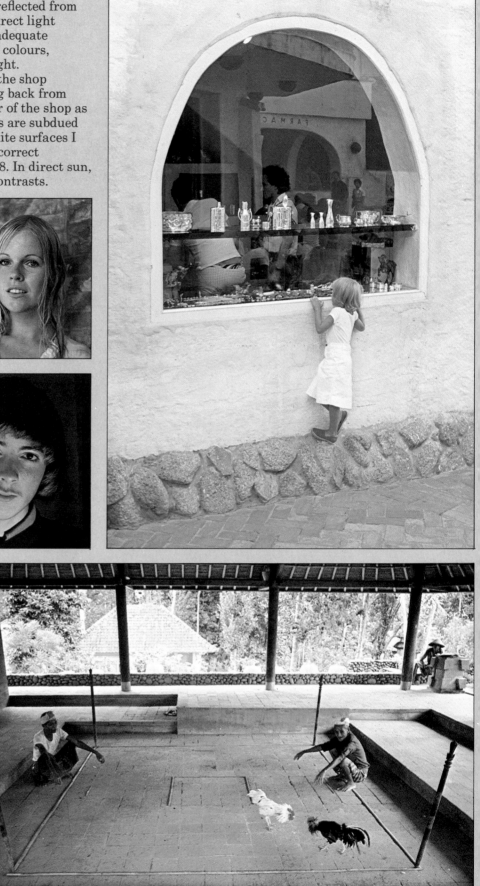

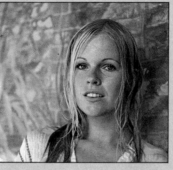

Reflected colour *from nearby objects always needs to be taken into account when working in colour. Although the brain corrects for colour cast, colour film cannot, and faithfully records the actual colours present. Bizarre effects can be produced when direct light shines on one side of a subject while reflected light with a colour cast shines on the other. The green surroundings in the shot of the girl are strongly reflected in her shirt, hair and skin. For the shot of the boy, light was filtering through windows and also being reflected from the red wall opposite. Although colour cast is usually best avoided it can, if used selectively, create mood and atmosphere and produce interesting changes of hue.*
Both pictures: Pentax, 55mm, Ektachrome 64, 1/125, f8.

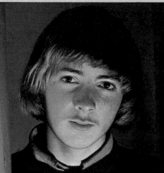

The diffused, even light *that illuminates this building in a village square in Bali clearly reveals the expressions of the two old men, the colours of the fighting cocks and the hues and texture of the brick floor. The softness of the light, in which the red of the cocks' combs and the men's hat tabs shows up well, contrasts markedly with the strong sunlight outside.*
Pentax, 28mm, Agfachrome 50s, 1/30, f8.

High backlight *falling on the top of the girl's head and circling her face has given a golden glow to her skin, an effect that is helped by upward reflection from her silver jacket. Exposing for the shadows I burned out the highlights and achieved a warm, sunny image.*
Pentax, 55mm, Ektachrome 200, 1/60, f8.

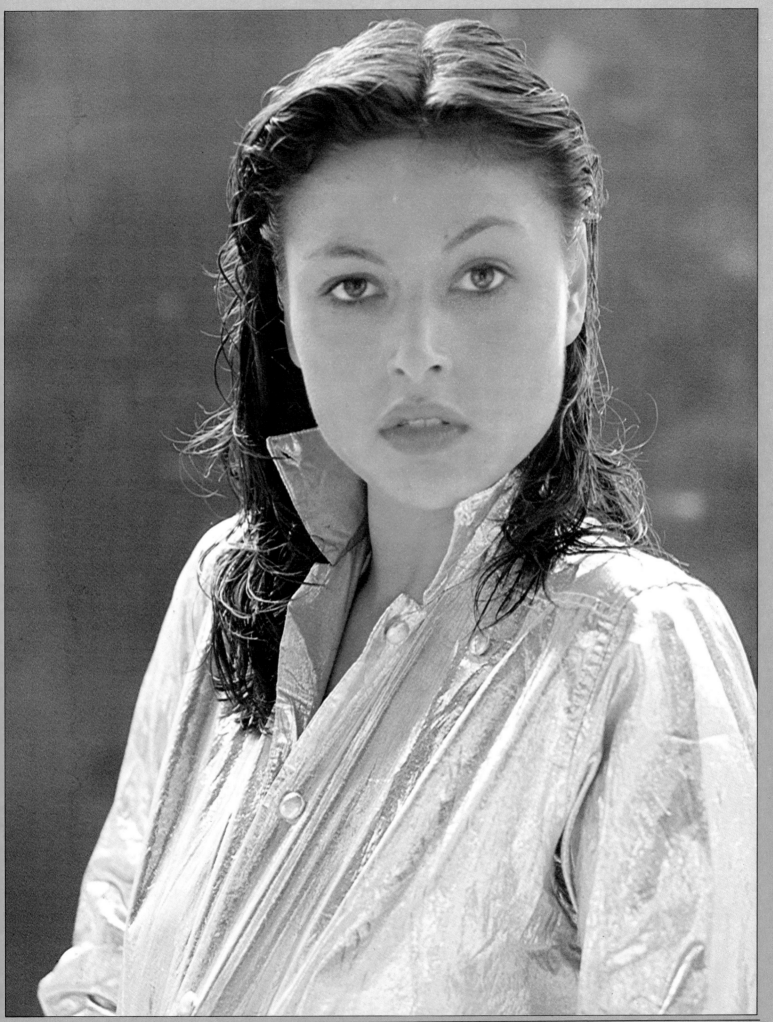

Diffused light

Under overcast skies, the world becomes more enclosed and intimate, and subtleties of tone and colouring begin to appear. Contrasts are less emphatic, but darker colours often take on a richness and density that is never apparent in direct sunlight. The picture opposite, a view of the pier at Saltburn, Yorkshire, is full of the gentle quality of diffused English light. Strong sun would have given the roofs and their sharp shadows too much importance. As it is, slight gradations of tone and colour can be explored as the eye is carried downwards by the rush of the cable-car line and follows the slow expansion of the pier into the blue-grey sea. The red and blue trim of the sheds is softly repeated in the asphalt area between them and in the muted colour accents along the pier.

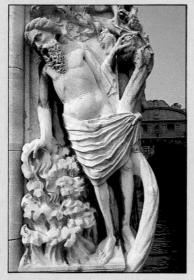

Weak directional light, *diffused here by a Venetian evening, is perfect for sculpture, showing this relief carving in subdued contrast with the shadowed Bridge of Sighs.* Nikon, 55 mm, Ektachrome 64, 1/60, f8.

The wide eyes of a Balinese boy *suggest one of the qualities of diffused light—it is easy for people to look at the camera without squinting. Contrast between the boy's shirt and dark skin is reduced, yet the detail of his rounded limbs is retained, even in shadowed areas such as the inside of his sleeve.* Pentax, 35 mm, Ektachrome 64, 1/60, f8.

Food *is often best photographed in light that casts little shadow, as shown by the detail in this basket of ripe strawberries.* Minolta, 135 mm, tripod, Ektachrome 64, 1/60, f8.

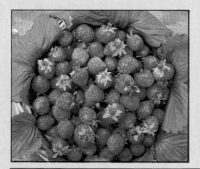

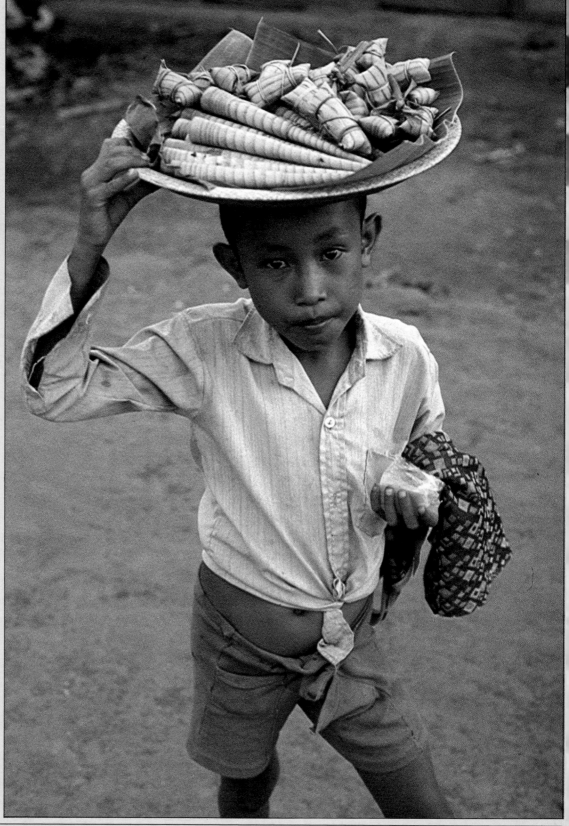

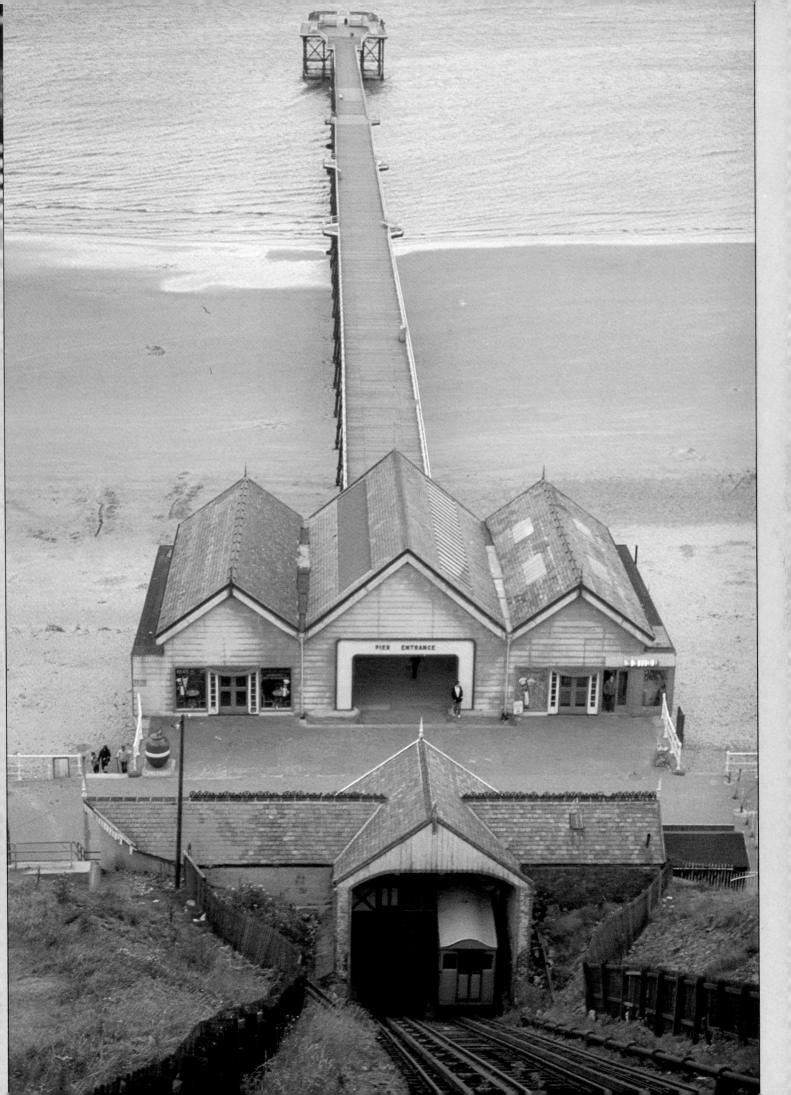

Early morning

The freshness and delicacy of early morning light, with its gradual deepening of pearly colours, is unlike any other. Minute by minute, a world composed entirely of tones of grey is tinted until colours intensify and glow even in the angular shadows. As temperatures rise, frost melts, dew evaporates and the air dries.

The atmosphere breathed out by a picture like the one opposite is compounded partly of autumnal light and colour and partly of the subject itself. Early morning is a time of preparation—of exercising horses, hosing them down and grooming them. Frail sunlight penetrates the mist, but the heavily coated soldiers, frosty park, pools of water and sodden leaves all convey the exhilarating coolness of the hour after dawn. The picture was taken with a Leicaflex, 35mm at 1/125, f8.

Early morning frost, *briefly preserved by the bars of a farm gate, has given substance to shadows in a picture that is almost an abstraction of dawn. The low sun directly behind me casts eerily long shadows, which, because of the pattern of frost, show clearly that I am standing behind the gate, not in front of it. The transformations effected when sunlight warms fields dusted by overnight frost can be swift and dramatic.* Leicaflex, 28mm, Ektachrome 64, 1/125, f8.

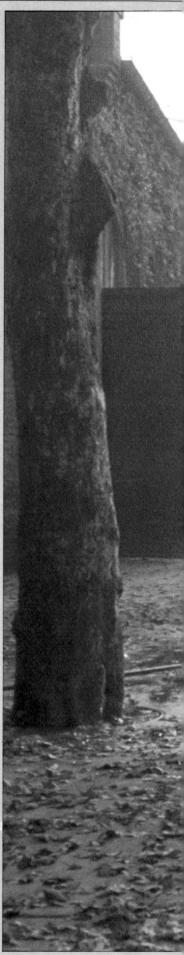

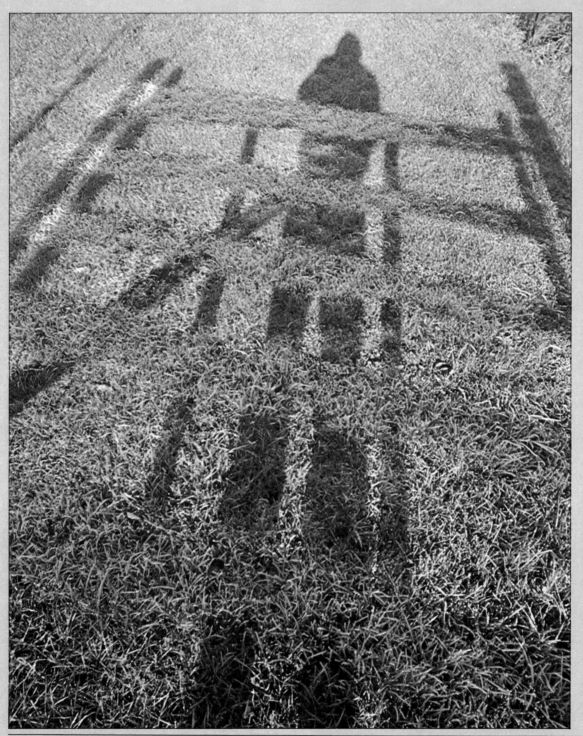

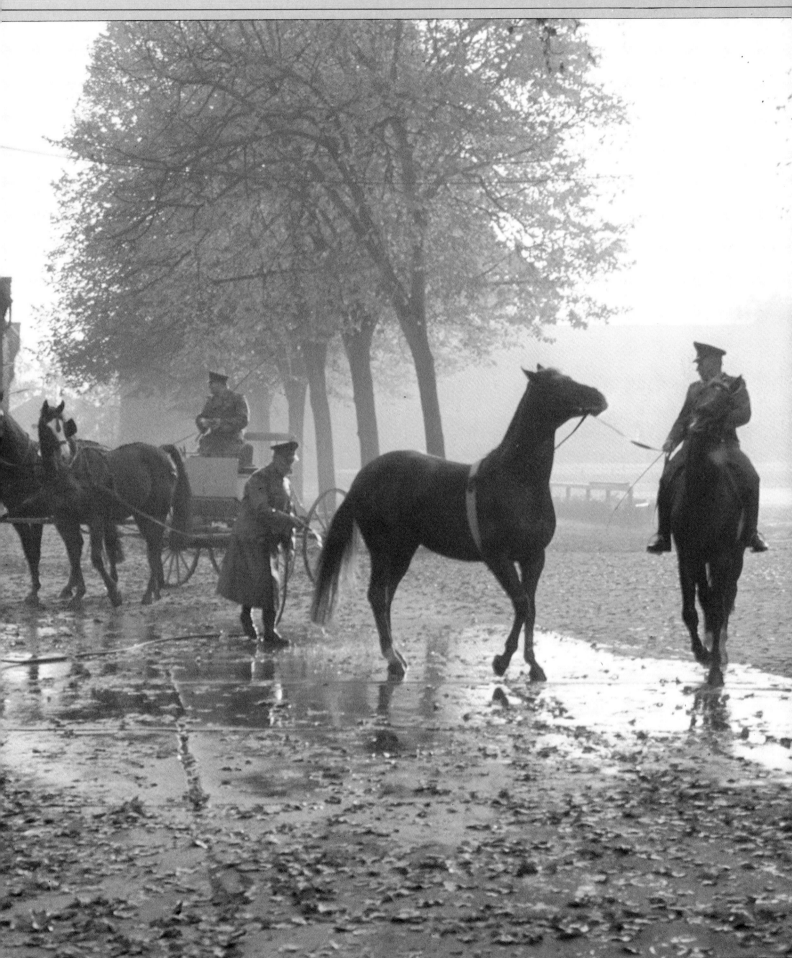

Midday

At noon the light of the sun is whiter than at any other time of day. If the atmosphere is clear, without heat haze, and if the strength of the light does not dissipate colours through glare, hues are at their brightest with the contrasts between them sharp. Tonal contrasts are even more marked, with intense highlights and dense, short shadows. The angle and quality of the light obviously changes from season to season. In cold climates, for instance, wintry midday light can resemble the pink softness of morning or evening light at other times of the year. But in summer, with the sun directly overhead, the angle of light tends to obscure form and emphasize pattern, making portraiture particularly difficult. Faces may be hidden in the shade of hats and eyes are usually lost in deep shadow.

Effects such as these give many noonday pictures a stark quality devoid of subtlety. Shadows should therefore be regarded as an essential compositional device and exploited for their capacity to set the mood of a picture. The patterns they make are not always hard, as shown in the photograph opposite of a woman in a coat resting against a tree. This time of day gives opportunities for showing people relaxing in the shade. Exposure for shadow areas, allowing the highlights to burn out, can effectively convey both the coolness of interiors and the intensity of heat outside.

If you are photographing intense light and cannot avoid it by positioning your subject against the light or in shadow, slow film will make it easier to control exposure. Ultraviolet, neutral density and polarizing filters can help to reduce haze, brightness or glare, and a yellow filter may sometimes be useful for colour accuracy if indirect light from an intense blue sky is likely to produce a blue cast. There are times, however, when the harsh quality of midday light in summer should not be avoided but rather used for its dramatic effects. Photography with high contrasts of light and shade may produce striking and evocative images.

The merciless quality of the noonday sun in Alice Springs, heart of the Australian interior, is summed up in the picture below of an Aboriginal couple and their children sitting outside the town's medical centre. Highlights have made the brown hair of one child look almost blond, while reflected light bouncing off the pavement has lightened the shaded concrete blocks. A light as intense as this would burn out detail on a white skin, but the sun-blackened faces and arms of the Aborigines show up fairly well. The strength of the picture comes from its uncompromising view, conveying as it does the harshness of the environment that has shaped the lives of these people. For the shot I used a 35 mm lens on my Pentax and exposed at 1/500, f16.

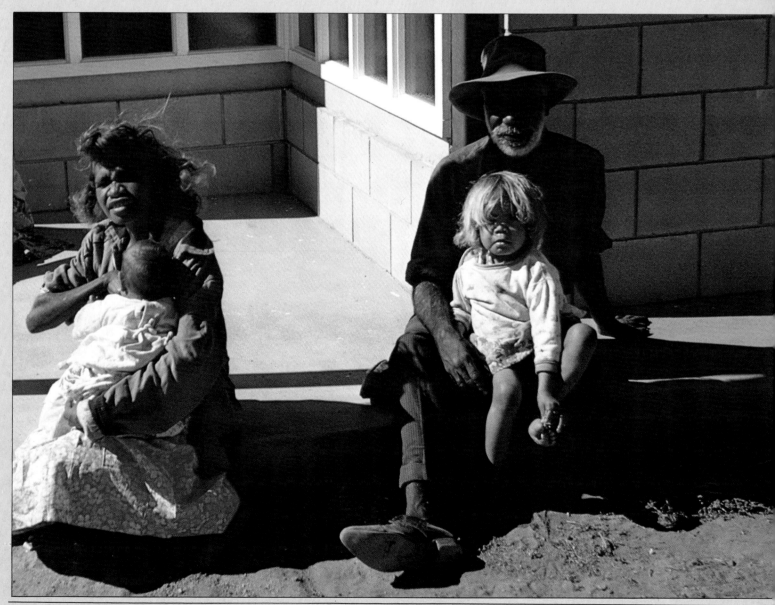

1

Seemingly imprisoned in a net of shadows, the woman wears colours that harmonize well with her surroundings in Hyde Park, London. Although it is midday and early summer, the air is still cool and the light that filters through the branches is soft and restful. The pattern of shade and muted hue is so effective that the figure could almost be overlooked. Nikon, 55mm, Ektachrome 64, 1/125, f8.

The bleached weatherboards and wrought-iron veranda of this Australian general store are well described by midday light. Highlights and deep shadow help capture the feeling of a small rural township where nothing much seems likely to happen until the heat lessens. Pentax, 50mm, Ektachrome 64, 1/500, f16.

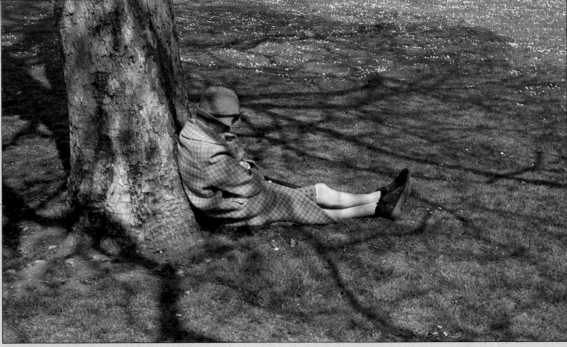

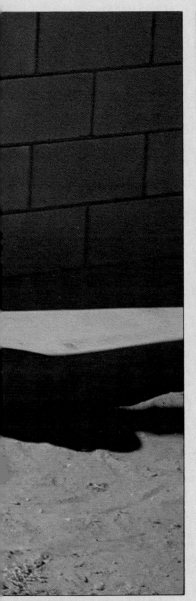

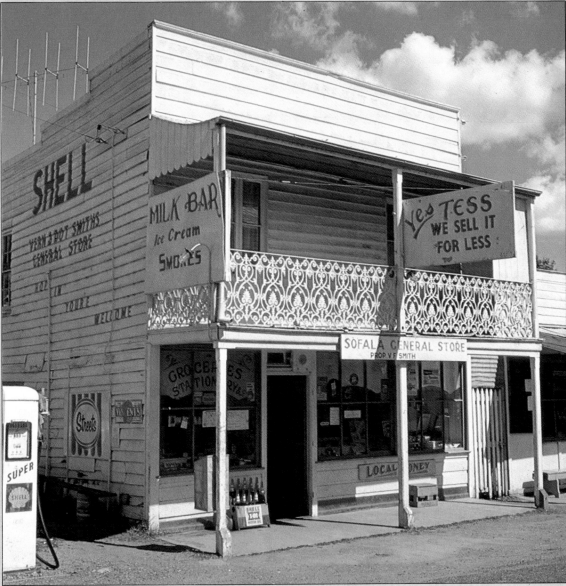

Dusk

Even after a solidly overcast day, skies tend to clear towards evening. Clouds, especially near the horizon, often break up, giving a beautiful diffused light tinged with gold if the sun is still setting or with blue as the night draws on. Colour film is particularly sensitive to blue light and can produce exciting images, as reds tend towards purple and whites or light yellows become almost luminous.

With today's modern emulsions almost anything you can see can be photographed, and an image intensifier can be used to photograph things you cannot see. Early evening is also an ideal time to take pictures that give the impression of night. In total darkness highlights tend to be harsh, with areas of halation surrounding light sources, and shadows display no details at all. To cope with the conditions you will encounter at dusk, a camera with a fast lens (f1 to f2.8) is essential if slow shutter speeds are to be avoided. For a speed slower than 1/30 a tripod, or some other support, will be necessary. If there is any artificial light in the picture, perhaps from lighted windows, you will need to make a choice between daylight and artificial light film, depending on the colour rendition you want.

For photographs of wildlife, dusk is often the best time to go hunting, as this is when shy, nocturnal animals begin to emerge in search of food. In the dimmer light they feel safe and confident and it is possible to photograph them using very slow speeds. It is always advisable to carry a pencil torch so that you can make camera speed adjustments easily yet not show too much light.

Maintaining definition *over the whole depth of your subject can cause problems when shooting at dusk. The poor light levels usually demand a wide aperture, and that means a shallow depth of field. In the picture of a Sumatran fisherman, the sun had almost completely set and the predominant blue light has emphasized the whiteness of his teeth and the blue of his shirt. Shooting at 1/30 and an aperture of f1.2, I did not attempt to keep his whole figure in focus. Definition was important in the picture of the girl to record the subtle colours of her scarf catching the last rays of sunlight. I chose an aperture of f5.6 with a 100mm lens and a shutter speed of 1/8, using a tripod to avoid camera shake.*

Late afternoon atmosphere *is encapsulated by birds flocking and skimming towards their roosts. The extraordinary, almost metallic gold of the corn against the blue sky is an example of the saturated colours that can be achieved in late light, here hinting at an approaching storm. Conica, 100mm, Ektachrome 200, 1/125, f2.8.*

The afterglow of dusk *is a marvellous light for photographs in the Mediterranean. With the sun nearly down behind this Greek island the village lights have just come on, and in the warm light the colours of whitewashed buildings blend with the older, more mellowed stone. An earlier shot would have shown glaring highlights and dense, featureless shadows, a later one more dramatic sunset colours. Instead, the atmosphere is soft and romantic, giving the impression of a village where time is unimportant. Contax, 35mm, Ektachrome 200, 1/30, f2.*

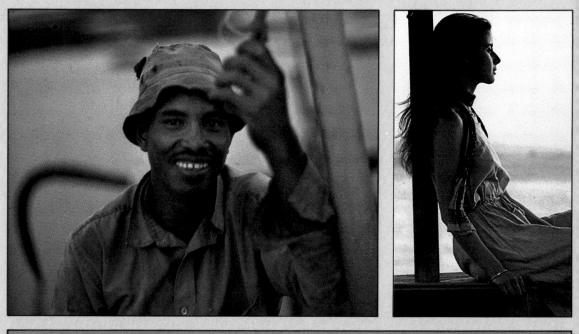

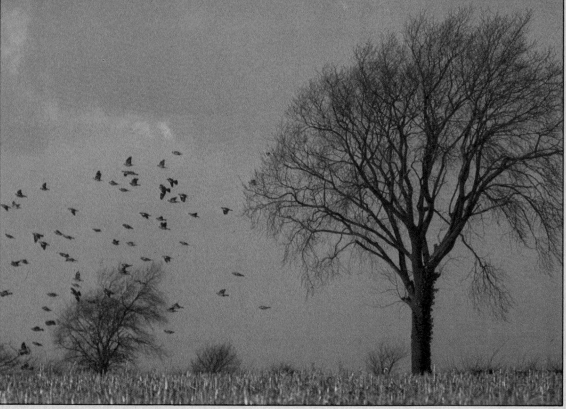

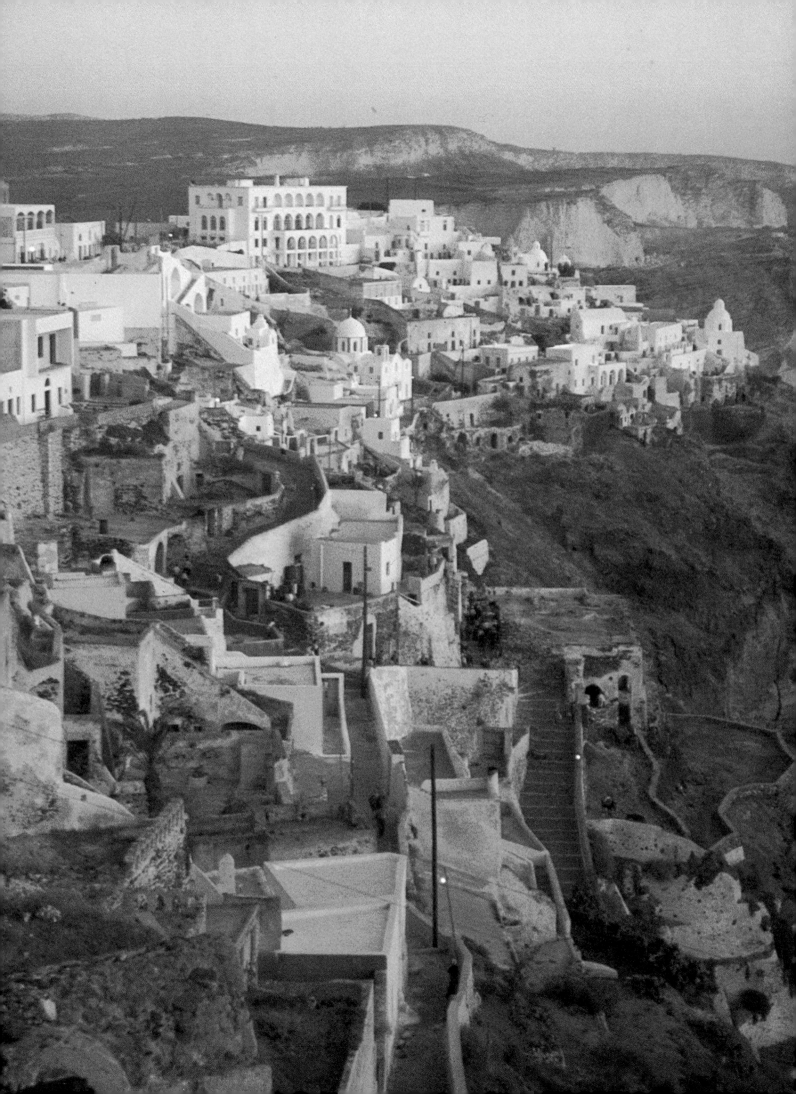

Night

A mysterious world is revealed to the photographer at night —a landscape in which illusion seems to become reality. Familiar scenes are reduced to their simplest elements and shapes are emphasized, especially against a skyline, while the intricate clutter of daytime is hidden. Artificial light can, of course, be used to replace some of the lost detail. But it evokes a mood rather different from that conjured up by night scenes in which natural light—from the moon, stars or sky—provides the main source of illumination. The possibilities of photography under these severe restrictions should be explored because it can teach you much about the handling of faint colours or simple monochromatic masses of blue, grey and black.

Normally, the best time for night photography is on a still evening when the sun has set but the sky remains luminous. If you have a scene in mind, establish your camera on a tripod and watch as the light ebbs and luminosity wells up from reflective surfaces such as roofs, roads or water. As the strength of light will vary rapidly, you will need to check exposure readings constantly. Although you should not be daunted by exposures of a minute or more, nothing will be achieved by an exposure longer than five minutes.

As colour film is designed for "normal" light conditions at shutter speeds ranging up from 1/30, unexpected colour casts may be produced by reciprocity failure at lengthy exposures. Remember, also, that movement will show up in the moon as well as in clouds. Inclusion of the moon, or another small source of light, such as a lamp, helps to evoke mood, however, particularly in contrast with dark areas. Little colour will appear, so you should look instead for interesting shapes or patterns, and for objects that will show up well against a skyline.

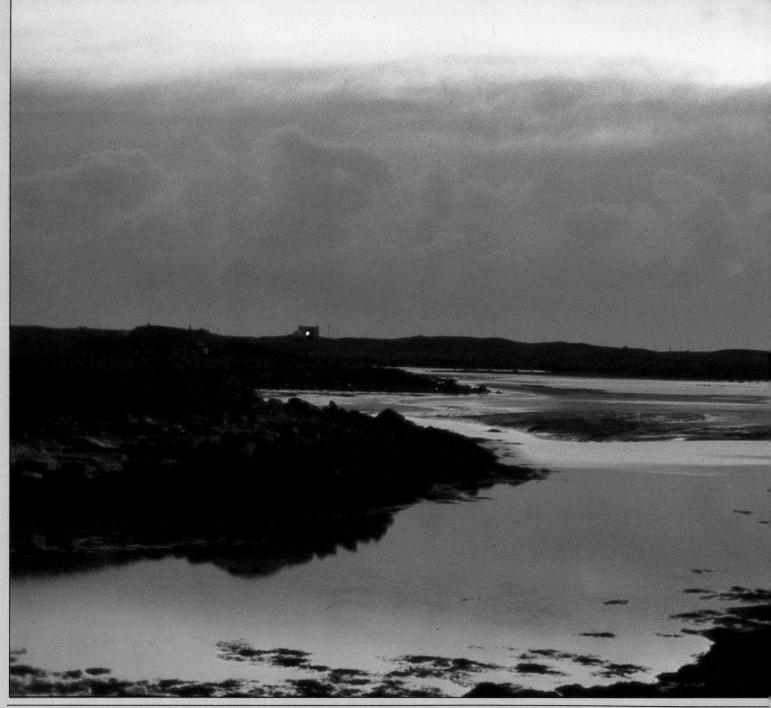

The moon *is best shot in the early evening to balance exposure between its bright surface and the land. Here the ghostly pink hues in the cliff help to evoke the romantic mood of a Mediterranean night* Pentax, 100 mm, Agfachrome 50s, 2 min, f4.

A cottage light *heightens the lonely beauty of a picture in which the dominant element is the patterns of tone around the dark strip of land between evening sky and estuary water.* Pentax, 28 mm, Ektachrome 64, 1 sec., f6.3.

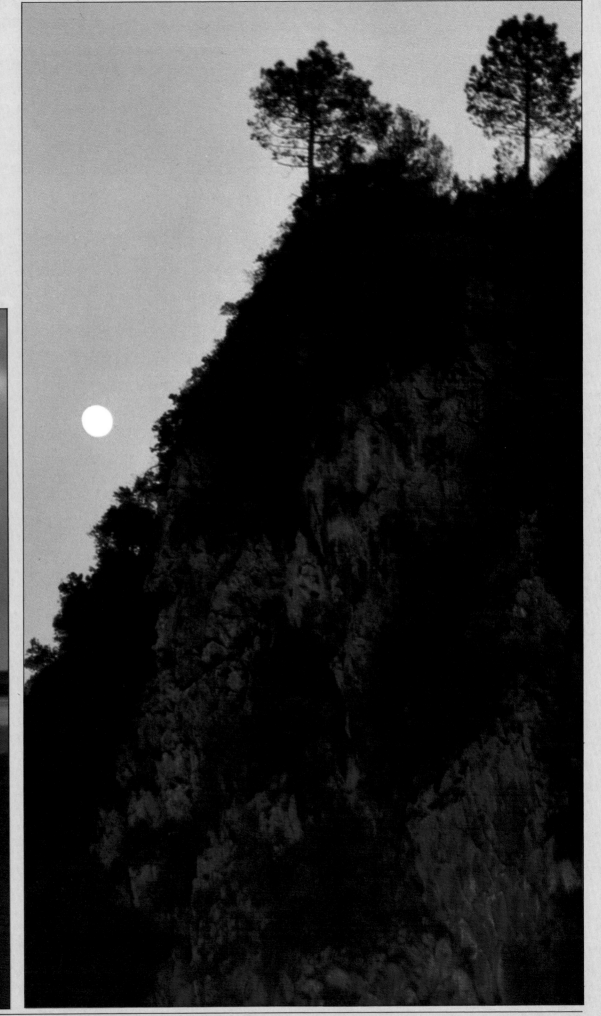

133

Spring

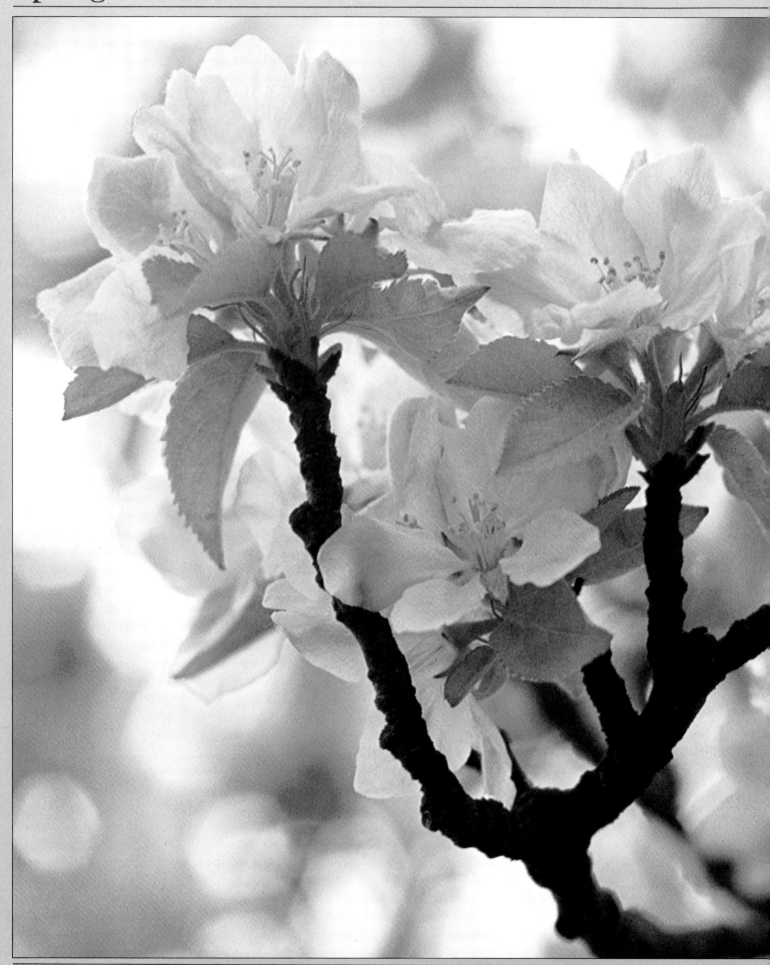

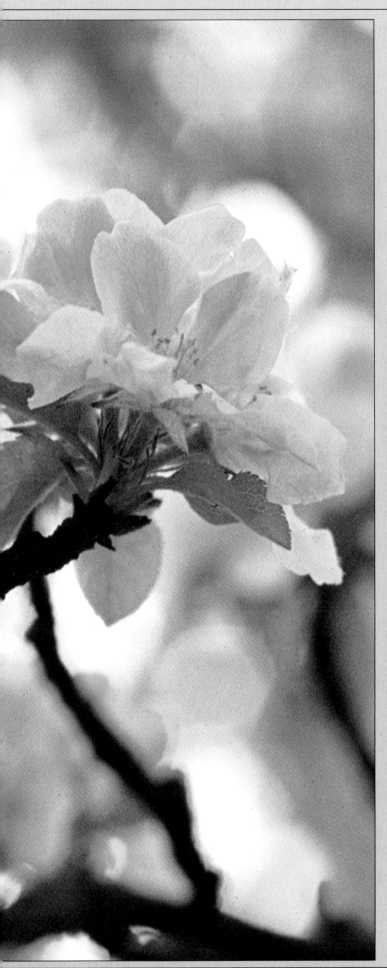

Perhaps by sheer contrast with the greyness of winter, the light and the colours of spring seem fresher than those of any other season. The countryside reawakens in a gentle explosion of new foliage and grass, early flowers, sprouting shrubs, buds and blossom. The pictures everybody likes to take of fledgling birds or wobbly legged animals are given a sparkling quality by the clear, angular light, and candid shots of people outdoors in spring weather tend to be characteristically relaxed and cheerful. Spring showers can heighten the colours of nature, but are often sudden and violent enough to destroy delicate blossom, so if you see an attractive display to photograph, you should take the picture as soon as possible. Early morning is the best time, especially when the buds have just opened after a calm night and are still damp with dew.

In the picture of apple blossom, I focused on a single bracket of flowers, their fragile pink emphasized by the white circles of confusion behind them and by the pale leaves and dark branches. I used a Pentax 105mm macro lens, high-speed film and an exposure of 1/250 at f5.6.

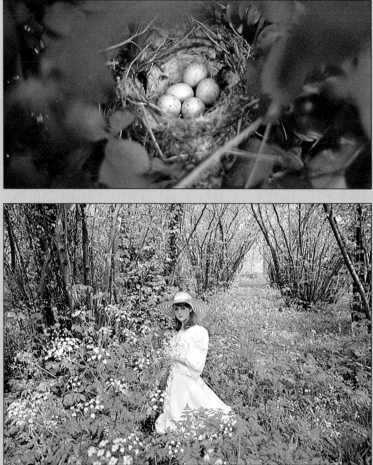

A cluster of bird's eggs *snuggled against the wall of a downy nest is framed by out-of-focus leaves, which add to the picture's feeling of undisturbed seclusion. I used a long lens and climbed on the roof of a nearby shed so that I could shoot downwards from a distance of about 20ft (6m).*
Pentax, 200mm, Ektachrome 64, 1/250, f5.6.

The prodigality of spring *is captured in the picture of a girl knee-deep in a carpet of wild flowers. Her romantic clothes and pose establish a delicate atmosphere that is well supported by the lush yet light greenery of the copse. The filtered sunlight increases in brightness in the background.* Pentax, 28mm, Ektachrome 64, 1/60, f11.

Summer

The months of summer are the most popular of all for photography. Yet the intense light is often the most difficult to handle, especially at midday, when forms can be obscured by heavy shadow and colours are often masked by glare from reflective surfaces. Backlighting and indirect lighting can be effectively used to reduce the level of contrast or provide a softer light for portraits. But the best course is to avoid the harsh, uncomplimentary light of full day and exploit instead the more gentle light of early morning or long evenings when people are more relaxed and the rich colours of nature are seen to the greatest advantage. Particularly after rain, green grass will look greener and blue skies bluer than at any other time. Shooting in the cooler part of the day will also reduce the problems of sun flaring into the camera lens or heat affecting exposed films. When going on holiday you should avoid the temptation to load yourself up with exhausting extra equipment. One camera and three lenses will cover most eventualities and a tripod is usually unnecessary.

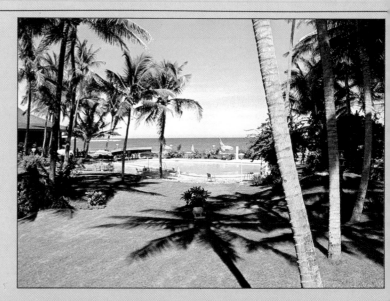

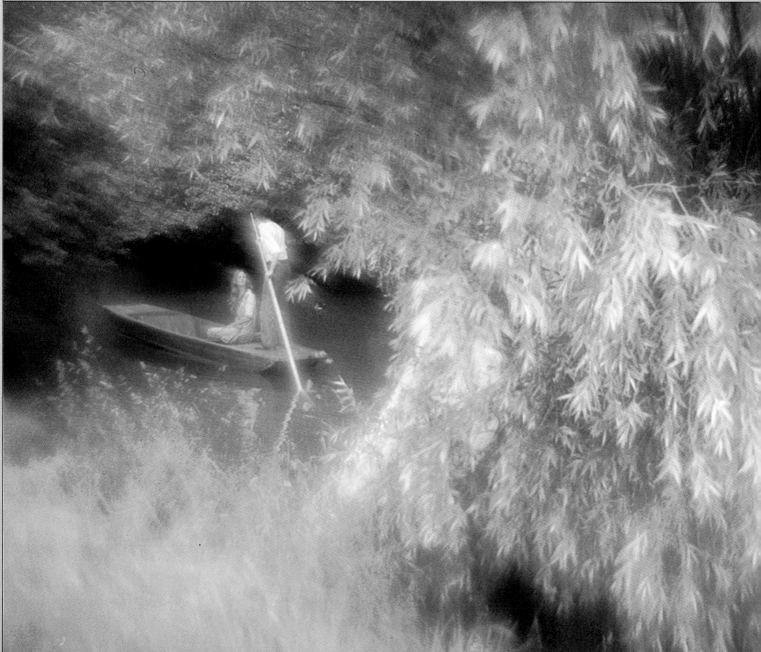

The atmosphere of summer *is often best evoked by using shadows as a main element in the picture. The deserted pool of an Indonesian hotel and the deck chair precisely positioned in the shade combine to convey the intense heat of midday. A more romantic image (helped by smearing butter on a u/v filter) is created by the punt gliding beneath willows in reflective light. The sun-dappled street suggests coolness, although it was photographed in the heat of Bombay, with reflected light illuminating the intricate façade of the tenement block. Pentax, 35 mm, Agfachrome 50s, 1/500, f11 (left); 1/250, f11 (below); 1/250, f11 (right).*

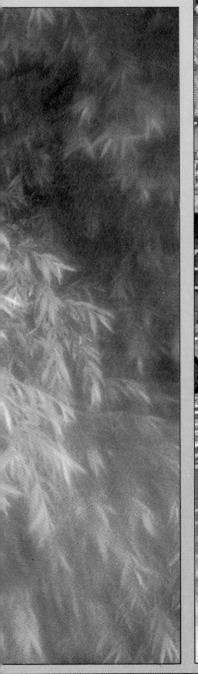

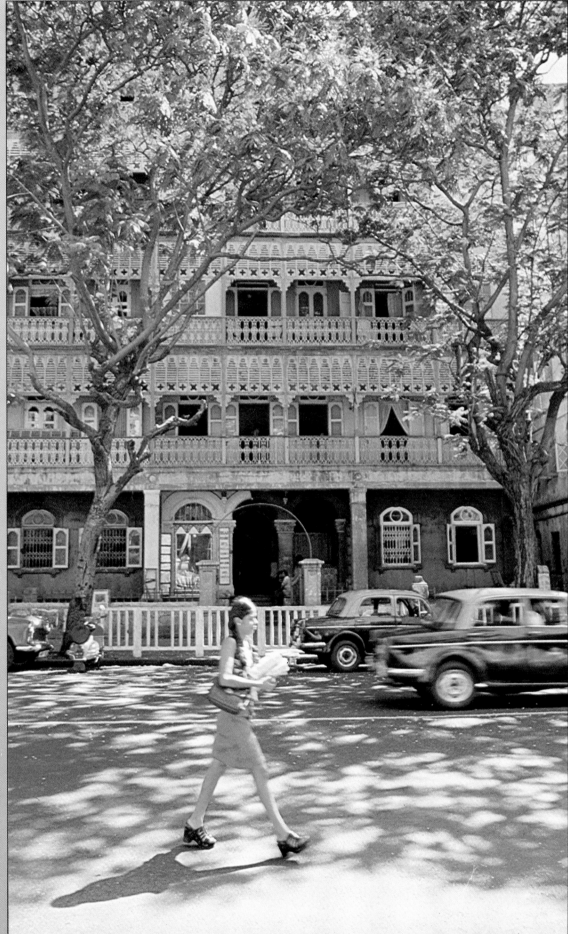

Autumn

The transition from ripeness to decay in autumn provides marvellous opportunities for colour landscape photography. Increasingly, towards winter, the weather becomes turbulent with strong winds, dense clouds, the first frosts and damp mists. Days shorten, while the light itself grows slightly redder than in summer and casts longer shadows, describing more searchingly forms, textures and colours. As the foliage of trees turns from full greens to vivid reds and golds, and as winds begin to expose the sculptural forms of the landscape, colour contrasts are at their most dramatic and glowing. The best time to take advantage of the uniquely soft light of autumn is in the early morning or late afternoon; and the full richness of the season's colours is effectively photographed not only in isolation but also against the darker greens of pastures or evergreen trees or the sober hues of bare soil, ploughed and ready for planting.

In North America, cold nights and fine, hazy days produce the brilliant tints and sharp contrasts of foliage seen in the early morning shot, opposite, of a lake in Vermont. A low angle of light gives sheen to the water, accentuating the thrust of the bank of tall trees, their colours varying from dark greens to greys, pinks and rusts, blending softly towards the top of the frame. I used a 100mm lens on my Pentax with an exposure of 1/125 at f8.

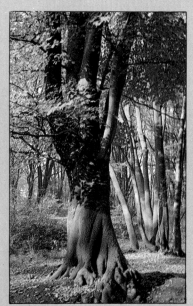

Soft but powerful angular light *sweeps across a wood to reveal the complex strength of a beech tree. Thinning leaves have let the light of the midday sun penetrate the whole scene, so that individual forms and colours can be seen clearly and a delicate interplay of light and shade contrasts with the bold image of the tree.*
Pentax, 35mm, Ektachrome 64, 1/60, f11.

The harvested field *swept clean, the straw in the barn, the huddle of buildings behind the trees and the subdued colours all evoke the idea of autumn as a time of preparation for winter.*
Pentax, 28mm, Ektachrome 64, 1/125, f8.

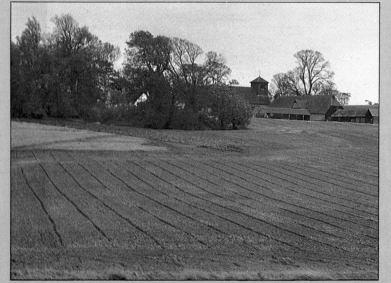

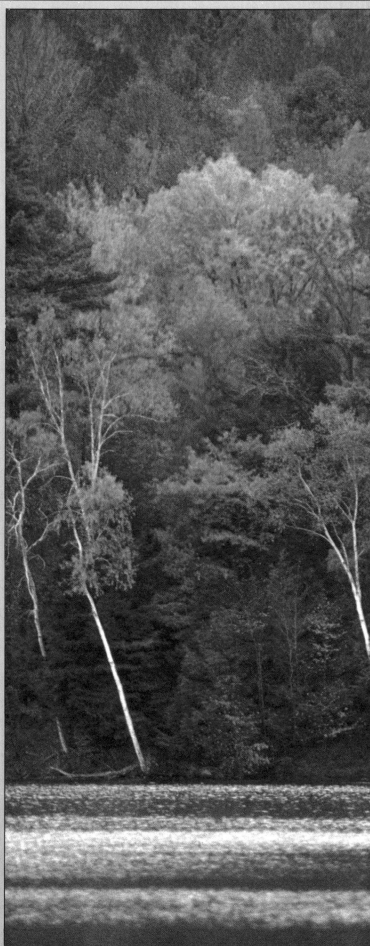

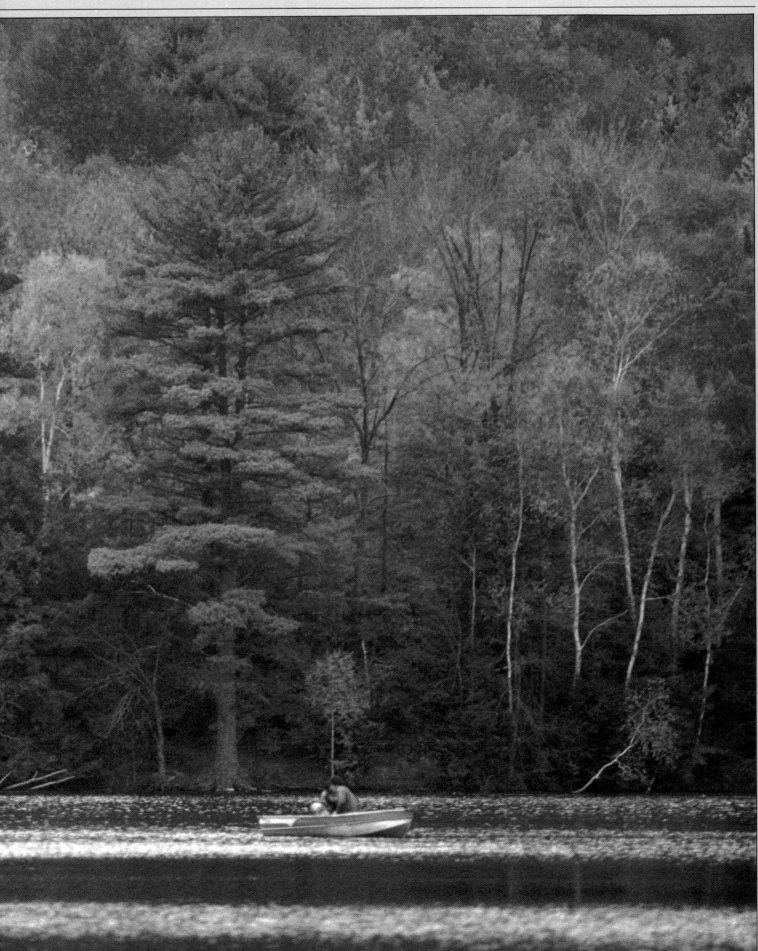

Winter

Rain, sleet, snow and fog—images of winter—suggest diminished light and muted colours. Yet on a fine winter's day the air has a cold, rinsed freshness that gives colours a particular clarity. In cold weather, with people huddled indoors, and fields or beaches empty, the bleakness of landscapes and seascapes can be evoked by powerfully atmospheric photographs in which the limited colours appear all the more vivid against sombre backgrounds.

As the hours of daylight lessen, the effects of changing light tend to be condensed. A winter's afternoon can give a low, orange-tinted light similar to that of a summer's evening, emphasizing textures and revealing surprising colours. In a snow-covered landscape, nature's outlines tend to soften, land and sky merging. But the shapes of man-made things are often accentuated, buildings standing out more blackly and boldly against snow or pale skies. As colours are subdued, tone and pattern become more important elements in the overall composition.

The moods of winter light can be discovered by recording the imagery of winter—bare trees, frozen water, cobwebs sparkling with frost, the crystalline fur of snow on a window ledge, the thick coats of animals, glowing fires and the bright woollens of people muffled in scarves and caps. Apart from the contrasts of colours against snow, delicate tints often appear, especially in the early morning or towards evening when the light is often a soft pink or orange.

In the view of an estuary that provides the main picture here, the strange, luminous warmth of the shaft of sunlight is characteristic of midwinter light in northern climates. The photograph was taken in the Hebrides during a momentary gap in leaden skies. Frost on the tussock is preserved by the long shadow of a building behind the camera. The exposure was 1/125, f8 with a 35mm Pentax.

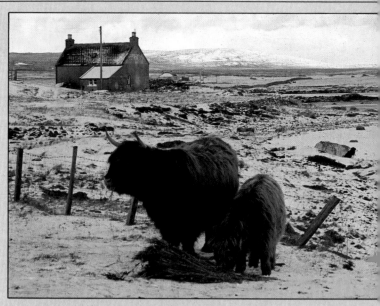

A child's snowfight *is full of the exhilaration produced by a fresh snowfall, and you need a fast shutter speed to capture the mood. The effect of soft shadows on the snow has been created by photographing through the branches of the bare trees. A slight grey-green cast gives the picture an unexpected quality and other colours have recorded well, especially the boy's reddened cheeks.*
Pentax, 200mm, Ektachrome 200, 1/500, f8.

The unity of form and tone *in this photograph of a house beside a Welsh lake would not have been apparent in a shot taken in summer, when green grass, white walls and blue water would have produced a rather more prosaic picture. As it is, the colours of the winter landscape and the light dusting of snow on the hillside are blended with the whites, greys and browns of the house in complete harmony.*
Pentax, 50mm, Ektachrome 64, 1/125, f8.

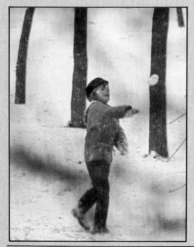

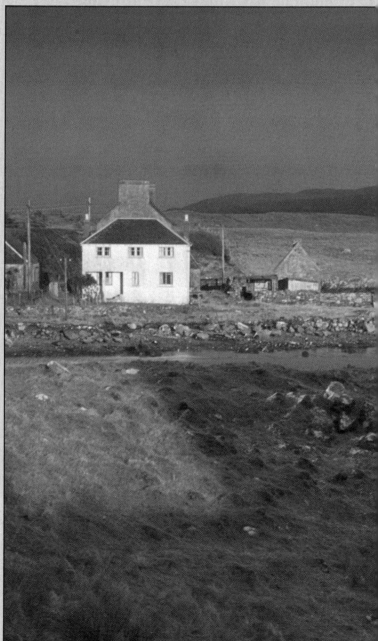

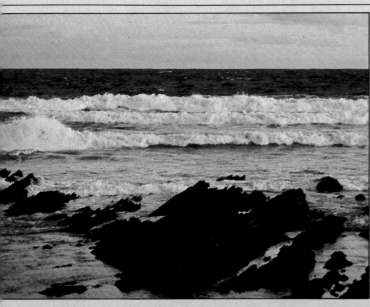

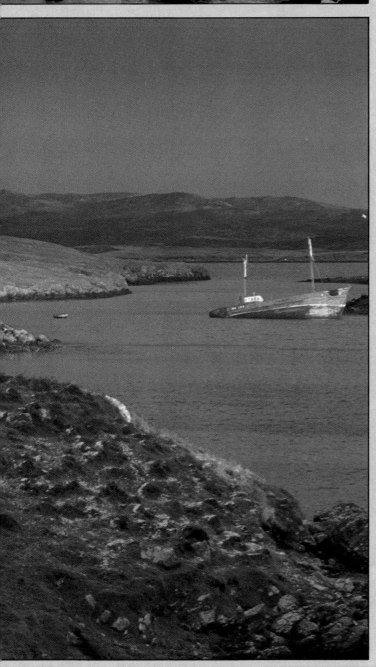

Mauve sky tints *reflected from the snow in the picture of Highland cattle create the impression of early morning or evening. Yet the shot was taken at midday. The shadowed plain, open to the wind, suggests a barren isolation in which the shaggy coats of the animals provide a comforting warmth.*
Pentax, 35mm, Ektachrome 64, 1/250, f8.

A dark green sea, *with surf frozen by shutter speed, and the pale, brittle light of a sunset at Dunbar, Scotland, evoke such a bleakness that it would be impossible to mistake the season.*

Pentax, 50mm, Ektachrome 200, 1/250, f8.

A road in Canada, *running to the skyline, appears to be spotlit by the white rim of the setting sun. In fact, the sun had already gone down and I waited until the headlights of a car appeared at the brow of the hill to give the impression of a wintry river flowing from the source of light. Although the wet road reflects the pink of the sky, the winter light is not strong enough at this time of the evening to give a similar tint to the snow, which has the blue cast typical of snow in shadow areas. A static landscape is avoided by the off-centre placing of the road and horizon.*

Minolta, 35mm, Agfachrome 50s, 1/125, f5.6.

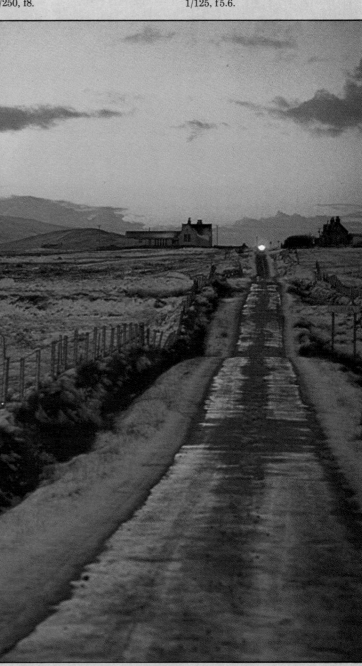

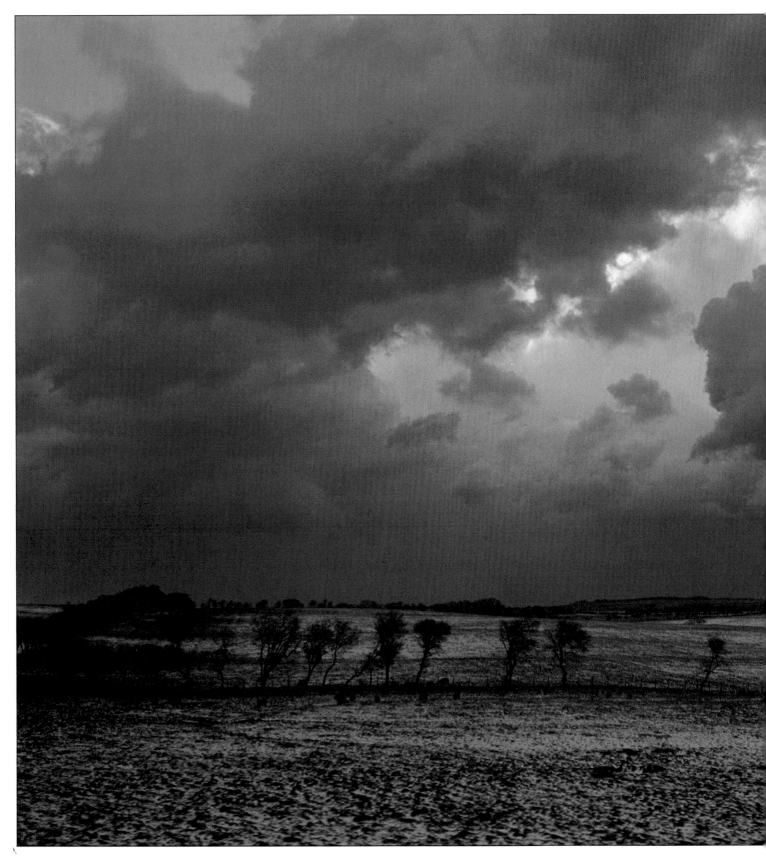

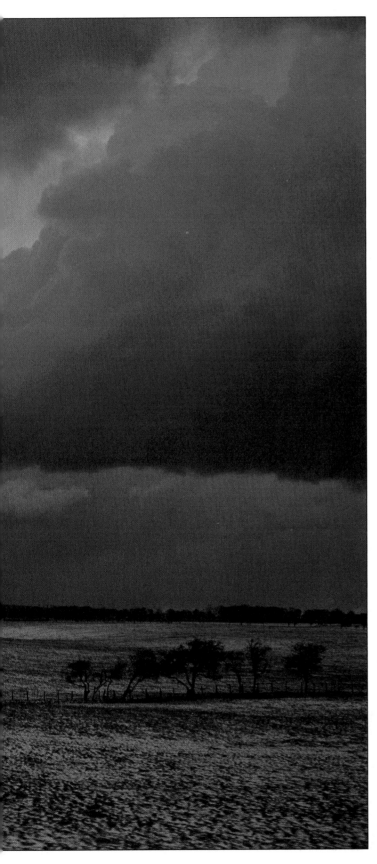

Adverse conditions

Pictures unique in power *and atmosphere are often produced in situations that seem most hostile to photography. The purple luminosity of this sky, lasting only a few minutes, was the aftermath of a driving storm that has left the fields covered with hailstones. A freezing wind tosses the trees and the clouds are massing again in the background. Yet the light is subtle and delicate, filtering down and tinting the whole scene with muffled pink accents. The photograph was taken in Northumberland.* Leicaflex, 50mm, Ektachrome 200, 1/500, f16.

Taking advantage of poor light

Poor light can mean anything from fog or rain to failing light. As light dims, colour values tend to darken and blend together and at this point many photographers put their cameras away. Yet in a sense there is no such thing as bad light for photography. Next time you are out in the open in a storm, look carefully at the objects around you and notice how different they appear. If there is a dark cloud base, the sky will have sealed in the available light like a lid closing, producing rich colour saturation despite the dulling of more brilliant hues. Photographers often overlook the ways in which changing light can bring alive subjects they might have dismissed as hardly worth a shot. You should be prepared to use every one of the many subtle colour variations produced by weather changes.

Successful photography in most kinds of poor light is more a matter of patience, experience and alertness than of special equipment. Basically, you need a light, easily handled single-lens reflex camera that, in rain, you can keep under your coat until the last possible moment, fast film (up to 400 ASA) and a lens that will allow you to photograph at the fastest possible shutter speed. Most good modern cameras have fairly fast lenses (at least f2 or f2.8) and these should be exploited. To use only the normal aperture range of f8 to f16 is like driving your car at only 30mph. If you do not want to use a wide aperture because of depth of field or focusing considerations, and time is available for a slow shutter speed, a tripod will help you to achieve maximum definition. Remember that in general, poor light will help you to balance your picture by blending colour and reducing contrasts of light and shade.

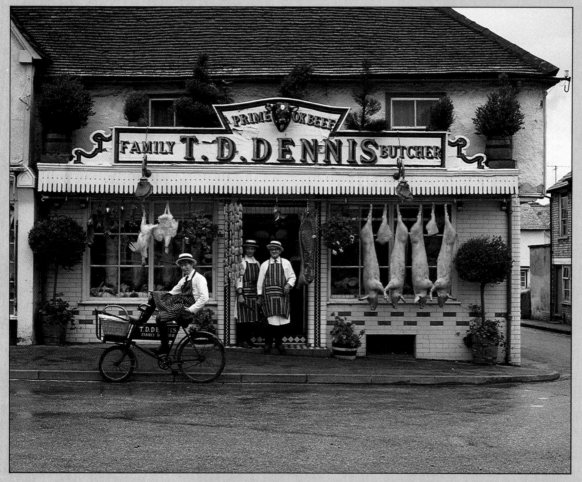

Poor light is almost inevitable in photographing animals, which are seldom seen posing in broad daylight. Light rain was falling when I took the picture of a tiger in an open zoo in Singapore, and I doubt whether the shot would have been possible otherwise. I arrived in sunshine to find that the tigers were keeping their distance from about 30 chattering people. It was only when the weather changed and the crowd headed for shelter that I had a chance to attract one of the animals. I was using a K2 Pentax loaded with Ektachrome 200 and with a 100mm lens. This gave me an exposure of 1/15 with a wide aperture (f4). At that slow speed I could expect blurring if I moved or the animal did. So I decided to shoot at 1/60 and push the film two stops in processing. I threw some pieces of meat into the water from a low bridge on which I was standing and the tiger entered the moat in a couple of gigantic bounds and swallowed the meat. I was able to get one shot at close range. The dim light has helped the picture, producing ominous dark tones in the water.

Clarity of detail *can actually be enhanced by poor light, as in this picture of an English butcher's shop, photographed between rain showers. The cloud cover has sealed in the little available light, creating a luminescence found on certain overcast days. In bright sun, with shadows and gaudy colours, the scene might have appeared discordant. Instead, the subdued colours, muted contrasts and sheen on the road give the picture an overall balance of tone.*

Hasselblad, 150mm, tripod, Ektachrome 200, 1/30, f5.6.

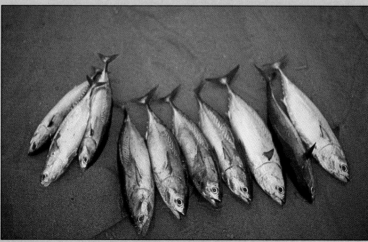

Colour harmony *in this picture of fish on a beach in Indonesia is the result of failing light in the early evening. With illumination coming only from an overcast sky, a blue cast has unified colours that actually ranged from yellow to silver. By shooting directly down on the fish I have caught the light reflected from the scales and sand, which has turned an almost metallic magenta. Depth of field was not a consideration, allowing me to use a very wide aperture.*

Pentax, 50mm, Ektachrome 64, 1/30, f2.

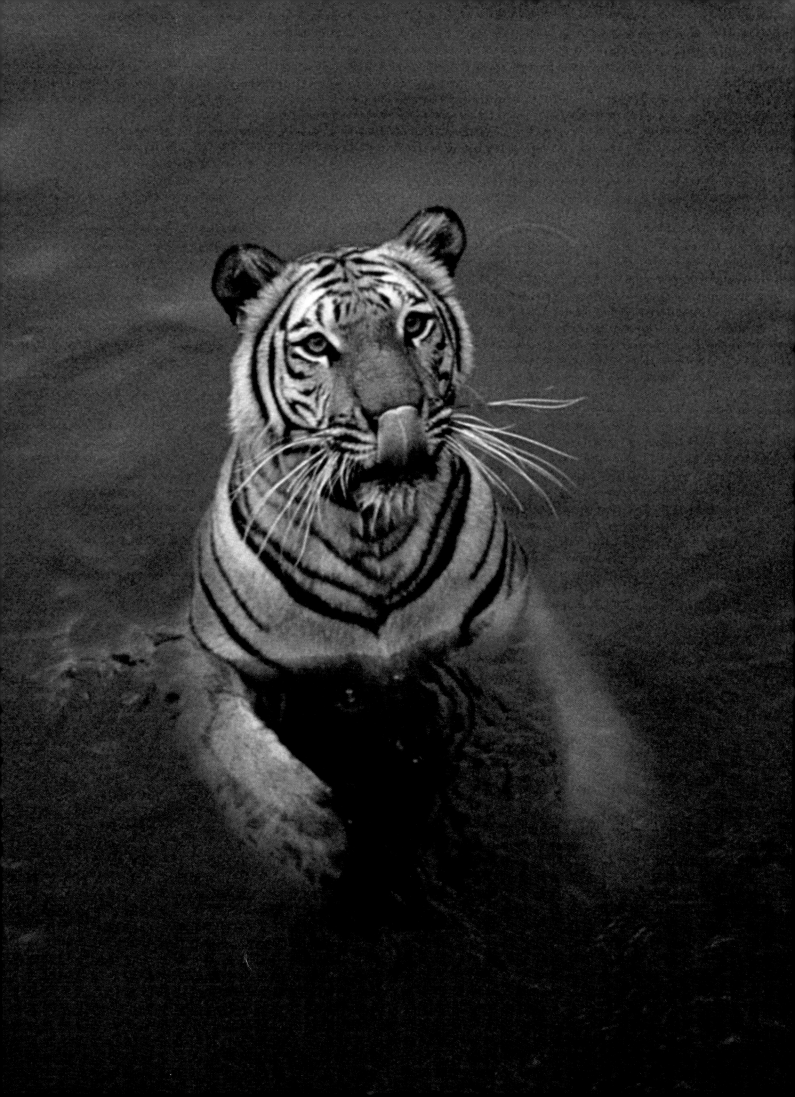

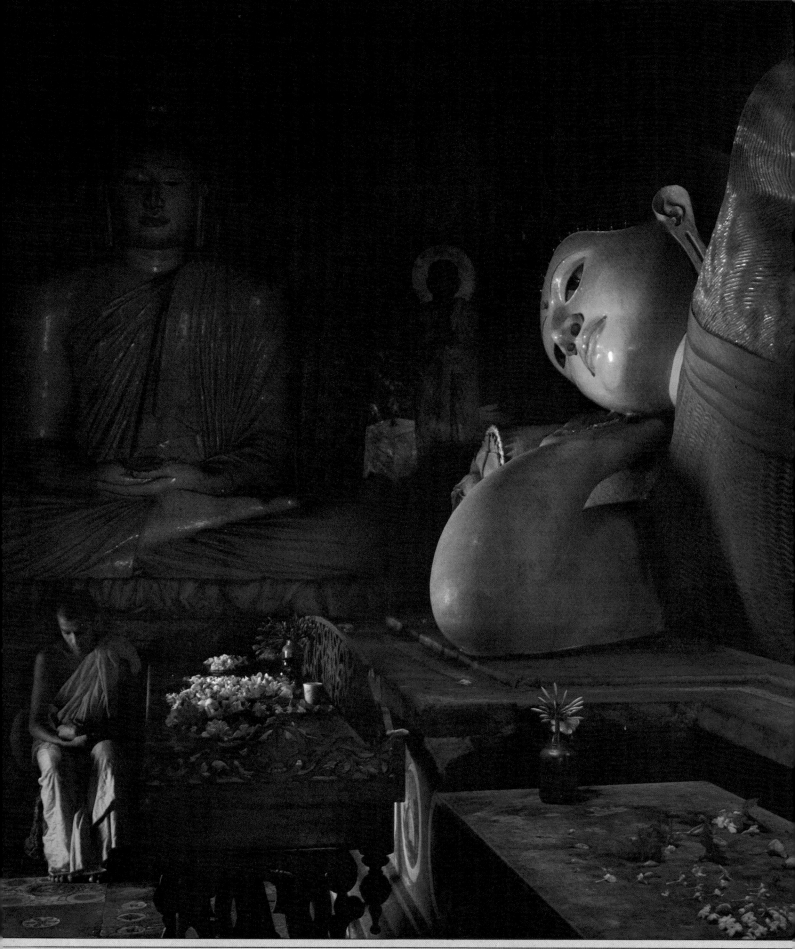

Interiors with limited lighting pose technical problems, but overlighting may be a mistake, destroying the very scene that attracted you. The subdued light characteristic of places of worship is most dramatically apparent if entry is made from full sun, when the eyes take time to adjust from brightness to darkness. When I entered a Buddhist temple in Sri Lanka I was immediately impressed first by bright colours glowing from out of the gloom and then by a penetrating quiet. This is the effect I sought to capture by using existing light. A shaft of weak sunlight passed across the young monk, accentuating the colours of his robes, and illuminated the serene face of the reclining Buddha. The statue against the far wall, with detail hidden in shadow, emphasized the atmosphere of mystery, serenity and personal communion. Not wishing to impose too much I simply braced myself against a wall for a long exposure.

Rolleiflex, 80mm, Ektachrome 200, 1/4, f2.8.

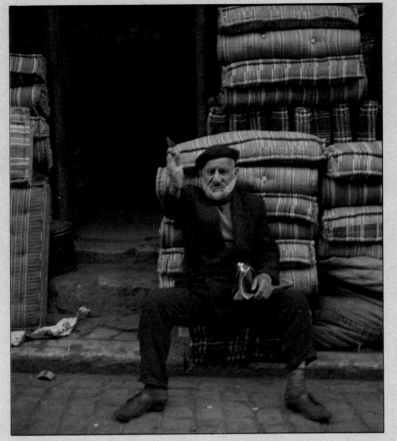

The irascible bedding sales-man *was photographed in the dim light of an Istanbul back street and I had to lean against a wall for a relatively long exposure. The bluish-magenta cast helps convey the area's slightly dilapidated ambience.*
Rolleiflex, 80mm, Ektachrome 200, 1/10, f2.8.

The stable *in which I found this smith at work with his assistant was so dark that an exposure of 2 seconds was needed with a wide aperture. The slow shutter speed has given a greenish cast, but this has not diminished the overall effect of the picture. Earlier in the day, with more light, the shot would have been hard and unsympathetic. As it is the texture and discoloration of the walls and floor are given added emphasis, while the slight softening of the image strengthens the atmosphere. The composition relies largely on the contrast between the stolid stance of the horse and the energetic positions of the men.*
Leicaflex, 21mm, Ektachrome 200, tripod, 2sec., f5.6.

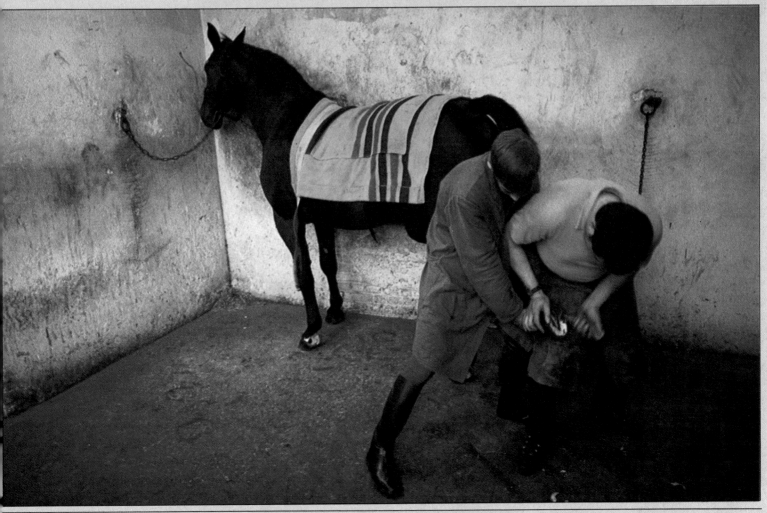

Fog and mist

Moisture in the air diffuses light and poses special problems that can, nevertheless, be overcome to give pictures full of atmosphere and interest. The quality of light on misty or foggy days is biased towards blue if totally overcast or red if there is morning or evening sun. The pale, fragile light reduces depth and form, increasing the tendency towards two-dimensional flatness. Colours and contrasts are softened alike, and because the light is scattered, scenes can have a duality of tone from light distance to darker foreground. To capture the mist, expose for highlights.

Slight overexposure will enable you to penetrate fog, but it is easy to miscalculate. Take a reading of your hand in the light and overexpose by half a stop. Keep your camera protected from wet, drifting fog in its case when you are not using it.

In the shot of a Spanish farm couple walking to work, the magenta cast comes from early morning sunlight filtered by mist, which screens an untidy background. Perspective is provided by the converging lines and receding colours of the road surface and the reddish soil. I used an 80mm lens on my Rolleiflex and exposed for 1/125 at f11.

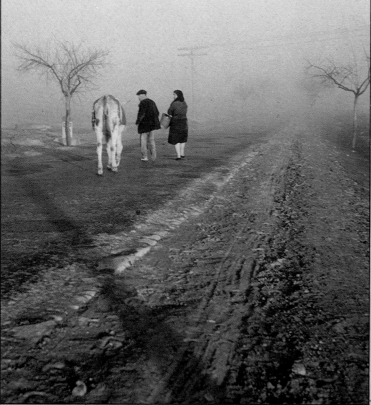

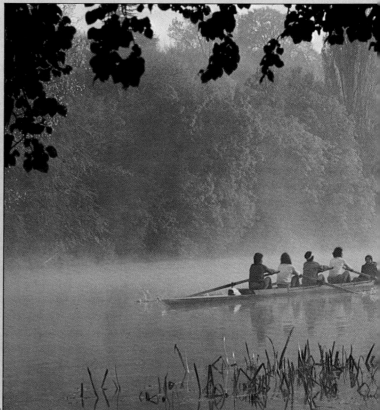

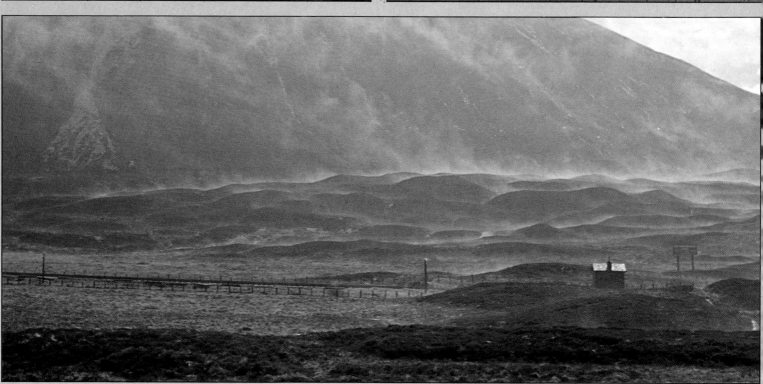

Rising mist *on a warm morning in early autumn dissipates the vivid colours of the trees along a river bank as a rowing crew glide by in training. A low angle of view, emphasizing the foreground reeds, helps the impression of the boat slicing easily through tranquil water.* Pentax, 35mm, Ektachrome 64, 1/250, f5.6.

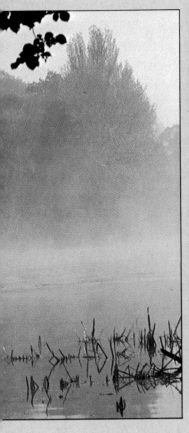

Thick midday fog *envelops a pylon set amid bush-fringed lakeland, draining the scene of colour to create an ethereal picture in monochrome with a hint of green and brown. Aerial perspective gives depth helped by converging wires, which add interest to the sky. I used a spot meter to calculate exposure for the pylon, then overexposed by half a stop in order to penetrate the murky foreground.* Leicaflex, 90mm, tripod, Ektachrome 64, 1/15, f5.6.

Mist creeps along foothills *in the Scottish Highlands shrouding the heather to create the effect of smouldering land. White wisps caught by the light bring out the rhythm of the hillocks, while the rectangular house stands small and insubstantial at the edge of a gently rocking landscape.* Leicaflex, 90mm, Ektachrome 64, 1/125, f8.

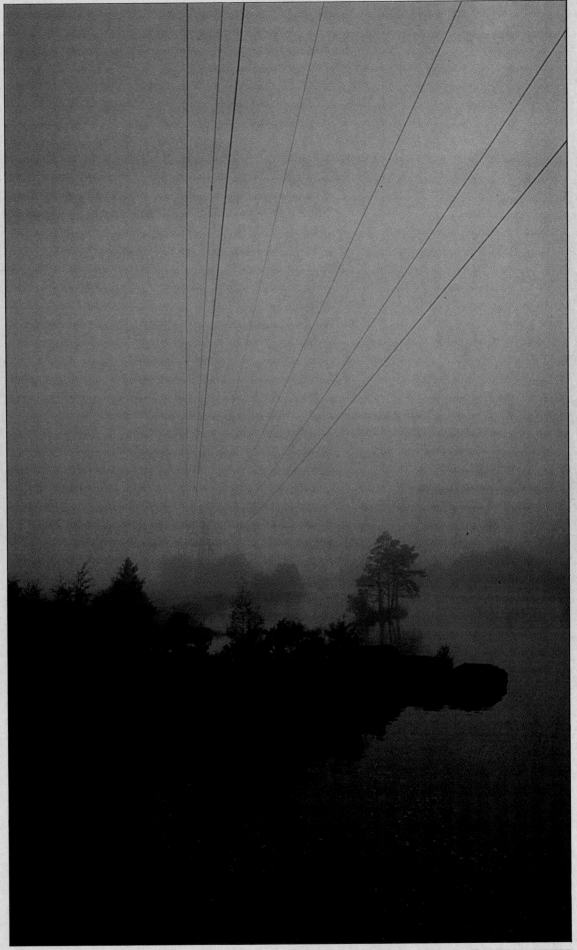

Rain

Falling rain can give colour pictures strong atmosphere, often with beautiful, subdued hues. You will need to dry a wet camera as soon as possible and avoid touching film with wet hands. Water on the lens will soften the image, so constantly check and dry. I usually keep my camera under my coat, or shoot from beneath a broad umbrella. But a cheap plastic bag with a hole for the lens is just as good. Rain, as such, is difficult to capture on film, though it shows up well against a dark background. A speed of at least 1/125 is usually needed to arrest its fall.

Vibrant colours of a sunbed, *of red tiles around a blue swimming pool and of an emerald bay in Sardinia are blurred and muted to convey, through colour alone, a sudden rainstorm. The shot records the weather without showing it, as the speed was too slow to stop the falling rain.* Nikon, 50mm, tripod, Ektachrome 64, 1/8, f8.

Shooting through a car window, *providing it is not steamed over, is one way of recording rain while keeping dry. Taken from a Singapore taxi, this picture contrasts the sharp image of the dashboard with a tropical storm, effectively capturing the local conditions.* Pentax, 28mm, Ektachrome 64, 1/125, f5.6.

A prosaic stretch of tarmac *is transformed into a fascinating pattern of circles forming and re-forming in heavy rain. The shallow water produces a good contrast of light and shade and a fast shutter speed defines the rings clearly. At a slower speed only a splatter would appear.* Pentax, 35mm, Ektachrome 200, 1/500, f2.8.

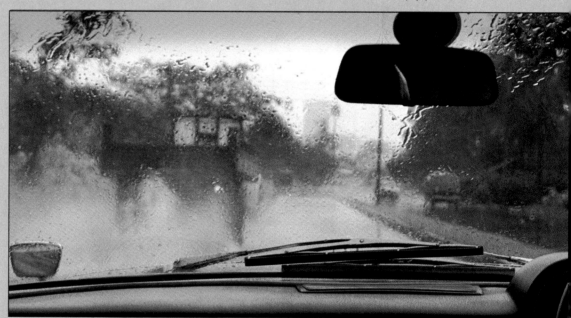

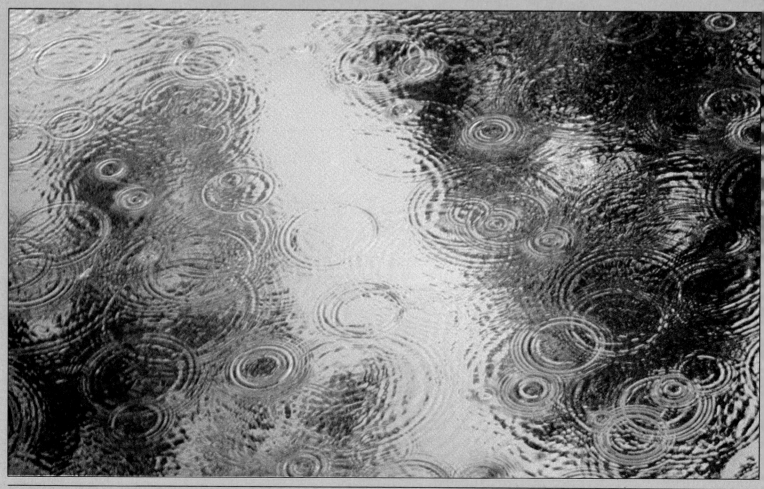

Storms

Startling, distorted and often beautiful hues appear under
storm conditions, when heavy clouds refract certain colours,
often producing an eerie greenish light. A variety of
atmospheric effects—clouds, wind, rain, snow, lightning, hail
and shafts of unexpected sun—transforms the appearance
of the world as light changes rapidly in intensity. Summer
storms are especially exciting when strong sun, rain-clouds
and wind all combine to alter the light, seemingly by the
second. Heavy clouds race across the sun, highlighting one
part of a scene then another, producing impressive contrasts
of tone and hue as areas are suddenly revealed in light then
just as quickly covered in gloom. To capture the turbulence
of a scene, expose for the highlights so that the areas in
shadow are left dark, giving a full range of contrasts.
Including the source of light in the picture will add to its
mood and impact, as will wet roads, swaying trees and people
scurrying for cover.

Taking pictures in stormy conditions can be uncomfortable,
but you should not be deterred by a bit of rain on the camera,
provided you keep drying off the lens before shooting. In
strong winds it may be difficult to hold the camera steady,
even with a tripod, for the relatively long exposures required.
You may need screws to secure the equipment, or clamps on
a car, or perhaps a companion can lean against your back to
steady you for the shot. It may be possible to shoot from the
inside of a car if the angle of view is appropriate.

The Scottish Highlands have a reputation for temperamental
weather. I took the picture opposite, shot partly against the
light, in total storm conditions with light moving across the
landscape as the clouds rushed along. A shaft of sun striking
a field has clearly revealed its shape and colour although it
was perhaps 3 miles (5 km) distant. The effect of looking at
brightness from an area of dark is accentuated by the murky
foreground with its wet leaves glistening in the light.
I used a 135 mm lens on my Leicaflex with an exposure of
1/125 at f5.6.

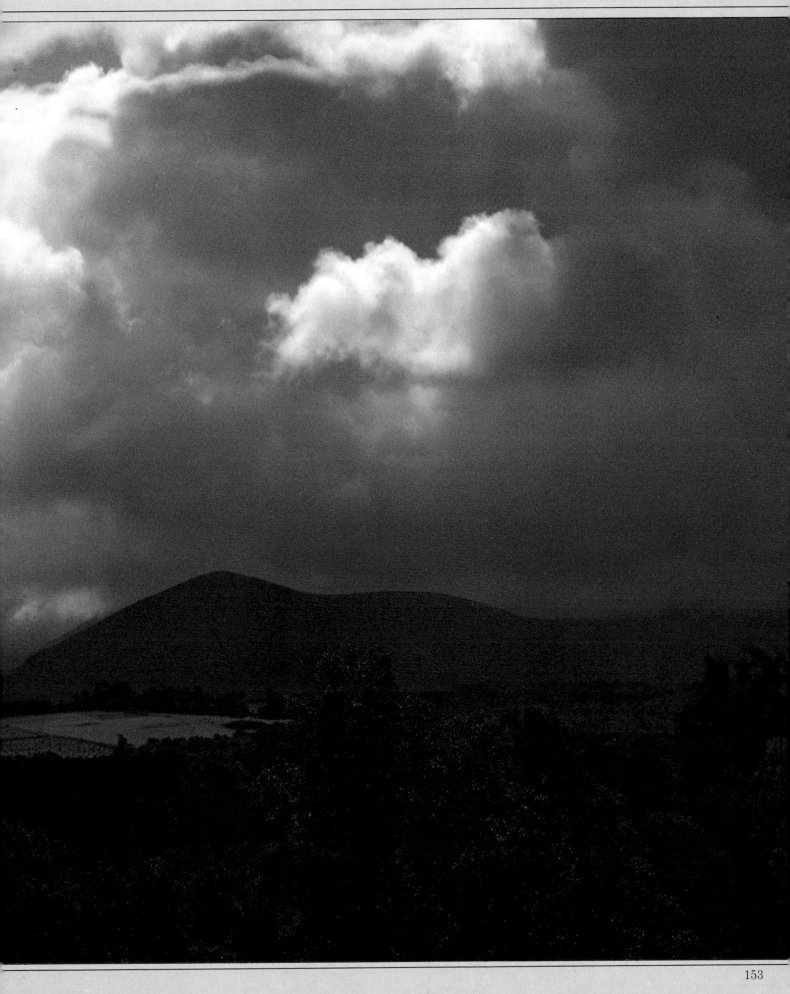

Snow and cold

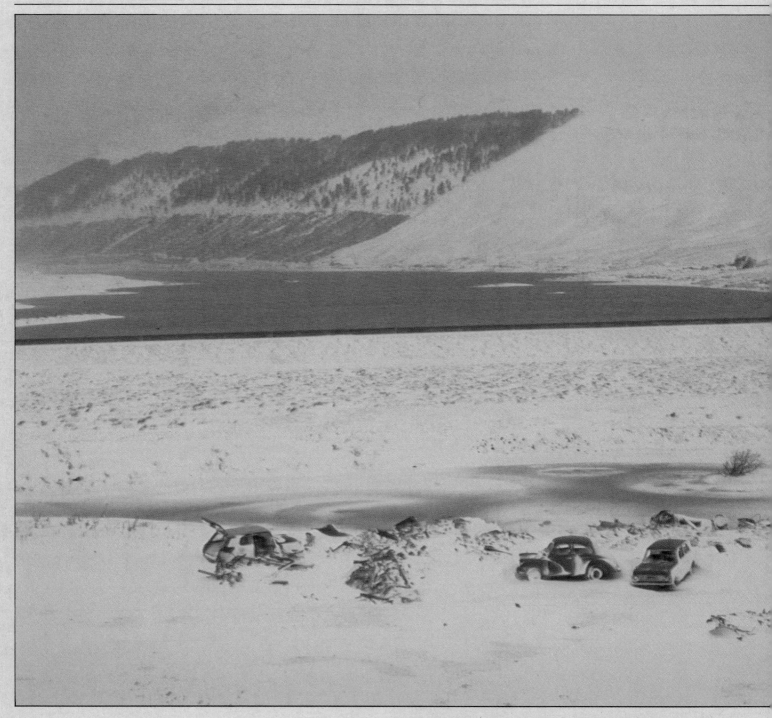

Apart from the difficulty of simply keeping warm and the discomfort of handling equipment or changing film with numbed fingers, photography in heavy snow raises several special problems. Perspective and other normal guidelines often vanish, making it hard to judge size, distance or height. The even quality of light and lack of tonal recession tend to flatten landscapes. Strong blue casts appear in shadows, especially under overcast skies just before a snowfall. Under bright skies, the intensity of light also produces meter readings that are too high, leading to underexposed shots. Although experience will help to overcome these problems, the best way of adapting to snow is to take pictures that exploit the beauty of its monochromatic tones and patterns. Falling snow can be photographed at fairly slow speeds to show streaks or fast speeds to arrest flakes. On the ground, its texture shows up best in the sweeping light of dawn or dusk.

The silence and isolation *of extreme cold is summed up in a monochromatic picture of abandoned cars beside a frozen lake in Scotland. Distance is impossible to judge. The pine-forested hill runs abruptly into a snow-covered ridge that disappears into the sky. Every-thing is composed in leaden tones of grey and white, and the enclosed feeling is completed by a background ominously darker than the foreground, where snow has already obliterated the roadway.* Pentax, 35mm, Ektachrome 64, 1/125, f8.

The colours of skiers' clothes *(top right) and a slate-roofed hut are brought out by light trapped between snow and cloud. Masking a Swiss mountain, the cloud darkens the background and defines the pleasantly irregular line of the horizon.* Pentax, 100mm, Ektachrome 64, 1/250, f8.

A line of sheep *heading for shelter gives a sense of warmth and sanctuary to an otherwise cold picture, which I took from the window of a train.* Pentax, 50mm, Ektachrome 64, 1/250, f5.6.

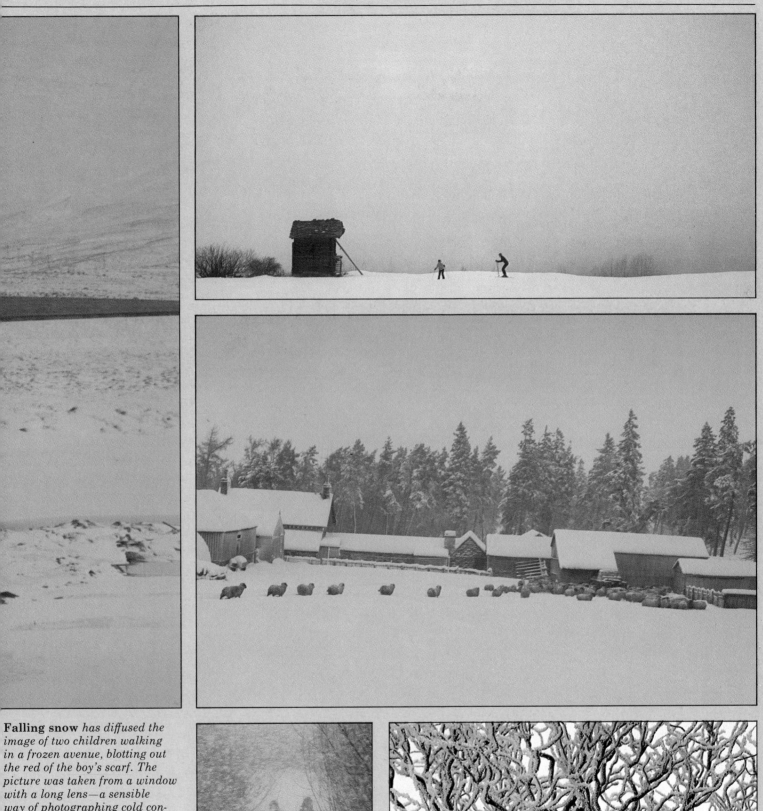

Falling snow *has diffused the image of two children walking in a frozen avenue, blotting out the red of the boy's scarf. The picture was taken from a window with a long lens—a sensible way of photographing cold conditions without enduring them.* Leicaflex, 400mm, Ektachrome 200, 1/250, f8.

The twisted branches *of a tree rimmed with frost were photographed against a misty sky at an exposure just sufficient to show their detail.* Pentax, 100mm macro, Ektachrome 64, 1/250, f5.6.

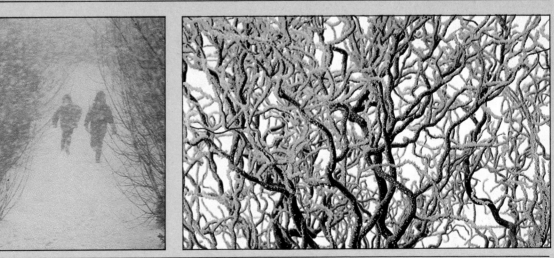

Heat

Colour photography in extreme heat is often affected by glare, haze, dust or blinding reflections, which tend to dissipate colour. A neutral density filter will cut down the amount of light reaching the film without upsetting tonal or colour balance. As a general guide, you should underexpose by half to two-thirds of a stop to increase colour saturation.

Most of the problems presented by hot climates are purely mechanical. To prevent dust or sand working its way into your camera and jamming the shutter or scratching film you should inspect and carefully clean the camera each night. An ultraviolet filter can be left on permanently to protect the lens. Spare lenses can be kept in a plastic bag inside a camera hold-all, with a couple of packets of silica-gel to absorb moisture. Remember that a camera lens left pointed too long at the sun can act as a magnifying glass and may burn the fabric of your shutter blind.

Condensation will form on camera equipment taken out of an air-conditioned room on a hot day. You can counter this by leaving equipment outdoors in the shade for half an hour before use. Not the least important thing to remember about photography in hot climates is to avoid burdening yourself with excess equipment.

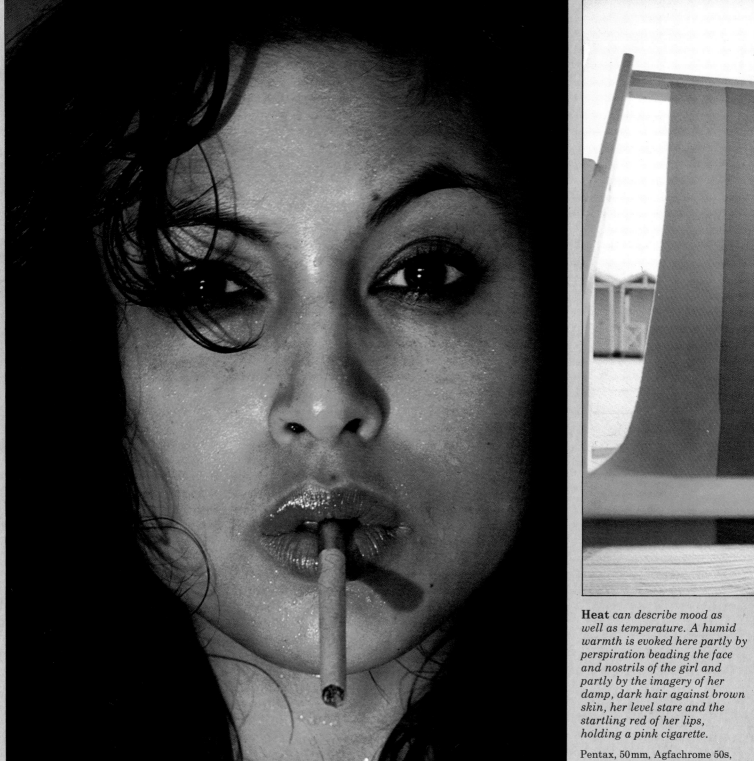

Heat *can describe mood as well as temperature. A humid warmth is evoked here partly by perspiration beading the face and nostrils of the girl and partly by the imagery of her damp, dark hair against brown skin, her level stare and the startling red of her lips, holding a pink cigarette.*

Pentax, 50mm, Agfachrome 50s, 1/250, f8.

An arid landscape *photographed in burning heat needs a touch of contrast to convey atmosphere. Here, the white reflecting roofs of a train crossing the Simpson Desert in Australia emphasize a barrenness in which the only other traces of life are marks left by excavators.*

Leicaflex, 50mm, Ektachrome 200, 1/500, f8.

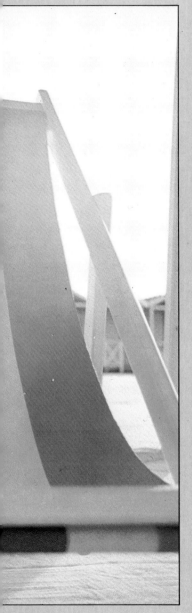

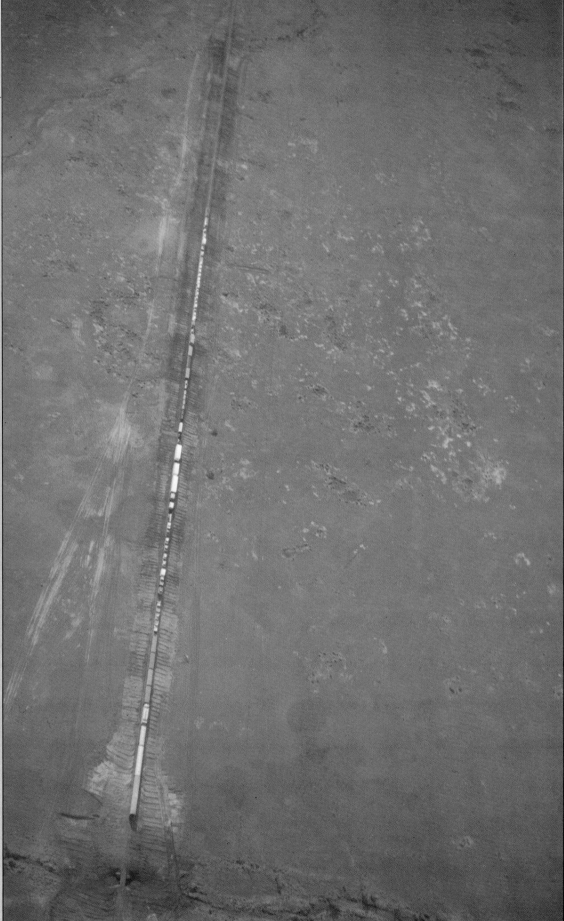

Intense midday sun *has bleached out the strong colours of this deckchair, suggesting a heat too fierce for sunbathing. The chair would have appeared in silhouette had I made a correct exposure for the sky. I chose an exposure for the shadows and left the glare of light to convey the strong Mediterranean sun.*

Pentax, 50mm, Agfachrome 50s, 1/500, f11.

Underwater photography

Underwater photography can be a startling experience, especially for a newcomer to diving. Apart from the cathedral-like silence, the vividness of colours and abundance of life in warmer and clearer waters are a revelation. As a novice with an aqualung the main problems I encountered were of unfamiliarity with diving techniques and difficulty in manoeuvring quickly and smoothly. But with a specially adapted camera, underwater photography is fairly straightforward, providing a few fundamental points are remembered for which allowances need to be made.

Chief amongst them is the reduced light levels you will encounter. Even in the clear waters of the eastern Mediterranean, seven-eighths of daylight is lost at a depth of only 35ft (about 11m). Much daylight in fact never penetrates below the surface, being bounced off the top to varying degrees depending on the roughness of the surface and the angle of the sun. Also, water, being many hundreds of times more dense than air, retains many more particles, such as sand, plankton and minerals, and these have the effect of scattering the little light that is available. By restricting yourself to the top 20ft (6m) most marine life is accessible using only a snorkel; and electronic flash and fast (400 ASA) film will overcome most of the problems associated with feeble light. As a rough exposure guide, divide the surface flash factor by four. It is often best to photograph fish at an angle rather than flashing them straight on, when their luminous colours may disappear. It is also worth remembering that you will get a more interesting picture by shooting fish against a background of rocks, weeds or sand, which will help avoid a flat image. Novice divers should preset the camera controls at a specific short distance and then simply wait for a likely subject to come within range. This will enable them to concentrate on diving technique without worrying about camera adjustments.

Because of the scattering and absorption of light in water, distant shots are not usually successful, and for a good-quality image it is best to shoot at approximately one-fifth of your visibility range. To improve contrast in the murky conditions move in as close as possible to your subject. A wide-angle lens is ideal because of its close-focus ability. Contrast can also be improved by underexposing your film and then extending the development time by an appropriate amount to compensate.

As light enters water it is refracted, or bent. This has the effect of making objects look larger and nearer than they in fact are. Do not attempt to remedy this in focusing the lens, but focus on the apparent distance of your subject as you see it, because this is the way the camera will see it also. The magnification also has some interesting effects on the focal length of the lenses. A 21mm lens has an effective focal length under water of only 28mm and its angle of view is correspondingly reduced from 92° to 75°; a 50mm lens becomes a 67mm lens and the angle of view is 36° instead of 47°. This strengthens the case for using a lens with a wide angle of view.

In clear shallow waters it is possible to take pictures straight down on the surface, or through a watertight, optically corrected glass-bottomed box. But I do not recommend swimming with an ordinary camera in a plastic bag. Many camera housings are available either for sale or hire that will be suitable for most conventional cameras. Those with autowinders have an obvious advantage. Nikon have produced a purpose-built underwater camera—the Nikonos—which is completely waterproof to a depth of 150ft (45m) and needs no additional housing.

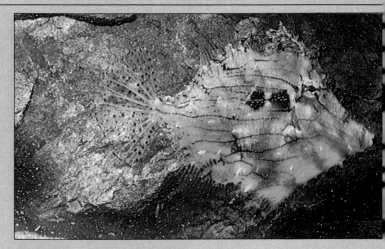

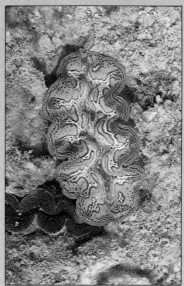

The remarkable camouflage *of this Prickly Leatherjacket from Southeast Asian waters, which looks almost like a cave painting, attracted my attention in an aquarium. To avoid reflections from the glass, I lit the tank from above.* Pentax, 100mm, Ektachrome 64, electronic flash, f11.

The sea anemone, *exposing its turquoise interior, was shot through a glass box in shallow water on the Great Barrier Reef.* Leicaflex, 90mm, Ektachrome 64, 1/125, f8.

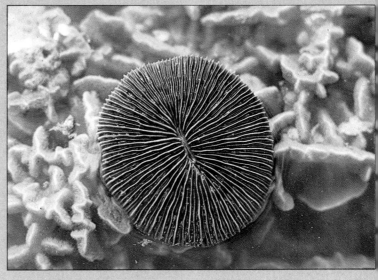

Marine life *in tidal pools or on coastal reefs can often be photographed with an ordinary camera. This dead coral with its shapely radiating spines had just been uncovered by a receding wave on the Great Barrier Reef of Australia.* Leicaflex, 90mm, Ektachrome 64, 1/250, f8.

The brilliant colours *of this Regal Tang show the advantage of photographing fish against a background that provides scale and contrast. I used a slow shutter to record the rocks and the movement of the fish prevents the shot looking static.* Nikonos, 35mm, Ektachrome 200, electronic flash, 1/30, f16.

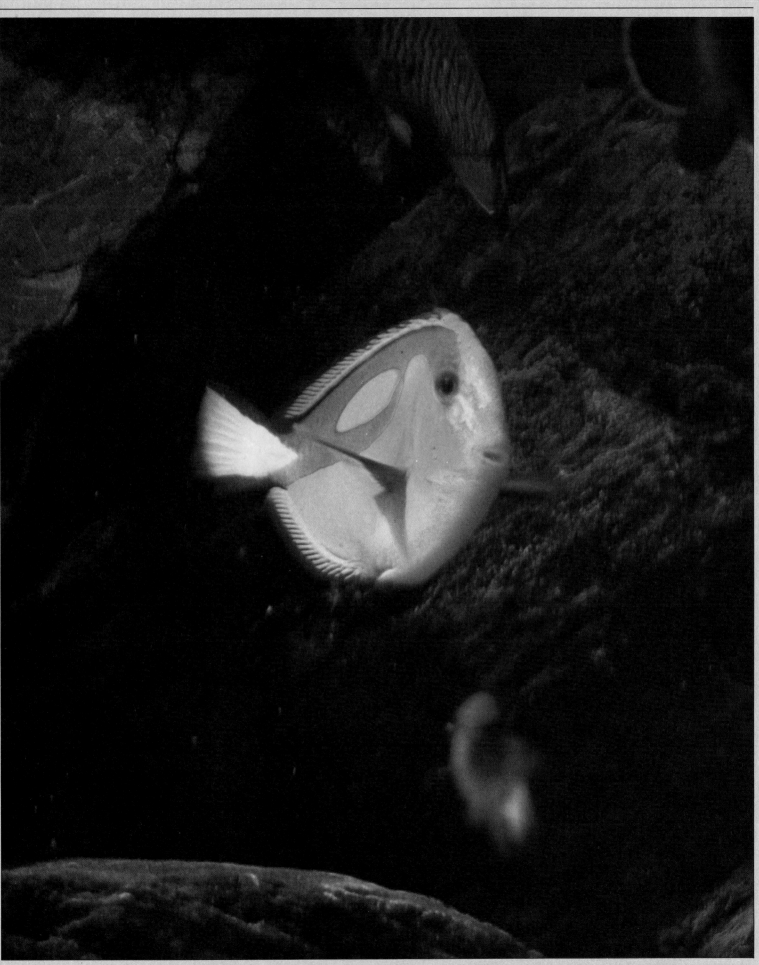

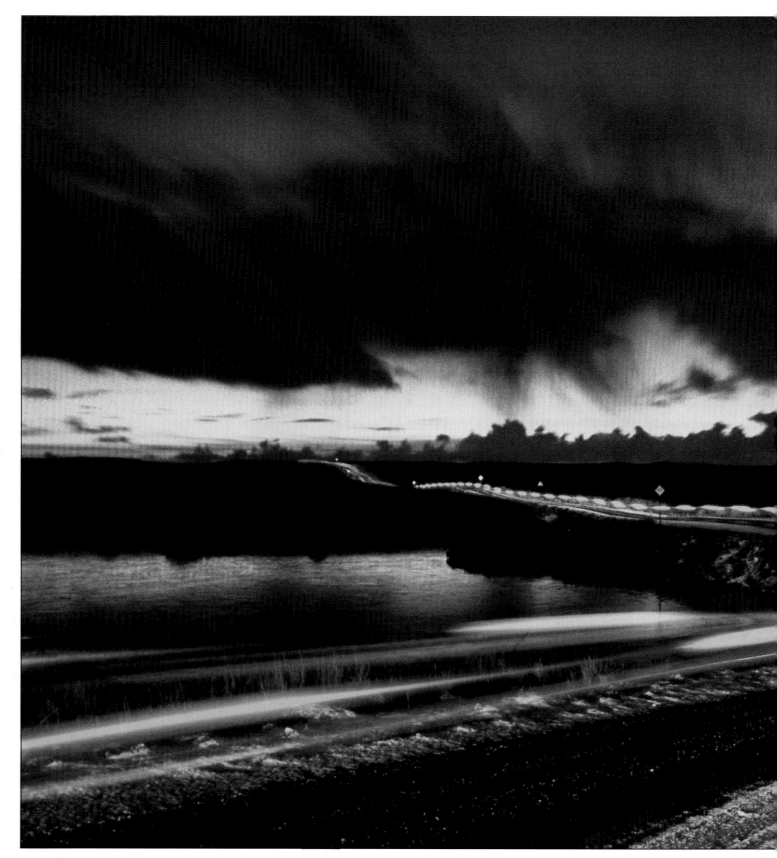

Artificial light

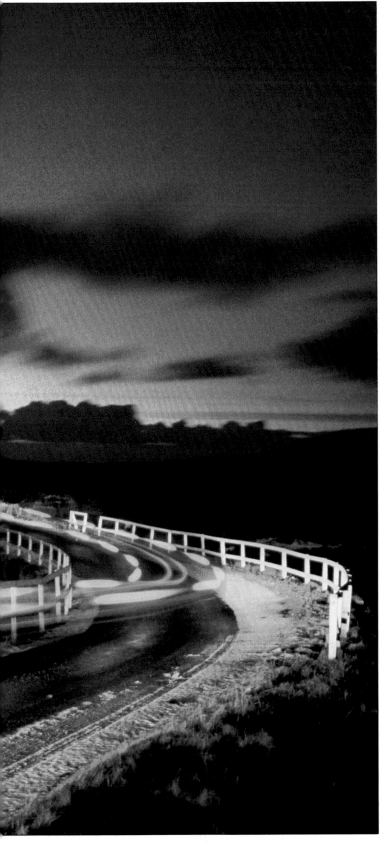

The brilliant effects *produced by artificial lighting, with its controllable colour, intensity and duration, greatly extend the range of photography. Although skill is needed to exploit the full range, spectacular pictures can be taken simply by seizing an opportunity offered. Here, a landscape has been painted with light in a chain of glowing reds and yellows strung across a darkened moor by a Range Rover with its headlights, fog lights and hazard warning lights all turned on. The headlights have picked out the snow on the road and tinted the railings a pure and delicate white. The red streaks were produced by the fog and rear lights, the yellow by the intermittent flashing of the hazard lights. I used daylight film to warm these colours and accurately to record the freezing evening sky, allowing four minutes for the car to cross the moor during the exposure.*
Pentax, 28mm, Ektachrome 64, 4min, f22.

Mixing tungsten and daylight

In the early morning and evening, no colour in nature is constant. Everything is changing from moment to moment and it is the fugitive quality of light that makes these times of day so exciting for colour photography. With colours either emerging from the night or ebbing into it, the "truth" of a particular hue is completely subjective. If there is any source of artificial light, the situation becomes still more complex and the colours of a scene will depend to a large extent on your choice of film. By using daylight film to record tungsten light or tungsten film to record daylight you can extend your ability to control the colour balance of a picture and to heighten selected hues.

The most beautiful effects are achieved when one source of light predominates, with just a touch of the other. Usually, the light that predominates should dictate your choice of film. If, for instance, an evening sky retains quite a lot of light while a few house lights are beginning to wink on, you should use daylight film. The effect will be to make the lights in the houses look a warmer orange. This is because daylight film is balanced to the colour temperature of standard midday light (about 5,500 to 6,000 kelvins), a mixture of direct sun and clear sky light that has a high content of blue. Artificial-light films are balanced to the more orange light produced by tungsten at a colour temperature of 3,200 kelvins (or 3,400 kelvins for some types of studio lights).

Daylight film used to photograph tungsten light strengthens reds and yellows in a scene and gives an orange cast to whites. Conversely, when tungsten film is used to photograph daylight it brings up the blues, subdues reds and yellows and gives a bluish cast to whites. In full daylight this produces an eerie, unnatural atmosphere. Tungsten film can sometimes be used effectively at sunset, turning reddish skies a dramatic magenta. But unless you want to achieve this kind of special effect, the rule of matching your film to the predominant source of light holds good. The brighter the minor light source, the more startling it will appear. Seen from a lighted room, a patch of daylight becomes a deep blue, while a lighted window seen from the outside looks cheerful and welcoming. The effect in both instances is to increase the atmosphere of the picture and give a stronger impression of dawn or of approaching night.

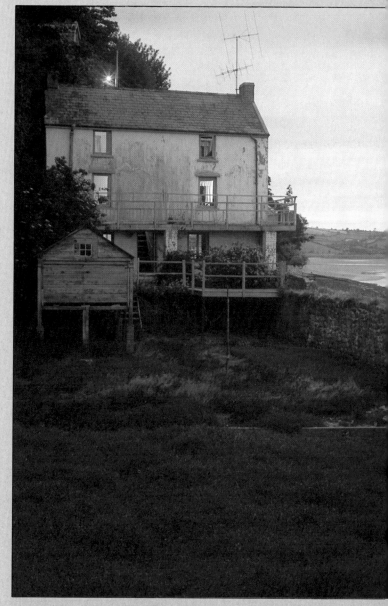

As a simple illustration *of the effect of mixing light sources and photographing them with different types of film, I made a sequence of shots of a tent on an autumn evening, using one Pentax loaded with film balanced for daylight and another loaded with film balanced for tungsten light. The top strip used daylight film (Ektachrome 64) and the first two shots closely reproduce the colours of the tent and surrounding field as I saw them. They lack interest, however, and exposure for the field and tent (1/4, f4) has burnt out the sky area, which is the main source of light. The first two shots on the lower strip were taken immediately after on high-speed tungsten light film (Ektachrome 160) at an* exposure of 1/8, f4. At these slow speeds it was essential to use a tripod.

When it had grown slightly darker I put a 100-watt bulb inside the tent and repeated the sequence. The top strip, using daylight film, now shows the true colour values in the sky area because the balanced illumination between the sky and the lighted tent allows a correct exposure for both light sources (1/2, f4). The light in the tent is a warm orange and a dramatic silhouette compensates for the loss of detail in the surrounding landscape. The tungsten film strip, at an exposure of 1/4, f4, is equally interesting, showing a bluer but more unnatural sky and more accurate rendering of colour inside the tent.

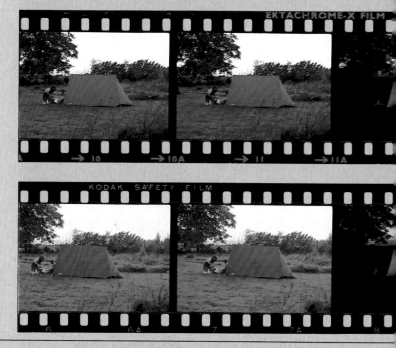

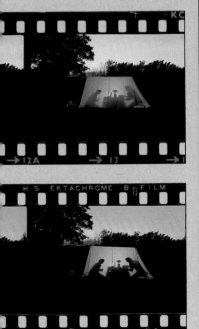

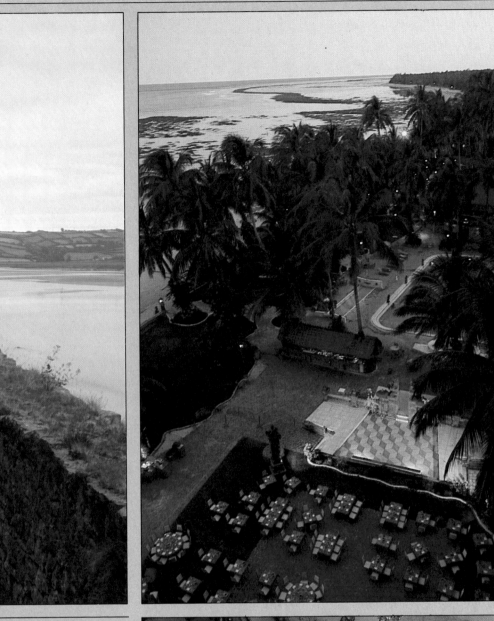

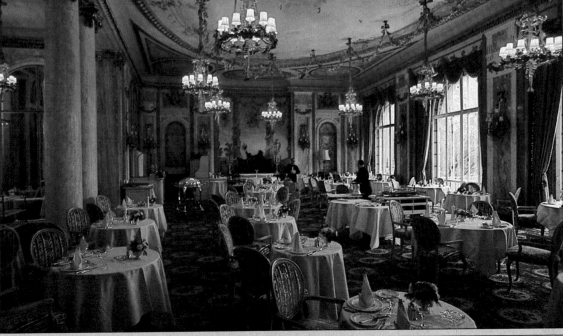

Tungsten film *has given a blue cast to Dylan Thomas's house at Laugharne, photographed at sunset. Balanced for the house lights, the film has produced purple tints that prevent the estuary setting looking prosaic. Rolleiflex, 80mm, Ektachrome 160, 1/30, f8.*

Either daylight or tungsten film *would have been effective in the shot from a hotel balcony. My choice of tungsten film has brought up the blues and reflections from table settings, catching the late sky light. Pentax, 28mm, tripod, Ektachrome 160, 1/8, f11.*

The richness and warmth *of the splendid dining-room in the Ritz Hotel, London, has been captured by using daylight film and carefully balancing the daylight and artificial lighting. I chose an overcast day so that illumination from the windows would not overpower the interior lights and destroy the intimate atmosphere. As the lighting balance seemed to be less suitable with the wall lights turned on, I used only the tungsten bulbs in the ceiling. Daylight film has warmed their light, strengthening the pinks in the table-cloths, pillars and murals. Colours become richer away from the right-hand side of the room, which is lit by the subdued daylight. Pentax, 28mm, Ektachrome 64, 1/2, f8.*

Mixing flash and daylight

Of all types of artificial light, blue flash bulbs or electronic flash can most effectively be used to simulate daylight or to support it without altering its character. Deployed with sensitivity, electronic flash is a form of portable daylight and can overcome a fundamental problem of photography in natural light—excessive contrast between highlights and shadows in the same scene. An exposure difference of two f-stops between highlights and areas of semi-shadow is about the widest range film will handle comfortably. Yet strong daylight falling into a room could indicate an exposure of f8, 1/500 in a sunlit area and f8, 1/30 in a shaded area only a step or two away—a sixteenfold fall-off in light intensity. A white or silverized reflector may be enough to lighten a small shaded area opposite a light source. But if this is not practicable, flash becomes essential to allow an exposure balanced to record detail in both highlights and shadows.

What is important to remember, however, is that the very high speed of flash (up to 1/50,000) and its harshness can produce contrasty, over-sharp images unless it is used with judgement. The aim should be to reinforce the existing light to capture a scene rather than dramatically changing it by over-lighting and killing the atmosphere. The use of flash with daylight should enable the camera to match more closely the eye's capacity to handle sharp contrasts of light and shade. This is done by lowering the contrast ratio while increasing the total amount of light, allowing you to stop

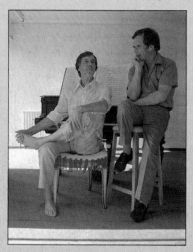

Composers Sir Michael Tippett and Antony Hopkins *were in a room divided by strong sunlight into areas of intense highlight and deep shadow. I placed them in the shade and reflected fill-in flash from a white umbrella to retain a sunny atmosphere while recording the important detail in their faces.*
Hasselblad, 60mm, Agfachrome 50s, 1/125, f11.

The diamond wedding *of this couple, both in their eighties, prompted me to try to duplicate the lighting of their original wedding photograph, taken in the north light of an English studio 60 years before. To the weak daylight I added studio window lighting with four flash tubes opposite a white reflector as shown in the diagram.*
Hasselblad, 80mm, Ektachrome 64, 1/30, f8.

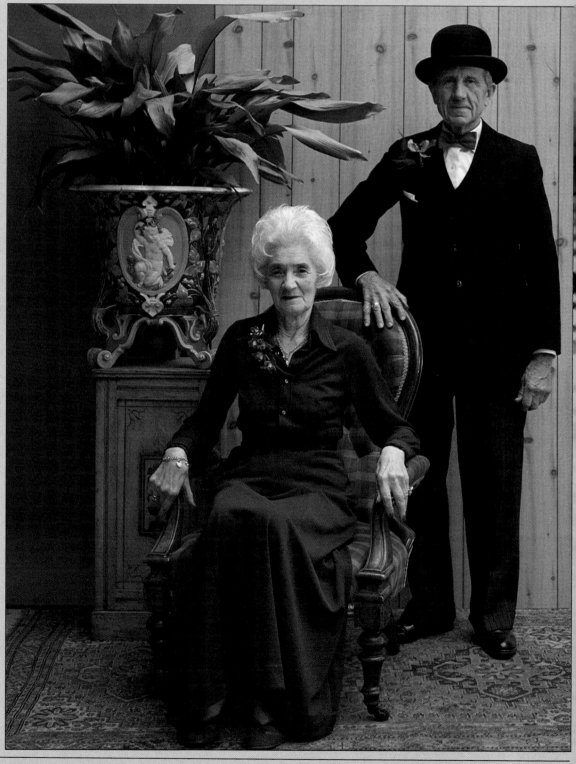

down perhaps to f16 or f22 for increased definition. And remember that highlights can be lit as well as shadows.

Electronic flash is cheaper, easier to use and more reliable than expendable flash bulbs. Compared with tungsten, it also uses little electricity and produces little heat. But when mixed with daylight, careful calculation of exposure is needed, especially when lighting large areas. A large number of flash units (I have used up to 36) can be effectively synchronized through photo-electric cells to fire simultaneously during a single exposure. In planning lighting, a large area is simply split up into smaller segments. A flash meter is used to calculate the exposure for the highlight in the first segment, aperture setting depending on the output of the unit, its distance from the subject and whether or not it is diffused, bounced or reflected. Then the illumination for the next segment is matched to the first, with the units being placed a little farther back to allow for some spill-over of light.

The final effect should be of one light source with shadows falling at the same angle. To soften the effect, or to avoid cluttering the scene, light can be redirected by means of umbrellas or white card reflectors, or bounced from a convenient wall or ceiling (provided it does not give a colour cast). Exposure for the areas in the scene lit by daylight can usually be adjusted by selecting the appropriate shutter speed after the aperture has been calculated for the flash.

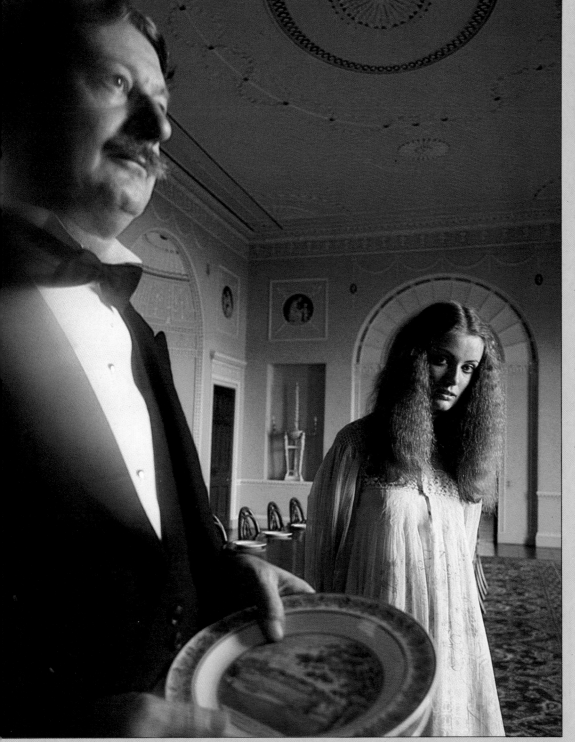

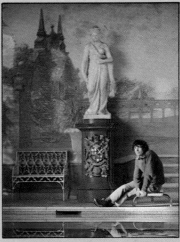

Subdued light *filtering through French doors provided the only natural light available for a pool-side shot of author Tom Chitty. The day was overcast and the effect flat, so for better modelling and a sunny atmosphere I fired an electronic flash through green and white glass in doors to the left.* Hasselblad, 80mm, Ektachrome 64, 1/125, f8.

The butler and the girl *provided an interesting contrast in imposing surroundings, but the room was too dark and unevenly lit. Electronic flashes boosted the lighting behind the man, on both faces and at the end of the room, allowing the rest of the scene to be relatively darkened. To soften the butler's shirt, I used a smear of gelatin.* Rolleiflex, 50mm, Ektachrome 64, 1/30, f8.

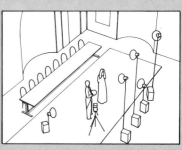

Mixing flash and daylight

Posing with a trumpet *against an evening sky, the girl made a striking silhouette. But when shot with flash at the same exposure, the scene was recorded more as the eye would see it. With flash providing the correct exposure for the girl, I could have lightened or darkened the sky by varying the shutter speed.*
Pentax, 100mm, Ektachrome 64, 1/30, f8.

In the pictures of the Indian hotel waiter, *flash was needed to balance the light inside the room with that outside. The first shot, at an exposure of 1/250, f8, showed the gateway to Bombay in the background but did not reveal the food, although it just managed to show the tray of drinks. In order to show the room itself an aperture of f11 was needed for an electronic flash bounced off the ceiling. Accordingly, I altered the speed for the outside view to 1/125, and this enabled me to achieve a successfully balanced result.*
Nikkormat, 35mm, Agfachrome 50s.

An oxy-acetylene welder *in a sculptor's workshop provided me with a lighting challenge, for the intense light given by the welding torch threw everything surrounding it into heavy shadow unrelieved by the presence of weak daylight. I used electronic flash as a fill-in, but did not want to overwhelm the scene or freeze the shower of sparks. An exposure measured from the torch gave a highlight reading of f16, while the reading from daylight on the man was f2.8. After calculating an aperture of f8 for flash I allowed two extra stops for the daylight and torch and shot at 1/15 to record the spark trails. The image has been effectively softened by slight movement.*
Hasselblad, 150mm, Ektachrome 64, 1/15, f16.

The pensive expression of the girl, *backlit by red evening light, was so appealing that I did not want to spoil the mood by asking her to face the light. The exposure reading on her face was 1/8 at f2.8, but I had slow film and no tripod. A portable flash diffused by two layers of white handkerchief gave me the necessary extra fill-in light with a wide aperture.*
Pentax, 50mm, Ektachrome 64, 1/30, f4.

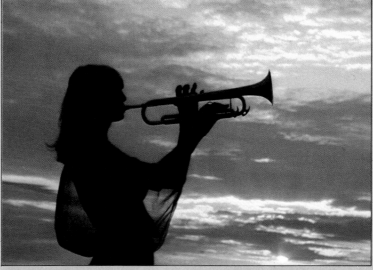

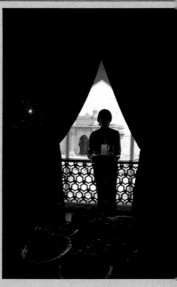

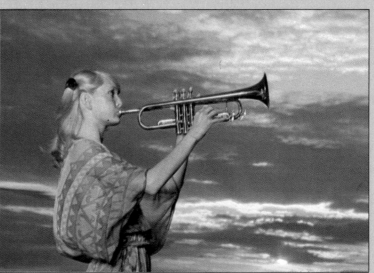

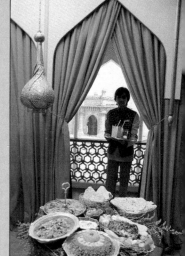

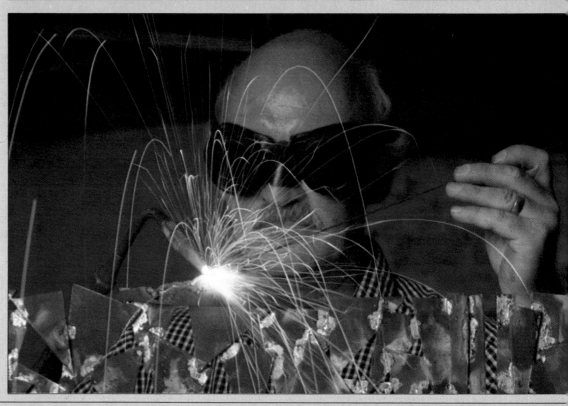

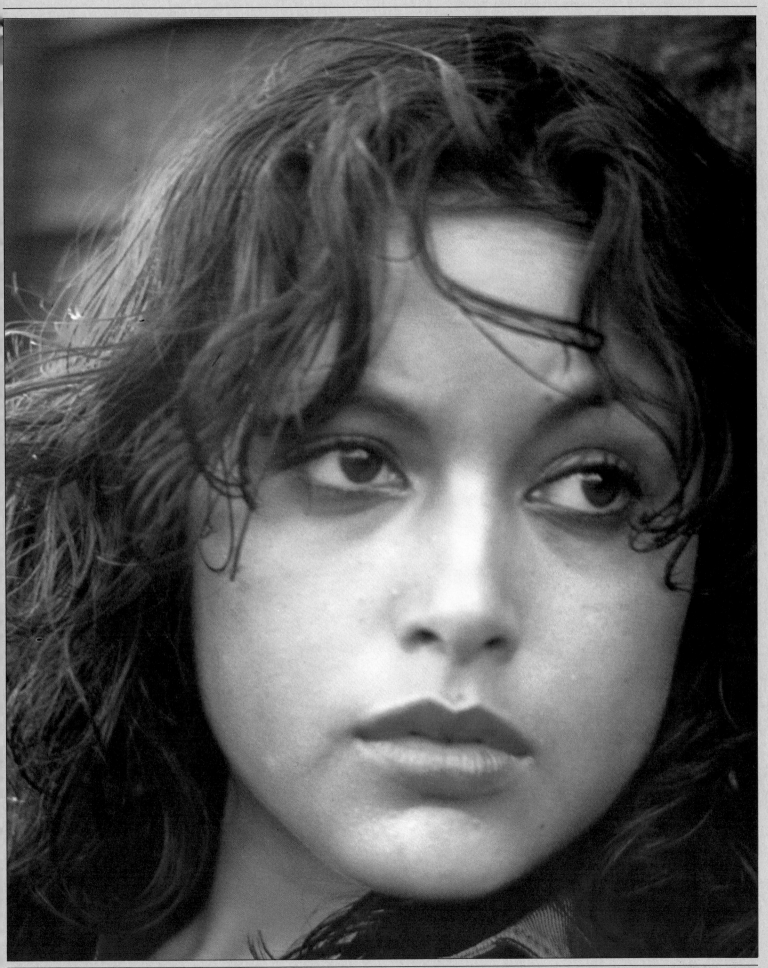

Mixing daylight and tungsten with flash

A mixture of daylight and tungsten light is one of the most common forms of lighting encountered in indoor photography, especially in winter, when daylight alone is usually too weak to adequately light even a small room or office. With the room lights switched on our eyes, being amazingly sensitive receptors, can perform exacting tasks. In photographic terms, however, the intensity of light may be too low to record detail properly, and the mixture of light sources will also produce a colour cast unless either daylight or tungsten light is predominant.

Light intensity can be increased by adding flash to the mixture. If electronic flash or blue flash bulbs are used, then balanced colour can be achieved by using daylight film, as this supplementary lighting will strengthen the daylight element in the scene. If, on the other hand, clear flash bulbs, balanced to the same colour temperature as tungsten light, are used, then tungsten light film is appropriate. It must be remembered, however, that although colours will reproduce well, the atmosphere of the room may be completely changed. To preserve a natural effect when lighting a scene with daylight flash, try to position your unit near a source of natural illumination, such as a window. In pictures relying on flash alone, the output of the flash and its distance from the subject will determine the aperture, and movement will be frozen unless several flashes are made. But with a mixture of light, the right exposure will record movement. For the shot below, taken with a Hasselblad, 150mm, at f16, the boy has been frozen by flash, but I then continued the exposure for one second with a tungsten light to show his moving hand. Notice the difference in the colour of his hand as it is recorded on daylight film, first by flash and then by tungsten light which has reddened it.

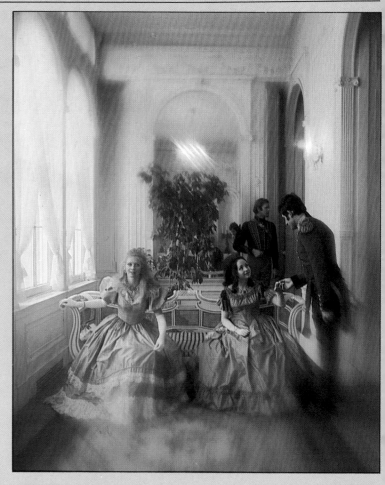

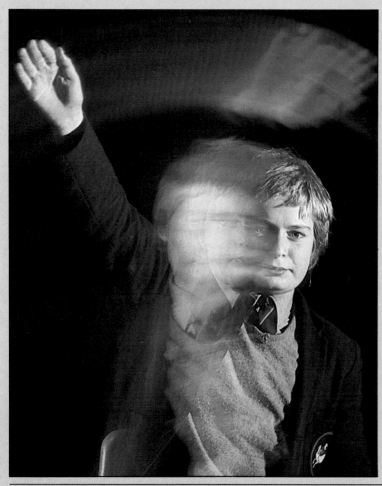

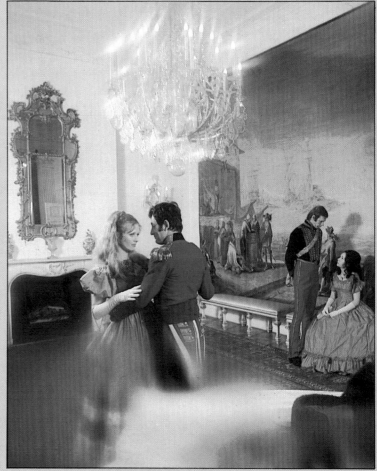

The Malayan bridal couple *were photographed in a mixture of weak daylight reinforced by electronic flash and tungsten light from the chandelier and wall lights. I positioned the flash mid-way between the camera and subjects at a 45° angle and used daylight film. The chandelier lights have given a strong green cast with this type of film, which has helped to harmonize the white background with the greens and golds of the couple's bridal costumes.* Pentax, 35mm, Ektachrome 64, 1/8, f8.

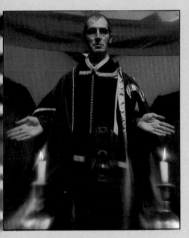

A combination *of existing room lights, candles and clear flash bulbs bounced off the white ceiling have all come together (above) to bring out the rich golds of the "priest's" vestments. I had to strike the right balance of illumination so as to give the impression of the room being lit by candle light and also to show the background without distracting areas of deep shadow.* Hasselblad, 60mm, Ektachrome 160, soft-focus filter, 1/4, f16.

The rich, warm colours *of the picture (left) taken in the Austrian Embassy, London, are the result of mixing four clear flash bulbs with existing light from the chandelier and wall lights. To soften the image, I breathed on my Hasselblad lens and shot at 1/15, f16. The picture above it was taken in the conservatory, and to support the existing daylight I used two electronic flashes outside the window and floodlights inside, bounced off the ceiling to strengthen the wall lights. For a natural effect I switched to daylight film at 1/10, f22 and a soft-focus filter.*

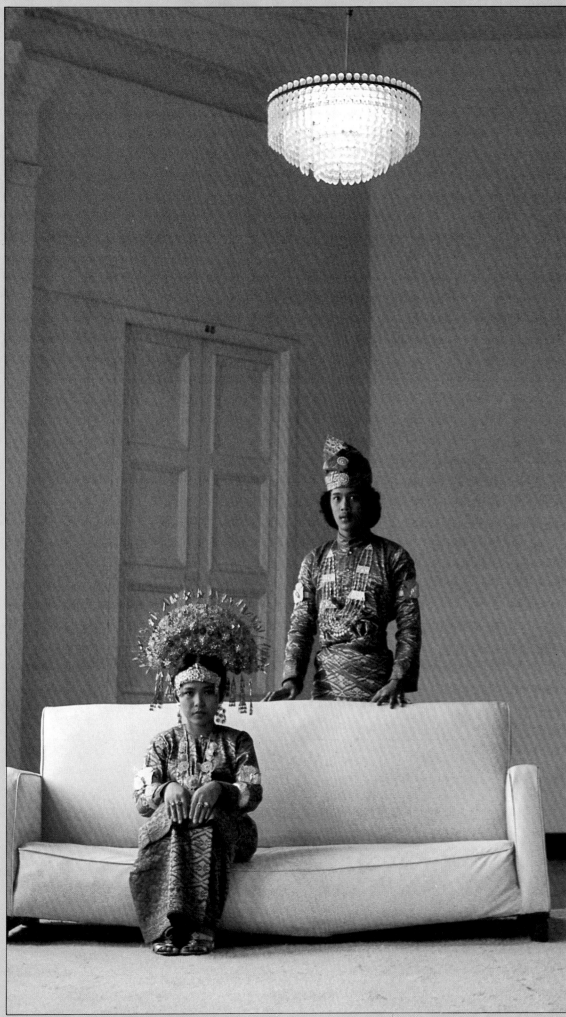

Tungsten and flash as complete sources

Flash is a sudden burst of light, tungsten, a continuous light at a lower colour temperature, and they create moods that are subtly different. The speed and bluer light of flash gives a harsher result unless it is diffused or reflected. It is often more convenient to use flash than tungsten. But if modelling is important, as in many still lifes or portraits, its effect is more difficult to determine, necessitating the use of Polaroid test shots or modelling lights. With tungsten, shadows and highlights can be seen before you shoot.

The picture below of Allen Jones in his studio, surrounded by his work, shows how flash can be used to simulate daylight. The natural light was so weak that I replaced it with four flashes, one at a 45° angle, two bounced off the white walls and one bounced off the ceiling, giving perfect, even illumination. I used a 60mm Hasselblad lens at an exposure of 1/125, f16.

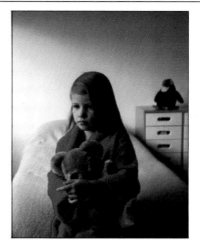

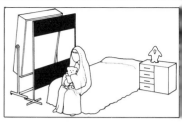

The illusion of a shaft of soft daylight *in a child's bedroom was created in a studio with a bank of 20 500-watt bulbs diffused with opal glass and masked (see diagram).* Hasselblad, 80mm, Ektachrome 160, 1/30, f8.

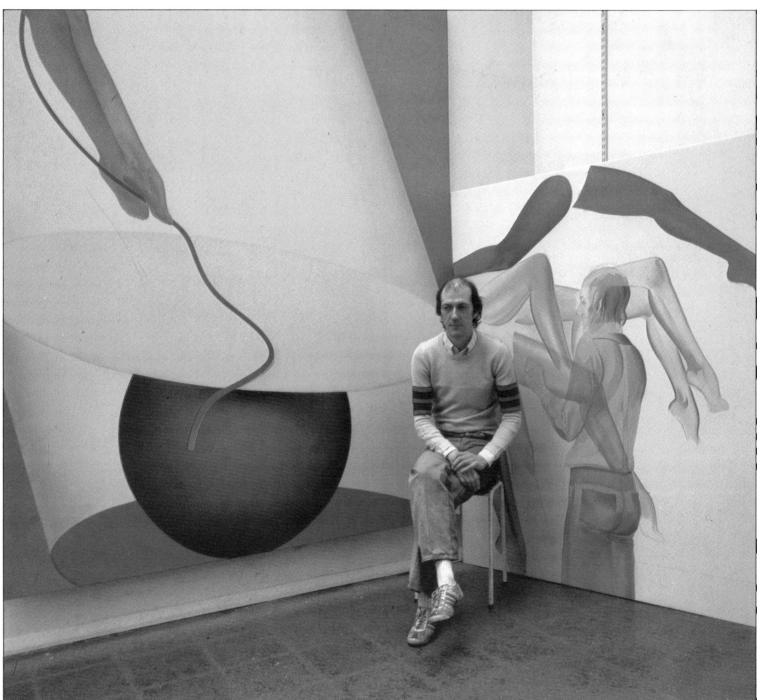

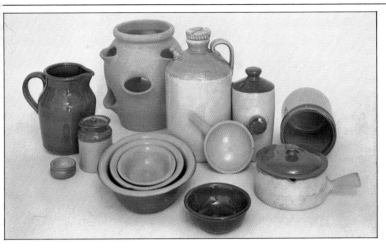

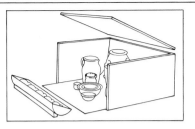

Lighting *for this still life of earthenware was provided by four 500-watt bulbs, positioned as shown in the diagram. For the mellow background, I put a red Wratten filter over the lens.* MPP 5 × 4 in, Ektachrome 160, 1/10, f11.

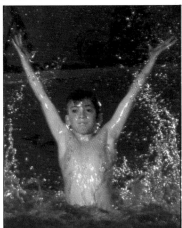

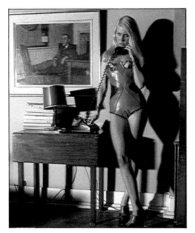

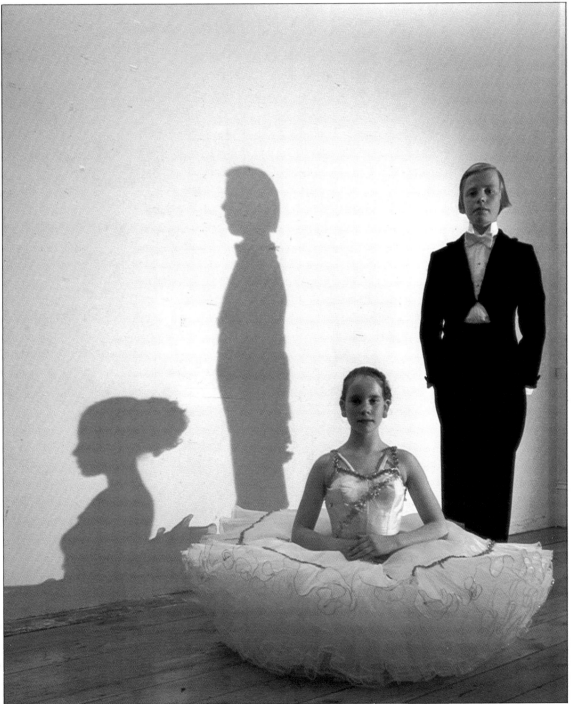

A single portable flash *(top) at short range has produced a bizarre picture of a boy jumping in a darkened pool. Although glistening liquid seems to flow on his body, the speed of the flash has arrested the spray in jewel-like globules. Many more flashes would have been necessary to light the whole pool. This kind of single flash is a good way of eliminating an unwanted background.* Pentax, 100mm, Ektachrome 200, f4.

The girl, *wearing an Allen Jones outfit, was lit by one electronic flash angled to give a hard effect suiting the leather costume. The shadow was used to exaggerate her figure.* Hasselblad, 80mm, Ektachrome 64, f11.

The shadows on the wall *(left) complement the frontal portrait of two youthful old-time dancers and emphasize the shape, grace and formality of their pose. One main photoflood provided the sidelight and the shadows, which I softened by bouncing another photoflood off the ceiling.* Pentax, 35mm, Ektachrome 160, 1/15, f8.

Fluorescent, mercury vapour and mixed light sources

Every type of colour film, either negative or transparency, is designed to be used with a particular light source in mind. If the film you choose matches the principal source of illumination in the scene, then the resultant colour balance will closely resemble the colours as you originally saw them at the time of shooting.

Problems start to arise when the light source available is not constant, has peaks of intensity or does not contain the full range of wavelengths in the visible spectrum. Fluorescent tube lighting and mercury vapour lighting fit into this classification. For fluorescent tube lighting, at least, there are colour correction filters available, but I have found them useful only under certain conditions, when the lighting is old, for instance. Modern daylight tubes can produce well-balanced results.

What all the pictures here show is that although the film and light sources were mismatched, and the colours represented are not "true", they are nevertheless interesting and evocative colour compositions in themselves. As photography is a form of abstraction anyway, this further abstraction matters little if used selectively and with appropriate subjects.

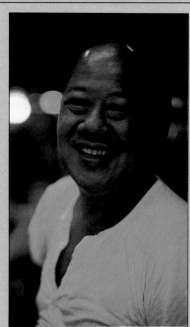

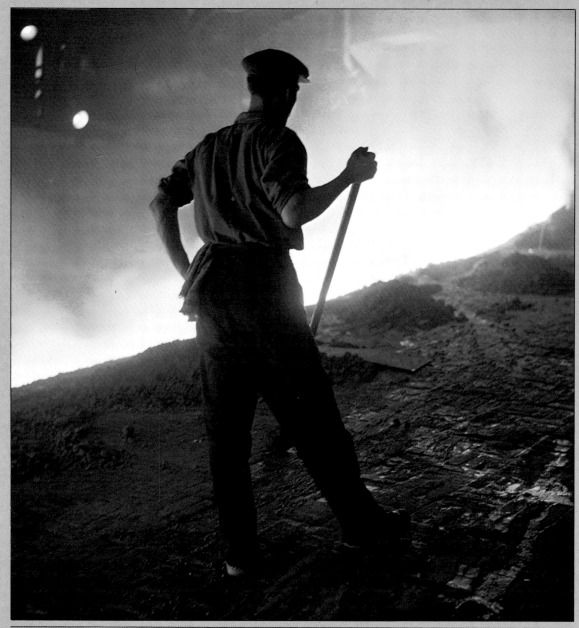

Mercury vapour lights *give a strong blue cast (left) to the skin and shirt of the proprietor of Fatty's Restaurant in Singapore. Although his lips appear an odd hue, the colours throughout the scene are quite acceptable and further interest is provided by the orange tones cast by the tungsten lights hanging on the stalls of the street market in the background. This combination of colours is repeated in the blue and yellow highlights alternating on his bald head.* Pentax, 50mm, Ektachrome 200, 1/30, f2.

The green carpet *(right) covering a vast hotel room was lit by daylight fluorescent tubes and was of such strong colour that I found it made little difference whether or not I used a fluorescent light correction filter. Some types of fluorescent lights do need filters, however, so it is best to experiment with and without.* Pentax, 28mm, Ektachrome 64, 1/15, f4.

The shot of telephone booths *(far right) in Montreal combines daylight fluorescent tube lighting with ordinary tungsten lighting in the booths. The colour contrast gives the impression that the girl is some distance from the booth. I used daylight film because it happened to be in the camera, but some colour cast would have appeared with either type of film.* Leicaflex, 35mm, Ektachrome 64, 1/30, f2.8.

The steelworker *(left) is lit mainly by the rich gold and red glow of the furnace he has tapped. Being high in infra-red, the light gives a strong colour cast entirely appropriate to the scene. Had I chosen to use flash the result would have been less dramatic and atmospheric.* Rolleiflex, 80mm, high-speed artificial light film, 1/30, f4.

The dusk shot *(right) of a whisky distillery shows how a combination of different coloured lights can enliven a scene. Adding to fading daylight, mercury vapour lamps glow green and ordinary tungsten bulbs cast a yellow light.* Pentax, 35mm, Ektachrome 64, 1 sec., f11.

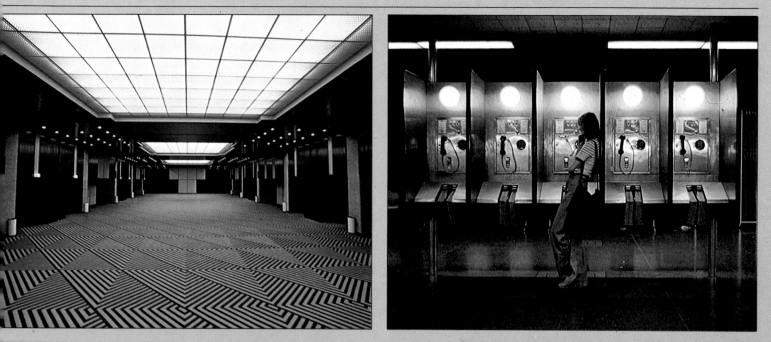

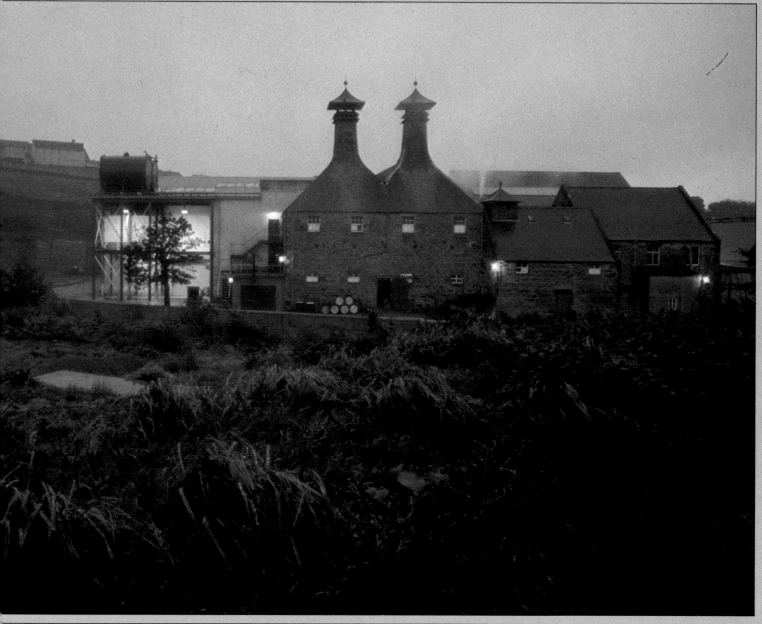

Oil lamps, torchlight and matches

As Georges de la Tour and other seventeenth-century painters understood, some of the most dramatic effects of light and shade are created by pictures in which the only source of illumination is a candle or dim lamp held by a figure half-obscured by darkness. With today's fast lenses and sensitive emulsions effective and evocative photographs can easily be taken with low-level sources of artificial light, such as lamps, torches or even by the dim light of a single match, providing the problem of finding an exposure balance can be overcome. For this type of photography a CdS meter is preferable to the less-sensitive and slower-reacting selenium meter. As in night photography, it is best to concentrate the restricted light source on the main point of interest in the picture and try to ensure that the area immediately surrounding it is no more than one f stop darker. This is normally only possible in the early evening, when the ebbing sun still provides enough ambient light to fill in a little detail in the shadowy areas around the light source. Exposure will depend on the nearness of the light to the subject and the amount of light being reflected back.

The graduation ceremony *at the University of St Andrews, Scotland, is traditionally followed by an evening parade around the harbour. The dramatic red robes of the graduates are emphasized (right) by the use of film balanced for daylight, although the main illumination is from the oil flares, their light diffused to a pale red by a breeze. The lighting suggests the re-enactment of some ancient ritual centring upon the occupants of the boat and watched by acolytes with raised flares. The brilliant evening sky and the lights of the distant university combine to form a spectacular backdrop.*
Hasselblad, 80mm, Ektachrome 64, 1/2, f8.

A single match *was the only source of illumination for the picture below, which says much about the versatility of modern lenses and films. Although artificial light film was used, the low colour temperature of the match has brought out warm tones in the girl's face. An easier light to work with, but one that produces a similar effect, is a candle. The only problem, apart from the length of exposures, is the excessive contrast caused by a localized area of relatively bright light.*
Pentax, 35mm, Ektachrome 160, 1/15, f4.

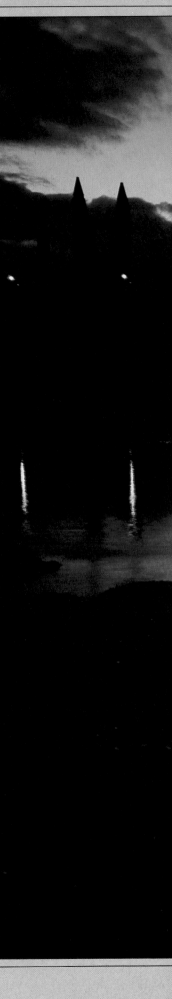

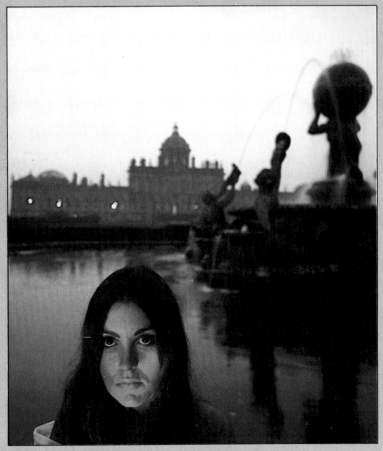

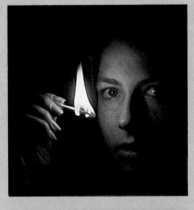

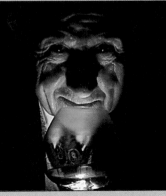

Castle Howard, *the imposing building behind the girl, would have overwhelmed the picture unless a careful lighting balance had been struck. I waited until the evening light had toned down the colours to a soft neutral grey and then lit her face with a hand torch. Daylight film has caused a slight warming of skin tone, highlighting her golden skin and dark brown eyes, without an unnatural effect.*
Hasselblad, 80mm, Ektachrome 64, 1sec., f5.6.

Low-angled lighting *(right) has created a melodramatic, almost theatrical, effect. Lighting from below is unusual and has to be used with discretion, for a less-obviously fatherly and good-natured face may look sinister. I set up this shot by darkening the room and shining a small but powerful torch up through the brandy glass. Tungsten light film was used to obtain the correct colour balance for the clothing.*
Pentax, 100mm, Ektachrome 160, 1/15, f4.

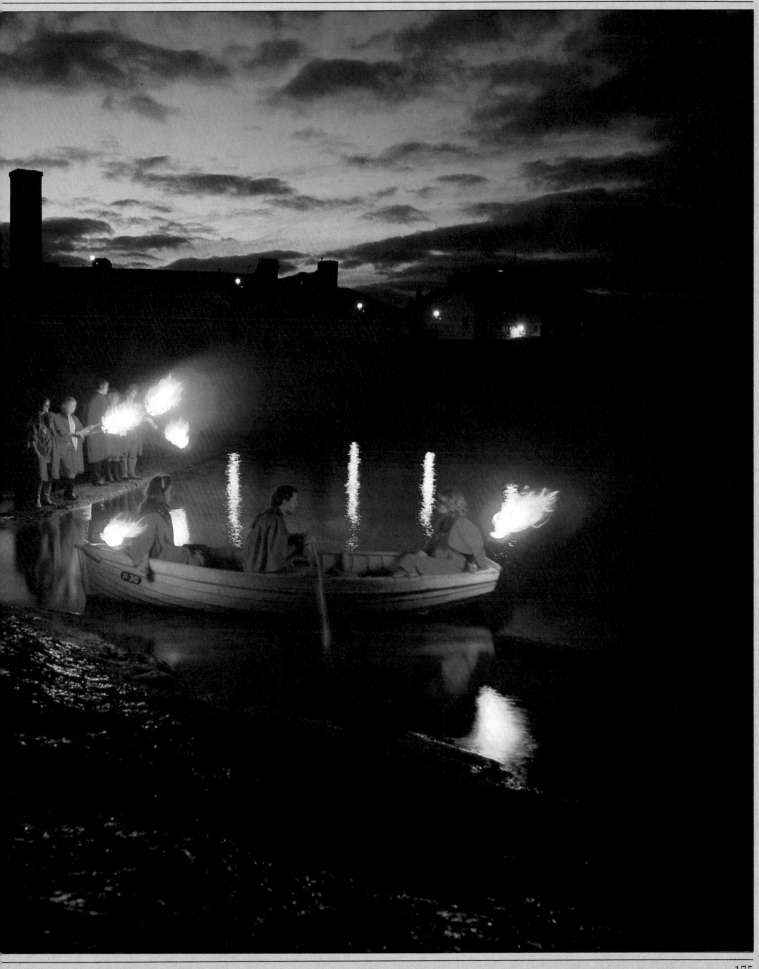

Alternative lighting

Photographs taken in lighting designed to entertain rather than to illuminate will often produce theatrical colours and dramatic contrasts but it is usually a mistake to try and overcome this by using flash. You may record more detail in this way, but you are likely to overwhelm coloured lighting effects that were carefully created and destroy the whole atmosphere of the occasion. In theatres or nightclubs, at concerts or fireworks displays, it is better to make use of the existing lighting if possible. There will often be a high point during the display when the lighting is strong enough to give a good result. Except in stroboscopic lighting, balanced to daylight, you will need high-speed artificial light film. Fast lenses are useful and you should not worry about long exposures producing movement. If the scene is full of activity —as it usually is at theatrical events—slight blur will probably help to convey the atmosphere. Long exposures can be particularly effective in photographing fireworks, capturing several explosions in one frame.

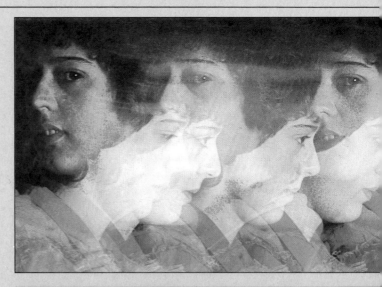

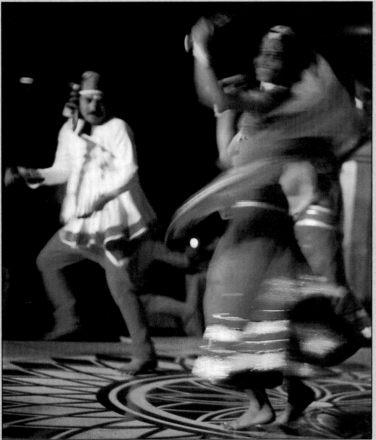

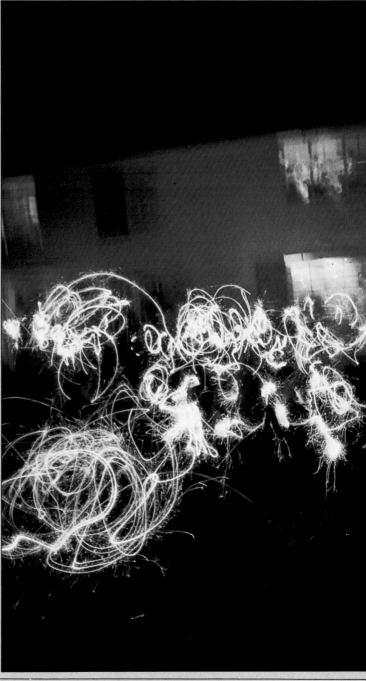

The whirling rhythm *of a dance company in Bombay has been captured here by a lengthy hand-held exposure in the low-level illumination of stage lighting. Flash would have frozen the dancers and produced a black background. Instead, the restaurant setting can be glimpsed behind the dancers and their vitality is emphasized by blur. The shot was timed for a peak moment as the woman spun her body around her almost motionless feet.*
Pentax, 50mm, Ektachrome 160, 1/15, f1.2.

Fireworks displays, *showing cascades of brilliant coloured lights, can make marvellous pictures, especially if you concentrate on a small area rather than the whole scene. Lengthy hand-held exposures can be made as definition is not so important, and double or triple exposures will allow you to capture multiple explosions. Apart from the house lights, these fiery patterns were made simply by a dozen sparklers.*
Pentax, 50mm, Ektachrome 160, 1/4, f2, hand held.

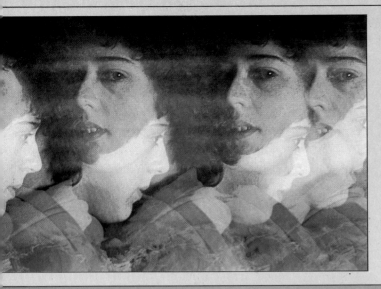

Stroboscopic lights *can give intriguing multiple images. A dark background is usually preferable, and to start with, the flashes should be fairly well spaced and the action simple. To demonstrate the effect of stroboscopic light in a studio, I positioned four clear flash units behind the camera and to one side, synchronized at 10 flashes a second. During a two-second exposure the girl walked briskly across the line of the camera, spun and rushed back again with her head bent. The 20 flashes produced 15 separate images, the other five firing while she was* turning round. The mauve tints that appear in the girl's blue dress are ghost images of her skin. Stroboscopic pictures like this can be used to analyse motion—an early preoccupation of photographers before the invention of moving pictures. Complicated set-ups were once needed but today stroboscopic lamps are available that have variable controls and will fire up to 20 flashes a second. These can be combined to give any number of flashes during an exposure, with flash frequency timed to suit the recorded movement.
Pentax, 50mm, Ektachrome 64, 2 sec., f8.

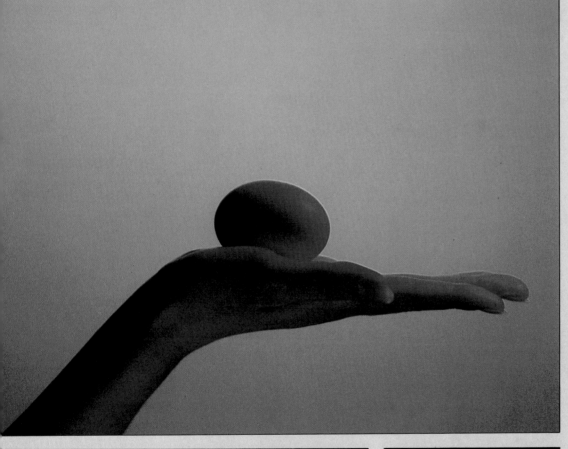

Coloured lights *are often used for theatrical effect to highlight particular areas of a scene. The simple picture of an egg lying in the palm of a girl's hand was lit with a red spotlight in the ceiling and a blue light aimed at the white screen that forms the background. The mixture of lights produced a white rim around the egg and made the nails appear translucent.*
Pentax, 100mm macro, Ektachrome 160, 1/30, f4.

A shower of sparks *from an oxy-acetylene welder shows how sensitive colour film is to the differing temperatures of light. The highlight from the welder is whiter than the daylight entering the studio, which has given a greenish cast to the background. But as the sparks lose heat they become yellower and this is accentuated by my use of daylight film. The man at work here is the sculptor Philip King.*
Pentax, 50mm, Ektachrome 64, 1/30, f8.

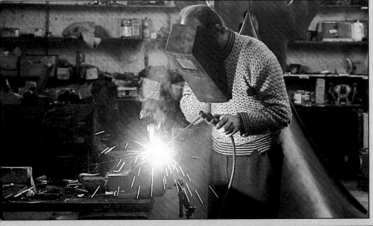

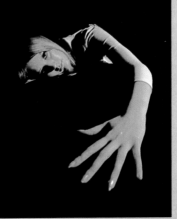

Infra-red film, *combined with coloured filters, produces a bizarre effect and completely changes the colours of the subject. The girl with the waxen-looking skin is leaning on a black tablecloth and wearing a yellow dress, but an overall greenish-blue cast has been created by using infra-red film with two electronic flashes fired separately, the second with a red filter placed over the light.*

Leicaflex, 21mm, infra-red Ektachrome, red filter, 1/60, f16.

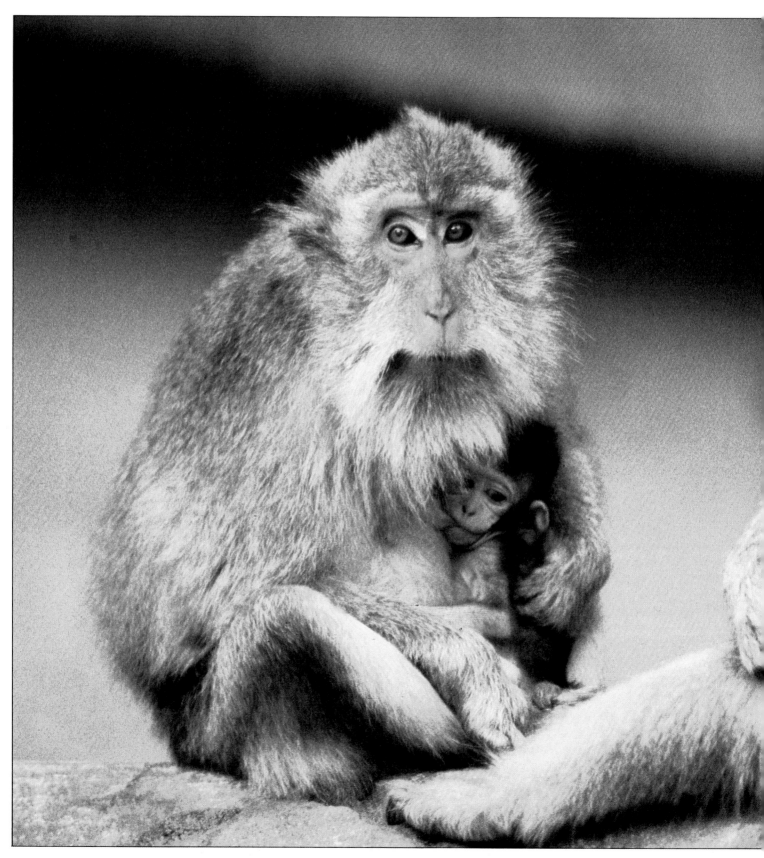

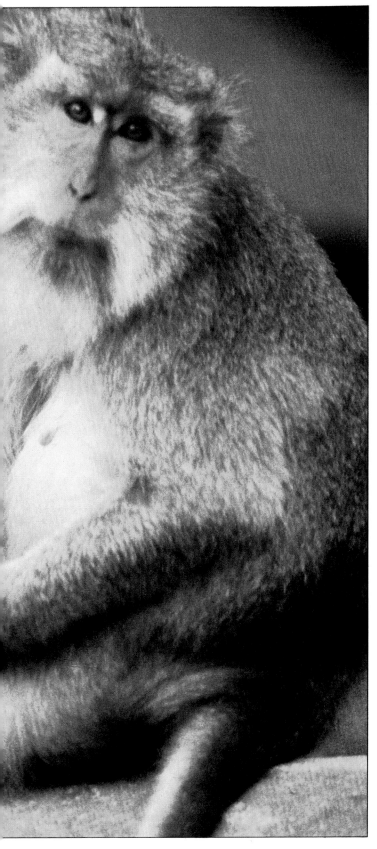

Subject lighting

When lighting is matched to subject, *the camera can be as sensitive as the brush of a painter. Here, in the diffused light of an overcast afternoon, it has blended together the gentle pinks and greys of the monkeys' fur and skins with the colour of terracotta tiles on the roof of an old Buddhist temple. Though focus is sharp on the baby monkey and its mother, the background is deliberately blurred, softening detail and helping to create an overall colour harmony.* Pentax, 250 mm, Ektachrome 64, 1/250, f4.

Portraits

Portraiture is one of the most enjoyable and rewarding areas of photography, and the simplest form of lighting is often the best. One lamp can produce a wide variety of effects. Used straight-on, it produces little form or modelling and flattens facial structure, but if it is angled at 45°, form and texture can be revealed. To reduce strong contrasts, a reflecting screen on the opposite side of the subject is preferable to another direct light, which can give cross-shadow. A second lamp, weaker than the main light source, can emphasize particular areas, such as the back of the head and the sitter's hands.

A successful portrait captures a person's essential character or style, which may be revealed in the face alone or indicated by pose, clothing and setting. The subject should always feel at ease, and you will need to learn to establish a rapport quickly with many different types of personalities. The background should support the subject, not distract attention. If the sitter is wearing elaborate clothes, choose a neutral backdrop; if the clothing is subdued, a contrasting background with colour and impact might be more effective. Avoid low camera angles, which accentuate the size of the nose and make the forehead shallow. Shooting downwards on to the face can result in foreshortening. If you want to minimize freckles or wrinkles, a soft-focus filter will help. When depth of field is tight, focus on the eye nearest the camera.

You should select a lens that will enable you to fill the frame with the subject without coming too close, otherwise distortion will occur. For head and shoulder shots using a 35 mm camera, a 90–135 mm lens is best, but a 150 mm lens is preferable for a $2\frac{1}{4} \times 2\frac{1}{4}$ in (6 × 6 cm) camera.

The portrait of E. M. Forster *was taken in his rooms at Trinity College, Cambridge, shortly before his death in 1970. He was a big man and because of age had to be seated, but I was able to show his size by placing him in the immediate foreground and cropping at the waist. Screening off some of the daylight ensured that the background was subdued, and cropping close to his head gave tension to the picture. I used his clasped hands to counterbalance his gaze out of the window. Chatting to him helped him to relax and allowed his expression to reveal his gentleness. The books supply the narrative element that can often be provided in portraiture by choice of background.*
Leicaflex, 50 mm, Ektachrome 200, 1/15, f5.6.

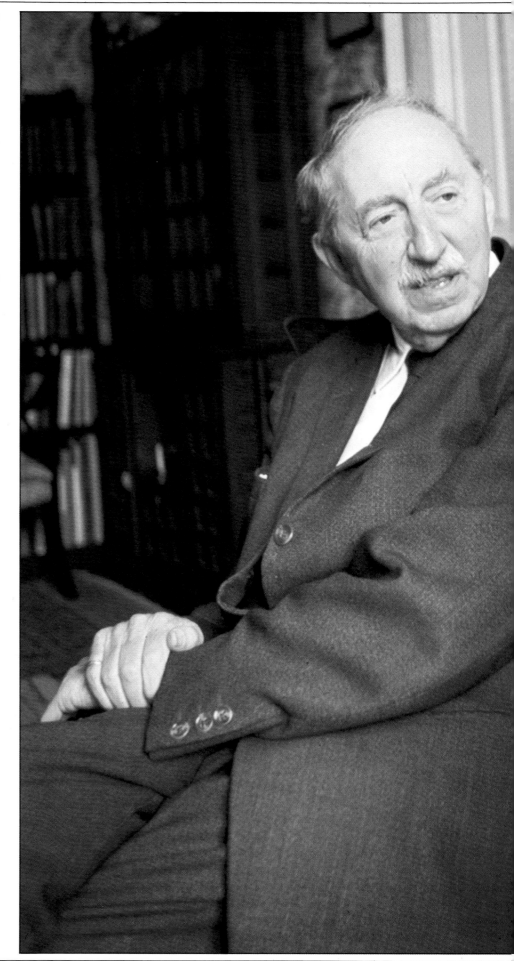

Agatha Christie *on her 70th birthday showed a sparkling and mischievous animation, caught by my use of high-speed electronic flash. I placed one unit to her right and bounced another off the ceiling (as shown in the diagram) to lighten the shadow areas. The light reveals much detail, but was not unkind and brought out the warmth and softness of her skin. I used a long cable release and chatted to her, waiting for this expression.* Hasselblad, 150mm, Ektachrome 64, f11.

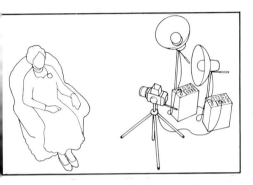

The simplicity and colour *of Cecil Beaton's clothes contrast strongly with the elaborate bust he leans against. Beaton's expression is enquiring, his pose nonchalant, suggesting the relaxed attitude of a man who is himself an outstanding photographer and perhaps more at ease with other photographers and their equipment than a normal sitter might be. Bright light from a window provided the only form of lighting, the rich burgundy background picking up the check in his suit.* Minolta, 35mm, Ektachrome 64, 1/30, f5.6.

For the portrait of Dr Michael Ramsey, *Archbishop of Canterbury from 1961 to 1974, I decided to break one of the rules: I shot from a low angle to emphasize both his commanding presence and moral authority, and so that his richly coloured vestments would show up well against a dark background. Daylight from the tall windows of Lambeth Palace provided the only source of light for this picture.* Hasselblad, 60mm, Ektachrome 200, 1/15, f8.

The King of Tonga, *shown in front of his palace, was given a sense of lightness and elevation, despite his considerable bulk, when daylight struck the steps in such a way that the straw-coloured mat seemed to float on either side of the black central strip. Symmetry can be useful for suggesting power in informal portraits such as this.* Hasselblad, 150mm, Ektachrome 64, 1/250, f8.

George Steiner, *an authority on language and literature, is placed behind a table with maps and looks directly at the camera to counterbalance the downward gazes of the women in the painting. He remains the focus of attention, his head showing up well in the area of white between two panels of black. To capture his alert look I bounced an electronic flash off the ceiling to eliminate background shadow and positioned another flash at a 45° angle to give modelling to his face.* Hasselblad, 150mm, Ektachrome 64, f16.

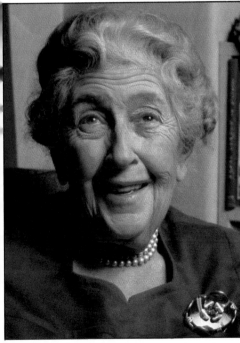

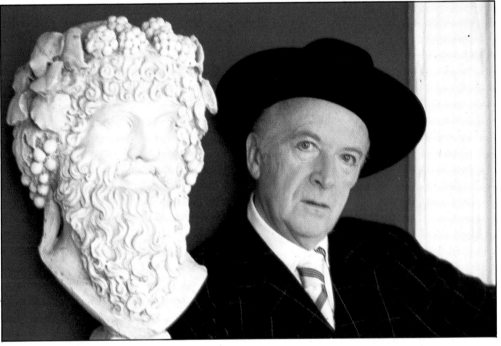

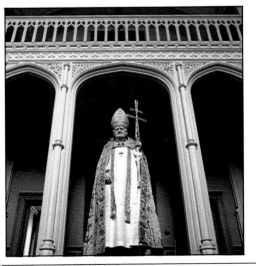

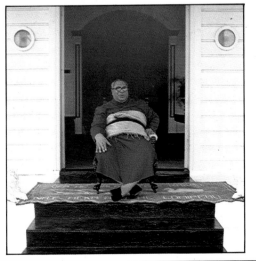

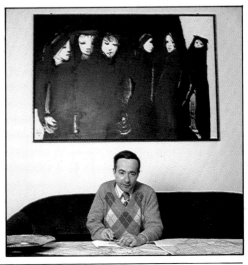

181

Portraits

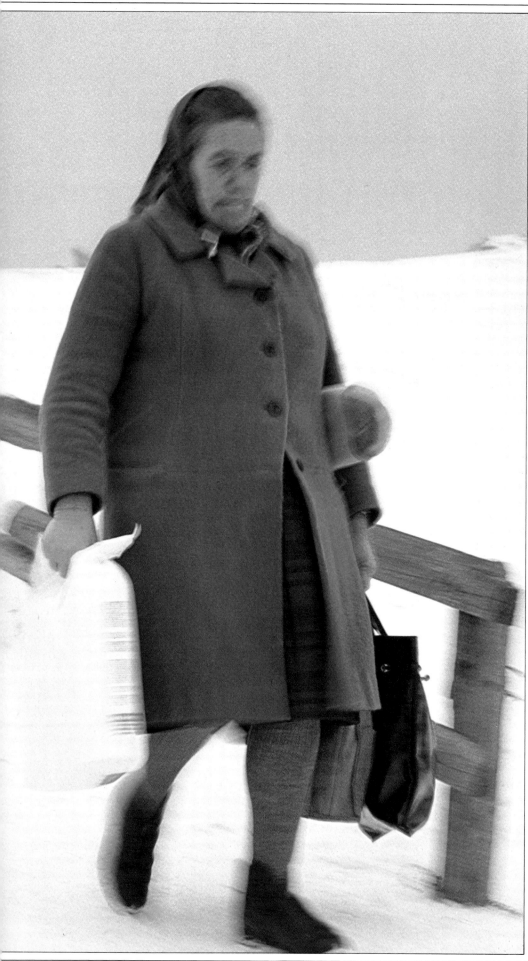

Heavily laden with shopping, *the Swiss woman (left) was intent on retaining her footing on a steep, icy path and gave me a completely candid shot at fairly close range. To convey a feeling of slight uncertainty, I shot at a deliberately slow speed and panned the camera down the line of the railings. The slow exposure in overcast light with a strong blue cast was perfect for her face and coat, the colour tones clearly describing the bulk of her figure, although at this speed the highlight on the snow is burnt out.*
Pentax, 50mm, Ektachrome 64, 1/15, f16.

The area of landscape *that forms a prominent element in the long-range picture of the painter Fred Dubery is included to suggest the subject of his work. Intended more as a study of the artist painting than as a record of his features, the shot exploits the flattened perspective of a long lens and the softness of morning light.*
Pentax, 200mm, Ektachrome 64, 1/250, f8.

The bluff, rugged face *of a Highland crofter in his heavy jersey and tweed cap was shot in overcast light using a normal lens. I focused on his eyes from a distance of only about 3ft (1m) and this has slightly exaggerated the squareness of his features, though without distorting them. The power of the portrait is emphasized by a shallow depth of field and the shadowless light brings out every seam of his weathered face.*
Pentax, 50mm, Ektachrome 64, 1/30, f2.

Duncan Grant, *the last great figure of the Bloomsbury set, whose stage designs had a powerful influence on theatre between the wars, was 91 when I took this picture of him leaning on the gate of his home in Sussex. In the late afternoon, the sun had gone behind the house, providing a soft side light well suited to the mood of seclusion I wanted to convey. Beneath the floppy straw hat, the artist's craggy features and keen eyes suggest the spirit of a man who has lived a full life and was still painting well into his 90s.*
Contax, 50mm, Ektachrome 64, 1/125, f8.

Ebbing light *at evening on a beach in Indonesia provided a sympathetic atmosphere for the portrait of the old fisherwoman, who is crowned by a piece of coral and the turquoise bowl she has been using to collect seafood and shells. She leans on her spiked stick as if it were a parasol, maintaining a considerable dignity in spite of her bare feet and ragged clothing.*
Pentax, 35mm, Ektachrome 64, 1/125, f11.

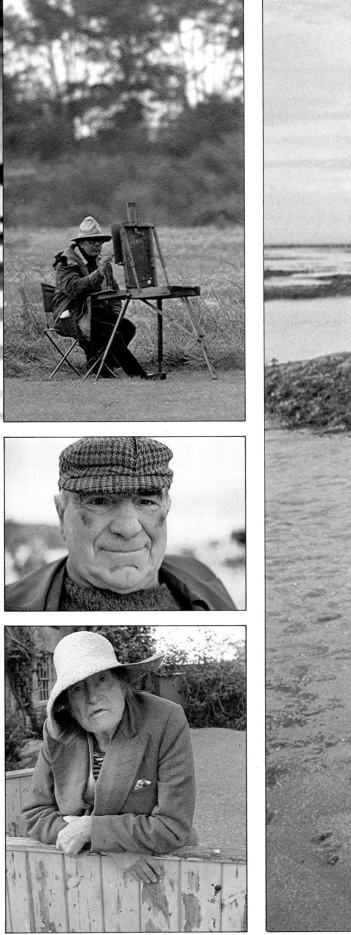

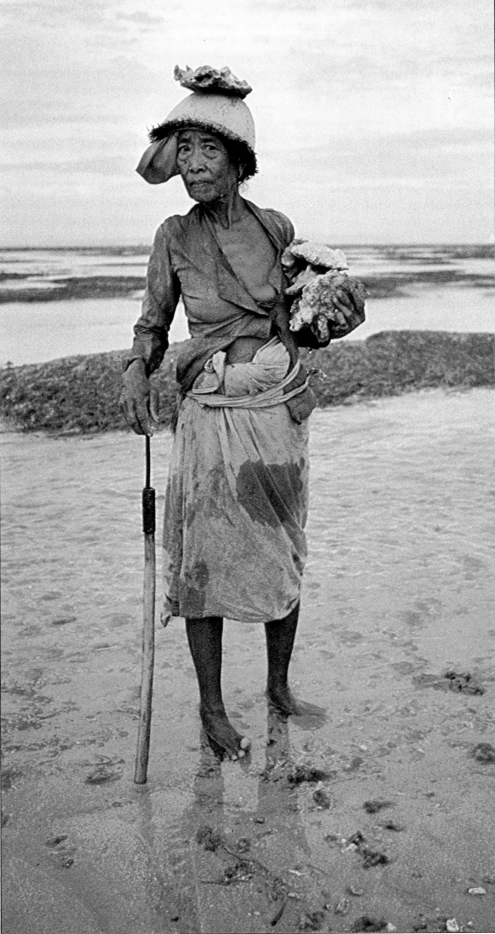

Portraits

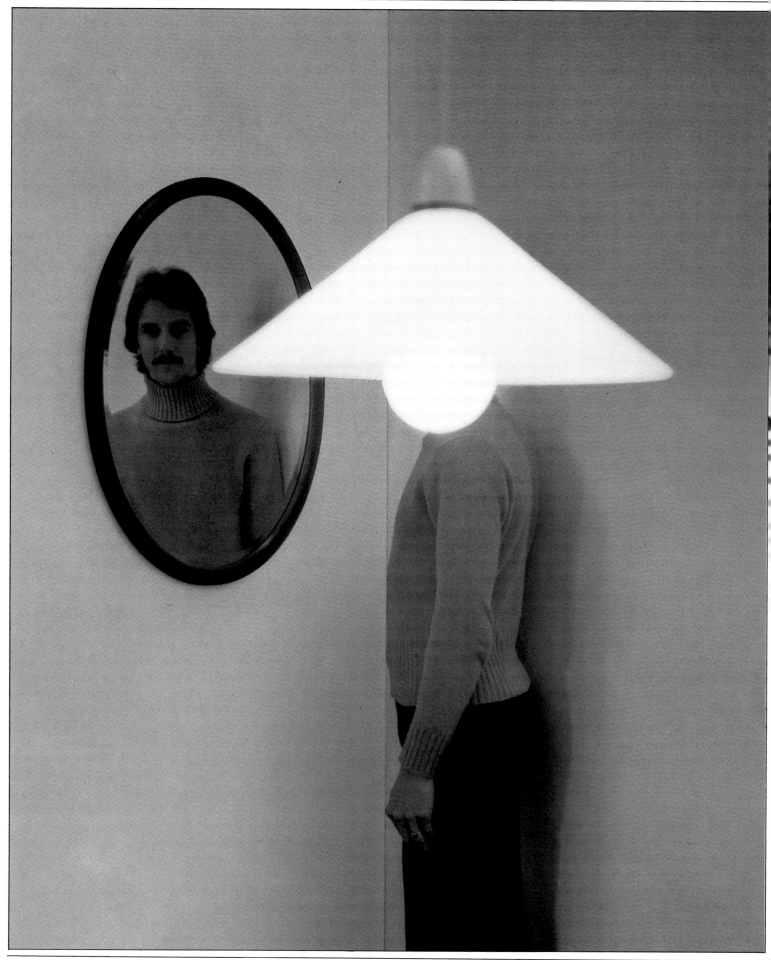

The mystery of human personality *is exploited by viewpoint and lighting (left) that hides the head of the subject but leads the eye to his reflected image— an intended irony in the portrait of the neurologist Colin Blakemore. Apart from the household bulb, daylight predominated and the film has warmed the colours.*
Hasselblad, 60 mm, Ektachrome 64, 1/30, f11.

A slender woman in a sari *holding a mirror before her face shows that a portrait can reveal character while hiding identity. Her dress and accessories, and the ornate mirror itself, all suggest someone meticulous about her appearance. I took the picture in diffused daylight across a hotel balcony in Singapore.*
Pentax, 100 mm, Ektachrome 200, 1/125, f11.

Photographed through the window *of a station waiting-room, the girl in the cowboy hat has a haunting softness. The lighter reflection on the right-hand side is from open country, while stronger colours on the left show up against the darker reflections of a building.*
Leicaflex, 80 mm, Ektachrome 64, 1/125, f8.

A photograph of W. B. Yeats *and the reflected image of his son, Senator Michael Yeats, form a double portrait that has some of the qualities of a still life. I placed the senator near a window in a position where he would be framed in the mirror yet be well modelled by the strong sunlight.*
Hasselblad, 150 mm, Ektachrome 200, 1/15, f8.

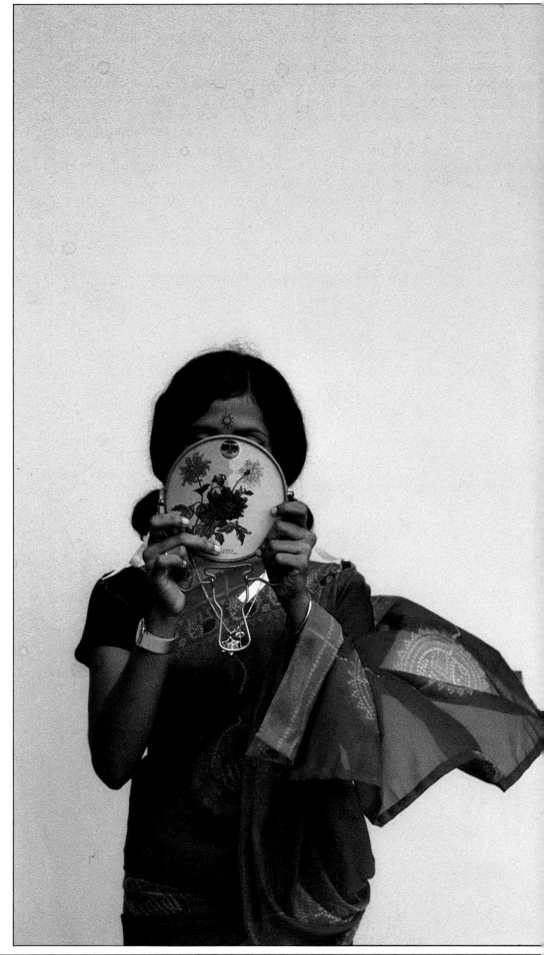

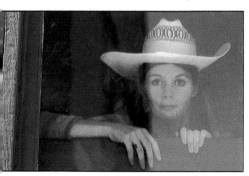

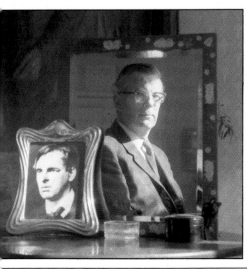

Groups

Balanced lighting is usually best in photographing groups, as each member will want to be identified clearly and strong shadows make this difficult. Overcast or indirect daylight is ideal. For indoor shots, flash units need to be positioned carefully and bounced or reflected. Lighting can be used to subdue clashing colours, often a problem. As an alternative, strong colours can be distributed evenly, as in the shot below of staff on a hotel balcony.

It is useful to work out positions and exposure before marshalling a group. Control is not always easy, as the group will tend to feel in command of the situation. You should give as few instructions as possible until ready for shooting. Then use a tripod and cable release to allow you to direct them with one hand and to talk freely without having to peer into the camera. Take a number of shots and you will usually find that the best one is somewhere in the middle of the series, when the group has begun to relax, but when you still have their attention.

Positions will often be determined by the hierarchy of the group. Be prepared to break the rules, though; use props if this is possible, exploit the terrain in outside shots to gain height, or position the group on a convenient stairway to avoid formal poses in which chairs or benches have to be used.

The picture of staff at Raffles Hotel, Singapore, is tied together by the strong pattern of the balcony, and diffused daylight shows them clearly against a dark background. I separated the two girls in blue and placed the brightest colour—pale green—at the focal point. To balance the strong contrasts of light and shade, I exposed at 1/125, f8, using a 28mm lens on my Pentax, with Ektachrome 64.

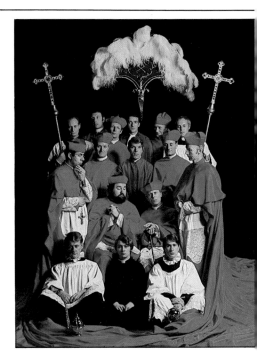

Actors at the Mermaid Theatre, London, *during a production of* Hadrian VII *are framed by their own ecclesiastical robes to give an effect of richness against gloom. The shot was intended for maximum front-of-house impact so I used dramatic flash lighting to give form to the faces and figures without obscuring any of the 16 players. Although the group is arranged symmetrically, changes of pose give an informal effect and allow the eye to move over the whole picture. I placed two electronic flashes behind the camera and two at the right for modelling.* Hasselblad, 80mm, Ektachrome 200, f16.

Morning sunlight on a beach *has created a sparkling picture of a group of young Japanese swimmers being photographed by a friend. He is finding it characteristically difficult to hold the attention of several people who have momentarily stopped their activity. I like the range of silvers and blues in this shot and the variety of poses and expressions. As the long shadows in the foreground show, I was shooting into a low, weak sun.* Pentax, 50mm, Ektachrome 200, 1/250, f8.

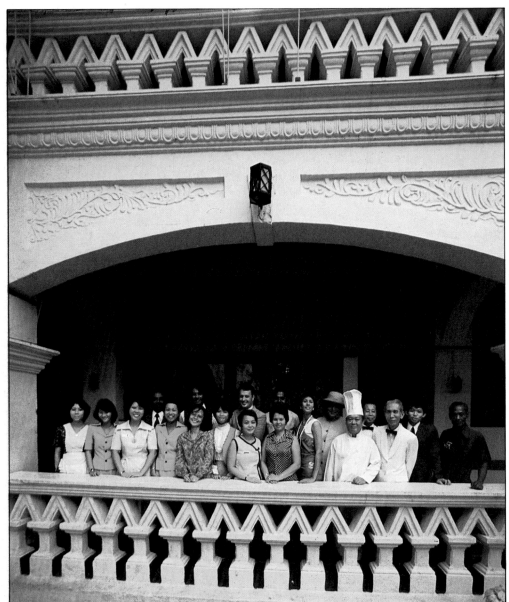

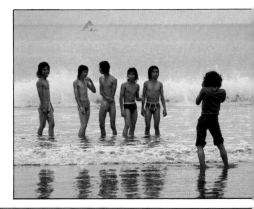

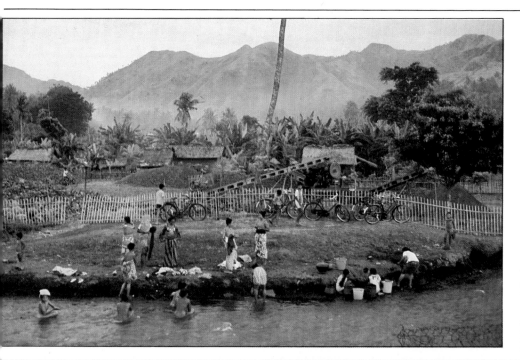

A scene of villagers bathing *outside a gravel works in Bali is given the romantic quality of a musical stage-set by soft evening light and rising mist above the trees. The bright blues and yellows of the plastic buckets blend with a range of subtle and beautiful greens in the background. A strong atmosphere encompasses foreground detail that, in a different picture, might simply have looked untidy.* Pentax, 50mm, Ektachrome 200, 1/250, f5.6.

The informal group *at a refreshment stall in Kuala Lumpur was photographed with a long lens in diffused sunlight. The pale pinks, yellows and greys, the relaxed pose of the man lighting his pipe and the slight movement on the figure of the child who has just slipped off his knee draw attention to the main group, yet the bamboo pole cleaving the figure on the right establishes a strange presence.* Pentax, 200mm, Ektachrome 200, 1/250, f8.

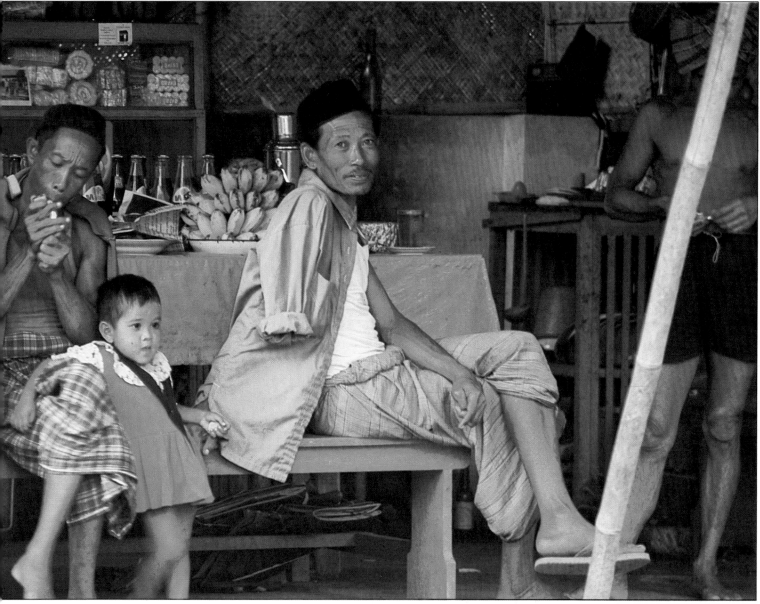

Nudes

Photographs that isolate facets of a nude figure through lighting or cropping can create striking abstract patterns. But in colour I prefer less depersonalized pictures, showing a woman in a light that caresses her skin. Indirect daylight can reveal all the subtleties of form through tonal gradations. Stronger, more directional light and harder shadows will create a bolder mood if that is your intention.

Background, viewpoint and lighting should all be related to the character of the model and the quality she conveys —innocent or sensual, romantic or erotic. Dim secretive lighting can be effective if the model herself feels vulnerable, while a confidently provocative woman may respond to a more revealing light with stronger contrasts. You should study your subject carefully to see how her body can be modelled with light and shadow, and remember that in avoiding blatancy, the expression is often more crucial than the pose.

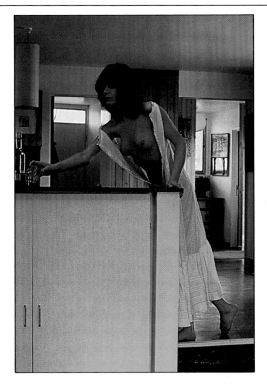

A graceful candour *can be captured at moments when a model is offguard and unselfconscious. I photographed the girl reaching for the drink while she was relaxing after a shooting session. Her open robe forms a natural frame revealing her breasts, and also reflects some light on to her body, helping to show form and texture. Her pose and position isolate her from a rather untidy and complicated background with several competing sources of light around the room.*
Pentax, 50mm, Ektachrome 64, 1/30, f2.5.

The unexpected quality *of the picture below is based on a series of paradoxes. The girl is both ethereal and statuesque, frozen and moving, warm and cool, seemingly linked to the statues around her. I used a wind machine to hold the robe against her breasts and thighs, and reflected a single electronic flash directly in front of her. A long exposure picked up the filmy movement of the robe.*
Pentax, 28mm, Ektachrome 200, 1/15, f11.

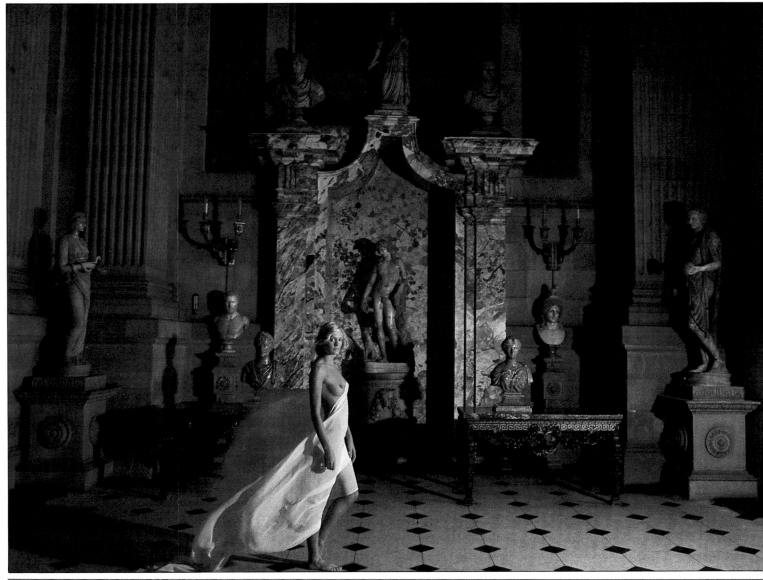

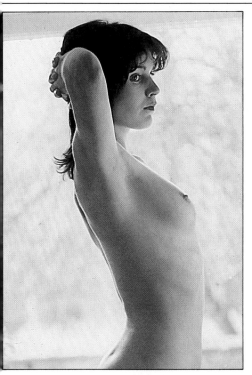

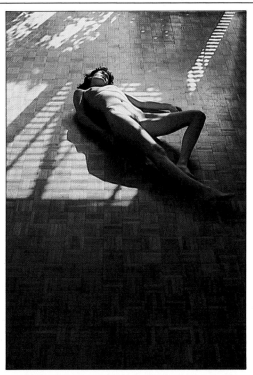

Delicate skin tones *are revealed in the picture of the girl with raised arms as light spreads around her body from either side. The simplicity and beauty of her stance is helped by her neutral expression.*
Pentax, 50mm, Ektachrome 64, 1/30, f8.

Patterns of sunlight *rake the body of a girl who seems almost a victim of the warmth in which she basks. The pose is unconventional, light flattening her breasts. But the picture is an intriguing composition in yellows and browns, light and shade, hardness and softness.*
Pentax, 28mm, Agfachrome 50s, 1/125, f8.

Silence and languorous warmth *suffuse the picture below, yet the girl is sensually aware of her body and of the settee. A golden light, reflected into the shadows from an Aubusson carpet on the floor, bathes her limbs, and its luminosity is counterpointed by gold-leaf decoration in the background. In this superb light for tone and form I exposed mainly for the shadows.*
Pentax, 50mm, Ektachrome 200, 1/125, f8.

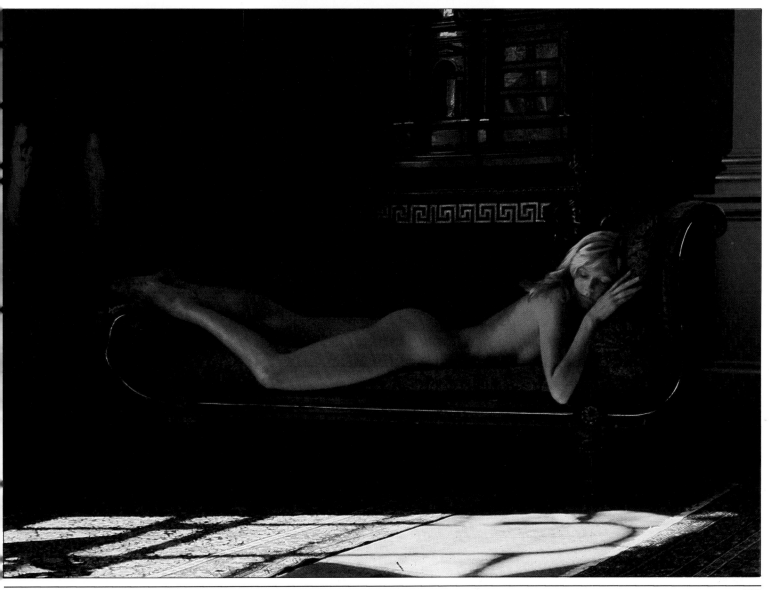

Nudes

A study in Victorian nostalgia, *the picture of the three girls has a romantic softness created by six photofloods diffused by a sheet and reflected to give an even illumination. The girls could move about the room without my needing to make lighting changes.* Pentax, 35 mm, Ektachrome 160, 1/30, f8.

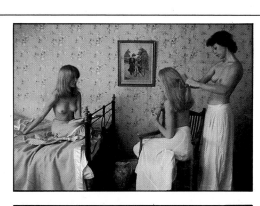

Looking bewildered, *even apprehensive, the girl trapped in the elaborate bedroom glances out of the frame, excluding the viewer from a scene that has a strong narrative interest. To avoid overpowering the room lights I masked an electronic flash to shine only on the girl herself.* Hasselblad, 50 mm, Ektachrome 200, 1/15, f8.

A poignant vulnerability *is conveyed by the woman with clasped arms. For the soft lighting, an electronic flash was diffused and masked so that it fell just in front of her body. I took the picture through a sheet of glass, using the steam from a kettle for condensation.* Hasselblad, 80 mm, Ektachrome 64, f8.

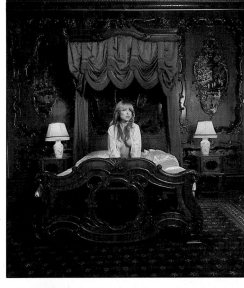

The combination of water and nakedness *can produce a mood of delicate eroticism. The girl floating in the glowing pool is lit by hard and powerful sunlight that gives the picture great luminosity and depth. The water conceals as much as it reveals, forming intriguing double images.* Leicaflex, 50 mm, Ektachrome 200, 1/125, f8.

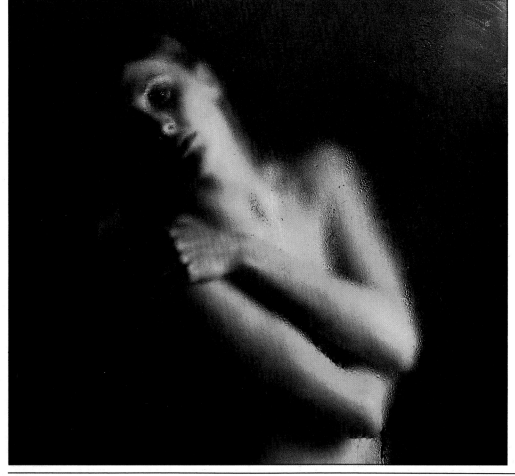

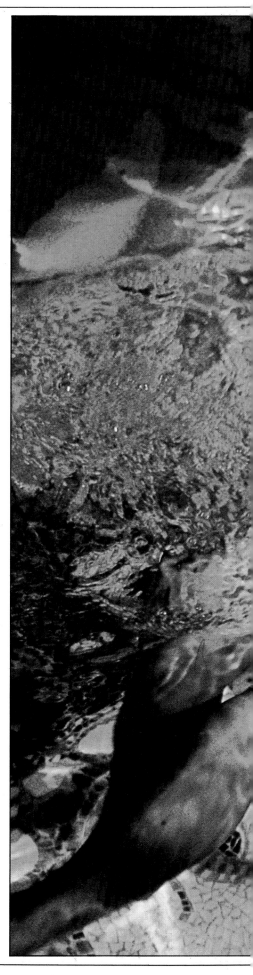

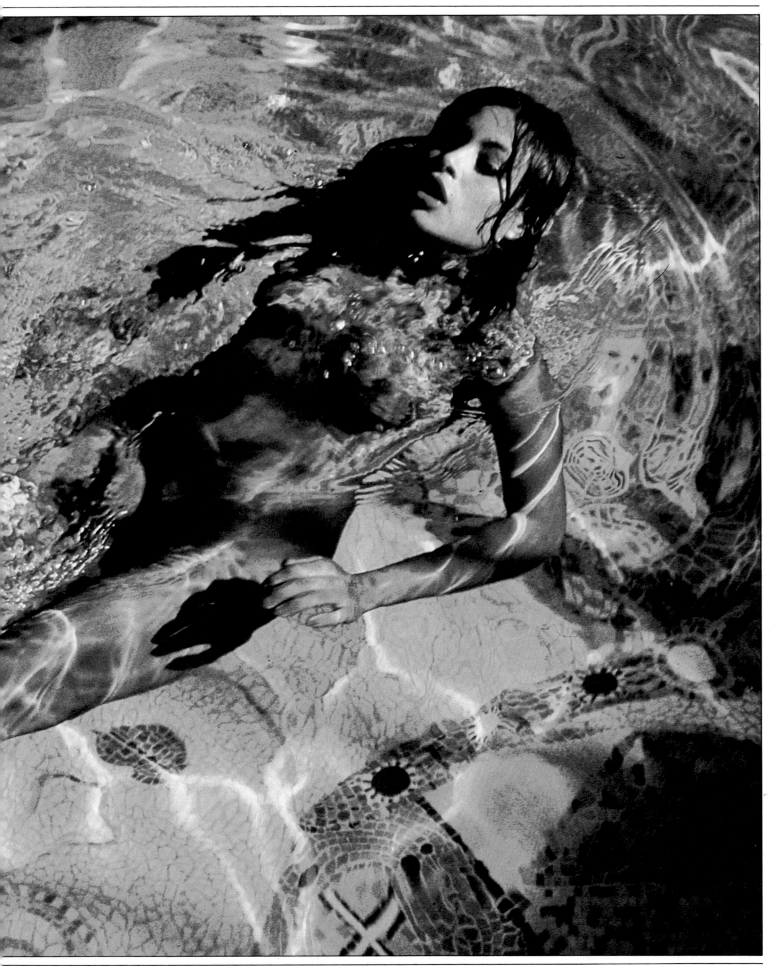

Fashion and beauty

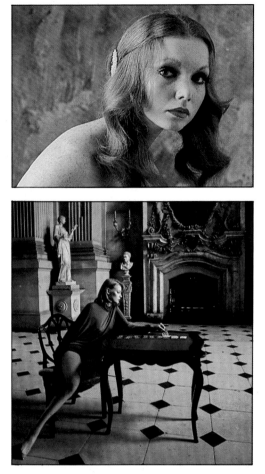

The challenge of fashion photography is to create pictures with mood and atmosphere that both show what the garments look like and make the viewer want to wear them. This is different from simply photographing clothes for a catalogue, where the aim is mainly to give detailed information. *Haute couture* clothes, particularly the more bizarre garments, allow the greatest creative freedom, because it is more important to suggest atmosphere and style than to show the garments in close detail.

In choosing the lighting, some knowledge of the qualities of different materials is essential. Silk and satin usually need a hard light bounced off the surface, while the texture of tweed is brought out by strong side lighting. Backlighting helps to show the transparency of gauze or chiffon and can also create a soft outline that suits angora. Daylight, electronic flash, or a combination of both, permit more rhythm and movement than can be achieved with tungsten lighting.

The style and cut *of the model's auburn hair was the most important feature in planning the beauty shot (top). To capture the rich tones in her hair and the delicacy of her skin I used an electronic flash window light, with a reflector about 3ft (1m) from her face. The background is rough-plastered hardboard, stained with coffee for colour harmony and shown in soft focus.* Hasselblad, 150mm, Ektachrome 64, 1/125, f11.

To reveal the silky texture *and the drape of the aubergine jersey evening dress I supported existing daylight with electronic flash. The girl's pose is provocative, but the card game and the formal setting help to keep the picture fairly impersonal.* Pentax, 28mm, Ektachrome 64, 1/15, f11.

The green swimsuit *is clearly made for sunning rather than swimming, so I placed the model against a background that would suggest sunshine and warmth without dissipating colour. Photographed in subdued daylight, with her face in shadow, she leans against a textured wall that helps to bring out the feel of the garment. This kind of fashion picture strikes an appropriate balance between atmosphere and descriptive information, giving enough atmosphere to persuade a customer that if she bought the costume she could look equally glamorous.* Pentax, 50mm, Agfachrome 50s, 1/125, f8.

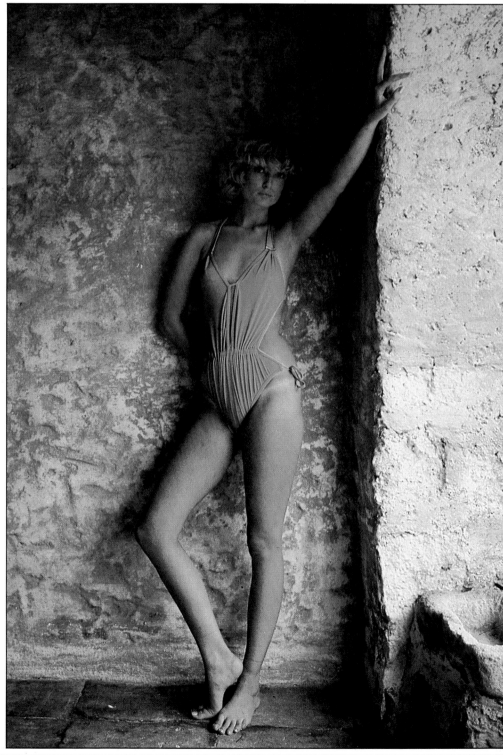

Ring flash, *a lighting technique developed for medical photography to produce shadowless pictures, is now often used in fashion and beauty photography. Because the flash is fixed around the lens, "red eye" appears in frontal portraits. But this can be used to effect, as in the delicate, etched portrait of a girl in white against a white background. I placed her close to the backdrop so she would be outlined by shadow and balanced the pattern of her hair against the fullness of her lifted sleeves. Hasselblad, 150mm, Ektachrome 64, f8.*

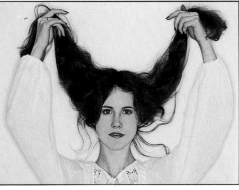

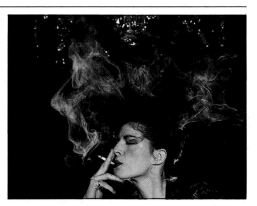

Dramatic lighting *heightens the bizarre style of the woman in the punk make-up, whose bicoloured lipstick repeats the colours in her embroidered silk jacket. I placed one electronic flash directly behind the camera and another about 6ft (2m) behind the model, angled to light the cigarette smoke and backlight the chandelier and her head. Hasselblad, 150mm, Ektachrome 64, 1/125, f16.*

The seductive-looking girl *in opulent surroundings seemed to need a fairly hard flash, which I positioned high up to the right at a 45° angle so that it would follow the line of her bias-cut evening dress and reveal her figure. At this angle, the texture and form of both the dress and jacket are well shown. Hasselblad, 80mm, Ektachrome 64, f11.*

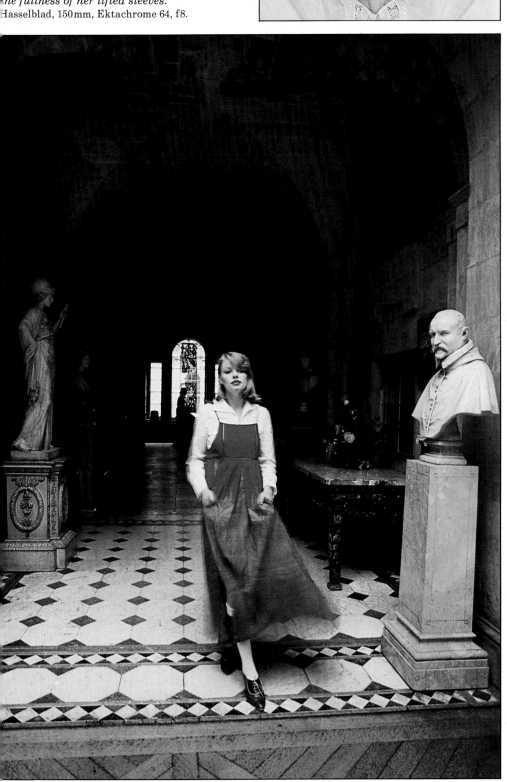

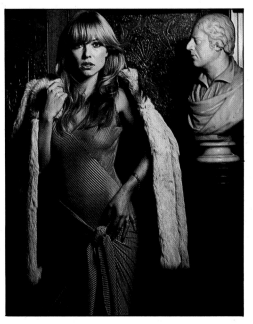

A casual mood *was suggested by the Indian-patterned pinafore worn with a white shirt and socks. Although the setting is formal, a slow shutter speed showing the hazy swing of the skirt conveys a sense of freedom and comfort. To strengthen the light in the foreground, I reinforced diffused daylight with a single reflected electronic flash, letting the background remain a stop or so darker. Pentax, 35mm, Ektachrome 64, 1/30, f11.*

Children

Spontaneity is the essence of child photography, and it is for this reason that I prefer to take pictures of children outdoors, where they can move around freely. Gentle directional sunlight is ideal, both because it allows you to work from any angle, with or against the light, and because its soft, even quality brings out the fresh colour and smooth texture of children's faces.

The volatility of a child's moods means that quick reflexes and a degree of preplanning are needed to capture a characteristic gesture or expression. For candid shots outdoors, it is useful to work out exposures on the basis of shooting at 1/250, or at least 1/125. The picture below of boys sliding on an icy road was taken with high-speed film at 1/250, f8. Intent on their game, the group paid no attention to me as I approached and I simply dropped to one knee for a shot that owes everything to their boisterous animation and varied positions.

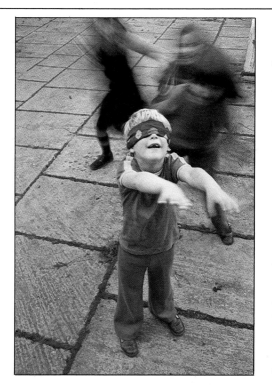

Blindman's-buff *is a child's game that combines excitement and fear. To capture the feelings of the stumbling boy in a circle of whirling friends, I shot at a very slow speed, bracing myself against a wall for a hand-held shot.*
Nikon, 35 mm, Agfachrome 50s, 1/15, f16.

A long lens *ensured that the camera did not disturb boy or rabbit. The colours were simplified by a slightly overcast light and narrow depth of field.*
Pentax, 200 mm, Ektachrome 64, 1/250, f5.6.

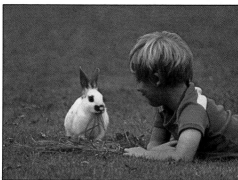

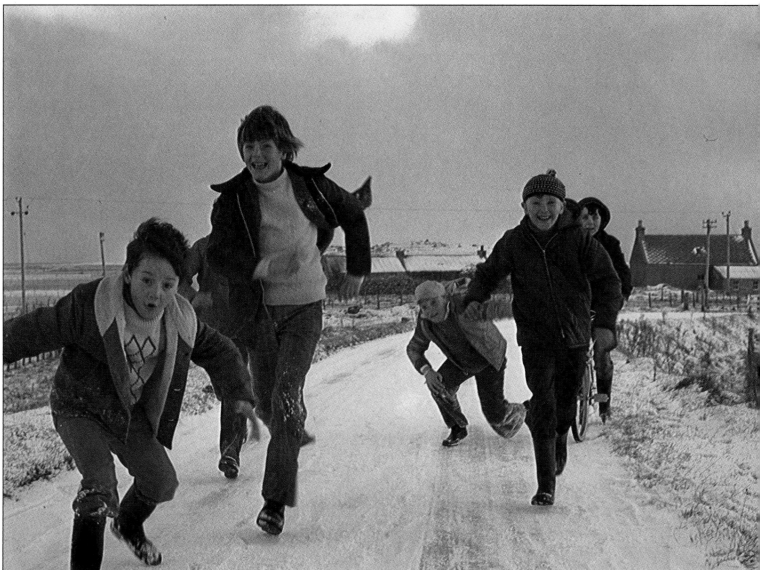

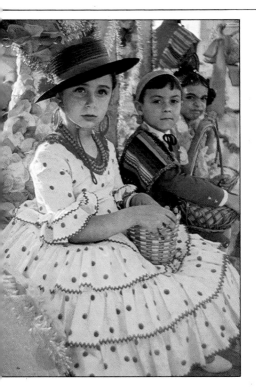

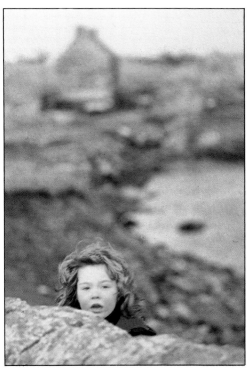

The carnival costumes *of the Spanish children (far left) were photographed against weak sunlight, which has subdued the bright colours and which allows attention to be focused on their different expressions—serious, detached and impish.* Pentax, 35mm, Ektachrome 64, 1/125, f5.6.

A bleak background *says everything about this lonely Hebridean child, but its dominance in the picture is lessened by my use of a shallow depth of field.* Minolta, 135mm, Agfachrome 50s, 1/125, f4.

The forlorn boy, *encountered in the hills of Bali, was worried because his father was late to meet him. I would have preferred to photograph him against a less strongly patterned background. But the power of his expression is able to dominate the picture because haze has diffused the sunlight and reduced tonal contrasts. I left the landscape slightly out of focus and exposed for the texture of his shadowed skin and the delicacy of his fingers and limp arms.* Pentax, 35mm, Ektachrome 64, 1/250, f4.

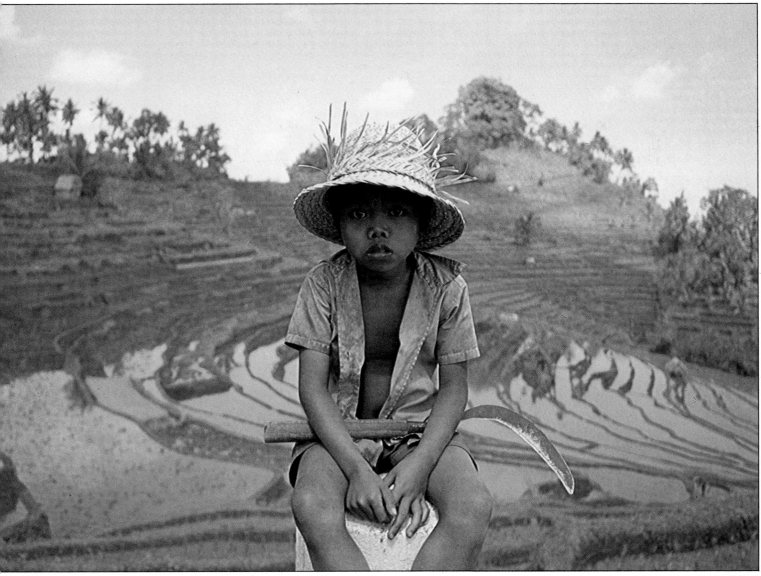

Children

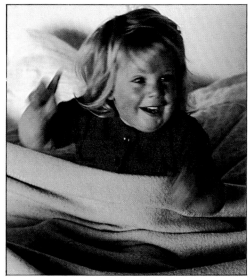

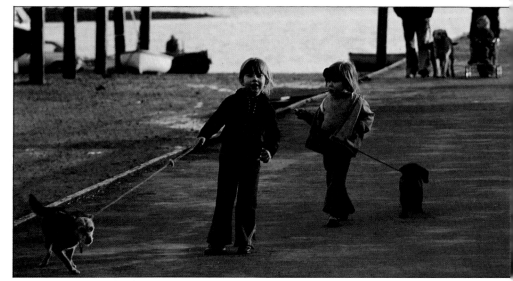

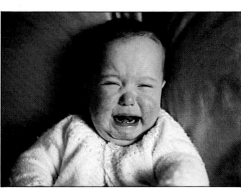

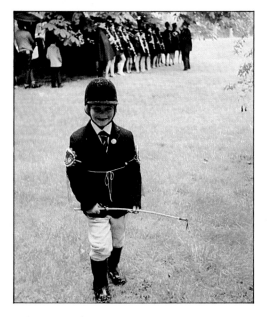

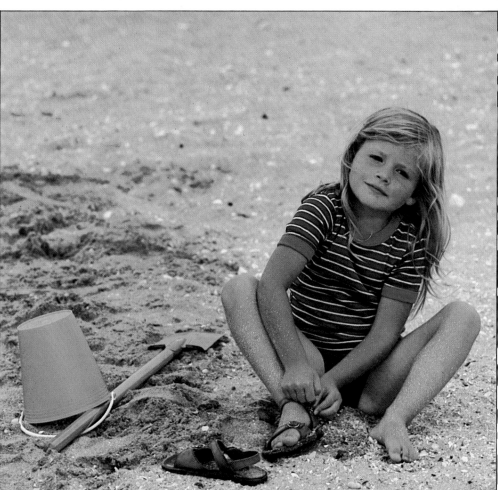

The exhilaration of the moment *is what counts in child portraiture. The crying baby and laughing boy were both photographed in soft, diffused daylight with a 50mm Pentax, high-speed film and an exposure of 1/30, f8. The boy's blurred arm adds to the sparkle. The vivid face of Lucy (above), posing in heavy rain, needed overexposure by one stop. I shot at 1/125, f5.6, lightening the picture a further stop in processing to give a sunny atmosphere.*

Pale winter sunlight *produces delicate shadows in the picture of the two girls taking their dogs for a walk—or being taken by them. The angle of the leads places the emphasis on the children, but the long diagonal of the kerb links them with their parents, whose legs can be seen at the top of the frame. This weak light is perfect for the soft pinks of the children's jerseys and in their glowing cheeks.*
Pentax, 35mm, Agfachrome 50s, 1/250, f8.

An overcast day at Deauville *gave me a good light for the picture of the girl with her sand bucket. The background beyond the frame was distracting so I used a long lens and focused on the girl's sweater. The narrow depth of field prevents the texture of the sand being too noticeable and it has become a perfect background for the delicate tones of the girl's sandy arms and legs.*
Hasselblad, 150mm, Agfachrome 50s, 1/125, f8.

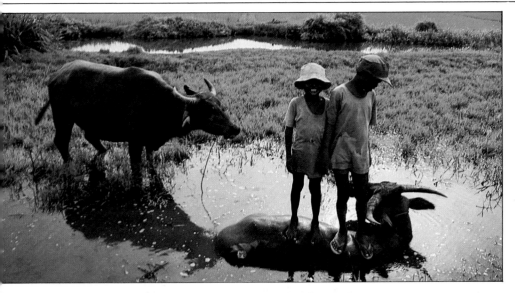

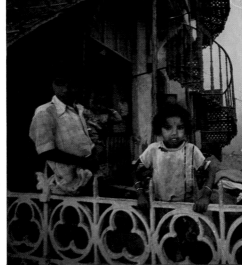

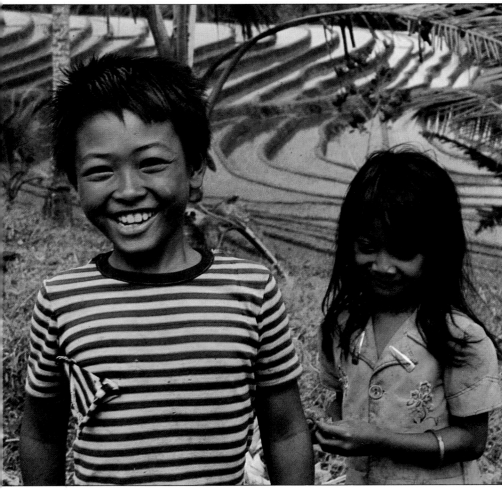

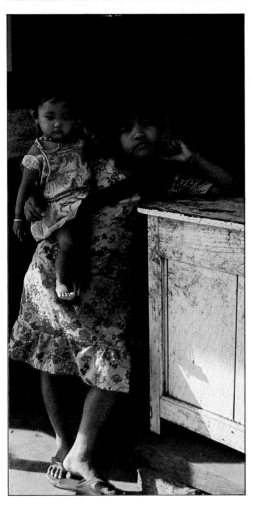

Wallowing water buffalo, *two grinning farm boys and low evening light, which brings out rich greens in the field behind them, make up a composition that balances subdued tones against a bright background and water reflections. I stood on my car roof to make sure the boys' heads did not become lost in the darker vegetation. Notice how their nails and teeth shine in the bluish light that predominates at evening.*
Pentax, 35mm, Agfachrome 50s, 1/250, f8.

The diffused evening light *in which I took the photograph of the boy in the tee-shirt with his shy sister was strong enough to give highlights on their hair but soft enough to show colours well. The luminosity of their skins adds to a spirited picture. Although the terraced paddy-field makes a complicated background, it is subdued and links up in a pattern with the lines of the boy's striped shirt.*
Pentax, 35mm, Ektachrome 64, 1/250, f8.

Close relationships *are brought out by the unselfconscious poses of the children in the pictures above. The group (top) was photographed in a dark Bombay alleyway, background colours harmonizing with their olive skins. I used high-speed film and exposed at 1/30, f8. In the lower picture the girl's positioning in the foreground shade helps to screen a complicated interior. Her sash links her with the baby she holds in her arms. The exposure was 1/250, f5.6.*

197

Still life

Still-life pictures are studied arrangements of inanimate objects that give the photographer the luxury of time and complete control. Such pictures may be assembled with patient care, or chanced upon. In making still lifes you can give full rein to creativity, selecting objects that are constantly used but rarely seen as shapes, forms and textures of intrinsic aesthetic interest. To give coherence to the picture it is necessary to have a clear idea of its central theme. I collect objects for days or even weeks, then choose one that seems characteristic or telling as the basis of an arrangement.

Lighting is of crucial importance. For identification, soft, shadowless, diffused light is most effective, and reflectors can be used to suggest form without producing hard shadows. If more contrast is needed, directional light will dramatize form and texture and a selective light source, such as a spotlight, allows precise control over the creation of shadows or highlights.

When building an arrangement it is advisable to view it constantly through the camera in the approximate lighting you will be using. A tripod is generally necessary and a firm surface is essential, preferably one that can be lit from all sides. The effect should be of only one light source, without conflicting shadows. If an interesting arrangement does not emerge, it is best to clear everything and begin again.

The collection of Victoriana shown opposite is so arranged that no one piece dominates. Light was diffused by greaseproof paper over a window on one side and a white card reflector on the other. I shot downwards on to the floor at an exposure of 1 second, f11, using an MPP 5 × 4 in and tripod.

A faded rose *caught my interest and provided the starting point for a still-life sequence. Dead for a week, the rose had a subdued richness of colour and a texture like frayed parchment. Its fragile quality would have been destroyed by harsh lighting, but a diffused winter sun, tinged with orange, gave sufficient form to convey the impression of natural beauty heightened by decay. For this shot I used a 100mm macro lens on my Pentax, with tripod, and exposed the Agfachrome 50s film for 1/15 at f8. When placed against a suitable backdrop the entire jug of spent blooms made a colourful display. The existing background was highly coloured and confusing, so I put weathered planks of neutral pink and grey hues and with an interesting texture behind the flowers, but out of focus so as not to detract from the main point of interest. Adding a bottle and glass of mineral water contrasted a sparkling clarity with the clouded water in the jug. A silvered reflector on the left-hand side, as shown in the diagram, brought out the glassy highlights. Before shooting I dropped some sugar into the glass to reactivate the bubbles. These two pictures were taken with a 50mm lens at the same aperture and speed as before.*

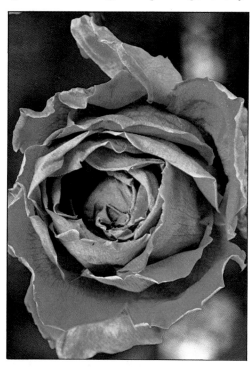

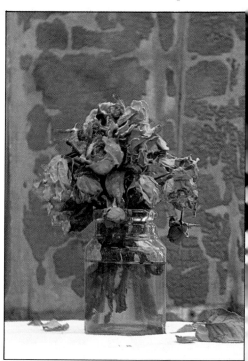

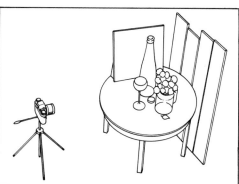

Adding domestic items *transformed a classically simple picture into one of narrative interest. Ferns, a box and a vase were added to the background and the old card, photograph and frame suggest the nostalgia of family life. I removed the reflector and placed a board against the right side of the table, blocking the light to subdue the background colours.* Pentax, 50mm, tripod, Agfachrome 50s, 1/15, f8.

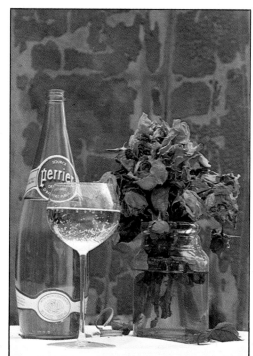

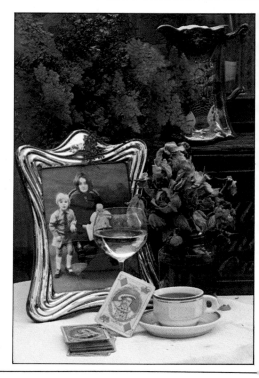

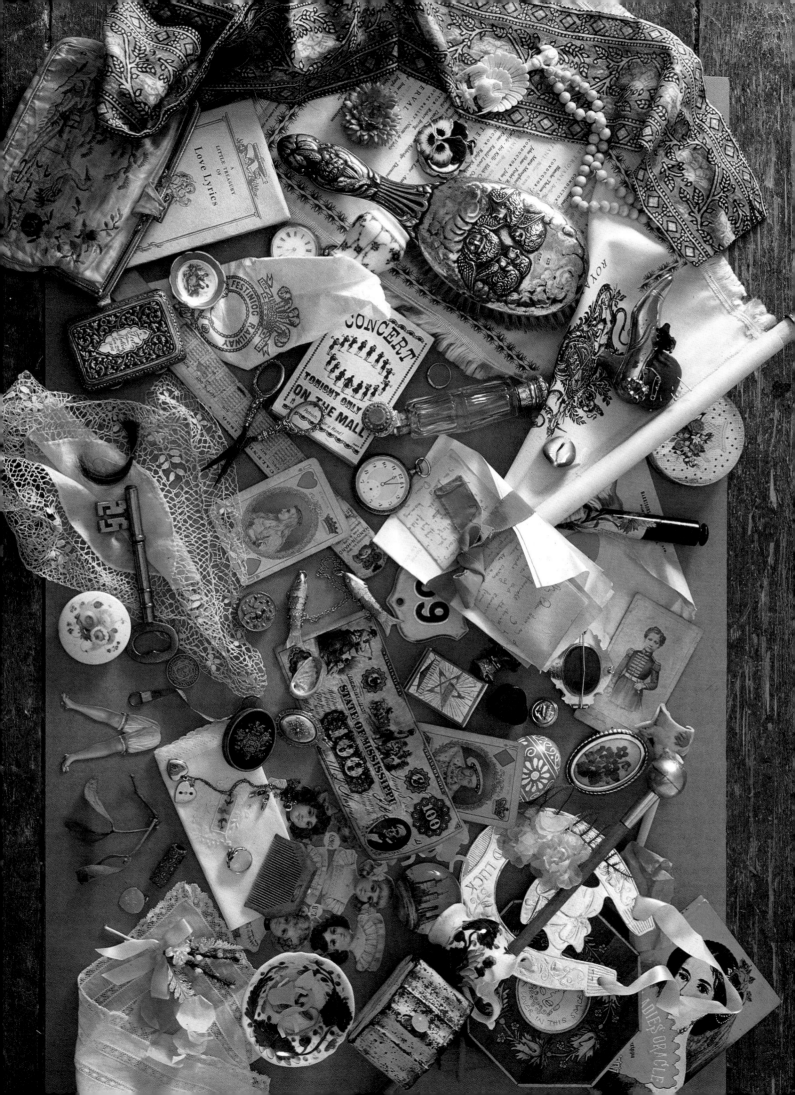

Still life

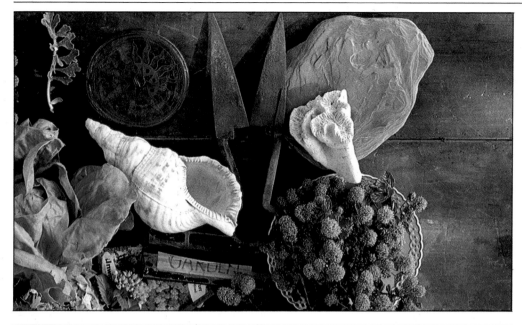

Emphasis can always be given *to particular objects by lighting for contrast. The shell and bone are here thrown into strong relief by diffused sunlight falling upon items lying on a potting shed bench. If you like an arrangement when you look down on it, photograph it the same way, as I did here by standing directly over the bench.*
Linhof, 150mm, tripod, Ektachrome 64, 1 sec., f16.

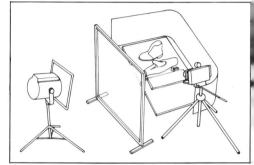

A worn leather boot, *grained wood, bark and stripped wood and a knotted rope end provide colour harmonies and contrasting textures that clearly describe the forms. A low, directional, 1,000-watt spotlight was diffused by a plastic screen and linen sheet. The spotlight was 3ft (1m) above the objects but 6ft (2m) away. As the diagram shows, white side reflectors were used to further reduce contrast.*
Linhof, 150mm, tripod, Ektachrome 64, 1 sec., f22.

A dressing-table *in the bedroom of Dylan Thomas's house at Laugharne, Wales, contained cherished memories of childhood and was so strongly evocative that I shot it as I found it. The only change I made was to hang a white sheet opposite the mirror in order to eliminate confusing detail in the back of the room. By replacing these reflections with a plain background I was able to increase the feeling of intimacy.*
Rolleiflex, 80mm, tripod, Ektachrome 200, 1 sec., f8.

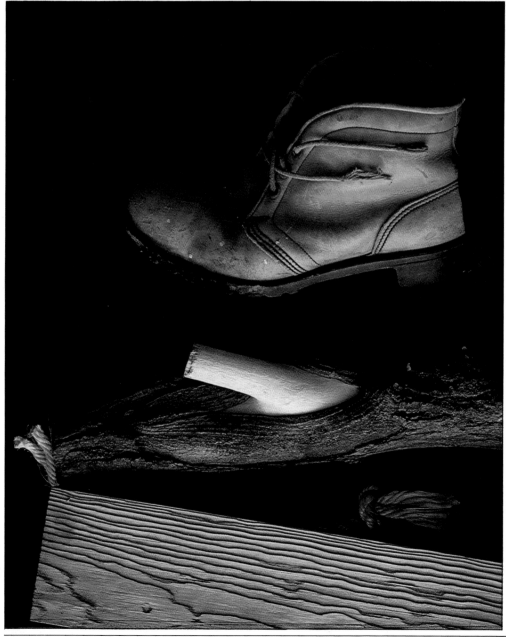

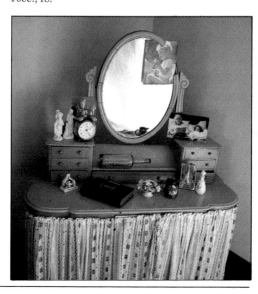

Cropping at the top *was essential to make a still life of this picture of a Graham Sutherland pen and wash drawing in progress. Space above the top of the pen would have given a strong sense of movement, but as it now appears the frame has pinned the pen, making the artist's hand an integral part of the picture.* Hasselblad, 150mm, tripod, Ektachrome 200, 1/2, f11.

People in still lifes *seem frozen in time, as if they were simply other inanimate objects in the picture. This table of food in Raffles Hotel, Singapore, caught my eye because of its intrinsic interest, but the presence of the man and woman, like silent observers, adds interest to the background and introduces an extra dimension to the picture. Some areas are given a green cast by light filtered through a sun-screen.* Pentax, 35mm, tripod, Ektachrome 64, 1/8, f11.

Careful lighting is needed *to enable a still life of small, interesting items, such as this collection of memorabilia, to be identified clearly. To avoid heavy shadows I used studio window lighting, but diffused daylight would have been even better. The table on which the objects rest is curved to eliminate any line between its horizontal surface and vertical back. A silver reflector helps diffuse the light.* Linhof, 150mm, tripod, Ektachrome 160, 5 sec., f32.

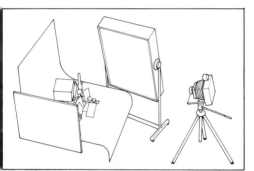

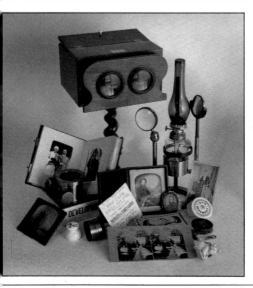

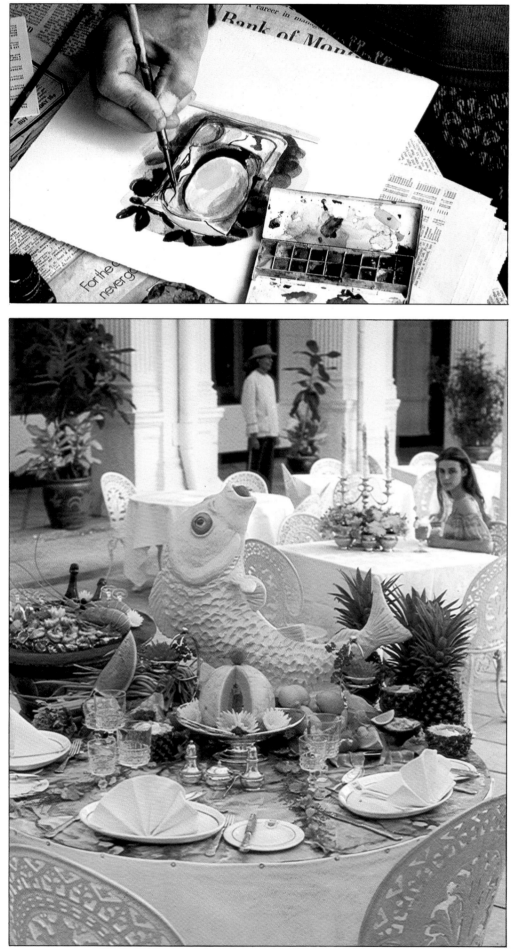

Architecture

To bring architecture to life, lighting is of paramount importance as it can dramatize a derelict building or make the most adventurous structure look dull. The response to light of each building material thus needs to be appreciated—the reflections in glass at different angles, for instance. Concrete structures often show up well in full sun with solid shadows; stone relief work needs more delicate light to reveal form; and iron or steel structures make striking abstract patterns when backlit. Strong sidelight, highlighting some surfaces and throwing others into shadow, provides modelling and texture, while diffused light may better reveal subtle colour.

Buildings such as cathedrals, often located on high ground, can frequently be shot from a distance with long lenses. A shift lens or a camera with a rising back and front is essential for photographing buildings of any height, and so is a steady tripod. The inclusion of one or two people can emphasize a point of interest and scale in a picture, but gaily dressed crowds are usually distracting. Provided they are moving, and not too strongly lit, people can be removed by using slow film with an exposure of about 5 seconds.

The setting *is often important in shots of period houses, such as the fine Jacobean mansion Bickling Hall, Norfolk. The link between the formal gardens and majestic architecture is captured by a Linhof wide-angle camera that produces a* $6\frac{7}{8} \times 2\frac{1}{4}$ *in image (shown to size) without distortion.* Linhof wide-angle, Ektachrome 200, 1/125, f22.

An aerial view *can reveal design features impossible to record from ground level. In the picture of an English country house the angle of view is forward of the building to show the elevations, rather than simply the layout. I was a few minutes late for perfectly symmetrical shadow.* Pentax, 50mm, Ektachrome 200, 1/500, f8.

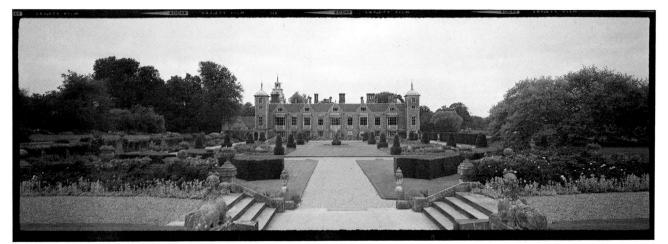

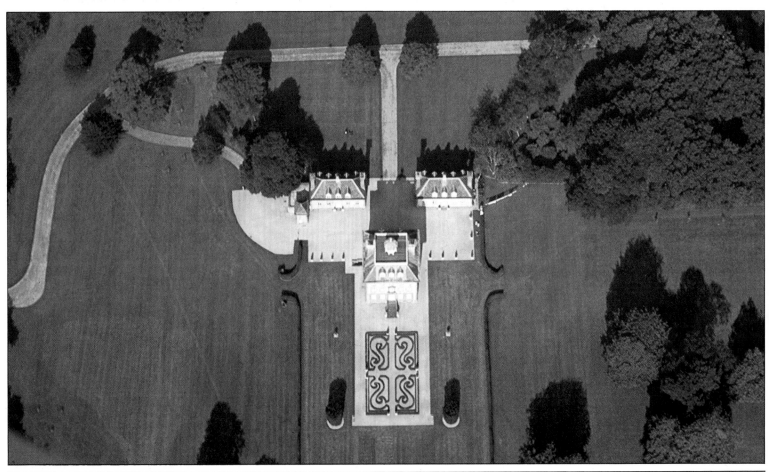

The glow of the setting sun *backlights a building under construction in California. It has created an exciting pattern from what was essentially an unremarkable box-like form.* Pentax, 100mm, Ektachrome 64, 1/125, f8.

A modern glass-covered building *in Ipswich, England, glimmers with light and colour that add interest and depth to a piece of striking architecture, leading the eye into the building as well as along its surface. To avoid the effect of a black wall, which a shot in full daylight would have produced, I waited for the softer evening light, when an impressive sunset was reflected at one end of the curved*

frontage with neon lights below. I felt that showing the entire façade was more important than achieving correct verticals, so I used a wide-angle lens and shot from a high camera position. Pentax, 15mm, Ektachrome 200, 1/15, f16.

Shot against late light, *the ponderous concrete spheres of the early warning defence system at Fylingdale, Yorkshire, are made to look as insubstantial as giant balloons yet also ominous against the darkened moor. Had the picture been taken in sunlight, more form and detail would have been recorded, but at the expense of the powerful atmosphere achieved here.* Pentax, 200mm, Ektachrome 64, 1/250, f8.

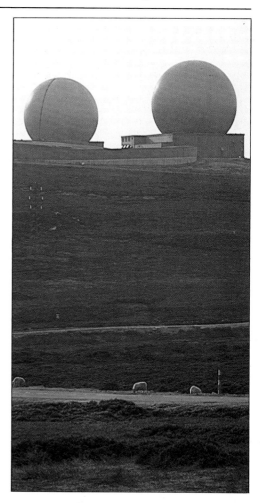

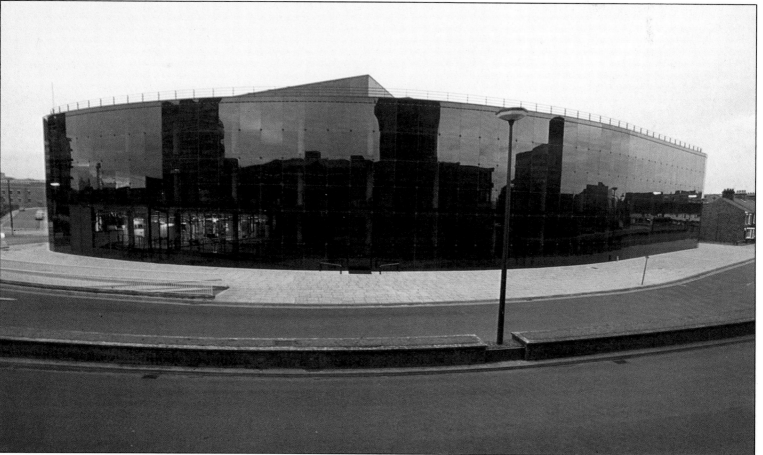

Architectural detail

Pictures of architectural detail, picking out the colour or texture of materials, the beams or girders of a construction or features of woodwork or stone carving, can often reveal much about the character of a building as well as the individual quirks of its designer or the craftsmen who worked on it.

Such functional or ornamental elements can provide fascinating studies. Soft directional light is most effective for showing the modelling of a detail without the confusion introduced by harsh shadows, although flat lighting may be suitable if the detail itself lacks form.

An observant eye coupled with imagination can find and pinpoint innumerable visual delights that are overlooked by most passers-by. Appropriate subjects can range from an intriguing painting on a dilapidated door to crisply painted drain pipes that neatly obscure part of a street sign. Pattern and harmony are evident in such things as sagging timbers centuries old or the window display of a French charcuterie.

Close-ups can be instructive in showing embellishments that would not be noticed in an overall view. They also provide a means of documenting things of a bygone era that may not survive much longer. Modern façades increasingly lack the charming touches that make old buildings so attractive.

For close-up shots it is advisable to underexpose by a stop in order to record the colours richly, especially where time has caused them to fade. Fine-grained film is also best, and you will need to allow for slightly longer exposures when using extension rings and bellows. After having shot in close-up, it is a good idea to take a view of the whole building to establish the location of the incidental detail that you have made into an entire picture.

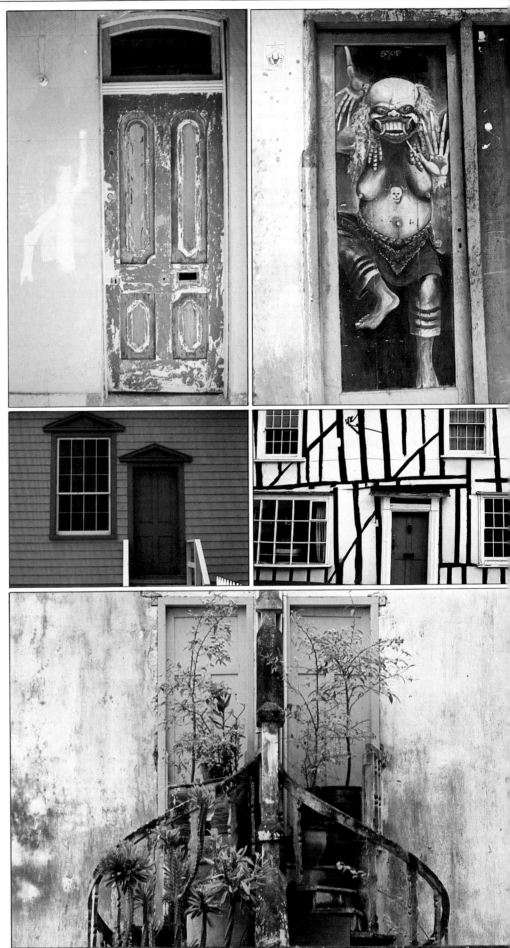

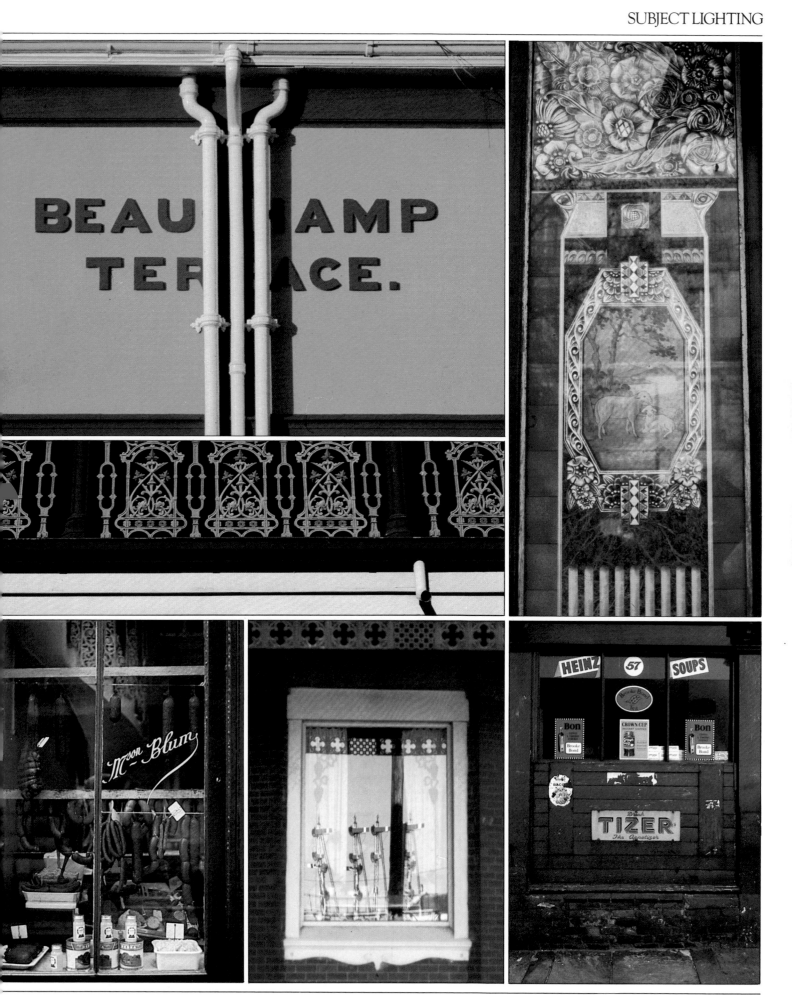

Interiors

Interior lighting is not usually planned or arranged for the convenience of photographers. As a result, some areas are lit well, others dimly. In particular, older churches were designed to give dramatic lighting contrasts rather than even illumination. Badly lit areas will need to be supported with flash, either by the judicious placing of several units or, during a long exposure, by "painting with light"—moving around in dark clothes so as not to register and firing the flash into shadows. If you are using only existing light, shoot with the light rather than against it and try to reduce contrasts by showing only small areas of windows in the view. In weak light with long exposures, colour shifts occur through reciprocity failure, but this is often acceptable. Overlapping forms of furniture make a room look crowded, so you may need to shift foreground furniture or shoot from a height, especially when using a wide-angle lens.

Faded fluorescent lighting *gives a greenish cast to a room in the old Charing Cross Hospital, London, now a hostel for the homeless. A tungsten bulb and overcast daylight from windows make up a lighting mixture that well conveys the atmosphere of Victorian shabbiness.*
Pentax, 28mm, Ektachrome 200, 1/4, f8.

Fan vaulting *in the ceiling of Wells Cathedral was difficult to photograph because of intense light from the high windows. I overcame the problem with a smear of petroleum jelly, which has diffused the light.*
Hasselblad, 150mm, Agfachrome 50s, 1/15, f16.

The Painted Hall, *Greenwich, is so vast that it would be a major undertaking to light it completely. To support the daylight I simply aimed two flash units at the ceiling from behind my tripod, set up on steps at the entrance.*
Pentax, shift lens, Ektachrome 200, 1/8, f11.

The baroque Bavarian church *is given luminosity by daylight reflected from snow outside, which often provides a good light for shots of church interiors.*
Pentax, 28mm, Ektachrome 200, 1 sec., f22.

A girl *and her reflected image, light creeping across the faded wallpaper from each side and the bareness of the hotel room all help to create a picture with a haunting atmosphere.*
Pentax, 15mm, Ektachrome 200, 1 sec., f8.

A designer's bedroom, *full of bizarre objects, needed even lighting. I turned off the room lights and bounced two electronic flashes from the ceiling.*
Hasselblad, 40mm, Ektachrome 64, f16.

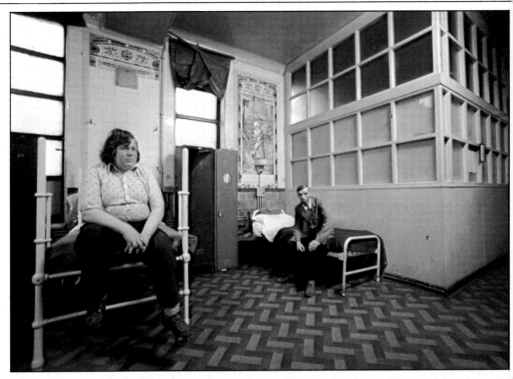

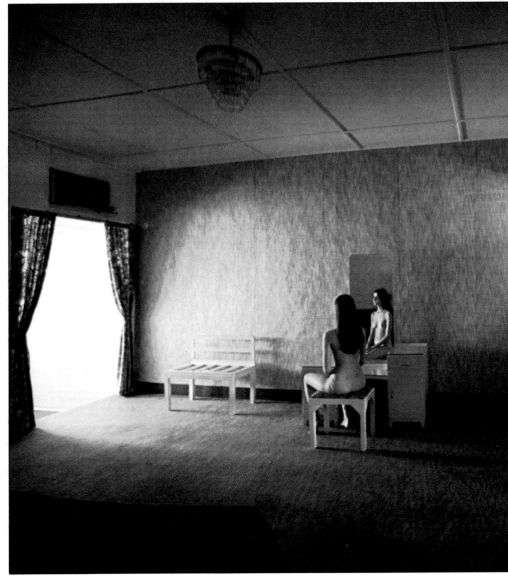

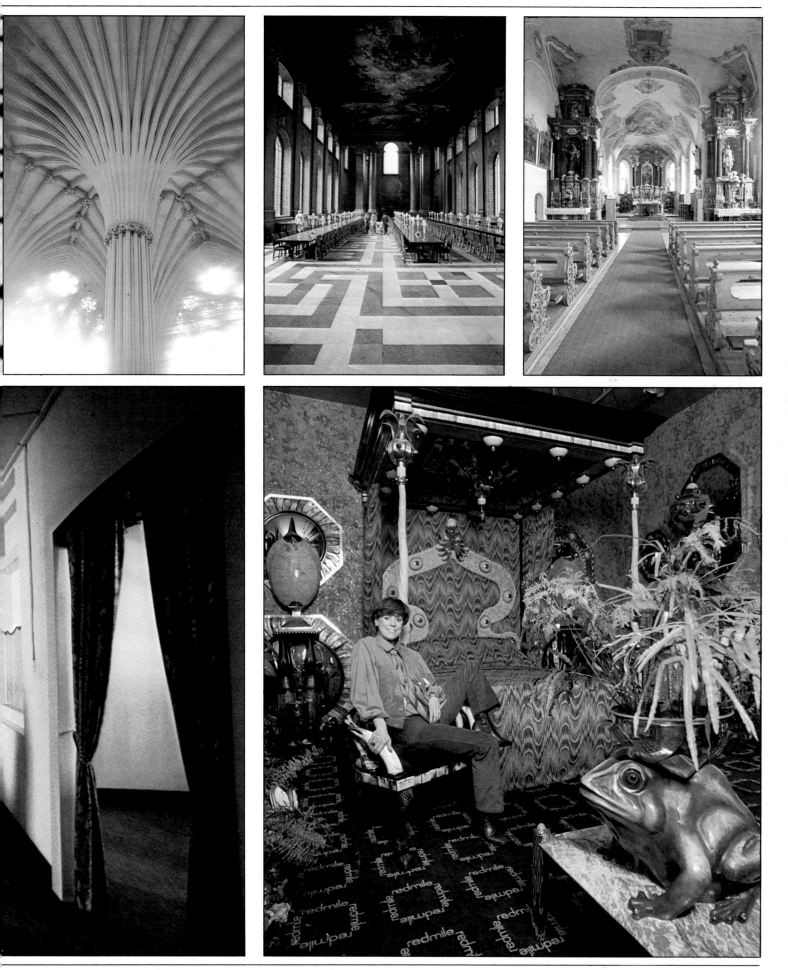

Animals

To succeed at animal photography you need to be something of a naturalist as well, because half the problem is understanding the behaviour of the animal you want to picture. In time, however, you can learn the habits of different animals and often come to anticipate their movements and recognize likely haunts. Quick reflexes, alertness and patience are required. Experience will also teach you the need to move cautiously and quietly. You may need to spend long hours in a hide or under natural cover waiting for the right moment to shoot, and may find that if luck is not on your side the wait is fruitless or the picture disappointing. But the frustration often involved is more than offset when you succeed in capturing a compelling study.

Light conditions for wildlife photography can be the most difficult of all. Many wild animals appear in the open only in poor light. Long exposures are rarely possible, for animals move quickly and often in an unpredictable way, so you have to rely on such aids as fast film, fast and long lenses, silent shutters, and remote-controlled motorized cameras. You may often have to shoot from a distance with telephoto lens and tripod. If it is an important shot, have two cameras ready and gauge the exposure in advance. If you cannot portray the animal against an unencumbered background, panning or the use of a shallow depth of field will enable you to isolate it. For zoo work you can either insert the camera between the bars of the cage or blur them out by moving close in and using a long lens at wide aperture. Domestic animals pose fewer problems simply because they are tame, recognize you as a friend and are close at hand.

The best animal pictures are those that show a characteristic pose. I took the picture of the fox one morning in early winter after having stalked it for two days. The animal was in peak condition with a splendid brush. I shot from behind a tree at a distance of about 25 ft (8 m), having let some chickens out of their run to attract its attention. I had tried to photograph the fox before, but it had always headed off in the wrong direction for me or else hugged the undergrowth. This time, with luminous white fur and glistening tongue and eye, it was intent on a chicken (rescued in time). A rapid pan has blurred the leaf-strewn field and given added vitality to the shot, taken with a 105 mm lens, high-speed film and an exposure of 1/60 at f16.

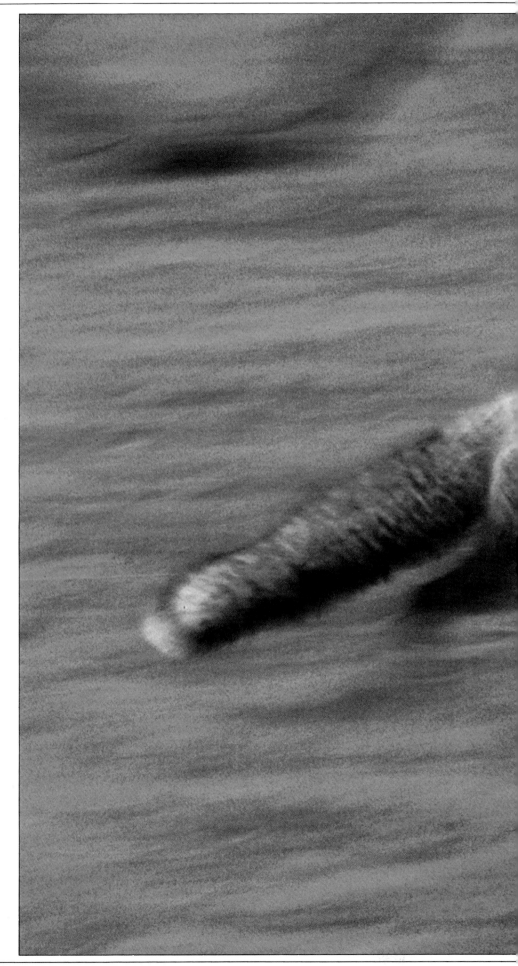

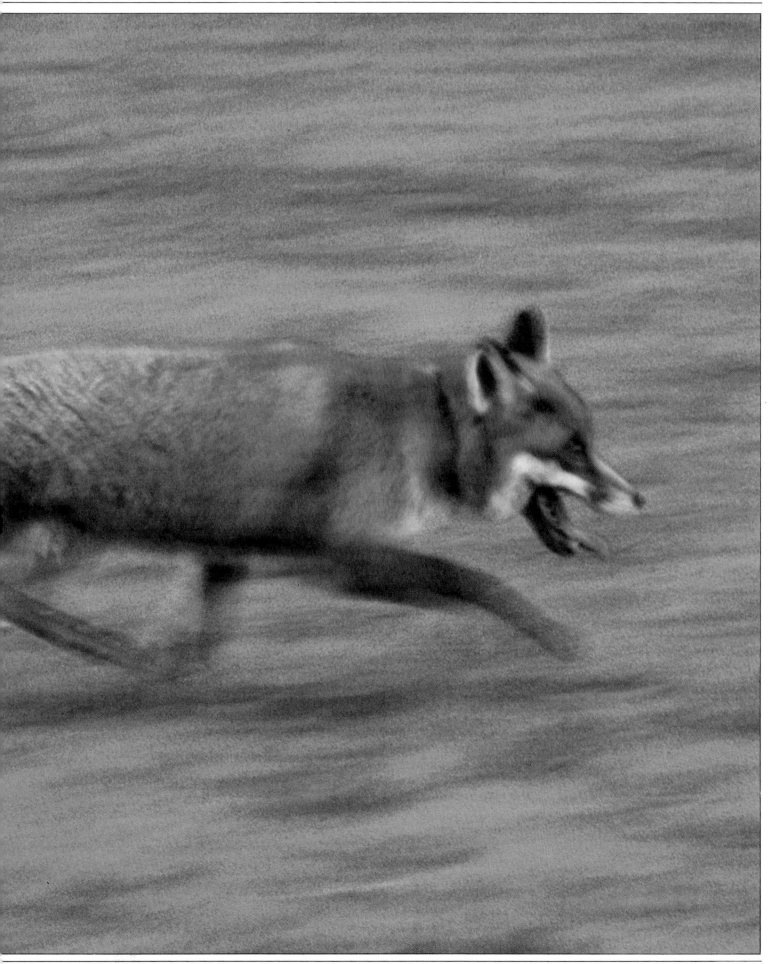

Animals

The vivid hues *of Australian parrots have been softened to take on the appearance of coloured chalks in this diffused light. The birds, nesting on Lindeman Island in the Great Barrier Reef, could have been photographed at close range, but I chose a telephoto lens and shot from 20ft (6m), wedging myself against a tree for a long exposure in evening light.*
Hasselblad, 250mm, Ektachrome 200, 1/60, f5.6.

The tousled English setter, *zipped into his red drying bag, has been for a walk in the rain. Zealous owners have done their best to make him warm and comfortable, but the dog is obviously feeling very self-conscious, even without a camera being pointed at him. Overcast afternoon light brings out the strong colour contrasts.*
Pentax, 50mm, Ektachrome 64, 1/60, f5.6.

A straightforward picture *(below) of pigeons is given a gentle atmosphere by a change of light and viewpoint. I moved into some trees and photographed through the leaves for the second picture, thus changing the background from brown to green. The softened light still reveals the form of the birds.*
Leicaflex, 400mm, Ektachrome 64, 1/250, f8.

Direct sunlight on a fallen tree trunk *and a sky streaked with wispy cloud provided the starting point for an oblique portrait of Captain Dudgeon, director of Burton Hall training school near Dublin. In order to stress his teaching role, I asked two of his students to jump their horses over the obstacle in such a way as to frame their trainer, an Olympic horseman, in the background. Having one enter the jump as the other left, added more sense of movement. By lying in the mud and using a wide-angle lens I emphasized the horses and distant man by portraying them against a large expanse of pale sky.*
Leicaflex, 21mm, Ektachrome 64, 1/500, f11.

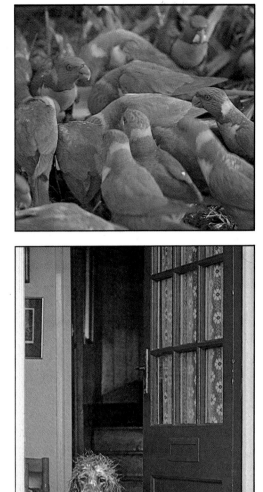

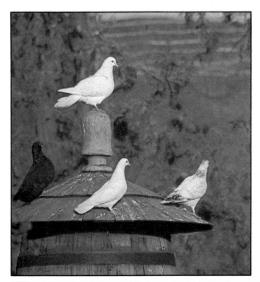

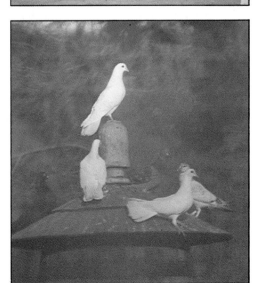

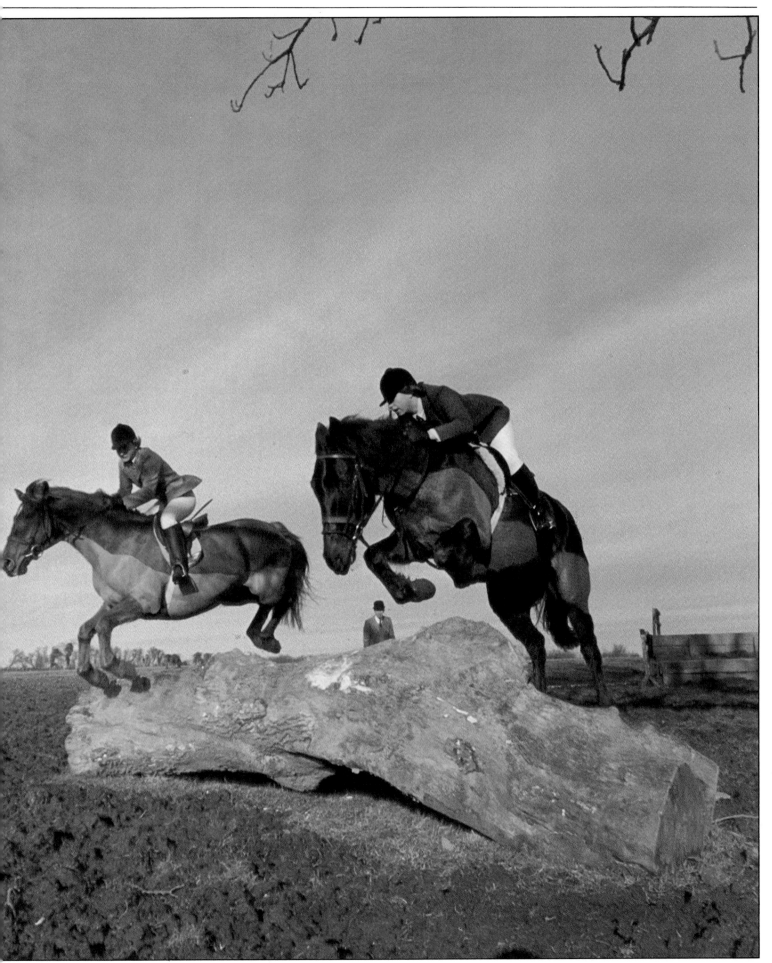

Indoor sport

Lighting levels for interior sporting events are seldom adequate to record fast-moving activities, and electronic flash must nearly always be used to support the spotlights or floodlights. Flash on the camera tends to give a rather flat image without much form. It is better to set up flash units at an angle. A dark background helps to hide the tangle of bars, wires or ropes often present, but you should try to avoid jet-blackness by shooting at slow exposures (1/60 or 1/30) to pick up existing light. Fast lenses and film are usually needed, and anticipation of the right moment to shoot is crucial.

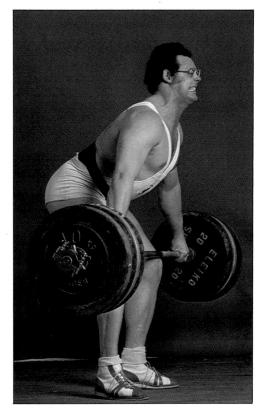

Weightlifting *is relatively easy to light and photograph, as the positions are fixed. To catch this moment of stress, I arranged a plain background and positioned one electronic flash close to the camera and another aimed towards the lifter's face from a fairly high angle.*
Hasselblad, 150mm, electronic flash, Ektachrome 64, f16.

The two shots of the gymnast *were lit from the rear right by a strong spotlight that established a suitable atmosphere but which did not provide enough light to arrest her movement. I supported this with an electronic flash from the same direction, with another at front left. An exposure of 1/30 picked out background flare, and flash froze the movement.*
Hasselblad, 150mm, tripod, electronic flash, Ektachrome 200, 1/30, f16.

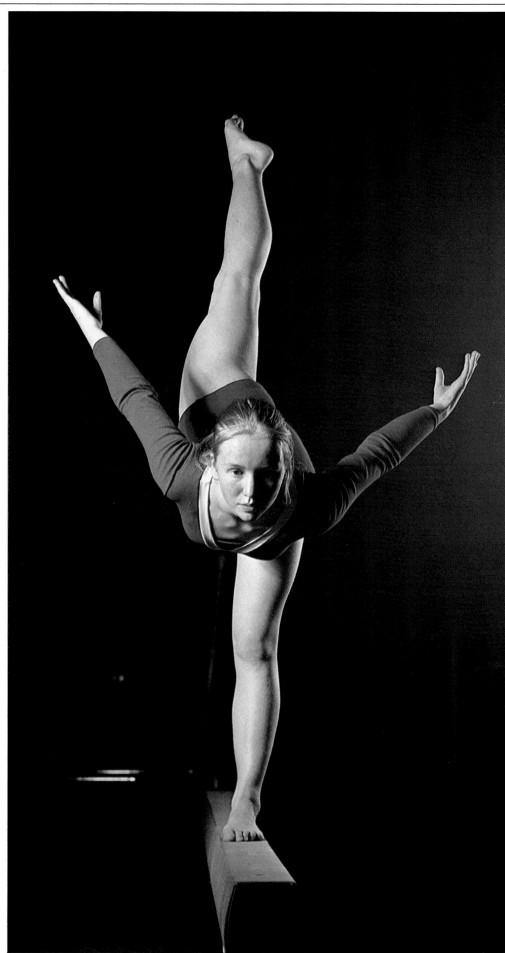

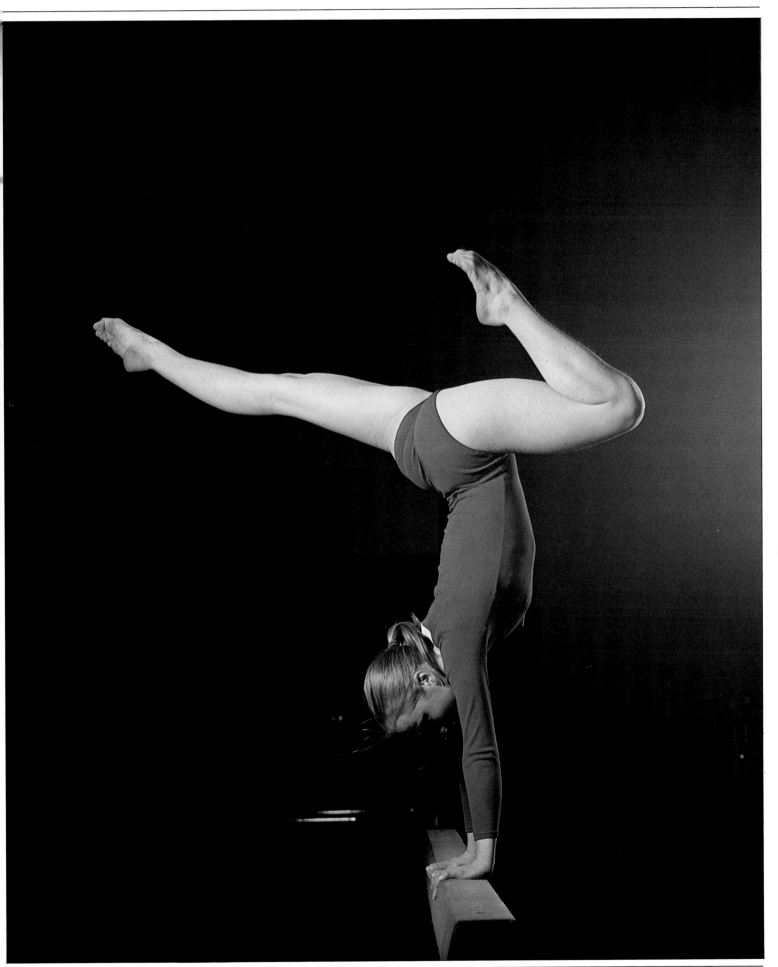

Outdoor sport

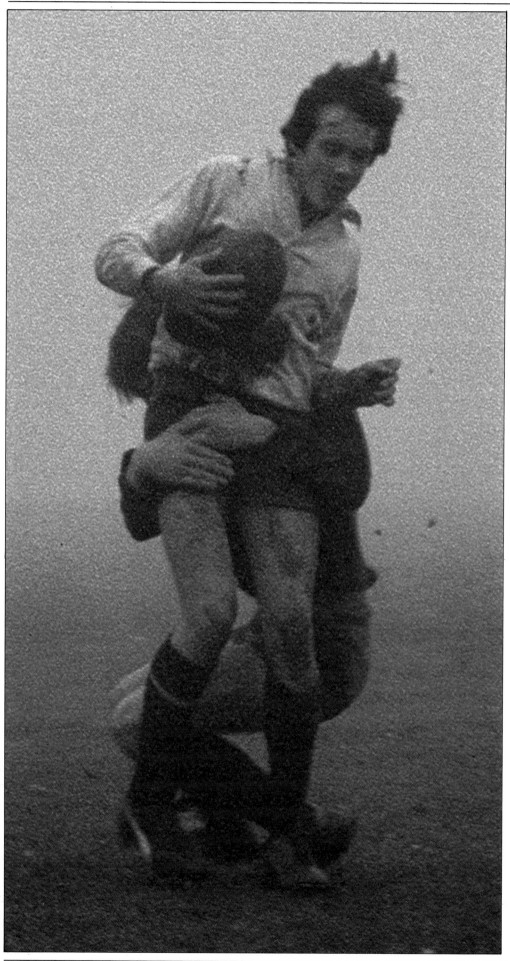

Sportsmen compete outdoors under conditions ranging from dazzling sun to near-blizzard. Strong light makes it easier to capture their energy and vitality because high shutter speeds are usually necessary and you may also have to stop down for maximum depth of field in fast-moving events. An instinct for the dramatic moment is essential and anticipation becomes still more crucial in poor light to allow accurate focusing at open aperture.

Apart from fast lenses and film, the basic technical requirement is a versatile camera with interchangeable lenses. A zoom with pistol grip is useful for changing focal lengths but requires considerable skill. Choosing the right position is the most important consideration of all. Obviously, it helps to know the sport, though you can learn much by watching professional photographers at work.

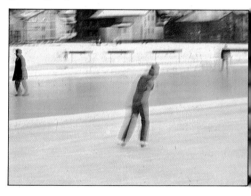

The graceful action of a skater *at Zermatt and the subtle blue tones in her clothing have been captured with an exposure slower than the movement of her body and swinging hand. Slight blur can effectively suggest both the speed and atmosphere of winter sport, indicating the whirl of snow and the cool colours of ice.* Pentax, 100mm, Ektachrome 64, 1/15, f22.

Taken in failing light and gathering fog, *the picture of a rugby tackle has a grimy quality that helps to evoke the mud and toil of the game. Locked together in equal exhaustion towards the end of the match, the two players could be seen clearly only from a distance of about 30ft (9m) but their movement made a longer exposure impracticable.* Pentax, 100mm, Ektachrome 200, 1/500, f4.

Yachting *can be photographed well either from water level or from a height, but if you are shooting from a distance you will need strong light to show form and motion. Sunlight gave good colour rendering in this picture, which exploits an angle of view that gives the yacht a powerful forward thrust through the V-shape made by the wake and the shadow.* Pentax, 200mm, Ektachrome 200, 1/500, f8.

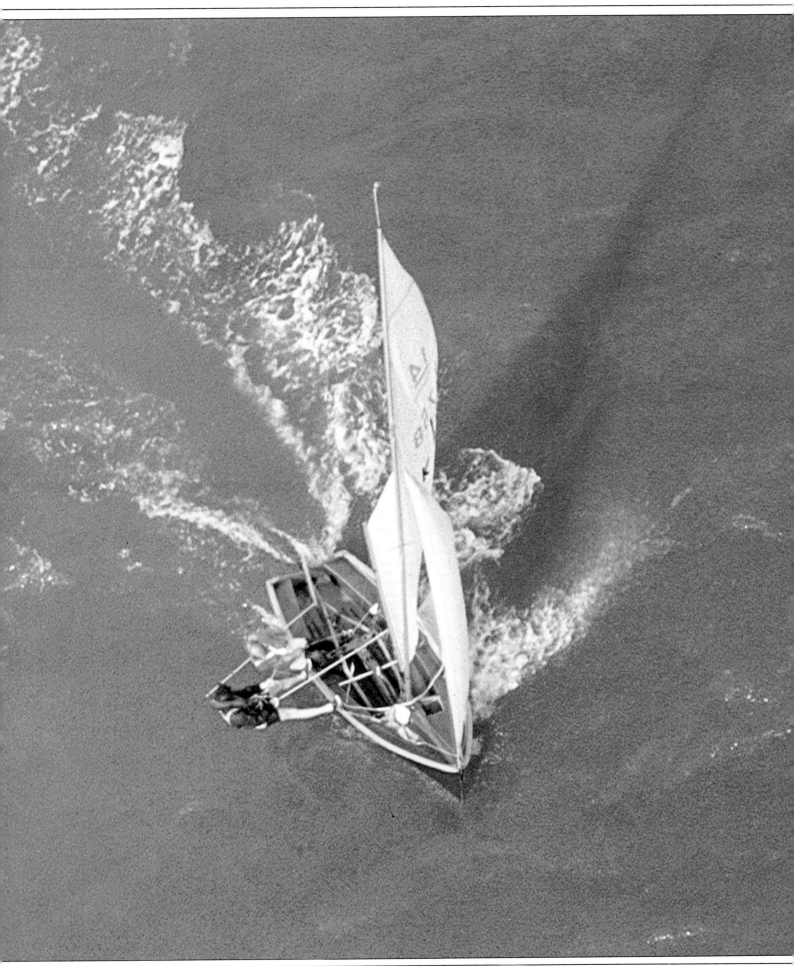

Copying

Reproducing an accurate facsimile of a work of art can be a simple matter in a studio or specially prepared room, but on site there are usually a number of difficulties to be overcome, not least that of lighting. The light should be perfectly even, and if possible a black velvet background should be used to define the edges of the work and absorb extraneous light. Copying can be done outdoors, but for good results the light should be diffused. You will need a steady tripod with the camera set absolutely parallel to the work you are copying and with correct verticals.

Indoors, ordinary floods can be used, but they should be kept at some distance from the subject. If the floods are circular, at least four will be needed to give even light. Better still are strips with daylight fluorescent tubes or electronic flash. Drawings with fine detail need subdued lighting.

Copying stained glass *presents special problems, partly because the glass will often be inaccessible, dirty and dimly lit and also because protective wire grids now tend to be placed behind many church windows and these show up clearly on sunny days. A slightly overcast day is better because the wire grids will be less evident then and lighting contrasts will also be reduced.*

If the stained glass is set into white glass, or if you want only a detail, it is best to mask off the surrounding area. Blocking extraneous light in this way will help you to capture the rich density and translucence of medieval glass seen in the larger of the two pictures below. As this window was set into the dark stone of a church vestibule, masking was unnecessary and luckily the wire frame behind can be seen only faintly. The glass was very dirty, but I was able to shoot it from a parapet directly opposite. I used a 150mm Hasselblad lens, with tripod, and high-speed film at 1/8, f8.

To photograph the coat of arms I had complete access from scaffolding, allowing me to place a white sheet behind the window and illuminate this backdrop with six 500-watt floods. The coat of arms was set in clear glass so I framed it with a black mask. To bring out the delicate etched tracery in the clear areas, I backed them with two layers of stencil paper. Exposure was 1sec., f8 using Ektachrome 160 and a 150mm lens on an MPP 5 × 4in camera.

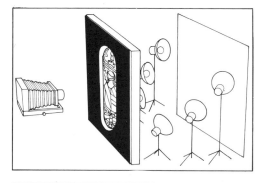

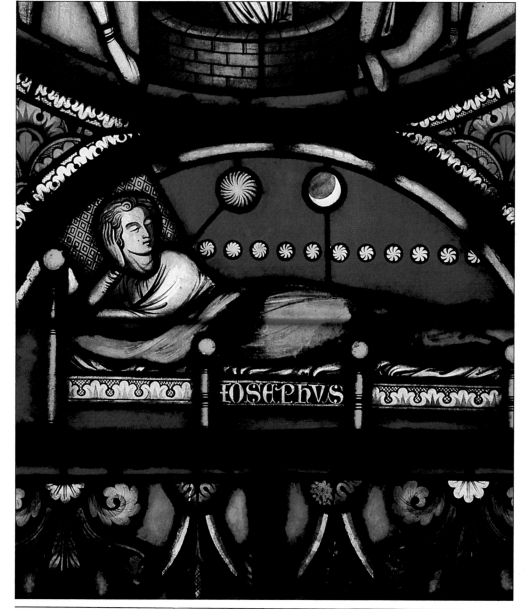

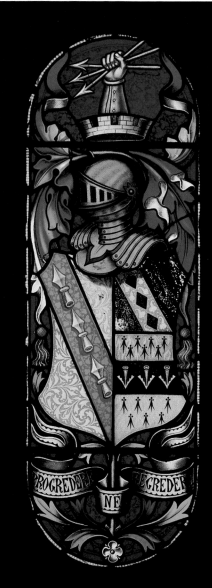

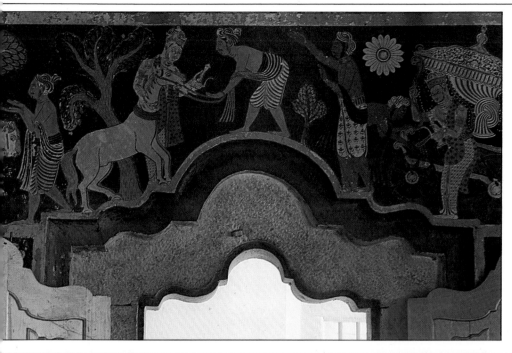

To photograph the mural *over a temple doorway in Sri Lanka, and also to show the attractive carved frame of the door, I had to balance strong light coming through the doorway from an anteroom. The feeling of heat outside the door and coolness inside would have been destroyed had I used flash. Instead, I hung two white sheets over an open doorway on the right of the anteroom, thus reducing the light reflected into the room with the mural.* Rolleiflex, 80mm, Ektachrome 200, 1/30, f8.

The old lady *in the mosaic kitchen is Madame Isidore, widow of a former guide at Chartres Cathedral who, in his spare time, decorated their house inside and out with murals, hand-painted furniture and elaborate mosaics of broken china. To achieve the effect of a moon over the spire, I switched on a light bulb. Strong diffused daylight shining through an open door behind me reveals pattern rather than form and I exposed for the darker areas.* Pentax, 28mm, Ektachrome 200, 1/30, f8.

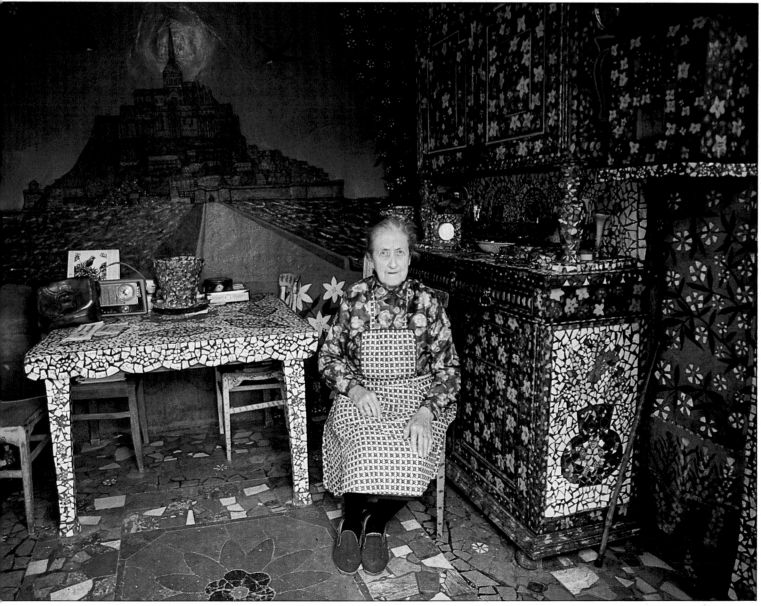

217

Copying

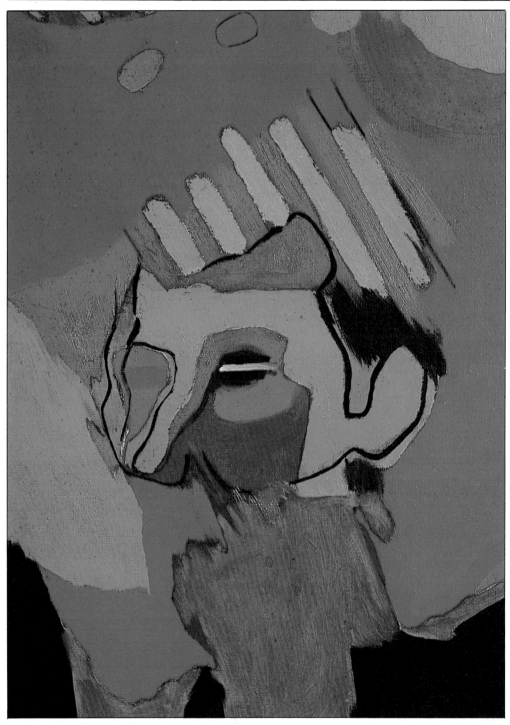

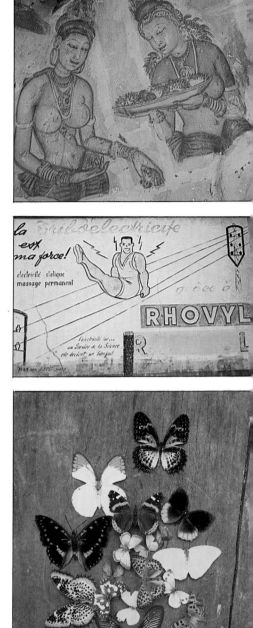

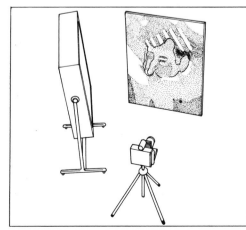

A **painting** *is normally copied by using flat, even lighting, which can be tested by holding a pencil near the subject to see if the density of shadow is equal on each side. When the texture is important, however, as in this detail of a self-portrait by Allen Jones, I prefer to use a directional light, placed at a 40° angle from the camera to show the surface of the canvas and brushmarks. The distance of the strip lights from the painting in the arrangement (shown right) was about 6ft (2m). A grey card is used for the meter reading to avoid variations produced by different areas of the work.* Linhof 5 × 4 in, 150mm, electronic flash, f22.

The **5th-century frescoes** *at Sigiriya, Sri Lanka (top), are painted under an overhang of rock in the open air, but the delicate colouring is remarkably intact. I took the picture in even, overcast light.* Rolleiflex, 55mm, Ektachrome 200, 1/125, f8.

Overcast light *reveals the subtle pinks and mauves of a French electricity advertisement, a more modern icon on a sun-bleached billboard in Lyons.* Pentax, 55mm, Ektachrome 200, 1/250, f8.

The butterflies *were arranged and lit for pattern and colour, with four photofloods bounced off a white ceiling.* MPP 5 × 4 in, Ektachrome 160, 1/30, f11.

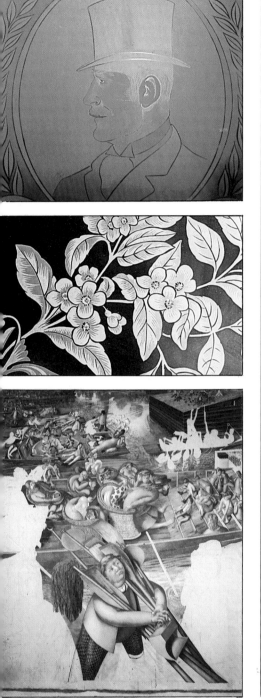

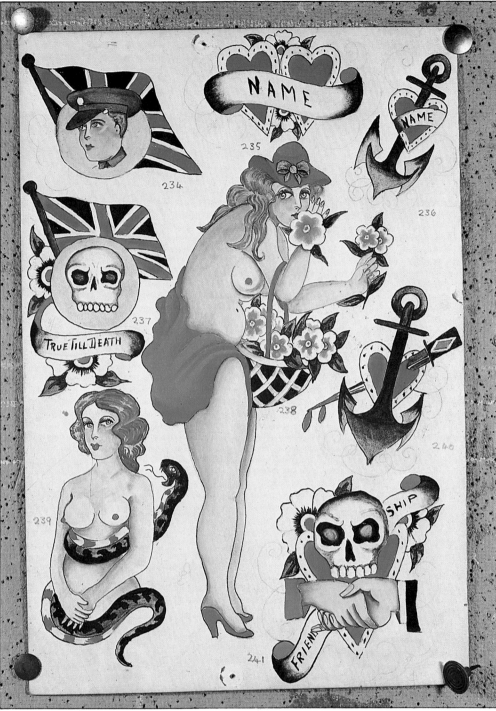

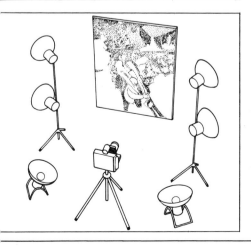

The diagram *shows the lighting needed to copy the painting above it, a large detail of* Christ at Cookham Regatta, *Stanley Spencer's last work. The small bedroom in which the artist was working made it impossible to light the painting from either side in the usual way. Using six 500-watt photofloods, I instead bounced the light from both side walls and the ceiling to achieve an even result. As soft light was essential to retain detail in pencil-sketched areas that were unpainted, I underexposed one stop. When copying paintings it is usual to show a grey and a standard colour chart for correct colour reproduction.*
MPP 5 × 4 in, 150 mm, Ektachrome 160, 1 sec., f8.

Increased contrast *is sometimes needed in copying. As the tattooist's chart (above) was faded, I underexposed half a stop in the light of two photofloods and lengthened development time.*
MPP 5 × 4 in, 150 mm, Ektachrome 160, 1/10, f8.

The top-hatted gentleman, *etched on a pub window, was lit by bulbs inside. I aligned a red lamp with his lips.*
Pentax, 50 mm, Ektachrome 160, 1/30, f4.

The etched flowers *were photographed in bright sun. I angled the camera so that the etched areas reflected light while the clear window showed a dark interior.*
Pentax, 55 mm, Agfachrome 50s, 1/250, f8.

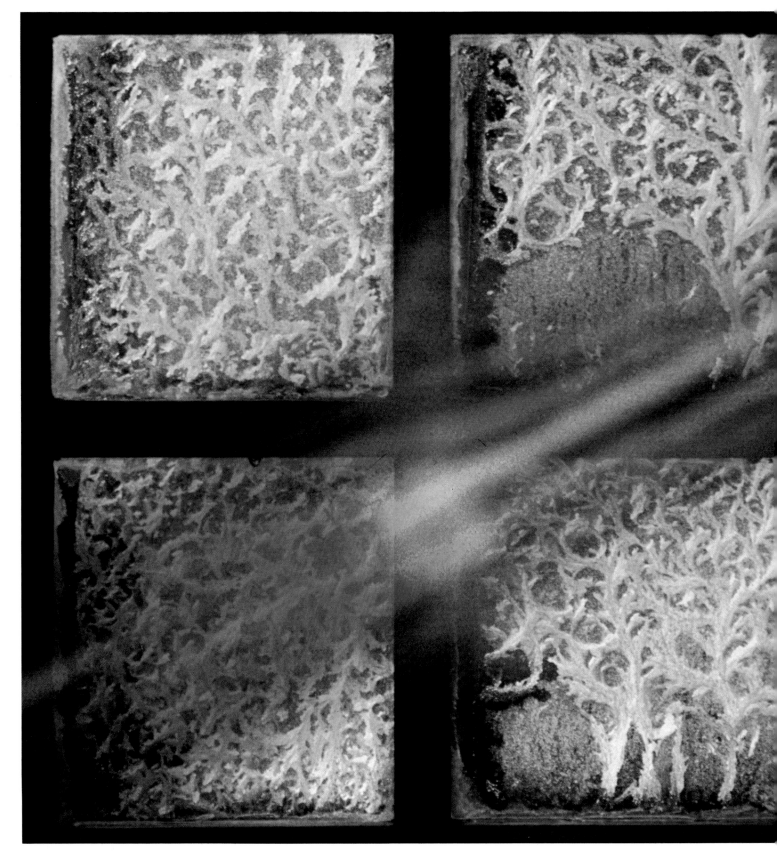

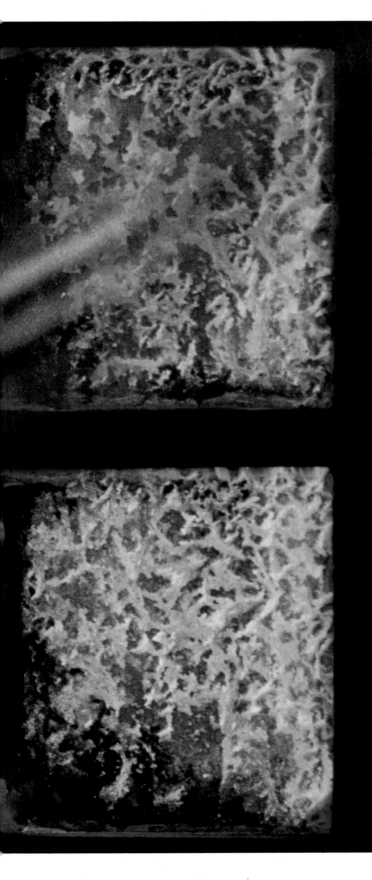

Colour materials and methods

Creativity in colour photography *does not end with the composition of an image in the camera. It is extended by variations of exposure and filtration, processing and printing, and by studio or darkroom techniques of altering the image. The mysterious flash of colour appearing through a window delicately etched by frost never existed until two images were sandwiched together and rephotographed. The window was projected on a screen simultaneously with a photograph taken through a microscope showing a pinpoint of light distorted by a lens into streaks of spectral colours.*

The colour process

All modern colour films have a "tripack" structure; they comprise a sandwich of three gelatin layers containing light-sensitive silver halides. When the camera shutter opens, each layer can record one of the primary colours of light—red, green or blue. Thus white light (a mixture of red, green and blue) forms a latent image in all three layers, while yellow (a mixture of red and green) forms latent images only in the red- and green-sensitive layers.

To understand how the colour process works in a transparency imagine that the colours of the subject include a strip of green. This will appear green in the final picture because in that part of the image, dyes of colours that are complementary to red and blue have been formed in two layers of the film during development. As a result, when that area of the transparency is viewed in white light, red and blue are subtracted from the light by the complementary dyes, leaving only green light to appear.

To form the coloured dyes, the film is first developed in much the same way as a black and white film. We follow only what happens in the strip of film that will finally appear green. The developer chemicals cause silver to form as grains in this area of the green-sensitive layer. Next, the film is treated so that silver will form in the same area of the other two layers during a second development, *together with* coloured dyes, either introduced in the developer materials themselves or formed through reaction with "couplers" present in the emulsion. The colour appears only where silver is being newly deposited.

In the strip that will finally look green, the blue- and red-sensitive layers of the film thus contain correctly positioned subtractive dyes, though hidden by the developed silver that now blackens all layers of the film. When this silver is removed the final image can be seen.

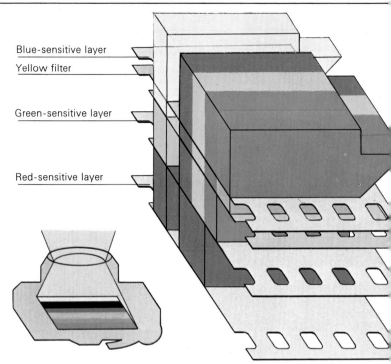

Blue-sensitive layer
Yellow filter
Green-sensitive layer
Red-sensitive layer

A beam of six colours entering the camera (above) is "seen" selectively by the three layers of a reversal film. The diagrams (right) open the film sandwich to show how the six colours affect each layer. Blue is absorbed by the top layer, green by the next and red in the lowest. Yellow has both red and green components, which are absorbed in the middle and lowest layers respectively. Black (no light) has no effect. Part of the white light is absorbed in all three layers. (The yellow filter below the top layer blocks stray blue.)

Colour negatives

Colour negative film differs significantly from transparency film in its processing, as the complementary dyes are formed in the areas where the film layers absorbed light when the photograph was taken, instead of in those where it was not absorbed. The negative thus shows the scene in its complementary colours—yellow where it was blue, magenta where it was green and cyan where it was red.

A positive colour print is made by shining light from an enlarger through the negative on to printing paper containing three emulsion layers on a white paper base. Complementary dyes formed in these layers ensure that the colours finally exhibited by the print are those of the original subject. Test prints enable the colours of the final print to be exactly controlled by varying the densities of coloured filters inside the enlarger, and hence the colour balance of the light.

The dyes used in colour films and colour papers are not perfect. Often the magenta dye absorbs some blue light as well as the intended green, and so is too yellowish (though not to the naked eye). Cyan dye may absorb some green and blue light in addition to the intended red, and so be pinkish. "Integral" masks in negative film correct for these defects. The magenta-forming coupler is made yellowish from the start instead of colourless. After processing, the magenta layer is yellow in clear areas and magenta in areas that absorbed light. Similarly, the cyan-forming dye coupler is coloured pink and, after processing, leaves a pink mask in the areas that did not absorb light. The combined colouring of the dye couplers gives the negative an overall orange cast that enables the final colour balance of the pictures to be checked and adjusted during printing.

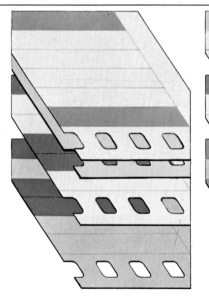

Development of negative film causes silver to form in areas that absorbed light from the photographed beam, together with dyes complementary to the colours in the beam. So yellow forms in the top layer in the strips that absorbed blue light. The magenta- and cyan-forming layers below this show yellowish and pink masks in clear areas of the emulsion.

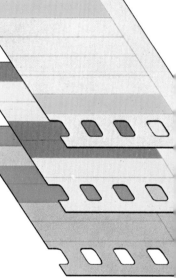

Bleaching and fixing remove silver so that complementary colour dyes appear clearly. In combination, the film layers form the colour negative seen at the top of the diagram on the right. This negative can then be projected through an enlarger on to the three layers of emulsion in the printing paper. The top layer absorbs red, the middle layer green and the bottom blue.

Silver development
A negative silver-grain image is developed in each layer of the film emulsion.

Colour development
Colour is now introduced in the formerly clear areas during a second development.

Bleaching and fixing
When silver and its salts are removed, dyes are left in the appropriate areas.

How a transparency works
Each film layer absorbs a primary colour from the viewing light in certain areas.

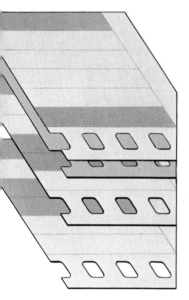
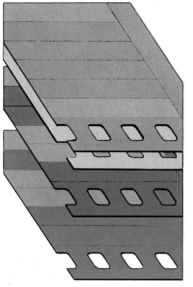
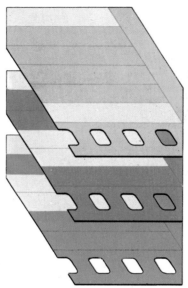
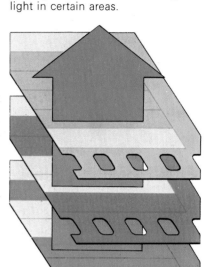

Silver grains appear wherever the film has absorbed light. Thus white in the original scene gives rise to a dark image patch in all three layers, while green creates an image in the middle layer only. At this stage of processing no dye is yet developed.

The first development is halted and the film is "fogged" so that silver grains can be formed throughout all emulsion layers. Special chemicals then develop the remaining silver, and where this happens dyes appear in colours that are still masked by the silver grains on all layers.

During the final stages of processing, silver is bleached out. With silver (and the yellow filter) removed, the layers now show dyes that are the complementaries of blue, green and red (yellow, magenta and cyan). These appear only where layers did not record light originally.

When white light is beamed through the layers, green light emerges in the correct strip, as shown. In this strip, the red component of white light has been subtracted by cyan dye in the bottom layer, the blue by yellow dye in the top layer.

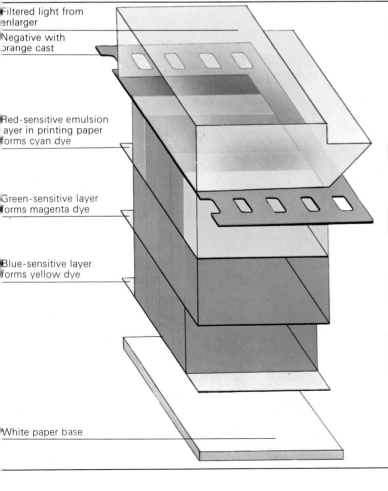

Filtered light from enlarger

Negative with orange cast

Red-sensitive emulsion layer in printing paper forms cyan dye

Green-sensitive layer forms magenta dye

Blue-sensitive layer forms yellow dye

White paper base

During print development, colour dyes and silver form where emulsion layers in the paper absorbed light from the negative. In the strip that was magenta in the negative (and green originally) the top (cyan-forming) layer and the bottom (yellow-forming) layer

now have dye patches darkened by silver. After bleaching and fixing, the strip looks green because these patches subtract the red and blue components of light entering the paper and being reflected up from the white base.

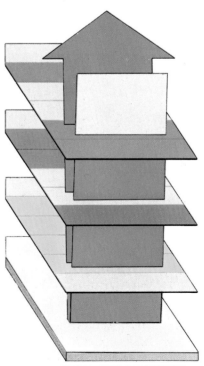

The colour process

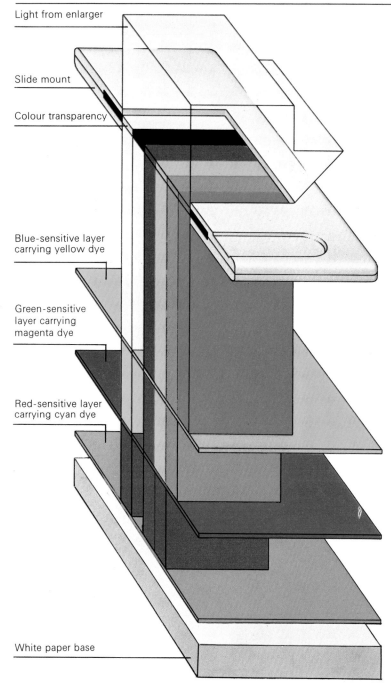

Light from enlarger

Slide mount

Colour transparency

Blue-sensitive layer carrying yellow dye

Green-sensitive layer carrying magenta dye

Red-sensitive layer carrying cyan dye

White paper base

Dye-destruction processes

Making enlarged colour prints directly from negatives has the disadvantage that the quality and colour cast of the negative cannot be assessed by the eye. It is also hard to judge the crop that will give the best picture. As a result test prints have to be made before the final print. Dye-destruction processes avoid these disadvantages for they form positive prints from colour transparencies directly. In the printing paper used, the layers of emulsion contain already-formed yellow, magenta and cyan dyes, and unwanted areas of dye are bleached during processing to leave only the coloured areas necessary to the subtractive colour synthesis described in the previous pages.

Before processing, the print looks completely black. White light falling on the paper would have each of its component primary colours subtracted by either the yellow, magenta or cyan dye. No yellow mask is needed beneath the blue-sensitive layer because the yellow dye is a sufficiently good absorber of blue light. The dye characteristics can be controlled so that they are longer lasting and transmit purer colours than dyes formed during processing of negative or reversal film. There is also less degradation of colour by internal reflection. The speed of the printing paper is improved by making each sensitive layer in a double structure. The lower part contains both silver halide and dye. But in the upper part the silver halide in the emulsion has no associated dye absorbing part of the light and there is more light available for the halide to absorb.

When the transparency is projected on to the dye-destruction paper, both parts of each layer form latent images in the areas that absorb light. The dyes are unaffected at this stage. Development causes silver grains to form in the image areas and grains migrate from the top part of each layer into the dye layer below to reinforce the images there.

During the subsequent bleaching process, the dye associated with each clump of silver grains is made colourless in each layer of emulsion as the silver itself is dissolved out. In areas where no silver formed, dyes remain in the correct patterns to show the original subject.

The tripack structure *of dye-destruction printing paper is shown above as it analyses light beamed through a six-banded colour transparency that is mounted in a slide. The top layer of the printing paper is dyed yellow and strongly absorbs blue light. Only green, red and a mixture of the two (yellow) passes to the next, magenta-dyed, layer. Here, green light is absorbed and only red light can reach the bottom layer, dyed cyan. The black area of the transparency blocks all light, so in this strip dyes are left unaffected in all the layers.*

Processing of dye-destruction prints *begins with development of silver grains in each layer where light from the subject has been absorbed. Dark images in two parts of the top layer (right) correspond to blue light from both the white and blue strips in the subject. The middle layer records the green, yellow and white strips and the bottom layer the red, yellow and white strips. Bleaching dissolves the silver and leaves dye only in the previously unsilvered areas. By subtracting complementary colours these combined dye patches will show the subject.*

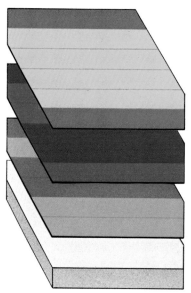

During development, silver images of each colour component of the subject appear in each layer of the printing paper.

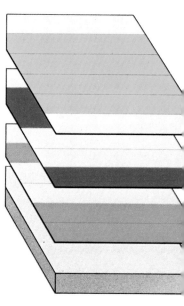

Bleaching and fixing removes the silver and associated dyes and leaves the dyes that remain to produce the positive image.

Instant colour

The structure of a typical instant-colour film is shown below at the left as it receives the image of a coloured band. There are three sensitive emulsion layers, each positioned just above a layer of primary-absorbing dyes whose molecules are linked to molecules of developer compound. These six layers together form the "negative layer" of the film—the area shown opened up here.

During processing, the development of silver controls the upward migration of dyes into an image-receiving layer. The final colours are formed by the mingling of these dyes, not their superimposition as in ordinary colour films and prints.

When a photograph is taken, light passes through a clear protective layer, an acid polymer layer that will "switch off" the processing and a "timing" layer. The light then forms a latent image of the blue component of the subject in the top, blue-sensitive, layer in the usual fashion. Remaining light passes through the yellow dye developer layer beneath and encounters in turn the green-sensitive layer, magenta dye developer, red-sensitive layer and cyan dye developer.

After exposure, the film is pulled from the camera or wound out by a motor. A pod containing fluid is burst by this action and its contents spread between the image-receiving layer and the negative layer. The fluid contains a pigment that during development protects the negative layer from light and thereafter provides a white backing for the final image. Other chemicals in the fluid rapidly soak through the negative layer and cause the dye developers to start diffusing upwards as shown in the right-hand diagram.

Where dye developer meets a sensitized area of emulsion (an area that has absorbed light), it causes silver to develop. The same reaction immobilizes the dye that is the immediate cause of this development. Thus, where silver is developed in, say, the green-sensitive layer (corresponding to a green area in the subject) the magenta dye developer is immobilized and does not contribute to the image. Silver developed here does not impede the upward diffusion of cyan from the lowest layer, however, as the development reaction has been stopped by the time this dye arrives.

In the area corresponding to blue in the subject, silver does not develop in the green-sensitive layer and the magenta dye is free to mix with the rising cyan and then continue up through the immobilized yellow dye to appear as blue. In the image-receiving layer, green appears where cyan and yellow are mixed, yellow where yellow rises alone, red where magenta and yellow mingle, black where all the dyes mingle and white where no dyes arrive at all—light is simply reflected back from the white layer formed as development began.

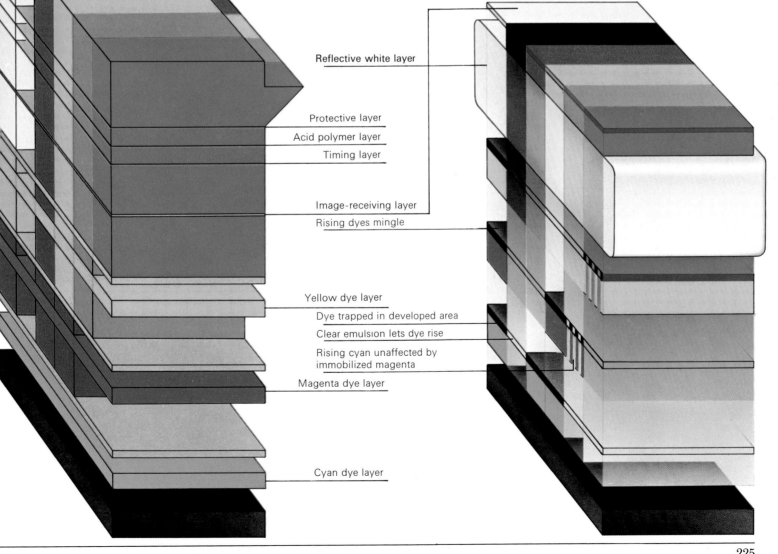

Reflective white layer

Protective layer
Acid polymer layer
Timing layer

Image-receiving layer
Rising dyes mingle

Yellow dye layer
Dye trapped in developed area
Clear emulsion lets dye rise
Rising cyan unaffected by immobilized magenta
Magenta dye layer

Cyan dye layer

Choosing colour film

The range and availability of colour film changes rapidly and no list can remain completely up to date for long. The great variety of packaging and brand names tends to obscure the fact that there are comparatively few manufacturers of film, for the same product may be sold under a dozen or more different names. While this chart does not list every make of film sold in every country, it does provide a good idea of the major brands available around the world.

*(Speeds marked * indicate arti-ficial light film. All others are balanced for daylight.)*

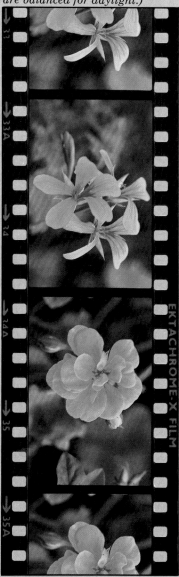

COLOUR REVERSAL FILM (for transparencies)

FILM NAME	ASA SPEED	SIZES	MANUFACTURER/DISTRIBUTOR
Agfachrome 50L Professional	*50	120, 135, sheet, 35 mm bulk film	Agfa-Gevaert, West Germany
Agfachrome 50S Professional	50	120, 135, sheet, 70 mm, 35 mm bulk film	Agfa-Gevaert, West Germany
Agfachrome 64	64	126, 135	Honeywell, USA
Agfachrome Pocket Special	64	110	Agfa-Gevaert, West Germany
Agfacolor CT 18	50	120, 127, 135, rapid	Agfa-Gevaert, West Germany
Agfacolor CT 21	100	135	Agfa-Gevaert, West Germany
Agfacolor CT-PAK	64	126	Agfa-Gevaert, West Germany
Alfochrome DC21	100	135	Ringfoto, West Germany
Boots Colourslide	64	135	Boots, Great Britain
Brillant HS	100	135	Neckerman, West Germany
Brillant Superchrome	50	135	Neckerman, West Germany
Cilchrome	125	135	Lumière, France
Diachrome SL 18	50	135	Foto-Porst, West Germany
Diachrome SL 20	80	126	Foto-Porst, West Germany
Diachrome SL 21	100	135	Foto-Porst, West Germany
Ektachrome Aero Infrared	125	120, 135	Kodak
Ektachrome 64	64	110, 126, 135	Kodak
Ektachrome 200	200	135	Kodak
Ektachrome 160 Tungsten	*160	135	Kodak
Ektachrome 64 Professional	64	120, 135, 220, 70 mm	Kodak
Ektachrome 50 Professional	*50	120, 135	Kodak
Ektachrome 200 Professional	200	120, 135, 35 mm bulk film	Kodak
Ektachrome 160 Professional	*160	120, 135, 35 mm bulk film	Kodak
Ektachrome Slide Duplicating Film 5071	*3	35 mm bulk film	Kodak
Ektachrome Duplicating Film 6121	*3	Sheet	Kodak
Ektachrome 64 Professional Film 6117	64	Sheet	Kodak
Ektachrome 50 Professional Film 6118	*50	Sheet	Kodak
FK Color RD-17	40	135	Fotokemika, Yugoslavia
Fortechrom	50	135	Forte, Hungary
Fujichrome R 100	100	126, 135	Fuji, Japan
Fujichrome RK	100	126	Fuji, Japan
Fujichrome Professional Type D	100	120	Fuji, Japan
Fujicolor R 100	100	120, 135	Fuji, Japan
Fujicolor Professional Type D	50	Sheet	Fuji, Japan
Fujicolor Professional Type T	*32	Sheet	Fuji, Japan
Gratispool Colour	64	126, 135	Gratispool, Great Britain
Kodachrome 25	25	135	Kodak
Kodachrome II Type A	*40	135	Kodak
Kodachrome 64	64	110, 126, 135	Kodak
Kodak Photomicrography Color 2483	16	135	Kodak
Negrachrome	50	135	Negra, Spain
Ogachrome	50	135	Obergassner, West Germany
Ogachrome	100	135	Obergassner, West Germany
Orwochrom UT 18	50	120, 135, sheet	VEB Filmfabrik, Wolfen, East Germany
Orwochrom UT 21	100	135	VEB Filmfabrik, Wolfen, East Germany
Orwochrom UK 17	*40	120, 135, sheet	VEB Filmfabrik, Wolfen, East Germany
Orwochrom Professional Type S	40	120, sheet	VEB Filmfabrik, Wolfen, East Germany
Peruchrome C 19	64	126, 135	Perutz, West Germany
Prinzcolor Slide Film	100	135	Dixons, Great Britain
Sakuracolor R 100	100	120, 126, 135	Konishiroku, Japan
Sears Color Slide	64	126, 135	Sears, Roebuck, USA
3M Color Slide Film	64	110, 126	3M, Italy
3M Color Slide Film	100	135	3M, Italy
3M Color Slide Film	400	135	3M, Italy
Technicolor Slide	64	126, 135	Technicolor, USA
Turachrome	50	135	Turaphot, West Germany
Turachrome	80	126	Turaphot, West Germany
Turachrome	100	135	Turaphot, West Germany
Turachrome	200	135	Turaphot, West Germany

COLOUR NEGATIVE FILM (for prints)

FILM NAME	ASA SPEED	SIZES	MANUFACTURER/DISTRIBUTOR
Agfacolor CNS 2	80	120, 126, 127, 135	Agfa-Gevaert, West Germany
Agfacolor Pocket Special	80	110	Agfa-Gevaert, West Germany
Agfacolor 80S Professional	80	120, 135, sheet	Agfa-Gevaert, West Germany
Agfacolor II N21	80	120, 135, sheet	Agfa-Gevaert, West Germany
Berkeycolor	80	126	Berkey, USA
Boots Colourprint II	100	110, 126, 135	Boots, Great Britain
Brillant	80	110, 135	Neckerman, West Germany
Brillant	100	120, 126	Neckerman, West Germany
Cilcolor	100	110, 126, 135	Lumière, France
Directacolor	80	110, 126, 135	PIAL, Canada
Dixons Colourprint II	80	110, 120, 126, 135	Dixons, Great Britain
Ektacolor ID Copy Film	100	135, sheet	Kodak
FK Color	64	120, 135	Fotokemika, Yugoslavia
Fortecolor	80	120, 135	Forte, Hungary
Fujicolor F-II	100	110, 120, 126, 135	Fuji, Japan
Fujicolor F-II 400	400	110, 120, 135	Fuji, Japan
Fujicolor Professional Type L	*50	120, sheet	Fuji, Japan
Fujicolor Professional Type S	100	120, sheet	Fuji, Japan
Gratispool Colour	80	120, 126, 127, 135	Gratispool, Great Britain
Hanimex-Color CNS80	80	126, 135	Hanimex, Australia
Kodacolor II	80	110, 120, 126, 127, 135	Kodak
Kodacolor 400	400	110, 120, 135	Kodak
Kodak Instant Picture Film PR-10	150	Film pack (6.7 × 9 cm)	Kodak
Ogacolor	80	110, 120, 126, 135	Obergassner, West Germany
Orwocolor NC 19 Mask	64	120, 135, sheet	VEB Filmfabrik, Wolfen, East Germany
Pacific Prestige	80	110, 135	Pacific Film Laboratories, Australia
Perucolor	80	110, 126, 135	Perutz, West Germany
Polacolor Type 58	75	Sheet	Polaroid, USA
Polacolor 2 Type 88	75	Film pack (8.2 × 8.6 cm)	Polaroid, USA
Polacolor 2 Type 108	75	Film pack (8.5 × 10.5 cm)	Polaroid, USA
Polaroid SX-70 Land Film	80	Film pack (8 × 8 cm)	Polaroid, USA
Porst Color	100	110, 120, 126, 135	Porst, West Germany
Prinzcolor Print	80	126, 135	Dixons, Great Britain
Revuecolor 3000	80	110, 120, 126, 135	Foto-Quelle, West Germany
Sakuracolor II N 100	100	110, 120, 126, 135	Konishiroku, Japan
Sakuracolor 400	400	110, 135	Konishiroku, Japan
Sakuracolor Professional Type L	*32	4 × 5 in sheet	Konishiroku, Japan
Sakuracolor Professional Type S	80	4 × 5 in sheet	Konishiroku, Japan
Sears Color Print	80	120, 126, 127, 135	Sears, Roebuck, USA
Svemacolor DS4	50	120, 135	Svema, USSR
Svemacolor DS5	40	120, 135	Svema, USSR
Svemacolor LW3	40	120, 135, sheet	Svema, USSR
Technicolor Print	80	126, 135	Technicolor, USA
3M Color Print	80	110, 126, 135	3M, Italy
TriFCA Colourprint	80	110, 126, 135	FCA, Great Britain/USA
Turacolor	80	120	Turaphot, West Germany
Turacolor	100	110, 135	Turaphot, West Germany
Valcolor	100	126, 135	Valca, Spain
Vericolor II Professional Type L	*80	120, 135, 220, sheet	Kodak
Vericolor II Professional Type S	100	120, 135, 220, 35 mm, 46 mm, 70 mm	Kodak

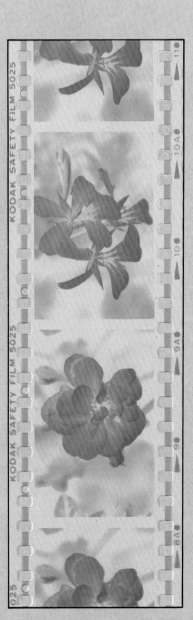

Selecting the exposure

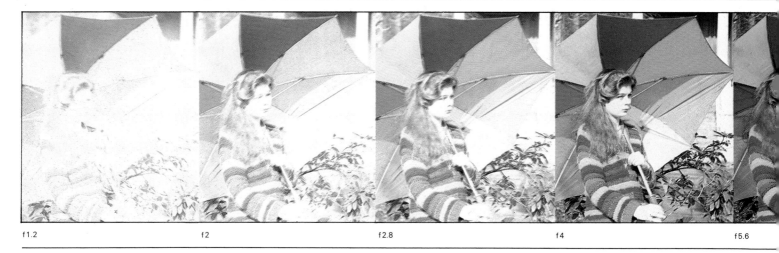

f1.2   f2   f2.8   f4   f5.6

Gauging the correct exposure for colour film is much more critical than for black and white, yet it is usually possible to vary the exposure by one stop on either side and still produce acceptable results. Printing allows further latitude for correction by at least a stop or two either way without much loss of colour fidelity or detail. Modern exposure meters are accurate enough to keep you well within these limits if you are photographing in flat, even lighting. Problems generally arise when you are shooting against the light, in extreme conditions, or if there are areas of strong tonal contrast, when you have to decide what balance to strike between bright highlights and shadow areas. On an overall reading the highlights will influence the meter most, leading to underexposure unless an allowance is made for the shadows.

Underexposure by up to half a stop generally produces a saturated colour in reversal film, and overexposure by a similar amount has similar results with colour negatives. It is a good idea not to send a whole batch of reversal film for development at once if you have shot a considerable amount at a single session. A test roll will show if any adjustment is needed for the remaining rolls of film during their processing.

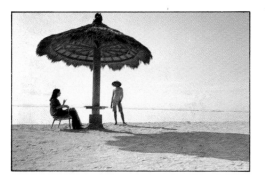

The photographs of the girl beneath the seaside parasol *evoke a feeling of isolation in the gathering heat. I took both shots in oblique morning light, exposing for the foreground sand in the smaller picture and for more detail in the shaded area in the other, burning out the sea and sky and creating a stronger impression of heat.*
Pentax, 50mm, Ektachrome 64, 1/500, f11, (above), f5.6 (right).

In the two pictures of the child, *the first was taken at the exposure that was indicated for the girl's skin and has an appropriately sunny atmosphere, but background colour is dissipated. The second shot strengthens the colour of the background, with greater contrast and increased sharpness, because I closed down one stop. The recording of colour is less accurate, however, and gives an overall impression of evening light.*
Pentax, 105mm, Ektachrome 64, 1/125, f8 (right), f11 (far right).

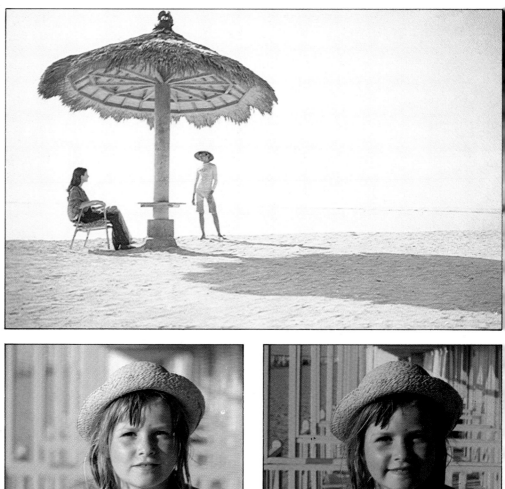

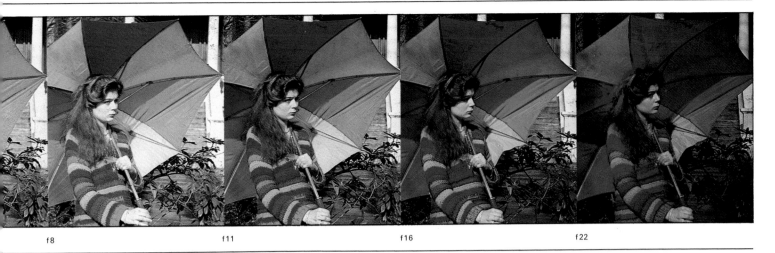

f8   f11   f16   f22

As the mood of a colour picture can be radically changed by such adjustments, exposure must be carefully considered. Landscapes will appear richer by underexposing half a stop or more, whereas portraits of women are often more effective with a slight degree of overexposure, as this will emphasize the delicacy of their features and subtleties of skin colouring.

The sequence of pictures of the girl holding an umbrella shows the difficulty of striking an ideal balance between colours when some are directly lit while others are in shade. The full range of aperture variations was shot in daylight with a Pentax, using a 50mm lens, Ektachrome 64 film and a shutter speed of 1/60. The first three, taken on apertures of f1.2, f2 and f2.8, are much too overexposed, but at f4 the result is almost acceptable for a high-key pic-

ture. At f5.6 the colours in the shaded area of the umbrella are almost perfectly recorded, but overall the picture is still too light. There is not much improvement with an aperture of f8. At f11 slight underexposure has produced extremely rich colour in the sunlit parts of the umbrella, and in the girl's jersey. Colours remain rich at f16, but the picture has started to darken. At f22 the result is too gloomy.

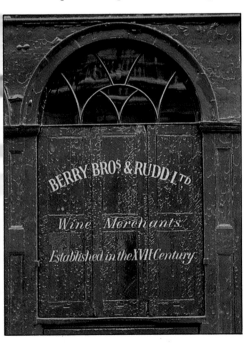

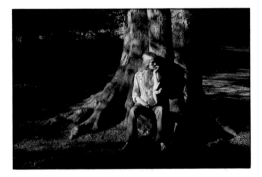

The pattern of light and shade *in the picture of the girl sitting against a tree was captured by exposing for detail and richness in the highlights. This resulted in the dense, encroaching shadows suggesting the secrecy of a forest. The bulk and form of the tree trunk is accentuated by the angular light. The reading for the general scene was f8, but I chose to stop down.*
Nikon, 50mm, Ektachrome 64, 1/125, f11.

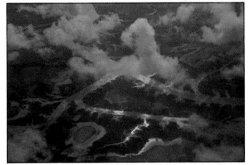

When shooting from an aircraft *it is usually best to hold the camera close to the window, brace yourself firmly and wait for the plane to bank. A dark coat or blanket held behind you will help eliminate reflections on the window. The picture of evening light on an Australian river was exposed for the highlights and a wide aperture lessened the possibility of window scratches diffusing the image.*
Minolta, 50mm, Ektachrome 200, 1/250, f2.8.

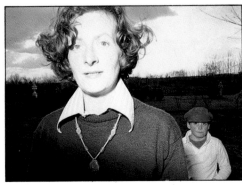

Anything black or dark brown *needs more exposure than usual, while reflections on a shiny black surface can give particularly misleading meter readings. For the wine merchant's shutter (above left) I chose an exposure in diffused light that fully recorded detail. To show detail in black areas you should increase exposure by one stop. White surfaces, on the other hand, give readings that are misleadingly high and you should close down by a stop.*
Pentax, 50mm, Ektachrome 64, 1/125, f5.6.

Selective exposure *can be used with flash, as in the shot at the left, where exposure has been varied on the faces, while the garden is greatly underexposed and the sky slightly overexposed. The shot was taken with a Pentax and 50mm lens at f11—the correct reading with electronic flash on the boy at 6ft (2m). His mother is 3ft (1m) away so is overexposed by two stops. At 1/30 the garden needed an aperture of f5.6 so is two stops underexposed, while the sky needed f16 and is overexposed by a stop.*

Exposure variations

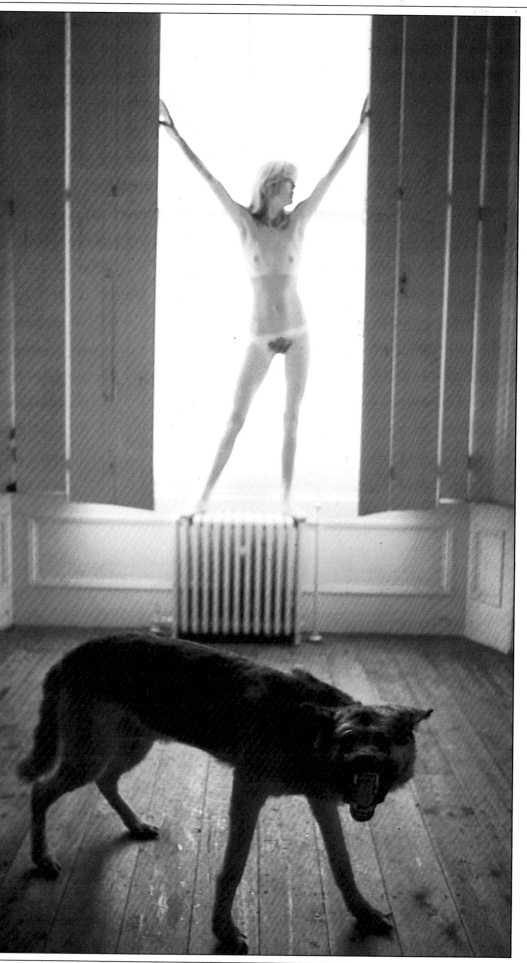

A deliberately "incorrect" exposure *accentuates the drama of the narrative picture (left). The girl is almost devoured by the light that frames her, and the intensity of the highlight draws the eye back from the foreground image of a snarling dog. A more even lighting balance would have destroyed the bizarre quality of the picture with its juxtaposition of shadowy menace and airy gracefulness. The shutters emphasize the height of the girl, who is fined down by the light bathing her body.* Pentax, 28mm, Ektachrome 64, 1/60, f5.6.

The man whittled away *by the intense light at the end of a corridor is the centre of interest in a picture I shot at a purposely slow exposure in order to strengthen the impression of a dwindling form. To reveal any of its detail, the passageway would have needed an exposure several stops greater, but the effect of leaving it dark is that the two highlight areas are played off against each other.* Nikon, 35mm, Ektachrome 64, 1/8, f8.

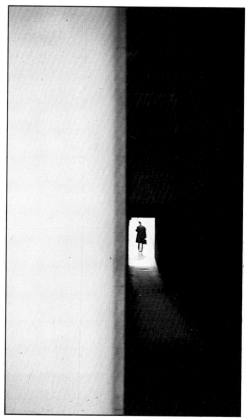

Underexposure *has brought out the emphatic baroque forms of the Fountain of Bacchus in the Boboli Gardens at Florence. The light falling on the statue of the dwarf Pietro Barbino was too flat for an effective picture at normal exposure, so I closed down an extra stop and a half. This darkened the purple and brown tones in the rough-textured background and accentuated the modelling.* Rolleiflex, 80mm, Ektachrome 64, 1/125, f11.

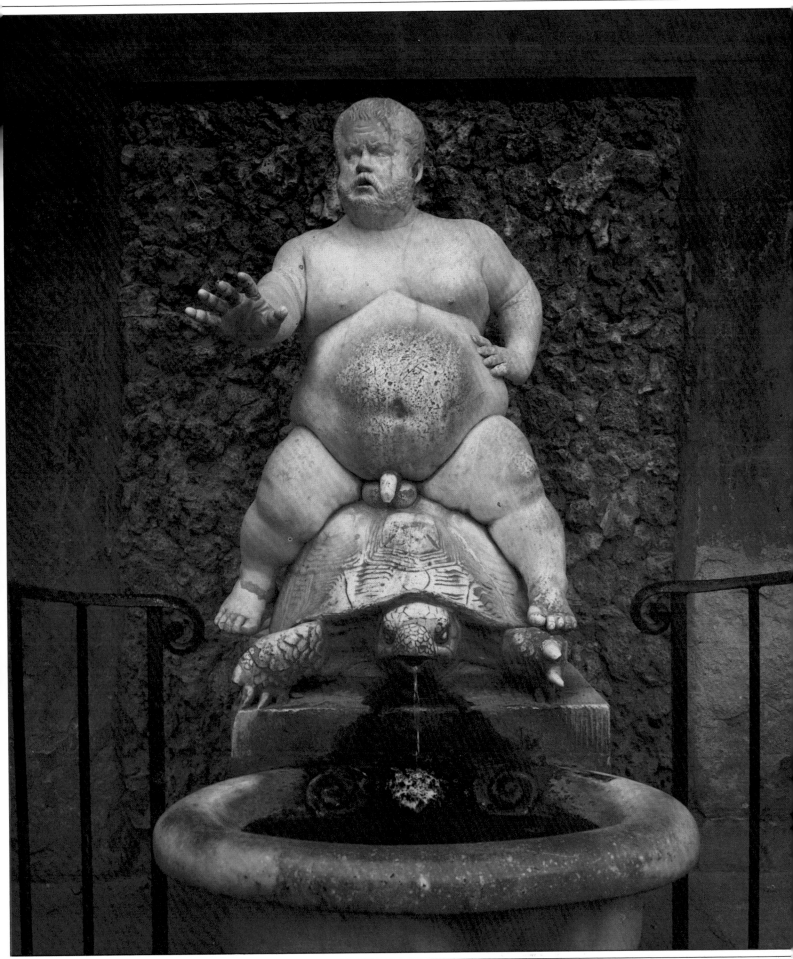

Altering the image

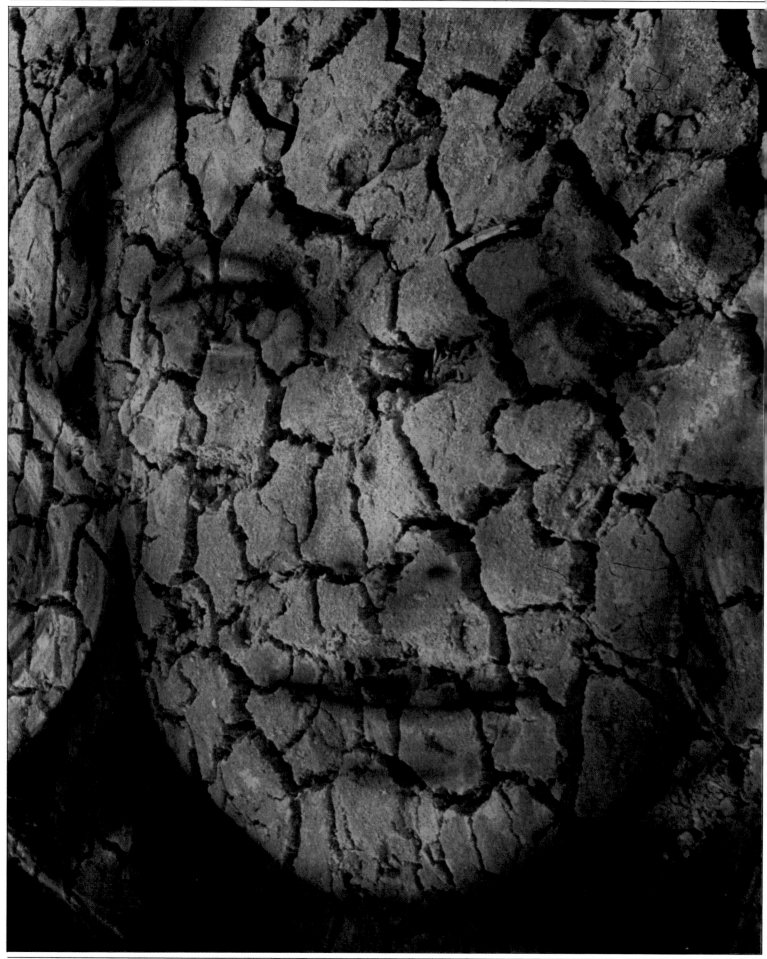

Effective manipulated images produced in the studio seldom emerge by accident but need careful thought and advance preparation. Almost any combination of pictures can be tried, as it is quite easy to select certain areas and mask out others. But simple images combined with patterned ones are the most effective. Imagination and perception are more important than complicated techniques. Apart from being fun, ex-periments with mixed or altered images provide a visual jolt that can force us to reassess familiar objects. Seen on a different scale and in a different setting, everyday things can take on an entirely new significance.

Sandwiching, where two or more transparencies are combined to make a composite image, can produce fascinat-ing and eerie effects. The technique can be used either in the studio, through a projector, or in the darkroom through an enlarger, when it can be combined with exposure variations and masking processes to alter tonal densities as well as subject matter. For the picture on the opposite page I simply brought together photographs of a young and pretty girl and of a landscape parched and baked open by the heat of an Australian summer. The result is a dis-turbing image of mortality.

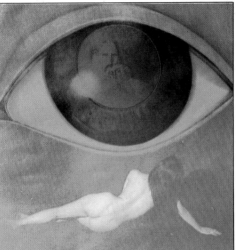

The eye *is an image cut out from a magazine which I photographed with a Hasselblad, marking the position of the bottom of the eyelid on the camera screen and underexposing by half a stop. Then with the girl posed against a black velvet background, I positioned her in the lower part of the viewfinder and re-exposed the frame. A camera technique available if you do not have facilities for front projection, double exposure also allows you to increase or reduce the apparent size of objects by contrasts of scale. The seemingly huge eye, for instance, was only about 4in (10cm) wide in the magazine illustration.*
Hasselblad, 80mm, Ektachrome 160, 1/30, f8.

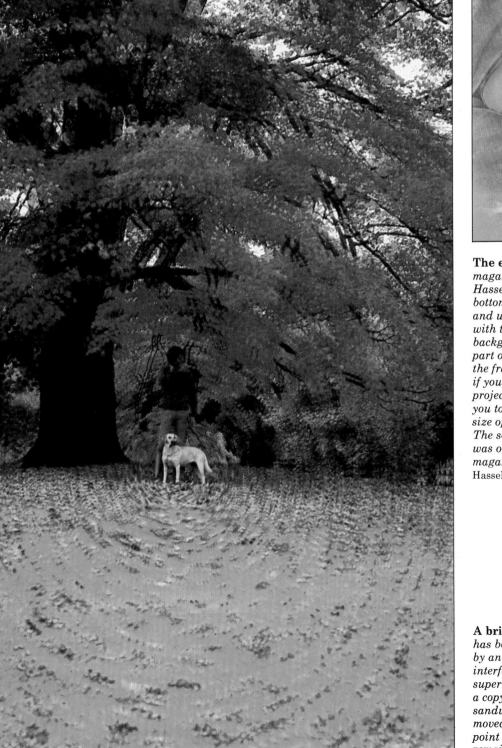

A brilliant autumn scene *in Vermont has been given the texture of watered silk by an effect known as moiré, produced by interference when identical patterns are superimposed almost in register. I made a copy of the original transparency, sandwiched the two together and then moved them slightly around the central point of the picture, where the image remains unaffected on the dog and is fairly sharp on the man himself.*

Altering the image

Outdoor locations can be suggested in a studio by using front projection. For the lingerie shot below, a street scene was projected on to a beaded screen by bouncing the image off semi-transparent glass. The camera was mounted behind the glass with its lens exactly in line with the axis of the projected image, ensuring that the model in front of the screen masked her own shadow. A flash unit lit her independently, to eliminate any projected image on her body. Hasselblad, 80mm, Ektachrome 64, electronic flash, f8.

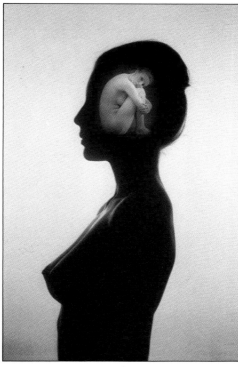

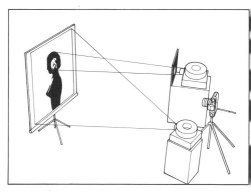

A simple arrangement was used to combine two images of the same girl on the left. Her silhouette was first projected on to a screen and a second projector with the image of her curled-up body masked by black paper was positioned to form a picture only in the selected area. The superimposed transparencies were then photographed. The size of the images can be varied by moving the projectors in relation to the screen. The diagram below shows the final set-up. Leicaflex, 90mm, Ektachrome 160; 1/15, f8.

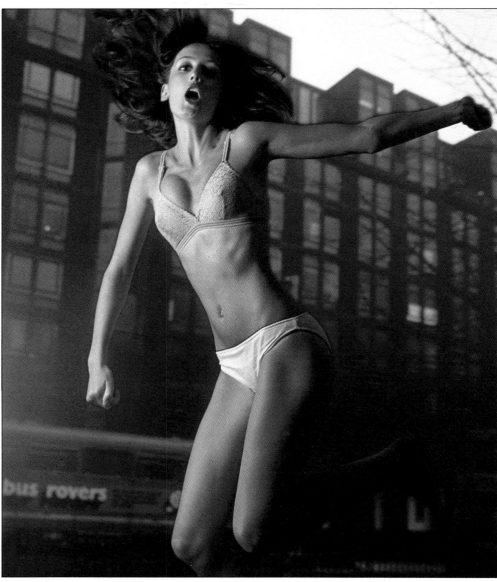

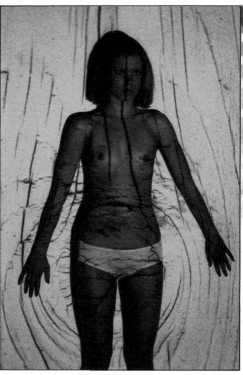

Projecting patterns on to the human form can produce effects ranging from a delicate and subtle alteration to powerful and surreal distortion. In the shot above, a pattern of wood grain thrown over the girl seems to pin her against the wall. By contrast, the girl on the opposite page seems to generate the lines radiating from her. This picture needed careful positioning so that the projected pattern would appear to emanate from the girl's eye without distorting it.

Above: Pentax, 85mm, Ektachrome 160, 1/4, f5.6.
Right: Nikon, 135mm, Ektachrome 160, 1/8, f4.

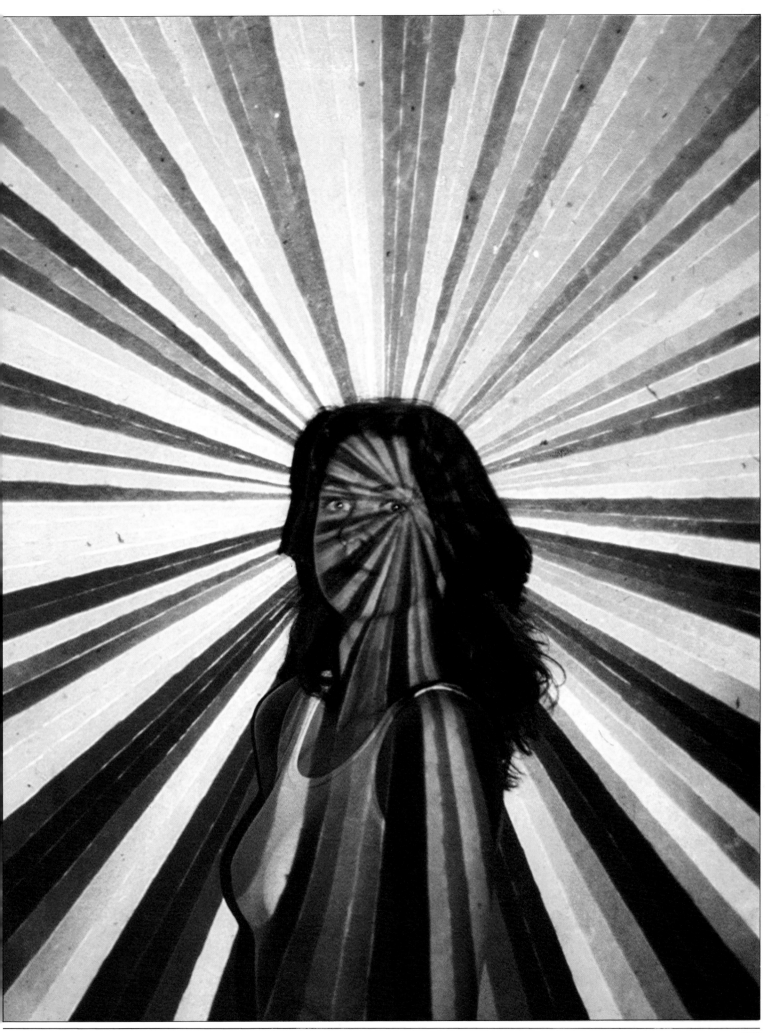

Altering the image

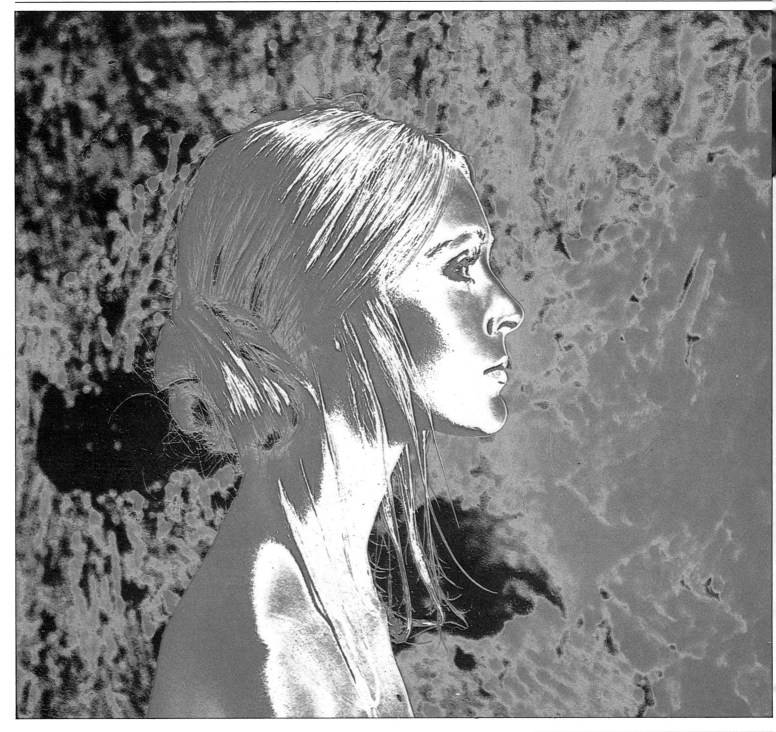

Most techniques of altering the image in the studio allow the final print to be seen and rephotographed—a relatively quick process. In the dark-room, however, laborious processes are often involved. The result is not so predictable either, although this is part of the fascination of experimenting with printing variations. The reward of painstaking work may be a picture that transforms an ordinary image into an exciting one—the product of imagination and perception as well as printing skill.

Altering the image effectively in the darkroom depends on an ability to visualize the final result and on the selection of the right image to start with. Simple, bold forms are usually best. A great variety of processes is available, only some of which are illustrated here. The range extends from mechanical processes to chemical ones such as toning and solarization, and from simple procedures, such as laying objects on bromide paper under the enlarger (photograms) to elaborate methods of controlling contrast by means of masking and converting continuous tones into separate ones.

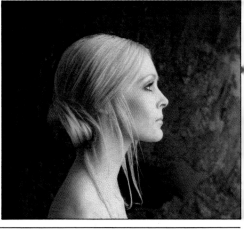

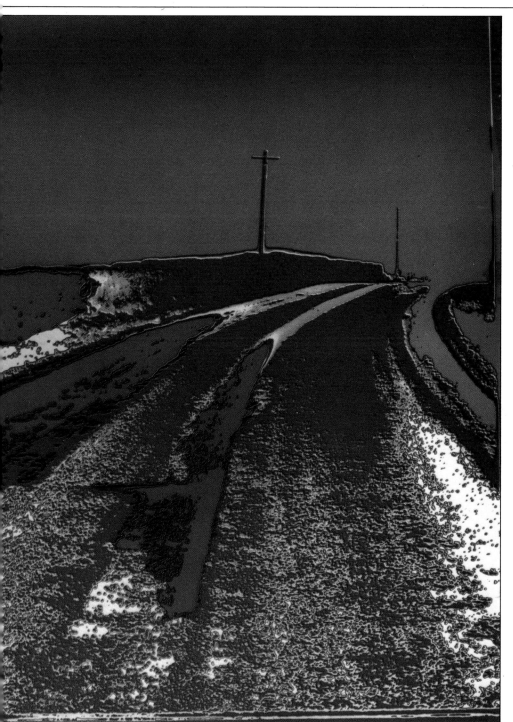

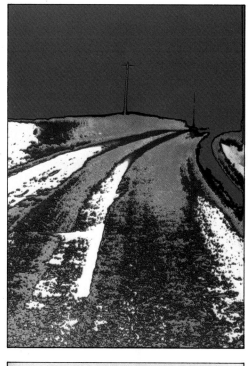

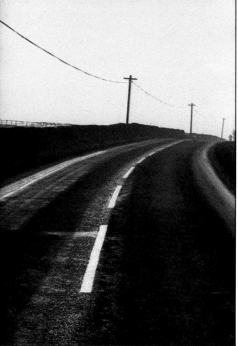

Posterization is a technique of turning ordinary negatives with continuous tones into images with distinctly separated flat tones. As realism is not the objective, the final colours can be as adventurous as you wish. Either a colour or a black and white negative can be used to produce a colour posterized image. The clear profile of a girl (left) provided a good foundation for the posterized image shown above her. The original was first copied on to high-contrast lith film three times, the first separation negative being under-exposed, the second normally exposed and the third overexposed. This provided a set of masks recording detail in only selected areas and blacking out others. (The overexposed mask, for instance, was mostly black except for highlight areas.) A contact copy was then made of each negative, all at normal exposure, and aperture, reversing the effect of the first masks. This second set of masks, screening certain areas, was used either singly or in combination to make a series of exposures on to colour paper through different coloured filters—the number of exposures determining the number of colours in the final image. To achieve precise colour register during all stages of the process, holes must be punched in each mask that fit over registration pins on the baseboard.

Equi-density film is a new medium which records both shadows and highlights as equally dense, leaving only the mid-tones clear. To achieve the startling colour compositions (above left and top), a low-contrast black and white negative was made from the original picture (above) and exposed on to equi-density (Agfa contour) film. This was used to produce a second equi-density negative, from which a third was made. The three negatives, all with a differing line effect, were printed in turn through coloured filters using the punched registration pin system followed in posterization. The final result depends on the filtration and the number of equi-density negatives used.

Altering the image

Solarized colour images *like the one below need a sharp and contrasty negative for an effective result. The process involves exposing the negative normally in the enlarger, but then interrupting the development process with a brief, even exposure to low-intensity coloured light. This has the effect of reversing or partly reversing the colours of the final print—most strongly in the undeveloped highlight areas. For instance, a red light will produce a blue-green cast. The length of exposure depends on the effect you want, the strength of the light source and its distance from the print. But the longer the exposure the more widespread the colour cast will be. Too long an exposure will produce a final print of virtually one colour, as the mid-tones and shadows will be affected.*

The patterned image *of Raffles Hotel, Singapore, began with a negative print that reversed the colours and densities of the original transparency. This print was used to make a contact positive on colour paper. The negative and positive prints were then sandwiched back to back with the images in precise register for a final contact print on colour paper.*

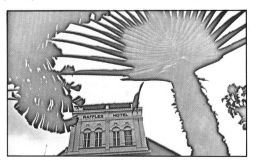

An action shot of a tennis player *has been given even greater impact by a printing derivation using high-contrast lith film. The colour negative was exposed on to the lith film, which was processed and dried normally, then sandwiched in precise register with the original negative. When the package was printed through the enlarger the lith film masking the image reduced the density without greatly altering colour, and enabled a heavy print to be made.*

The still life *of fish on a plate also makes use of a lith film mask. Positive and negative lith images were copied from the original negative and sandwiched together to make a third copy. This thin-line image was then sandwiched with the original negative and printed normally on colour paper.*

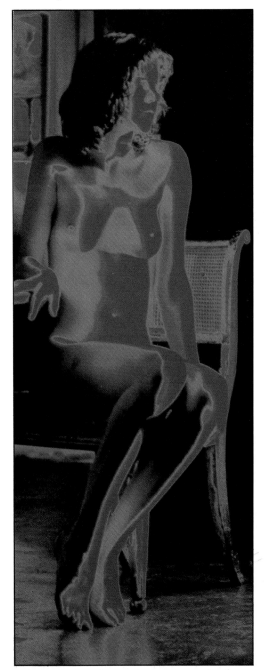

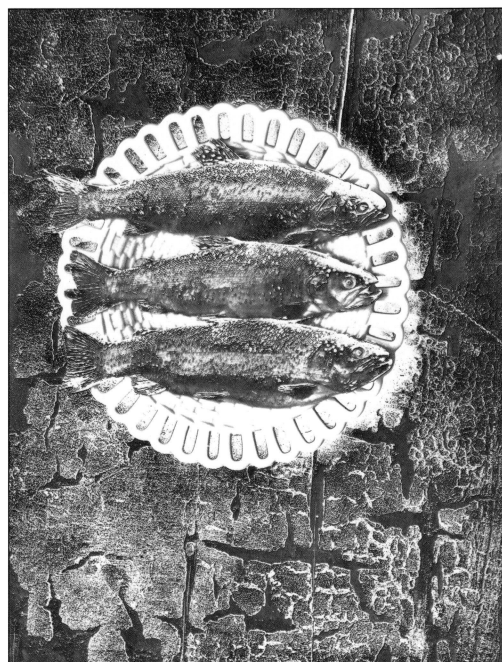

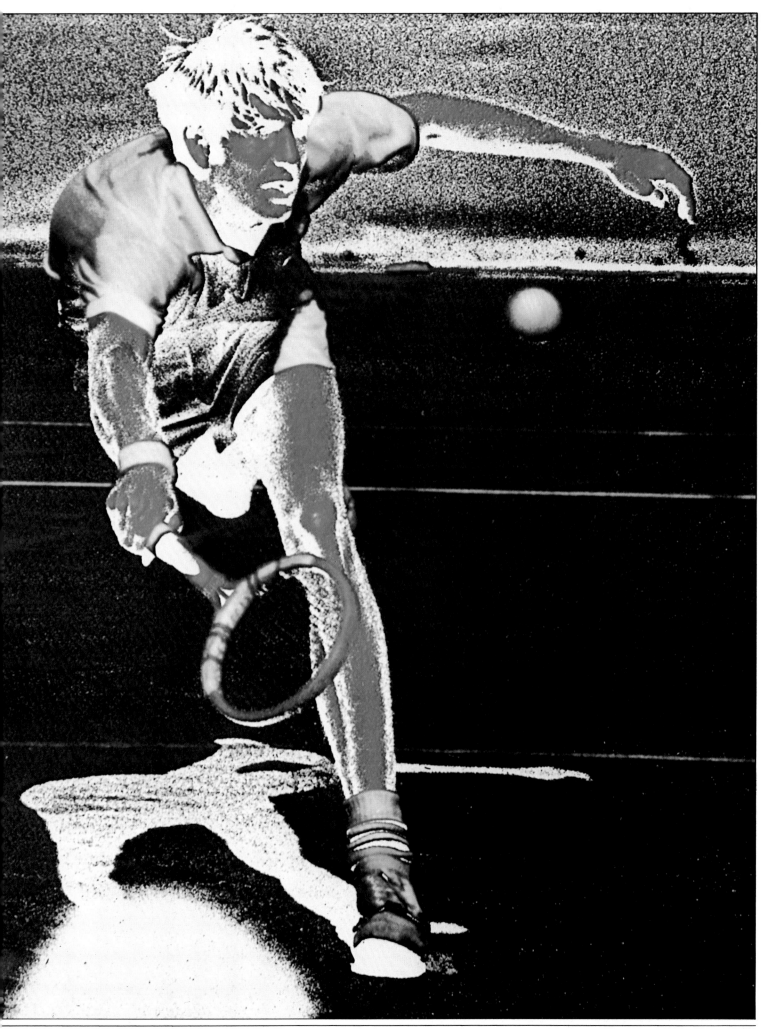

Retouching, toning and colouring

Retouching on a major scale to remove unwanted detail or change the relative position or scale of objects is a skilled and demanding task, especially if the retouching is carried out on the negative. Unless sheet film is used, professionals usually find it necessary to work on an enlarged image. Creative retouching, as distinct from the removal of print blemishes discussed on pages 284–5, can produce striking pictures.

The crisp image of the apparently headless horse below began with the 35mm transparency (right) showing a field of well-trampled snow. From this, an 8 × 10 in (20.3 × 25.4 cm) colour negative was made and the entire snow area was deleted with black dye. On a positive of the same size, an air brush was then used to paint in the unblemished snow, accentuating the horse's shape.

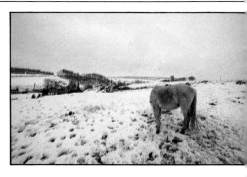

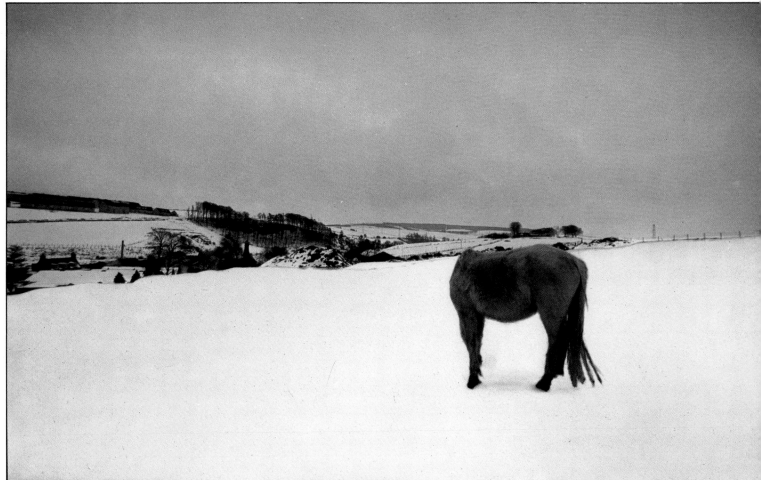

The hang glider *in the right-hand of these two pictures was enlarged and shifted down in a transparency made from the first shot. Photographed from the Swiss side of the border, the left-hand picture shows the hang glider high above the Matterhorn a few moments after it had been launched from the peak. As I was using a wide-angle lens, I was unable to include the Matterhorn in a later close-up of the glider as it turned and swept directly overhead. To recreate this moment using the shot I had taken slightly earlier, an 8 × 10 in positive and two black and white overlay masks were made. The positive was reshot twice, using one overlay to hold back the sky and the other to hold back the peaks. The sky area containing the hang glider was further enlarged and superimposed over the area showing the mountains only.*

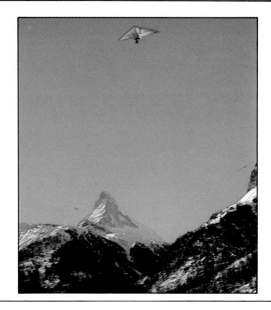

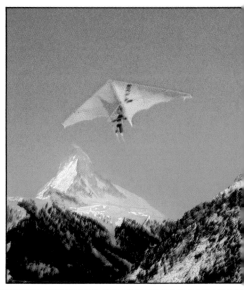

Toning a black and white print to produce a coloured image involves introducing a chemical that reacts with the black part of the image only, changing it into a colour corresponding to the colour former being used. Four colour formers are available: yellow, magenta, cyan and brown. Unlike chemical dyeing the reaction is selective. The process is quite straightforward and is carried out in normal room lighting.

A four-bath multitoning process was used to produce the monochromatic examples below and left. In each case the black and white print was immersed in a bleaching solution for between three and five minutes and then thoroughly washed. The bleached print was then held about 1 ft (30 cm) away from a 100-watt light bulb for 60 seconds and soaked in a solution made up of two colour developers and the colour for-

mers, a mixture of yellow and cyan for the river and trees and brown for the bridge. The print is usually bleached again to remove the silver nitrate, leaving the colour pigment only, but this step was omitted to give a fuller image. A final bath stabilized the prints. By masking parts of the image with rubber cement, multicoloured pictures can be produced. The processing steps are repeated for each new colour.

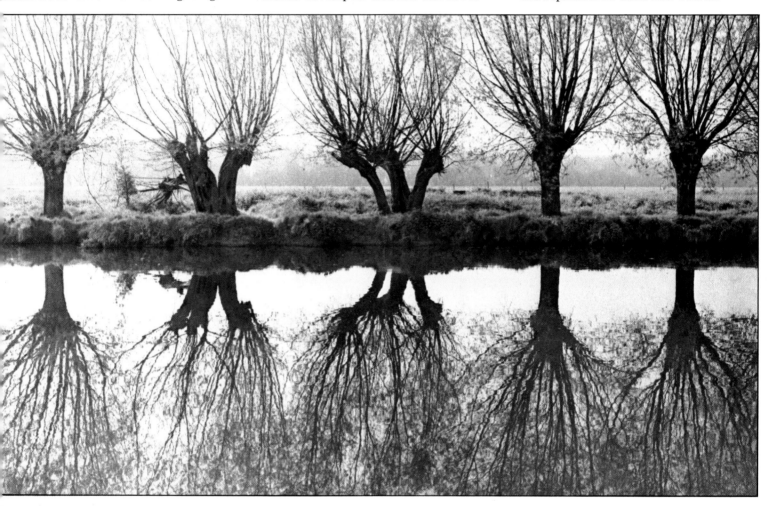

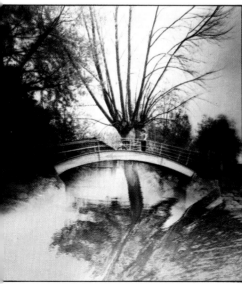

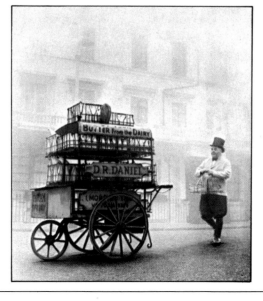

Hand colouring *allows much finer control of the final coloured image than chemical toning does, as any number of colours can be introduced in the strength and proportion that suit the image on which you are working. In the nostalgic picture of a milkman from another era, water-based colour dyes have been added with a fine sable brush to highlight particular details only, leaving most of the scene its original black and white. For this type of work a lighter-than-normal print is necessary as heavy dark tones will show through and dilute the colour effect. The grade of paper is not crucial as long as the surface is unglazed. Resin-coated papers are unsuitable as the dyes are not absorbed into the surface. In general, it is best to start with large areas of flat tone, working down to areas of fine detail.*

Using lenses

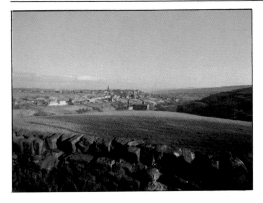

Effective colour pictures can be taken with any lens, although the less sophisticated single-element lenses will produce soft images and colour inaccuracies. Design advances have greatly extended the accuracy of modern lenses, bayonet fittings allowing you to change from one lens to another in a few seconds. The problem of flare has also been largely overcome by multi-coated lenses.

At least 90 per cent of the pictures in this book were taken with lenses between 28mm and 150mm. The most useful range of lenses lies between 15mm and 200mm, although a 400mm or 1,000mm lens has advantages if you are specializing in sport or nature photography. The capacity of extreme telephoto lenses to record colours when focused on infinity is affected by atmospheric haze dissipating hues and reducing contrast.

The pictures on these pages provide a guide to the average range of lenses for a typical SLR, the Pentax.

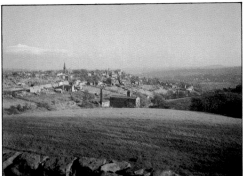

These five pictures *of a mill town in Yorkshire were all taken within a few minutes of each other on a sunny winter's day and from a fixed position. The pictures differ only through a change of lenses. Exposure in each case was 1/125, f11.*

A 15mm lens *shows a broad expanse of countryside. Although its angle of view includes a stone wall only 3ft (1m) in front of the camera as well as a church spire 1 mile (1.6km) away, definition is perfectly sharp throughout.*

A 28mm lens *eliminates most of the foreground wall, making what remains seem much larger and nearer. The hill on the right has disappeared and the distant buildings are now more easily recognizable than before.*

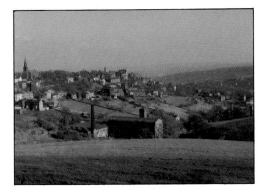

A 50mm lens *cuts out the immediate foreground and shows a more confined area, but produces excellent colour definition in the foreground. A tonal change begins to appear in the distance due to aerial perspective.*

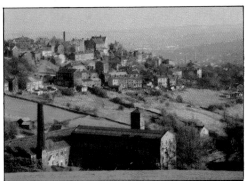

A 105mm lens *narrows the angle of view even further and cuts out the church on the left of the picture. The town has been reduced to the immediate surroundings of a wool mill that now begins to dominate the scene. Haze seems to thicken in the valley as the lens brings up more distant features.*

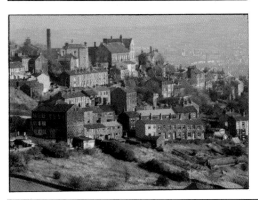

A 200mm lens *includes only the central parts of the scene, softening the colours to mainly blues and greys, but shows the form of the distant buildings well. Only the flagpole of the mill remains.*

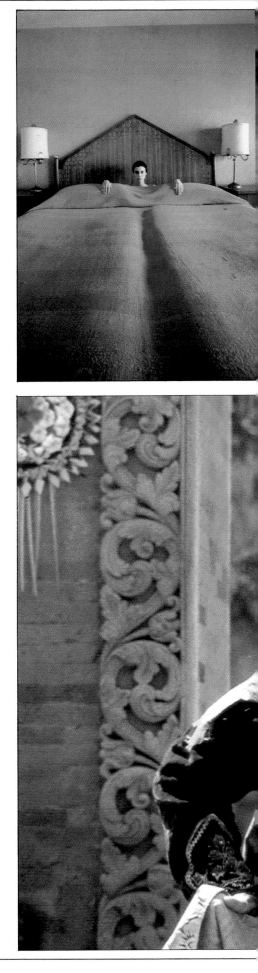

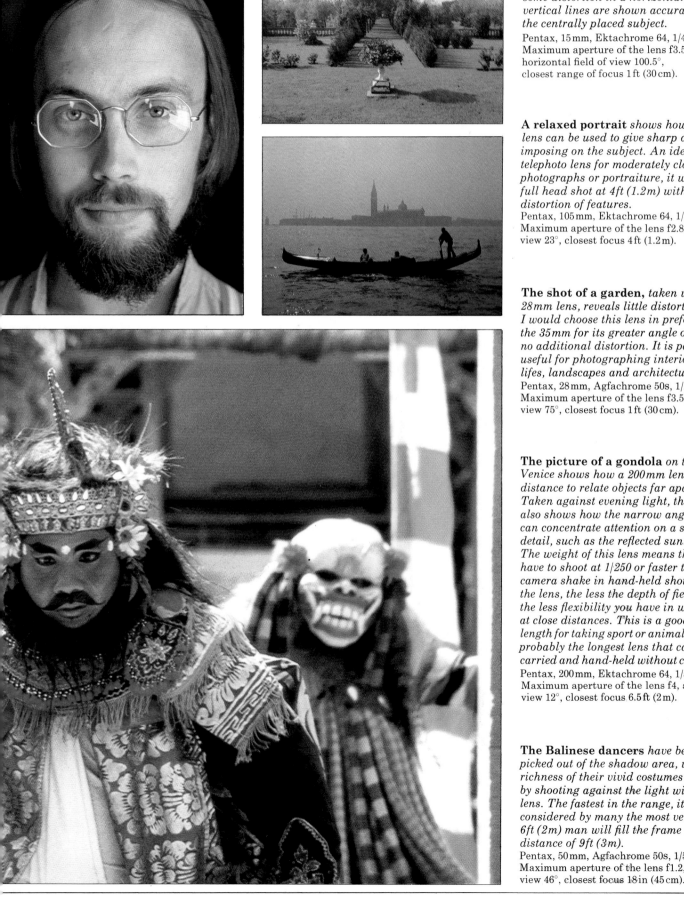

The photograph of a girl in bed *shows how a 15mm lens tends to result in extreme distortion of the foreground, making the bed seem endless. Although it produces some distortion in a horizontal plane, the vertical lines are shown accurately, as is the centrally placed subject.*
Pentax, 15mm, Ektachrome 64, 1/4, f8.
Maximum aperture of the lens f3.5,
horizontal field of view 100.5°,
closest range of focus 1ft (30cm).

A relaxed portrait *shows how the 105mm lens can be used to give sharp detail without imposing on the subject. An ideal medium telephoto lens for moderately close animal photographs or portraiture, it will take a full head shot at 4ft (1.2m) with no distortion of features.*
Pentax, 105mm, Ektachrome 64, 1/250, f5.6.
Maximum aperture of the lens f2.8, angle of
view 23°, closest focus 4ft (1.2m).

The shot of a garden, *taken with a 28mm lens, reveals little distortion. I would choose this lens in preference to the 35mm for its greater angle of view with no additional distortion. It is particularly useful for photographing interiors, still lifes, landscapes and architecture.*
Pentax, 28mm, Agfachrome 50s, 1/250, f5.6.
Maximum aperture of the lens f3.5, angle of
view 75°, closest focus 1ft (30cm).

The picture of a gondola *on the lagoon at Venice shows how a 200mm lens compresses distance to relate objects far apart. Taken against evening light, the picture also shows how the narrow angle of view can concentrate attention on a small detail, such as the reflected sunlight. The weight of this lens means that you have to shoot at 1/250 or faster to avoid camera shake in hand-held shots. The longer the lens, the less the depth of field and the less flexibility you have in working at close distances. This is a good focal length for taking sport or animal photographs, probably the longest lens that can be carried and hand-held without causing strain.*
Pentax, 200mm, Ektachrome 64, 1/500, f5.6.
Maximum aperture of the lens f4, angle of
view 12°, closest focus 6.5ft (2m).

The Balinese dancers *have been picked out of the shadow area, with all the richness of their vivid costumes revealed, by shooting against the light with a 50mm lens. The fastest in the range, it is considered by many the most versatile. A 6ft (2m) man will fill the frame at a distance of 9ft (3m).*
Pentax, 50mm, Agfachrome 50s, 1/500, f4.
Maximum aperture of the lens f1.2, angle of
view 46°, closest focus 18in (45cm).

Using lenses

The array of lenses and lens attachments available to the photographer today is vast. Outside those commonly used by the average photographer, with focal lengths between 28mm and 200mm, specialist shops sell lenses ranging from 2,000mm with an angle of view of less than 2° to the 6mm fish-eye with an angle of view of more than 180°. Unless you have settled on a particular field of photography that demands constant use of specialized lenses, it is probably not worth while buying them because they can easily be hired for specific situations.

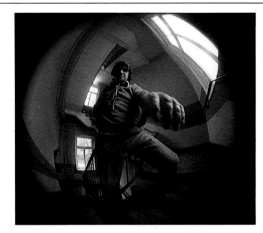

The image produced by a fish-eye lens *is a reminder that all lenses produce a circular image, although the picture format usually crops it to a rectangle. The depth of field with this lens is so enormous that no focus control is needed, and filters are built in to avoid the filter mount appearing in the picture. Although its applications are limited the lens can produce spectacular images, exploiting the interest of fun-parlour mirror grotesqueness. This self-portrait, with a comparatively normal central area, shows the lens's close-focusing ability—my hand is only about 6in (15cm) away.* Nikon, 6mm, Ektachrome 64, 1/30, f8.

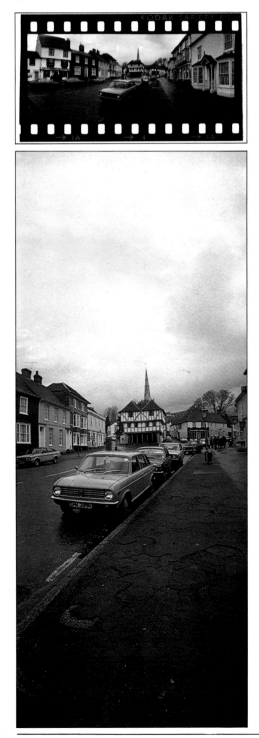

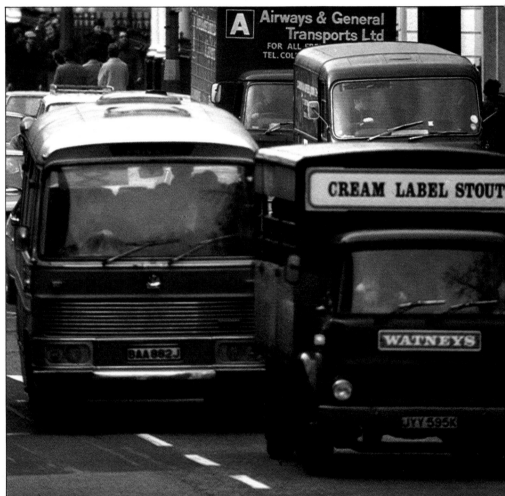

Horizontal and vertical shots *of an English village were taken from the same spot using a Widelux camera. As with most panoramic cameras, it is hard to detect distortions, except in close-ups, although someone familiar with the scene would notice marked changes in the positions of objects in the field of view. This type of camera was developed for school or other large group photographs. Subjects positioned in an arc around the camera appear to be in one line as the lens itself travels in an arc. On a 36-exposure film the camera takes 21 pictures.* Widelux, 26mm travelling through a 140° arc, Ektachrome 64, 1/125, f8.

Compression of space *is a feature of extra-long telephoto lenses. Taken from 400yds (365m), the vehicles above seem to be caught in a traffic jam. In reality they were well spaced and travelling at about 30mph (50km/h). The apparent closing up of distance can be seen most easily in the two delivery vans. Although they are several lengths apart, the advertising signs on them appear to be roughly the same size. This telephoto lens is excellent for sport or nature photography but demands accurate focusing as its depth of field is much less than that of normal lenses.* Leicaflex, 800mm, Ektachrome 64, 1/125, f5.6.

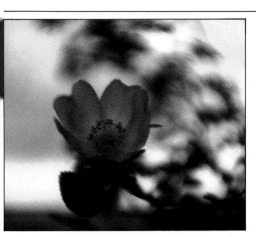

As a cheap alternative to a wide-angle lens, attachments are available that screw into the end of an ordinary lens. An accessory of this type can widen the acceptance angle of a lens from 43° to 104°. These attachments produce more aberrations than normal wide-angle lenses do but can give interesting results, as in the picture of a dog rose (left). The increase in the close-focus ability of the lens enables the stamens and petals to be picked out clearly, but the leaves show colour fringes and background hues have merged.

Hasselblad, 150mm with Maxwider, Ektachrome 64, 1/125, f8.

A prism lens is an attachment that enables you to split an image vertically or horizontally to produce overlapping or wholly separate images. For best results a strong central subject is needed with a plain or uncluttered background. The sequence of three pictures below of County Hall, London, shows two effects of a prism lens, basically a multi-faceted glass filter. The normal view is seen in the first picture. For the next I attached a three-band prism lens and for the last I turned the lens during the exposure.

Pentax, 50mm, Ektachrome 160, 2sec., f5.6.

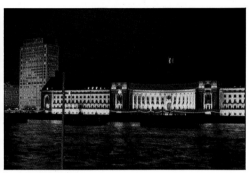
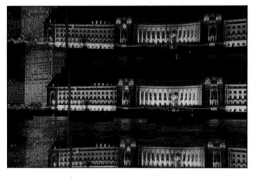
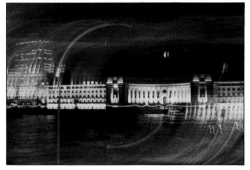

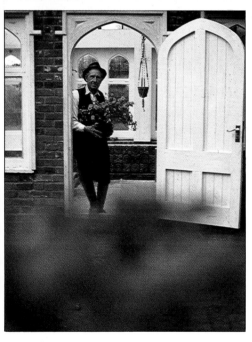
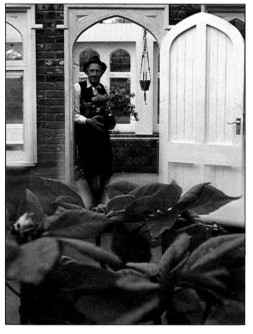

A half-lens consists of a semi-circle of magnifying glass, covering half the prime lens, which brings near objects into focus while the prime lens focuses farther back. In the shot (far left) the flowers in the foreground are too close and out of focus, but in the next shot a half-lens has brought them up sharply. Notice the soft-focus at the boundary of the half-lens.
Pentax, 50mm, Ektachrome 64, 1/30, f16.

An anamorphic lens attachment has been used in two of the pictures of the conservatory below. Compared with the normal view (centre), it has stretched the building lengthwise in the left-hand picture through compression of the vertical plane. Rotation of the lens attachment has squeezed the whole image horizontally in the other shot. Little distortion is apparent as long as the lens is kept parallel to the subject.
Hasselblad, 80mm, Ektachrome 64, 1/125, f11.

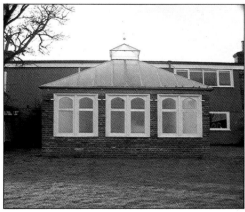
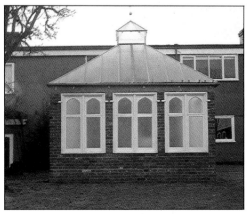
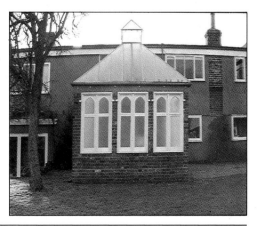

245

Using filters

Although the value of filters in general photographic work is limited, familiarity with the range can help you to record colours accurately in difficult conditions or to enliven scenes that might otherwise be dull. Correction filters, which alter the colour temperature of light entering the camera to match the type of film being used, form the largest group. Others, including star-burst and dual-colour filters, are designed for special effects. Soft-focus filters diffuse the image, and similar results can be achieved by breathing on the lens or smearing petroleum jelly on a plain glass filter.

Of the correction filters, the most generally useful are skylight and ultra-violet filters, which help to take blue cast out of shadow areas and generally "warm up" the picture. Either can be left on the camera permanently for outdoor photography. Polarizing filters are invaluable for eliminating reflected glare. Many filters require exposure adjustment, as recommended by the manufacturers, to compensate for reduced light. Glass filters are more durable than gelatin ones. If definition is not essential, filters can also be improvised from coloured tissue, scarves or other suitable materials.

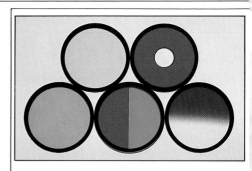

Correction and special effects *filters illustrated above are (clockwise): solid yellow, fog, "color-spot", graduated and "dual-colour" filters.*

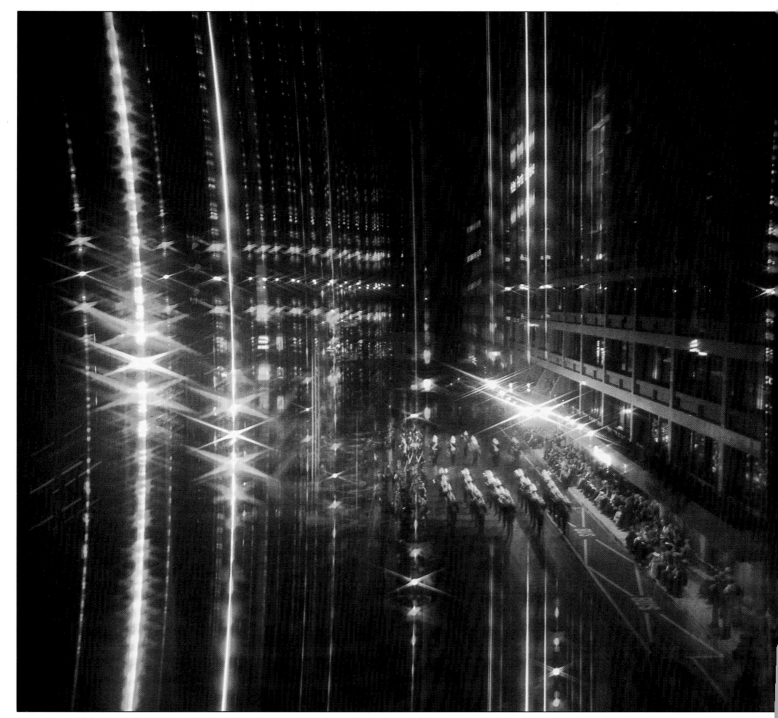

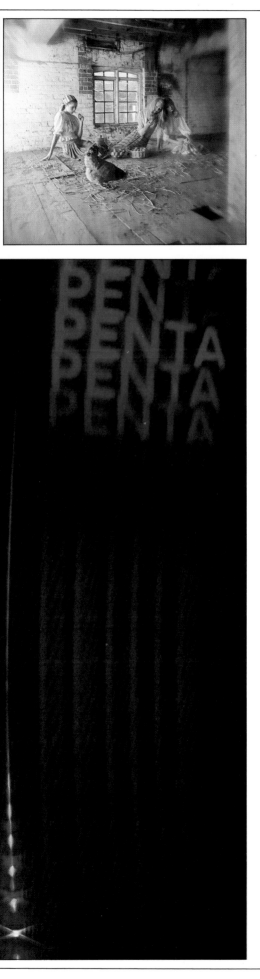

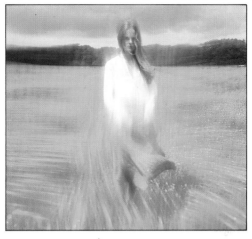

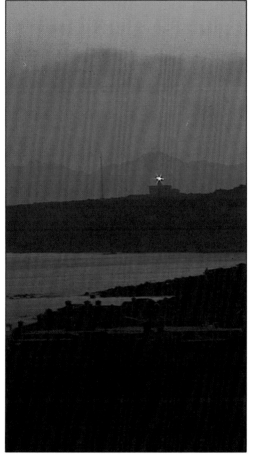

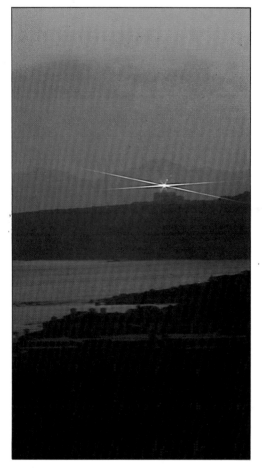

The romantic atmosphere of the barn
(far left) has been heightened by the use of a variable soft-focus filter to diffuse the indirect light, but only around the perimeter of the lens. A mistake often made with this filter is to stop down too far, destroying the desired effect. It is best to use a fairly wide aperture and to adjust exposure by means of shutter speed.
Hasselblad, 80mm, Ektachrome 64, 1/30, f5.6.

The hazy warmth of a summer's day
and a strong sense of movement have been conveyed (left) by smearing petroleum jelly on a glass filter.
Hasselblad, 80mm, Agfachrome 50s, 1/60, f5.6.

A marching band *and a neon-lit street are transformed into a glittering cascade of multi-coloured lights by the combination of two diffraction filters with slightly different effects. The bandsmen are seen in the centre of a "colorburst" filter, which does not add or subtract colour but bends light entering the camera into its component colours. To create the explosions of light from the street lighting and on the buildings I added a "vario-starburst" filter to the first. With reflex focusing cameras these variable effects can be easily seen, allowing appropriate adjustments to be made.*
Pentax, 28mm, Ektachrome 160, 1/4, f5.6.

Photographed at sunset, *the two shots above illustrate the natural effect that can be achieved with a small area of intense light and a "vario-starburst" diffraction filter. The first picture of the lighthouse was a straight shot and the glowing lamp has been recorded simply as a pinpoint of light. For the second shot I attached the starburst filter and achieved a picture much closer to what the eye would see, with a beam of light penetrating the softly coloured sky and the darkness of the headland. This filter does not require adjustments to the exposure so both pictures were taken using the same camera settings.*
Nikon, 35mm, Ektachrome 64, 1/30, f5.6.

247

Using filters

Strongly coloured filters *need to be used with discretion if they are not to overwhelm the picture. The green and orange dual filter used for the two shots on the right works effectively in the picture of the pylon as the colour division coincides with a natural division, strengthening the perspective. Turned on its side, the same filter gives a more unnatural, theatrical effect.* Pentax, 50mm, Ektachrome 64, 1/125, f8.

The effect of lush, wet greenness *surrounding the small girl below was created by using a green filter with a clear centre. She is positioned so that the colour of her hair is quite natural.* Nikon, 50mm, Ektachrome 64, 1/250, f5.6.

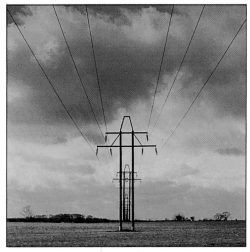

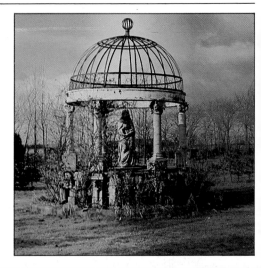

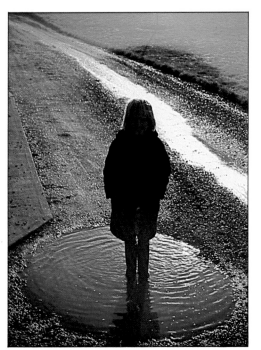

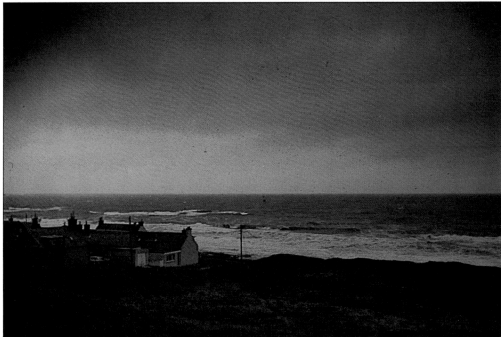

Graduated filters, *particularly if their colours are not too strong and if they are judiciously exploited, can help to reduce contrast between highlights and darker areas in landscape pictures, a problem that cannot always be met by averaging the exposure. These filters have half clear glass and half coloured, with diffused colour around the division between the two areas. In the lower of the two seascapes the ominous sky, suggesting a storm gathering over the headland, is darkened by a blue graduated filter, tilted slightly to the left so that the blue spreads down into the clear lower area. For the upper picture, I chose a red graduated filter, rotated to cover the foreground, and also tilted the colour slightly. The illusion here is of a strange, wintry light and the lurid glow of a sinking sun on the horizon. The colour is less natural than the blue of the other filter, which corresponds more with the sea and sky.* Pentax, 50mm, Ektachrome 64, 1/250, f5.6.

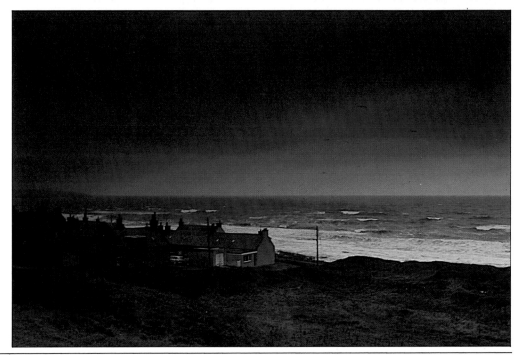

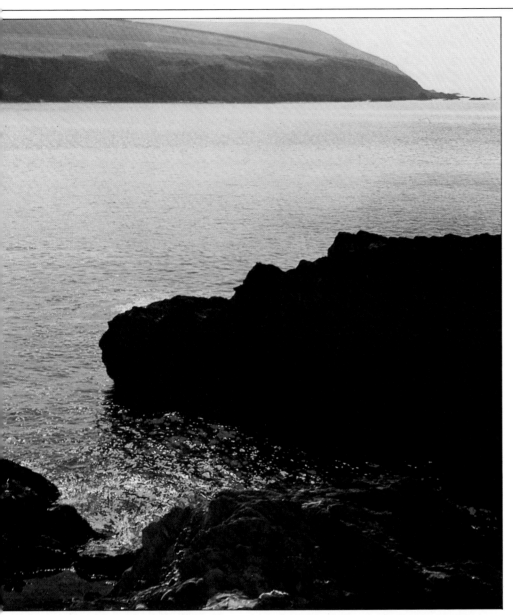

Red, green and blue filters *were used successively in a triple exposure to produce the striking image (left). In combination they gave normal colour through most of the picture, but the moving water recorded their colours separately on highlights in the inlet.*
Rolleiflex, 80mm, Vericolor 2, 1/125, f8.

A red graduated filter *rotated to darken the sky has helped to balance the picture of the bollard (below).*
Nikon, 50mm, Ektachrome 64, 1/250, f5.6.

The dramatic storm light *in the landscape picture was deepened by an orange-brown graduated filter.*
Pentax, 50mm, Ektachrome 64, 1/60, f8.

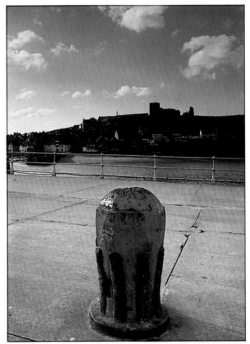

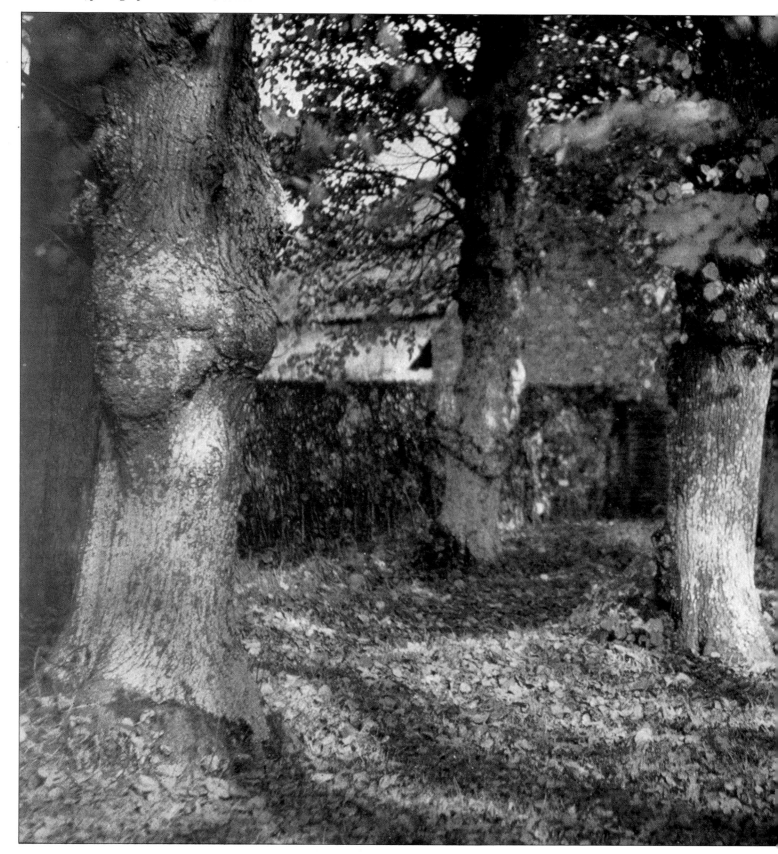

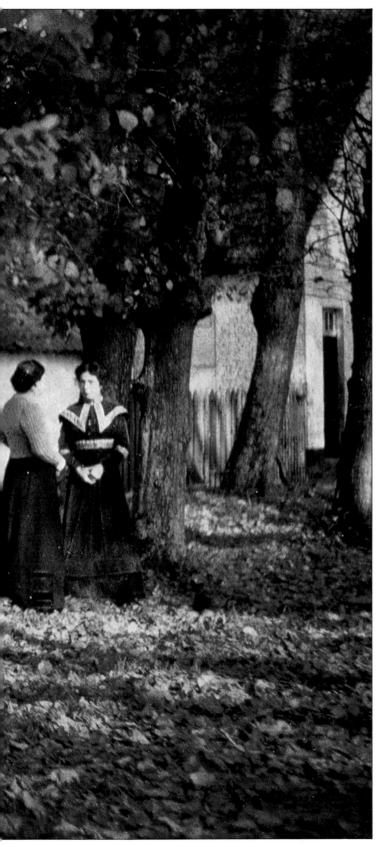

The history of colour photography

Colour photographs are almost as old as black and white. No sooner had the pioneers of photography astounded the world by producing permanent black and white images of their surroundings than they began to try to make colour pictures as well. Some took a short cut and simply added colour tints to black and white photographs by hand. The earliest untinted colour pictures, made in the 1830s, showed a limited range of hues and quickly faded—but they were colour just the same, and pointed the way towards greater realism. Nearly a century would elapse, however, before colour photography would take its place both as a powerful force in visual communication and as a pastime of mass appeal.

The nature of light is the foundation stone of all photography, and a discovery of fundamental importance was made by Johann H. Schulze in 1725 when he proved that light, not air or heat, caused silver nitrate mixed with chalk to go dark. Carl W. Scheele, a Swedish chemist, verified Schulze's work 52 years later with silver chloride. This also went black when exposed to light and was unaffected by heat. But Scheele took matters a step further. He found that light from the violet end of the spectrum darkened the silver chloride faster than light of other spectral colours.

In 1826, Joseph Nicéphore Niepce obtained his first fuzzy but permanent camera image of the roofs and chimneys visible from his work-room—a photograph taken on a sunny day with an exposure of about eight hours, using pewter plate coated with a light-sensitive varnish of asphalt (bitumen of Judea) and using oils as a fixing agent. Even before this in 1810, Johann T. Seebeck, a German physicist, had observed that colours of the spectrum could be recorded in moist silver chloride that had first been darkened by exposure to white light. This effect was later shown to be the result of interference of light waves, a phenomenon subsequently pursued by Gabriel Lippmann using photographic emulsion. The pioneers of black and white photography, Niepce himself and Louis Jacques Mandé Daguerre, whose process for producing finely detailed one-off images was announced in 1839, each tried to make permanent colour pictures, but they could not fix the images they obtained. Further developments were soon to come.

Early colour images

Early attempts to achieve colour photographs by direct methods culminated in 1891 in the work of Gabriel Lippmann, a physicist at the Sorbonne. Lippmann's photographic plate had a virtually grainless emulsion in contact with a layer of liquid mercury. When light fell on the photographic emulsion to form the image, it passed through and was reflected from the mercury. The incoming light "interfered" with the outgoing light and formed "standing waves"—a stationary pattern of brightness and darkness—and a corresponding silver grain pattern in the developed emulsion. The developed negative was backed with black material and then viewed by reflection. White light shone on to the negative, passed through the emulsion and was reflected by the pattern of silver grains in the emulsion, causing the light emerging after reflection to be coloured in the correct proportions. The processed plate showed accurate and shining colours—but they could be seen only from directly in front.

Lippmann succeeded in producing the most faithful rendering of colour to that time, but the exposure required was lengthy and so great were the technical obstacles that the method was then incapable of practical development. Lippmann showed, in effect, that scientists would need to concentrate on more indirect methods.

This was happening already, of course. Back in 1802 the physicist Thomas Young had announced his theory that the eye contains three kinds of colour receptor, responding most strongly to red, blue and yellow light respectively. He suggested that from the responses to these, in varying combinations and proportions, the sensations of all visible colours could be created. It was Young's ideas that formed the basis of James Clerk Maxwell's contribution to the advance of colour photography.

In 1855 Maxwell showed that by mixing red, green and blue light in different proportions any other colour could be reproduced. He realized that this could form the basis of a method of colour photography if the subject's colour was analysed in terms of black and white records taken through red, green and blue filters.

Six years later Maxwell demonstrated his method, nowadays known as an additive method, to a gathering of

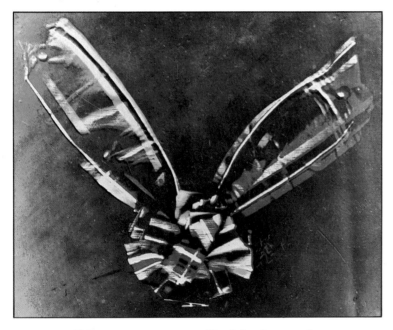

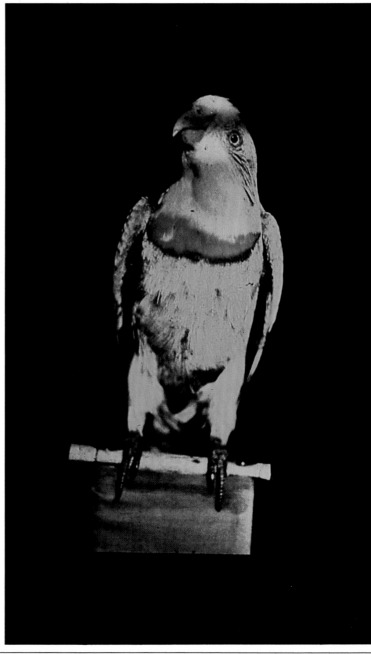

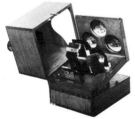

The faint image of a tartan ribbon (above), *beamed through coloured filters by James Clerk Maxwell in 1861, showed colours accurately enough to greatly impress his audience.*

The Kromskop, *a box-like projector (left), was made by Frederic Ives to display pictures such as his bowl of fruit, taken with a camera in which three negatives were carried on one plate. Filters and mirrors in the Kromskop enabled the positive separations to be viewed as a single image of superimposed colours.*

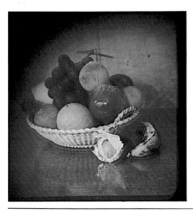

Gabriel Lippmann *won a Nobel Prize for developing a plate that produced colour by light interference. The parrot is a sample of his work.*

scientists in London. What he did was to show how a coloured image could be obtained of a tartan ribbon. A photographer made three separate exposures of the ribbon, one with a red filter, one with a green and one with a blue. From each negative a positive black and white transparency was made. Each transparency was then projected on to a screen with light of the appropriate colour. The red, green and blue images coinciding on the screen formed a naturally coloured picture of the original scene.

How Maxwell succeeded proved a mystery to later scientists, for no photographic emulsion at that time was sensitive to light other than blue, violet and ultraviolet. Only in 1873 did Hermann Vogel find a way of making a plate sensitive to green; and not until 1906 did the panchromatic plate, sensitive to all parts of the spectrum, become available commercially. It is now known, however, that Maxwell was unwittingly helped by two fortunate coincidences. The reds in his ribbon reflected ultraviolet light that registered on the plate, and his green filter in fact let some blue light through.

In France, in the late 1860s, Louis Ducos du Hauron, working doggedly away in the countryside, and Charles Cros, a gregarious Parisian with a head full of ideas, revealed independently their theories on colour processing. Each suggested a new approach, using dyes, that came to form the basis of the subtractive colour process. Du Hauron's ideas were published and amounted to an extensive compilation of principles that included both additive and subtractive methods (see pages 38–9). Many subsequent advances can be traced back to suggestions made by du Hauron. He proposed, for example, a screen plate consisting of primary coloured dots; he also suggested a photographic plate with three layers, each sensitive to a different primary colour. But the development that was to have the greatest impact ultimately was the decision to use dyes.

Like Maxwell, du Hauron obtained three separate black and white negatives for the primary colours with coloured filters, but he then made separate colour positives with a gelatin coating containing dyes that were complementary in colour to the corresponding filter. (For example, the positive made from the red-filter negative would contain a blue-green dye, which subtracted red.) All that remained was for these coloured images to be superimposed in register and illuminated with white light to give on paper a colour print or on glass a colour transparency. Each layer subtracted appropriate amounts of red, green or blue from the white light. This was the method du Hauron used to make both prints and transparencies. Du Hauron thus followed Maxwell's additive method part of the way, but foresaw the possibilities that subtractive methods held for colour processing. Further development of his ideas, however, had to wait for progress in chemical research that would eliminate the need for three separate colour positives and the problem of registration.

There were many difficulties in the way of photographers working in colour. One of the most obvious was simply the need to take three separate exposures through three different filters. It was a fiddly and time-consuming business, although much less so from the 1870s as the collodion wet plate process, which was not only messy but required a photographer doing outdoor work to carry a portable darkroom around with him, gave way to commercially produced dry plates that came pre-sensitized. Another difficulty was the very long exposures required, which meant that sudden changes in the light or weather or position of the subject ruined the balance of colours in the final picture. The

position was eased somewhat by the introduction of cameras capable of exposing three negatives at the same time. For example, in the 1890s an American camera invented by Frederic Ives accommodated the three negatives on one plate.

The great demand for George Eastman's Kodak hand camera, offered to the American public in 1888 for $25, gave further impetus to the search for a practical form of colour photography. Black and white pictures were now easily accomplished by people with no photographic skills, yet colour too was on the point of further advances in practice as well as in theory.

The additive method of recreating colour remained the only workable means available. John Joly, a Dubliner, invented a process in 1893 that was similar to one described earlier by du Hauron. Instead of three negatives he made one; in place of an image combined from three colour positives he projected a single transparency through a three-coloured screen to show one multi-hued picture. Screen plates of one kind or another were to provide acceptable and often extremely beautiful colour until the 1930s.

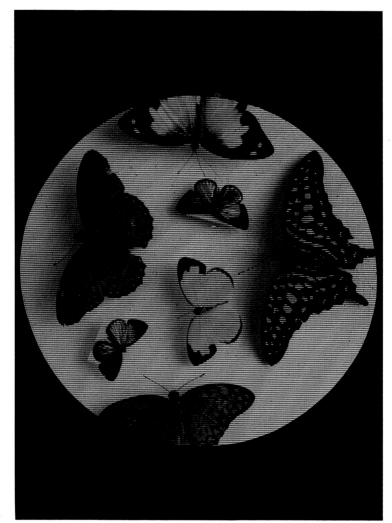

John Joly *photographed these butterflies in 1893 using a screen plate. He made a combination filter by ruling across glass microscopic and transparent bands of red, green and blue, about 200 to the inch (2.5 cm). Placed against the plate in the camera, the screen filtered the light transmitted on exposure and registered its tonal values in black and white on the plate. A positive transparency was then obtained and bound up in register with the same screen so the image would show its original colours on projection.*

From Autochrome to Polacolor

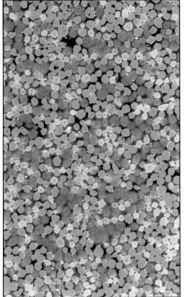

A print taken from a photo-micrograph *(above) shows the randomly scattered particles of starched dye, in the three primary colours, that formed the screen filter on the plate developed by the Lumière brothers and successfully marketed by them in 1907.*

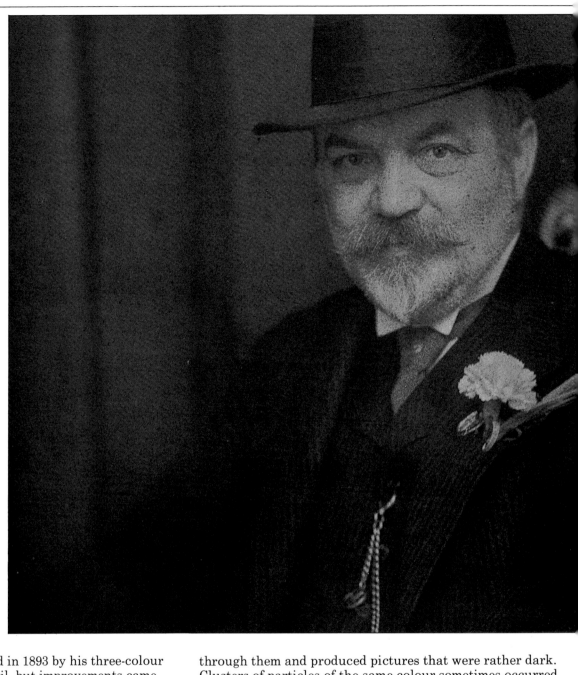

The delicate colouring of the portrait *(right), taken by an unknown photographer in about 1908, is typical of pictures made by the Lumière brothers' Autochrome process.*

The picture John Joly obtained in 1893 by his three-colour screen method lacked fine detail, but improvements came before long from the workshops of Auguste and Louis Lumière, pioneers in the public projection of moving pictures. At their factory in Lyons, the Lumière brothers developed their own screen plate, which they sold from 1907 as the Autochrome process. For their screen filter they coated one side of the glass plate with tiny rounded particles of transparent starch, dyed in primary colours, which were scattered randomly then compressed. They filled any remaining gaps with carbon black, and a covering of varnish gave a watertight seal. By this time panchromatic emulsion had been introduced, so the Lumières placed a layer on the plate's reverse. The process was almost identical to Joly's, except that the Lumière screen consisted of a mosaic of dots rather than parallel lines. Exposures were usually between one and two seconds in good light, and the exposed plate was processed by reversal to give a positive, colour picture.

Several other screen plate processes were subsequently devised, but a common failing was that the screens them-selves absorbed two-thirds or more of the light passing

through them and produced pictures that were rather dark. Clusters of particles of the same colour sometimes occurred in Autochrome plates, giving a blotching effect, yet the Lumières were manufacturing 6,000 plates a day in 1913. Autochrome plates provided photographers with the first genuinely simple method of taking colour pictures. They had a wide circulation and remained in production for 30 years.

While the Autochrome additive process attracted many to colour, research in Germany was pointing in a totally new direction. In 1912 Rudolf Fischer disclosed that chemicals existed which, when used in the development of film, reacted with the light-sensitive halides in the emulsion to convert other compounds into insoluble dyes. These colour-forming ingredients—dye couplers—could be included in the emulsion. As development of the film proceeded dyes would be released to produce colour images that could then be superimposed. Whereas du Hauron had added dyes to separation positives, Fischer now showed that dyes could be produced within the emulsion. Fischer's work prompted renewed scientific research into subtractive methods of colour reproduction involving dyes that would work by

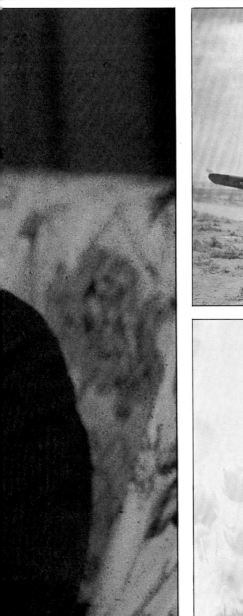

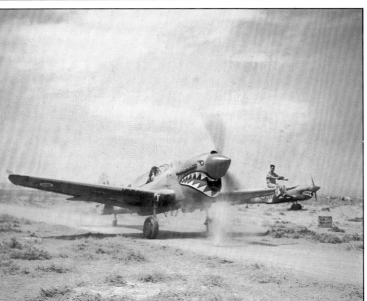

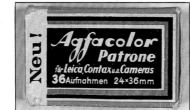

Agfa *advertise their new colour film in 1936.*

Kodacolor, *introduced in the middle of World War II, was used for this picture of a Kittyhawk fighter in service with the RAF in North Africa.*

A Polacolor portrait *shows the speed and accurate colour reproduction of the instant-print process introduced in 1963.*

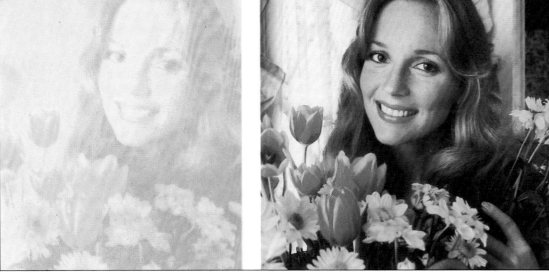

absorbing some primary components of light—a line of approach that opened the door to modern colour processing.

Researchers about this time were using standard dyes and experimenting with films of more than one emulsion layer. In the United States Leopold Mannes and Leopold Godowsky, friends from school days, patented in 1924 a two-layer emulsion that had one layer sensitive to green and blue-green, the other sensitive to red. To put colour into the image they connected the double negative to a black and white positive and then infused it with dyes. But when, in the 1920s, they learned of Fischer's pre-war work they changed course and began to investigate the use of dye couplers in triple-layer emulsions.

The Americans found, however, that they were unable to prevent the dyes "wandering" from one layer of emulsion to another, so they switched them to the developer instead. The tactic provided the breakthrough they needed, and in 1935 the first subtractive colour film using three layers of emulsion appeared under the name of Kodachrome. It was a film for home movies, but the following year a 35mm slide version became available. Because the dye couplers for these

films were added at the developing stage the purchaser had to send his exposed film to the manufacturer for processing. Customers who used the 35mm film had their slides returned in cardboard mounts ready for the projector.

In 1936 Agfa marketed a 35mm colour transparency film, Agfacolor, with dye couplers in the emulsion, allowing photographers for the first time to process their own colour films. A further six years elapsed before the Kodacolor process was marketed in the United States, giving paper prints in rich, clear colours. A colour negative as opposed to a colour reversal film, Kodacolor ushered in an age of colour snapshots. The colour print became hugely popular, but equally dramatic was the development of the *instant* colour print. The Polaroid Corporation had first sold their 60-second black and white instant picture package in the late 1940s and by 1963 the adaptations required to market a camera able to take and process colour shots in a minute were completed. Using Polacolor film, the Polaroid camera enabled a fascinated public to click the shutter, pull the tab and watch, intrigued, for a minute as the likenesses of people and things transformed a piece of white paper into a full-colour picture.

255

Time chart

The evolution of photography

Photography traces its origins to the camera obscura, a dark room or box with a tiny hole that admitted an inverted image. Known to Aristotle, the device with a lens added was developed from the 16th century onwards as an aid to artists. By the late 18th century, chemical advances brought the realization that the camera could be used to capture a permanent image through the action of light itself.

A box camera obscura, as used by Fox Talbot.

James Clerk Maxwell (below) pioneered colour photography in 1861 by separating and recombining the light reflected from a tartan ribbon.

Developments in colour

In 1777 Carl W. Scheele noted that silver chloride was most quickly blackened by light from the violet end of the spectrum. The idea that colour images could be achieved by direct means was pursued by some of the pioneers of photography throughout the 19th century, but it was gradually realized that some indirect method involving colour filters or subtractive dyes was more feasible.

Year	The evolution of photography		Developments in colour	
1800	1802 Thomas Wedgwood and Sir Humphry Davy announce success in achieving contact images on paper	and leather that had been sensitized with silver nitrate; they were unable to fix the images.	1802 Thomas Young delivers a lecture at the Royal Society of London on his theory that the eye responds to only three colours.	
1810	1812 William Wollaston invents meniscus lens. 1819 Sir John Herschel proposes sodium thio-sulphate as fixing agent.		1810 Johann T. Seebeck discovers that silver chloride assumes natural spectral colours when	exposed to white light.
1820	1826 Joseph Nicéphore Niepce makes first photograph from nature, which he fixes with bitumen of Judea.			
1830	1835 William Henry Fox Talbot produces negative photograph of window at Lacock Abbey, Wiltshire, using paper sensitized by	silver chloride. 1837 Louis Jacques Mandé Daguerre makes daguerreo-type using copper plate sensitized with silver	iodide, a mercury vapour developer and a solution of sodium chloride as a fixer. 1839 Sir John Herschel coins word "photography".	
1840	1840 Josef Max Petzval makes a lens suitable for portrait photography. 1840 Alexander Wolcott opens world's first portrait	studio in New York. 1841 Fox Talbot patents negative–positive calotype process for paper prints, and produces book of photo-	graphs in 1844. 1847 Claude Niepce de St Victor uses glass negative coated with an albumen-based emulsion.	1848 Edmond Becquerel's experiments result in colour impressions on plates coated with silver chloride.
1850	1851 Frederick Scott Archer invents collodion wet-plate process. 1853 John Benjamin Dancer	builds binocular camera.		
1860	1861 William England makes focal plane shutter with a variable aperture.		1861 James Clerk Maxwell obtains a three-colour image. 1869 Louis Ducos du Hauron publishes *Les Couleurs en Photographie*, listing	principles of additive and subtractive colour theories. 1869 Charles Cros announces theories of three-colour printing separation.
1870	1871 Richard Leach Maddox uses dry plate coated with gelatin containing silver bromide. 1875 Leon Warnerke makes	roll film with gelatin on paper. 1878 Eadweard James Muybridge photographs action of galloping horses.	1873 Hermann W. Vogel makes emulsion, prev-iously sensitive only to blue, sensitive to green. 1878 Du Hauron, with his	brother, publishes *Photographie des Couleurs*, which describes their original methods for making colour pictures.
1880	1887 Edward Bausch designs shutter that has iris diaphragm and blades. 1887 Hannibal Goodwin files patent for celluloid	roll-film. 1888 Kodak sell roll-film camera with 100 exposures. 1889 Paul Rudolf designs anastigmat lens.	1882 Orthochromatic plates (sensitive to blue and green light but not red) are successfully manufactured.	
1890	1891 Kodak introduce daylight-loading roll film.		1891 Gabriel Lippmann achieves natural colours by interference principle. 1891 Frederick Ives invents one-shot colour camera.	1892 Ives designs the Kromskop for viewing pictures in colour. 1893 John Joly invents linear screen filter.
1900	1900 Kodak "Brownie" camera available in the United States, price $1.		1902 Arthur Traube and Adolf Miethe discover ethyl red as sensitizer for red. 1903 Lumière brothers produce Autochrome process.	1904 Benno Homolka discovers pinacyanol as sensitizer for red. 1906 Panchromatic plates available commercially.
1910			1910 Louis Dufay produces his own screen process for additive colour. 1912 Rudolf Fischer discovers chemicals that	produce dyes during the development process. 1919 Discovery of crypto-cyanine as sensitizer for infra-red light.
1920	1924 Leica 35 mm camera, designed by Oskar Barnack of Ernst Leitz, in commercial production. 1925 Flashbulbs invented.	1928 Rolleiflex twin-lens reflex camera manufactured.	1921 Discovery of sen-sitizer for ultraviolet using fluorescent layer on the emulsion. 1924 Leopold Mannes and	Leopold Godowsky patent two-colour subtractive process using film with two layers of emulsion.
1930	1935 Development of electronic flash. 1937 Production of the first 35 mm single-lens reflex camera, the Exacta.		1935 Kodachrome film on sale: three-colour subtractive film for use in cine cameras. 1936 Kodachrome 35 mm film	on sale. 1936 Agfacolor 35 mm film on sale: dye couplers in emulsion, allowing processing by the user.
1940	1948 Polaroid Land camera launched, producing developed black and white prints in 60 seconds.		1942 Kodacolor film commercially available; the first film to allow colour paper prints to be produced.	
1950				
1960			1963 Polaroid instant-picture colour camera commercially available for colour prints developed in a minute.	

Gabriel Lippmann (above) explored interference methods later important in hologram photography.

The Lumière brothers, who marketed Autochrome in 1907, were notable photographers in colour.

Equipment
and darkroom techniques

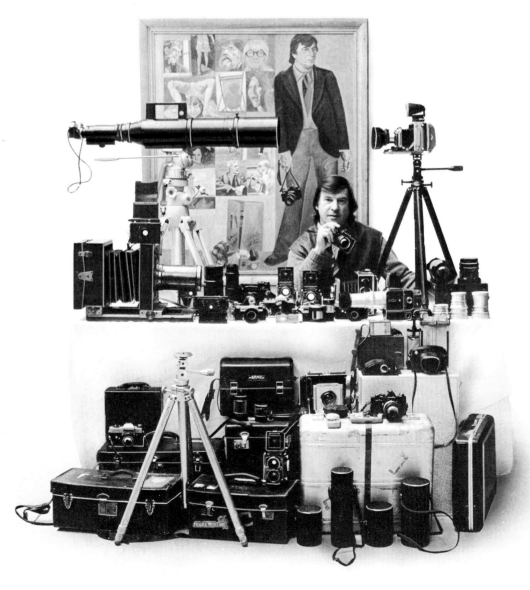

Cameras

Cameras for colour film are no different from those used in black and white photography and, in general, any piece of equipment capable of producing a sharp picture in one medium will give good results in the other. The very cheapest cameras, however, in addition to producing softer images, will not be able to register colours correctly.

All cameras have a lens that forms an image on light-sensitive material. They also have a shutter for controlling the length of time light reaches the film, and an aperture, which determines the quantity of light entering the lens. The versatility of cameras and the character and quality of the image they produce vary enormously. But a basic way of categorizing them is in terms of the size of film they use and their method of focusing.

Film sizes
110 The smallest film size in popular use, 110 gives an image size of 12×17 mm on 16 mm cartridge-loaded film. Most 110 cameras are used for making enprints—standard enlargements about 9×12 cm.

35 mm By far the most widely used size, 35 mm film, with an image size of 24×36 mm, can produce transparencies large enough for high-quality projection, and negatives that allow for enlargements many times greater than 110 negatives will permit. The largest range of films is made in this size.

120 roll film (or 220, its double-length version) is used by professional photographers and serious amateurs, partly for the larger image size that can be achieved. The size of the image, or format, varies according to the camera. The Hasselblad and the Rolleiflex, for example, produce images

that are $2\frac{1}{4} \times 2\frac{1}{4}$ in (6×6 cm), while the Mamiya 645 and the Pentax 6×7 both give rectangular pictures, one being 6×4.5 cm, the other 6×7 cm. These sizes are only approximate —the actual image sizes may be slightly smaller.

Most photographers now use 35 mm or 120/220 film except for specialized work, when they may use larger sizes of sheet film such as 6×9 cm, 5×4 in (12.7×10.2 cm) or 10×8 in (25.4×20.3 cm).

Methods of focusing
Very simple cameras such as the cheaper 110 models have fixed-focus lenses. Slightly more advanced cameras have zone-focusing lenses—instead of marked distances, they usually have pictorial symbols such as a head or a group of people to indicate the proper camera-to-subject distance. Both of these are direct view cameras; the window used to frame the picture is quite separate from the lens, but is constructed to give approximately the same viewpoint.

A more accurate form of direct view camera may incorporate a rangefinder focusing device. The viewfinder is still not optically connected to the lens, so the image is not exactly the same as that "seen" by the lens, a disparity known as parallax error, but sophisticated rangefinder cameras such as the Leica M4 have built-in parallax correction.

With large-format cameras such as the Sinar, you focus on an image formed on a ground-glass screen behind the lens. The image on the screen is inverted, but at least the eye can see exactly what the final photograph will look like. After the image is composed and focused, the ground-glass screen is moved back and a sheet of film in a holder is inserted.

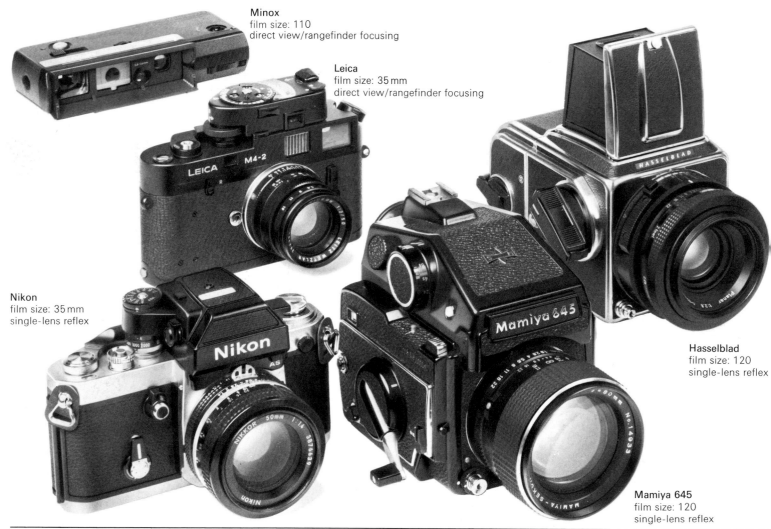

Minox
film size: 110
direct view/rangefinder focusing

Leica
film size: 35 mm
direct view/rangefinder focusing

Nikon
film size: 35 mm
single-lens reflex

Hasselblad
film size: 120
single-lens reflex

Mamiya 645
film size: 120
single-lens reflex

The most common focusing system in modern high-quality cameras uses a mirror positioned between the film and the lens. Because the mirror reflects the light coming through the lens upwards on to a screen, cameras using this system are known as reflex cameras. Twin-lens reflex (TLR) cameras, such as the Rolleiflex, view the image through one lens directly above a second lens, which actually transmits light to the film when an exposure is made. Cameras of this type have waist-level viewfinders and the images seen through them are upright, but reversed left to right.

Single-lens reflex (SLR) cameras operate on the same principle, but have only one lens with a mirror that swings out of the way when the shutter is released.

On some roll-film SLRs, such as the Hasselblad, the image is viewed from waist level and is, like the image on the TLR, upright but laterally reversed. In 35mm SLRs, such as the Nikon, the image is reflected from the mirror up to a penta-prism at the top of the camera. The pentaprism alters the orientation of the reflection so that the viewfinder, at eye level, shows the image as both upright and laterally corrected. Most roll-film cameras are constructed so that a pentaprism can be fitted as an optional accessory.

One of the main advantages of SLRs, whether 35mm or roll-film, is that lenses of different focal length can be fitted quickly and easily. TLRs are mechanically less complex than SLRs and so are generally less expensive. But only one manufacturer, Mamiya, produces TLR cameras with a range of interchangeable lenses. There are a few costly rangefinder cameras with interchangeable lenses.

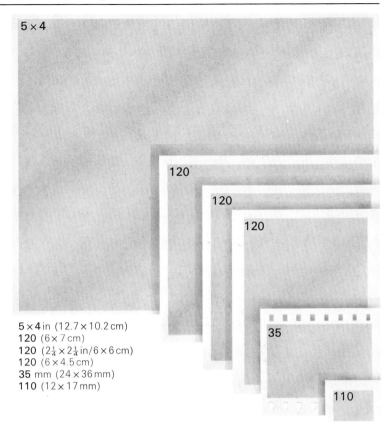

5×4 in (12.7×10.2 cm)
120 (6×7 cm)
120 (2¼×2¼ in/6×6 cm)
120 (6×4.5 cm)
35 mm (24×36 mm)
110 (12×17 mm)

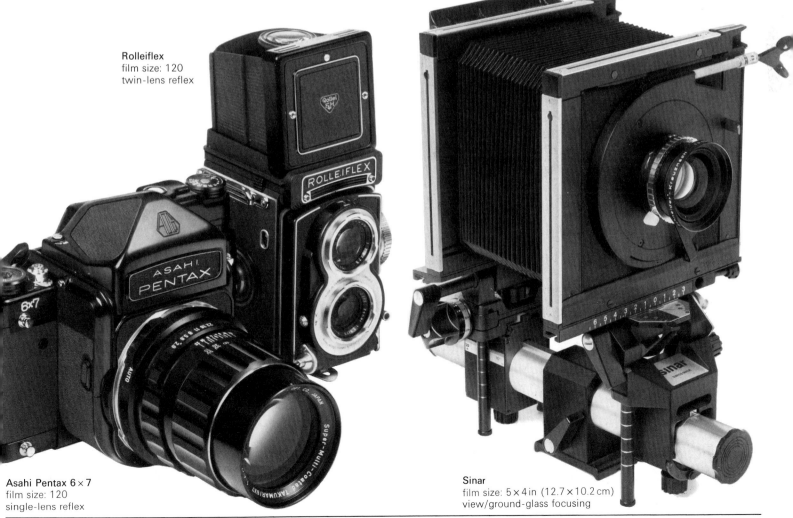

Rolleiflex
film size: 120
twin-lens reflex

Asahi Pentax 6×7
film size: 120
single-lens reflex

Sinar
film size: 5×4 in (12.7×10.2 cm)
view/ground-glass focusing

Cameras

Exposure is governed in the camera by two essential mechanisms, the lens diaphragm, which controls the intensity of light reaching the film (see pages 264–5), and the shutter, which determines the length of exposure time. There are two main kinds of shutters—leaf shutters (also known as between-the-lens shutters or diaphragm shutters) and focal plane shutters.

Leaf shutters are usually built into the lens, positioned between the optical components and immediately behind the iris diaphragm, which controls the size of the lens aperture. They consist of a number of thin metal blades that open outwards from the axis of the lens to allow light through and immediately spring back together again after the exposure has been made. The standard range of speeds found on cameras with leaf shutters is 1 second, 1/2, 1/4, 1/8, 1/15, 1/30, 1/60, 1/125, 1/250 and 1/500. Some have speeds up to 1/1000 second, while others have slightly slower maximum speeds. Each speed, from 1/2 onwards, is approximately twice as fast as the one preceding it and therefore gives half the exposure. For excessively long exposures there may be a "B" setting (indicating that the shutter will remain open as long as the shutter release button is depressed) and a "T" setting (indicating that the shutter will open when the release is depressed and will remain open until the release is depressed a second time).

One advantage of leaf shutters is that they allow synchronization with electronic flash at any speed (see pages

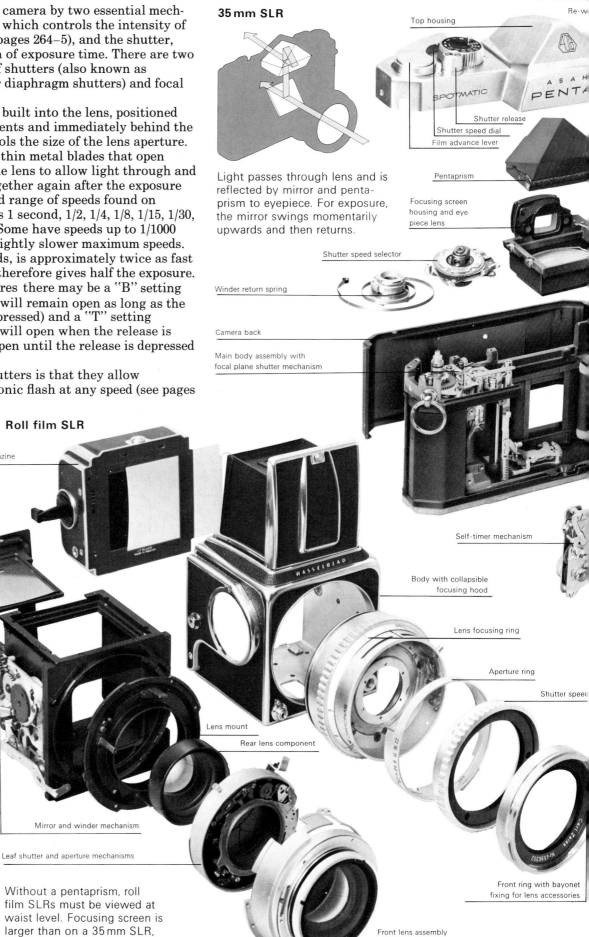

35 mm SLR

Light passes through lens and is reflected by mirror and pentaprism to eyepiece. For exposure, the mirror swings momentarily upwards and then returns.

Top housing

Re-w

Shutter release

Shutter speed dial

Film advance lever

Pentaprism

Focusing screen housing and eye piece lens

Shutter speed selector

Winder return spring

Camera back

Main body assembly with focal plane shutter mechanism

Self-timer mechanism

Body with collapsible focusing hood

Lens focusing ring

Aperture ring

Shutter speed

Lens mount

Rear lens component

Front ring with bayonet fixing for lens accessories

Front lens assembly

Roll film SLR

Interchangeable film magazine

Interior of film magazine showing film path

Instant-return mirror housing

Film advance crank

Mirror and winder mechanism

Leaf shutter and aperture mechanisms

Without a pentaprism, roll film SLRs must be viewed at waist level. Focusing screen is larger than on a 35 mm SLR, but image is laterally reversed.

274–5). But there are also drawbacks. Each lens must have its own integral shutter, so, while leaf shutters are excellent for cameras with permanently fixed lenses, they are comparatively expensive when designed as part of an interchangeable lens system. This is the reason why nearly all cameras having interchangeable lenses (most models of the Hasselblad are a notable exception) are fitted with focal plane shutters.

Focal plane shutters are built into the camera body immediately in front of the film plane. They are made of rubberized fabric or metal blades and work rather like roller blinds, moving horizontally or vertically across the front of the film. Cameras fitted with focal plane shutters can usually accept a wide range of lenses. Although focal plane shutters permit higher speeds than leaf shutters (up to 1/2000 on some cameras), they can be synchronized to electronic flash only at a low speed—generally 1/30 or 1/60.

Many cameras of recent design have electronically controlled shutter speeds for greater accuracy. The shutter, whether leaf or focal plane, opens as it would normally, but is prevented from closing by tiny electromagnets. At the end of the exposure time, the current stops and the shutter closes.

An exposure sequence with a typical 35mm SLR camera consists of the following stages. After the shutter speed and aperture are selected, the image—reflected by a mirror from light passing through the lens—is focused at full aperture and composed. The shutter release is depressed and, in rapid succession, the mirror swings upwards, the lens diaphragm closes down to the pre-selected aperture, the shutter opens and the film is exposed. When the shutter closes the mirror returns and the diaphragm opens. The film is wound on a frame and the camera is ready for another exposure.

Varying levels of automation achieved through the use of miniaturized electronics have made cameras easier to use than ever before. Through-the-lens (TTL) metering systems have been developed to the point where they can compute and set exposures automatically (see page 271). Even more astonishing is the advent of automatic focusing, which enables a camera lens to be focused by means of an electric motor. Automatic focusing is useful for photographing moving subjects whose distance from the camera changes.

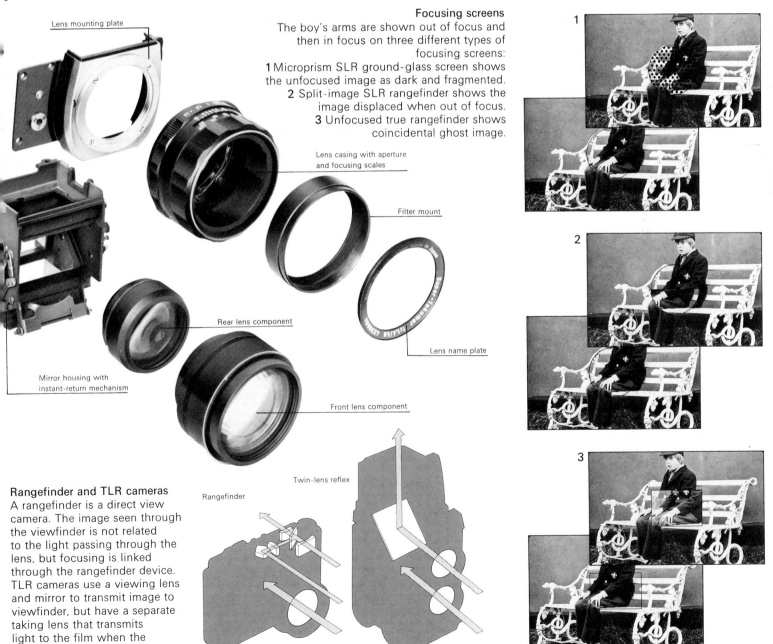

Focusing screens
The boy's arms are shown out of focus and then in focus on three different types of focusing screens:
1 Microprism SLR ground-glass screen shows the unfocused image as dark and fragmented.
2 Split-image SLR rangefinder shows the image displaced when out of focus.
3 Unfocused true rangefinder shows coincidental ghost image.

Lens mounting plate

Lens casing with aperture and focusing scales

Filter mount

Rear lens component

Lens name plate

Mirror housing with instant-return mechanism

Front lens component

Twin-lens reflex

Rangefinder

Rangefinder and TLR cameras
A rangefinder is a direct view camera. The image seen through the viewfinder is not related to the light passing through the lens, but focusing is linked through the rangefinder device. TLR cameras use a viewing lens and mirror to transmit image to viewfinder, but have a separate taking lens that transmits light to the film when the shutter release is pressed.

The system camera

Any single camera, however well designed, is inevitably a compromise and cannot be expected to suit every photographer's needs. Therefore most manufacturers, particularly of SLR cameras, produce a system of additional lenses and accessories, such as the range illustrated here.

Each system camera has its own lenses, but you may wish to use one lens on another make of camera or decide to buy cheaper alternatives offered by independent lens manufacturers. A prime consideration in using different lenses is their method of coupling to the camera body. There are three basic kinds of lens mount—screw thread, bayonet and breech-lock bayonet. As a rule, the bayonet mounts will take only lenses made specifically for that camera. Most screw-threads, however, are of a standard size (usually known as the Pentax or Praktica mount), allowing a degree of inter-changeability with other cameras.

The matter of interchangeability is complicated by the fact that the size and position of the pins and levers at the back of the lens which couple its diaphragm to the camera's shutter and metering system frequently vary from make to make. To get around this, the independent lens manufacturers produce adapters that allow their own products to fit most cameras. Special adapters also enable screw-thread lenses to fit bayonet-mount cameras (and vice versa) and can convert one type of bayonet mount to another. Even so, the automatic diaphragm controls may be partly affected.

Viewfinders and focusing screens

A number of available attachments allow the camera to be held and focused in various positions. Some permit waist-level or eye-level viewing, while others magnify the image.

Many SLR cameras have interchangeable focusing screens. Ground glass screens are good for general photography; they usually have a focusing aid in the centre that may be a disc of microprisms, a split-image rangefinder or a combination of both. Screens ruled with rectangular grids are especially helpful when, as in architectural photography, it is essential to line up horizontals or verticals accurately.

Backs and motor drives

Some camera makers produce different backs for their cameras. Bulk film holders can be fitted in place of the ordinary back to enable you to take 250 exposures without having to change film. Other backs can convert the size and type of film used or record numerical reference data on each frame of exposed film.

In recent years power winders have become popular accessories. Attached to the base-plate of the camera, these allow you to shoot up to two frames per second without the distraction of having to wind the film on manually between each frame. Motor drives are generally larger and more expensive units that can shoot five or more frames per second.

Other accessories, such as supports, attachments for photographing through microscopes, underwater housings, carrying equipment, flash, and so on, are peripheral to a camera's system and in most cases your choice is not confined to the manufacturer's own products. Many professional photographers find it pays to hire specialized equipment.

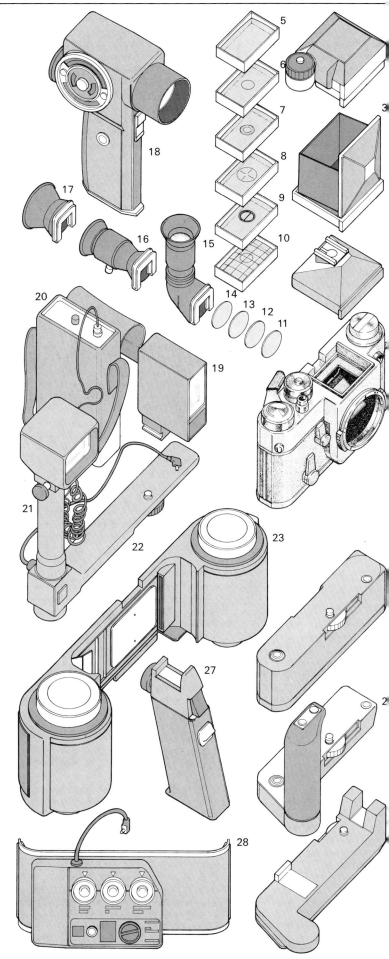

1 camera body 2 standard pentaprism 3 waist-level finder 4 meter prism 5 focusing screen: ground glass 6 focusing screen: ground glass with clear centre spot 7 focusing screen: ground glass with microprism surrounding clear centre spot 8 focusing screen: ground glass with centre cross hairs 9 focusing screen: ground glass with microprism surrounding split-image rangefinder 10 focusing screen: ground glass with clear centre spot and grid 11–14 eyepiece correction lenses 15 right-angle finder 16 magnifier 17 rubber eyecup 18 spot meter 19 auto flash 20 portable power pack 21 heavy-duty flash 22 flash bracket 23 bulk-film back 24 power winder 25 motor drive 26 motor drive power unit 27 pistol grip power unit 28 data back 29 converter lens 30 200mm lens 31 400mm lens 32 catadioptric (mirror) lens 33 fish-eye lens 34 28mm lens 35 50mm lens 36 85mm lens 37 75mm – 150mm zoom lens 38–40 lens hoods 41–43 extension rings 44 bellows 45 bellows focusing rail 46 reversing ring 47–55 filters 56 tripod 57 cable release 58–60 filter holders 61–63 lens caps 64 eveready case 65 holdall 66 spare lens 67–68 bulk film magazines 69 lens pouch 70–72 lens cases 73 underwater housing

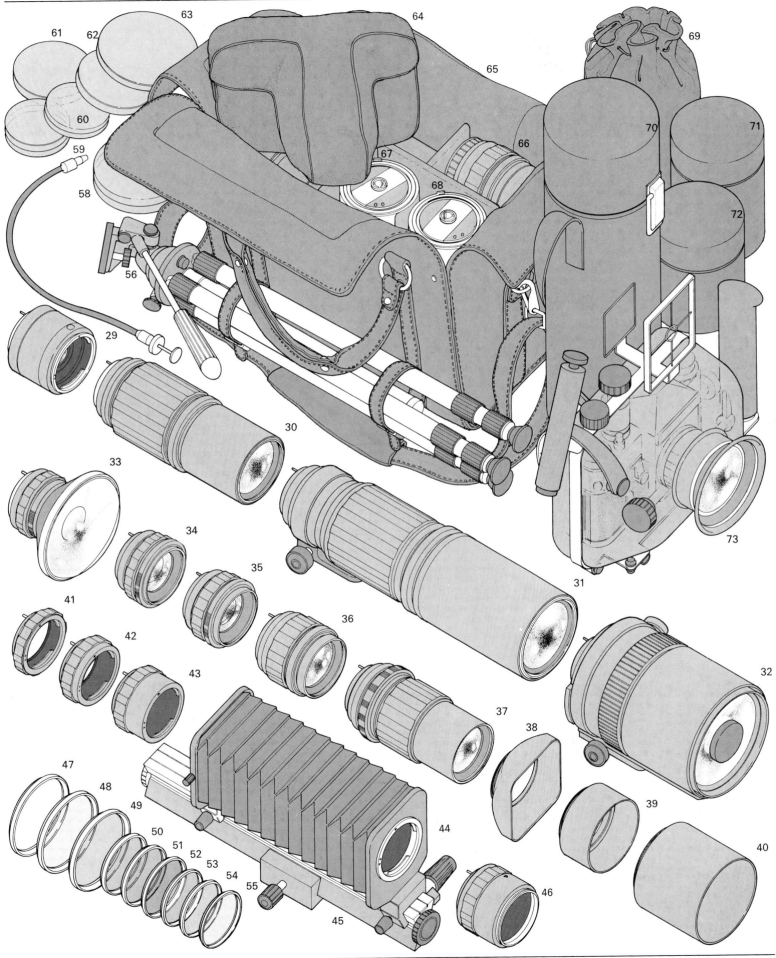

Lenses

No single camera lens is as adaptable as the lens of the human eye. But there are specific lenses that can record more detail than the unaided eye can perceive. Selecting the proper lens and using it to full advantage is possible only if certain basic optical characteristics are properly understood.

Focal length and angle of view

When choosing a lens, a photographer has to know its focal length—the distance behind a lens at which a sharp image will be formed when the lens is focused at infinity—and the effect it will have on the image. The longer the focal length the larger will be the image size. If, for example, a 50mm lens produces a 3mm image of an object, a 100mm lens will produce a 6mm image of the same object. In doing so the 100mm lens will reduce the total area of the scene proportionally. On the other hand, a 25mm lens will include a greater area but on a smaller scale.

By convention a "normal" or "standard" lens is one with a focal length approximately equal to the diagonal of the format of the film it covers. On 35mm film, with a format of 24 × 36mm, the diagonal is about 45mm. Lenses with focal lengths in the region between 45mm and 55mm are therefore described as standard. The diagonal of $2\frac{1}{4} \times 2\frac{1}{4}$ in (6 × 6cm) film is about 85mm and lenses between 75mm and 90mm are considered standard for that particular format. Lenses shorter than the standard focal length are designated as wide-angle lenses, while those with longer focal lengths are telephoto lenses. Therefore, an 80mm lens used with 35mm film would be considered a telephoto, while a 50mm lens used with $2\frac{1}{4} \times 2\frac{1}{4}$ in (6 × 6cm) film would be a wide-angle lens.

Another approach is to consider the angle of view taken in by a lens. A standard lens, regardless of the film size, has an angle of view of between 45° and 55°. Telephoto lenses take in angles of 30° down to 2°, while wide-angle lenses have an angle of view of 70° up to 180°.

The scale of the image can be controlled in one of two ways, either by altering the distance between the camera and the subject or by changing the focal length of the lens. A 2mm image, for example, can be magnified to a 4mm image by doubling the focal length of the lens or by halving the camera-to-subject distance. But these two methods produce different results, a fact that enables photographers to exercise a large degree of creative control over the images they record. Different lenses also have varying perspective effects, with wide-angle lenses tending to increase the apparent depth between objects on different planes and telephoto lenses decreasing depth.

Depth of field and f number

The amount of light reaching the film is controlled by the iris diaphragm, which can be opened up to allow in more light or closed down to restrict the amount of light. The size of the diaphragm's aperture is important not only because it affects exposure times but also because it determines to some extent the depth of field, or range of object distances, over which the image is sufficiently sharp.

The aperture is measured in f numbers (or f stops) which range from a maximum opening of f1 or larger to a minimum opening of perhaps f64 or less, with intermediate stops of 1.4, 2, 2.8, 4, 5.6, 8, 11, 16, 22, 32, 45. Stopping down, each f number allows in half the light of the preceding one and twice as much light as the one following—f2 will allow half as much light through the lens as f1.4 and a quarter of the light of f1, but twice the light of f2.8 and four times the light of f4. Intermediate stops such as 1.2, 1.8 or 3.5 can also be chosen. A typical 50mm lens for a 35mm camera may have f numbers from 2 to 16, and be referred to as a 50mm f2 lens.

Lenses that have wide maximum apertures in relation to their focal lengths are known as fast lenses and are useful when light intensities are low and long exposures are not practical.

When a lens is focused at a particular distance, only objects at that distance are recorded with maximum sharpness, although objects both in front of and behind that point may still be acceptably sharp. Three factors determine the depth of field, or range within which objects appear to be in focus—the focal length of the lens, the f number selected and the camera-to-subject distance. Depth of field *increases* as the focal length of the lens becomes shorter, as the aperture is stopped down and as the camera-to-subject distance approaches infinity. It *decreases* with lenses of longer focal length, when larger apertures are selected and when the subject in focus is closer to the camera.

Most camera lenses have depth-of-field scales engraved on them, but these are worked out on the basis of a pre-determined degree of format enlargement. The scale on lenses made for 35mm cameras, for example, may be relevant for a print size of $8\frac{1}{2} \times 6\frac{1}{2}$ in (21.6 × 16.5cm). If larger prints are made, then the depth of field will be less than indicated on the scale and with smaller prints the depth of field will be greater. It is important to note that depth of field does not begin and end abruptly, but changes gradually from a blur to acceptable sharpness, and also that the notion of what is not "acceptably" sharp is a highly subjective one.

Nearly all lenses improve in performance when stopped down. A 50mm lens at f2, for example, would increase in sharpness, especially towards the edges of the picture, when

Depth of field/aperture
A 50mm lens focused on the boy at 14ft (4.3m) shows the depth of field at three apertures. (Top) f2, depth of field 13–15ft (4–4.6m), ladders out of focus. (Centre) f5.6, depth of field 11–18ft (3.3–5.5m), ladders slightly out of focus. (Bottom) f11, depth of field 9–29ft (2.7–8.8m) ladders sharp.

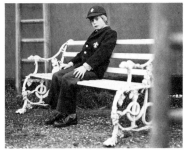

Above: 1/1000, f2.

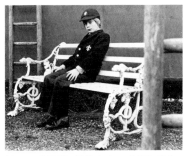

Above: 1/125, f5.6; below 1/30, f11.

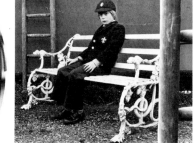

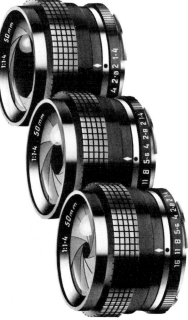

stopped down to f5.6 or f8. At very small apertures though, such as f16 or f22 with the same lens, the narrower aperture would begin diffracting light, causing some fall-off in definition. The longer the focal length of the lens, the greater the f number permissible before the problem of diffraction begins to arise.

Although most of the light entering a lens is passed through to the film, some is inevitably reflected out of the lens and within the lens barrel itself. This internally reflected light degrades the image by reducing contrast, a fault known as flare. To prevent this, lens manufacturers take great care to black out all metal surfaces in the lens. Another means of reducing flare is by covering the lens surface with an anti-reflective coating. Flare can also be reduced by using a lens hood, which blocks out unwanted light from outside the picture area. Deep and effective hoods can be fitted to lenses that have narrow angles of view.

135 mm telephoto lens

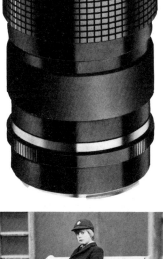

How lenses affect an image
Three lenses typically used on a 35 mm camera are a 28 mm wide-angle, a 50 mm "standard" and a 135 mm telephoto. Each in its characteristic way affects the appearance of the image in terms of size and the scale relationship of objects on different planes. Equally important is the extent to which each lens can sharply record objects in front of and behind the point of focus.

28 mm wide-angle lens

50 mm standard lens

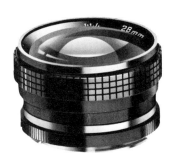
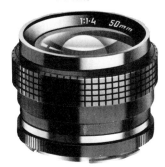

Depth of field/focal length
Camera distance was varied to keep image size about equal. All three lenses were set at f4. (Left) 28 mm focused at 8 ft (2.4 m) —everything appears sharp. (Centre) 50 mm focused at 14 ft (4.2 m)—ladders slightly blurred. (Right) 135 mm focused at 30 ft (9 m)—foreground and background blurred.

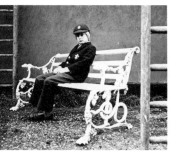
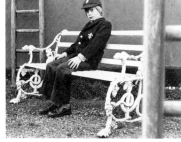
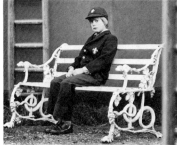

Angle of view/image size
All shots were taken from the same camera-to-subject distance. (Left) 28 mm with a 74° viewing angle, takes in a wide scene but the image is small. (Centre) 50 mm has a 45° coverage, roughly equivalent to the angle of view of the human eye. (Right) 135 mm has an 18° viewing angle and magnifies the image.

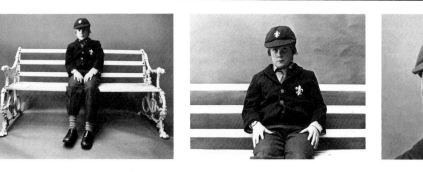

Angle of view/perspective
Camera-to-subject distance was varied so that the side of the bench nearest to the camera remained the same size. (Left) 28 mm steepens perspective; the bench looks deceptively long. (Centre) 50 mm registers perspective normally. (Right) 135 mm flattens perspective so that the bench appears shorter.

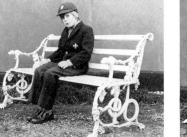
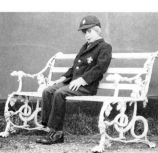

Lenses

Most subjects can be recorded with a selection of three lenses —a moderate wide-angle (28–35 mm for 35 mm cameras), a standard lens (45–55 mm) and a medium telephoto lens (90–135 mm). There will be times, though, when you may need a special-purpose lens to extend the image-recording ability of your camera.

With cameras that have interchangeable lenses, it is possible to take extreme close-ups by increasing the distance between the lens and the film with bellows attachments or extension tubes. Macro lenses are also available for working at very close distances and can record images that are on the same scale as the object they photograph.

Very wide-angle lenses are difficult to design, one of the problems being the effects of distortion. Fish-eye lenses, which can have angles of view as wide as 180°, attempt to make a virtue of distortion by producing circular pictures with straight lines appearing as concentric curves. The effect can be dramatic, but few subjects suit this kind of treatment.

Shift lenses are wide-angle lenses, made primarily for 35 mm cameras, that can be moved off their normal axis to provide a certain degree of control over perspective. The results are similar to those obtainable on a studio camera with swinging and rising front controls. They are most widely used in architectural photography, particularly to encompass tall buildings without the sides of the building appearing to converge as they would if photographed with an ordinary lens tilted upwards.

Zoom lenses are useful for their variable focal lengths. Once the subject is in focus, focal length can be changed at will to alter the scale of the image. Most zoom lenses have 13 or more elements and are consequently heavier, and more expensive, than any comparable lens of fixed focal length.

But one zoom will still be cheaper and lighter than a set of, say, four separate lenses that cover the same focal lengths. For 35 mm cameras, zoom lenses with variable focal lengths between 60 and 300 mm are the most useful. Those with longer focal lengths tend to be too heavy for hand-held photography, while high-quality wide-angle zooms are difficult to produce. Some zoom lenses can be locked in at a macro setting, giving yet a further dimension to an already versatile lens.

One way of providing a single camera lens with wide-angle or telephoto capability is by fitting adaptor lenses. They usually allow for an increase or decrease of only one-third of the focal length of the lens to which they are attached, a change many photographers may consider to be negligible. Converter lenses, on the other hand, can actually double or treble the focal length of a lens. Fitted between the camera body and the lens, converters work by magnifying the centre

Macro, fish-eye and perspective control lenses *enable photographers to achieve effects they might not be able to obtain by using lenses of standard focal length. The shot taken with a standard lens (1) provides a basis for comparison. A macro lens is used for close-up photography (2), for example in copy work or when shooting plants and insects. Fish-eye lenses produce distorted circular images (3). Perspective control, or shift, lenses solve the problem of converging parallel lines (4, 5).*

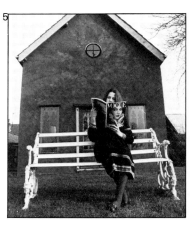

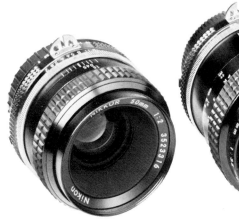

Standard lens

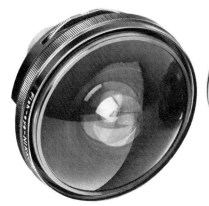

Macro lens

Fish-eye lens

Perspective control (shift) lens

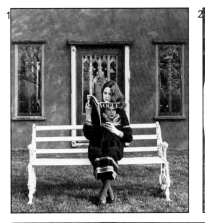
1

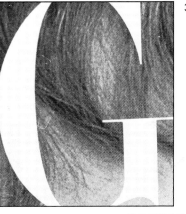
2

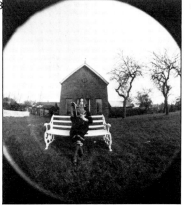
3

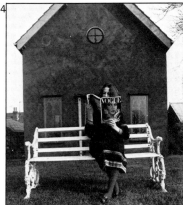
4

of the image formed by the existing lens and therefore produce the best results when that lens is itself of good quality. Converters are most often used with telephoto lenses. You may, for example, have a 250mm lens and consider that a 500mm lens would be too heavy or used too seldom to be worth buying. By fitting a 2× converter, however, you can effectively double the focal length of the 250mm lens and achieve results comparable with those of a separate 500mm lens. The advantage is that the converter is cheaper, lighter and far more compact. But there are disadvantages as well, for converters decrease the amount of light reaching the film —a 2× converter reduces light transmission by two stops— and they increase the likelihood of flare (although a good converter with perhaps four elements should not cause an excessive drop in image contrast).

Telephoto lenses are, of course, used for photographing distant subjects, but their limited depth of field also makes

them excellent for isolating a subject from its background. Accurately focused and at maximum aperture, a telephoto lens can pick one face out of a blurred crowd. But generally, the longer the lens the heavier it is, and some can only be used when mounted on a tripod. To get around this problem of size and weight, lens manufacturers devised catadioptric, or mirror, lenses. These use a combination of lenses and mirrored surfaces to reflect light backwards and forwards inside the barrel so that focal length is, as it were, folded up. As a result, the physical length of mirror lenses can be much shorter than their actual focal length. One drawback, however, is that the f number is fixed (usually at f8).

Catadioptric (mirror) lens

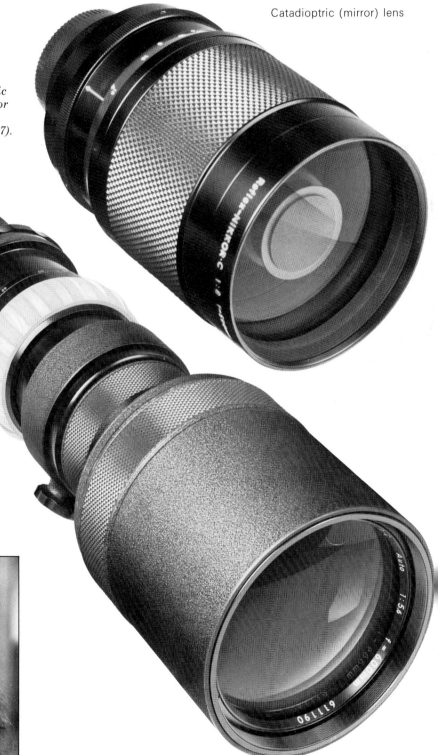

Zoom, ultra-telephoto and catadioptric lenses *can all be used to pull in far-off subjects. The zoom has variable focal lengths, from wide-angle to* *telephoto. Zooming during exposure (6) can create dynamic effects. Ultra-telephoto or mirror lenses allow close-up images of subjects far from the camera (7).*

Zoom lens (above)　　Telephoto lens (right)

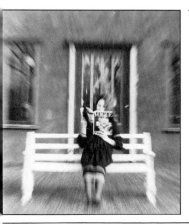

7

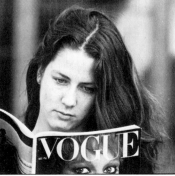

Filters

Although colour films are balanced for particular light sources, they can be used with other sources of light if appropriate correcting filters are selected.

The colours of various light sources are described in terms of their colour temperature, measured in kelvins (see pages 26–7). With colour reversal film, from which transparencies are produced, the matching of the colour temperature of the film to the colour temperature of the light source is critical as there is no stage between the exposure and processing of the transparency at which any correction can be made. This is why there are three types of reversal film available— *Daylight* (balanced for about 5,500 K, corresponding to mid-day sunlight), and two kinds of artificial-light films, *Type A* (balanced for 3,400 K, the colour temperature of photofloods) and *Type B* (balanced for 3,200 K, the colour temperature of studio lamps). Unless corrected by filters, the mis-matching of these films and their recommended light sources will produce transparencies with varying degrees of colour cast. Daylight film exposed under artificial light will have a yellow cast, while Type A and Type B film exposed outdoors will have a strong blue cast. Colour negative films, on the other hand, are all approximately balanced for daylight. If used under artificial lighting any imbalance in colour can usually be corrected at the printing stage.

The three colour temperatures for which reversal film is balanced by no means cover the wide range of different colour temperatures actually encountered in different lighting conditions. To cope with variations in light, there are close to a hundred different correction filters from which to choose. And apart from sheer numbers the problem of selection is further compounded by the fact that various manufacturers use different codes for their products.

Kodak, for example, have CC (colour compensating) filters in varying densities of blue, cyan, green, magenta, red and yellow, which are used to make very slight changes in colour. For larger changes, they produce Wratten filters, which consist of four series within two main groups. The two groups are conversion filters and light-balancing filters. Conversion filters are used to make the largest changes in colour, and they consist of series 80 (blue) and 85 (amber) filters. Light-balancing filters are used to make smaller changes and consist of series 81 (amber) and 82 (blue) filters. There is no readily discernible connection between the coding of the series and their effects. Agfa name their filters in a more consistent manner—CTB (colour temperature blue) and CTO (colour temperature orange); an Agfa CTO 12 filter is equivalent to a Kodak Wratten 85B.

One way of simplifying the choice of Wratten filter is by using the mired system. Mireds (an acronym for micro-reciprocal degrees) are obtained by dividing 1,000,000 by the colour temperature. Mired values can be calculated for the light source and the film being used. The difference between the two results is what is known as the mired shift value. Each filter in the Wratten series is assigned a mired shift value so all one need do is calculate the mired values of light and film (or consult tables that list them), work out the difference between them and match that to the shift values assigned to each of the filters. For example, daylight—with a colour temperature of 5,500 K—has a mired value of $\frac{1,000,000}{5,500}$, approximately 182. Type A film—balanced for light having a colour temperature of 3,400 K—has a mired value of $\frac{1,000,000}{3,400}$, approximately 294. A filter with a shift value of +112 (294 minus 182)—which corresponds to a Wratten no. 85—would then be used to convert Type A film for use in daylight. (Mired shift values are quoted in positive and negative numbers. Positive ones indicate that the filter is yellow/orange and is to be used with films balanced for lower colour temperatures than the illumination, while negative ones indicate that the filter is blue and is to be used with films balanced for colour temperatures higher than the illumination.) Thus, an 85 filter, which is amber, has a mired shift value of +112 and would be used to balance Type A film to daylight, while an 80B filter with a mired shift value of –112 is blue and would be used to balance daylight film to artificial light.

Filters can be used not only for colour correction but also for dramatic and artistic control of colour (see pages 246–9). A blue filter used with daylight film might be used to convey a feeling of coldness or to simulate moonlight in an otherwise unremarkable outdoor scene. (A similar effect could be achieved by using artificial light film unfiltered in daylight.) Some filters have a single colour of varying density. With a graduated red filter that varies from clear glass to red it is possible to produce a red sky in a landscape photograph without unduly affecting the colour of the land in the bottom half of the picture.

Neutral density (ND) filters control the overall level of brightness of a scene without altering the colour. They are manufactured in various densities of grey and are used to prevent overexposure of film in exceptionally bright lighting conditions. Polarizing filters are often used in colour photography to intensify certain colours and to eliminate reflections from shiny surfaces (see pages 28–9).

Some light loss occurs with most filters and extra exposure must be given to compensate for this. Manufacturers always quote a filter factor, which must be converted to the number of f stops the aperture needs to be opened.

Selecting the right filter for a given lighting condition is no easy task and, wherever possible, it is always best to use film in the lighting conditions for which it is intended.

Mired values

Converting colour temperature to mireds

Mireds, or micro-reciprocal degrees, are obtained by dividing 1,000,000 by the colour temperature.

Kelvins	5,500	5,000	4,000	3,500	3,000	2,500
Mireds	150	200	250	300	350	

Approximate mired shift values for Wratten filters

Amber filters		Blue filters		
81	+10	82	—10	To find the mired shift needed, subtract the mired value of the illumination from the mired value of the light for which the film is balanced. If the resulting value is positive, a yellow orange filter is indicated; a negative shift value indicates a blue filter. The larger the shift value, the darker the filter.
81A	+18	82A	—18	
81B	+27	82B	—32	
81C	+35	82C	—45	
81D	+42	80D	—56	
85C	+81	80C	—81	
85	+112	80B	—112	
85B	+131	80A	—131	

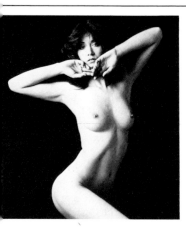

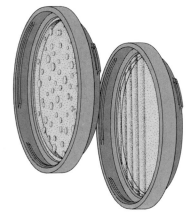

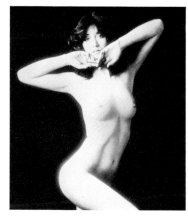

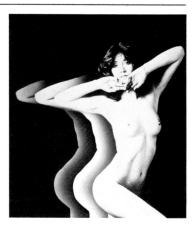

Special effects attachments

There is a range of special lens attachments and filters that can create striking photographic effects. Soft-focus attachments are used to give photographs a misty, diffused appearance. Prismatic, or multi-image, attachments are usually made of clear optical plastic and each faceted surface produces a separate image. Popular attachments of this type may have parallel or triangular prisms. Star and cross attachments split point sources of light into four or more streaks of radiating light (see pages 246–7 for a colour effect). Unlike most of the filters used for correcting colour, none of these attachments requires any compensating exposure increase.

A straight image (left) is altered by a soft-focus attachment and a six-surface repeater prism (above).

Soft focus may be used to create a glowing halo around highlights in the image.

A repeater attachment can suggest movement by repeating part of the image.

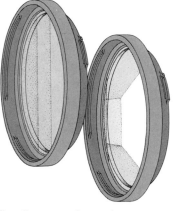

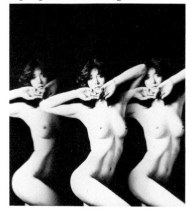

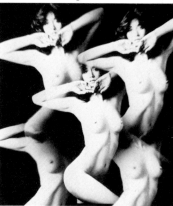

The diagrams above show a three-surface parallel prism (left) and a five-faceted prism (right).

A three-surface parallel prism multiplies the image linearly in a well-spaced pattern.

A faceted prism creates radial patterns that are made up of multiple images.

Which filters to use

Light source	Colour temperature	Correct for these films	If used with these films	Colour cast will be:	Use these filters	Filter colour	Increase f stop
Domestic tungsten bulbs 100W	2,860 K		Daylight Type A Type B	yellow yellow	82C + 82A 82C	blue blue	1 $\frac{2}{3}$
500W	2,950 K		Daylight Type A Type B	yellow yellow	82C + 82 82B	blue blue	1 $\frac{2}{3}$
Studio lamps (also early morning or late afternoon)	3,200 K	Type B	Daylight Type A	yellow slight yellow	80A 82A	blue blue	2 $\frac{1}{3} - \frac{1}{2}$
Photofloods	3,400 K	Type A	Daylight Type B	yellow slight blue	80B 81A	blue yellow	1$\frac{2}{3}$ $\frac{1}{3}$
Clear flashbulbs	3,800–4,200 K		Daylight Type A Type B	yellow slight blue slight blue	80C 81C 81D	blue yellow yellow	1 $\frac{1}{3} - \frac{1}{2}$ $\frac{2}{3}$
Midday sunlight Electronic flash Blue flashbulb	5,000–6,000 K	Daylight	Daylight Type A Type B	may be slight blue cast strong blue strong blue	Skylight 1A or B, Haze or UV 85 85B	slight pink orange orange	no increase $\frac{2}{3}$ $\frac{2}{3}$
Cloudy or hazy sky	6,000–9,000 K		Daylight	blue	81A	yellow	$\frac{1}{3}$

Light meters

Exposure is determined by three factors—the speed of the film, the shutter speed and the lens aperture. Exposure meters measure the intensity of light and indicate the possible f stop and shutter speed combinations that will give the proper exposure for any given film speed.

All exposure meters have light-sensitive cells that convert the light falling on them into an electrical current. One type uses a selenium cell that generates its own current without needing batteries. It is the least sensitive of meters and not very responsive to poor light. Cadmium sulphide (CdS) cell meters are much more sensitive; the cell acts as a battery-powered resistor that allows current to increase as light reaches it.

With some meters the current causes a needle to move across a numbered scale, and the control dial is then turned to the number indicated by the needle. Once this is done, the f stop and shutter speed combinations can be read off another segment of the dial. Other meters have a match needle system. The first needle moves according to the light falling on the cell; when it stops, another needle attached to the control dial is aligned with it and the correct exposure combination is read directly off the dial.

Exposure meters can be used to take over-all, or average, light readings from a subject. Alternatively, more selective readings can be taken of the most important parts of the subject—either the shadow areas so that the film can be exposed to give detail in dark areas, or the highlights.

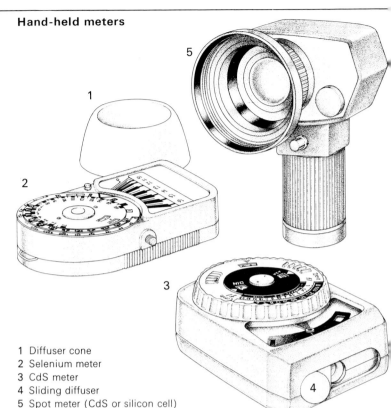

1 Diffuser cone
2 Selenium meter
3 CdS meter
4 Sliding diffuser
5 Spot meter (CdS or silicon cell)

Using a meter

Meters are usually employed to take reflected light readings. Unless used selectively, they average out highlight and shadow areas. Diffusing cones can be placed in front of the cell for incident light readings of high-lights—measuring the light falling on the subject. Spot meters are excellent for taking reflected light readings from far-off subjects. Their narrow angle of view, in some cases as little as 1°, gives highly selective readings of tonal areas in the subject.

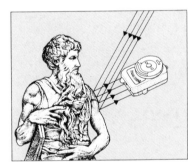

Reflected light readings measure light coming off the subject. Point the metering cell towards the subject.

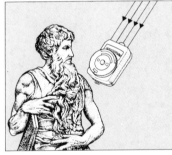

Incident light readings measure light falling on the subject. Point the metering cell back towards the light source.

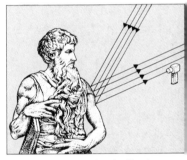

Spot meters are basically the same as reflected light meters, but they measure light from a very selective area.

Care and maintenance

Camera repairs are costly and the best way of avoiding them is by regularly examining and carefully cleaning your equipment. Lenses easily collect dust, grit and grease, but if they are cleaned too often, the lens elements may become scratched, reducing the quality of your photographs more than the original dirt would have done. When cleaning is really necessary, use a rolled-up lens tissue with a ragged edge to brush away any loose particles. Blower brushes can also be used, but quickly become greasy. Unless the brush is absolutely clean, use only the bulb part to blow dust away. Lens cloths should generally be avoided as they tend to pick up grit and grind it back into the lens. If cleaning fluid is used, never apply it directly to the lens as it may work its way around the edges and dissolve the cement holding the lens elements together. First clean off any loose dirt with tissue or blower brush; then squeeze a drop of fluid on to a clean tissue and *gently* remove the grease.

The question of how often a camera should be cleaned depends how and under what conditions it is used. At the very least it should be inspected before any assignment, otherwise once a month. With cameras that have removable lenses, take off the lens, open the back of the camera and keep the shutter open with the B or T settings. Inspect the interior and note any scratches or exposed metal. These can cause internal reflections, so should be blacked out by a qualified repairman. To avoid hairs being left inside, remove the head of the blower brush and blow out any loose dust particles. Check the film guide rails and pressure plate; grit in these areas can scratch the film. When the camera is not used for a couple of weeks remove any batteries powering the metering system. They contain a corrosive acid that may leak out if the cells become exhausted. It is unwise to wind on the film after the last shot of the day, as the shutter spring may stretch if left tensioned for a long period.

Through-the-lens metering
Many cameras are now built with integral light-metering systems. The system used in most 35mm SLR cameras is through-the-lens (TTL) metering. Adding to this some cameras are automatic; the cell controls shutter speeds

Viewfinder displays
The viewfinder of many SLRs is a complete information centre, where the subject is focused and exposure adjustments can be made by noting the shutter speed and aperture read-outs. With all the information in the viewfinder your eye need not leave the subject to alter camera controls while you are composing the picture.

or lens apertures. With one type, the speed is set manually and aperture is adjusted by the camera; with another aperture is selected and the camera adjusts the speed. Most TTL metering systems are either averaging, centre-weighted or

spot systems. Averaging meters are most sensitive at the centre of the screen, but they nevertheless give an integrated reading over the entire picture area. Centre-weighted meters have concentrated sensitivity at or near the centre, but take some account of the rest of the picture area. Spot readings are limited to a small area.

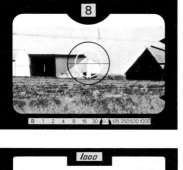
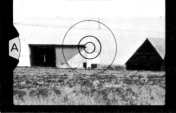

Top: Viewfinder of the non-automatic, match-needle type.
Above: Viewfinder employing light-emitting diodes (LEDs).

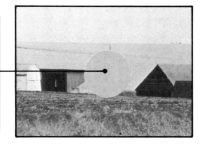
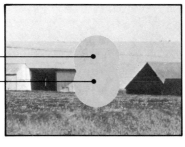
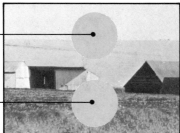

Maximum sensitivity areas for
Top: Spot metering
Centre: Centre-weighted metering
Above: Averaged metering.

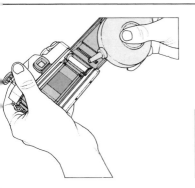
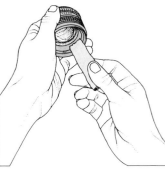
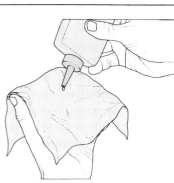
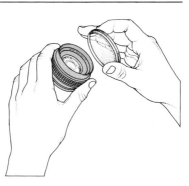

Remove the lens, open the back and blow out loose dust from the inside of the camera. Tilt the camera body downwards so that the dust falls away.

Roll up a lens tissue and tear it to form a ragged edge. Use this to brush away loose dust from the front and rear lens elements instead of a blower brush.

To avoid damaging your lens, use a minimum of cleaning fluid. Wet the tissue with the fluid first; then apply the tissue to the lens and gently polish.

The best way of protecting the front element of the lens is by fitting a UV or Skylight filter on it permanently. This will not alter exposure or colour values.

Supports

Camera supports are used to prevent camera shake and to fix the camera position so that all the photographer's attention can be concentrated on choosing the right moment to make the exposure. Generally, cameras with wide-angle and standard lenses can be hand held at speeds down to about 1/30 before the effects of vibration can be seen on the photograph. With telephoto lenses, however, vibration will be more noticeable. When shooting with long lenses some photographers use a tripod if their shutter speed falls below 1/250. Much depends on how firm your grip is on the camera. Very large and bulky cameras—or, for that matter, ultra-miniature 110 cameras—are difficult to hold steadily. The stability of the photographer's stance and the way the camera is held may also determine whether or not a tripod should be used. A camera held at waist level, for example, shakes less than one at eye level because the effect of body sway increases from the feet upwards.

The most stable supports are those used in film and television studios, where steadiness is more important than portability. These are far too heavy to lift, so they are mounted on castors or wheeled trolleys. At the other extreme are pocket tripods with multi-sectioned telescoping legs. While easy to carry around, they are worse than useless for holding a camera steady as they quiver in the slightest breeze. A good compromise is an aluminium alloy tripod with three- or four-sectioned tubular or U-shaped legs that are lockable at any extension. This type of tripod usually has a centre column that can be raised or lowered for rapid height adjustment. For added rigidity, some tripods have umbrella-like struts joining the legs to the centre column.

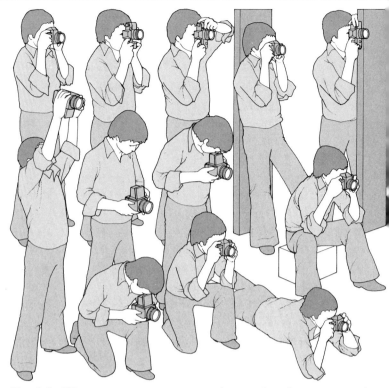

Hand-holding a camera
Either hand can be used to support the camera, depending on style. Extra stability can be achieved.

by pressing the camera against face or body, distributing your weight evenly, or using a conver door or wall as an aid.

Lights

Illumination from ordinary domestic light bulbs may seem bright to the naked eye, but it is inadequate, in terms of colour temperature, for most colour photography. There are, however, incandescent lamps constructed so that their filaments burn at a higher temperature than those in ordinary bulbs. These types of lamps, known as photofloods, give out more light, but do not last for long as the filaments tend to burn out in a few hours. Photofloods are available in two sizes and wattages, the smaller lamp carrying a 275-watt bulb, the larger a 500-watt bulb. Both produce light with a colour temperature of 3,400 K, the temperature for which Type A reversal film is balanced.

Studio lamps provide another form of photographic tungsten lighting. These have a longer life than photofloods and can last for about 100 hours, but they are also considerably more expensive. Studio lamps produce light with a colour temperature of 3,200 K and are used with Type B reversal film.

A third type of photographic lamp, providing continuous, high-intensity illumination, is a tungsten-halogen lamp.

The angle over which light from all these lamps travels is controlled by the type of reflector used. The deeper the reflector, the more narrow the angle of reflection and the stronger the shadows produced. Polished reflectors give a harder light than semi-matt ones. A good all-purpose reflector is shaped like a soup bowl, while a very shallow reflector fitted with a cap that goes over the top of the bulb is excellent for giving a soft, almost shadowless light. Spot lamps are constructed so that their light can be focused by adjusting a movable lens built into the lamp housing.

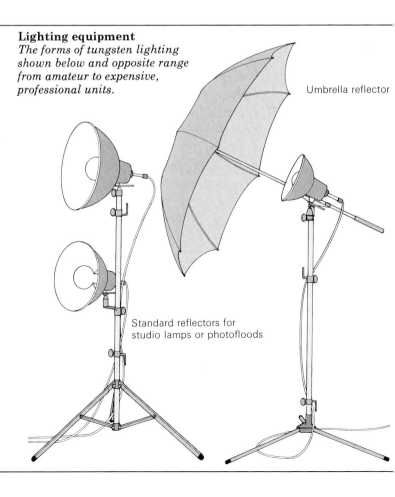

Lighting equipment
The forms of tungsten lighting shown below and opposite range from amateur to expensive, professional units.

Umbrella reflector

Standard reflectors for studio lamps or photofloods

Supporting a camera

Camera supports range from heavy studio tripods weighing upwards of 10lb (5kg) to G-clamps and monopods, which can be easily pocketed. Heavy tripods offer the best support, but their weight makes them less portable.

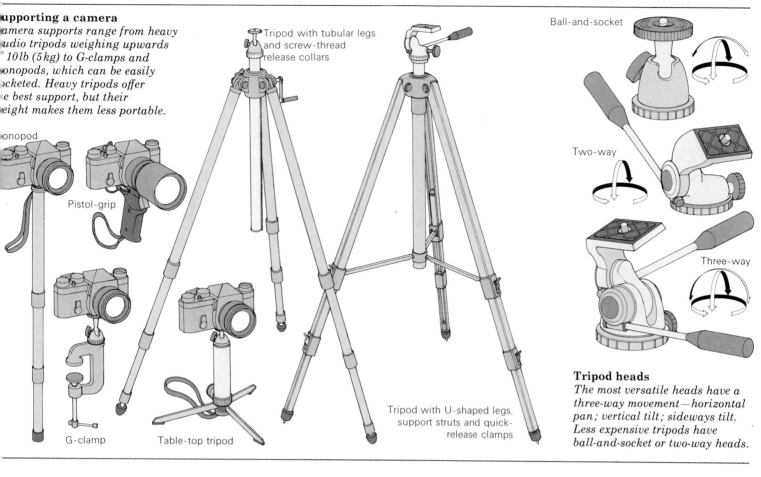

Monopod

Pistol-grip

G-clamp

Table-top tripod

Tripod with tubular legs and screw-thread release collars

Tripod with U-shaped legs, support struts and quick-release clamps

Ball-and-socket

Two-way

Three-way

Tripod heads
The most versatile heads have a three-way movement—horizontal pan; vertical tilt; sideways tilt. Less expensive tripods have ball-and-socket or two-way heads.

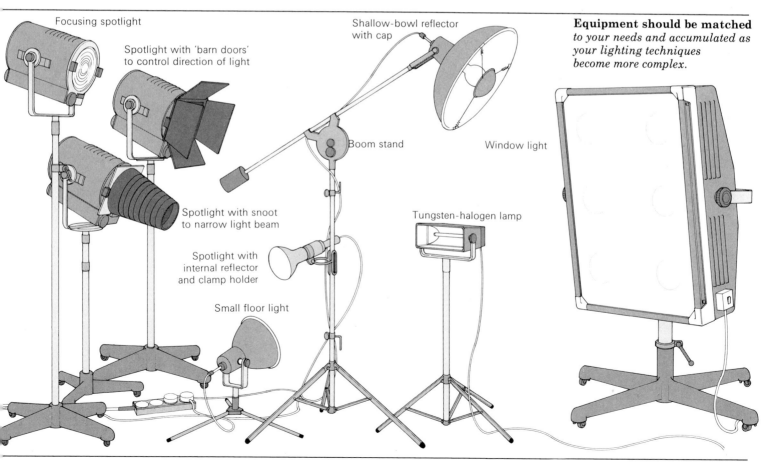

Focusing spotlight

Spotlight with 'barn doors' to control direction of light

Spotlight with snoot to narrow light beam

Spotlight with internal reflector and clamp holder

Small floor light

Shallow-bowl reflector with cap

Boom stand

Tungsten-halogen lamp

Window light

Equipment should be matched *to your needs and accumulated as your lighting techniques become more complex.*

Lights

The simplest form of flash is a single flashbulb—a plastic-coated glass envelope containing oxygen and fine aluminium of magnesium alloy or zirconium wire. When electricity passes through the bulb, the wire ignites. This type of flashbulb is seldom used except with outdated equipment. Simple cameras now use flashcubes—four bulbs with reflectors built into the sides of a cube. A variation is the magi-cube, which fires mechanically instead of electrically like a flashcube. Other bulb assemblies—known as "flipflash" and "topflash"—are also available and may consist of rows of five, eight or ten bulbs. All bulbs are tinted blue so that the light they emit is corrected for daylight-balanced film.

Most flashbulbs have effective burning times of between 1/25 and 1/50 and are known as type M. Special longer-burning bulbs, known as type FP, are made for use with cameras employing focal plane shutters.

Using electronic flash

Although electronic flash equipment is more expensive than bulbs, the actual cost per flash is much cheaper, amounting to no more than a fraction of a penny. Another advantage is that the duration of the flash is so short that no trace of subject movement or camera shake should be evident.

Electronic flash equipment can vary from compact models the size of a large matchbox to substantial professional units with separate power packs. The power to run them may come from expendable batteries—either ordinary zinc-carbon ones or the longer-lasting but more expensive manganese alkaline type of cell. Rechargeable accumulators, whether nickel-cadmium (NiCad) or lead-acid are also popular as power sources, but they are more expensive. Both kinds are rechargeable from mains electricity. Recent advances in circuitry design allow more flashes from a set of expendable batteries or one accumulator charge, and also shorten the recycling time between flashes.

The reflectors of electronic flashguns are built to cover a specific angle of view, usually less than the coverage of a wide-angle lens. Unless a diffuser is placed over the flashgun, there will be a fall-off in illumination towards the extremities of the film frame. Some units have zoom heads to match the angles of view of different lenses.

To obtain softer lighting and avoid harsh background shadows, flash can be bounced from reflective surfaces such as ceilings or walls. If the surface is coloured, the light reflected from it will be similarly tinted, so neutral white surfaces are obviously best if colours are to be recorded accurately. Some flash units have reflectors that tilt to facilitate bouncing.

A well-known effect that may appear with bulb or electronic flash is "red eye". It occurs in portraiture when the flash is fired near the axis of the lens with the subject looking at the camera, and is caused by light reflecting from the blood vessels at the back of the eye. The darker a room is the stronger will be the effect as the pupils of the eyes will be dilated. "Red eye" can easily be avoided by moving the flash away from the lens axis.

Flash equipment in the studio

Studio flash systems are run from the mains; their power packs may be built into the flash heads or contained in separate units. In addition to the flash tubes, the heads have incandescent lights (known as modelling lights) built into them. If daylight is excluded, this allows the photographer to anticipate to a certain extent the eventual effect of the flash on his subject. Of the many types of reflectors used in conjunction with studio flash equipment, the most popular is

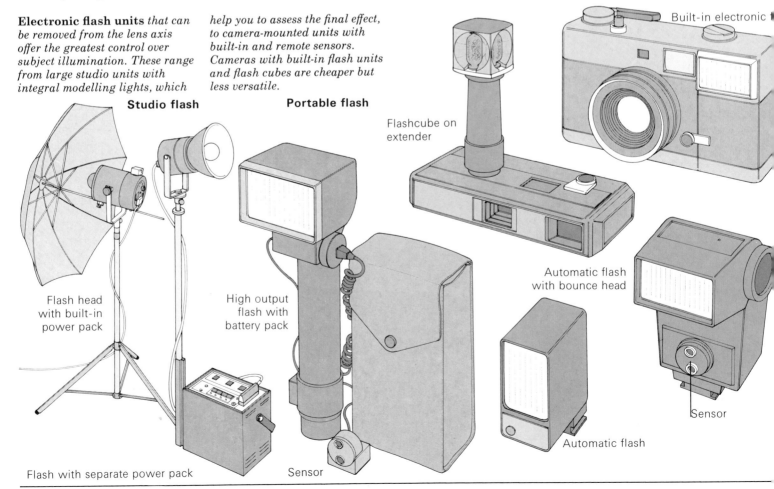

Electronic flash units that can be removed from the lens axis offer the greatest control over subject illumination. These range from large studio units with integral modelling lights, which help you to assess the final effect, to camera-mounted units with built-in and remote sensors. Cameras with built-in flash units and flash cubes are cheaper but less versatile.

Studio flash

Portable flash

Built-in electronic

Flashcube on extender

Flash head with built-in power pack

High output flash with battery pack

Automatic flash with bounce head

Sensor

Automatic flash

Flash with separate power pack

Sensor

a large white umbrella that bounces a soft, almost shadow-less light on to the subject. More often than not, a number of flashes are used simultaneously.

These may be interconnected by wire leads to ensure that they fire together, but it is more convenient to use photo cells (known as "slave" units), which are triggered by the light of the main flash. Exposures for studio flash have to be measured with a separate flash meter.

Flash synchronization

Bulb or electronic flash can be synchronized with the camera shutter either by a contact in the accessory (or hot) shoe, or by a lead that plugs into a socket. Focal plane cameras often have two such sockets, one marked x (for electronic flash) and the other marked F for FP-type bulbs. Cameras with between-the-lens shutters usually have one socket with a lever that selects the appropriate setting, either x or M (for normal small bulbs).

Cameras with between-the-lens shutters can use electronic flash at any speed, but those with focal plane shutters can be synchronized to electronic flash only at speeds of 1/30, 1/60 or fractionally higher, depending on the type of shutter design. These are the fastest speeds during which all of the frame is exposed at once. Often a special setting, symbolized by a lightning flash, will be engraved on the shutter speed dial. If a higher speed is selected, only part of the film will be exposed. If a slower speed is chosen then two images of the subject will be recorded on the film—one from the flash and the other (usually much less distinct) from existing ambient light.

Calculating exposure

Exposure with flash is controlled mainly by the aperture of the lens, the speed of the film, the power of the flash and its distance from the subject. Calculating exposure can either be done by the guide number (or factor) system, or by using the calculator dial found on most flash units.

Guide number method. If a flash is rated at a guide number of 80, it means that the distance from the flash to the subject multiplied by the f stop should equal 80. If the distance is, say, 20 ft then the correct exposure would be obtained with the aperture set at f4. Guide numbers are always given in conjunction with a specified film speed, for example, "guide number 80 for a film speed of 100 ASA". But if the flash is used with a faster film, say 400 ASA, then you need to calculate the new guide number. This can be done by multiplying the original guide number by the square root of the ratio of the new film speed to the old. The equation would therefore be $80 \times \sqrt{\frac{400}{100}}$ or $80 \times \sqrt{4}$ which equals 160. The same distance $\times$ f stop rule pertains to the new guide number indicating an exposure of f8 at 20 ft.

Calculator dial method. Determining the correct exposure with a calculator dial is somewhat simpler than with the guide number system. Set the film speed and then read off the possible subject distance/f stop combinations.

Automatic flash. With automatic flash, correct exposure is ensured by a sensor, which, after the selected f stop is set, measures the light reflected from the subject and automatically cuts off the flash when sufficient light has been emitted from the unit.

Exposure for bounced flash. Calculating exposure for bounced flash is not always easy, for the flash-to-subject distance is cumulative, made up of the distance from the flash to the ceiling and the ceiling to the subject. With automatic flash the sensor must be aimed at the subject to avoid a reading based only on the flash-to-ceiling distance—possible in units where head and sensor point in the same direction.

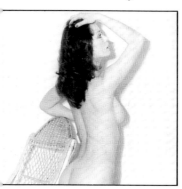
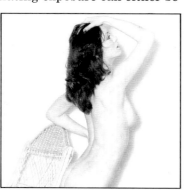
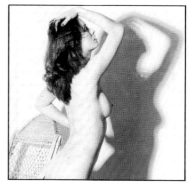
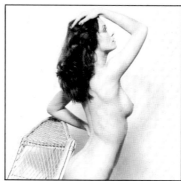

Direct flash *makes exposure calculation easy, but produces hard and generally unflattering shadows. Because of this it is not recommended for portraiture unless there is no alternative.*

Diffusing direct flash *with a cloth gives a softer effect. Unless using automatic flash, increase the exposure by two stops to compensate for the fall-off in the intensity of light.*

Directional flash *can be used to accentuate texture, but it also produces hard shadows rather than showing subtleties of form. Exposure is calculated in the same way as for direct flash.*

Bounced flash *is best for soft shadowless light. When using automatic flash, aim the sensor towards the subject, not the ceiling; otherwise the photograph will be underexposed.*

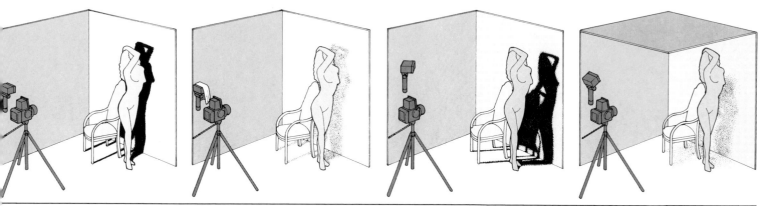

Darkroom layout and equipment

The layout of a darkroom can best be planned by considering the flow of work in terms of step-by-step sequences and organizing the equipment accordingly within the available space. To begin with, all outside light must be excluded. Windows can be covered with overlapping black felt curtains or with black polythene fixed to light wooden frames or on roller blinds. Then decide where specific jobs will be done in the room. Consider any part of the room where chemicals or water will be used as a "wet" area and separate it from the "dry" area, where enlarging and related activities will be carried out. All work-surfaces should be resistant to chemicals, free from cracks or joins and easily cleanable, so a covering of laminated plastic, such as Formica, would be ideal. A heavy, firmly supported bench should be used to support the enlarger. A small fan heater fitted with a thermostat is useful for maintaining an even temperature in the darkroom, but make certain that the room is well ventilated. Dish heaters and water baths will be necessary to keep the chemicals at the correct temperatures, as will accurate thermometers. Check that the thermometers have a safety margin of a few degrees in excess of the highest temperatures likely to be needed.

The safest way to handle colour materials is in total darkness. Although some materials can be used with safelights these lights do not provide a sufficient level of illumination to be really useful. Colour prints can be processed in dishes, but it may be more convenient to use a print drum. This is initially loaded in the dark, and subsequent steps can be carried out with the lights turned on. Films are also processed in tanks—preferably made of stainless steel rather than the cheaper plastic tanks and spirals. A precision timer is needed to ensure correct timing at each processing stage.

Choosing the right enlarger

Most of the equipment needed for printing from colour transparencies or negatives is the same as that used for black and white printing, but in any darkroom specifically set up for colour printing a colour enlarger is by far the biggest investment. While almost any black and white enlarger fitted with a filter drawer is suitable, there are enlargers with special colour heads carrying dial-in filters that are more effective.

If you are buying an enlarger for the first time, choose one with a column as long and as rigid as possible. Even if you do not wish to make giant prints, there are times when an enlargement is needed from a small portion of a negative or transparency and when the head of the enlarger has to be raised to the top of the column. Some enlargers are constructed to allow the head to be swung round so that enlargements can be made on the floor. Examine the position of controls such as the column lock and focusing knob. Some enlargers are built with all the controls on the right side, which may be awkward if you happen to be left-handed.

Negative carriers are used to hold the film in the enlarger. Some have glass to prevent the film from curling, while others do not. With small-format films such as 35mm, dust is invariably a problem and glass carriers, which provide four additional surfaces on which dust can collect, are not recommended. Some carriers have masking devices—metal strips that can be adjusted so that only the exact part of the negative or transparency being printed will be projected. The size of the baseboard should correspond to the largest size of print likely to be made. Choose a print easel with adjustable borders and clearly marked scales.

The quality of the enlarger lens is obviously important and a good colour-corrected one is essential. The sharpness of the

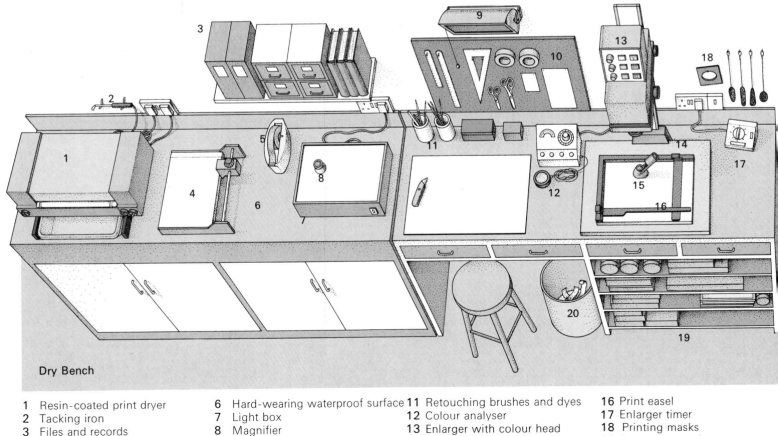

Dry Bench

1 Resin-coated print dryer	6 Hard-wearing waterproof surface	11 Retouching brushes and dyes	16 Print easel
2 Tacking iron	7 Light box	12 Colour analyser	17 Enlarger timer
3 Files and records	8 Magnifier	13 Enlarger with colour head	18 Printing masks
4 Print trimmer	9 Safelight	14 Enlarger baseboard	19 Storage space for paper
5 Tape dispenser	10 Pinboard	15 Focusing magnifier	20 Waste bin

lens is more critical than its speed, so an f4.5 lens will usually be sufficient. The lens is focused at full aperture, then closed down two or three stops for the exposure. Some enlargers have automatic focusing; after being focused manually, the image remains in focus as the height of the head is altered.

Filters for colour printing

Colour printing may be done either by the additive or subtractive method. The additive system uses only three coloured filters—red, green and blue, along with a UV filter. The paper is given three separate exposures, one under each filter. Printing-in and shading are very difficult and the final print can be ruined if there is even the slightest shift in the position of the film or paper between exposures. It is not a common method of printing except in large, automated laboratories operating on a commercial scale.

Most colour printing is now done by the subtractive system, which uses yellow, magenta and cyan (Y, M, and C) filters that are combined during a single exposure. For this method, a set of acetate or gelatin filters of various densities is required, in addition to a UV filter. A typical set has a density range of 05, 10, 20, 40, 80 and 100 for each colour.

Meters and analysers

There are two critical factors in the initial stages of producing a colour print—exposure and colour balance. Exposure can be measured by printing meters, which may either take spot readings from a small area of the projected image, or integrated (average) readings from the unfocused light just beneath the enlarger lens. The device used for measuring colour balance is known as an analyser. It, too, can take either spot or integrated readings. The information is translated into a set of numbers that appears on a metered scale or digital display and these figures determine the filtration.

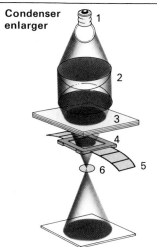

Condenser enlarger

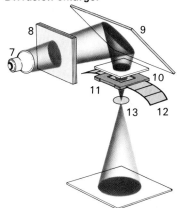

Diffusion enlarger

Enlargers for colour printing

Simple enlargers use acetate or gelatin filters that are placed in a drawer between the film and the enlarger lamp. These enlargers usually employ a condenser system. Unless fitted with a diffusion screen or a pearl lamp they can emphasize scratches and dirt on film, producing spotty prints.

1 tungsten light 2 condensers
3 filter pack 4 negative carrier
5 negatives 6 lens

More expensive enlargers use dichroic filters permanently incorporated in the head. Almost infinite variations in filtration can be made by dialling-in increasing or decreasing densities of Y, M or C. Exposure times can vary according to the degree of enlargement, the lamp used, the degree of filtration and the type of print material. Generally they are kept between 10 and 60 seconds. Less time does not allow for shading, while more may alter the colour response of the paper.

7 quartz-halogen light 8 dichroic
filters 9 reflex mirror
10 diffuser 11 negative carrier
12 negatives 13 lens

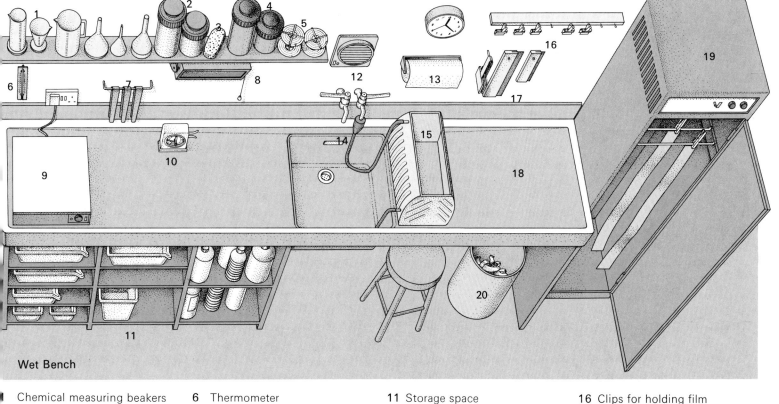

Wet Bench

1	Chemical measuring beakers	6	Thermometer	11	Storage space	16	Clips for holding film
2	Print drums	7	Print tongs	12	Ventilation fan	17	Squeegees
3	Sponge	8	Safelight	13	Paper towels	18	Draining board
4	Film-processing tanks	9	Tray warmer	14	Water filter	19	Film-drying cabinet
5	Stainless-steel spirals	10	Processing timer	15	Print washer	20	Waste bin

Chemicals

Chemical kits containing crystals, powder or concentrated liquid are available for processing a limited number of films or prints. Unless otherwise indicated, only the process recommended on the film cassette, the outer wrapping of roll film or the package of printing paper should be followed. Many kinds of colour film and paper are available, and developers, bleaches and baths, while formulated to do similar jobs, are designed primarily for a specific manufacturer's product. So the best policy always is to buy the kit suggested for the type of film or paper you are using.

All colour chemicals conform to rigid safety standards, but this is not a licence to handle them haphazardly. Read the mixing instructions thoroughly and handle the chemicals only in the recommended manner. Some chemicals can cause minor skin or eye irritation. Others, notably those in the Cibachrome process, include a neutralizer, which must be added to ensure that used chemicals are rendered harmless before being discarded. Aside from this aspect, improperly mixed chemicals can cause difficult-to-trace processing faults that can ruin films and prints.

Processing faults can also arise from contamination. When solutions are accidentally mixed together they are prevented from working properly. To avoid contamination, thoroughly clean your mixing area and always mix the chemicals in their order of use—first the developer, then the bleach, and so on. As a rule, less harm is caused if contamination is from a preceding chemical in the process rather than a following one. Bleach, for example, will become slightly neutralized when contaminated with developer, but developer contaminated with even a few drops of bleach will be ruined.

Mixing and preparation of chemicals

Manufacturers always specify the temperatures at which their chemicals should be mixed—usually ranging from 20°C to 40°C (68°F to 104°F). These temperatures must be followed to ensure that powders and crystals dissolve entirely and that liquid chemicals are completely homogeneous.

Mix the chemicals in polyethylene, glass or stainless steel containers. Never use containers made of tin, copper, iron, brass or their alloys as these materials can cause either contamination and deterioration of the processing solutions or fogging or staining of films and prints. Containers should be cylindrical in shape as the corners of square ones can trap undissolved particles. Often chemicals for a solution come in two or more parts, usually labelled A, B, C and so on. Always mix these chemicals in the order recommended. Another mixing rule is always to add the chemicals to water, never the other way round. The equipment required for mixing is a stirring rod, funnel, thermometer, vessels with graduated markings, storage bottles (labelled and colour coded), waterproof gloves and clean sponges.

Storing chemicals

Chemical kits can be stored for a long time if kept away from extremes of temperature. When particular storage conditions are necessary, the label will say so.

Problems with storing chemicals usually arise after the chemicals have been mixed. Consequently chemical solutions should never be stored for periods longer than those recommended or at temperatures other than those used during mixing. In warm weather, solutions will evaporate and, in so doing, become more concentrated, while lower temperatures can cause some chemical solutions to precipitate or crystallize. Over a period of time, developers tend to oxidize.

To prevent oxidation and evaporation, mixed chemicals should be stored in air-tight containers filled to the brim. With small volumes it is better to use three or four little bottles rather than one large container that is only three-quarters full. There are special concertina-shaped collapsible containers that are excellent for storing chemical solutions. As the volume of solution decreases with each processing session, the container can be squeezed down to bring the remaining solution to the brim and then stoppered.

Some form of coding is necessary to prevent choosing the wrong chemical. Once bottled, solutions can be colour coded, the most conventional system being to use blue for developer, red for bleach, green for fix and white for any others. Alternatively they can be stored in differently shaped bottles (say, round containers for developers, square for bleach or bleach/fix and triangular for other solutions).

Replenishment

Processing chemicals diminish in strength with each roll of film developed or each sheet of paper printed. You may be better off discarding used chemicals after each darkroom session if you process only the occasional colour film. On the other hand, you may compensate for the decreasing strength of the chemicals by extending processing times. The solution will, however, eventually become exhausted. You may also maintain the consistency of chemicals by regenerating them with additional chemicals known as replenishers. Over a period of time, replenishing regularly used solutions is worth while in terms both of cheapness and results.

Replenishment rates are determined by the areas of film and paper that have been through a particular volume of processing solution. The rates are listed by the manufacturer and are expressed in millilitres of replenisher per square metre of film or paper. The following chart will help you calculate the area of the film you process so that you will know how much replenisher is needed.

A Guide to Film Areas

Film size	Number of films and area			
	1	2	5	10
35mm (20 exposure)	0.355 ft² 0.033 m²	0.71 ft² 0.066 m²	1.775 ft² 0.165 m²	3.55 ft² 0.33 m²
35mm (36 exposure)	0.581 ft² 0.054 m²	1.162 ft² 0.108 m²	2.905 ft² 0.27 m²	5.81 ft² 0.54 m²
120	0.538 ft² 0.05 m²	1.076 ft² 0.1 m²	2.69 ft² 0.25 m²	5.38 ft² 0.5 m²
220	1.076 ft² 0.1 m²	2.152 ft² 0.2 m²	5.38 ft² 0.5 m²	10.76 ft² 1.0 m²
5×4 (10.2×12.7 cm)	0.140 ft² 0.013 m²	0.28 ft² 0.026 m²	0.7 ft² 0.065 m²	1.4 ft² 0.13 m²

Silver recovery and regeneration

Recovering silver from photographic chemicals is an important means of conserving a diminishing natural resource, and it can save you money. Exhausted fix or bleach/fix solutions containing silver can either be sold directly to an agent or, if the volume of work you do warrants it, you can recover the silver yourself with special recovery cartridges, sell it and reuse the chemicals. After desilvering, the chemicals must be thoroughly aerated and then mixed with a small bottle of regenerater solution. They will then become a replenisher for a freshly mixed batch of bleach.

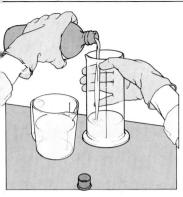

1 Wearing waterproof gloves, pour required amount of chemical into measuring beaker. Make sure the room is ventilated.

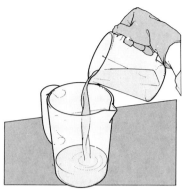

2 Pour water into a mixing jug. Use a polyethylene, glass or stainless steel container, preferably one that is cylindrical.

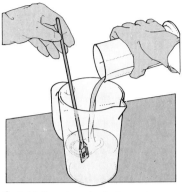

3 Add the chemicals to water, never the other way round. The mixing temperature is not critical within the recommended limits.

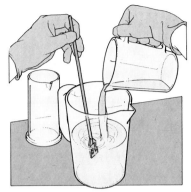

4 Add water to bring solution up to correct volume. Stir with a circular motion, but avoid creating bubbles.

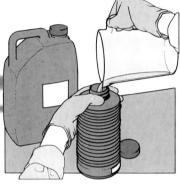

5 To prevent oxidation use collapsible container for developer solution. Not necessary for fix and bleach solutions.

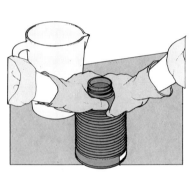

6 If there is not enough solution to fill container, press down until the solution reaches the top, so leaving no space for air.

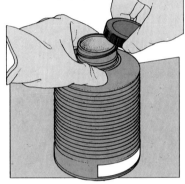

7 After expelling the air, screw the lid down tightly. Remember to compress the container to expel air each time.

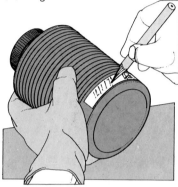

8 Clearly label each container with the name of the solution and the date it was mixed. Store in a cool, clean, dry place.

Functions of chemicals

Each manufacturer's set of chemicals is formulated to suit a particular type of film or paper, so different products are not always compatible: Fuji and Kodak products, for example, are, while Kodak and Agfa products are not. Some systems, such as Cibachrome, require a unique set of chemicals. Although the chemical compounds may differ, they share a common set of functional names.

First developer	much like an ordinary black and white film or paper developer; converts the exposed silver halides (the latent image) into clumps of black metallic silver, forming a black, negative image
Stop bath (or first wash)	an acid solution (usually acetic acid) or running water used to stop developer activity
Re-exposure	a chemical fogging solution to produce a latent image in the undeveloped parts of the film. (This part of the process is often achieved by a physical exposure to light)
Colour developer	converts exposed silver halides to black metallic silver and simultaneously produces a dye "cloud" around each crystal
Wash	stops chemical contamination between stages
Conditioner	(some reversal processes only) prepares metallic silver (both negative and positive images) for bleaching
Bleach and Fix	(sometimes combined) converts metallic silver to a halide similar to the thiosulphate solutions used in black and white processes; reduces silver halides to water-soluble salts
Wash	removes all traces of silver salts and chemicals
Stabilizer	mild acid that helps harden the emulsion, thereby improving dye stability

Storing chemicals

Chemicals	if unused last longer than if partially used
Developers	have shorter useful lives than other solutions
Containers	if full and tightly stoppered will preserve chemicals longer than if partially full
Exhaustion	of solution can be reliably assessed only by processing a test film, print or control strip
Replenishment	and careful filtering of chemicals extends their working life almost indefinitely, but the usual practice is to change them after several months

Factors governing chemical activity

1 The *strength* of solution affects the *energy* of reaction.
2 *Temperature* affects the *speed* of reaction.
3 *Time* affects the *completeness* of reaction.
4 *Agitation* affects *uniformity* of reaction on emulsion surface.
5 *Washing* halts chemical activity, preventing unwanted reactions in succeeding solutions.

Processing

Processing your own film adds enormously to the satisfaction of photography, giving you greater control over the quality of work you produce. With a small darkroom you can process most films, whether colour reversal (from which transparencies are produced) or colour negative. A few films, however, notably Kodachrome, can only be processed by specialized laboratories.

Read the instructions packed with processing kits carefully before you start and keep them handy for constant reference. Your choice of chemicals will depend on the make and type of film being developed and you will get the best results by working within the recommended latitudes of time and temperature.

No matter how many rolls of film you are developing, it helps to carry out processing in three distinct phases, beginning with preparation. Clean the area you will be working in, arrange all the equipment so that it is near to hand and set the timer. The next phase is the processing itself. If you are not used to working in total darkness, it may be helpful to prerecord a tape giving step-by-step instructions and play it back on a tape recorder during the processing cycle. The final stage is the drying and storage of the film.

Loading the film
Colour film has to be loaded on to spirals and placed in processing tanks in total darkness. Stainless-steel spirals and tanks are preferable to plastic or nylon ones as they are easy to keep clean, allow a maximum flow of chemical round the loaded film and will last a lifetime.

Because of short developing times, it is essential that film is both quickly immersed into the chemical solution at the beginning of processing and quickly removed and drained at the end of each stage.

When processing a single roll of film it is usual to place the loaded spiral into the tank and then pour in the chemicals. The ten seconds or so it takes to do this will not affect development. With two or more rolls in a larger tank, however, pouring and draining take appreciably more time. To avoid this problem, the film must be placed in a tank into which chemicals have already been poured. This ensures that the chemicals make contact with the film evenly.

Drift-by technique
Once the film has been immersed, the tank needs to be agitated periodically to ensure even distribution of the chemicals. Small light-tight tanks need only be inverted. Larger tanks have a rod that threads through the centre of the spirals. Agitate by raising and lowering the rod.

Developing temperatures are critical. In less than ideal conditions, it is difficult to keep the temperature of any solution constant throughout the period it is in the developing tank. To overcome this problem, you can use the "drift-by" technique, which involves raising the temperature of the developer to its upper limit just before it is used and then allowing it to drop towards the lower limit during the time it is in the tank. Say, for example, the manufacturer recommends a latitude of 0.5°C above and below a specified temperature. This means, in effect, that there is a one degree safety margin through which the temperature of the chemicals can drift between the time they are poured in at the upper temperature limit and the time they are poured out.

Re-exposing reversal film
Some reversal films need to be exposed to light before the colour developer stage of processing. To do this, open the tank and remove the film from the spirals. Hold the film at both ends 2 feet (30 cm) from a 250-watt lamp. Expose each side of the film for about 15 seconds. Do not let the heat from the light dry the film.

Drying and storing
Wet film has a milky, opaque look, which disappears as it dries. Immediately after removing the film from its final wash, clean it down with a squeegee or chamois leather to ensure that it dries evenly and without any water spots. Then hang the film in a warm, dust-free area or, better still, in a thermostatically controlled drying cabinet.

Take care to avoid splashing partially dry film with water. If the film does get splashed, quickly place the whole roll in water and dry it again. To avoid damaging the emulsion and to stop the film curling excessively, make sure the drying temperature does not exceed about 38°C (100°F). When it is dry, cut the film and store it in moisture-proof sleeves or, if reversal film, mount the transparencies.

Equipment
Processing tanks and spirals *stainless steel and/or plastic*
Thermometer *accurate to within 0.25°C*
Timer *luminous face with minutes and sweep second hand*
Measuring cylinders *twice as large as volumes needed*
Waterproof gloves
Drop rod *stainless steel—longer than the depth of the tank*
Short hose *with tap connection for washing film*
Deep trays *for controlling temperature*
Squeegee or chamois leather *for wiping film*
Film clips or clothes pegs
Drying cabinet
Tape recorder *optional*

Volumes of chemicals needed to cover film in cylinder tanks
The volume of chemical solution required for each stage of processing depends on tank size and the number of rolls being developed. One roll of 35mm film, for example, needs 250ml of solution; two rolls of 35mm (or one roll of 120) need 450ml; two rolls of 120 need 800ml and four rolls of 35mm need 950ml. Choose storage bottles and processing tanks large enough to suit the amount of work you can handle at any one time, but not so large that chemicals are wasted.

Techniques may vary somewhat according to the number of rolls you are going to process. If you are doing only one roll, place the film in the tank and then pour the chemicals in. At the end of each stage drain the used chemicals out and pour the new batch in. But if you are processing two or more rolls, first pour the chemicals into one tank and then immerse the films. At the end of each processing stage, lift the films out and re-immerse them quickly in another tank that has been prefilled with the next chemical bath.

Choosing the most efficient tank

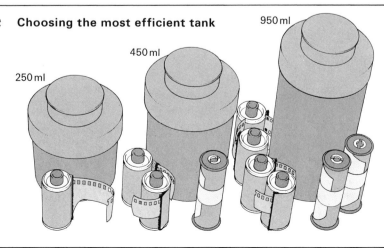

250 ml   450 ml   950 ml

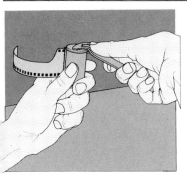

1 Lift the end off the 35 mm cassette with a tin opener. Unroll the paper backing of 120 film to the start of the film.

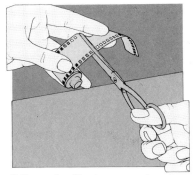

2 Drop the film into your hand and holding it by the edges, let it unwind slightly. Cut off the tapered end for a straight edge.

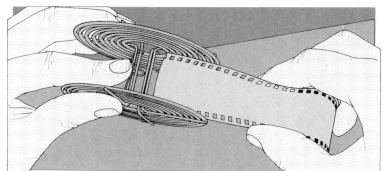

3 Insert the end of the film under the spring clip on the spiral. Bow the film so it will fit between the sides of the spiral, keeping your wrists in a straight line to ensure even loading. To prevent the film from buckling, pull rather than push it on to the spiral.

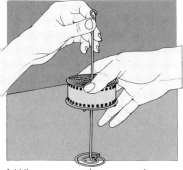

4 When processing more than one roll, load each spiral on to a drop rod. Hold each spiral by its edges to avoid touching the film.

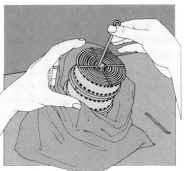

5 Lift the loaded drop rod and place it in a light-tight container. Use either a spare tank or an opaque polythene bag.

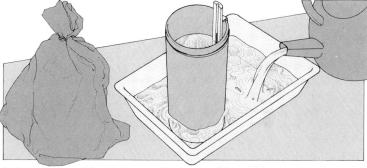

6 Seal the bag. Then turn on the lights. Pour a measured amount of processing solution into a processing tank and place it in a tray filled with warm water. Check that the chemicals have been brought up to the recommended temperature.

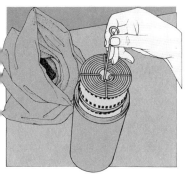

7 Turn off the lights and lift out the loaded drop rod. Immerse the film in the tank and start the timer immediately.

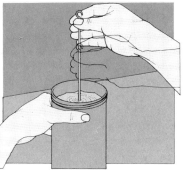

8 Raise and lower the drop rod slightly every second for the first 15 seconds. Follow the instructions for further agitation.

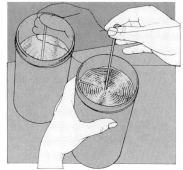

9 Ten seconds before the end of developing time, lift the film from the tank, drain, and quickly place it in the second bath.

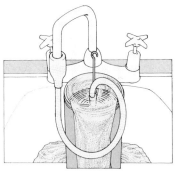

10 After all the processing stages have been completed, turn on the lights and wash the film. Then hang it up to dry.

Deep tank processing

Sheet film 5 × 4in (12.7 × 10.2 cm) and larger can be processed in deep tanks holding 3, 5, or 7 litres. Unload the film from its holder in the dark and clip it by the corners on to stainless-steel hangers. Fit the hangers into grooves on the tank so that the film is immersed. Agitate by lifting a hanger from the tank and tilting it. Processing solutions are normally kept in the tanks instead of being stored in bottles. Between processing sessions, floating lids are placed on the tanks to inhibit evaporation.

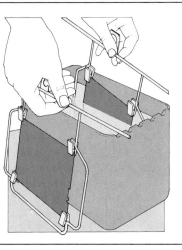

Rotary drum processing

A rotary processor consists of a motor-driven light-tight drum that rotates at a constant speed. It has a built-in timer and a thermostatically controlled water jacket that maintains the temperature of the chemicals. It also uses less chemicals than an ordinary tank of equivalent size. Rotary processors provide constant agitation, so processing times may be shorter than with conventional tanks. Appropriate instructions for temperatures and times will come with the processor or with the chemical kits.

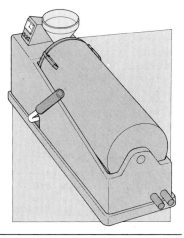

Making prints from transparencies

Recent improvement and simplification of processing techniques have now made it possible to produce exhibition-quality prints directly from transparencies. Although most photographers still consider that colour negatives produce the finest quality prints, others think this is offset by the distinct advantages of shooting with reversal, or transparency, film. For one thing, processed reversal film gives positive images, immediately ready for viewing. There is no difficulty in telling whether or not the transparency colours are accurate, which is always a problem when viewing colour negatives. Even more important—for the professional photographer, at least—is that magazine and book editors prefer to use transparencies for reproduction in their publications. Apart from showing a wider range of tones than it is possible to achieve from negatives, transparencies give a better result in photomechanical printing processes.

Two manufacturers—Kodak and Ciba Geigy—provide materials and chemicals for direct colour printing, which can be done in any small, adequately equipped darkroom. The two systems illustrated below appear to be similar, but it is important to note that they are *not* interchangeable. One is a chromogenic system, where colours are created by chemical reaction with the developer. The other is a dye-destruction system where colourfast dyes are incorporated into the emulsion of the printing material. Whatever the method used, always follow the manufacturers' instructions.

The ideal transparency for reversal printing is one that is slightly underexposed—that is, one with a greater-than-normal saturation of colour. But, however perfect the transparency, exposure times and filtration still have to be determined through a process of trial and error. This is because different types of film vary in their colour characteristics and, similarly, enlargers vary in the nature and output of light. Once the first print satisfactorily matches the original for colour and density, exposure and filtration for subsequent prints made from the same batch of film need not be varied.

Because of the sensitivity of the materials, colour printers have to discipline themselves to work in total darkness during the time of exposure and loading, and for at least part of the processing cycle. Safelights are not recommended.

Reversal printing should always be done in volume, so on average, aim to complete six to ten prints from the same number of transparencies during a three-hour session in the darkroom. Obviously this will depend, among other things, on the capacity of your equipment, but experience and a methodical approach will increase the number of prints you can complete in any given time.

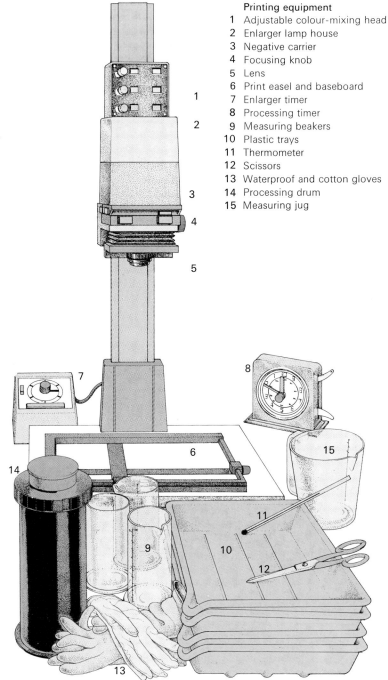

Printing equipment
1. Adjustable colour-mixing head
2. Enlarger lamp house
3. Negative carrier
4. Focusing knob
5. Lens
6. Print easel and baseboard
7. Enlarger timer
8. Processing timer
9. Measuring beakers
10. Plastic trays
11. Thermometer
12. Scissors
13. Waterproof and cotton gloves
14. Processing drum
15. Measuring jug

Methods of processing

Dye-coupling (Kodak Ektachrome Paper)	Process	Time	Temperature
	1 First developer	1½ min	38°C ± 0.3° (100.4°F ± 0.5°)
	2 Stop bath	½ min	38°C ± 0.6° (100.4°F ± 1.1°)
	3 First wash	2 min	38°C ± 1.0° (100.4°F ± 1.8°)
	4 Colour developer	3 min	38°C ± 0.6° (100.4°F ± 1.1°)
	5 Wash	½ min	38°C ± 1.0° (100.4°F ± 1.8°)
	6 Bleach/fix	1½ min	38°C ± 0.6° (100.4°F ± 1.1°)
	7 Final wash	1½ min	38°C ± 1.0° (100.4°F ± 1.8°)
	8 Stabilizer	1 min	38°C ± 0.6° (100.4°F ± 1.0°)
	9 Rinse	½ min	38°C ± 1.0° (100.4°F ± 1.8°)
Dye-destruction (Cibachrome-A)	1 Developer	2 min	24°C ± 1.5° (75.2°F ± 2.7°)
	2 Bleach	4 min	24°C ± 1.5° (75.2°F ± 2.7°)
	3 Fix	3 min	24°C ± 1.5° (75.2°F ± 2.7°)
	4 Wash	3 min	24°C ± 1.5° (75.2°F ± 2.7°)

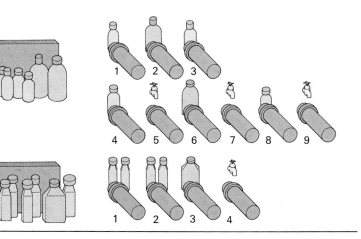

Exposure

Establish the proper exposure and filtration by exposing a test strip on one-third of a sheet of paper. Suggested settings for exposure and filtration come with all processing kits. Adjust the enlarger accordingly. Compose the enlarged image; then turn out the lights, lay the test strip across the easel and expose it section by section at 15-second intervals. The first part of the test strip will thus receive a 45-second exposure, the middle 30 seconds and the final section only 15 seconds.

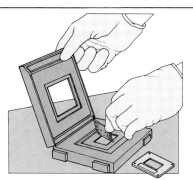

1 Place transparency in carrier emulsion side down. Handle carefully—even tiny specks of dust reproduce as black spots.

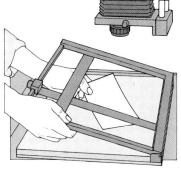

2 Position test strip, emulsion side up, over the enlarged area of the projected transparency that has the most representative tones.

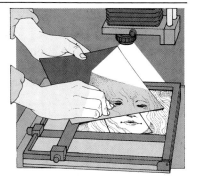

3 Cover two-thirds of test strip with black card and expose. Move card up one-third; expose again. Repeat for the last third.

Drum processing

Many types of rotary drum processor are available. All are tubular containers with light-tight lids, designed to use a minimum of processing solution. The amount of liquid needed will vary according to the volume of the drum and the size of the paper being processed. Precise information is included in the manufacturers' instructions. Care should be taken to remain always within the recommended tolerances. Mix the chemicals in measuring beakers and bring them up to the recommended temperature, cleaning all equipment between solutions to avoid contamination. Temperature can be maintained throughout by standing the beakers in a shallow tray of warm water. All colour printing materials must be used in complete darkness. It is therefore essential to place the necessary equipment close to hand so that it can be located quickly and safely after the print has been exposed and during the processing stages. The illustrations show the main steps of the cycle where special attention is needed in handling the materials to avoid processing faults.

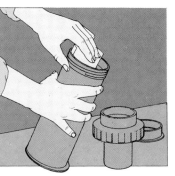

4 Load the drum in total darkness. Carefully curl the paper with the emulsion side inwards. Cover securely with the light-tight lid.

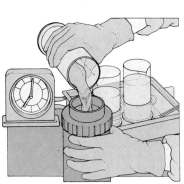

5 Turn the room light on. Wearing gloves, quickly pour exact measures of chemical solution into the drum. Start timer.

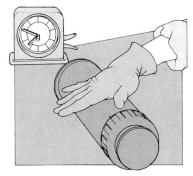

6 Agitate the chemicals by slowly and continuously rolling the loaded drum backwards and forwards over a flat surface.

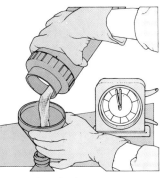

7 Return chemicals to container. Consider the draining time (5 to 15 seconds) as part of the total processing time.

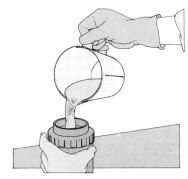

8 Wash print between chemical baths with water at suggested temperature. Repeat stages 5 to 8 for each chemical process.

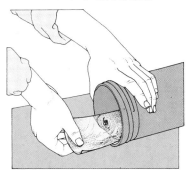

9 Handle the printed strip by one edge as the wet emulsion is very soft. Air-dry the print in a warm and dust-free area.

Assessing colour

Compare the test strip result with the transparency. Decide which of the three exposures is correct and check the colours in that area. Remember that colour will appear darker if the print is wet. Note also that the effects of exposure and filtration are opposite to those in printing negatives, whether black and white or colour. If, for example, the print is too light, it has been overexposed rather than underexposed. See the correction chart on the right of the page for altering filtration.

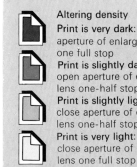

Correction chart

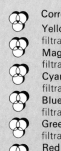

Altering density
Print is very dark: open aperture of enlarger lens one full stop
Print is slightly dark: open aperture of enlarger lens one-half stop
Print is slightly light: close aperture of enlarger lens one-half stop
Print is very light: close aperture of enlarger lens one full stop

Correcting colour balance
Yellow cast: decrease filtration by 20Y
Magenta cast: decrease filtration by 20M
Cyan cast: decrease filtration by 20C
Blue cast: decrease filtration by 20M + 20C
Green cast: decrease filtration by 20Y + 20C
Red cast: decrease filtration by 20Y + 20M

Making prints from negatives

A transparency is the most simple medium on which to record a colour image. But it is a medium that is not ideal for all purposes. Colour negatives, for example, generally produce the best prints. Colour negative film is also much more forgiving than reversal film. Underexposed or overexposed shots that on reversal film would have to be discarded may, on negative film, produce an acceptable image. A large degree of control can be exercised over the final print. Areas can be burned in or shaded during exposure, just as in black and white printing, and specific colours can be altered by the selective use of filters. An added bonus is that the cost of producing several copies by negative—positive printing is far less than that of making duplicate transparencies or reversal prints. Also, negative—positive printing produces a better-quality image than can generally be obtained by making duplicate transparencies.

If you are starting with a roll of processed film, the first thing to do is make a set of contact prints. Not only is this the least expensive way of seeing everything you have shot, but it also provides you with a permanent positive record of your negatives. Begin by exposing and processing a test strip of the contacts, using the filtration recommended by the paper manufacturer and altering the exposures in steps of 15, 30 and 45 seconds. Then, adjusting the filtration and exposure according to your assessment of the test strip, produce a final full set of contacts. Since they are only an intermediate stage, the contacts need not be exact for colour or density as you will, in any case, be able to make further corrections on test strips of the negatives you subsequently decide to enlarge.

Keep an account of exposure and filtration details, beginning with the very first test strip of the contacts and following through to the assessments and adjustments made at each step along the way to producing the final print. You will then have all the relevant data as reference should you ever wish to reprint that negative.

Assessing and correcting colour

When you have processed and dried the first test strip, find an area that appears to be properly exposed. Examine the colour in that part of the strip only, as underexposed and overexposed areas will not give you an accurate enough guide to colour correction.

Colour is best assessed by comparison, so ensure that a portion of the test strip includes a colour that can be readily checked, such as a flesh tone that can be matched with your hand, or a neutral grey area that can be compared with a grey reflectance card. Accurate judging of colour calls for a degree of discrimination that comes only with experience. The eye very quickly adapts to give the impression that something is the "correct" colour even though it may not be. Because of this and other factors influencing colour perception (see pages 32–3), make a habit of assessing test strips and contact sheets within the first few seconds of looking at them. Examine them well away from bright colours, preferably against a neutral grey background, and, when possible, under the same lighting conditions as those in which the final print will be seen.

Unwanted colour cast can be removed by increasing or decreasing yellow (Y), magenta (M) and cyan (C) filtration. Place the filters of required colour and density in the drawer located above the negative carrier or, if the enlarger is fitted with a dial-in colour head, simply adjust one or more of the Y or M dials (the C filter is rarely used). The initial recommended filtration provides a starting point when you make the first test strip, but serves only as a rough guide. Due to a number of factors, including the quality of light in the original photograph, the age of the film or paper or slight variations in their emulsions, instability of the paper dyes, inconsistencies in the temperature of process chemicals, and the age of the enlarger bulb, some degree of correction always needs to be made.

One way of assessing the degree of filtration needed is by viewing the test strip through filters. But bear in mind that the photographic effect will be greater than the visual effect, so adjust the enlarger filtration by only half the amount indicated by the viewing filter.

Any addition to the filtration will reduce the amount of light passing through the lens of the enlarger, while a decrease in filtration will let more light through. Details of exposure adjustments for specific filters are given by the filter manufacturers or included in the instructions that come with the enlarger.

Retouching colour prints

Dust spots on colour prints can be concealed with special photographic dyes, available in both liquid and solid form. These dyes should never be applied directly to prints. Instead, put a few drops of liquid dye on a white china saucer, or transfer solid dye to the dish with a wet brush.

Allow the dyes to dry. Then moisten the brush with equal parts of print stabilizer and water. Remove excess liquid on a sheet of blotting paper, rotating the tip of the brush at the same time to get a fine point on it. Mix the dyes on the dish and test the colour on a piece of paper to see if it matches the print. A neutral dye with only a minimal amount of the basic colour will usually be sufficient. Lightly touch the spot with the tip of the brush, repeating the movement to build up the density of colour.

To remove excess dye, carefully rub the spot with cotton wool soaked in a non-methylated spirit, such as isopropyl alcohol. Then buff clean with dry cotton wool. Dyes can also be gradually removed with a dye-reducing agent.

Paper

Paper for colour printing is manufactured in only one contrast grade, but you do have a choice of surface. A glossy finish helps to reproduce specular highlights in shots of water or jewellery, while many photographers choose a semi-matt surface for printing portraits or landscape shots. Textured surfaces, such as a stipple or silk finish, are less visually brilliant but involve no loss of colour quality and are often used for wedding photographs.

All colour papers are coated first with a synthetic resin, then with a light-sensitive emulsion layer. The emulsion is particularly susceptible to fingerprints, so the paper should be handled only by its edges or with clean cotton gloves. Special dryers can dry resin-coated papers in a matter of minutes, but an ordinary hair-dryer or fan-heater can do the job just as well. If you use a drum-type dryer, do not let the temperature exceed 99°C (212°F) or the resin will melt.

Variations in the sensitivity of the emulsion are unavoidable. Each batch of paper is tested by the manufacturer and any deviation from the ideal will be labelled on the package. Although basic filtration information is included in the packaging, this should be used only as a rough guide. When changing from one package to another it is still necessary to process a test strip to check for any variation in the dyes of the paper.

Improper storage causes changes in the colour balance and speed of paper. To minimize these changes, keep unexposed paper refrigerated. When a package has been partially used, squeeze out the air, fold the end and place the package in a plastic bag to prevent damage from humidity.

Making contact prints

Before producing a full set of contacts you first have to print a test strip to assess correct exposure times and the type and extent of filtration needed. Enlargers designed specifically for colour work, incorporating dial-in filtration, are preferable. A methodical approach is essential for printing, so use a notebook to keep records of all exposure times and filtration. It is far too easy to make mental corrections as you proceed, only to forget them when it actually comes to the critical point of adjusting the enlarger controls.

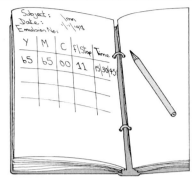

1 Record the subject, date and the emulsion number of the paper. Below this note the filtration selected, aperture and exposure times.

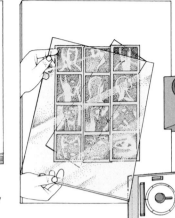

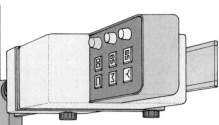

2 Dial in recommended filtration. Then place a strip of paper across the enlarger baseboard. Lay the negatives (preferably in their protective sleeves) emulsion side down on the paper. Cover the negatives with a clean sheet of glass.

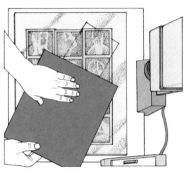

3 Place a black card over two-thirds of the test strip and expose. Move the card down one-third, expose again. Repeat for last third.

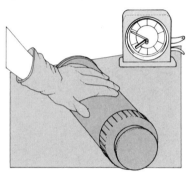

4 Process test strip in chemicals suitable for the paper. Instructions for times and temperatures will be included in the chemical kit.

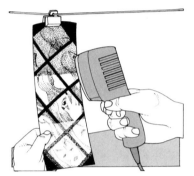

5 Remove test strip from the drum (see previous article for a typical drum processing sequence) and dry with a fan heater or hair dryer.

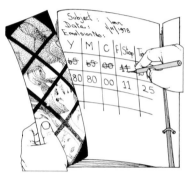

6 Find an area that seems closest to the correct exposure and assess the colour. Strike out previous figures and note down necessary adjustments.

Correcting filtration

If the colour cast is only slight, adjust the filtration by ± 5 to 10 units of density; if moderate, by ± 20 units; if considerable, by ± 30 or more units. You can, of course, select intermediate densities of filtration for fine colour corrections.

Colour cast:

yellow	+Y	or −M and C
magenta	+M	or −Y and C
cyan	+C	or −Y and M
red	+Y and M	or −C
green	+Y and C	or −M
blue	+M and C	or −Y

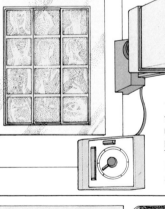

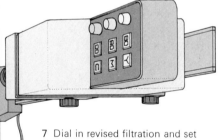

7 Dial in revised filtration and set timer to new exposure. Lay the negatives down on a full sheet of paper and again cover with glass. Turn on the enlarger and expose. Process and dry the contact sheet as shown in the previous stages.

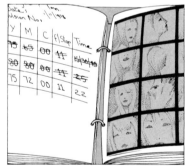

8 File contacts with your records after noting down any additional adjustments needed to correct exposure and filtration.

Test strip for enlargements

Before printing an enlargement, another test strip is made. The size of the enlargement depends mainly on the quality of the negative and the enlarger lens, the maximum height of the enlarger column and the degree of graininess acceptable. Pearl, stipple or silk finish papers, because of their texture, help to disguise graininess. As a rough guide the largest print from a 35mm negative is about 10 × 12in (25.4 × 30.5cm) and from a 2¼ × 2¼in (6 × 6cm) negative, a 16 × 20in (40.6 × 50.8cm) print.

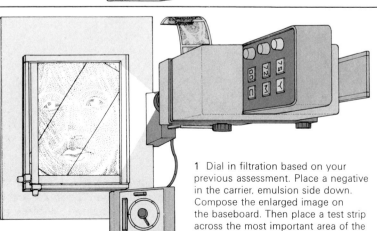

1 Dial in filtration based on your previous assessment. Place a negative in the carrier, emulsion side down. Compose the enlarged image on the baseboard. Then place a test strip across the most important area of the image. Expose, process and dry.

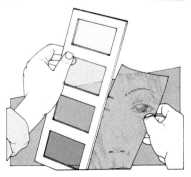

2 Check test strip against neutral background. If there is any colour cast, determine degree of correction by viewing through gelatin filters.

Projectors and viewing

Simple hand-viewers for small-format films consist of a plastic or glass lens and a slide holder that is held up to a light source. More sophisticated viewers have integral lamps powered by torch batteries or, more rarely, mains electricity. Hand-viewers do not give magnification and only one person can view the slide at a time, but they are useful for previewing and organizing transparencies for a slide-show. Large transparencies from 5 × 4 in (12.7 × 10.2 cm) upwards, are best examined on a light box—a shallow frame fitted with fluorescent tubes covered by translucent glass or plastic.

The best way to view slides is through projectors, which throw an enlarged image on to a screen or white wall. Choose a projector made for the size of slide being used. If, for example, a 110 slide is used in a 35 mm projector, the image will be small. If the projector-to-screen distance is increased to achieve an enlarged image, screen brightness will be lost.

Depending on the type of projector, slides can be fed in individually with simple push–pull carriers, but straight magazines holding 30–40 slides are more convenient. Circular magazines have a greater capacity, holding up to 100 slides. Slide changing can also be automatic, actuated by a button on the projector, a cable, or a remote control panel, which may have provision for adjusting the focus. With automatic focus machines, the focus is first set manually on the screen and the projector subsequently makes any adjustments if the slide "pops" (changes its curvature as it heats up in the projector gate).

Tungsten-halogen lamps are used in sophisticated slide projectors as they are more robust and efficient than ordinary incandescent bulbs—a 150-watt lamp of this kind can, for example, produce light as bright as that from a 300-watt domestic bulb. Projectors with these lamps run off low voltage using a step-down transformer and are fan-cooled.

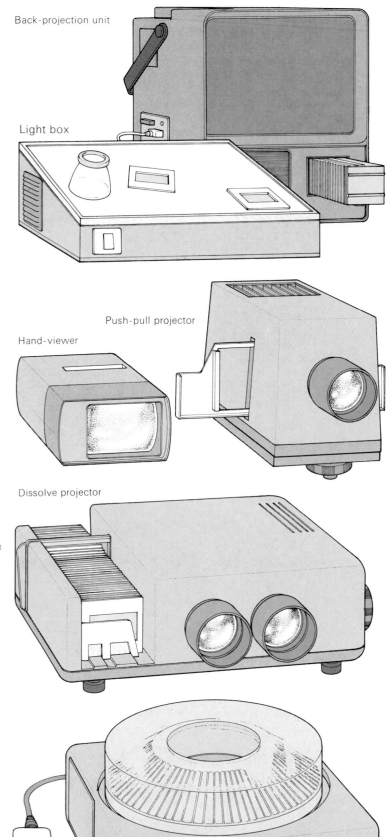

Back-projection unit

Light box

Push-pull projector

Hand-viewer

Dissolve projector

Carousel projector with remote controls

Projection screens
Screens are available in various surfaces. Glass beaded ones are the most reflective, but the audience must face the screen squarely. In an average room the best surface is matt white, giving a wide angle of reflectance and an acceptable level of brightness.

To fill a 40 × 40 in (100 × 100 cm) screen with a 35 mm slide, use these combinations of projector lenses and screen distances: 75 mm at 7.5 ft (2.3 m), 100 mm at 10 ft (3 m), 125 mm at 12.4 ft (3.8 m). Dividing the focal length of the lens by 10 gives the approximate screen distance in feet.

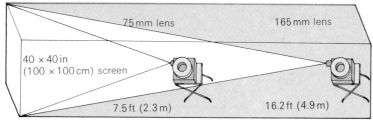

75 mm lens   165 mm lens

40 × 40 in
(100 × 100 cm) screen

7.5 ft (2.3 m)   16.2 ft (4.9 m)

Audio–visual presentations
Some equipment allows slides and tape recordings to be synchronized and slide changes to be made automatically via a signal on the tape. Two projectors can be used to dissolve one image gradually into another so avoiding blanks between slides and allowing smoother continuity.

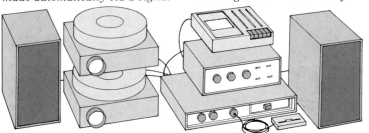

Processing errors are usually the result of handling materials incorrectly or failing to follow manufacturers' instructions. Sometimes these faults can be corrected after processing, but more often the fault is irreversible once the film is developed or the print made. To avoid repeating errors, examine the film or print for abnormalities at the end of every processing session. Physical damage often appears as scratches or abrasions, while chemical faults or damage caused by improper storage of materials, can be identified by blotches or stains. Once a defect is discovered it will probably be necessary to process test films or prints to isolate the cause (or causes).

The tables on this page, while not exhaustive, show some common faults and remedies for low-volume processing.

Transparencies

fault	Dark, round magenta or red spots
cause	Air bubbles during first developer
remedy	Tap tank on bench during agitation
fault	Too dark, magenta/red colour cast (Agfa film); highlights smoky
cause	First development inadequate or developer exhausted
remedy	Increase first development time (if recommended) or re-mix developer
fault	Very blue to cyan; D-max smoky (D-max, or maximum density, is the deepest black an emulsion can achieve when processed)
cause	Agfa: first developer contaminated with stop bath. Kodak: reversal bath too concentrated or colour developer too weak
remedy	Agfa: re-mix developer. Kodak: dilute reversal bath or re-mix colour developer
fault	Green cast; D-max smoky and coloured
cause	Re-exposure omitted or reversal bath inadequate
remedy	Check re-exposure procedures or replenish reversal bath
fault	Too light and cyan; D-max very weak and cyan
cause	Colour developer contaminated with first developer
remedy	Re-mix colour developer and clean equipment
fault	Film milky and cloudy
cause	Incomplete fix
remedy	Re-fix, wash and dry immediately
fault	Pink highlights
cause	Inadequate wash after colour development
remedy	Check wash time, agitation or temperature
fault	Yellow/brown coloured stain on emulsion
cause	Inadequate bleach
remedy	Re-bleach, fix, wash and dry immediately
fault	Light patches or tear-shaped spots with dark outlines
cause	Uneven drying or film splashed with water during drying
remedy	Re-wash immediately and dry normally

Prints from Transparencies
1 Cibachrome–A process

fault	Light image with low D-max (green edges)
cause	Development time too long
remedy	Follow correct processing times
fault	Too dark and flat
cause	Underexposed print or developing time inadequate
remedy	Increase print exposure, open lens aperture or check development time and temperature of chemicals
fault	Dull print with overall foggy look
cause	Bleach time too short
remedy	Increase bleach time or check temperature (possibly exhausted bath)

fault	As above, but with stripes across the print
cause	Contaminated drum
remedy	Rinse drum thoroughly before reprinting
fault	As above, but dark
cause	Bleach/fix contaminated
remedy	Re-mix bleach; clean measuring cylinders more thoroughly
fault	Flat, yellowish print
cause	Fix bath exhausted or omitted
remedy	Repeat fix step or mix fresh fix

Prints from Transparencies
2 Kodak R–14 process

fault	Dark print with magenta cast
cause	Inadequate first development
remedy	Check time, temperature or agitation
fault	Bluish shadows
cause	Inadequate colour development (or diluted colour developer)
remedy	As above or re-mix colour developer
fault	Veiled-over or foggy highlights
cause	Inadequate bleach/fix (or contaminated first development)
remedy	As above or re-mix bleach/fix
fault	Overall blue (especially in black areas)
cause	Inadequate first wash
remedy	Follow recommended time, temperature or increase flow of water
fault	Overall red (highlights pink)
cause	Inadequate second wash
remedy	As above
fault	Overall cyan
cause	Contamination of first developer with bleach/fix
remedy	Re-mix first developer

Negatives

fault	Heavy, dense negatives (orange mask on Agfa will appear normal; orange mask on Kodak will be denser than normal)
cause	Overdevelopment
remedy	Process within manufacturers' tolerances
fault	Heavy, dense negatives (with denser than normal mask on Agfa)
cause	Excessive bleach
remedy	Check bleach time and temperature or prepare fresh bleach
fault	Excessive contrast (Kodak)
cause	Inadequate bleach
remedy	Re-bleach, fix, wash and dry normally
fault	Spots with orange mask colour only
cause	Air bubbles during development
remedy	Increase agitation; tap tank on bench
fault	Streaks from perforations on edge of film
cause	Developer trapped in perforations, especially during draining time
remedy	Check agitation during development; avoid excessive draining times

fault	Predominant overall purple colour with dark image
cause	Fogged film
remedy	Turn safelight off during loading and processing or make sure that your darkroom is completely light-tight

Prints from Negatives

fault	Dark prints with high contrast
cause	Overdevelopment
remedy	Check time, temperature, possible over-replenishment
fault	Cyan stains
cause	Slight contamination of developer
remedy	Re-mix developer
fault	Magenta, red or pink overall stain
cause	Oxidized developer, improper storage of replenisher or inadequate wash after bleach/fix stage
remedy	Use fresh developer or extend wash after bleach/fix (Agfa prints can be treated with 20 per cent solution of Agfa M23)
fault	White spots
cause	Air bubbles on print surface
remedy	Increase agitation during development
fault	Red fingerprints
cause	Emulsion touched before processing
remedy	Handle prints by edges or with clean cotton gloves
fault	Blue or cyan streaks
cause	Excessive carry-over of developer into bleach/fix
remedy	Drain drum thoroughly after development
fault	Large white areas (with sharp edges) or very light, diffused print
cause	Paper improperly loaded into drum (emulsion touched drum walls)
remedy	Load drum with emulsion side of paper facing inwards
fault	Uneven processing
cause	Inadequate solution level
remedy	Increase volume of chemical
fault	Mottling, yellowish tinge to whites
cause	Paper improperly stored or out of date
remedy	Store paper in cold, dry, moisture-proof packages
fault	Multi-coloured small circles
cause	Interference rings (called Newton's rings) from glass negative carriers
remedy	Use anti-Newton ring glass above negative
fault	Inconsistent density from one print to another
cause	Fluctuations in voltage or timer not working properly
remedy	Control exposure current with voltage stabilizer; test consistency of timer
fault	Totally unexpected colour cast
cause	Wrong filtration (possibly from transposing Y and M filters)
remedy	Check records of last consistent result against filters in the colour head

Storage and mounting

The purpose of any negative or slide storage system is to make the retrieval of a particular image quick and easy. Proper storage will also reduce the risk of deterioration due to damp, heat or fumes. Where damp is persistent, a drying agent, usually silica gel, should be used.

Storing negatives

35mm and roll film negatives are best cut into strips rather than individual frames, and stored in sleeves or special envelopes made of transparent or translucent material. Ordinary paper envelopes should not be used as the acid content of the paper may react adversely with the emulsion. Complete rolls of film or images of the same subject can be filed on one page in special ring binders and a contact sheet made and filed alongside, on which can be written the date the film was exposed, any technical information and a reference number. Large format negatives from sheet film need to be stored in individual sleeves inside a drawer or filing cabinet well protected from heat and moisture.

Storing transparencies

Conditions for storing transparencies should be the same as those for negatives—dry and cool. Transparencies, too, can be cut into strips and placed in acetate sleeves, or put into plastic or card slide mounts. If only a limited number of slides is involved they can be kept in magazines in correct order and ready for projection. But as films accumulate, this method becomes prohibitively expensive. A cheap and practical alternative is to use the plastic boxes most film processors return slides in. To maintain the correct order for projection, a diagonal line can be drawn across the top of the mounts—any slide that is positioned out of order can then be seen at a glance. Binders similar to those described for storing negatives are available with plastic sleeves to accommodate mounted slides. For large numbers of slides, metal storage boxes are popular. These hold slides in numbered slots and have index cards on the inside of the lid on which data can be noted.

Presentation

When presenting your work for possible sale, it is necessary to show many images quickly and attractively. Artists' portfolio cases offer the most versatile option as both photographs and slides can be displayed together. Plastic view-packs allow a large number of slides to be viewed together. They are not so popular for domestic use as it takes too long to remove and replace each separate slide for projection. With a metal strip inserted into the top, they can be hung in a filing cabinet. Matt black presentation boards made of rigid card with apertures that show only the image are a particularly effective way of presenting pictures attractively.

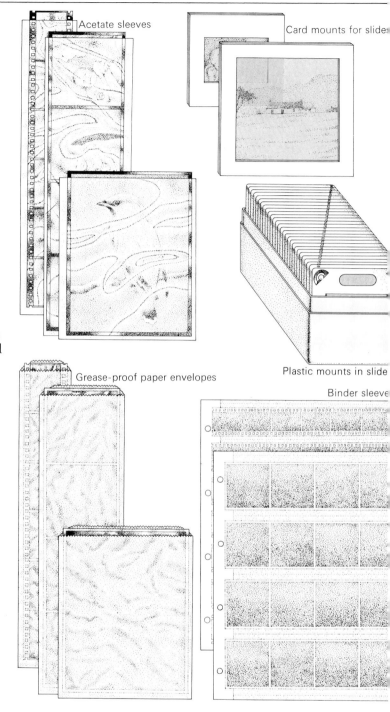

Acetate sleeves

Card mounts for slides

Plastic mounts in slide

Grease-proof paper envelopes

Binder sleeve

The traditional method of mounting photographs in albums does not allow them to be put on permanent display. Mounted on heavy card, however, they can either be framed, or hung on a wall as they are. Prints can be fixed to card with a rubber-based glue or with a spray adhesive. Other—perhaps less messy—ways of mounting make use of resin-impregnated mounting tissue or double-sided tape. For most purposes mounting tissue is the best choice. Sandwiched between the print and the mount, the tissue will bond the two surfaces together when heat and pressure are applied. An ordinary domestic iron will suffice for most prints and a small tacking iron or soldering iron is useful for initially securing the tissue to the print, but a dry-mounting press will make the process virtually foolproof. Whatever the method used, make sure the print and card are absolutely dry.

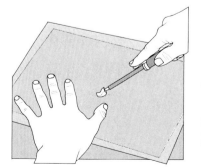

Place the print face down on a clean surface. Lay mounting tissue on it and secure to centre of the print with a tacking iron.

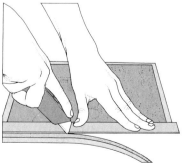

Turn the print over and, using a straight edge and a craft knife, trim off excess tissue so that it is flush with edges of the print.

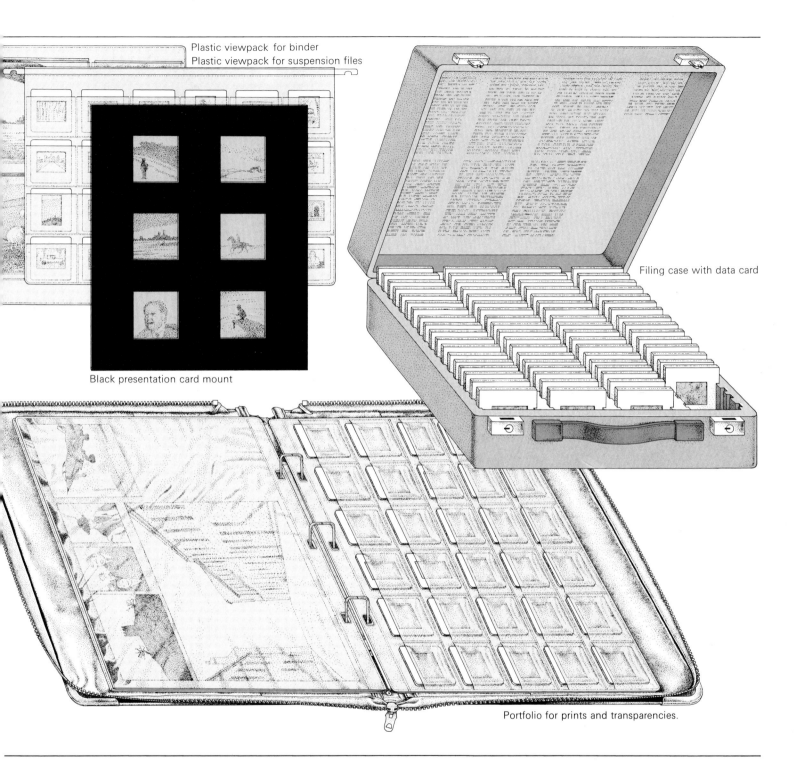

Plastic viewpack for binder
Plastic viewpack for suspension files

Black presentation card mount

Filing case with data card

Portfolio for prints and transparencies.

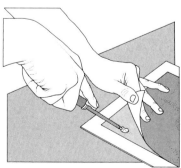

Turn the print over again and lay it on the mounting card. Lift up each corner of the print and tack the loose tissue to the card.

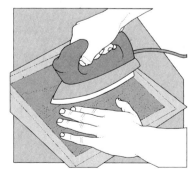

Lay a sheet of clean paper over the print and, with the iron at a low setting apply even pressure from the centre outwards.

Dry mounting press

One of the most efficient ways of mounting prints is with an electrically heated mounting press. Thermostatic controls ensure that the mounting tissue is melted at the correct temperature, and the size of the press beds enables uniform pressure to be applied over the whole of the print. Tack the tissue to the print and trim in the manner described previously. Clean the plates of the press and remove any dirt from the print. Then place the print, picture-side up, in the press. For large prints, several "bites" can be made.

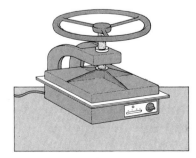

Follow recommended time and temperature. (Double-weight paper may require 5–10 seconds pressure at about 85°C (185°F).)

Glossary

Aberration General term for image faults caused by an imperfect lens. See also Astigmatism, Barrel and Pincushion distortion, Chromatic aberration, Coma, Spherical aberration.

Absorption Taking up of light energy by matter and its transformation into heat. Surfaces that are seen as coloured usually absorb some of the components of light falling on them and reflect others. For example a red surface absorbs green and blue light, reflecting red.

Accelerator Alkaline chemical used in developing solutions to increase activity and shorten development time.

Achromatic Describes colours that contain equal mixtures of the three primary colours of light and so display no hue but vary only in lightness. These range through the greys from white to black.

Achromatic lens Lens that brings two colours of the spectrum, usually blue and green, to the same point of focus.

Acid fixer Stabilizing solution containing a weak acid that neutralizes any residual developer in the final stages of processing.

Actinic Describes the ability of light to produce changes in materials exposed to it, for example, photographic emulsions. Blue light is especially actinic.

Acutance Scientific term for the sharpness with which a photographic material can record images at various levels of contrast.

Additive colour process A means of producing a colour image by mixing blue, green and red coloured lights in proportions corresponding to those reflected by the original subject.

Additive primaries Blue, green and red lights of a saturated hue, which mixed together in varying combinations or intensities can give any other colour.

Aerial perspective Effect of depth produced by haze in a photograph. Distant objects are recorded with lighter zones and with colours distorted towards blue, giving a three-dimensional impression.

After image Persistence of an image after the original stimulus to the retina of the eye has ceased. Because of cone fatigue, the colours of the after image may be complementary to those registered initially.

Agitation Movement set up between photographic material and processing solutions to ensure uniform action.

Air-bells Bubbles of air clinging to the emulsion surface during processing and thus preventing chemical action.

Airbrushing Retouching of prints by dyes or pigments sprayed on with high-pressure air from small hand-sprays.

Alum Class of compounds frequently used to harden photographic gelatin. Potassium aluminium sulphate is often included in hardening fixing baths.

Ammonium thiosulphate A fixing salt used as an activator in rapid fixing solutions, replacing the customary, slower acting, sodium thiosulphate or hypo.

Anaglyph Two photographs dyed and printed on the same support as a stereoscopic pair. Generally one image is blue-green and one red. The viewer looks through spectacles with one red and one blue-green filter to receive an impression of a three-dimensional picture.

Anamorphic lens Lens with prisms or cylindrical elements producing an image with a wider angle of view in one dimension than the other. The narrower dimension can be widened to match the other by using a similar lens for printing or projection, as on a wide screen in the cinema.

Anastigmat A lens designed to correct optical faults, including astigmatism. Often loosely applied to lenses with three or more elements.

Angle of incidence The angle between a ray of light striking a surface and a right angle drawn from the point at which the ray meets that surface.

Angle of reflection The angle between a reflected ray of light and a right angle drawn from the point at which the ray leaves the reflecting surface.

Angle of view The angle formed between the lens and the most widely separated points on a distant subject that the lens images sharply on the film format. Usually the diagonal from opposite corners of the film is taken as the base.

Ångström Unit sometimes used to express the wavelength of light. There are 10 million Ångström units to a millimetre.

Anti-halation backing Coating of dye or pigment to prevent the reflection of light from the near surface of the film support.

Aperture Area of lens through which light enters the camera, controlled by the diaphragm.

Apochromat Lens bringing three colours in the spectrum, usually blue, green and red, to the same point of focus.

ASA film speed Arithmetical system of rating the emulsion speed of photographic materials laid down by the American Standards Association.

Aspherical A curved surface that is not spherical. Lenses are sometimes ground with an aspherical surface for improved correction.

Astigmatism Off-axis aberration causing vertical and horizontal lines to be focused in different focal planes.

Autochrome Early colour material utilizing a screen made of starch grains over the emulsion. The grains were dyed red, blue and green, and mixed at random.

Backlighting Lighting from behind the subject. Often produces a fringe or halo of light separating subject from background.

Back projection Projection of a picture on to the back of a translucent screen rather than on to the front of a reflecting screen.

Ball-and-socket head Mounting on the top of a tripod that permits the camera to be pivoted in any direction by the loosening of one control.

Barium sulphate White chemical used as a pigment in the reflective layer below a print emulsion in most photographic papers. Common name baryta.

Barn doors Hinged flaps surrounding a spotlight to control the spread of light.

Barrel distortion A distortion of the image where straight lines at the edge of the field bend inwards at the corners of the frame.

Bas-relief Sculpture carved in low relief. Prints giving this effect can be produced by combining negative and positive images slightly out of register and printing through an enlarger.

Batch numbers Serial numbers marked by manufacturers on each batch of photographic film or paper. Can be invaluable in tracing and proving faults of manufacture. For consistency, photographers order film with the same batch numbers.

Beaded screen Projection screen covered with minute glass beads giving a narrow angle of reflection. Used in front projection.

Bellows Light-tight folding sleeve between lens and camera body. A bellows focusing unit can be used to provide additional extension between lens and body when taking close-ups.

Between-the-lens shutter Shutter with light-obscuring blades placed between the lens elements close to the diaphragm. Also known as an interlens shutter.

Binocular vision Visual perception using two eyes to provide a sensation of depth. The basis of stereoscopic photography.

Bitumen of Judea A naturally occurring form of asphalt which hardens in light and was used by Niepce for the first photograph taken in 1826.

Bleaching The process of converting metallic silver into an almost colourless compound such as a silver halide, which can then be dissolved, reduced or dyed.

Bloom Transparent coating on lens glass to suppress reflections. *See* Coated lens.

Bounced flash Flash illumination reflected from a surface such as a wall or ceiling before reaching the subject, thus being diffused.

Bracketing Taking extra shots of a subject, doubling and halving the exposure judged to be correct. Prudent where a shot is important and there is an uneven balance of light.

Brightness range The difference in brightness between the lightest and darkest areas of a scene or image.

Bromide paper Printing paper coated with light-sensitive salts of hydrobromic acid.

B setting Mark on the shutter speed ring indicating that the shutter will open when the release button is depressed and stay open until pressure is released.

BSI British Standards Institution, which rates emulsion speed similarly to the ASA system but expresses it logarithmically as well as arithmetically (BS 100 is the same as BS 5°).

Bulk loader A device for loading film from a large reel into cassettes or other containers.

Burning in Extra exposure given to particular areas of a print as a means of selective darkening.

Cable release A wire moving within an outer sheath allowing the camera shutter to be triggered from a distance and reducing vibration.

Calotype Print made from a paper negative that was brushed with silver iodide and other chemicals and exposed in the camera—a process patented by Fox Talbot in 1841.

Camera movements Means of altering the relative planes of the camera back and lens panel. Also of moving the lens at right angles to its axis. Movements are generally found only on large cameras, but lenses with rise and fall are made for the 35 mm film size.

Camera obscura Ancestor of the modern camera that formed an image of an outside scene inside a darkened enclosure by means of a pinhole entry for light.

Candle metre The illumination per square metre of a surface one metre from a point light source of one candle power. Also known as lux.

Cartridge A container for film, such as 110 and 126, that can be placed in the camera to deliver the film from one side and store it in the other side after exposure.

Cassette A light-tight container for 35 mm film. In the camera, film is wound back into the cassette after exposure.

Cast Overall shift of colours in an image towards a particular part of the spectrum, often due to a disparity between the colour temperature of a light source and the colour balance of the film.

Catadioptric lens Lens utilizing a mirror and reducing the overall lens dimensions in extreme long-focus designs.

CdS cells Light-sensitive cells that alter their electrical resistance when light falls upon them. The letters CdS are the chemical symbols for cadmium sulphide. An external source of current is needed for these cells.

Changing bag Bag made of opaque material that allows film to be loaded into cassettes or tanks outside a darkroom.

Characteristic curve A graph showing the density of a sensitized material that will result from a given exposure to light.

Chroma Term used in the Munsell system of colour classification to describe the degree of saturation or purity of a hue.

Chromatic aberration Image fault caused by the inability of the lens to bring light of all colours to a common point of focus.

Circle of confusion An image disc produced by a lens from a point source of light. The smaller the disc the sharper the image.

Close-up lens An auxiliary lens used in conjunction with a normal lens for close focusing.

Coated lens A lens with surfaces coated with thin layers of a hard substance, such as magnesium fluoride, to minimize light loss or fogging caused by reflection from the lens. The thickness of the coating is a precise fraction of an average wavelength of light, so that reflection from the coating material is intermediate between that of air and glass.

Cold cathode enlarger An enlarger with a tubular fluorescent light source providing even, diffuse illumination with slightly softened contrast. This type of light source, with its low working temperature, is particularly suitable for large format work.

Collodion process Wet plate process introduced in 1851 and in general use until the 1880s. The plate was coated with iodides and exposed in the camera while still wet. Its fine grain gave good results but it required bulky equipment.

Colour analyser Device for measuring the colour of a projected colour image in order to make corrections with colour filters when printing.

Colour blindness Inability to distinguish between different hues. Most commonly, the defect is partial—a failure to discriminate certain pairs of colours because either the red- or green-sensitive cones in the retina do not function normally.

Colour compensating (CC) filters Comparatively weak colour filters used to correct for small differences between the colour temperature of the illumination and that for which the film was manufactured.

Colour conversion filters Fairly strong colour filters used for exposing film in light of a type markedly different from that for which the film was made.

Colour negative film Film that records the colours of the subject in complementary hues that are subsequently reversed again in the printing paper to give the correct colours.

Colour reversal film Film that produces a direct positive by effectively "reversing" the negative image during processing. In transparency film, which is of this type, colour dyes are developed in image areas wherever a layer of the tripack emulsion did not record light from the subject. By subtracting colours from the white light in which they are viewed, these dyes reproduce the original colours of the subject.

Colour synthesis The formation of colours by mixing lights, dyes or pigments of other colours.

Colour temperature The measurement of a light source in terms of the energy distribution over the spectrum and hence the colour quality. Theoretically related to the appearance of a heated "black body", it is expressed in degrees kelvin.

Coma An off-axis lens aberration resulting in a point of light being reproduced as a disc with a comet-like tail.

Complementary colours Any two colours that, when mixed, will produce an achromatic colour, white, grey or black. The complementary colour pairs used in most colour film and printing processes are red-cyan, green-magenta and blue-yellow.

Condenser A lens, usually of simple construction, used in an enlarger to focus light, through the negative, on to the enlarger lens.

Cones Tiny cone-shaped organs in the retina containing pigments that absorb certain wavelengths of light. Signals from these light receptors, analysed in the nervous system, lead to the sensation of different colours. The cones are of three main classes, responding most strongly to either blue, green or red light.

Continuous tone Variation in density within a negative or print, matching the graduated range of lightness or darkness in the subject.

Contrast Differences between light and dark tones in a subject or image, and also between colours that lie opposite each other on the colour wheel.

Contre jour Against the light, an alternative term for backlighting.

Converging lens A lens that is thicker in the middle than at the edges, making parallel rays of light converge to a point of focus. All camera lenses are converging.

Converging verticals An effect produced when the camera is pointed away from a parallel position. Vertical lines, such as the sides of buildings, appear to lean in towards the top of the photograph.

Converter An auxiliary lens used in conjunction with the camera lens to produce a lens system of different focal length.

Cooke triplet An early design of lens with three elements. Ancestor of many modern types.

Correction filter General term for filters used to alter colours to suit the colour response of the film.

Coupled rangefinder Device that focuses the camera lens as the rangefinder is adjusted to the correct distance by making two images of the subject coincide.

Covering power The maximum size of film on which the lens produces an image of acceptable quality.

Cross front Camera movement that allows the lens to move horizontally across the camera.

Curvature of field Lens aberration that causes the image to be focused on a curved plane instead of a flat surface.

Cut film Large-format film supplied in flat sheets for individual exposures.

Daguerreotype Photograph taken on a copper plate coated with polished silver, sensitized with silver iodide and developed with mercury vapour. This photographic process, developed by Daguerre in 1839, was the first to be marketed successfully.

Dark cloth Light-absorbing material to exclude unwanted light from the focusing screen of a studio-type camera.

Dark slide The container in which cut film is stored before being placed in the camera.

Daylight film Reversal film balanced for use in average daylight illumination of about 5,500 K, suitable also for electronic flash, or blue flash bulbs.

Definition Sharpness of the image produced by a lens or recorded by a film.

Delayed action Operation of a camera mechanism that produces a delay between pressing the shutter release and the exposure being made. Used to reduce vibration and to enable the photographer to be included in the picture.

Densitometer Instrument that measures the density of a negative, for instance to assess contrast and exposure for enlarging.

Density The light-absorbing power of a processed photographic image (measured quantitatively and expressed logarithmically). A density of 0 refers to complete transparency, 0.3 means 50% transmission, 1.0 is 10% and so on.

Depth of field The distance over which objects remain acceptably sharp behind and in front of the point on which the lens is focused. Within this zone, the distance behind the plane of focus is usually twice as great as the distance in front of it.

Depth of field tables Tabular presentation of values of depths of field for various focal lengths, apertures and focusing distances.

Depth of focus Focusing latitude—the distance through which the film can be moved, parallel to the optical axis, after the lens has been focused while still producing an acceptably sharp image.

Developer The chemical bath that produces a visible image of metallic silver sometimes with associated dyes, from the latent image formed on film or print emulsion by light.

Diaphragm The adjustable aperture of a lens, usually controlled by a set of curved metal blades that open and close around a central hole.

Dichroic fog A processing fault consisting of a deposit of finely divided silver. Literally means "two-coloured" because the image appears red by transmitted light and greenish by reflected light.

Diffraction Scattering of light rays around the edge of an opaque substance, particularly noticeable when light passes through a small hole. Diffraction softens the edge of shadows, as some light bends around the edge.

Diffusion Scattering of light passing through a translucent but not transparent medium such as tracing paper or a smoky atmosphere. Diffused light is softer and lower in contrast.

DIN film speed Emulsion rating as specified by the German standards association (Deutsche Industrie Norm). 21 DIN = 100 ASA. A doubling of speed is indicated by an increase of 3 DIN.

Distortion An alteration in the geometrical shape or relative proportions of a photographic image, whether intentional or accidental.

D-max Scientific term for the maximum density of a processed photographic image.

Dodging A term for shading when exposing a print on the enlarger baseboard.

Double exposure The result of exposing a film twice. With many cameras the film advance and shutter setting are interlocked to prevent accidental double exposure.

Double extension Mechanism permitting the lens to be moved up to two focal lengths away from the film, which makes possible an image the same size as the subject.

Drift-by technique A means of using the latitude available in maintaining the temperature of processing solutions, by starting a few degrees above the correct temperature and finishing a few degrees below.

Drying marks Blemishes left by the evaporation of droplets of water on the film or the print surface.

Dry mounting A method of fixing prints on to mounts by using heat-sensitive adhesive usually in the form of tissue.

Dye coupler Chemical that reacts with oxidized developer to form dyed images in colour transparencies or prints from colour negatives.

Dye sensitizing The process of rendering a silver halide emulsion sensitive to colours of light other than the blue to which they have an inherent response.

Dye transfer prints Almost obsolete method of producing colour prints involving the making of three separate negatives, one for each primary colour, and the subsequent registration of a positive dye image from each.

Eberhard effect An effect of development resulting from insufficient agitation. Appears as a dense line along the edge of a high density image area or a clear line along the border of a low density area.

Electronic flash Lighting unit utilizing the flash of light produced by discharging a current between two electrodes in a gas-filled tube.

Emulsion General term for the light-sensitive layer, consisting of silver halides in gelatin, used in the production of films and printing papers.

Enlargement A print larger than the original negative or transparency. Once uncommon, now almost universal.

Expiry date Manufacturer's stamp indicating the working life of sensitized material. As films age the fog level rises, speed falls and the colour balance alters.

Exposure The amount of light that is allowed to reach sensitized film or printing paper. The product of time, controlled by shutter speed, and light intensity, controlled by aperture.

Exposure counter Device on a camera showing the number of photographs taken.

Exposure latitude The range over which exposure can be varied and still produce an acceptable result.

Exposure meter Device for measuring the light falling on or reflected from the subject. Usually the measurement is expressed in terms of shutter speeds and apertures.

Extension tubes Tubes that can be attached between lens and film to facilitate close focusing.

Fast lens A lens with a wide aperture capacity in relation to its focal length, for instance a 50mm lens with a maximum aperture of f1.2, or a 400mm lens with a maximum aperture of f4.5.

Fill-in Light directed on a subject to illuminate shadows cast by the principal light.

Film plane The plane on which the film is positioned in the camera.

Film speed A means of representing numerically the response of a photographic emulsion to light.

Filter A material that absorbs certain portions of incident light and transmits the remainder. Colour filters absorb selected wavelengths while neutral density filters absorb equal portions of all visible wavelengths.

Filter pack Assembly of filters used in an enlarger when making colour prints. Normally consists of any two of the three subtractive primaries (yellow, magenta, cyan) in appropriate strengths.

Fish-eye lens Extreme wide-angle lens covering an angle of about 180° and producing a distorted image with central objects at a larger scale than those towards the edges.

Fixed focus lens A permanently focused lens usually permitting acceptably sharp pictures beyond about 5ft (1.5m).

Fixing Stabilizing an image by removing excess silver halide or converting it to a soluble complex.

Flare Scattered light produced by reflections inside the lens and camera. Flare reduces image contrast.

Flashbulb Plastic-coated expendable glass bulb containing metal foil that burns to emit light of an intensity ranging from 3,800 K (clear bulb) to

5,000 K (blue bulb). Duration of the flash ranges from 1/20 to 1/200 depending on type.

Floodlight In photography, a general, overall, artificial light providing soft, even lighting, usually consisting of a tungsten filament lamp or lamps mounted in a reflector.

Fluorescence The re-emission of absorbed light converted to a longer wavelength. Fluorescent dyes are incorporated in the white base of some printing papers.

F number Numerical expression of the light-passing power of a lens at its different stops. Equal to the focal length divided by the effective aperture of the lens.

Focal colours Blue, green, red and yellow, the colours generally regarded as fundamental psychologically.

Focal length In the case of a simple lens, the distance between the lens and the position of a sharply focused image when the lens is focused at infinity.

Focal plane Plane on which a lens forms a sharp image when correctly focused.

Focal plane shutter Type of shutter where the blinds or blades are placed behind the lens, as near to the focal plane as possible.

Focusing The adjustment of the lens-to-film distance to produce a sharp image of the subject. Closer subjects require greater lens-to-film distance.

Focusing screen Etched glass or plastic used on a camera as an aid to observing and focusing the image before exposure.

Fogging In reversal film processing, the deliberate production of an overall veil of silver on the film during the second stage of development after silver has first been developed in areas of the emulsion that received the latent photographic image. This may be done by exposure to light or chemically. Unwanted fog may also appear accidentally as a visible deposit or density in the negative or print that is not part of the photographic image.

Fog level Measurement of the basic density of fog produced when unexposed film is developed.

Forced development Development that is extended beyond the normal level to counteract underexposure. Also known as "pushing" the film.

Fresnel lens Lens consisting of a series of concentric stepped rings, each a section of a convex surface. This construction produces a very flat lens of light weight. Normally used only for spotlights and viewing screens because the rings are visible.

Gamma Figure expressing the ratio of contrast in the processed film to that in the original subject.

Gelatin Colloid of animal origin used as the binding medium for silver halides in photographic emulsions.

Graininess Visual impression of the irregularly distributed silver grain clumps or their associated dye images, which form the photographic image.

Granularity Scientific assessment of grain as opposed to the subjective impression that is termed graininess.

Ground glass screen Translucent screen used for viewing and focusing in large format and reflex cameras.

Guide number An indication of the power of a flash unit, enabling the correct aperture to be selected at a given distance between flash and subject. The number divided by the distance gives the f stop that should be used. A film speed is specified with the guide number, and recalculation is needed for different speeds.

Halation Diffused secondary image caused by light reflected from the film support.

Halogen Generic term for elements in the iodine, bromine, chlorine and fluorine group. Compounds of metals with these elements are called halides. Light-sensitive silver halides form the basis of photographic films and papers.

Hardener Chemical used to increase the mechanical toughness of gelatin and raise its melting point.

High key Describes an image consisting mainly of light, delicate tones.

Highlights Bright parts of the subject, which reproduce as the densest areas in the negative and as the lightest areas in prints or transparencies.

Hologram Photographic image recording the interference of two beams of light from a laser, one of which has been reflected from the subject. When illuminated by a similar light, this gives a three-dimensional image of the subject.

Hot shoe An accessory shoe, usually on top of a camera, with a contact for flash synchronization that matches another contact on the foot of the flash-gun.

Hue The quality that distinguishes one colour from another and which changes when a surface reflects a different mixture of spectral light.

Hydroquinone Common developing agent. Normally used in conjunction with metol and phenidone.

Hyperfocal distance The distance from the lens to the nearest point that is acceptably sharp when the lens is focused at infinity. By refocusing on this point the depth of field can be extended in front of it by half the hyperfocal distance.

Hypo Popular name for sodium thiosulphate, once the universal fixing agent for dissolving un-

wanted silver halides. A hypo eliminator (HE) is an oxidizing agent that converts the hypo into harmless sodium sulphate.

Image plane Plane, normally at right angles to the lens axis, where a sharp image is formed.

Incident light Light that falls upon a subject or surface as distinct from light that is reflected from it.

Incident light reading Measurement of light falling on the subject by a meter that faces the light source or camera position. Now an uncommon method.

Infinity Setting that places the lens as close as possible to the film plane, giving a sharp image of distant objects.

Infra-red Radiation with a wavelength longer than that of visible red light—roughly 700 to 15,000 nanometres. Special films can record this radiation.

Integral tripack Film or printing paper with three main emulsion layers inseparably coated on the same base, each sensitized to one primary colour of light. Almost all modern colour films are of this type. In addition to the three main layers, the tripack includes a yellow filter below the blue-sensitive emulsion.

Interference Alteration of the wavelength of light resulting from the meeting of two wavefronts, as when light reflected from the back of a thin film meets light reaching the front.

Inverse square law A mathematical formula for working out the increase or decrease in light intensity falling on a surface as the distance between the surface and a point source of light changes. The change of intensity is calculated by inversely squaring the change of distance. At twice the distance the light is one-quarter as intense. If the distance is reduced three times the intensity is increased nine times.

IR setting Special focus setting, often marked in red, for infra-red photography. Infra-red radiations are focused further from the lens than visible light.

Iris diaphragm Aperture mechanism with adjustable metal leaves forming a circular opening.

Irradiation Scattering of light through the emulsion caused by multiple reflections from the minute silver halide crystals.

Joule Strictly speaking a unit of measurement, equal to one watt-second, of the energy stored in an electronic flashgun for conversion into light. Used to indicate the output of light from an electronic flash.

Kelvin (K) Unit of temperature measurement, starting from absolute zero at minus 273°C, used to indicate the colour balance of light.

Lamphouse Part of an enlarger containing the lamp or light source.

Laser Acronym for light amplification by stimulated emission of radiation. Source of bright, pure and controllable light moving in coherent waves.

Latent image The invisible image stored in a photographic emulsion after exposure but before development.

Lens Optical device for forming an image of an object by bending light rays. Made of a transparent medium with at least one curved surface.

Lens hood Shielding, usually funnel-shaped, designed to prevent stray light from outside the picture area reaching the lens and causing internal reflections.

Line image Image consisting of pure black and white, or intense colour and white, without intermediate tones.

Local control Printing technique involving burning in or shielding particular areas.

Long focus Refers to a lens with a focal length greater than the diagonal of the film format it covers.

Long Tom Colloquial term for a large, high-powered telephoto lens.

Low key Describes a picture composed mainly of dark, rich tones.

Lumen Unit of light intensity falling on a surface. A lumen-second refers to light of one lumen intensity for a duration of one second, or the equivalent, such as two lumens for half a second.

Macro lens Lens designed to work at close distances, giving images up to life-size.

Macrophotography Photography with image scales from 1:1 (same size) up to about ten times magnification.

Magnification Relationship between the size of the object photographed and a larger image formed by the lens.

Masking In colour reproduction, the technique of using negatives or positives made from the original and printing them in combination in order to alter tone, contrast or colour in the image. In its general sense, masking prevents light from reaching selected areas.

Matrix Relief image used for making dye or pig-ment print by transferring colour from the raised part of the relief to a suitable paper or other base.

Mercury vapour lamp Enclosed arc lamp producing a bluish light generated by passing a current through a tube full of mercury vapour.

Metol Popular developing agent. By itself tends to form a low-contrast image. Frequently used with the other developing agents such as hydroquinone.

Micrometre One millionth of a metre. The wavelengths of visible light are just below this measurement.

Microphotography Optical reduction of photographs to a microscopically small scale. The term is used in some European countries for the technique of photographing through microscopes.

Microprisms Small prisms moulded into focusing screens, usually within a central circle, to assist focusing. The image appears discontinuous when out of focus.

Mired shift value A filter's ability to change the colour quality of a light source, expressed as a plus or minus number of micro-reciprocal degrees. The mired value of a light source is found by dividing one million by its colour temperature in degrees kelvin. Filters are assigned fixed mired shift values by which they will modify the mired value of the light source. Yellowish filters have positive mired shift values, which means that they raise the mired value of the light source and lower its colour temperature. Bluish filters have negative values, lowering the mired value of the light source and raising the colour temperature. A decamired is ten mireds—a colour shift just detectable by the human eye.

Moiré The effect produced when two identical patterns are superimposed slightly out of register, giving a shimmering, concentric appearance.

Montage A composite picture made from several images edge-to-edge or overlapping.

Motor drive Device for winding-on the film and re-tensioning the shutter by means of an electric motor.

MQ/PQ developers Popular developing solutions containing metol and hydroquinone or phenidone and hydroquinone.

Nanometre (nm) One thousand millionth of a metre. A unit for measuring the wavelength of electromagnetic radiation.

Negative Image in which light areas of the subject are recorded as dark and, conversely, dark areas as light.

Negative carrier Holder for negatives and transparencies in an enlarger. Films may be held by the edges or between glass.

Negative lens A diverging lens, with at least one concave surface. In photography normally used only in conjunction with converging lenses.

Newton's rings Coloured rings appearing when two transparent surfaces are not quite in contact. This interference effect can be troublesome when negatives are held between glass.

Nodal point Intersection between the optical axis of a lens and an imaginary "principal plane of refraction" within a compound lens. This plane is near the front of the lens for incoming rays of light and near the back of it for emerging rays. The rear nodal point is found on the plane where parallel light rays entering the lens would meet lines diverging from the point where they were brought to focus behind it. Focal length is the distance from the rear nodal point to the focal plane when the lens is set at infinity.

Non-substantive Refers to colour films that do not have colour-forming couplers incorporated into the emulsion.

Opacity Describes a material's lack of transparency. An image transmitting half the light falling on it has an opacity of 2.

Open flash Non-automatic flash, fired manually between opening and closing the shutter.

Optical axis Imaginary line through the centre of an optical system at right angles to the lenses and image plane.

Orthochromatic film Sensitive to the blue and green regions of the spectrum but not to red or orange light.

Overdevelopment Excessive development, producing dense negatives of high contrast that will give featureless highlights when printed. Overdeveloped prints are fogged or stained.

Overexposure Excessive exposure, producing dense, flat negatives and pale transparencies with burnt-out highlights. Overexposure in printing negatives produces darkened images.

Over-run lamps Incandescent lamps used at a higher voltage than normal to increase light output at the expense of lamp life.

Oxidation Chemical reaction relating to combination with oxygen. Developers should be protected from oxidation by storage in sealed bottles.

Pan and tilt head Tripod head with separate locks for horizontal (pan) and vertical (tilt) movements of the camera.

Panchromatic Describes emulsions that are sensitive to light of all colours.

Panning The action of swinging the camera to follow a moving subject. Can produce a sharp image of the subject against a blurred background, thus providing an impression of movement.

Panoramic camera Camera with lens that travels in an arc during exposure to make a record on a long strip of film that receives successive parts of a wide view. Once popular for large group photographs.

Parallax Difference between the image seen in a viewfinder and that recorded by the taking lens. Most pronounced at close distances with TLR and rangefinder cameras. Single-lens reflex and studio cameras are free from parallax error.

Paraphenylenediamine Developing agent which, in many derivative forms, is particularly suitable for colour development.

Partitive colour mixing The technique of placing small areas of separate colours so close together that the eye combines them, making other colours.

Pentaprism Five-sided prism which, in combination with the lens and mirror, can show an unreversed, upright image for eye-level viewing.

Perspective The relationship between objects in a scene in terms of scale, position and shape when seen from one viewpoint. Because three-dimensional objects appear in this same perspective in a two-dimensional image, such as a photograph, an impression of depth is created. The main elements of perspective in photography are diminishing size, converging lines and overlapping forms, together with the recession of tone and colour known as aerial perspective.

Petzval lens Lens invented by Josef Petzval in 1840 based on two widely-spaced colour-corrected combinations. Originally a fast portrait lens, now used in modified forms for projection.

pH Strictly defined as the logarithm of the concentration of the hydrogen ion in grammes per litre. In practice a useful scale denoting the degree of acidity or alkalinity, with water being neutral at pH 7.

Phenidone Developing agent. Not used alone but always in combination with hydroquinone or similar developing agent. More active than metol and smaller quantities are required.

Photo-electric cell Light-sensitive cell that either generates electrical current when light falls on it (as in a selenium cell) or reduces its electrical resistance (as in a cadmium sulphide cell).

Photoflood Photographic lamp designed to be over-run in order to produce a high output of light during a comparatively short life.

Photogram Originally referring to artistic photographs, the term is now applied to photographs made without a camera, usually by arranging translucent or opaque objects on sensitive material and then exposing them to light.

Photogrammetry The measurement of subjects such as buildings from photographs. Applies also to survey work and astronomy.

Photometer Instrument for measuring light by comparing subject illumination with a standard light source.

Photomicrography Photography that records magnified images of small or minute objects, generally by means of a camera attached to a microscope.

Physiogram Photographic recording of the pattern traced out by a point-source of light attached to a complex moving pendulum.

Pincushion distortion Image distortion in which straight lines near the edge of the field appear to bend in the middle towards the lens axis.

Pinhole camera Camera that uses, instead of a lens, a small sharp-edged hole in an opaque diaphragm. Requires very long exposures and gives fuzzy pictures.

Plano-concave lens A lens with one flat side and the other concave. Similarly a plano-convex lens has a flat side and a convex one. Used in constructing compound lenses.

Plate Glass coated with light-sensitive emulsion. Once universal, now available only for scientific purposes.

Plate-camera Camera, usually of large format, originally intended for use with plates and now utilizing cut film.

Polarized light Light vibrating in one plane instead of in all directions at right angles around its line of motion. The polarization of specularly reflected light produces glare.

Polarizing filter Filter that passes on only polarized light and can be rotated to block polarized light reaching it, cutting down glare from polished surfaces or from blue sky.

Positive Print or transparency in which tones and colours correspond to those in the original subject.

Positive lens A converging or convex lens. Usually simple in construction.

Posterization Pictorial technique of tone separation in which a continuous range is split up into a few main tones with intermediate detail suppressed.

Potassium bromide Chemical used as a restrainer in developers and as a source of bromide ions in silver bleaches.

Potassium carbonate Alkali, similar to sodium carbonate, used as an accelerator in developers, especially those supplied as concentrated liquids.

Potassium ferricyanide Important constituent of many silver bleaches in conjunction with potassium bromide.

Potassium hydroxide Powerful alkali with a basic similarity to sodium hydroxide (caustic soda) but of greater solubility.

Potassium metabisulphite Useful as a mild acid in fixing solutions as the sulphurous acid produced when it dissolves does not decompose hypo.

Preservative Chemical, usually sodium sulphite, that preserves developing agents from oxidation while in solution by itself utilizing oxygen.

Primary colours Blue, green and red, the regions of the spectrum that, in various combinations, can form any other colour by additive mixing.

Prism Transparent medium, often of basic triangular shape, capable of bending or refracting light.

Process lens Highly corrected lens used for copying illustrations for subsequent photomechanical reproduction. Normally a macro type that covers a large format.

Pushing Prolonging development of film beyond the normal duration in order to compensate for underexposure or increase contrast.

Quartz-iodine lamp Incandescent lamp with a quartz envelope containing iodine.

Rack and pinion Mechanism for focusing used on many large-format cameras. The focusing wheel is fixed to a pinion wheel that engages in a toothed rack along the baseboard of the camera. When the wheel is turned the lens panel is slid along the baseboard.

Rangefinder Any device that measures the distance to an object by optical means. Now usually coupled to the focusing movement of the lens.

Rapid rectilinear Obsolete lens design consisting of two identical components, each of two or more cemented elements, placed each side of the iris to cancel out basic distortions.

Reciprocity law States that the effect of exposure is equal to light intensity multiplied by duration. With extremely low intensities of light, or very high ones, this rule fails and extra exposure must be given in compensation. Very long exposures may have unpredictable results on colour balance.

Reducers Substances capable of reducing deposited silver on a negative or print, thus decreasing the density of the image.

Reflected light reading A measurement of light reflected from the subject to the meter. Virtually all meters built into cameras utilize this principle.

Reflector Surface capable of reflecting on to a subject light that is travelling away from it. White or grey cards are used in addition to metal reflectors.

Reflex camera Type of camera utilizing a mirror to reflect image-producing light rays on to a viewing screen for viewing and focusing.

Refraction The bending of light as it passes from one transparent medium to another of different density, a lens element, for example. The amount of bending a medium produces is described numerically by its refractive index.

Rehalogenization Technique of converting silver deposits back to silver halides.

Relative aperture Refers to the f number marked on lens barrels and is obtained by dividing the focal length of a lens by the actual size of the aperture.

Replenishment The regeneration of processing solutions by the addition of those chemicals that have become altered or used up in the solutions.

Resin-coated paper Printing paper treated with a synthetic resin to prevent the paper base from absorbing water or processing solutions. Results in shorter processing washing and drying times.

Resolution The ability of the lens and film to record adjacent fine detail.

Restrainer Chemical used in very alkaline developers to inhibit fog formation.

Reticulation Regular crazed pattern in gelatin caused by any significant change in temperature between solutions. Has largely been overcome.

Retina Light-sensitive area at the back of the eye containing specialized cells known as rods and cones. Light absorbed by these cells triggers electrical signals for further analysis by a chain of cells leading to the cortex of the brain.

Retouching Handwork, on film or print, using a brush, pencil or knife, to remove flaws or otherwise improve or alter the image.

Reversal film See Colour reversal film.

Reversal ring A ring that attaches to the camera body of an SLR, into which the lens is secured with the front element next to the body. The reversed lens allows greater image magnification and is used in close-up photography.

Ring flash Electronic flash arrangement that fits round the front of the lens and produces virtually shadowless pictures. Used in close-up shots.

Rising front Lens arrangement that can be moved vertically so that the lens rises above, or drops below, its normal position. Invaluable in architectural photography to prevent distortion of verticals in tall buildings when the camera is tilted.

Rods Light-sensitive cells in the retina responsible for vision at low light levels. The rods are sensitive to light at low intensities but do not discriminate colours.

Sabattier effect Partial reversal of an image produced by exposing a partly developed film or print to white light, affecting only the previous shadow areas. Similar to solarization.

Sandwiching The projection or printing of two or more negatives or slides together to produce a composite image.

Saturated colour A pure spectral colour reflecting light of only one or two of the three main areas of the spectrum with no admixture of the third which would desaturate the hue towards white, grey or black.

Saturated solution The condition of a solution when no more soluble substance can be dissolved at a given temperature.

Secondary colours Colours resulting from mixing together any two of the primary colours, red, green or blue. The principal secondary colours used in colour film and printing processes are cyan (blue-green), magenta (red-blue) and yellow (red-green).

Selenium cell Light-sensitive cell used in exposure meters. Need no battery as the cell generates electrical current when exposed to light.

Sensitometry Scientific measurement of the relationship between exposure and density for any photographic material.

Separation negative A negative that records one of the three primary colours of a subject or, more usually, a transparency, as a silver image. For photomechanical printing a set of three separation negatives is produced, recording the red, green and blue components respectively, together with a negative recording the tones of the whole scene. These are used to produce four plates in cyan, magenta, yellow and black-and-white.

Shades Hues with an admixture of black.

Shading Prevention of light from the enlarger reaching some portions of the printing paper during exposure in order to make part of the image lighter.

Sheet film Individual pieces of film available in normal plate sizes. Also known as cut or flat film.

Shellac A naturally occurring resin once used for varnishing negatives and as an adhesive for dry mounting. Now generally superseded by synthetic resins.

Shutter Mechanical device used to expose film to light for an exact period of time. Between-the-lens leaf and focal plane shutters are the two main types.

Silhouette The recording of a subject basically in terms of its shape. Usually achieved through backlighting or by illuminating a background while preventing light falling on the subject.

Silver halides Generic name for light-sensitive compounds of silver with a halogen (iodine, bromine, chlorine, fluorine). Silver bromide is the main constituent of photographic emulsions but silver chloride and silver iodide are also used. The latent image produced on these compounds by the action of light can be converted to metallic silver by developers.

Single-lens reflex Camera system utilizing a hinged mirror between the lens and the film, which swings out of the light path when the shutter is open, allowing the taking and viewing functions of a lens to be combined.

Slave unit A photo-electric device, which, when activated by light from the main flash, fires one or more auxiliary flashes.

SLR Abbreviation for single-lens reflex.

Snoot An attachment (often tubular) for lamp reflectors or spotlights used to control the spread of light.

Sodium carbonate Alkali used in developers. The unpurified grade is known as washing soda.

Sodium hydroxide Powerful alkali used in developers. Impure grade known as caustic soda.

Sodium sulphite Chemical used to prevent oxidation of developing agents in solution. Absorbs oxygen and becomes inert sodium sulphate.

Sodium thiosulphate Popular solvent for silver halides. Used in fixing baths. Known as hypo.

Soft-focus image A photographic image that is not critically sharp. Any lens incapable of pinpoint definition will produce this effect, or a soft focus attachment, which diffuses light, can be added to the front of a lens. A soft-focus effect can also be achieved by printing through a diffusing screen.

Solarization Reversal of image produced by grossly excessive exposure of film or plate. True solarization requires about 1,000 times the exposure needed to produce a normal negative and the effect was first noticed in images of the sun. Partial image reversal by re-exposure to white light at the development stage (more correctly termed Sabattier effect) is used for special effects in printing.

Spectral sensitivity The response of a light-sensitive surface to the different colours of the spectrum.

Spectrum The range of colours in the visible part of electromagnetic radiation that can be produced by dispersion or diffraction. The spectrum is customarily divided into regions of red, orange, yellow, green, blue, indigo and violet. The wavelength band ranges from violet at about 380 nanometres to red at 700 nanometres.

Specular reflection Reflection of light rays from a smooth surface at the same angle. The slight unevenness of most surfaces normally produces diffuse reflection with rays bouncing off in all directions.

Spherical aberration The inability of a lens to bring light passing through its edge to the same point of focus as light passing through its centre. Controlled spherical aberration is used in soft focus lenses and attachments.

Spotlight Lamp unit with reflector and lens that can focus light into a small concentrated circle or give a wider beam.

Spot meter An exposure meter that measures reflected light from a small area of the subject, useful for high-contrast subjects.

Spotting Technique of retouching small spots and similar blemishes on prints or negatives.

Stabilization Chemical process of making superfluous silver halides stable in prints. Used instead of fixing and washing when speed is more important than permanence.

Standard lens Lens with a focal length approximately equal to the diagonal of the negative format of the camera.

Stand camera A camera intended to be used on a stand or tripod. Usually a large-format camera with movements.

Stop bath A bath, usually containing a weak solution of acetic or citric acid or potassium metabisulphite, used between the developer and a subsequent bath to prevent contamination by carry-over of alkali.

Stopping down The action of decreasing the lens aperture to control exposure or increase depth of field.

Stress marks Marks visible on a photographic image after processing, caused by pressure or friction before processing.

Strobe light American term for an electronic flash unit. Also used as an abbreviation for stroboscopic light, a flash unit that fires repeatedly at predetermined intervals.

Subminiature camera Not necessarily a very small camera but a still camera that takes a tiny negative such as 16mm or smaller.

Subtractive colour process A means of producing a colour image by using filters or dyes to absorb some primary components of light, allowing only others to form the image. The subtractive primaries used in most colour reproduction processes are cyan (blocking red), magenta (blocking green) and yellow (blocking blue).

Swing back/front Camera movement permitting the camera back (front) to swing at an angle to the vertical axis, and occasionally also to the horizontal axis, to extend depth of field and give perspective accuracy.

Synchronized flash Flash automatically fired at the moment when the shutter is fully open.

Telephoto lens Compact type of lens with a focal length greater than the diagonal of the film it covers.

Test strip Strip of printing paper that receives several different exposures section by section so that when it is developed exposure and filtration can be assessed without the need for a lengthy and expensive series of trial prints.

Tint A colour that has been made lighter by the addition of white.

TLR Abbreviation for twin-lens reflex.

Tonal range The range of tones between the lightest and darkest areas, usually of a positive image.

Tonal separation A technique for increasing the visual contrast between some tones and eliminating others either through processing or printing techniques. Shadows and highlights may be printed separately.

Toners Agents used to change the black silver image of a black and white print into a colour. Main toners are: sulphide and selenium, metal, dye and colour developers.

Transmitted light Light that has passed through a transparent or translucent medium.

Trichromacy Sensitivity to three fundamental colours which, in varying combinations, produce other colour sensations. People with normal vision are trichromats.

T setting Time setting—a device fitted to some shutter mechanisms that allows the shutter to open when the release is depressed, and remain open until the release is depressed a second time. Used for long exposures.

TTL Abbreviation for through-the-lens. A TTL metering system uses cells inside the camera body that react only to the light transmitted by the camera lens. Most modern SLR cameras have this type of metering.

Tungsten-halogen lamp Incandescent lamp with a tungsten filament and a halogen (either iodine and/or bromine) contained in a glass or quartz envelope. The halogen prevents the glass from blackening.

Twin-lens reflex Camera system with separate, but identical, viewing and taking lenses. The upper (viewing) lens has a mirror behind it that reflects light to a focusing screen.

Ultraviolet Invisible, electromagnetic radiation of a shorter wavelength (10–400nm) than blue light. Photographic materials are sensitive to this radiation which, on hazy days, can increase aerial perspective unless counteracted by an ultraviolet filter.

Uprating Rating of a film at a higher speed index than normal. In practical terms, means underexposing. A 400ASA film uprated to 800ASA represents a one stop underexposure and is usually compensated for by increasing development time.

Variable focus lens A lens system with movable elements allowing the focal length to be continuously varied within design limits. Also called a zoom lens.

View camera Camera of large format with main camera movements. Usually takes cut film. Also known as a field camera or technical camera.

Viewfinder A screen built into a camera or a separate, simple frame by means of which the photographer can see the field of view of the lens. Most viewfinders incorporate a focusing system.

Viewpoint The relationship between camera position and subject when a photograph is taken. The viewpoint is the primary factor in determining the perspective of a photograph.

Vignetting Darkening or lightening of a picture at the edges. A darkroom technique using a mask to shield the central area of a print and allowing the edges to go black, or a mask with a central

aperture, ensuring that light is faded out towards the edges of the print.

Water softeners Chemicals that remove or render harmless the calcium or magnesium salts present in "hard" tap water. These impurities react with developers and may cause a scum to be deposited on films or plates.

Watt-second Unit of electrical energy equal to one joule. Used for measuring the energy discharge of an electronic flash unit (watt-second = watts × seconds).

Wavelength Distance between two successive similar points on an alternating wave. Inversely proportional to the frequency of radiation.

Wetting agents Chemicals that reduce the surface tension of water allowing a solution to spread evenly and quickly over a surface. Generally used in developers to prevent air-bells and in the final rinse water to promote even drying.

Wide-angle lens Lens with a focal length shorter than the diagonal of the negative in use, giving a field of view of 60° or more.

Working solution Processing solution at a strength suitable for use without being further diluted, as opposed to a concentrated stock solution.

X-rays Electromagnetic radiation in the wavelength region 0.0001–10nm. It is shorter than ultraviolet and longer than gamma radiation and can fog photographic material through normal wrappings. At airports it is prudent to carry film in hand luggage to avoid X-ray examination of baggage spoiling unexposed or exposed film.

Zone system A method of predetermining focus settings, especially in sports photography. Once the aperture has been determined, the focus of the lens is set so that everything within a particular zone will be rendered as acceptably sharp. Also a simplified method of focusing used on some simple types of modern cameras. Possible subjects are split up into a few zones, such as portraits, groups and landscapes, with the corresponding focus position of the lens indicated by symbols on the lens barrel.

Zooming Moving a variable focus lens during an exposure.

Zoom lens Alternative term for a variable focus lens.

Index

Credits

The author and publishers wish to thank the following people and organizations for their help in producing this book:

Tom Boddy; Brian Coe of the Kodak Museum; Mel Francis of the Imperial College; Julia Hedgecoe; Graham du Heaume of the British Museum of Natural History; Imperial War Museum; Indonesian Government; Langham Studios; Munsell Color, Baltimore; Dr K. H. Ruddock of the Imperial College; Singapore Airlines; Singapore Tourist Board.

Retouching
O'Connor Dowse
Roy Flooks
Sally Slight

Mitchell Beazley Studio
Alan Suttie
Mike Saunders
Marilyn Bruce
Chris Forsey

Darkroom techniques
Roger Bounds
Fred Dustin
Michael Pearcy

Picture research
Karin Liebrecht
Sue Pinkus
Paddy Poynder
Sarah Snape

Equipment
Nikon
Pelling & Cross Ltd,
Baker Street, London W1.
Pentax
Rank Photographic,
Brentford, Middlesex.
West One Camera Ltd,
108 Shaftesbury Avenue,
London W1.

Photography for artwork
Kim Sayer
David Strickland

Photographic services
Negs Photographic

Index
Michael Gordon